Education of Children and Adolescents with Learning Disabilities

Abraham Ariel

California State University, Los Angeles

Merrill, an imprint of
Macmillan Publishing Company
New York

Maxwell Macmillan Canada
Toronto

Maxwell Macmillan International
New York   Oxford   Singapore   Sydney

Cover art: Cathy Watterson
Editor: Ann Castel
Production Editor: Sheryl Glicker Langner
Art Coordinator: Ruth A. Kimpel
Photo Editor: Anne Vega
Cover Designer: Thomas Mack
Production Buyer: Pamela D. Bennett

This book was set in Melior by Compset, Inc. and was printed and bound by Book Press, Inc., a Quebecor America Book Group Company. The cover was printed by Lehigh Press, Inc.

Macmillan Publishing Company
866 Third Avenue
New York, NY 10022

Macmillan Publishing Company is part of the
Maxwell Communication Group of Companies.

Maxwell Macmillan Canada, Inc.
1200 Eglinton Avenue East, Suite 200
Don Mills, Ontario M3C 3N1

Library of Congress Cataloging-in-Publication Data
  Ariel, Abraham.
    Education of children and adolescents with learning disabilities   /
  Abraham Ariel.
        p.   cm.
    Includes bibliographical references and index.
    ISBN 0–675–20544–1
    1. Learning disabled children—Education—United States.
    2. Learning disabled youth—Education—United States.
    3. Metacognition.   I. Title.
  LC4704.A75   1992
  371.9—dc20   92-2871
                                                                    CIP

Printing: 1 2 3 4 5 6 7 8 9   Year: 3 4 5 6 7

Photo credits: pp. 3, 31, 63, 149 by Jean-Claude Lejeune; pp. 45, 53, 237, 421, 475 by Robert Finken; p. 71 by Trinity Sunrise Photos; pp. 87, 167, 249 by Ulrike Welsch; p. 119 by Macmillan; p. 183 by Andy Brunk/Macmillan; p. 206 by Gale Zucker; pp. 227, 315, 372, by Larry Hamill/Macmillan; p. 361 by Skjold Photographs.

*To my dear wife Ayala
and my children Orit, Sheira, and Danit
and
in memory of my querida imma Buli
and my beloved brother Haim*

Preface

The recognition of children with otherwise normal intelligence who have problems in learning brought forth the formation of the field of learning disabilities nearly 50 years ago. Theoretical constructs, diagnostic materials and procedures, intervention approaches, and teaching strategies were developed. What seemed to be, at that time, a scientific approach to the treatment of, and intervention with learning-disabled individuals—primarily the theoretical constructs underlying process deficits and their amelioration—was challenged in the 1970s. The 1970s and the 1980s can be described as a critical period during which the practices of the past were questioned and a search for new direction was intensified.

Issues in assessment, intervention approaches, and service delivery practices have since generated a great deal of research, resulting in a new body of knowledge regarding learning disabilities. New concepts about the nature of learning disabilities have emerged and have contributed to the search for new directions. Influenced by information-processing theories, cognitive psychology, applied behavior analysis, cognitive behavior modification, and the newly acquired knowledge in the field of learning disabilities, this search has led to the formulation of new constructs and the development of new intervention approaches such as strategy intervention models and metacognitive approaches.

This text is intended for undergraduate and graduate students who are developing expertise in working with those with learning disabilities. It may also serve as a basic comprehensive reference source for prospective special and regular educators, school psychologists and counselors, and school administrators, and as a handbook for other practitioners who may desire additional knowledge in the field of learning disabilities.

The reader will find up-to-date information on learning disabilities. The text provides an objective look at theories, curricula, teaching approaches, classroom management strategies, and materials applicable to the learning disabled. The author has provided practical intervention approaches based on sound theories, empirical research, and data-based observations. The work presented in this text has been influenced by the accumulated knowledge and research in the field of learning disabilities, and by the author's experience in working with individuals with learning disabilities, their parents, learning disability specialists, school psychologists, and counselors for nearly 30 years. In addition, this text represents the content delivered by the author in a main course on learning disabilities for prospective credential learning disability teachers at California State University, Los Angeles, for nearly 20 years. A conscientious attempt has been made to provide content based on clinical observations and empirical evidence. Information-processing paradigms, metacognition, and strategic learning are emphasized throughout the book.

This text provides comprehensive and practical information for the education and management of those with learning disabilities from preschool to adulthood. The content is organized into four parts with 15 chapters. It provides background knowledge and detailed descriptions of teaching approaches and intervention strategies intended to maximize teachers' effectiveness in providing learning-disabled students with an optimal learning situation in the least restrictive environment. The first part introduces the reader to the concept of learning disabilities—its historical perspectives, definitions, characteristics, etiology, current constructs, concepts, and issues. The second part discusses a service delivery framework and introduces the reader to approaches commensurate with the least-restrictive environment philosophy. Consideration is given to the provision of a comprehensive and integrated intervention program, with emphasis on metacognition and strategic learning, in order to meet the needs of the learning disabled throughout their life span. The third part presents material on identification, assessment, and instructional programming, including general principles and specific assessment and programming procedures. The fourth part is a how-to section on program implementation, including descriptions of classroom setups and variables that contribute to an optimal learning environment. This section deals in detail with teaching methods and strategies in various curriculum areas, as well as classroom management intervention strategies. Throughout the text, anecdotal reports of a variety of real-life situations involving individuals with learning disabilities from preschool to adulthood are presented. In-depth case studies designed to synthesize knowledge derived from assessment to program implementation and evaluation are also presented.

The author considers himself fortunate in choosing learning disabilities as his field of study. In fact, it can be said that his personal experiences in working with individuals with learning disabilities reflect the enthusiasm, success, frustration, and changes that have occurred in the field. The author began as a special-class teacher for so-called "mentally retarded children" in the latter part of the 1950s. His work as a learning disabilities specialist, supervising teacher, and school director at the Marianne Frostig Center of Educational Therapy during the 1960s and the early 1970s introduced him to "process training." At about the same time, he was exposed to prescriptive teaching, task analysis, and other behavioristic approaches. For many learning disabilities specialists, the 1970s posed great challenges as previous practices were questioned and new approaches had yet to be developed. The realization of the importance of integrating associative, cognitive, and self-directed approaches to learning and the author's conviction that those with learning disabilities are capable of active learning, of assuming control over their destiny and maximizing their potential have led to his intensive work in metacognition. The metacognitive procedures and strategies advocated throughout this text have been developed and tested over a period of more than 10 years in individualized and classroom settings. Much of the work reflects many teachers' and students' contribution to what seems to be a sound and viable approach supported by research.

Throughout his career, the author has been actively involved in promoting the welfare of individuals with learning disabilities, their parents, and teachers. He was instrumental in program development and in shaping the course of the Resource Specialist Program in California while chairing numerous task forces at the local and state level during the 1970s. His concern for professionalism in the field of learning disabilities led him to be one of the founders and the second president of the California Council for Learning Disabilities (CLD/CEC) in the early part of the 1980s.

This text is the culmination of Dr. Abraham Ariel's lifelong dream. Tragically, it will also stand as his last and final contribution to the field of Learning Disabilities.

Abraham Ariel

August 2, 1938—March 23, 1992

Acknowledgements

While a single name appears on the binding, this book represents a cumulative body of knowledge of many LD specialists who, over the years, have put their efforts into trying to help learning disabled individuals and their parents. The influence of their writing is evident throughout the text. Most noteworthy is the work of the pioneers in the field from whom I have gained much knowledge and understanding of learning disabilities. In its essence, this work represents the collaborative efforts of many LD specialists, school psychologists, and counselors with whom I have worked closely for nearly 30 years. These individuals have had the welfare of learning disabled students in mind and have tried utmostly to help them. It also represents my first hand experience in working with individuals with learning disabilities and their parents. To all of these children and their parents who have shared their experiences, anxiety, and frustration, as well as their exuberant feelings when they met with success, I take my hat off. They were the real teachers who taught me to understand learning disabilities and provided me with a source of inspiration for new knowledge and the development of the many approaches advocated in this book.

I am also indebted to my students at California State University, Los Angeles, who have continued to challenge me, particularly to those students who provided assistance and input: Ann Ruegg, Sandra Scovil, Patricia Dolan, Mike Biery, and Carole Seedman.

A number of individuals provided feedback and critiques as they reviewed the manuscript at the various stages of its development. I would like to thank the following persons for their advice, criticisms, and contributions: David Anderson, Lock Haven University; Synnone Heggoy, Georgia Southern University; Diane Woodrow, West Virginia University; Paula J. Smith, Illinois State University; Doris J. Johnson, Northwestern University; Charleen D. Peryon, University of Dubuque; Robert S. Sloat, Texas Woman's University; Katherine

Greenberg, University of Tennessee, Knoxville; Rhoda Cummings, University of Nevada, Reno; and Phyllis Maslow, Cal State University @ Long Beach.
Their input was invaluable. I also would like to thank Judith Margolis for her suggestions for Chapters 1 and 2.

I am especially indebted to Jack Little, my colleague of many years, who, during the final stages of the manuscript, carefully read every page and offered comprehensive comments and suggestions for improvement.

Special thanks are due to Margaret Clark for her dedicated work in locating and verifying the references, and to Dori Stuchinsky, my computer trouble shooter who would come to my aid, even at late hours of the night.

I am especially grateful to my administrative editor, Ann Castel, for her encouragement and support. I would also like to thank my production editor, Sheryl Langner, and my copy editor, Mariellen Hanrahan, for their proficient skills.

Finally, but certainly not least, I wish to express my gratitude to my immediate family who have always been the source of my enthusiasm, sacrifice, and support. The marvelous patience and understanding of my wife, Ayala, has sustained me along every inch of the long road to the completion of this textbook. Her contributions and sacrifices are an integral part of it. My daughters, Orit and Sheira, my private "grad assistants," have understood the difficulty of achieving the efforts and sacrifices one must make in the process of contributing to a better world. To their "editorial assistance" and exhilaration, I say thank you. Finally, the delightful exuberance of my youngest daughter, Danit, has also been an unwitting contribution. Her smiles and her zest for life have provided me with inspiration, even at the most difficult times, when I took ill and it seemed as the world was closing in on me. To them my deepest gratitude.

Abraham Abastado Ariel

Contents

PART
1

Overview of Learning Disabilities

Part 1 introduces the concept of learning disabilities (LD) as a phenomenon that continues throughout an individual's life span. It provides insight into the characteristics, etiology, and definitions of learning disabilities. A discussion of the historical development of the field provides the reader with a realistic perspective of its evolution, a review of current practices and approaches, and a look toward the future.

Understanding Learning Disabilities

Questions to Consider

1. **Who are the individuals with learning disabilities and what is the prevalence of learning disabilities in the United States?**

2. **What are learning disabilities?**

3. **How are learning disabilities defined?**

4. **What are the characteristics of individuals with learning disabilities?**

5. **What are learning disabilities subtypes?**

6. **What are the causes of learning disabilities?**

The phenomenon of learning disabilities has been studied and investigated extensively, with numerous professional and parent organizations advocating the rights of individuals with learning disabilities to receive appropriate educational services in the least restrictive educational environment. Extensive research and development regarding the nature of learning disabilities, service delivery models, and instructional approaches have taken place. In addition, the federal government and individual states have provided considerable support through legislation and funding sources.

An increasing consensus attributes learning disabilities to neurological dysfunction or central nervous system pathology. Learning disabilities constitute a heterogeneous set of conditions with no single syndrome nor a single etiology (Keogh, 1990). Individuals with learning disabilities represent a diverse group with multiple characteristics. As a group, they tend to exhibit (a) a discrepancy between ability and achievement (Keogh, 1990; Swanson, 1991); (b) failures in some, but not all, academic or educational tasks (Keogh, 1990); and (c) inefficient information-processing functions, including monitoring and regulating of production (Swanson, 1988c, 1990). Although learning disabilities pose an impediment to an individual's ability to function in school or society, they should not prevent anyone from becoming successful in school and in life. Those with learning disabilities can be taught in our school programs in the least restrictive environment. They can learn effectively when appropriate teaching methods are used and when they are provided with tools that facilitate their learning. Profiles and case studies of individuals with learning disabilities are presented throughout the text to bring into focus the realities associated with the condition.

PEOPLE WITH LEARNING DISABILITIES

Individuals with Learning Disabilities: Who Are They?

A Profile of Jim

Jim is a 9-year-old who is behind academically. He can't, or won't, read, and his writing is illegible. His pencil grasp seems weak, and writing numerals and letters is hard for him. He is easily distracted and has difficulty attending to a task for any prolonged period of time. He repeatedly interrupts his classmates and is constantly in and out of his seat.

Jim's sensory motor functions are markedly impaired. His dominance is confused—he uses his left hand for some activities, such as writing, but uses his right hand for others, such as throwing a ball. He has serious problems with fine motor coordination. His difficulty in grasping a pencil results in slow and shaky writing. Jim's gross motor coordination is also poor. He has trouble jumping and playing handball, and he often appears clumsy.

Jim's ability to memorize is quite strong, enabling him to remember correctly the order in which he has seen and heard information. Although he understands what he hears, Jim exhibits difficulties in verbal expression. His somewhat short sentences are awkward and syntactically incorrect. Overall, he seems to function at the high average range of intelligence.

Although only 9 years old, Jim is hesitant in his approach to learning. He apparently sees himself as the least successful child in his family and therefore as undeserving of any positive rewards. His self-image is so low that he cannot express any of his positive qualities. Situations in school and life are generally too threatening for him to cope with.

According to the teacher's observations of his academic functioning, in reading, Jim is unable to discriminate between short and long vowels. He knows all the letters of the alphabet but occasionally confuses the various sounds. He knows some sight words at one time but misses them at another. In written expressive language, Jim becomes quite frustrated when asked to write or even copy from the board. In arithmetic—his stronger area—he functions at about the third-grade level. Emotionally, Jim is very anxious about his learning difficulties.

A Profile of Adam

Adam is a 14 ½-year-old who is in the ninth grade, but who is functioning at approximately the fourth-grade level in most academic areas. Passive in his approach to school as well as in his interpersonal relationships, Adam seems to have given up. His teachers complain that it is impossible to teach him, and his father continuously claims that he is simply lazy. On the playground, Adam always seems to get into trouble. He easily explodes during simple social interactions.

Adam is of average intelligence. His fine and gross motor coordination are age appropriate. He enjoys sports and would like to participate in his school's athletic program; however, his peers reject him because they think that he "looks strange." His language functions, both expressive and receptive, are impaired: His verbal expression and articulation are not clear, and he sometimes reacts as though he does not understand what is being said to him. Adam has extreme difficulty remembering information presented to him auditorily, but because of his excellent ability to reproduce visual patterns, he easily retains information presented to him visually.

Emotionally, Adam experiences feelings of inadequacy. He is bewildered by his inability to perform well in school and claims that he is dumb. Adam is basically a loner; he has no friends. His social behavior is inappropriate and often awkward. He does not understand why he cannot get along with his peers. He tries his utmost to make friends with them, and consequently they take advantage of him. Adam would easily give his own possessions to others in exchange for their affection.

A Profile of Larry

Larry is a 21-year-old student with a history of learning disabilities who is attending a junior college. He is fully aware of his handicaps, yet he has a strong desire to succeed in school. He has tremendous difficulties in writing and performs well only in courses in which he can record the lectures. Larry feels that he is being discriminated against by professors who, for example, will not allow him to take verbal rather than written tests. He is always seeking teachers who can understand his situation.

Larry's overall disposition is that of a young adult who is shy, hesitant, and unsure of himself. He has never dated. He is generally lonely and spends a great deal of his leisure time at the movies. Larry resents the fact that his parents are overly protective of him and doubt his ability to function independently as an adult. His intellectual functioning is in the high average range. Despite his difficulties in the language areas (reading, writing, and spelling), he does not allow himself to feel defeated. Because his knowledge of mathematics is excellent, Larry hopes to be an accountant.

These are just a few examples of individuals with learning disabilities. They represent a heterogeneous group in which each individual manifests different strengths and weaknesses in the skills and abilities related to learning and life in general. Some complete high school, go to college, and even earn advanced degrees, whereas others give up and drop out of school. They may be of near-average, average, or above-average intellectual ability. With proper educational interventions, these individuals can function effectively, and may even excel and contribute significantly to society.

Eminent People with Learning Disabilities

Individuals such as Jim, Adam, and Larry, as well as prominent people with learning disabilities, have existed throughout history. Various eminent individuals have been presumed to suffer from learning disabilities. Many have exhibited developmental delays, extreme difficulties in reading, and problems in writing. Those often named include Thomas Edison, Auguste Rodin, Woodrow Wilson, Hans Christian Andersen, Leonardo da Vinci, Nelson Rockefeller, and Albert Einstein. Questions still remain, however, as to the true nature of their learning disabilities and the validity of these suppositions (Adelman & Adelman, 1987). Following an in-depth study of some of these people using four sources of information (biographical information, cognitive characteristics, neuropsychological characteristics, and biological characteristics), Aaron, Phillips, and Larsen (1988) pointed out that the resolution of the uncertainty of the learning disabilities of these individuals depends partially on one's definition of learning disabilities. Post-hoc analysis indicates that they were able to manage, overcome, or circumvent their learning disabilities due to several factors, including their unusually intense interest and perseverance in a particular area and the positive parental support that they received. These and other successful individuals with learning disabilities provide a source of inspiration to many people with the same condition.

Prevalence of Learning Disabilities

In 1969, public schools classified only 120,000 students as learning disabled. During the formulation of the guidelines for the implementation of Public Law 94–142 (1975–1977), it was estimated that approximately 2% of the school-aged population was learning disabled. At the time, that figure represented 17% of the total population of handicapped children. According to a 1987 report to the U.S. Congress, of the 39 million students in public schools, approximately 4,373,000, or 11%, are eligible for special education services for various handicapping conditions. Per the same report, the number of children identified as learning disabled rose to 1,872,399, or 4.78% of the total school-age population between the ages of 5 and 17, exceeding the 2% allotted under Public Law 94–142 (United States Department of Education, 1987). These figures indicate that 42.8% of identified and served handicapped children are classified as having specific learning disabilities.

DEFINING LEARNING DISABILITIES

The definition of a term or the description of a disease is intended to facilitate an understanding of the disorder, the identification of individuals who exhibit the disorder, and communication among parents, professionals, and service delivery agents. In order for a definition to be viable, previous knowledge is essential, that is, knowledge of the characteristics and etiology of the condition. The definition of learning disabilities is complex and perplexing due to their nature and their heterogeneity. Examining the origin of the definition and its evolution will aid our understanding of learning disabilities.

Historical Perspectives

The majority of definitions of learning disabilities strongly reflect the origin of the LD field. The precursor to such definitions was the description of a brain-injured child by Strauss and Lehtinen (1947):

> A brain-injured child is a child who before, during, or after birth has received an injury to or suffered an infection of the brain. As a result of such organic impairment, defects of the neuromotor system may be present or absent; however, such a child may show disturbances in perception, thinking, and emotional behavior, either separately or in combination. These disturbances can be demonstrated by specific tests. These disturbances prevent or impede a normal learning process. Special educational methods have been devised to remedy these specific handicaps. (p. 4)

The first acknowledged definition of learning disabilities was that proposed by Kirk (1962):

> A learning disability refers to a retardation, disorder, or delayed development in one or more of the processes of speech, language, reading, spelling, writing, or arithmetic resulting from a possible cerebral dysfunction and/or emotional or behavioral disturbance and not from mental retardation, sensory deprivation, or cultural or instructional factors. (p. 263)

Thus the term *learning disabilities* represented a departure from the terms *brain injured* or *mental retardation*. This definition "has also shifted away from an etiological focus to a behavioral focus emphasizing the primary difficulties-reduced learning performance manifested in academic achievement deficits" (Kavale & Forness, 1985, p. 46).

In 1966, a task force on terminology and identification of the "child with minimal brain dysfunction" (sponsored by the National Society for Crippled Children and Adults, Inc. and the National Institute of Neurological Diseases and Blindness of the National Institutes of Health) proposed the following definition:

> The term "minimal brain dysfunction syndrome" refers to children of near average, average, or above average general intelligence with certain learning or behavioral disabilities ranging from mild to severe, which are associated with deviations of function of the central nervous system. These deviations may manifest themselves by various combinations of impairment in perception, conceptualization, language, memory, and control of attention, impulse, or motor function. (S. D. Clements, 1966, pp. 9–10)

In 1967, the Association for Children with Learning Disabilities (ACLD) adopted the following definition:

> A child with learning disabilities is one with adequate mental ability, sensory processes, and emotional stability who has a limited number of specific deficits in perceptual, integrative, or expressive processes which severely impair learning efficiency. This includes children who have central nervous system dysfunction which is expressed primarily in impaired learning efficiency. (Proceedings of ACLD Annual Conference)

In 1968, in an attempt to develop an acceptable definition, the National Advisory Committee on Handicapped Children (NACHC) suggested the following:

> Children with special (specific) learning disabilities exhibit a disorder in one or more of the basic psychological processes involved in understanding or in using spoken or written language. These may be manifested in disorders of listening, thinking, talking, reading, writing, spelling, or arithmetic. They include conditions which have been referred to as perceptual handicaps, brain injury, minimal brain dysfunction, dyslexia, developmental aphasia, etc. They do not include learning problems which are due primarily to visual, hearing, or motor handicaps, to mental retardation, emotional disturbance, or to environmental disadvantage. (As cited in Public Law 91–320, "The Learning Disabilities Act of 1969," p. 14)

In 1985, the Association for Children and Adults with Learning Disabilities (ACALD) adopted the following definition:

> Specific Learning Disabilities is a chronic condition of presumed neurological origin which selectively interferes with the development, integration, and/or demonstration of verbal and/or nonverbal abilities. Specific Learning Disabilities exists as a distinct handicapping condition in the presence of average to superior intelligence, adequate sensory motor systems, and adequate learning opportunities. The condition varies in its manifestations and in degree of severity. Throughout life the condition can affect self-esteem, education, vocation, socialization, and/or daily living activities. (Association for Children with Learning Disabilities, 1986, p. 15)

Contemporary Definitions

Definition in Public Law 94–142

The definition developed by the NACHC in 1968 was incorporated into legislation in Public Law 94–142. This definition has been the applied standard in determining eligibility for services under the law:

Specific learning disability means a disorder in one or more of the basic psychological processes involved in understanding or in using language, spoken or written, which may manifest itself in an imperfect ability to listen, think, speak, read, write, spell, or to do mathematical calculations. The term includes such conditions as perceptual handicaps, brain injury, minimal brain dysfunction, dyslexia, and developmental aphasia. The term does not include children who have learning problems which are primarily the result of visual, hearing, or motor handicaps, of mental retardation, of emotional disturbance, or of environmental, cultural, or economic disadvantage. (*Federal Register*, Dec. 29, 1977, p. 65083)

The 1981 National Joint Committee on Learning Disabilities Definition

In an attempt to address the shortcomings of the PL 94–142 definition, the National Joint Committee on Learning Disabilities (NJCLD) developed a new definition. Members of the NJCLD include the American Speech-Language-Hearing Association (ASHA), the Council for Learning Disabilities (CLD), the Division for Children with Communication Disorders (DCCD), the Division for Learning Disabilities (DLD), the International Reading Association (IRA), the Learning Disabilities Association of America (LDA), the National Association of School Psychologists (NASP), and the Orton Dyslexia Society (ODS). According to Hammill, Leigh, McNutt, and Larsen (1981), the NJCLD definition (a) reinforced the idea that learning disabilities occur across the life span, (b) deleted the controversial phrase *basic psychological processes*, (c) drew a distinction between learning disabilities and learning problems, and (d) made clear that "the 'exclusion clause' did not rule out the coexistence of learning disabilities and other handicapping conditions" (Hammill, 1990, p. 78). The NJCLD definition reads as follows:

Learning disabilities is a generic term that refers to a heterogeneous group of disorders manifested by significant difficulties in the acquisition and use of listening, speaking, reading, writing, reasoning or mathematical abilities. These disorders are intrinsic to the individual and presumed to be due to central nervous system dysfunction. Even though a learning disability may occur concomitantly with other handicapping conditions (e.g., sensory impairment, mental retardation, social and emotional disturbance) or environmental influences (e.g., cultural differences, insufficient/inappropriate instruction, psychogenic factors), it is not the direct result of those conditions or influences. (Hammill et al., 1981, p. 336)

Despite their shortcomings, the NJCLD definition and the PL 94–142 definition are currently the most widely used in the field. One focuses on the heterogeneity and neurological etiology of learning disabilities, and the other emphasizes a disorder in underlying basic psychological processes without reference to an underlying neurological disorder.

Issues in the Definition

The locus of the problem in defining learning disabilities lies in postulates emanating from the work of Strauss and Werner that have been incorporated into the definitional conception of learning disabilities. Learning disabilities have been viewed from a medical perspective as caused by neurological dysfunction and not due primarily to other handicapping conditions. In addition, learning problems experienced by individuals with LD were related to process disturbance, most notably in perceptual-motor functioning. The existence of learning disabilities was also associated with a discrepancy between ability and achievement (Kavale, Forness, & Bender, 1987).

In the 1987 report by the Interagency Committee on Learning Disabilities (ICLD) to the U.S. Congress, concerns were expressed regarding the shortcomings of the PL 94–142 and 1981 NJCLD definitions. The shortcomings of the PL 94–142 definition were expressed as follows: (a) the definition wrongly implies that learning disabilities is a homogeneous condition rather than a heterogeneous group of disorders; (b) the use of the term *children* in the definition indicates its failure to recognize the existence of these conditions throughout adulthood as well; and (c) it does not indicate that "whatever the etiology of learning disabilities, the final common path is an inherently altered process of acquiring and using information, presumably based on an altered function within the central nervous system" (ICLD, 1987, p. 220).

According to the same report, the ICLD believed that the NJCLD definition represents a substantial improvement and reflects the conceptual advances that have emerged from research in the past 2 decades. However, the definition does not address itself to social skills, nor to the relationship between attention deficit disorders (ADD) (with or without hyperactivity) and learning disabilities.

The major flaws in most definitions of learning disabilities, which were subject to continuous debate, were summarized by Kavale et al. (1987) as follows: (a) they overemphasize etiology; (b) the presumed physiological correlates, that is, central nervous system dysfunctions, are unidentifiable at the present time and of limited usefulness for educational purposes; (c) the psychological process deficiency lacks construct validity; (d) the discrepancy between expected and actual achievement is fraught with complex issues related to its implementation; and (e) the exclusion component in the definitions has not isolated a unique and distinct LD category.

Proposing a New Definition

In an attempt to deal with the various definitional concerns, the ICLD presented the following modified definition:

> Learning disabilities is a generic term that refers to a heterogeneous group
> of disorders manifested by significant difficulties in the acquisition and
> use of listening, speaking, reading, writing, reasoning or mathematical
> abilities, *or of social skills.* These disorders are intrinsic to the individual
> and presumed to be due to central nervous system dysfunction. Even
> though a learning disability may occur concomitantly with other handi-

capping conditions (e.g., sensory impairment, mental retardation, social and emotional disturbance), *with socio* environmental influences (e.g., cultural differences, insufficient or inappropriate instruction, psychogenic factors), *and especially with attention deficit disorders, all of which may cause learning problems, a learning disability* is not the direct result of those conditions or influences. (1987, p. 222)

The proposed definition was accepted by all member agencies of the ICLD except the Department of Education (DOE). Two major concerns were voiced by the DOE: (a) The inclusion of the "significant difficulties in the acquisition of and use of . . . social skills" would necessitate a change in the Education of All Handicapped Children Act (EHA), and (b) the last phrase of the proposed definition—"a learning disability is not the direct result of those conditions or influences"—was questioned by the department's legal advisors (Silver, 1988, p. 78).

The New NJCLD Definition

In 1988, the NJCLD modified its earlier definition both to reflect the current state of knowledge in the field of learning disabilities and to respond to the definition developed by the ICLD (Hammill, 1990). The revised definition acknowledges that problems in self-regulating behavior and social interpersonal difficulties as concomitant to learning disabilities do exist, but states that by themselves, they do not constitute a learning disability. This definition further reinforces the idea that learning disabilities exist across the life span (Hammill, 1990). The revised definition reads as follows:

Learning disabilities is a general term that refers to a heterogeneous group of disorders manifested by significant difficulties in the acquisition and use of listening, speaking, reading, writing, reasoning, or mathematical abilities. These disorders are intrinsic to the individual, presumed to be due to central nervous system dysfunction, and may occur across the life span. Problems in self-regulatory behaviors, social perception and social interaction may exist with learning disabilities but do not by themselves constitute a learning disability. Although learning disabilities may occur concomitantly with other handicapping conditions (for example, sensory impairment, mental retardation, serious emotional disturbance) or with extrinsic influences (such as cultural differences, insufficient or inappropriate instruction), they are not the result of those conditions or influences. (NJCLD, 1988, p. 1)

Current Status of the New NJCLD Definition

This new definition received the endorsement of the majority of the organizations represented on the NJCLD and is now the committee's official definition (Hammill, 1990). Two organizations did not endorse the new definition: The LDA voted against it, and the DLD declined to act on it. This definition does not meet the requirements of the LDA definition, which places stronger emphases on self-esteem, vocation, and socialization. The position of the DLD is that (a) the new definition could not be operationalized any more easily than could the several definitions currently used in federal and state laws and regulations; (b) the definition broadens the concepts of learning disabilities and differs in significant ways from the current PL 94–142 definition, which may pose a problem in the reauthorization of PL 94–142 and jeopardize the current status of LD in the Public Law; and (c) as yet, there is no empirical evidence that nonverbal learning problems constitute a learning disability.

Common Elements and Disagreements in Contemporary Definitions

In analyzing the definitions of PL 94–142, the 1981 NJCLD definition, and the new NJCLD definition, one can find the following common components: (a) disorders in the acquisition of academic skills, (b) implied etiology, and (c) exclusionary factors. An additional analysis of these definitions with their major concepts is presented in Table 1–1.

Table 1–1 Major Concepts in the PL 94–142, 1981 NJCLD, and New NJCLD Definitions

PL 94–142 Definition	1981 NJCLD Definition	New NJCLD Definition
1. Term refers to psychological processing disorder.	1. Generic term refers to heterogeneous group.	1. General term refers to heterogeneous group.
2. Disorders are manifested in the acquisition of academic skills.	2. Disorders are manifested in the acquisition of academic skills.	2. Disorders are manifested in the acquisition of academic skills.
3. Term includes conditions such as dyslexia and developmental aphasia.	3. Disorders intrinsic to the individual presuppose a CNS dysfunction.	3. Disorders intrinsic to the individual presuppose a CNS dysfunction.
4. Learning disabilities resulting from other handicapping conditions and/or environmental, cultural, or economic disadvantage are excluded.	4. Learning disabilities resulting from other handicapping conditions and/or environmental influences such as cultural differences or inappropriate instruction are excluded.	4. Learning disabilities resulting from other handicapping condition or extrinsic influence such as cultural differences or inappropriate instruction are excluded.
	5. Learning disabilities are not the same as learning problems.	5. Learning disabilities are not the same as learning problems.
		6. Problems in self-regulatory behavior, social perception, and social intervention may exist.
		7. Learning disabilities occur across the life span.

NOMENCLATURE: LABELING AND TERMINOLOGY

The study of nomenclature, that is, using terminology to define and/or explain a disorder, is essential for communication in the LD field. "To this end, terminology must define accurately and in so doing, distinguish clearly one condition from another" (S. D. Clements, 1966, p. 8). The use of appropriate terminology facilitates communication among clinicians, researchers, other professional groups interested in individuals with learning disabilities, parents, and the learning-disabled individual (S. D. Clements, 1966).

The Labeling Hodgepodge: What's Wrong with Our Child?

The account that follows illustrates the current state in labeling individuals with learning disabilities.

David is a 13½-year-old boy attending a special education program for individuals with learning disabilities in the public schools. In addition to David's public school testing, his parents consulted three private psychologists before agreeing to place their son in a special class for students with LD. Each of the professionals they saw provided them with the best information from his or her own vantage point. Yet the parents are confused and bewildered by the inconsistencies of the psychologists' findings. One psychologist told them that David has psychoneurological difficulties that are exhibited by his learning disabilities. The second psychologist told them that their son is dyslexic. The third psychologist told them that David has attention deficit disorders without hyperactivity. The frustrated parents are still asking what is wrong with their child.

Most Common Diagnostic Labels

In its early period, the field was deluged with diagnostic labels attempting to describe individuals with learning disabilities. A review of the early literature reveals a plethora of terms used to describe or distinguish among the conditions known as "minimal brain dysfunction" (S. D. Clements, 1966): "minimal brain damage," "perceptually handicapped," "hyperkinetic behavior syndrome," "character impulse disorder," "psychoneurological learning disorders," "dyslexia," "hyperkinetic syndrome," "specific reading disabilities," and "learning disabilities." Ariel (1975) listed the most common diagnostic labels used to describe learning disabilities: "minimal cerebral dysfunction," "neurologically handicapped," "neurologically impaired," "educationally handicapped," "learning handicapped," and "perceptual problems."

In a more recent study, Ariel (1985) pointed out that the professional use of labels and diagnoses to describe individuals with learning disabilities continues to be inconsistent and in disarray and that, in fact, very little if any change has occurred in the use of labels over the last 3 decades. The major difference is that the 1975 study showed "perceptual problems" to be the most frequently mentioned diagnosis, followed by "minimal brain damage" and "hyperactivity," and the 1985 study revealed that "attention deficit disorder" was the most frequently mentioned diagnosis, followed by "hyperactivity," "learning disabilities," and "dyslexia."

Generally, parents seem to accept the diagnosis of learning disabilities and resent the statement "He will grow out of it." Parents oppose the "minimal brain dysfunction" diagnosis. The confusion in the use of terminologies to describe the learning-disabled individual makes it difficult for both professionals and parents to effectively communicate regarding the nature of learning disabilities.

ATTENTION DEFICIT DISORDER

Attention-deficit hyperactivity disorder (ADHD) and undifferentiated attention-deficit disorder (UADD) classifications appear in the most recent version of the *Diagnostic and Statistical Manual of Mental Disorders* (DSM–III–R) (American Psychiatric Association, 1987). They replace the previous classifications of attention-deficit disorder (ADD) with hyperactivity and attention-deficit disorder without hyperactivity described in the DSM–III manual, and their predecessor category of hyperkinesis or minimal brain dysfunction.

Confusion between hyperactivity and learning disabilities has prevailed in the literature since its inception. The two conditions share historical roots as manifestations of minimal brain dysfunction syndrome. Although hyperactivity has been cited in most studies as a behavioral symptom of learning disabilities (Ariel, 1975, 1985; S. D. Clements, 1966) and attention deficit disorder was an appealing term to many professionals in the field as a diagnostic label for individuals with LD, the terms ADD and ADHD are not synonymous with learning disabilities (Duane & Leong, 1985). The overlap that exists reflects the use of vague and inconsistent criteria for both LD and ADD (Shaywitz & Shaywitz, 1988). Even though ADHD is prevalent in 15% to 20% of children and adolescents with learning disabilities, it is not a learning disability (Silver, 1990). According to Silver, learning disabilities are neurological disorders that impact the psychological processes of learning, and ADHD causes hyperactivity, distractibility, and/or impulsiveness, which do not impact the psychological processes necessary for learning.

Traditionally, the hyperactive syndrome included the following symptoms: "a) excessive physical activity, b) impulsiveness, c) aggressiveness, d) poor learning despite normal I. Q., e) clumsiness, f) soft neurological signs, g) low frustration tolerance, and h) poor relationships" (Aman, 1984, p. 40). The perception of this syndrome has undergone significant changes as a result of research studies that point to attentional problems as the primary symptom of hyperactivity, accompanied by secondary symptoms that include "deficits in academic performance despite normal intelligence, low self-esteem, sleep-related problems, difficulties in social interactions particularly with peers, fluctuations in performance, and aggression" (Ross & Ross, 1982, p. 2). The secondary symptoms result from the hyperactive child's interaction with the environment. Recent studies focusing on the cognitive styles of underachieving hyperactive children point to inefficient strategic employment in problem solving accompanied by impulsivity, negative self-statements, and mal-adaptive attributional beliefs that are characterized by an external locus of control (Cotungo, 1987; Reid & Borkowski, 1987).

Attention-deficit Hyperactivity Disorder

The current description of attention-deficit hyperactivity disorder firmly establishes inattention, impulsiveness, and hyperactivity as the essential features of this disorder (DSM–III–R, 1987). Some impairment in social and school functioning is also common, with school failure as its major complication. This disorder may occur in as many as 3% of children, and it is 6 to 9 times more common in males than females. The disorder is believed to be more common in first-degree biologic relatives of people with the disorder than in the general population. In addition, central nervous system abnormalities, including "the presence of neurotoxins, cerebral palsy, epilepsy, and other neurologic disorders, are thought to be predisposing factors. Disorganized or chaotic environments and child abuse or neglect may be predisposing factors in some cases" (DSM–III–R, 1987, p. 51).

The essential features and diagnostic criteria of attention-deficit hyperactivity disorder, as described in the *Diagnostic and Statistical Manual of Mental Disorders (DSM–III–R)*, are shown in Figure 1–1.

Undifferentiated Attention-deficit Disorder

Undifferentiated attention-deficit disorder is defined as a residual disturbance "in which the predominant feature is the persistence of developmentally inappropriate and marked inattention that is not a symptom of another disorder, such as mental retardation or attention-deficit hyperactivity disorder, or of a disorganized and chaotic environment" (DSM–III–R, 1987, p. 95). Some of the disturbances referred to in DSM–III (1980) as attention-deficit disorder without hyperactivity are included in this category. The DSM–III–R statement that this diagnostic category warrants further research to determine its validity expresses the confusion and uncertainty of this designation.

SYMPTOMATOLOGY: CHARACTERISTICS OF INDIVIDUALS WITH LEARNING DISABILITIES

Symptomatology is the study of symptoms and characteristics. This term, borrowed from the medical sciences, attempts to identify and describe symptoms or characteristics that are associated with a specific disease or disorder. Symptoms are overt reactions or manifestations of the body to a disease. The symptoms or the general behavior patterns of individuals are assumed to be indicative of their disorder. From this perspective, one would assume that there are typical behavioral patterns associated with learning disabilities and, therefore, the presence of such symptoms confirms the existence of learning disabilities.

"They too can succeed." Students with learning disabilities can be taught effectively in an educational environment which takes their characteristics into account and provides them with instruction commensurate with their abilities.

Descriptions of behavioral characteristics of learning-disabled individuals are based on clinical observations and empirical findings. The study of these characteristics is influenced by the theoretical construct and the source of information regarding learning disabilities. Because of the heterogeneity of the learning-disabled population, the characteristics of learning-disabled individuals are numerous. Because of the heterogeneous nature of learning disabilities, different behavior patterns are exhibited by various learning-disabled individuals, including variations across age, that is, the characteristics exhibited by the primary school child are not the same as those of an adult.

Figure 1–1

314.01 Attention-deficit Hyperactivity Disorder (ADHD)

The essential features of this disorder are developmentally inappropriate degrees of inattention, impulsiveness, and hyperactivity. People with the disorder generally display some disturbance in each of these areas, but to varying degrees.

Manifestations of the disorder usually appear in most situations, including at home, in school, at work, and in social situations, but to varying degrees. Some people, however, show signs of the disorder in only one setting, such as at home or at school. Symptoms typically worsen in situations requiring sustained attention, such as listening to a teacher in a classroom, attending meetings, or doing class assignments or chores at home. Signs of the disorder may be minimal or absent when the person is receiving frequent reinforcement or very strict control, or is in a novel setting or a one-to-one situation (e.g., being examined in the clinician's office, or interacting with a videogame).

In the *classroom or workplace,* inattention and impulsiveness are evidenced by not sticking with tasks sufficiently to finish them and by having difficulty organizing and completing work correctly. The person often gives the impression that he or she is not listening or has not heard what has been said. Work is often messy, and performed carelessly and impulsively.

Impulsiveness is often demonstrated by blurting out answers to questions before they are completed, making comments out of turn, failing to await one's turn in group tasks, failing to heed directions fully before beginning to respond to assignments, interrupting the teacher during a lesson, and interrupting or talking to other children during quiet work periods.

Hyperactivity may be evidenced by difficulty remaining seated, excessive jumping about, running in classroom, fidgeting, manipulating objects, and twisting and wiggling in one's seat.

At *home,* inattention may be displayed in failure to follow through on others' requests and instructions and in frequent shifts from one uncompleted activity to another. Problems with impulsiveness are often expressed by interrupting or intruding on other family members and by accident-prone behavior, such as grabbing a hot pan from the stove or carelessly knocking over a pitcher. Hyperactivity may be evidenced by an inability to remain seated when expected to do so (situations in which this is the case vary greatly from home to home) and by excessively noisy activities.

With *peers,* inattention is evident in failure to follow the rules of structured games or to listen to other children. Impulsiveness is frequently demonstrated by failing to await one's turn in games, interrupting, grabbing objects (not with malevolent intent), and engaging in potentially dangerous activities without considering the possible consequences, e.g., riding a skateboard over extremely rough terrain. Hyperactivity may be shown by excessive talking and by an inability to play quietly and to regulate one's activity to conform to the demands of the game (e.g., in playing "Simon Says," the child keeps moving about and talking to peers when he or she is expected to be quiet). (DSM–III–R, 1987, p. 50)

Figure 1–1   Continued

Diagnostic criteria for 314.01 Attention-deficit Hyperactivity Disorder
Note: Consider a criterion met only if the behavior is considerably more frequent than that of most people of the same mental age.

A. A disturbance of at least six months during which at least eight of the following are present:
   1. often fidgets with hands or feet or squirms in seat (in adolescents, may be limited to subjective feelings of restlessness)
   2. has difficulty remaining seated when required to do so
   3. is easily distracted by extraneous stimuli
   4. has difficulty awaiting turn in games or group situations
   5. often blurts out answers to questions before they have been completed
   6. has difficulty following through on instructions from others (not due to oppositional behavior or failure of comprehension), e.g., fails to finish chores
   7. has difficulty sustaining attention in tasks or play activities
   8. often shifts from one uncompleted activity to another
   9. has difficulty playing quietly
   10. often talks excessively
   11. often interrupts or intrudes on others, e.g., butts into other children's games
   12. often does not seem to listen to what is being said to him or her
   13. often loses things necessary for tasks or activities at school or at home (e.g., toys, pencils, books, assignments)
   14. often engages in physically dangerous activities without considering possible consequences (not for the purpose of thrill-seeking), e.g., runs into street without looking

   Note: The above items are listed in descending order of discriminating power based on data from a national field trial of the DSM–III–R criteria for Disruptive Behavior Disorders.

B. Onset before the age of seven.
C. Does not meet the criteria for a Pervasive Developmental Disorder.
   Criteria for severity of Attention-deficit Hyperactivity Disorder:
   Mild: Few, if any, symptoms in excess of those required to make the diagnosis and only minimal or no impairment in school and social functioning.
   Moderate: Symptoms or functional impairment intermediate between "mild" and "severe."
   Severe: Many symptoms in excess of those required to make the diagnosis and significant and pervasive impairment in functioning at home and school and with peers. (DSM–III–R, 1987, pp. 52–53)

From: American Psychiatric Association: *Diagnostic and Statistical Manual of Mental Disorders, Third Edition, Revised,* Washington DC, American Psychiatric Association, 1987.

Earlier Descriptions of LD Characteristics

Earlier, the most common set of characteristics used to describe the "brain-injured" child was known as the "Strauss Syndrome." These characteristics included

1. erratic and inappropriate behavior on mild provocation.
2. increased motor activity disproportionate to the stimulus.
3. poor organization of behavior.
4. distractibility of more than ordinary degree under ordinary conditions.
5. persistent faulty perceptions.
6. persistent hyperactivity.
7. awkwardness and consistently poor motor performance.
   (Stevens & Birch, 1957, p. 348)

The characteristics of learning-disabled individuals were studied in the early part of the 1960s by a task force sponsored by the National Society for Crippled Children and Adults, and the National Institute of Neurological Diseases and Blindness of the National Institutes of Health. The task force listed, in order of frequency, the 10 characteristics most often cited by various authors in the field of learning disabilities:

1. hyperactivity
2. perceptual-motor impairments
3. emotional lability
4. general coordination deficits
5. disorders of attention
   (short attention span, distractibility, perseveration)
6. impulsivity
7. disorders of memory and thinking
8. specific learning disabilities:
   reading
   arithmetic
   writing
   spelling
9. disorders of speech and hearing
10. equivocal neurological signs and electroencephalographic irregularities
    (S. D. Clements, 1966, p. 13)

Parents' Perception of LD Characteristics

Research and common sense tell us that parents are an important source of information in understanding the nature of learning disabilities. Parents observe their children grow, and react to their accomplishments with joy and excitement. A very definite set of interactions exists between parents and their children. A child with learning disabilities affects the family as a whole, and the child, in turn, is affected by the environmental atmosphere created in the family. Earlier studies of parents' perceptions of learning disabilities were carried out by Owen, Adams, Forrest, Stolz, and Fisher (1971) and by T. H. Bryan and J. H. Bryan (1975). Studies by Ariel (1975, 1985) pointed out that parents of a learning-disabled individual are cognizant of the existence of their child's learning disabilities. These parents seem to understand the disorder and are quite aware of various characteristics and symptoms associated with the disability.

In Ariel's 1975 study, socialization difficulties were perceived by parents as very important and second only to attention disorders. These earlier findings were consistent with the results of a follow-up study of 180 families (Ariel, 1985), with a notable exception—visual perceptual difficulties were noticed by about 20% of the sample population. In addition to socialization difficulties, parents also pointed out the prevalence of emotional overlay/emotional lability, but they did not consider their children emotionally disturbed. These findings are suggestive of an "adjustment reaction to learning disabilities," reflected in socialization as well as in emotional adjustment difficulties.

Following are the 10 most common behavioral characteristics, in order of frequency, as reported by parents of learning-disabled individuals:

1. attention and concentration difficulties
2. socialization difficulties/emotional overlays
3. low frustration tolerance
4. poor impulse control
5. perceptual difficulties
6. poor speech and language development
7. hyperactivity/continuous restlessness
8. poor self-concept
9. learning/studying difficulties
    specific difficulties in reading, spelling, writing, and math
10. poor gross motor development

Other characteristics frequently mentioned include disorders in cognitive processes, poor memory, and perseveration/resistance to change (Ariel, 1975, 1985).

Classifying Characteristics of Individuals with Learning Disabilities

The characteristics of learning disabilities described in the following section are derived from empirical findings, clinical observations, information from parents of learning-disabled individuals, and self-reports of learning-disabled adults. No single characteristic can point to the existence of the condition of learning disabilities; a combination of various characteristics may indicate its presence. To facilitate an understanding of the characteristics of learning-disabled individuals, while considering the constitutional and environmental factors, two major categories of characteristics have been identified—primary and secondary. The reader must recognize that at times an interaction occurs between the constitutional and environmental factors, making it difficult to delineate the origin of the characteristics.

Primary Characteristics

The primary characteristics are associated with constitutional/neurophysiological factors of learning disabilities. These constitutional factors influence the capacity of the individual to interact with the environment. They include sensory receptors, attention, perception, channels along which information travels, and various memory stores in which information is held (J. Clements, 1987). In addition, they affect the individual's development and capacity in language and cognition.

The primary characteristics are listed as follows:

1. Difficulties with attentional processes, including distractibility, short attention span, impulsivity, and perseveration (Bryan, 1974a; Forness & Esveldt, 1975; Richards, Samuels, Turnure, & Ysseldyke, 1990; Hallahan & Reeve, 1980; McKinney, McClure, & Feagans, 1982; Richey & McKinney, 1978).
2. Deficit in memory processes, including short- and long-term memory (Bauer, 1979; Borkowski, Peck, & Damberg, 1983; Ellis, 1963, 1970; Torgesen, 1988).
3. Pervasive global problems in general language functioning, including communication deficits (Vellutino, 1986; Vellutino & Scanlon, 1982).
4. Cognitive and organizational deficits (Deshler, 1978; McKinney et al., 1982; Swanson, 1988c; Torgesen, 1979, 1980).
5. Poor impulse control and hyperactivity (S. D. Clements, 1966; Gail et al., 1990).
6. Perceptual-motor difficulties (Frostig, 1972; Marsh & Price, 1980; Wilcox, 1970).
7. Inefficient information processing (J. Clements, 1987; Maisto & Baumeister, 1984; Swanson, 1988c, 1989).

Secondary Characteristics

Secondary characteristics can be attributed to the interaction of the constitutional elements of learning disabilities with the individual's environment. They result from years of repeated failure (Goodman & Mann, 1976). Social-emotional problems are concomitant with repeated failure and produce low self-concept, social immaturity, and poor self-perception (McKinney, 1989; Thompson, 1986). This class of secondary characteristics can be divided into the following subcategories: (a) adjustment reactions to learning disabilities, (b) characteristics associated with the learning-disabled individual's interaction with the learning environment and instructional interventions at school, and (c) characteristics associated with the overall interaction of learning disabilities and the individual's environment.

Adjustment reactions to learning disabilities include interpersonal relationships/socialization difficulties and poor social judgment (Benson, Reiss, Smith, & Laman, 1985; Bryan, 1974b; J. H. Bryan & T. H. Bryan, 1983; T. H. Bryan & J. H. Bryan, 1990; Stone & LaGreca, 1990); fluctuation of behavior and changes in mood or disposition (S. D. Clements, 1966); behavior inappropriate to situations (J. H. Bryan & T. H. Bryan, 1983); and poor self-control (S. D. Clements, 1966).

The characteristics associated with the learning-disabled individual's interaction with the learning environment and instructional interventions at school include deficiencies in task-oriented behavior (Fine & Zeitlin, 1984); specific difficulties in reading, spelling, writing, and arithmetic (Ariel, 1975, 1985; S. D. Clements, 1966); inefficient use of information-processing strategies (Sternberg, 1987; Swanson, 1989); deficiencies in the use of strategic processing (Bauer, 1982; Sternberg, 1987; Torgesen, 1982); difficulties in automatizing learning routines (Garnett & Fleischner, 1983); learned helplessness (Torgesen, 1977, 1980; Torgesen & Licht, 1983); and high test anxiety (Bryan, Sonnefeld, & Grabowski, 1980).

The characteristics associated with the sum total variance in the individual's environment include lower self-concept (Rogers & Saklofske, 1985); low frustration tolerance (Ariel, 1975, 1985; Fine & Zeitlin, 1984); general passivity to learning (Torgesen, 1977, 1980; Wong, 1979); inefficient information processing (McKinney & Feagans, 1983; Torgesen, 1979, 1980, 1988); metacognitive deficiencies (Wong, 1982b); deficiencies in using strategic behaviors (Swanson, 1988c, 1989); poor regulation and monitoring of behavior (Brown & Palincsar, 1982; Owings, Peterson, Bransford, Morris, & Stein, 1980); and consistently less active, planful, and organized approaches to learning (Bauer, 1979; Fine & Zeitlin, 1984; Torgesen, 1986).

The behavior patterns of individuals with learning disabilities may reflect numerous characteristics which result from the interaction of the constitutional factors of learning disabilities with the environment of the individual. Thus children with the same constitutional factor may in fact demonstrate different characteristics. Yet these individuals are distinguishable from others with a handicapping condition. The prevailing characteristic is that these individuals exhibit difficulties in learning despite near-normal, normal, and above-normal intelligence.

CLASSIFYING LEARNING DISABILITIES: SUBTYPES

Heterogeneity of the Learning-Disabled Population

Both clinical observations and empirical research point to the heterogeneity of the learning-disabled population (Keogh, 1990; Lyon & Flynn, 1991). It has become increasingly clear that the learning disabled as a group is composed of various subtypes. The identification of these subtypes could provide insight into the assessment and instructional approaches for individuals with learning disabilities (Lyon & Flynn, 1991; Lyon & Moats, 1988). While the search for learning disabilities subtypes and attempts to formulate a taxonomy of learning disabilities based on these subtypes have increased in recent years, the notion that learning-disabled individuals constitute a heterogeneous group is not new. As early as 1963, in the initial symposium that laid the groundwork for the formation of the ACLD under the leadership of Samuel Kirk, the multitude of handicapping conditions and the manifestations of these conditions resulted in the adoption of the term *learning disabilities* to describe the various learning problems that are due not to mental retardation but to other unknown causative factors. The phrase was meant to serve as an umbrella term for the different conditions that manifest themselves as variations of learning disabilities. It was used to describe "a broad collection of disorders related to school failures that could not be attributed to any other known forms of exceptionality nor to environmental disadvantage" (Lyon, 1988, p. 33).

Thus the earlier definitions of learning disabilities point out the manifestations of learning disabilities in (a) language disorders, that is, oral expression and listening difficulties; (b) reading and writing problems; and (c) mathematics problems (Kirk & Chalfant, 1984). The earlier writings examined the field from various perspectives: (a) visual perceptual disorders, (b) disorders of auditory language, (c) disorders of written language, (d) disorders of reading, (e) disorders of arithmetic, and (f) nonverbal disorders of learning (Johnson & Myklebust, 1967). Early attempts at remediation, such as matching methods and techniques to sensory modalities, tried to make a distinction among learning-disabled individuals who exhibit different behavioral patterns and characteristics.

Similarly, early specialists attempted to link learning disabilities with various processing constructs; visual-perceptual processing perspectives (Benton, 1975; Frostig, 1968; Hallahan & Cruickshank, 1973); deficits in linguistic processes (Kirk & Kirk, 1971; Myklebust, 1968; Satz & Van Nostrand, 1973; Shankweiler & Lieberman, 1976; Vellutino, 1978); attention deficit disorder hypotheses (Hallahan & Reeve, 1980; Ross, 1976); and/or deficiencies in memory processes (Torgesen & Kail, 1980). These conceptualizations have provided the impetus for subtype research in recent years. Subtype research holds the greatest potential for the diagnosis and treatment of learning disabilities (Bender & Golden, 1990).

Subtype Classification

Despite recent attempts to classify individuals who have been identified as learning disabled into discrete subtypes on the basis of common characteristics and the nature of the disorder, a review of LD subtype research produces a plethora of subtypes that reflect the specific research methodology used and the researcher's theoretical construct of learning disabilities. The study of learning disabilities subtypes can be viewed from various perspectives: (a) neurophysiological perspective, (b) information-processing perspective, and (c) behavioral subtypes. These various perspectives, as well as the various subtyping techniques employed, produce a multitude of subtypes that have not been helpful for classification or instructional purposes.

In summarizing the research on learning disabilities subtypes, McKinney (1984), points out that the study of subtyping learning-disabled children is still in its embryonic stage. There are shortcomings and limitations to the empirical classification studies; in fact, "statistical classification procedures are simply designed to group individuals into homogeneous clusters: they do not ensure that the clusters are meaningful, or that they have any prognostic value" (p. 24). This research on learning disabilities subtypes has led some researchers, such as Kavale and Forness (1985), to call for a moratorium on LD classification research until a greater corpus of descriptive information has been obtained. Despite this current state of affairs, learning disabilities subtype research offers the promise of providing a meaningful picture of the learning-disabled individual's adaptive abilities and deficits and thereby providing a framework for successful diagnosis and treatment practices (Fisk & Rourke, 1984).

ETIOLOGY: THE STUDY OF CAUSATION

The study of etiology is the study of the conditions or factors that contribute to or cause a disorder or a disease. The goal of science is to identify the symptoms/characteristics of a disorder, to identify the cause of that disorder, and to discover a means of preventing and/or treating that disorder.

The constellation of behavioral characteristics of learning-disabled individuals does not stem from a single etiology. In addition, this constellation of behaviors is not associated with any specific neurological sign that leads to the cause of learning disabilities. The array of possible explanations and the fact that the learning disabilities phenomenon has become almost exclusively the interest of educators have led some to take a pragmatic stance on etiology by adhering to the position that teaching students with learning disabilities requires no more than knowing what the youngsters need to learn (Adelman & Taylor, 1983). Moreover, some assert that since learning disabilities are primarily an educational problem, etiology may be a secondary concern, and teachers may be better trained and equipped to deal with the observable behaviors than to explore possible causes (Wallace & McLoughlin, 1988).

Several factors have contributed to the current state in the study of LD etiology: (a) consideration of the field of learning disabilities as an educational problem, with very little involvement from other disciplines; (b) no interest by pediatricians and the field of medicine by and large in school problems or learning disabilities, or no time to spare from medical practices (Richardson, Kloss, & Timmons, 1971); (c) the complexity of the "science" of learning disabilities; (d) lack of knowledge of neurophysiology by learning disabilities specialists; (e) the attempts by many educators to underplay the importance of causation; and (f) the general state of the science of neurology.

While the study of etiology has been neglected (Brackbill, McManus, & Woodward, 1985), complete abandonment of the search for factors contributing to learning disabilities can result in wasteful and unproductive intervention practices. To a large degree, the prevention and treatment of learning disabilities depend on adequate scientific answers to the causes of cerebral dysfunction (Gallagher, 1984; Kirk & Chalfant, 1984). One cannot fully ignore the constitutional/neurological factors as well as the environmental factors affecting learning disabilities. The understanding of some of the plausible causes of learning disabilities and the knowledge of an individual's background can facilitate the LD specialist's understanding of what a learning-disabled individual might be experiencing.

Etiological Factors in Learning Disabilities

The nature of learning disabilities suggests no single etiology but rather a wide range of etiologies. A number of theories have been formulated to explain the causes of specific learning disabilities. These various etiologies can be classified under two main headings: neurophysiological/organic and psychosocial/environmental, as shown in Table 1–2.

Neurophysiological Organic Factors: Constitutional or Acquired

The current definition of learning disabilities adopted by the NJCLD and the definition included in PL 94–142 both infer organic causation. Among the neurological factors considered are genetic factors, reproductive causality, brain anatomical variations and dysfunction, developmental or acquired brain damage, and biochemical factors.

Genetic Factors

Studies of familial patterns of learning-disabled individuals and recent research in genetics point to an inheritability factor in learning disabilities. Most genetic studies of learning disabilities have concentrated on specific reading disabilities, that is, dyslexia. Family and twin studies have suggested a genetic component (Critchley, 1970; Hallgren, 1950; Hermann, 1959). As early as 1950, Hallgren reported that in a genetic study of 276 children and their families, 88% of the individuals with dyslexia had other family members with similar disorders. Studies of families of learning-disabled individuals point to a genetic basis of reading, spelling, and writing difficulties among the LD population (Ariel, 1975, 1985; DeFries, 1985; DeFries & Decker, 1982; Goldberg & Schiffman, 1972; Ingram, 1964; Naidoo, 1972; Owen, 1978).

Recent studies in genetics suggest the influence of genes on learning disabilities at several levels. While it is known that genes appear to influence normal development and variations among individuals, it has been found that certain genes may have an effect in producing a specific disability. For example, a gene influencing dyslexia is found on chromosome 15 (Smith & Pennington, 1987). Thus children inheriting that

Table 1–2 The Etiologies of Learning Disabilities

Neurophysiological/ Organic	Psychosocial/ Environmental
Genetic factors	Traumatic experiences
Reproductive causality	Prolonged stress
Brain anatomical variations and dysfunctions	Dyspedagogia
Developmental or acquired brain damage	Impaired home environment
Biochemical factors	

gene are at risk of developing reading disabilities. The β_2 microglobulin gene, which is thought to influence both the immune system and male sexual development, is also found on chromosome 15 (Smith & Pennington, 1987). This may explain the high prevalence of males among the learning-disabled population. Furthermore, according to Smith & Pennington (1987), "a genetic component may also account for the possibility of fairly subtle learning disabilities of bright children who are not identified by the schools because they do not meet the schools' criteria for learning disabilities" (p. 70).

Reproductive Causality

Reproductive causality refers to causes of learning disabilities that are not genetically inherent but rather are due to environmental factors during the prenatal and postnatal periods (Pasamanick & Knobloch, 1960, 1973). During the prenatal period, factors that may contribute to learning disabilities include maternal-fetal blood type incompatibility, maternal endocrine disorders (such as hypothyroidism and diabetes), maternal reproductive readiness, infectious diseases, anoxia (oxygen deprivation), prematurity, and substance abuse (Gray & Yaffe, 1983; Sever, 1985; Streissguth, 1983).

Factors that may contribute to learning disabilities during and/or about the time of birth—referred to as perinatal—include labor complications and anoxia. Birth histories of learning-disabled individuals indicate that 25% of the mothers in Ariel's (1975, 1985) sample experienced problems during pregnancy, and 35% experienced various problems during delivery. Prolonged labor and respiratory problems were the most frequently mentioned problems (Ariel, 1975, 1985). Postnatal variables include factors such as malnutrition, infectious diseases, and general undetected metabolic disorders.

Brain Anatomical Variations and Dysfunctions

The brain, more than any other organ in the body, is vulnerable to environmental influences, primarily during gestation, embryonic and fetal development, and development in the early years. Among the variables involved are anatomical variations in brain development. Anatomical variations suggest that in some children "the normal asymmetrical structure of the temporal lobes develops differently both structurally and sequentially during life" (Gaddes, 1985, p. 26). According to Smith & Pennington (1987), "dyslexics show deficits in particular 'left hemisphere' temporal processing abilities with comparative strengths in 'right hemispheric' spatial strategies" (pp. 67–68). Furthermore, dyslexic individuals show predominantly right hemispheric cognitive styles. While this research is in its embryonic phase, it may have significant implications for intervention approaches and methodologies.

Other aspects of brain dysfunction have been implicated as possible bases for learning disabilities. These include temporal lobe dysfunction, diencephalon dysfunction, cerebral and vestibular dysfunction, cortical and subcortical imbalance, delayed lateralization of brain function, disorders of brain metabolism, and maturational lag in the central nervous system (Kavale & Forness, 1985). Kavale and

Forness further conclude that "no one theoretical formulation has proved more valid than any other and, thus, the idea of a single deficit underlying the MBD [minimal brain dysfunction] condition is not supported" (p. 64).

Developmental or Acquired Brain Damage

The field of learning disabilities originated from the study of brain-injured individuals. While the term *brain damage* in its pure sense usually connotes direct destruction of nervous tissue, as in a lesion, the brain may become dysfunctional for other reasons. Brain injuries or brain damage may result from external causes, that is, external impact of the environment on the individual, such as brain damage resulting from an accident, brain injury resulting from infectious conditions such as encephalitis, meningitis, Reye's syndrome, and anoxia (D. J. Johnson, 1988), and brain damage resulting from poisoning due to aversive chemicals, including substance abuse. Brain injury also results from a continuous deprived and malnutritional environment. It has been known for a long time that malnutrition impairs mental development and causes damage to the brain, and such damage has been well documented in the literature (Gaddes, 1985). Brain injury is not limited to cognitive processing dysfunction but also affects the normal development of goals, attitude, and the emotional reaction to experiences (Cotman & Lynch, 1988).

Biochemical Factors

Various metabolic disorders such as hypoglycemia, hypothyroidism, nutritional deficits, and additive weaknesses (allergies) have been suggested as possible causes for learning disabilities. Metabolic irregularities have been found among dyslexics, including increased amounts of monoamine oxidase in the blood and higher thyroxine levels (Hughes & Park, 1968; Tansley & Panckhurst, 1981). Metabolic irregularities may also result from nutritional deprivation, which directly affects the molecular environment of the brain (Cott, 1972; Houck, 1984). Further scientific studies in this area are essential in order to better understand biochemical causations of learning disabilities.

Psychosocial/Environmental Factors

While the current definition of learning disabilities excludes learning disabilities due to environmental influences such as cultural differences, economic disadvantage, and insufficient/inappropriate instruction, one cannot eliminate environmental/psychosocial factors as contributing agents to learning disabilities. Environmental variables as possible etiological agents of LD have been suggested by Breitmayer and Ramey (1986) and Martin (1980). These also include traumatic experiences, prolonged continuous stress, faulty school experiences, and faulty home experiences.

Traumatic Experiences

One of the most notable environmental factors is emotional disturbance resulting from traumatic experience and/or prolonged continuous stress. The individual's adaptation to emotional stress produces effects very similar to those of brain-injured individuals (Kephart, 1968). The first type of emotional disturbance results from one or more traumatic experiences in which an individual faces an event that is intensely emotional and disrupts normal functioning and behavior, such as having a parent die or being the victim of a crime. However, when the event is dealt with properly through immediate emotional support and/or appropriate professional help, the individual may overcome these difficulties. After a relatively short period of time during which the traumatic experience interferes with the individual's normal behavior, the individual resumes normal functioning without any long-term effect on the general learning patterns.

The second type of emotional disturbance results from experiences that are less highly charged emotionally but are extended over a period of time, such as being neglected by parents or living in a war-torn country. The individual adapts behaviorally to the prolonged stress, which results in general abnormal behavior patterns and affects the individual's capacity to learn and interact with her or his environment (Kephart, 1968). This interference with learning is very similar to the interference observed in a brain-damaged child. Family crises, such as breakdown of the family, separation, divorce, death, or alcoholism, affect the individual's ability to learn (Goldberg & Schiffman, 1972).

Faulty School Experiences: Dyspedagogia

Behavioral manifestations similar to those of individuals with primary learning disabilities are also noticed in individuals with secondary learning disabilities. This similarity is evident in behavioral manifestations resulting from environmental factors such as traumatic school experiences due to faulty teaching (also referred to as dyspedagogia [Kauffman & Hallahan, 1976]). Faulty teaching may result from poor teaching methods and a conflict between a teaching style and a student's learning style.

Impaired Home Experience

The effect of an enriched or impoverished home environment on the future learning of children has been well documented in the literature. Home environment stress, stemming from high parental expectations and disapproval of one's efforts commensurate with abilities, may lead to discouragement and resignation. Other home environmental factors include poor management, chaotic life-style, and breakdown in the family. While these conditions may not necessarily produce learning disabilities, the behavioral adaptations of the individual may be manifested in behavioral characteristics very similar to those stemming from neurophysiological dysfunction.

SUMMARY AND CONCLUSIONS

The LD specialist must be aware that those with learning disabilities comprise a heterogeneous group of individuals displaying various behavioral patterns. Likewise, no single etiology accounts for all learning disabilities subtypes. The behavioral patterns of individuals with LD, according to the literature, affect the way they interact with the environment. Influenced by both constitutional and environmental factors, these behavioral patterns affect the way individuals with learning disabilities approach learning tasks as well as the manner in which they process information. This suggests the need for the adaptation of instructional methodologies and approaches to accommodate the idiosyncratic mode of the learning-disabled individual.

Learning Disabilities: A Perspective

Questions to Consider

1. **When did the field of learning disabilities appear and what were its historical antecedents?**

2. **What influenced the evolution of the field of learning disabilities?**

3. **What changes have occurred in the way we view and treat individuals with learning disabilities?**

4. **What may the future hold for the field of learning disabilities?**

LEARNING DISABILITIES IN PERSPECTIVE

The field of learning disabilities is relatively new. As late as the 1950s, until professionals and parents acquired knowledge and understanding of learning disabilities, many of the individuals who are now considered as having learning disabilities were not receiving special help, or at best they were placed with "educational misfits" in one or two special classes usually housed on the perimeter of the school grounds. These classes consisted of children who did not perform well in school, were academically behind, and were problematic in the regular classroom. Based on current knowledge, these individuals were primarily the educable retarded, learning disabled, behavior disordered, and even severely handicapped. Slowly it became apparent that many of these children exhibiting school problems were not mentally retarded or emotionally disturbed. They did not show clear evidence of brain damage nor demonstrate any physical disability (Reid, 1988); they simply were not able to function adequately in school despite their apparent normal or above-normal intelligence.

Yet as we look at the field of learning disabilities today, we must acknowledge the significant progress achieved during the last 4 decades. Now, students with learning disabilities, for the most part, are receiving free services in their local schools, usually in resource rooms or special classes designed to accommodate their needs. Support services are also available in some community colleges and universities.

The Chronology of Learning Disabilities

The historical development of the field of learning disabilities must be viewed within the context of society, societal needs, changes, philosophical convictions, and legislative mandates. The historical events in the field serve as specific landmarks with influences that cross all geographic borders and generations. The chronological development of the field can be viewed from the following perspectives:

1. Historical antecedents
2. The "brain-injured" phase (1935–1955)
3. The formation of the field of learning disabilities (1955–1965)
4. The expansion and proliferation phase (1965–1975)
5. The changing directions phase (1975–1985)
6. The contemporary phase: emerging directions and future perspectives (1985 to present)

Table 2–1 presents the chronology of the field of learning disabilities with its major demarcating events.

Historical Antecedents

Four aspects can be considered historical antecedents to the development of the LD field: (a) the evolution of the field of special education, characterized by work with individuals with mental retardation and by the contributions of Itard, Seguin, Montessori, and Decroly; (b) the brain research of Gall, Jackson, and Hinshelwood, and the work of Head and Goldstein with brain-injured adults; (c) the influence of 20th-century developments in psychology; and (d) the early attempts to remediate learning problems in reading and other areas by professionals such as Fernald, Orton, Gillingham, Stillman, and Monroe.

Beginning as early as 3000 B.C., accounts of handicapping conditions have appeared throughout history. However, concern with handicaps was minimal until the late 18th century. Then the French and American revolutions with their philosophy of individual human rights, scientific advances, and sweeping technological and economic changes led to changes in society's perception of handicapped individuals. An increasing awareness of the existence of handicapped individuals prompted the belief that with proper treatment these individuals could be helped. In the renowned case of the "wild boy of Aveyron," for example, Itard (1774–1838), a physician for the deaf, was convinced that education could transform the boy into a normal human being. Having used sensory training to teach speech to the deaf, Itard decided to employ sensory training methods with the wild boy (Itard, Trans. 1962 by Humphrey & Humphrey). Belief in the power of education was common during a time when science had begun to make giant leaps and when philosophy placed no limits on the possibilities inherent within the human race. Seguin (1812–1880), a physician, neurologist, and educator influenced by the work of Itard, further developed Itard's sensory training approaches (Seguin, 1866). The inclusion of sensory motor training in educational methods was further advocated and developed by Decroly (1937) and Montessori (1912). They refined sensory training and developed teaching approaches that emphasized the integration of sensory motor and perceptual training in academic teaching.

Brain research and studies of specific disorders related to brain dysfunction by Broca (1824–1880), Gall (1758–1828), Jackson (1835–1911), Goldstein (1878–1965), Head (1861–1940), and Hinshelwood (1859–1919) have influenced the course of the field of learning disabilities. These physicians were interested in the discovery of a relationship between brain functions and behavior. They were par-

Table 2–1   The Chronology of Learning Disabilities: Highlights of Major Events & Issues

Historical Antecedents

- Sensory Training
- Brain Research
- Work with Brain-Injured Adults/Children
- Early Attempts at Remediation of Learning Problems
- Interdiscipline Influences

Brain-Injured Phase 1935–1955

- Wayne County Training School
  Exogenous retarded
- Brain-Injured Concept
- Work with Cerebral Palsied Children
- Montgomery County Project

Formation of the Field of Learning Disabilities 1955–1965

- Origin of LD Term
- LD Definitions
- Formation of ACLD (now LDA)
- Formulation of LD Constructs
- LD Studied from Different Perspectives
  Communication/language disorders
  Perceptual-motor disorders
- Development of Diagnosis and Intervention Approaches
- Process Training

Expansion & Proliferation Phase 1965–1975

- Formation of DCLD within CEC
- Proliferation of ACLD
- Passage of PL 94–142
- Service Delivery Models
- Development of Diagnosis/Intervention Approaches
- Process Training

Changing Directions Phase 1975–1985

- Questioning the Practice
  Process Training
  Assessment and placement
  LD definition
  LD or not LD
- Mainstreaming/Least Restrictive Environment Alternatives
- Secession of DCLD (CLD) from CEC
- Formation of DLD within CEC
- Formation of IARLD

Contemporary Phase 1985 to Present

- Reaffirmation of LD Construct
- Mainstreaming/Least Restrictive Environment Alternatives/REI
- Collaborative Multiple Discipline Research
- Search for a Taxonomy of LD
- Diagnosis and Intervention based on
  Information processing
  Metacognition/learning strategies
  Curriculum-based assessment
  Systematic teaching
- Delivery of Services Emphasis
  Integrated/comprehensive curriculum
  Strategies for learning
- Collaboration and Consultation with Regular Educators

ticularly interested in discovering the etiological factors in communication disorders, that is, thinking, speaking, listening, and reading (Kirk, 1971). Their research provided the foundation for the development of intervention approaches for disorders of spoken and written language, as well as of perceptual and motor processes by Orton and others in the early part of the 20th century.

The work of Head and Goldstein with soldiers who had suffered brain injuries during World War I was influential in the conceptualizing of learning disabilities being caused by brain injury. In 1942, Goldstein published a report on his observations of brain-injured adults, *Aftereffects of Brain Injuries in War*. These brain-injured veterans exhibited disordered behaviors, which included emotional lability, perceptual disturbances, and distractibility. Goldstein referred to these behaviors as the catastrophic reaction of a brain-injured organism. During the same period, Europeans suffered through an epidemic of encephalitis that left many individuals, including children, with brain damage. These children exhibited behaviors similar to Goldstein's brain-injured adults, including irritability, restlessness, and emotional lability. The description of these characteristics provided support for the brain-damaged etiology of learning disabilities.

During the early part of this century, professionals from various backgrounds were preoccupied with a puzzling problem of children with otherwise normal intelligence who had difficulties in acquiring academic learning. In the 1920s, Grace Fernald was concerned with the difficulties these children had in reading and spelling. Through her efforts and clinical work at the Fernald School, University of California, Los Angeles, she developed a multisensory approach to remedial reading that has come to be known as the Fernald reading method (Fernald, 1943). Marione Monroe (1932) developed a diagnostic reading test and a program to remediate reading difficulties. Samuel T. Orton (1937), a neurologist, suggested that language problems and reading and spelling problems are due to lack of cerebral dominance. Along with Anna Gillingham and Bessie Stillman (Gillingham & Stillman, 1936, 1960), he developed a multisensory reading method quite often referred to as the Orton-Gillingham or the Gillingham-Stillman reading method. The Orton Dyslexia Society is named in honor of Samuel T. Orton.

Many disciplines have influenced the field of learning disabilities. These include Gestalt psychology, of which Goldstein was a disciple (Hallahan & Kauffman, 1976); psychoanalysis, which treated learning disabilities as an emotional disturbance; and developmental psychology—primarily the concept of developmental diagnosis (Bühler, 1935), the work of Bruner (1966) and other cognitive psychologists, and the work of the neuropsychologist Hebb (1949, 1958) and his concept of cell assembly.

The "Brain-Injured" Phase

The "brain-injured" phase (approximately 1935–1955) was noted for the distinguished work of Alfred Strauss and Heinz Werner at the Wayne County Training School, Northville, Michigan, and their subsequent influence on the field of learning disabilities. The term *gehirnverletzt* was widely used in Germany in the post-World War I period. It was literally translated into English as "brain injured" and was introduced to this country through the work of Werner and Strauss. The term implied that behaviors of individuals and their various disorders, such as disorders of spoken and written language and disorders of perceptual motor functions, were attributable to brain injury or brain dysfunction. These disorders manifested themselves in the individual's inability to read, write, solve mathematical calculations, accomplish other school work, participate in general activities, and adjust to life. It thus became common to refer to this condition from the point of view of etiology. The term *brain injury* and/or *brain damage* was used to explain the basis for disorders in learning and for the behavior of these individuals.

Strauss, a physician who was greatly influenced by the work of Head and Goldstein, observed and treated World War I veterans who demonstrated observable brain injuries that were typified by their catastrophic reactions. Working with mentally retarded children, Strauss along with Werner (1943) distinguished between endogenous (familial) and exogenous retardation. Exogenous retardation was presumably due to an external cause, that is, brain injury; individuals with exogenous retardation exhibited behaviors very similar to those of Goldstein's adult subjects. Children with exogenous retardation were described as hyperactive, emotionally labile, perceptually disordered, impulsive, destructible, and perseverative. This collection of symptoms came to be known as the "Strauss syndrome," or the "brain-injured" syndrome (Stevens & Birch, 1957).

In his later years, Strauss turned his attention to brain-injured children of normal intelligence. The characteristics of children with exogenous retardation were extended to children with normal levels of intelligence. Brain injury resulting from exogenous etiologies could be assessed and diagnosed and appropriate remedial techniques developed. The behavioral syndromes of these exogenous brain-injured individuals were described by Strauss and Werner (1943) in terms of disturbed perception, disordered conceptual processes, language disabilities, thinking disorders, attention deficits, and behavior problems. These characteristics were similar to the pathological characteristics found in the brain-injured adult. The brain injury etiology in learning disabilities is attributed to Strauss more than to any other individual. His books, *Psychopathology and Education of the Brain-Injured Child*, Volume I, coauthored with Laura Lehtinen in 1947, and Volume II, coauthored with Newell Kephart in 1955, and *The Other Child* (1951), written by Richard Lewis with Strauss and Lehtinen, became landmarks and served to legitimize the concept of brain-injured children. The Wayne County Training School for brain-injured children was "a hotbed of professional activity, inquisitiveness, research and excellence" (Cruickshank, 1976, p. 102) and served as a reference point, a model, and a home base for many of the pioneers in the field of learning disabilities, including William Cruickshank, Newell C. Kephart, Samuel Kirk, Ray Barsch, and Elizabeth Freidus, and has directly or indirectly affected the work of other specialists such as Marianne Frostig and Gerald Getman.

During the latter years of this phase, Cruickshank (1953) published the results of a replication study of Werner and Strauss' work with cerebral-palsied children of near-normal, normal, and above-normal intelligence. According to Hallahan, Kauffman, and Lloyd (1985), this research project was significant because it was "the first major extension of the research of Werner and Strauss to children with normal

was critically reviewed to examine practices in the field. The main issues of concern were process training, assessment and diagnostic practices, referral and placement procedures, the heterogeneity of learning disabilities, and learning disabilities subtypes.

The most notable issue, with far-reaching impact, was that of process training. Researchers have questioned the efficacy of process training and have challenged its basic assumptions. They have maintained that there was no empirical support for the contention that sensory-motor, perceptual, and psycholinguistic training or remediation is a necessary prerequisite to the attainment of academic skills (Ysseldyke & Salvia, 1974). Further, they doubted the fractioning of behavior through tests with questionable validity and poor reliability, which were developed to fit theoretical constructs without adequate empirical support (Mann, 1971; Mann & Phillips, 1967; Ysseldyke & Salvia, 1974). A review of research studies that attempted to remediate sensory-motor and visual perception deficits failed to support the value of sensory-motor perceptual training and the assumption that the lack of sensory-motor and perceptual adequacy cause academic failures (Goodman, 1973; Hammill, 1972; Hammill, Goodman, & Wiederholt, 1974; Larsen & Hammill, 1975). Similarly, Hammill and Larsen (1974) reported the results of their analysis of 38 studies that purported to train psycholinguistic abilities based on the ITPA. The authors concluded that "the efficacy of training psycholinguistic functioning has not been conclusively demonstrated" (p. 12).

The conclusion based on the analysis of the psycholinguistic training studies did not remain unchallenged. Minskoff (1975) presented a critique of the Hammill and Larsen (1974) review and delineated the variables that must be described and controlled in all efficacy studies. Minskoff warned against the skepticism resulting from such inadequate analysis of the efficacy studies, stating that "such skepticism can be lethal to the field of learning disabilities" (p. 143). Similarly, Lund, Foster, and McCall-Perez (1978), in their reanalysis of the same efficacy studies of psycholinguistic training, concluded that the "efficacy of psycholinguistic training is far from being encapsulated in a definitive black and white statement" (p. 317). Ensuing studies by Sowell et al. (1979), Kavale (1982), and Larsen, Parker, and Hammill (1982) have not resulted in the resolution of the issue.

The efficacy studies and the subsequent professional discourse have placed many learning disabilities specialists in a quandary. Many practitioners discontinued process training, but new approaches were lacking. For a while, LD specialists abandoned the use of any specialized teaching approaches with learning-disabled individuals. A gradual shift toward approaches based on task analysis and direct instruction began to take place.

The Council for Learning Disabilities seceded from the Council for Exceptional Children in 1983, and the Division for Learning Disabilities was formed within the CEC. The International Association for Research in Learning Disabilities (IARLD) was established. The Association for Children with Learning Disabilities first changed its name to the Association for Children and Adults with Learning Disabilities, to reflect commitment to adults with learning disabilities, and then in 1989 to Learning Disabilities Association (LDA). At the same time, this period underwent its broadest expansion, with almost 2 million individuals identified as learning disabled nationwide, comprising about 4% of the school population and 40% of the total handicapped population served in the public schools.

The Contemporary Phase: Emerging Directions and Future Perspectives

This contemporary phase (approximately 1985 to the present) is characterized by the affirmation of learning disabilities as a valid construct (Keogh, 1987) and by the recognition of the need for both basic and applied research in learning disabilities. Problems in eligibility criteria, assessment and identification procedures, instructional variables, and service delivery practices have fostered many discussions and research symposia (D. J. Johnson, 1988; Vaughn & Bos, 1987). In addition, more experimental studies have been conducted, and a new body of knowledge has emerged, resulting in new volumes on theory and research on learning disabilities, such as the work of Ceci (1986), Kavale (1988), Kavale et al. (1987, 1988), Kavanagh and Truss (1988), Swanson and Keogh (1990), Torgesen and Wong (1986), and Vaughn and Bos (1987). The reader is encouraged to refer to these volumes for in-depth coverage of various topics of current concern in learning disabilities.

Studies in cognitive function and information processing and their implications for individuals with learning disabilities have guided research and practice in implementing strategic learning and metacognitive approaches with learning-disabled students. Principles of applied behavior analysis and cognitive behavior modification have guided the use of task analysis, curriculum-based assessment and instruction, and behavior management systems. The integration of these approaches has served as the basis for the development of a direct strategy instruction approach with learning-disabled students. Emphasis is placed on LD individuals as active learners capable of learning strategies and of being engaged in strategic production and able to monitor and regulate their activities. This period has resulted in a large expansion of service delivery models and approaches for adolescents and young adults with learning disabilities. The regular classroom, with support services from the resource room, remains the most prevalent placement for LD students. Collaboration and consultation with regular educators have begun to take place. The Regular Education Initiative (REI) has called for the merger of special and regular education (see also chapter 5). Additionally, a concern for the quality of intervention frameworks for LD students has resulted in a call for more comprehensive intervention programs that extend beyond the teaching of the three R's to the teaching of social and life adjustment skills and strategies for learning and problem solving that generalize across all domains in school and life. At the same time, teaching in the three R's curriculum and the content areas is perceived from an integrated perspective exposing these students to the core curriculum and to conceptual knowledge appropriate to their age. Thus the remedial reading program involves literacy experiences along with basic skills acquisition, and math concept instruction is integrated with practical math. The present growth in research is supplying new and innovative approaches for individuals with learning disabilities.

Future research is essential for continued progress in the field. The need for collaborative efforts between university-sponsored research programs and professionals in the field, involving multiple disciplines, to effectively carry out long-term basic and applied research is essential (Keogh, 1986; C. R. Smith, 1986). On a research level,

> . . . we need to provide a systematic way of organizing and describing the range of individual attributes which characterize LD individuals . . . identify causes and correlates of various LD conditions, and to document the sequences over time . . . [on an applied level] we need to determine which interventions or treatments are effective with which kinds of LD . . . consider institutional arrangements for services, to develop and evaluate training programs for professionals, and to improve the quality and content of diagnosis and assessment. (Keogh, 1986, p. 459)

A major concern is to develop an LD classification system, that is, a taxonomy of learning disabilities based on learning disabilities subtypes. Such a system is necessary for the development of a sound theoretical basis for learning disabilities. Such a basis should facilitate the identification of learning disabilities and their primary problems, thereby leading to intervention approaches most appropriate to specific learning disabilities. The purpose of a taxonomy and classification system is (a) to understand the nature of the problem and thus provide direction for the remediation technique; (b) to facilitate the delivery of services; (c) to maximize professional communication; (d) to facilitate advocacy and to direct support and attention to the problem; and (e) to guide further research in the field. Furthermore, Lyon (1988) stated:

> Attempts should be made to reclassify the heterogeneous group of learning disabilities objectively into smaller homogeneous subtypes to promote more precise study of the learner reading behavior and thus effects of different forms of instruction on improving such behaviors. The virtue of a reliable classification of learning disabilities is that for each subtype identified, differential intervention, prognosis, a specific correlation with educational, behavioral, physiological, and neuropsychological functions are far more reliable than what has been accomplished so far. Thus, detailed studies of LD subtypes and their responses to different types of educational interventions can help to identify and describe relations among cognitive skills, information-processing characteristics, linguistic and perceptual capabilities, and reading skill development far more precisely than if the LD population was investigated as a heterogeneous whole. (p. 35)

One would expect that the emergence of homogeneous subtypes of learning-disabled individuals will facilitate the identification of specific disorders and their causes and will eventually guide both prevention and intervention programs. "Although at present no commonly agreed-upon subtypes of LD appear to exist, a subtyping system that produced clear, reliable, and educationally relevant results should be the focus of LD research in the future" (Scruggs, 1988, p. 30). Thus the identification of learning disabilities subtypes offers much promise in guiding the development of the LD field.

If those in the field are to continue to make progress, they must have vision. Looking into the 1990s and beyond, one can foresee (a) the laying to rest of the controversies about learning disabilities; (b) increasing contribution from the field of neurology to the understanding of learning disabilities and learning disabilities subtypes (specifically the use of new neurophysiological diagnostic procedures such as computerized tomography [CT] scans, magnetic resonance imaging [MRI], and the use of brain electrical activity mapping [BEAM]); (c) the development of a taxonomy of learning disabilities; and (d) the study of different intervention strategies and their effects on different subgroups of learning-disabled individuals (C. R. Smith, 1986). On the applied level, the merging of behavioral, cognitive, and information-processing perspectives will direct our intervention approaches. Emphasis will be placed on (a) effective intervention strategies in the least restrictive environment; (b) systematic remedial instruction procedures; (c) information-processing approaches to assessment, combined with task analysis and curriculum-based assessment; (d) instructional approaches that emphasize metacognitive and learning strategy procedures; (e) increased emphasis on social skills training; and (f) the preparation of learning-disabled individuals for independent and productive adult lives. Service delivery models will continue to place emphasis on serving students with LD in the least restrictive environment with increased collaboration and consultation with regular educators.

Considering its brief history, the field of learning disabilities has made giant leaps. Despite the problems currently facing it and the individuals it serves, the LD field has an optimistic future (McCarthy, 1989; Smith, 1986). Within the historical context of special education, learning disabilities is known as "the avant-garde field of specialization" (Hallahan & Kauffman, 1976, p. 2), and as such, it must continue its course of new and innovative developments.

SUMMARY AND CONCLUSIONS

This chapter presents a historical account of the field of learning disabilities and the contributions made by its pioneers. Those pioneers have faced many critical issues related to the formulation of the LD construct, identification and labeling, and the nature of intervention approaches for LD individuals. The field has continued to be dynamic, and in attempting to resolve many of the issues, those in it have embarked on new and innovative undertakings at both the research and applied levels.

CHAPTER
3

Learning Disabilities in Adolescents and Young Adults

Questions to Consider | 1. **Do learning disabilities disappear as an individual reaches adolescence?**

2. **What are the characteristics of adolescents and young adults with learning disabilities?**

3. **What are the ramifications of learning disabilities for adolescents and young adults?**

4. **Is there a relationship between learning disabilities and juvenile delinquency?**

In chapter 1, we discussed the characteristics of individuals with learning disabilities. The purpose of this chapter is to provide a more in-depth understanding of adolescents and young adults with learning disabilities. These individuals pose a challenge to the LD specialist. The pioneers in the field focused on children of elementary school age and directed their major efforts toward the young child with LD (Mann, Goodman, & Wiederholt, 1978). Theoretical formulations about the nature of learning disabilities, identification, assessment, and treatment approaches were all formulated from the perspective of the young child. Several factors accounted for this trend: (a) it was hoped that proper remedial intervention would "cure" the elementary school child's problem so that he or she would be able to function without much difficulty in the mainstream of the secondary school environment; (b) the early grades—primarily the third—were the source of most referrals to classes for LD individuals (Ariel, 1975); (c) parents of young children took active interest in and provided input to the LD field; (d) for the most part, the pioneers of the field chose to concentrate on and work with young children; and (e) adolescence, as a period of growth, has its own mystique and is difficult to study, even without the additional dimension of handicapping conditions.

LEARNING DISABILITIES IN ADOLESCENTS

A youngster's learning disabilities do not disappear when adolescence begins. While there are variations in the LD characteristics of adolescents, certain traits are more common than others. The plight of the adolescent with learning disabilities is exemplified by the following profile.

Sam is a 14½-year-old youngster classified as learning disabled who currently attends a junior high special day class for students with learning disabilities. He has been attending special programs for LD students since Grade 3, when initial referral was made to special education and he was diagnosed as having learning disabilities. Sam still cannot read, spell, or write. His performance on the Peabody Individual Achievement Test-Revised (PIAT-R) shows him to be at a grade level of 1.8 in reading recognition, 1.7 in spelling, and 3.1 in math. At school, Sam is responsive and exhibits no significant behavior problems. He gets along well with his peers in the special day class. At home and in the neighborhood, Sam is a loner, spending most of his time in the garage fixing and polishing his moped. His parents say that when they are invited to friends' houses, Sam prefers to stay at home. This is especially true when the family friends have a son or daughter Sam's age.

There is a general apathy in Sam's approach to school and life. He is very discouraged and has dim hopes that he will ever read or write, yet he expresses a willingness and a desire to learn those skills. His math teacher reports that Sam quite often says he cannot do the assigned arithmetic problems when in fact he can do them. With teacher prompts, he usually completes his work.

Sam's intellectual abilities are within the normal range. His WISC-R Full Scale IQ is 91 with a Verbal IQ of 85 and a Performance IQ of 92. His subtest scatter shows a range of 4–11, with the low-functioning subtest scores primarily in the verbal areas. Sam does exhibit some gross motor deficiencies, reflected by his awkward walking and running. He speaks very softly and displays a moderate lag in his communication skills.

The preceding profile and clinical observations of other such adolescents confirm that the LD characteristics associated with younger ages do not disappear as children reach adolescence. While some characteristics appear in a more subtle manner, others are exaggerated. Moreover, new characteristics evolve as a direct result of adolescent development and the LD adolescents' interaction with the environment. At the same time, these youngsters also exhibit characteristics common to all adolescents.

In general, adolescents with learning disabilities develop as their peers do. Because of their handicapping condition, however, they have to deal with more than the usual adolescent developmental patterns and growth—their disabilities confound the usual patterns. The child with LD enters into adolescence carrying the burden of his learning disabilities which magnifies the frustrations, challenges, and rewards usually associated with this period (O'Connor, 1984). While the baggage differs with each LD adolescent, there are certain common denominators: a deep sense of being defective, a suspicion of helpful adults, and a fear of change. The child with learning disabilities who has experienced a prolonged history of school failure, inappropriate social and peer relationships, bitter interactions with adults, and general feelings of pervasive incompetencies enters the adolescent period with a disadvantage.

Studying normal aspects of adolescent development can help the LD specialist to understand adolescents with learning disabilities, and thus to view them from a general perspective. Behaviors that are usually considered "normal" can be viewed as maladaptive by an LD specialist unaware of typical adolescent developmental patterns. Adolescents are expected to challenge their environment, to challenge parents and teachers, and not to accept everything dictated by adults. Likewise, it is expected that adolescents with LD will resist parental coaching in an attempt to achieve social and psychological independence. Understanding such typical aspects of adolescent development and how they interact with learning disabilities allows us to offer LD adolescents a more effective intervention program.

CHARACTERISTICS OF ADOLESCENTS WITH LEARNING DISABILITIES

The literature on adolescents with learning disabilities contains various descriptions of these individuals. Most are based on clinical observations rather than on empirical research and "reflect unknown degrees of variability among both the youngsters studied and observer's judgements" (G. Smith, 1983, p. 262).

The characteristics of the learning-disabled adolescent can be viewed from two main perspectives: (a) characteristics associated with adolescent developmental patterns, and (b) characteristics associated with adaptations to the environment.

Adolescent Developmental Patterns

Physical Development

Most adolescents with LD are not distinguishable from their peers in terms of physical development. Physical changes during this period require all adolescents to adjust their perceptions of themselves and others. Some adolescents with learning disabilities may have more difficulty adapting to their physical development. A successful integration of the physical self into an individual's self-identity has a far-reaching effect on overall self-concept. Development of body image contributes to the development of self-concept and affects the general functions of the adolescent with learning disabilities in school and in life. Some learning-disabled adolescents may exhibit general motor awkwardness, hyperactivity, poor fine motor coordination, and deficits in body image.

Perceptual-Motor Development

Perceptual-motor difficulties manifest themselves in a more subtle manner, as hyperactivity, distraction, poor attention, uncoordination, and some perceptual irregularities (Deshler, 1978). Marsh and Price (1980) note the variations in the characteristics of adolescents with learning disabilities, including some compensations in perceptual-motor impairments. Adolescent hyperactivity is exhibited by finger tapping, grimacing, and tics (Marsh & Price, 1980; Wilcox, 1970). Emotional lability is expressed by inappropriate responses to stimuli. General coordination deficits are reflected in students' handwriting. Attention deficits appear as difficulties in listening to lectures and attaining information in class. Impulsivity manifests itself with overreaction to stimuli. According to Weiss and Weiss (1976), basically all general symptoms noted in a younger child appear in a somewhat altered manner in an adolescent with learning disabilities.

Language Development

Immature speech patterns, mild speech irregularities, and articulation problems are generally noted in the learning-disabled adolescent (A. J. Harris, 1970). Specific oral language disorders include distinct limitations in acquisition and comprehension of syntax, error patterns in sentences of higher grammatical complexity, and quantitative delay in acquisition of morphology. Findings show that both oral and written deficits associated with individuals with LD may persist into adolescence and may relate to earlier observed difficulties in language processing (Sitko & Gillespie, 1978). Many adolescents and young adults experience the most difficulties with written expressive language—compositions and other written outputs necessary to meet course requirements.

Cognitive Development

Adolescent cognitive development is marked by formal intellectual operations—the capacity for reasoning and abstract thinking, reflective thinking, and symbolization. Piaget (1966) asserts that between the sixth grade and the junior year of high school, most individuals enter a period of formal operations and acquire the tendency to formulate and test hypotheses. Adolescents are able to analyze their own thinking and construct theories that furnish the cognitive and evaluative basis for the assumption of adult roles. Furthermore, adolescents can look at themselves with some objectivity and evaluate themselves with respect to personality, intelligence, and appearance (Elkind, 1970). They become intellectually more mature. They are able to think more abstractly than children, and they can make hypotheses and utilize abstractions, reasoning, ideals, inventions, and mathematical logic (Piaget, 1963). According to Conger and Peterson (1984), "the development of hypothetico-deductive thinking and related aspects of formal operations makes adolescent thought much richer, broader, and more flexible than that of the concrete-operational child" (p. 162). Furthermore, at this stage, formal and abstract thinking abilities are developed that enable young adults to participate in philosophical thinking, plan for the future, and understand the historical past (Elkind, 1972).

Adolescents with learning disabilities exhibit general delay in abstract thinking and hypothetical reasoning, which stems primarily from production deficiencies (Torgesen, 1979, 1980; Wiens, 1983) rather than from deficiencies in cognitive abilities. They do not structure and organize their thoughts (Wiens, 1983). In addition, they exhibit production deficiencies (Torgesen, 1972, 1980) and deficiencies in control-executive functions, which involve such activities as planning and organizing (Deshler, Schumaker, Alley, Warner, & Clark, 1982).

Social and Emotional Development

The period of adolescence is marked by significant social and emotional development. As youngsters grow older, they move from dependency, with all needs and wants fulfilled by significant adults, to maturation and independency, directing their own activities and being accountable for their own actions. This process of moving from a nurtured immediate environment to a larger environmental sphere that must meet one's social and emotional needs is crucial for the development of a healthy individual with a healthy personality and sound interpersonal relationships.

According to Sabatino and Mauser (1978), "the psychological adaptation of a given individual to one's environment represents a total adjustment process; that is, each person is molded by how well one thinks he or she feels" (p. 6). It also represents the totality of events that is happening in one's immediate family, school, and work, including interpersonal relationships with parents, teachers, peers, and significant others. It portrays the individual's psychological adjustment mechanism and coping behaviors. Sabatino and Mauser (1978) further contend that "it seems necessary to develop systematic ways of looking at human adjustment and/or how each aspect interacts to promote or inhibit that process. . . . [T]he adaptation of man to his world is dependent on . . . the biological, socio-cultural, and psychological [factors which] form the complex whole involved in adaptation" (p. 6).

The psychological adaptation of adolescents with LD is often hampered by continuous failure experiences along various domains of life. They are continuously thwarted by an inability to achieve success in school, to meet parental expectations, and to interact and/or behave appropriately in other interactive environments. These adolescents may develop a negative self-concept that directly affects their approaches to new learning situations and new experiences. They develop poor social perception and have difficulties maintaining interpersonal relationships (Bryan, 1977; Kronick, 1978; Sisterhen & Gerber, 1989). Social/emotional maladjustment thus becomes concomitant to learning disabilities (McKinney, 1984; Thompson, 1986). In addition, such adolescents may acquire passive learning patterns (Torgesen, 1977, 1980) and exhibit the learned helplessness syndrome. These behavioral patterns associated with a prolonged history of failure and frustration, along with the production deficiencies of learning-disabled adolescents, may render individuals incapable of conquering the demands of the school environment, the home environment, and the community at large.

Many concomitant emotional and personality difficulties beset adolescents with LD (Deshler 1978). According to Deshler, factors related to their social/emotional adjustment include (a) inability to generalize from one situation to another, (b) oversensitivity, (c) inflexibility, and (d) difficulty in interpreting verbal and nonverbal communication patterns.

The relationship between the family and the adolescent also changes. For the "normal" adolescent, the family, while maintaining a powerful influence on the individual, is no longer the primary source of influence (Gullotta, 1983), although parents usually do continue the role of socializing agent while facilitating autonomy and separation of their children (Newman & Newman, 1986). Relationships with peers take on primary importance, and with maturity, the adolescent establishes a separate identity with his or her peer group.

Because of handicapping conditions and the situations resulting therefrom, learning-disabled adolescents tend to depend strongly upon parents for assistance in coping with school and life in general. Parents in turn are frequently very protective and do not allow the flexibility and elasticity associated with the development of independence typical of adolescence. In addition, because of their poor interpersonal relationships, low self-esteem, and the restrictive nature of their interpersonal relationships and peer interactions, adolescents with LD have more difficulty forming peer identity and fitting into peer groups than do other adolescents. This lack of appropriate social skills has been viewed by parents, teachers, and other professionals as a very serious handicapping factor (Wanant, 1983).

Most adolescents with learning disabilities are likely to have difficulty with all stages of psychosocial development (Blanton, 1984). The negative effects of academic failure on self-esteem and emotional development have been well documented. It is only reasonable to assume that consistent failure in academics, with the accompanying frustration, ridicule, and criticism, would contribute to the development of some secondary emotional problems.

Adaptation to the Environment

As they get older, learning-disabled individuals develop adaptive behaviors to their handicapping condition in an attempt to cope with the demands of the immediate environment. These adaptive and/or maladaptive behaviors can be seen as protective mechanisms.

Fine and Zeitlin (1984) contend that such adolescents often learn maladaptive coping behaviors to protect themselves from the stress of failure. These maladaptive academic coping strategies include lack of organizational skills, passivity in learning situations, excessive reliance on external cues for feedback, lack of flexibility, inability to generalize, difficulties in sustaining attention, poor tolerance for frustration, and inadequate social skills.

Kay (1986) concurs that adolescents with LD develop ineffective coping mechanisms that limit their academic success and thwart their emotional development. Some of these ineffective coping skills, used for protection, include not asking questions, resisting making choices, exhibiting discomfort when given a compliment, having poor eye contact, being poor risk takers, failing to use effective study skills, failing to use self-monitoring techniques and, after completing a task successfully, usually being unaware of having used any strategies at all.

Those individuals who struggle with learning problems and continue to experience failure for months or years become deficient in fundamental skills as well as in their approach to learning. In addition to experiencing feelings of inadequacy and worthlessness, they become unable to pursue learning appropriately. They develop feelings of learned helplessness, quite often characterized by the "I cannot do" syndrome. "Learned helplessness can be acquired early. The child's objective knowledge of his own cognitive processes is obviously contaminated by his feelings of competence" (A. L. Brown, 1978, p. 92).

As a result of the negative interactions with learning experiences, such an individual becomes an "inactive learner" (Torgesen, 1977, 1980; Wong, 1979), dependent upon others for regulating learning. "Thus the LD adolescent has particular reason for being a passive learner and, as a result, has often learned to be dependent on others. This passivity and dependence cannot help but interfere with and even negate purposive thinking. . . . [Furthermore] this learned helplessness and passivity are obvious liabilities when it comes to dealing with tasks requiring active structuring of information and problem solving, which is what most school learning requires" (Wiens, 1983, p. 146). Research further points to a production deficiency (Flavell & Wellman, 1977) of individuals with learning disabilities. The "learning disabled children as a group do not engage readily in certain organized, goal directed strategies that aid performance on intellectual tasks" (Torgesen, 1982, p. 46). The individual with LD does not perform well in school because of a failure to "adapt to task through the use of efficient and organized strategies" (Torgesen, 1980, p. 19).

Academic Development

By the time children with LD reach adolescence, they still have deficits in basic skills. Schumaker, Deshler, Alley, and Warner (1983) contend that these adolescents reach a plateau of basic skills during the secondary grades—by about the 10th grade they are at a 5th-grade level of ability. However, this plateau should not be viewed as the maximum potential, but as the result of less than adequate learning environment and instruction. Kronick (1981) reports that learning-disabled adolescents are disorganized in planning how to use their time to complete a task; limited in their ability to look at problems, analyze them, and select reasonable alternatives; rigid in their habits; disorganized; egocentric in their judgment; and unrealistic in setting goals, which results in expecting too much or too little. Schumaker et al. add that such adolescents frequently have deficits in study skills and strategies and that the deficit in their ability to create and apply strategies is caused by immature executive functioning.

Many adolescents with learning disabilities have low academic self-concept and do not expect to do well in school. According to Hiebert, Wong, and Hunter (1982), teachers and parents of these individuals also held low academic expectations for them, and the teachers saw them as engaging in more socially unacceptable behaviors than nondisabled adolescents. In contrast, normally achieving students had higher academic expectations and higher academic self-concept.

Individuals often base their self-esteem on others' reactions to their behaviors. An individual who receives negative feedback from peers, teachers, and parents is likely to have a negative sense of self-worth. Low self-esteem is said to be a cause of anxiety in learning-disabled adolescents. Anxiety is high when a person has a poor self-opinion and feels easily threatened (Peck, 1981). Anxiety can interfere with academic functioning and the development of peer relationships; excessive anxiety has even been associated with reduced physical growth and development (Newman & Newman, 1986). This may account for the smaller stature that is sometimes mentioned as a characteristic of adolescents with LD.

LEARNING DISABILITIES IN YOUNG ADULTS

During the past several years, learning disability professionals have become interested in the young adult with LD. There is growing evidence that learning disabilities do not disappear when a student leaves the school system. This is exemplified by the following profile of Tim.

Tim is a 20-year-old young adult with learning disabilities. After receiving special educational services during most of his life, he has finally managed to graduate from high school and is now faced with the bleak prospect of not knowing what to do. He is tired of schooling, yet unable to find employment. Tim's cognitive abilities are at the normal range. In academic areas, he functions at about the sixth-grade reading level and about the fourth-grade level in math. He has tremendous difficulties in writing, and his spelling is at about the third-grade level. He has difficulties in initiating and maintaining social-interpersonal relationships and as a result spends most of his time at home watching TV. He wanders aimlessly and dreams about taking a trip down the coast to South America while deciding what to do with his life.

Tim's profile and those of other such adults seem to indicate that learning disabilities persist into adulthood (Blalock, 1981), manifesting themselves in various aspects of life. "It seems that a type of learning may change with different demands, but inability to profit from experience remains a problem even when a 'curriculum' is no longer an obstacle" (Blalock, 1981, p. 45). In their study of 100 adults with learning disabilities, McCue, Shelly, and Goldstien (1986) found that the patterns and levels of performance obtained did not appear to deviate greatly from what one would expect to find among learning-disabled children.

The handicap of learning disabilities is life-long and intrinsic to the individual. Young adults with learning disabilities continue to experience academically related problems which require specialized assistance.

Characteristics of Young Adults with Learning Disabilities

The characteristics of individuals with LD support the conclusion that learning disabilities persist into adulthood. While there are some inconsistencies in descriptions of the characteristics, the following has been reported in the literature.

Young adults with LD exhibit mild neurological deficits characterized by poor performance on attentional and language-related tasks (McCue et al., 1986). They also exhibit processing deficits that interfere with higher education and vocational goals. These include residual auditory discrimination problems, memory and retrieval problems, and problems at the level of metacognitive abilities and automaticity in integrative use of skills (Blalock, 1981). In addition, subtle auditory language problems, which include discrimination, comprehension, memory, retrieval, sequencing, syntax, formulation, and articulation, appear to persist into adulthood (Blalock, 1982).

Learning-disabled young adults continue to experience academically related problems in reading, written language, and arithmetic (Blalock, 1981; Hoffman et al., 1987). They also exhibit general organization problems, usually evident in taking notes, organizing tasks on the job, planning a project, and scheduling and developing priorities (Blalock, 1981). Furthermore, they encounter difficulties in coping with daily living, career/vocational demands, and personal goals (Alley, Deshler, Clark, Schumaker, & Warner, 1983).

These young adults exhibit low motivation, distractibility, self-concept problems, emotional lability, and lack of organization (Buchanan & Wolf, 1986). They feel frustrated, have no self-confidence, and have difficulties controlling emotions and/or temper followed by depression (Hoffman et al., 1987). Such individuals, Buchanan and Wolf (1986) assert, view themselves as nervous, disorganized, moody, easily discouraged, having self-image problems, shy and self-conscious, insecure, overly passive, and withdrawn.

In studies by W. J. White (1985) and White et al. (1982), young adults with LD were found to be holding jobs with less social status and to be less satisfied with their employment situations when compared to their non-LD peers. More prescriptive drugs and a greater number of arrests and criminal convictions were reported for young adults with LD than for non-LD young adults. The young adults with LD were found to be less satisfied with their school experiences and to have lower aspirations for future education and training. They also reported receiving less support from parents and relatives than their nondisabled peers.

LEARNING DISABILITIES, JUVENILE DELINQUENCY, AND INCARCERATED YOUTH

Learning Disabilities and Juvenile Delinquency

Since the inception of the field of learning disabilities, professionals working with both adjudicated and learning-disabled youth have searched for a causal link between learning disabilities and juvenile delinquency (JD). The reports of similarities between adults with LD and juvenile delinquents, at least on the surface, have provided further reason for the search.

Although there is a paucity of research related to juvenile delinquency and learning disabilities, the search for the link has intensified during the last decade. Charles Murray of the American Institute for Research (AIR) was commissioned by the Office of Juvenile Justice and Delinquency Prevention (OJJDP), U.S. Department of Justice, to review research findings related to possible links between LD and JD through 1975. The AIR report—a major publication in this area—classified the empirical findings into two main data analysis formats: analysis based on qualitative data and analysis based on quantitative data. The qualitative data consisted primarily of case studies of delinquents reported either by the delinquents themselves or by professionals, whereas the quantitative data looked into empirical research studies related to LD and JD. The quantitative data was further classified into three groups: "(1) studies reporting on the simple association between conditions of being delinquent and those of being learning disabled; (2) studies reporting on the magnitude of the difference in the incidence of learning disabilities among delinquent and non-delinquent populations; (3) studies reporting on the incidents of learning disability among delinquents without reference to a non-delinquent group" (Lane, 1980, p. 22).

According to Lane (1980), the AIR report represented a critical milestone in the LD/JD controversy. Although the AIR report contended that studies in the search for a causal link between LD and JD often operate on two major assumptions or explanations of possible relationships (namely, the school failure rationale and the susceptibility rationale), it concluded that a causal relationship between learning disabilities and delinquency has not been established because of feeble evidence (Murray, 1976).

Moreover, the AIR report recommended that research regarding LD and JD links be based upon valid theoretical constructs, sound research definitions, and good methodological procedures (Lane, 1980). The study also recommended that carefully controlled research investigations on the possible link between LD and JD be undertaken by implementing an effective remediation program to assess the efficacy of remediation strategies with the delinquent population. In response to these recommendations, a federal grant was awarded jointly to the ACLD and the National Center for State Courts (NCSC) in October of 1976. The ACLD was responsible for providing the remedial program, and the NCSC was responsibile for program evaluation and other research components associated with the project (Cellini & Snowman, 1982).

According to Keilitz and Dunivant (1986), the project consisted of three studies. Two were designed to investigate the possible link between LD and JD and consisted of a cross-sectional study and a longitudinal study, and the third study was designed to evaluate the effectiveness of the ACLD remediation program. The authors concluded:

> The results of cross-sectional and longitudinal studies of samples of adolescent males from public schools, juvenile courts, and correctional facilities confirm the school failure theory, the susceptibility theory, and the

differential treatment theory—theories positing a causal relationship between learning disability and juvenile delinquency. Adolescents with
learning disabilities had significantly higher rates of general delinquent
behavior; they engaged in more violence, substance abuse, and school
disruption than non-learning disabled adolescents. The likelihood of ar-
rest and adjudication was also substantially higher for adolescents handicapped by learning disabilities. An evaluation of the academic treatment
program demonstrated that remedial instruction was effective in improving the academic skills and decreasing the delinquency of learning disabled youth who had been officially adjudicated. (p. 18)

While the preceding is a statement of the general findings of the studies, the authors
further state, "In contrast to the results in the cross-sectional study, however, the LD and
non-LD boys in the longitudinal sample did not differ in their attitudes toward school.
Thus, the hypothesized indirect effect of LD on delinquent behavior through school
failure posited by the school failure theory could not be confirmed" (pp. 22–23).

Many experts choose to doubt the concept of a causal link between LD and JD.
According to Spreen (1981), the presence of learning disabilities generally did not
confirm an increased likelihood of encounters with the police or a greater number of
offenses committed. Furthermore, the study is "even less supportive of the notion
that organicity or neurological impairment plays more than an accidental role as a
precursor or cause of delinquency" (p. 798). The findings of a recent study by
Sternig-Babcock (1987) have failed to demonstrate LD/JD causal links and point to
multiple risk factors as causes of delinquency.

Prevalence of LD Youth within the Adjudicated Population

Prevalence figures of learning disabilities among juvenile offenders have ranged
from 12% or less (Bullock & Reilly, 1979; Lenz, Warner, Alley, & Deshler, 1980; D. J.
Morgan, 1979; Pasternack & Lyon, 1982), to more than 50% (Duling, Eddy, & Risko,
1970; Jacobson, 1976; Love & Bachara, 1975; Podboy & Mallory, 1978; Swanstrom,
Randle, & Offord, 1981), to as high as 70% (Berman, 1974, 1975), 75% (E. M. R.
Critchley, 1968), 77% (Sawicki & Schaeffer, 1979), and 90% (Compton, 1974).

In the ACLD/NCSC study, 36% of the adjudicated delinquents were learning disabled. In a recent study of 90 adjudicated youths (Sternig-Babcock, 1987), the range
of prevalence varied according to the definition applied to LD. When the broadest
definition was applied, 38% of the sample were considered learning disabled. However, when the strictest definition was used (having both a significant discrepancy
and processing dysfunction), only 21% of the sample were classified as learning
disabled.

The inconsistency of the prevalence figures is due to problems in operational
definitions of LD and JD, the heterogeneity of the samples, and the methodological
limitations, as well as the extension of the concept of learning disabilities into
reading difficulties and/or learning problems in general. For instance, the General
Accounting Office (GAO) report (Comptroller General of the United States, 1977)
found that nearly 100% of a group of randomly selected juveniles exhibited learning

problems; of 129 juveniles, only one was found to be functioning at grade level. Both the E. M. R. Critchley report (1968) in France, which indicated that 75% of the juvenile delinquent population had reading difficulties, and the study by Compton (1974), which indicated that 90% of the juvenile delinquent population needed special individual attention, have quite often been quoted as prevalence figures in the JD population. Prevalence figures still remain inconsistent, and further research is still needed in this area.

Similarities Between LD and JD Characteristics

The background and school histories of learning-disabled youth and juvenile delinquents are, in many ways, quite similar. Both populations show a history of learning problems at school, including difficulties in attention span, temper control, social/interpersonal relationships, and relating to authority figures. In reviewing the literature on the traits of these two populations, Mauser (1974) listed the following common characteristics:

1. Both the learning disabled and juvenile delinquent populations evidence a negative self-concept and low frustration tolerance.
2. Both delinquency and learning disabilities are problems that have been primarily associated with males.
3. Both adolescents with LD and juvenile delinquents have similar levels of intelligence.
4. Most delinquents and children with learning disabilities tend to have difficulties in school, beginning in the primary grades.
5. Juvenile delinquency and learning disability appear to have no single cause and no single cure, but are associated with a variety of etiological factors and a multitude of treatment strategies. (pp. 393–394)

Because of the similarities between the two populations, some researchers have had a compelling need to describe the linkage between LD and JD. Unger (1978), in trying to establish such a link, states:

> Two things come into play in explaining how learning disabilities contribute to delinquent behavior. Frustration in school often leads to aggressive behavior. The child becomes more and more frustrated as his needs go unmet and the aggression spreads to all facets of his life. He calls attention to his unmet needs by delinquent behavior. Secondly, because many learning disabled children are impulsive and lack good judgment, they are unable to anticipate the consequences of their acts. They often cannot control their behavior and they do not learn from experience. (p. 27)

Theories Linking LD and JD

Three theories attempting to describe the possible link between LD and JD are commonly found in the literature: (a) the school failure theory (Berman, 1974, 1975;

Murray, 1976); (b) the susceptibility theory (Murray, 1976); and (c) the differential treatment hypothesis (Zimmerman, Rich, Keilitz, & Broder, 1981).

In elaborating on the school failure rationale as described by Berman (1974, 1975), Keilitz and Dunivant (1986) enumerate the following factors as contributing to delinquency:

1. The negative self-image and sense of frustration resulting from failure in school could motivate students with LD to strike back at society in anger and retaliation.
2. As a result of school failure, children with LD might be labeled as problem students and grouped with other children who have behavioral problems.
3. Failure in school may decrease a child's attachment or bond to school as an institution and to teachers as significant adults.
4. Teenagers with LD may experience incentives to commit crimes.
5. If caused to be unsuccessful at school, children with LD could foster the general tendency to attribute blame for negative events to others instead of to themselves.

The susceptibility theory attempts to explain how certain characteristics of individuals with LD make them more susceptible to be involved in delinquent behaviors, and consequently to be adjudicated.

> Such characteristics—which are components of or caused by LD—include lack of impulse control, inability to anticipate the future consequences of actions, poor perception of social cues, irritability, suggestibility, and the tendency to act out. Proponents of this view argue that these traits, which are frequently associated with LD, directly contribute to the development of delinquent behavior. (Keilitz & Dunivant, 1986, p. 19)

The third explanation, the differential treatment hypothesis, maintains that one or more elements of the juvenile justice system treat learning-disabled children differently from non-LD children. The results of the study by Zimmerman et al. (1981) indicate that:

> proportionately more adjudicated delinquent children than public school children were learning disabled. Self-report data, however, showed no differences in delinquent behaviors engaged in by learning disabled and non-learning disabled children within either the adjudicated or public school samples. Public school children who have learning disabilities reported that they were picked up by the police at about the same rate as non-learning disabled children, and engaged in about the same delinquent behaviors. Charges for which learning disabled and non-learning disabled adjudicated delinquents were convicted followed the same general patterns. In light of these findings, it was proposed that the greater proportion of learning disabled youth among adjudicated juvenile delinquents may be accounted for by differences in the way such children are

treated within the juvenile justice system, rather than by differences in their delinquent behaviors. (p. 1)

Broder, Dunivant, Smith, and Sutton (1981) provided further support for the differential treatment theory. In a sample of 1,617 teenagers—633 boys who had been adjudicated delinquents or status offenders by juvenile courts and 984 boys who had no record of previous adjudication by juvenile courts—36.5% of the adjudicated youth were learning disabled as compared to 18.9% of the nondelinquent group. This study also pointed out that "the learning disabled youth do not evidence more delinquent behaviors than non-learning-disabled youth, but they are more likely to be found delinquent by juvenile courts" (p. 838). Broder et al. (1981) further state the following:

> The behavioral characteristics and deficits associated with learning disabilities, often combined with long standing records of poor school performance, operate to the detriment of the learning disabled youths in their interactions with the system. . . . [T]he expressive deficits exhibited by some learning disabled youths could make them more vulnerable than non-learning disabled youths to formal processing by justice system officials simply because they are less able to present their perception of events. . . . [Their] inability to comprehend the significance of abstract ideas could significantly affect a youth's understanding of and response to the juvenile justice system. (p. 848)

The literature review thus far has failed to demonstrate a causal link between LD and JD. The differential treatment hypothesis seems to be the more acceptable, logical explanation of the disproportion of youth with LD among the adjudicated youth in our nation's juvenile justice system.

SUMMARY AND CONCLUSIONS

The plight of adolescents and young adults with learning disabilities is presented in this chapter. Because of their handicapping condition, they have to deal with more than the usual societal demands associated with these developmental stages. They are faced with tremendous challenges both at school and in everyday life. They need all the support they can get from parents, teachers, and other professionals with whom they come in contact. The importance of understanding normal development and the impact of LD on adolescents and young adults must be stressed.

PART
2

Service Delivery Framework and Intervention Approaches

This section provides the reader with a service delivery framework and intervention approaches for individuals with learning disabilities in the least restrictive environment. We discuss a comprehensive, integrated intervention framework that goes beyond the three R's curriculum. Emphasis is placed on a systematic approach to remedial teaching, including metacognition and strategic learning that ranges from preschool to adulthood.

A Framework for Service Delivery and Intervention

Questions to Consider

1. *How does adopting an intervention framework enhance the remedial program?*

2. *What are the basic assumptions that underlie the intervention program?*

3. *What should be the nature of the intervention program?*

4. *What is clinical teaching?*

5. *What is the role of the learning disability specialist in the remedial process?*

DEVELOPING AN INSTRUCTIONAL DELIVERY FRAMEWORK

Taxonomy of Educational Remediation Procedures

As a result of the increased knowledge regarding learning disabilities and the advent of new approaches for treatment, which were discussed in part 1, recognition of the need for a systematic framework for delivery of services has emerged.

A greater realization of the remedial potential of schools has resulted in the development of special programs for individuals with learning disabilities—programs designed to provide students with an appropriate educational environment, including curricula and methods adapted to their individual abilities and disabilities. One of the major areas of innovation in special education has been the development of delivery systems and taxonomic concepts and their application to the teaching-learning process. A taxonomy provides an organizational frame of reference. It delineates the numerous components involving various planes, which are usually hierarchical and interactional in nature. Taxonomies can be best described as blueprints that outline the organizational aspects and the specific procedures and methodologies of the remedial process.

Recognition of the need for this taxonomy grew out of experience in training learning disability specialists. Those who teach learning-disabled individuals must have an understanding of the broad spectrum of the remedial process. The taxonomy indicates that remedial teaching involves making a wide range of decisions. This taxonomy is by no means new, and its various elements can be easily recognized in other models of remedial education. It provides uncomplicated conceptualization and a systematic approach to the remedial process for individuals with learning disabilities. The taxonomy outlines the numerous areas of emphasis and the elements necessary for effective remedial teaching. It suggests how various teaching and learning conditions are interrelated and gives both general and specific guidelines for instructional procedures, thus facilitating an understanding of the remedial process. The aim of this taxonomy is to provide an optimal learning environment for individuals with learning disabilities, which includes educational programs adjusted to individual needs and appropriate motivation to enhance active learning.

The taxonomy of educational remediation procedures involves nine educational variables that predominate in terms of their remedial relevance:

1. Functional assessment procedures
2. Educational placement in the least restrictive environment (LRE)
3. An individualized educational program (IEP) and objectives
4. Prescriptive educational procedures, methods, and techniques
5. A developmental curriculum
6. Educational management and an intervention strategy
7. Individualized instruction
8. Parent involvement
9. Evaluative procedures

These variables are clustered into the five main phases of the taxonomy:

1. Analysis of the learner
2. Analysis of the educational environment
3. Programming
4. Program implementation
5. Evaluation

The relationship of these variables and phases is illustrated in Figure 4–1.

Analysis of the Learner

Functional Assessment Procedures

Functional assessment implies the utilization of assessment procedures relevant to the remedial education program. Its sole purpose is to provide assessment information input for the development of an effective instructional program. The individualized remedial education program should be based on comprehensive assessment procedures that provide information on the overall functional level of the student. These procedures should involve formal and informal measures conducted by a multidisciplinary team, including the school psychologist, other specialists, and the LD specialist. LD specialists play a major role in assessment. (Assessment procedures, the selection of assessment tools, and the role of the LD specialist in assessment are discussed in depth in chapter 8.) No standardized test can pinpoint what a student can and cannot do, but by using informal assessment procedures, the LD specialist can tap a student's specific skills. The elements of task analysis and curriculum-based assessment provide a framework for the teacher's informal assessment and observations as well as for the development of teacher-made informal assessment material. The blending of formal and informal assessment measures ensures adequate evaluation of a child's present level of functioning, including specific skill areas, strengths and weaknesses, and the most appropriate individual learning style and reinforcement mode.

Figure 4–1 Taxonomy of Educational Remediation Procedures

Analysis of learner	Functional assessment procedures
Analysis of educational environment	Educational placement in the LRE
Programming	Individualized educational program and objectives
Implementation	Prescriptive educational procedures, methods, and techniques
	Developmental curriculum
	Educational management and intervention strategy
	Individualized instruction
	Parent involvement
Evaluation	Evaluative procedures

(Feedback)

Analysis of the Educational Environment

Placement in the Least Restrictive Environment

Diagnostic and assessment information should assist in the identification of a student's educational needs in the various areas of school functioning and, accordingly, should determine a child's ability to benefit from regular classroom instruction. Placement of learning-disabled individuals should be consistent with the least restrictive environment mandate of PL 94–142. Section 4(c), 19 of the law requires that the individualized education program include a statement of "the extent to which such child will be able to participate in regular education programs." Most learning-disabled students are placed in regular classrooms, with support services from resource room programs.

Placement in special classes should be recommended when it is necessary to provide students with intensive remedial programs adjusted to individual needs for the ultimate purpose of participation in the mainstream of the school environment.

As much attendance as is possible in regular classrooms is recommended, for it allows students to remain integrated with peers, enhances self-respect, and facilitates emotional and social adjustments. Most students should be able to attend nonacademic regular classroom programs. As soon as students reach an achievement level that enables them to function in regular classrooms with support services from resource rooms, they should be able to make the transition. Throughout the process, continuous communication and feedback should be maintained between the LD specialist and regular classroom teachers. The LD specialist should have at least weekly contacts, should be informed of students' academic and social progress, and should be notified when special projects or examinations are to take place or when any crisis occurs. The continuous support that the LD specialist can provide during the period of transition may determine the difference between success and failure. Thus the mediating role of the LD specialist is of immense importance.

Programming

The Individualized Education Program, Goals, and Objectives

The written part of the individualized education program mandated by PL 94–142 requires the selection of annual goals and objectives and the specification of short-term objectives. An effective educational program must be based on functional assessment information. A sequential program must be carefully planned for each child to allow opportunities for appropriate behavior and personal success. The LD specialist needs to be familiar with both the core curriculum of the regular classroom and the teaching process. The more carefully tasks are adjusted to a child's abilities, the greater the possibility that the student will learn them. (These programming procedures are discussed in depth in chapter 9.)

In an environment in which each student is continuously taught at an individual pace and level, there will be few experiences of failure, and motivation will increase accordingly. Both short-term (daily, weekly) objectives and interim objectives (per month, per term/semester) must be formulated by the teacher. A teacher's knowledge of task analysis and curriculum-based assessment procedures can facilitate this process. The specification of skill acquisition in each of the content areas, as well as areas such as study skills and strategic learning, can ensure that a student is placed at a proper instructional level. The LD specialist who aims to bring a child up to the level of performance for children of his age must know the sequence of tasks by which this can be accomplished.

Program Implementation

Prescriptive Educational Procedures, Methods, and Techniques

Children do not all have the same patterns of abilities and disabilities, nor do they all learn in the same manner and at the same pace. No particular approach or material is appropriate for all students. Each student's functional assessment plan should indicate the specific methods and approaches that are to be used in each area of instruction. The following is an account of a sixth-grade student with learning disabilities.

Douglas exhibited auditory discrimination problems as well as visual perceptual difficulties. Because of his severe visual perception difficulties, his teachers attempted to teach him reading using a phonic approach, but to no avail. An inspection of work samples and classroom observations pointed out some strengths in visualization despite his visual perception difficulties. Because Douglas had a relatively intact visual memory, one teacher proposed the color-coded linguistic approach, which uses visualization. Within 1 year, Douglas was able to read the Scholastic Action series, which is approximately a 3.5 grade level.

Consideration must be given to a student's information-processing style and cognitive learning style. Although the research is equivocal in this respect, classroom observations indicate that appropriate selection of teaching methods and strategies can make the difference between success or failure in learning experiences.

The Developmental Curriculum

The educational goals must fit the needs of the student, and the educational material selected by the teacher must fit those goals. The degree of a student's success increases when the tasks presented are appropriate for that individual's level of functioning. If tasks are too high for abilities, feelings of success and adequacy are supplanted by feelings of helplessness and frustration. As early as 1939, the Report of the Joint Committee on Health Problems in Education, emphasized that "the curriculum should be so selected, organized and administered that the children would be given worthwhile activities of interest to learn, adapted to their abilities and fitted to their needs" (p. 46). Despite efforts in recent years to develop appropriate commercial remedial instructional materials, there is still a paucity of such items, and the lack is particularly severe at the upper elementary and secondary school levels. Adaptation of commercial materials and development of instructional materials geared to an individual's level of functioning, which take into account the scope and sequence of the curriculum, are necessary.

Classroom Management

The implementation of classroom management procedures that promote social and emotional development is essential to remedial teaching. The classroom environment and management approach must be designed to meet the needs of all students, from highly structured to least restrictive approximating the parameters of the regular classroom. The LD specialist should attempt to create a learning environment that provides opportunities for new experiences that ensure success—an environment in which a student feels accepted by the teacher and the group, which fosters a self-image as a valuable individual having worthwhile interests and ideas and the ability to accomplish tasks. Using successful experiences, the teacher attempts to build a student's self-confidence and circumvent the learned helplessness syndrome.

In an interactive learning environment, students feel that the teacher is an approachable individual, someone upon whose acceptance, understanding, and judgment they can rely. Students should not feel that a teacher is authoritarian or detached but rather that the teacher actively likes them and wishes to help them. However, students should not be encouraged to become dependent upon the teacher. On the contrary, when appropriate, a teacher should stress the students' ability to work out their own problems and help themselves; a teacher's goal should be to help children become active learners. The LD specialist should promote self-evaluation and, through the development of students' sensitivity to the learning situation, through the heightening of students' knowledge of the factors affecting learning, and through strategic learning acquisition and effective utilization of control executive functions, assist the learners to become *active* learners who are in control of their own learning and responsible for their own behavior. (For specific classroom management approaches, refer to chapter 12.)

Individualized Instruction
The effectiveness of the remedial program can be enhanced through individualized instruction. Section 140 (19) of PL 94–142 mandates the development of an individualized education program (IEP). The architects of this public law emphasized meeting the needs of each exceptional child and recognized the need to tailor instruction and teaching approaches for such students (see also chapter 9). Individualized instruction refers to the creation of an educational environment and instructional programs that meet the needs of students according to each one's level of functioning. The tailoring of approaches and instructional strategies to individual student needs are also implied in this definition. The IEP serves as the basic implementation plan for delivery of instruction.

While educators generally advocate and support the idea of individualized instruction, this concept means different things to different teachers. According to Lloyd (1984), "Individualization of instructional program . . . rests in part on the assumption that some kind of instructions are better for some students while other kinds are better for other students. . . . Implicit in our beliefs about individualization is an expectation that adapting instruction to the characteristics of students will benefit them" (p. 7). Individualized instruction does not always mean working individually; in fact, grouping and regrouping students according to their needs can maximize the learning process of each student.

Truly individualized programs depend first upon a teacher's awareness of individual needs, and then on the development and initiation of the programs appropriate to those needs. The teacher will be helped in the task of providing individualized instruction if self-corrective materials can be provided. In many instances, it may be necessary to devise or construct such materials.

Parent Involvement
The inclusion of a parent involvement component in the taxonomy of educational remediation procedures reflects this author's view that parents can be an asset to, as well as powerful reinforcers of, the remedial process. Traditionally, the educational process was seen as the sole responsibility of the school and of its personnel who played specific educational roles, and parent participation was discouraged. The signing of PL 94–142 in 1975 and its regulations for implementation provided a

framework for a closer partnership between parents and teachers. Sections 614iii and 615(b) of the public law mandate "participation and consultation" of children's parents and guardians and provide procedures to protect the rights of children and their parents. These regulations and the change of attitudes point toward more cooperation between the home and the school.

Research and common sense both indicate that parents serve an important role in educating their children. Parents are seen as the primary agent of change in their children's lives. They play a vital part in determining the nature of the growth and progress made and maintained by their children. Therefore, the process of educating parents and facilitating their understanding of the various aspects of their child's learning, both in school and at home, can make the difference between a successful and an unsuccessful educational program. According to Hampton and Fernandez (1985), parental involvement has been widely recognized by experts as a criterion for effective programming for handicapped children.

The literature reveals the important role parents can assume in the education of their children and the factors that support such an active role. These factors are (a) the increased interest and fund of information of the general public regarding the educational process, which enable parents to have meaningful participation in the education of children; (b) the call by educators for more parent involvement; (c) the passage of PL 94–142; and (d) the increased likelihood that individuals will share responsibility for solving problems if they are involved in the process (Witt, Miller, McIntyre, & Smith, 1984).

In general, involvement of parents can enhance the quality of their child's program. The term *parent involvement* in the literature incorporates fairly diverse areas that relate the parents to the school arena. Parental involvement ranges from minimal involvement, quite often referred to as passive involvement, in which the parents' role is limited to participation in parent education and training programs (McKinney & Hocutt, 1982), to active involvement, which includes parent participation in, and contribution to, the assessment, placement, and instructional processes of their child and usually involves shared decision making between parents and educators.

According to McLoughlin, Edge, and Strenecky (1978), the role of parents has been enhanced by increased recognition of the significance of the home and community as settings in a child's total learning environment. Furthermore, when parents actively participate in the remedial process, three things occur: (a) The parents and the professionals exchange information, (b) the parents are encouraged to grow in their role, and (c) trusting, productive relationships between parents and teachers are established.

By actively participating, parents not only aid the teacher within the school environment, but also reinforce at home what is taught in the classroom. It is thus important for the learning disability specialist to develop and encourage a collaborative relationship between parents and teachers in order to maximize the remedial process and formulate a more stable and diffused bond between home and school. Schools can view parents as important partners in a child's educational process and facilitate parental involvement in various phases of the remedial process, that is, identification, assessment, programming, implementation, and evaluation (McLoughlin et al., 1978).

Evaluation

Evaluative Procedures

Initially, an assessment of a child's level of functioning provides the basis for a remedial program. It is equally important to ensure an adequate evaluation of a child's progress. Remedial teaching cannot be considered adequate without ongoing evaluative processes.

There are two broad aspects of evaluation to be considered, and they are very much interrelated. One aspect is an assessment of the student's progress, that is, whether the child has mastered what the teacher has attempted to teach. The other aspect is an assessment of the educational procedures, methods, and techniques. In other words, one aspect is an evaluation of the learning outcome—the products of instruction—and the other aspect is an evaluation of the teaching/learning process—

Homework can be a positive experience when it's geared to the interests and functional level of the student.

the process of instruction. Product evaluation tells us something about how well the student is doing. Process evaluation tells how the student might perform better (Ariel, 1974). The LD specialist must review and modify the educational procedures, methods, and techniques in order to determine the extent to which the program has been effective. Quite often a change of approach might be indicated.

These evaluation procedures must be ongoing. Short-term evaluation should be conducted each month and/or each semester, and long-term evaluation is required in most states annually and triannually and involves the efforts of the school assessment team. The LD specialist needs to develop and implement procedures for determining criteria and methods for evaluating students' progress, and has to determine whether or not the intended instructional objectives were reached and accordingly outline the instructional goals and objectives for students. Moreover, the evaluation of students' progress should follow the guidelines of the functional assessment procedures and use both formal and informal measures (see chapter 8).

Ongoing Evaluation and Feedback Loop

Though the taxonomy is hierarchical in nature, one must also realize its interactional nature. As the LD specialist moves through the taxonomy, evaluation of information and direct observations of student performance provide the basis for an ongoing evaluation of the instructional procedures, methods, and techniques. Thus, as a teacher works with a learning-disabled student, the student's performance serves as additional input to modify the program and/or to confirm or nullify previously obtained information.

Program Components and Curriculum Considerations

Providing Comprehensive Intervention Programs

The characteristics and developmental needs of individuals with learning disabilities indicate the selection and inclusion of instructional program components. A program must take into account students' needs and their capacity to learn from experiences in and out of school. It must also consider each individual's adjustment in school and in life in general. Both practical observations and empirical research support the development of a comprehensive intervention program for individuals with learning disabilities (Deshler, Schumaker, & Lenz, 1984). For too long, programs for the learning disabled have had too narrow a treatment approach, focusing only on academic remediation (Pihl & McLarnon, 1984; Wanant, 1983). Programs must go beyond the narrow academic parameters to a broader framework of life adjustment (Fafard & Haubrich, 1981). Serious concerns have also been voiced regarding the nature of remedial teaching, which too often places emphasis on teaching basic skills without giving attention to the core curriculum. Consequently, students with learning disabilities are deprived of exposure to both age-appropriate concepts in science and social studies and literary experiences. The curriculum should relate to the skills and knowledge that those with learning disabilities need to function competently as students in school and eventually as adults in society, with the necessary strategies for learning and problem solving (Wiederholt, 1978b).

Most school districts have adopted a common core curriculum for all their students. The core curriculum refers to the district- or school-adopted course of study required for grade level promotion. All students, including those with learning disabilities, should be instructed in the concepts of the core curriculum in accordance with their functional level. In addition, the curriculum of learning-disabled individuals needs to be expanded to include such areas as study skills, metacognition and strategic learning, career/vocational preparation, independent living, and social and communication skills.

One may distinguish between program components (elements) that are common to all age groups and those that take into account the developmental aspects of the individual and are particular to a specific age range. The following common program components must be considered and integrated into the remedial teaching process:

1. academic skill development—basic skills and core curriculum
2. study patterns development, that is, study habits and study skills
3. metacognition and strategic learning
4. social skills and emotional growth and development
5. development of conceptual knowledge and life adjustment skills, including recreation and leisure skills
6. readiness skills across all areas

Thus the LD specialist must be concerned with areas that go beyond the three R's curriculum in order to meet the overall needs of individuals with learning disabilities.

In addition, the inclusion of program components (elements) that address the developmental age needs of the group must be considered. For example, at the preschool and primary levels, one would want to include a program component that deals with school readiness, whereas at the secondary level, one would include training in career/vocational preparation, the development of sound interpersonal relationships, and preparation for transition to postsecondary schooling and/or employment. Figure 4–2 illustrates the program components and curriculum considerations for individuals with learning disabilities.

The school should attempt to work closely with the home by providing guidance and training to parents in home management and home enrichment techniques. Specific counsel on assisting the learning-disabled individual at home through incidental learning and providing guided help with homework and other activities must be provided to parents.

The realities in the public schools are such that much of the responsibility of providing a comprehensive program for students with learning disabilities is left to the LD specialist. Therefore, in order to assist teachers in the provision of such a comprehensive program, an attempt should be made to enlist the resources available in the school system. An integrated intervention program, involving the work of professionals, can provide better services to learning-disabled individuals (Sapir, 1985).

Figure 4–2   Program Components and Curriculum Considerations for Individuals with Learning Disabilities

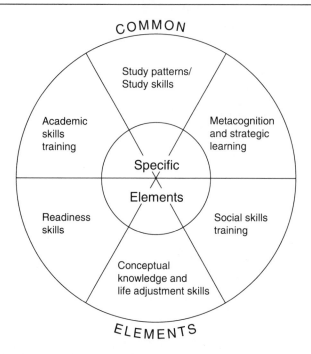

The Role of the LD Specialist in the Remedial Process

The LD specialist is viewed as a highly trained individual who has the knowledge, skills, and competencies to provide a comprehensive remedial teaching program for individuals with learning disabilities. Although emphasis is placed on school-related items such as academic knowledge, the LD specialist's concerns go beyond the teaching of the three R's. The LD specialist has to supply the social/emotional climate and supportive learning environment that nourish successful behavior—a classroom environment that both enhances an individual's academic skills and develops self-concept and self-esteem. In order to ensure success, the specialist must prepare an educational program geared to individual functional and interest levels. That educational program has to provide step-by-step instructions for the learning process and take into account the variables associated with an individual's information-processing style.

Also fully involved with other aspects of the student's functioning in school and general life, the LD specialist must furnish students with guidance, social skills training, training in metacognition, strategic learning, and problem-solving strategies. In addition, the specialist in learning disabilities must be cognizant of the developmental aspects of students and be able to deal with specific individual needs associated with development.

Through the provision of a feedback mechanism and an appropriate reinforcement mode, the LD specialist can enhance the development of a student's success-oriented identity and hence the student's positive self-concept. In a true sense, an LD specialist gears the daily activities to promote successful experiences and positive mental hygiene.

Toward Clinical Teaching: A Rationale and Process

Why Clinical Teaching?

Some concerns have been voiced about the role that learning disability specialists are currently assuming in the field. Although they have been trained to provide specialized education, many LD specialists are now engaged in educational practices that minimally utilize specialized instructional methodology. This situation is more severe at the secondary level, where learning disability and resource room teachers are "chasing" the regular classroom curriculum in their attempts to help students function in the mainstream of the school environment. The emphasis on the three R's curriculum is reinforced by the fact that the curriculum does not direct special educators to deal with social/emotional or other needs of learning-disabled students, nor does it address individual differences and broader aspects of the remedial program, such as strategic learning and problem-solving strategies. To make the situation worse, in many cases teachers who have received adequate training are limited by their school administrators in making any decisions related to educational remediation of their students.

The following profile illustrates the need for teaching procedures that can meet the requirements of individuals with learning disabilities. Michael is a 12-year-old who has been attending a regular classroom, with two periods of instruction for reading and written language in the resource specialist program, for the past 4 years. He currently functions at a low second-grade level in the language arts. Michael exhibits difficulties in sound blending, that is, he can sound all the letters of the alphabet in isolation but has difficulties in putting the sounds together to form words. He tends to memorize sight words and can spell sight vocabulary easily, but he has great difficulty with phonic words.

Michael's present program consists of reading the state-adopted Basal series at the second-grade level. He is also using a phonics book. Michael spends about an hour a day on reading instruction in the resource specialist program. He is a bright, normal child and, with the exception of the language arts areas, is performing at about grade level.

A review of Michael's reading program makes it quite apparent that he is not progressing in accordance with his abilities. As a matter of fact, one is amazed to learn that this child, who is bright and of normal intelligence, has made no significant progress in reading, even though he has participated in the resource specialist program for 4 years, nor has he benefited from the phonic approach used by the resource teacher. Because Michael is at the sixth-grade level, it is imperative that an effective reading program be developed that will produce immediate successful experiences. Michael is motivated, eager to learn, and, though he has a low self-concept, does not yet feel defeated.

Obviously, Michael's educational program neither meets his requirements nor maximizes his potential to learn. His situation points to a need for a more systematic approach in the instructional process and illustrates the necessity to use teaching procedures based on sound principles of learning and remedial education. The main questions, then, are: What should Michael's reading program be? How can he be helped to learn to read? Should the teacher consider other reading instructional approaches? What teaching methods and instructional materials should be used?

The LD specialist must know what to observe, what to assess, what to do with the assessment results, how to program, how to select approaches and methodologies, how to go about implementing appropriate teaching practices, and how to apply sound principles of teaching. A framework for working with learning-disabled individuals must be adopted. When teachers lack a framework and a road map on which to base their instructional procedures, they have no objective basis for evaluating the process of instruction. Thus a call for a clinical teaching approach based on current knowledge in the field and on sound principles of remedial education for learning-disabled individuals is essential. Learning disability specialists must attain knowledge and skills in clinical teaching and be permitted to utilize specialized approaches and methodologies in order to maximize the effectiveness of the remedial program. Programs must be designed as scientifically as possible, based on current knowledge in the field, and continuously modified as knowledge becomes more available.

Defining Clinical Teaching

Clinical teaching is defined as an instructional procedure that denotes a systematic approach to the remedial process and usually involves procedures set in advance to maximize the effectiveness of a remedial program. Clinical teaching employs sound principles of teaching and remediation. It is a specialized teaching technique tailored to an individual's needs in order to make the most of one's potential. It proposes careful steps and procedures that facilitate the identification, programming, and treatment of learning-disabled individuals. The LD specialist who uses clinical teaching sets goals for students and follows specific procedures that help them reach those goals. In contrast to other teaching procedures, clinical teaching involves a higher level of accountability aimed at optimizing the teaching process and the student outcome. Johnson and Myklebust (1967) refer to clinical teaching as a method that uses appropriate methodologies to produce the greatest gains possible for an individual student, and that involves the adaptation of teaching approaches to an individual's idiosyncratic characteristics.

Clinical teaching provides a systematic, hierarchical approach to the remedial process that incorporates techniques such as task analysis, curriculum-based assessment and instruction, and criterion-referenced and informal assessment (Sapir, 1985). Clinical teaching is essentially a continuous test-teach-test process that can be used in any classroom setting (C. R. Smith, 1983). Lerner (1989) points out that clinical teaching involves continual decision making by the teacher and that the clinical teaching process can be viewed as a cycle consisting of five phases: (a) diagnosis; (b) planning; (c) implementation; (d) evaluation; and (e) modification of the diagnosis, which leads to new planning, new forms of implementation, and a continuing cycle of clinical teaching. According to Lerner (1989), an important aspect of clinical teaching is the skills of the teacher in interpreting feedback information and the need for continuous decision making; clinical teaching is seen as an alternating teach-test-teach-test process.

Basic Assumptions

The clinical teaching approach advocated by the author makes the following basic assumptions:

1. An interactive and reciprocal relationship exists between a learner, the conditions of learning, the process of learning, and the teacher.
2. Clinical teaching denotes an awareness of individual differences that includes knowing that (a) not all individuals have the same patterns of abilities and disabilities, (b) not all individuals learn in the same manner and at the same pace, and (c) no particular approach or material is appropriate for all individuals.
3. The remedial process for individuals with learning disabilities can be maximized through effective use of sound principles of learning and remedial education.
4. Learners are perceived as active information processors who will bring to bear upon the learning process all available resources in order to ensure success (see chapter 6).
5. Learners' increased awareness of the learning process and of their own abilities, strengths, and weaknesses can contribute to the learning process.
6. The remedial process is perceived as a systematic procedure based on observation of strengths and weaknesses in skill development across various planes, including academics and social skills.
7. The remedial process can be used to the utmost through direct instruction of skills and guided teaching that leads to individual self-directed learning.
8. The teacher is viewed as a facilitator and a helping agent who is acquainted with principles of clinical teaching and who has a sound knowledge of the overall needs of learning-disabled individuals.
9. Learners can effectively be taught strategic learning and the use of control executive functions, that is, planning, organizing, monitoring, and checking outcomes, thus promoting a sense of realistic appraisal and self-evaluation (see chapter 6).
10. Learners can assume responsibility for their own learning and ultimately be in control of their destiny.

A New Perspective

With today's increasing concerns about educational accountability, the quality of the individualized educational program, and the general quality of our educational services to individuals with learning disabilities, it behooves the learning disability specialist to provide quality remedial programs based on clinical teaching procedures. The need for systematized teaching procedures was discussed earlier in the chapter. It seems imperative that we get back to basics in the remedial approach, namely, to apply sound principles of teaching and greater scrutiny to instructional procedures and methodologies. In addition, we must utilize procedures that will heighten the accountability and the quality of the remedial program—assessment, programming, and evaluation.

The new clinical teaching approach is founded on sound principles of teaching; it emphasizes functional assessment, both formal and informal, and the creation of an educational program based on assessment data. In contrast to the clinical teaching approach of the 60s and 70s, this new approach stresses skill teaching and strategic learning. Significance is given to direct observation, assessment, and the information-processing style of the individual. With the use of task analysis and curriculum-based assessment, emphasis is placed on a child's current level of skill development, the next skill to be mastered, and the behavioral component of each skill (Ysseldyke & Salvia, 1974). It is a direct teaching approach based on assessment information, in which the instructional procedures are monitored and reflect students' responses to the instructional methods and procedures. The LD specialist attempts to develop self-directed learners who can assume responsibility for their own learning and who are active learners, engaging in strategic productions, knowing when and how to apply appropriate strategies, and utilizing control executive functions effectively. Thus this new clinical approach stresses the teaching of strategic behaviors that regulate such activities in a well-rounded intervention program.

The LD specialist is perceived as an individual who is highly trained in assessment, programming, and implementation skills, one who is in a position to continuously observe students and make decisions as to the course of actions to be taken. The LD specialist is viewed as a teacher-technician who follows scientific procedures as closely as possible in the teaching process—procedures amenable to accurate definition, systematic scrutiny, and consequent improvement. The teacher-technician conception of instruction is essentially empirically based. It involves the gathering of empirical evidence regarding which instructional variation results in the most student achievements (Popham, 1966). The LD specialist bases teaching procedures on sound, scientific instructional procedures as a result of appropriate diagnosis, continuous measurements, and feedback. This approach requires stringent teaching procedures and usually involves the recording of students' performances and progress. It also involves the recording of students' reactions to the instructional process in order to improve the quality of instruction. In this context, the clinical teaching approach provides guidance for the remedial process that promotes understanding of learning-disabled individuals and in turn facilitates the provision of an effective individualized education program.

Using the Taxonomy in Clinical Teaching

There is always a relationship between the past, present, and future experiences of children. From each experience, children incorporate that which has personal meaning. What is incorporated depends upon previous experiences, that is, upon the meaning already developed. As Burham (1924) states: "If a child believes that he can do a thing he is likely to attempt it; and if he begins, the amount of effort put forth depends largely on his belief in the power to succeed" (p. 141).

Children who struggle with learning problems are likely to establish negative patterns of behavior. When the failure pattern continues for months or years, children actually become deficient in fundamental skills, as well as in their approach to learning, and exhibit production deficiencies. They lack the ability to evaluate themselves realistically and encounter tremendous difficulties in organizing their wants and goals. They develop feelings of inadequacy, worthlessness, and helplessness and perceive themselves and whatever they do as "no good." Failure, however, can be viewed as lying not within the children, but rather within the instructional procedures that have failed to meet their needs.

Consider 12 ½-year-old Howard, who cannot read or spell and functions at about the second-grade level in arithmetic computation. He has been in special classes since the second grade. He has low self-esteem and low self-confidence, feels frustrated and defeated, and has given up on learning how to read. His truancy rate at school is nearly 60%. However, Howard's mother has not given up hope and has continually sought assistance and help for her son.

The urgency of finding appropriate intervention approaches for this child cannot be stressed enough. The teacher who is going to help Howard cannot afford to waste any additional time, nor can Howard tolerate any additional failure experiences in the course of the remedial process. It thus behooves the LD specialist to have a framework of operation and a clear direction as to what steps and procedures must be taken in order to help Howard. How shall one go about reviewing the situation, conducting additional assessment and observations, and coming up with program recommendations appropriate to this student? The taxonomy of educational remediation procedures is aimed at providing the LD specialist with general guidelines and specific steps and procedures to enhance the quality of services delivered to learning-disabled individuals.

INSTRUCTIONAL MODELS AND APPROACHES FOR THE LEARNING DISABLED

Specialists whose mission is to assist individuals with LD must know and be able to use current practices for assessing students and providing remedial instruction. Some models and approaches are complementary to clinical teaching procedures. Although they employ different terms, these models and approaches have attempted to incorporate systematic instruction principles in their constructs, suggesting definite steps and procedures in the remedial process. These models and approaches include academic skill mastery approaches, that is, curriculum-based assessment and instruction and direct instruction, task analysis, precision teaching, and metacognition.

Academic Skill Mastery Approaches

Academic skill mastery emphasizes analysis of the teaching task and the learning task, rather than analysis of the student. It involves analysis of the academic task in terms of the underlying skills needed to accomplish that task and to help students acquire unmastered subskills (Lerner, 1985). Two academic skill mastery approaches—curriculum-based assessment and instruction, and direct instruction—are discussed in this section.

Curriculum-Based Assessment and Instruction

Curriculum-based assessment and instruction attempts to provide a systematic approach for teaching and for the remedial processes and to develop a manageable assessment framework for the individual functional level. This teaching approach is based on the assumption that the best way to assess children is in relationship to the curricular requirements of their schooling. Utilizing the materials to be learned as the basis for assessing the degree to which they have been mastered is the fundamental concept of curriculum-based assessment and instruction. In this approach, the essential measure of success in education is a student's progress in the curriculum of the local school. Furthermore, Tucker (1985) points out that each student's needs are best defined in terms of the context of the local educational program and the curriculum that a given student is expected to follow. (Curriculum is defined as a course of study adopted by a particular school system [see chapter 8].) A total special education system founded on curriculum-based assessment and instruction includes (a) a formal, organized problem-solving system; (b) a classification and service delivery system that emphasizes educational needs; (c) a measurement system that is direct and environmentally or curriculum based, continuous, and locally norm-referenced; and (d) outcome based at both the individual level and system level (Tucker, 1985).

Direct Instruction

Direct instruction is defined as "systematic, explicit teaching of academic strategies to students" (Gersten, Woodward, & Darch, 1986, p. 17). It is a step-by-step approach in which students are provided with direct instruction in basic academic skills based on the students' learning needs. "This is done through teacher-directed activities, presented with controlled practice in sequential steps, low level questions, opportunities for high success, and immediate corrective feedback" (Morsink, Soar, Soar, & Thomas, 1986, p. 34). Direct instruction programs usually involve (a) explicit instruction to students; (b) demonstration and modeling of new material; (c) guided practice, which allows a teacher to ask questions of students, check for understanding, and give corrective and sustaining feedback; and (d) independent practice, in which students work independently on activities directly related to new material (Gersten et al., 1986). Direct instruction evolved from the work of Breiter and Englemann (1966) which emphasized engaged time, frequent student response, immediate teacher feedback, and error correction (Rosenshine, 1976).

In describing the advantages of direct instruction related to correction and feedback procedures, Gersten et al. (1986) state:

> Because of the explicit, step-by-step approach used in Direct Instruction sequences, the teacher is in an excellent position to diagnose any problems that a student may have when applying the strategy. If a student makes an error, or fails to respond at all, the teacher can immediately intervene with a model of how to answer correctly or some type of instructional prompt based on a previously taught rule. Once students are again secure in their knowledge of the steps in the problem-solving strategy, teacher questions and instructions are gradually dropped from the instructional presentation, and the students are no longer required to respond overtly at each step. (p. 20)

The Task Analysis Approach

One of the greatest contributions of applied behavior analysis to special education, and specifically to the field of learning disabilities, is the task analysis approach (see chapter 9). Applied behavior analysis focuses on objectively defined, observable behaviors. It seeks to improve specific behaviors and to determine precisely the teaching procedures that are responsible for the desired change (Hallahan & Kauffman, 1976). Furthermore, it uses the methods of science-description, quantification and analysis through direct, continuous, and precise measurement of behavior (Cooper, Heron, & Heward, 1987; Hallahan & Kauffman, 1976). This approach, which emphasizes the antecedents and consequences of behavior, has resulted in a renewed focus on accountability (Howell & Morehead, 1987). Accountability implies the delineation of goals, procedures, and results so that they may be evaluated, and applied behavior analysis lends itself to such accountability (Alberto & Troutman, 1990).

The task analysis approach emphasizes assessment of the student's skills and instructional procedures that involve direct teaching of necessary skills. The approach assumes that a student must learn the subcomponents or prerequisites of a task in order to learn the task (Howell & Morehead, 1987). While tasks may vary, they have common elements, namely, the behavior, the conditions, and the criterion measurements (Mager, 1962). According to Guerin and Maier (1983), in task analysis "a skill is reduced to units and sequenced in teachable subskills, each with a hierarchy of tasks and subtasks. . . . [Furthermore, the strengths of this approach] . . . lie in its selection of a target objective, identification of the steps needed to reach an acceptable level of success, and breakdown of the tasks into learning units that the student can manage" (p. 27). The chief purpose of task analysis is to help a teacher determine the optimal learning conditions for task mastery (DeCecco, 1968) and to identify tasks and subtasks that must be acquired in the process of learning.

Task analysis requires the LD specialist to pinpoint students' skills and deficiencies, and to delineate the specific objectives of instruction by setting achievable goals that are observable and measurable. The goal statements must clearly specify the outcome of behavior and the evaluative criteria.

Precision Teaching

The precision teaching approach emphasizes the study of human behavior by both the teacher and the learners. The teacher becomes competent as a behavior analyst, and the students' awareness of their behavior is heightened by self-monitoring procedures. According to O. R. White (1986), "The fundamental guiding principle of precision teaching is simply that the learner knows best, and that through self-monitoring mechanisms, the learner can view his progress and internalize related factors" (p. 522).

Precision teaching is based on the traditional concept of measuring and recording students' progress. It involves continuous measurement and charting (Kunzelmann, Cohen, Hulten, Martin, & Mingo, 1970; Lindsley, 1963, 1990). It facilitates the pinpointing of student behavior through basic functional units referred to as "movement cycles" measured against time and produces the individual output rate. Precision teaching has three main characteristics: (a) It is a direct measure; (b) it is a continuous or daily measure; and (c) it uses rate or frequency as a unit. Both the teacher and the students have ongoing records of output behaviors, thus heightening the students' rate of progress and providing indicators when learning is not occurring at expected levels, which may indicate difficulty with the task at hand.

Implications of Applied Behavior Analysis Approaches

The LD specialist must know the scope and sequence of the curriculum. Anyone attempting to help students bridge academic gaps has to know the goals those children must reach. The preceding practices can be incorporated into aspects of informal assessment and into the instructional procedures of the LD specialist. A teacher should know specifically what skills students can and cannot perform and, accordingly, determine specific levels of performance in order to arrive at an instructional procedure based on the levels of the students' performance. This specificity of knowledge of students' skill levels can only heighten the remedial approach and minimize trial-and-error teaching or teaching at inappropriate levels. Thus the LD specialist must engage in direct instruction, utilize appropriate methodology, and address specific skill acquisition in the various academic areas. In addition, a direct instruction approach can also be employed in the teaching of learning strategies and study skills.

Metacognitive and Learning Strategy Approaches

Metacognitive and learning strategy approaches for individuals with learning disabilities have become topics of prime interest in the LD field. The metacognitive approach attempts to develop the sensitivity of students to learning situations, to heighten students' awareness of their own cognitive repertoire and the factors that affect the learning process and contribute to successful learning, to teach strategies for learning, and to develop students' capacity to regulate and monitor their activities (see chapter 6).

Several strategy training approaches for learning-disabled individuals have been reported in the literature. These approaches include Lloyd's Academic Strategy Training, Torgesen's Strategy Training, and the Strategy Intervention Model developed by Deshler and his colleagues (deBettencourt, 1987). The Lloyd strategy approach involves the teaching of specific strategies for use with specific academic tasks (Lloyd, 1980). The Torgesen strategy training recognizes various levels of learning strategies—specific, more general, and control executive—the use of mnemonic strategies, and the provision of guidance to students to promote strategic production (Torgesen, 1980, 1982). The Strategy Intervention Model is designed specifically for use with learning-disabled adolescents, and it emphasizes the application of learning strategies to curricular content at the secondary level. It stresses learning how to learn rather than remediating specific academic skills (Schumaker, Deshler, & Ellis, 1986). (See chapter 7.) In this respect, the goals of metacognitive strategic training are the same as the goals of strategic training employed by the Strategy Intervention Model (Schumaker et al., 1986), Lloyd's Academic Strategy Training (Lloyd, 1980) and Torgesen's Strategy Training (Torgesen, 1982).

In addition, in recent years professionals from various disciplines have engaged in the development and utilization of strategic learning across a wide range of domains and areas (Borkowski, Weyhing, & Carr, 1988; Ellis & Lenz, 1987; Englert, Raphael, Fear, & Anderson, 1988; McLoone, Scruggs, Mastropieri, & Zucker, 1986; Palincsar & Brown, 1984; Smith & Friend, 1986; Torgesen, Dahlem, & Gerenstein, 1987; Wong, 1979; Wong & Jones, 1982). The general goals of these approaches are to assist those with learning disabilities in the learning process by providing strategies for learning and by training individuals to regulate and assume control over the learning situation.

Metacognition and Clinical Teaching

The basic tenets of clinical teaching and metacognition are very similar. Namely, clinical teaching emphasizes following sound principles of teaching and viewing individuals as active processors of information who have the ability to bring upon the learning situation all available resources and to become active learners through the use of control executive functions. In addition, the learning environment is viewed as being interactive in nature, with a reciprocal relationship between a learner, the learning conditions, and a teacher. Like clinical teaching, the metacognitive approach is success oriented and involves development of student sensitivity to the learning environment, heightening of student awareness of the conditions of learning, including the task and strategy variables, and acquisition of both basic academic skills and strategies for learning. As stated earlier, the LD specialist must go beyond the teaching of basic skills to include a broader spectrum of the training program—to include intensive remediation of academic skills, training in strategic learning, training in metacognition and control executive functions, training in study skills and study habits, training in career/vocational aspects, and training in life-coping and problem-solving skills.

Operating from a metacognitive perspective, clinical teaching places emphasis on students' understanding of, and participation in, the learning process. Teachers and students develop cooperative learning situations in which aspects of each individual's functional level and needs are discussed in order to arrive at appropriate learning plans that are joint products of both teachers and students. Students are encouraged to become active learners involved in the learning process and ultimately assume responsibility for their learning.

EDUCATIONAL THERAPY

The term *educational therapy* is prevalent in the private sector that provides remedial and support services to individuals with LD. Some states (e.g., California) have a state organization for educational therapists. Educational therapy denotes the inclusion of therapeutic aspects in the remedial process. The term *educational therapy* was derived from the European term *educateur*. It referred to an educational specialist who was equipped to deal with children having learning and emotional problems and who was trained in education, psychology, and sociology (Linton, 1969).

Educational therapy is defined by Ashlock and Stephen (1966) as "the treatment of learning disorders through the application of educational and psychological principles of learning and adjustment. Such treatment is usually used as a prelude to, or in conjunction with, specialized educational techniques and materials employed to diminish the discrepancy between the learner's academic potential and level of attainment" (pp. 3–4).

Educational therapy is provided in clinical settings and hospitals throughout the nation. Its major purpose is to assist learning-disabled individuals in adjusting to a classroom environment and to supplement schools' remedial programs. In hospital settings, the purpose of educational therapy is to provide interim intervention and to facilitate the transition from a hospital to a school setting.

The goals of individualized educational therapy services are the same as those of clinical teaching, mainly to provide the learning disabled with remedial programs commensurate with their functional levels and abilities and tailored to their needs. The primary goal is to develop independent-active learners who can assume responsibility for their own learning and effectively utilize control executive functions. In addition, individualized educational therapy is intended to facilitate the functioning of individuals in the mainstream of the school environment.

Purpose and Functions

The purpose and functions of individualized educational therapy are as follows:

1. To ameliorate academic deficiencies
   a. in basic skills and content areas
   b. in study skills
2. To provide training in strategic learning
   a. guidance in work habits
   b. training in strategies for learning
   c. assistance in generalizing strategic learning to various aspects of school functions and home environment

3. To provide training in the use of control executive functions
    a. guidance in planning, organizing, and scheduling activities throughout a week
    b. guidance in monitoring activities
    c. assistance in developing realistic self-evaluation
4. To provide emotional support
5. To provide training in areas of developmental deficits where deemed appropriate.

Structuring the Educational Therapy Session

Arranging the Physical Setup

Educational therapy in an individualized setting usually occurs in a specially designated area and/or office. The setup should be flexible and amenable to learning, and should include a desk area, a resting area, and a free activity area. The educational therapist should maintain a professional learning environment with formal procedures and routines, yet allow enough flexibility to address a student's immediate needs.

Organizing the Session

Several distinct phases make up an individual educational therapy session. A session normally lasts 50 minutes and can be utilized effectively if structured as follows:

Phase 1: Developing an educational therapeutic relationship. During the first 5 to 10 minutes, through a discussion of general events both in and out of school, the educational therapist aims to develop the sensitivity of the student to learning situations, to heighten awareness of factors affecting performance and development of control executive functions (planning, organizing, monitoring progress, and evaluating outcomes). Using a metacognitive approach, the student and the therapist apply effective strategies to problem solving. Specific problems that the child has encountered in school, both in academic areas and in social-interpersonal relationships, are raised for discussion and resolution. The use of individualized metacognitive task cues and monitoring devices is recommended.

Phase 2: Planning the session. Although the therapist should have advanced planning, input from the student should be sought to identify and prioritize areas of emphasis. This should be done through assignment sheets and a feedback format.

Phase 3: Giving intensive remediation of academic skills and assistance in areas that pose difficulties at school.

Phase 4: Training in strategic learning and integrating such training with academic skills development, study habits, study skills, and problem-solving skills.

Phase 5: Working on special assignments and projects. The therapist provides guidance and assistance in the development of a student-directed project. Supplemental academic and study skills are taught as needed in order to complete the output.

Phase 6: Evaluating the session and planning for follow-up activities (done by both the therapist and the student). Metacognitive student task cues and monitoring devices should be used.

Note: The educational therapist should incorporate short, fun activities or games during the various segments of a therapy session.

Monitoring Student Progress

The monitoring of student progress should consist of students recording their personal progress, using specific formats and observations by the therapist. Monitoring schedules and devices can be helpful in the process. Continuous formal and informal communication with the regular classroom teacher should be maintained. Specific written communication forms can facilitate this process.

Metacognition in an Individualized Setting

The use of the metacognitive approach in an individualized educational therapy session can prove effective in developing the student strategic learning repertoire and the utilization of control executive functions. (Also see chapter 6.) Unlike a teacher in a school, who sees students for many hours, an educational therapist is limited to a number of sessions with a student. As previously stated, in addition to assisting a student in the remedial process, an educational therapy session is aimed at developing a student's independent/active learning. The use of control executive functions can assist both the educational therapist and the student in developing the necessary skills for independent learning and in monitoring the student progress.

An educational therapist must follow the steps and procedures for metacognitive training. As in a classroom situation, the educational therapist must prepare the learning environment and the student for the metacognitive approach. The prerequisite for its application is the formation of a sound educational therapeutic relationship.

SUMMARY AND CONCLUSIONS

The development and delivery of a comprehensive intervention program for individuals with learning disabilities are stressed in this chapter. Intervention practices must go beyond the narrow academic parameters to a broader framework of school and life adjustment. The curriculum should relate to the skills and knowledge individuals with LD need in order to function optimally in school and society with the necessary strategies for learning and problem solving.

The need to adopt an intervention framework that delineates the numerous areas and elements necessary for effective delivery of remedial teaching has also been emphasized. The LD specialist must have knowledge of clinical teaching procedures—must know what to observe, what to assess, how to program, how to select appropriate teaching methods, and how to implement an effective remedial program using advanced techniques and procedures. The LD specialist is viewed as a highly trained professional who has specialized teaching skills and is in a position to make decisions that will maximize the benefits of a remedial program.

Serving Individuals with Learning Disabilities in the Least Restrictive Educational Environment

Questions to Consider

1. **What do "least restrictive environment" (LRE) and "mainstreaming" mean?**

2. **What are the goals and objectives of mainstreaming?**

3. **How does the resource room program serve the needs of individuals with LD in the LRE?**

4. **What are the roles of regular classroom teachers, LD specialists, school psychologists, and school counselors in mainstreaming?**

5. **What is collaborative consultation?**

6. **How can the LD specialist develop a framework for effective consultation?**

7. **What does "transitioning into mainstreaming" mean?**

MAINSTREAMING AND THE LEAST RESTRICTIVE ENVIRONMENT MOVEMENT

Adopting a service delivery framework and providing appropriate intervention for students with learning disabilities, as discussed in chapter 4, must be viewed within the structure of the school environment. A key provision in PL 94–142 is an educational program in the least restrictive environment for handicapped individuals. Traditionally, students with LD were served primarily in self-contained special classes. Since the implementation of PL 94–142 and the mandate of a least restrictive environment, school systems throughout the nation have developed programs to serve learning-disabled students in the LRE.

Public Law 94–142 section 4(c), 19 requires that the IEP include a statement of "the extent to which such child will be able to participate in regular education programs." According to Fiscus and Mandell (1983), "In making this stipulation, Congress espoused the important principle that handicapped children should be educated in the least restrictive environment possible" (p. 12). Furthermore, section 612(5)(b) states the following:

> To the maximum extent appropriate, handicapped children, including children in public and private institutions or other care facilities, are educated with children who are not handicapped and that special classes, separate schooling, or the removal of handicapped children from the regular education environment occurs only when the nature or severity of the

handicap is such that the education in regular classes with the use of supplementary aids and services cannot be achieved satisfactorily.

Mainstreaming is a term created by educators to describe the process of reintegration of handicapped learners into regular classes from special classes. The term *integration* was initially used to refer to this process during the 1950s and 1960s. It was later replaced by the term *mainstreaming*, which became popular in the 1970s and is more prevalent in schools today than "least restrictive environment." However, "least restrictive environment" should not be equated with "mainstreaming." "For some handicapped children mainstreaming may be the least restrictive environment, while for others it may be a barrier for learning" (Fiscus & Mandell, 1983, p. 113). For many students with learning disabilities, the least restrictive environment is a regular classroom with support services from a resource room program; for others, it may be a self-contained classroom.

The following profile illustrates the plight of some learning-disabled students who are attempting to receive their education in the least restrictive environment.

Mary is a 16-year-old 10th-grade student with learning disabilities. In accordance with her IEP, she is enrolled for two periods of her day in a resource room for basic math and English and studies history, science, physical education, and drama in a regular classroom. Mary has been diagnosed as learning disabled since third grade and has spent most of her time in special day classes. However, for the past 2 years, attempts have been made to enroll her in regular classes. Her reading levels in both word recognition and reading comprehension are at about the sixth-grade level. She functions at the third-grade level in math and spelling. Mary is disorganized, but she tries hard to please her teachers and generally is very cooperative. On a recent report card, her history teacher noted, "Mary is a hard working student, and it is a pleasure to have her in my classroom." She is doing OK in her classes, with the exception of science.

The resource teacher in Mary's school usually works very closely with the regular classroom teachers and constantly seeks their cooperation and support in modifying instructional procedures for her students whenever necessary. Mary is having extreme difficulties in her science class. Her teacher assigns an average of two chapters per week to read, requests written projects, and also expects the students to know the material covered in class, which is quite often not in the textbook. Requests to permit Mary to use a tape recorder for lectures and to allow her to make oral rather than written reports, have met with continued refusals by the science teacher. Mary is frustrated, and since she realizes that she has no chance to pass the class, she has decided to "ditch" science. Equally frustrated is her resource teacher, who feels helpless in this situation because the principal left the decision to the science teacher, who claims that changing the standards and requirements for Mary is inappropriate.

Like Mary, many learning-disabled individuals in the regular classroom are encountering extreme difficulties. Although some of these problems can be attributed to their disabilities, others stem from inadequate modifications of instructional routines and styles of student output—modifications that are not commensurate with LD students' ability to benefit from the regular classroom experience.

While the research findings on the effectiveness of mainstreaming practices for students with learning disabilities are equivocal (Bersoff, Kabler, Fiscus, & Ankney, 1972; Caparulo & Ziegler, 1983; Gottlieb, 1981; Jenkins & Mayhall, 1976; Polloway, 1984; Rust, Miller, & Wilson, 1978; Sabatino, 1971; Stainback, Stainback, Courtnace, & Jaben, 1985), few people question the underlying philosophical values inherent in the mainstream movement. Turnbull and Schultz (1979) refer to it as "the most humanizing practice." The concept of mainstreaming is supported by the National Education Association and the American Federation of Teachers (Mori, 1979).

Mainstreaming in Perspective

Defining Mainstreaming

There are numerous definitions of mainstreaming in the literature. They vary in degree of specificity and professional involvement, as well as degree of services implemented. In April 1976, a delegate assembly at the 54th Annual International Conference of the Council for Exceptional Children adopted the following definition of mainstreaming:

> Mainstreaming is a belief which involves an educational placement procedure and process for exceptional children, based on the conviction that each such child should be educated in the least restrictive environment in which his educational and related needs can be satisfactorily provided . . . and that special classes, separate schooling or other removal of an exceptional child from education with nonexceptional children should occur only when the intensity of the child's special education and related need is such that they cannot be satisfied in an environment including nonexceptional children even with the provision of supplementary aids and services. (p. 43)

A generally accepted definition of mainstreaming is as follows:

> Mainstreaming means enrolling and teaching exceptional children in regular classes for the majority of the school day under the charge of the regular class teacher, and assuring that the exceptional child receives special education of high quality to the extent it is needed during that time and at any other time it is needed. (Birch, 1978, p. 1)

The important elements in this definition include the following requirements: (a) enrolling in regular classes for the majority of the school day and (b) the availability of special education support services.

Probably the most widely cited definition that adds clarity and operational guidelines is one offered by Kaufman, Gottlieb, Agard, and Kukic (1975):

> Mainstreaming refers to the temporal, instructional, and social integration of eligible exceptional children with normal peers. It is based on an ongoing individually determined educational needs assessment, requiring clarification of responsibility for coordinated planning and programming

by regular and special education, administrative, instructional, and support personnel. (pp. 40–41)

This definition contains three major components: (a) integration (i.e., temporal integration); (b) educational planning and programming (instructional integration); and (c) clarification of responsibility (social integration). Kaufman et al. (1975) stress that mere physical time in the classroom is not enough and argue that mainstreaming must involve services that lead to integration in the other dimensions.

Schultz and Turnbull (1984) described mainstreaming as an educational arrangement of placing handicapped students in a regular class with their nonhandicapped peers to the maximum extent possible. For a handicapped student to be mainstreamed requires a physical inclusion in a regular class for an unspecified portion of the day, and a functional inclusion demonstrated by social and instructional integration with nonhandicapped students (Schultz, Carpenter, & Turnbull, 1991). Furthermore, according to Schultz and Turnbull (1984), mainstreaming is (a) the creation of alternatives; (b) a systematic process; (c) the social and instructional integration of students; (d) a strategy to advance learning—not to penalize nonhandicapped students; (e) a shared responsibility; and (f) an opportunity to learn new skills.

The Council for Exceptional Children (1975) provided us with a description of both what mainstreaming is and what it is not. Accordingly, mainstreaming is

- providing the most appropriate education for each child in the least restrictive environment.
- looking at the educational needs of children instead of clinical or diagnostic labels such as mentally handicapped, hearing impaired or gifted.
- looking for and creating alternatives that will help general educators serve children with learning or adjustment problems in the regular setting. Some approaches being used to help achieve this are consulting teachers, methods and materials specialists, itinerant teachers, and resource room teachers.
- uniting the skills of general education and special education so that all children may have equal educational opportunity.

Mainstreaming is not

- wholesale return of all exceptional children in special class to regular class.
- permitting children with special needs to remain in regular classrooms without support services that they need.
- ignoring the need of some children for a more specialized program than can be provided in the general education program.
- less costly than serving children in special self-contained classrooms. (Caster, 1975, p. 174)

Mainstreaming Goals and Objectives

Underlying the process of mainstreaming is the normalization of handicapped students so that they may learn to cope with later real-life situations (MacMillan & Semmel, 1977). These students must become an integral part of regular classroom activities and be accepted by nonhandicapped students. Then the anticipated benefits of mainstreaming are possible in that the classroom environment is enriched for all students. More specifically, the goals of mainstreaming include the following:

1. To facilitate the normalization process so that individuals with handicaps may function in the mainstream of society
2. To provide, as far as possible, a normal educational environment
3. To provide an educational program in the least restrictive environment
4. To facilitate modeling of normal behavior patterns
5. To provide a cognitively stimulating learning environment
6. To provide interpersonal interaction with nonhandicapped peers
7. To remove stereotypes and stigmata attached to handicapped individuals
8. To provide a broader base and a more cost-effective educational environment

The Regular Education Initiative

During the second half of the 1980s, mainstreaming received a new interpretation with the introduction of the General Education Initiative (GEI) or, as it is more often called, the Regular Education Initiative (REI). Rather than aiming for integration of students with handicapping conditions into the mainstream, it seeks to restructure mainstreaming (Skrtic, 1987). The contention is that students with mild to moderate handicapping conditions can be fully served in regular classrooms, using assessment and intervention techniques directly related to the expectations and operations of those classrooms (Lilly, 1986). This call for the merger of special and regular education was brought into the forefront at the 1985 Wingspread Conference on Education of Students with Special Needs: Research Findings and Implications for Policy and Practice at Racine, Wisconsin. A keynote address given by Madeleine C. Will, the assistant secretary for the U.S. Office of Special Education and Rehabilitative Services, and entitled "Educating Children with Learning Problems: A Shared Responsibility" called into question the efficacy of "special," "compensatory," and "remedial" education programs in America's schools. Will (1986) stated:

> At the heart of the special approach is the presumption that students with learning problems cannot be effectively taught in regular education programs even with a variety of support. Students need to be "pulled-out" into special settings where they can receive remedial services. Although well-intentioned, this so-called "pull-out" approach to the educational difficulties of students with learning problems has failed in many instances to meet the educational needs of these students and has created, however unwittingly, barriers to their successful education. (p. 412)

At the same conference, Maynard Reynolds, Margaret Wang, and Herbert Walberg presented a position paper containing a rationale and support for the REI (Wang, Reynolds, & Walberg, 1986). Like Will, they challenged the categorical system for providing services to exceptional students and pointed to the failure of the pull-out programs. They contended that the "current classification systems for students with special needs are educationally ineffective and burden schools with excessive administrative, teaching, and financial costs" (p. 26). They proposed a two-part initiative to merge special and regular education. First, they recommended

> joining practice, from both special and general education into a coordinated educational delivery system. This system will combine methods that have a strong research record of effectiveness with comprehensive systems of instruction that have evolved from both general and special education such as the Adaptive Learning Environments Model (ALEM). [They urged the federal government] to collaborate with a number of states and local districts in experimental trials of more integrated forms of education for students who are unjustifiably segregated in separate programs. These trial efforts should assure accountability to parents of students in protected classes according to federal and state legislation. (p. 28) (see discussion of ALEM further in this chapter).

The REI is based principally on philosophical convictions and societal values of equality and fair treatment for all individuals, and the inclusion of persons with handicapping conditions into the mainstream of school and the community (Stainback & Stainback, 1988). It recommends wholesale mainstreaming of mildly handicapped students as well as those in compensatory programs (McKinney & Hocutt, 1988). This movement advocates that "the general education system assume unequivocal, primary responsibility for all students in our public schools—including identified handicapped students as well as those students who have special needs of some type" (Davis, 1989, p. 440).

The REI has generated a great deal of discussion and controversy. While recognizing its merit, the Executive Committee of the Council for Exceptional Children, Teacher Education Division also acknowledges the powerful complexities and dimensions inherent in the changes that are suggested. The critics of the initiative have questioned the assumptions underlying the initiative and have pointed to the lack of empirical evidence to support its basic assumptions (Kauffman, Gerber, & Semmel, 1988). They have questioned the use of efficacy studies that have serious methodological flaws (Hallahan, Keller, McKinney, Lloyd, & Bryan, 1988). They point out that although the initiative is called the REI, most of the professional dialogue is conducted by special educators, with a lack of involvement on the part of regular educators. Furthermore, they point out that the short history of the mainstreaming movement suggests a less than enthusiastic support for exceptional students in regular classrooms. Teachers are less tolerant of these students and at time resist any attempts to recommend instructional modifications for them. This situation is much more severe at the secondary level. The organizational structure of secondary schools, the degree of skill deficits of these individuals, and the curriculum demands placed on them preclude any implementation (Schumaker & Deshler, 1988). The learning and behavior needs of many exceptional students make their education in an extraordinary learning environment essential. Students with exceptional needs make extraordinary demands on regular classroom teachers—demands that those teachers are not trained, prepared, or willing to accommodate in their classrooms.

The REI movement ignores the fact that there is a realistic limit to what can be expected of regular classroom teachers (Newcomer, 1989).

If the initiative is enacted, special education services for individuals with learning disabilities who are considered by some as mildly handicapped will be reduced, perhaps even eliminated (Bryan, Bay, & Donahue, 1988). Whereas the early stages of the initiative called for experimental trials to develop adequate educational programs in the mainstream, politicians and administrative personnel in some states are quick to advocate and propose changes in the name of the REI (Schumaker & Deshler, 1988).

The REI must be placed in proper perspective; as a Platonistic ideal, it serves its purpose. Yet it could lead to a more cooperative working relationship between regular and special educators. Common goals of serving individuals with exceptional needs in the least restrictive environment could be developed. All the support these students need from both special and regular educators in order to succeed in school and to receive the maximum preparation to function as independent and contributing adults in our society could be accomplished. As stated by Davis (1989),

> The REI debate must be placed in proper perspective. . . . Issues and concerns currently being addressed as part of the REI debate are important ones. They provide us with a rare opportunity to rigorously evaluate public education's commitment to serving handicapped and other special needs, at-risk students, as well as to assess its present level of organizational readiness necessary to not only accommodate but also to respect and value individual student differences. Most important, however, the REI debate is focusing, in part, on quality-of-life issues—basic human needs issues that are much more global and significant than simply P.L. 94–142 compliance issues. (p. 445)

To date, the REI still basically remains a matter of professional discourse between special and regular educators. Silver (1991), in his article titled "The Regular Education Initiative: A Deja Vu Remembered with Sadness and Concern" points out the elements that make it difficult to implement the concepts of the REI which include more than just the involvement of the school and educational community. In essence, if any of the concepts of the REI are to be effectively implemented, politicians must see that money must be poured into the educational system to improve the quality of education by reducing class size, providing effective educational programs, and training regular classroom teachers to handle mildly disabled students. This contention is reinforced by Semmel, Abernathy, Butera, and Lesar's study (1991) on teachers' perceptions of the regular education initiative. Results favored the current special education practices and pull-out programs in elementary schools. "A relatively high percentage of respondents believed that full-time placement of students with mild disabilities in the regular classroom could negatively effect the distribution of instructional classroom time. Teachers felt that the rate at which district curriculum objectives are met may be decreased as a function of full-time placement of these students in the regular classroom" (p. 19).

While philosophically no one would disagree with the concepts bestowed by the REI, collaborative work must be done between regular and special educators to develop effective models that will emulate the concepts inherent in the REI. This can only be done with state and federal support. However, any move in that direction must be done cautiously to guarantee the rights of each individual student to receive the kind of educational services that take into account his/her needs and provide an educational environment conducive to learning.

Mainstreaming Models

Basic Components

Meisgeier (1976) provides us with a summary of major definitions and essential mainstreaming components identified in them. These include the following:

1. Modification of mainstream delivery systems, curriculum management systems, instructional strategies, professional roles, and other environmental variables
2. Appropriate pre-service and re-education programs for mainstream teachers, managers, supervisors, and other staff
3. Modification of special education delivery systems, curriculum management systems, instructional strategies, professional roles, and other environmental variables
4. Appropriate pre-service and re-education programs for special education teachers, managers, supervisors, and other staff
5. Change and modification of related support and parallel systems
6. A change to a teacher training-consultation model for special education, supervising, and psychological staff with deemphasis of elaborate, irrelevant, categorically oriented diagnostic procedures and systems
7. An emphasis on continuous progress, success oriented programs for all children
8. Precision programming and daily accountability for basic program and support system interventions
9. Pro-active programming that is responsive to educational needs of all students, as opposed to programming for economic, political, or managerial convenience. (pp. 258–259)

Thus one would expect that teachers in optimal mainstream classrooms would (a) provide for flexible physical setups and arrangements; (b) provide for grouping and regrouping of students based on functional levels and student interest; (c) provide instruction in a manner appropriate to students' needs in both the group and individual settings; (d) utilize learning and media centers and individual working areas; (e) establish structural routines, scheduling and pacing activities so that they are geared to the needs of individual students; (f) select instructional materials that are geared to students' functional levels and provide self-corrective materials; (g) utilize innovative and the most advanced instructional approaches; (h) provide support to handicapped individuals both in school and in the home; and (i) be open to communication with special educators and other support personnel.

Various mainstreaming models and programs are in use in schools around the country today. Three such models are discussed in this chapter: the Parallel Alternate Curriculum, the Adaptive Learning Environments Model, and the resource room program. While they may not necessarily include all the aspects previously discussed, they represent programs with promising practices.

The Parallel Alternate Curriculum

The Parallel Alternate Curriculum (PAC), which was developed at the Child Service Demonstration Center at Arizona State University in cooperation with the Mesa, Arizona, public schools, is designed to provide secondary teachers with alternative methods for meeting the educational needs of all students. The PAC program facilitates teaching of required high school courses in a nonreading format, using taped books, videotaped materials, movies, slides, lectures, and various forms of discussion. The PAC courses cover the same material as the regular curriculum but adhere to the individualized needs of the mildly handicapped and other low-achieving students (Hartwell, Wiseman, & Van Reusen, 1979). The PAC program combines alternative teaching strategies with schoolwide study skills training to facilitate mainstreaming (G. Smith, 1988).

The Parallel Alternate Curriculum provides four options within its program:

1. Total PAC—all content and assignments are presented to students in a non-reading format.
2. Mini PAC—only low achieving students use PAC materials in a regular class.
3. Partial PAC—only a particular topic or unit is presented in a PAC format.
4. Preference PAC—students are presented with a choice of instructional procedures; the classroom is divided into learning style stations such as reading, discussion, listening, etc. (Hartwell et al., 1979, p. 29)

Steps and procedures for implementation of these four options are described by the same authors:

Step 1—Learning outcomes are identified, knowledge to be acquired by the student;

Step 2—Possible alternatives for presentation are identified and considered for use, for example, taped textbooks;

Step 3—Available materials and equipment are identified for possible use;

Step 4—Students are evaluated for learning style, learning preference, and/or achievement level;

Step 5—Alternatives for presentation (i.e. taped books, discussion methods) are decided upon and matched with students' learning styles or preferences;

Step 6—Software are developed for future use (i.e. slides are collected, transparencies made, or textbooks are taped);

Step 7—Presentation is implemented;

Step 8—Student progress is evaluated in a traditional and/or alternative manner, such as oral or multiple choice tests. (Hartwell et al., 1979, pp. 29–30)

The Parallel Alternate Curriculum program has three areas of focus: (a) Teachers are trained to use methods that insure academic success for low-achieving students in the mainstream; (b) the learning environment includes innovative programs such as Math Labs, which use hands-on approaches to teaching math application skills; and (c) students are offered courses in study skills. In addition, it implements schoolwide study skills programs that integrate the teaching of study skills in all academic areas so students' skills can be improved and reinforced by all teachers (Smith & Smith, 1985).

Paramount to the implementation of the PAC program is the administrative support system that provides for (a) small class size (not exceeding 25 students); (b) scheduling of teachers into one room instead of having them travel to several rooms a day; (c) paid professional days to obtain training; (d) substitute teachers so that teachers can get together with participating colleagues and plan cooperatively; (e) special funds for materials and school-based coordinators at each secondary school; and (f) clerical assistance available for the exclusive use of teachers participating in PAC (Smith & Smith, 1985).

The Adaptive Learning Environments Model

The Adaptive Learning Environments Model (ALEM) is a mainstreaming program developed and studied at the University of Pittsburgh's Learning Research and Development Center over the past 15 years (Wang & Vaughn, 1985). The underlying assumption that guided the development of the program is "that students learn in different ways and at different rates and, as a result, effective school programs require both the inclusion of a variety of instructional techniques and learning experiences that match the needs of each student and the allocation of adequate amounts of time for all students to learn" (Wang & Walberg, 1983, p. 604). The ALEM program incorporates principles of diagnostic prescriptive instruction and provides an instructional-management support system designed to maximize the use of available classroom and school resources (McDowell, 1986). Its objectives are "to foster students' successful acquisition of basic academic skills and simultaneously, to develop students' confidence in their ability to learn and to cope with the social and intellectual demands of schooling" (Wang & Vaughn, 1985, p. 6).

In their *Handbook for the Implementation of Adaptive Instruction Programs,* Wang and Vaughn (1985) describe the ALEM in detail. The conceptual ALEM includes 12 critical dimensions related to the provision and support of adaptive instruction in the classroom, and 4 dimensions related to school and district-level support. The 12 classroom dimensions include 9 classroom-level instructional program dimensions and 3 support program dimensions. The 9 classroom-level instructional program dimensions, which have been identified as critical design features for effective provision of adaptive instruction, include (a) creating and maintaining instructional materials, (b) developing student self-responsibility, (c) using diagnostic testing, (d) instructing, (e) using interactive teaching, (f) monitoring and diagnosing, (g) motivating, (h) prescribing, and (i) keeping records. The 3 program dimensions critical for supporting implementation at the classroom level include (a) arranging space and facilities, (b) establishing and communicating rules and procedures, and (c) managing aides.

The 4 program dimensions related to school and district-level support include (a) using multi-age grouping, (b) doing instructional teaming, (c) having personal preparation, and (d) involving the family.

The ALEM systematically integrates individualized instruction in the basic skills with a classroom management system that provides a flexible organizational structure for adapting instruction to student differences. In this system, the instruction of exceptional students rests primarily with regular classroom teachers, who are provided with support and consultation from special educators and other resource personnel. Special educators are moved into the mainstream along with exceptional students to provide diagnostic services, intensive instruction, and consultation with regular classroom teachers and parents as needed. The program also includes for ongoing staff development and a delivery system for achieving an effective interface between special and general education services. The role of the principal is clearly defined as an instructional leader who works actively with teachers to (a) influence instructional strategies, (b) solve problems in the classroom, (c) participate in in-service activities, (d) conduct both formal and informal staff development, (e) observe in classrooms and provide feedback to teachers, and (f) identify instructional goals and means for teachers' achievement (Wang & Reynolds, 1985; Wang & Vaughn, 1985).

According to McDowell (1986), in schools that have been properly implementing the ALEM programs, one would expect to observe the following:

- students busily working individually or in small groups
- students of all ability levels taking charge of their own achievement
- students tutoring students
- teachers working as a team to provide instruction and feedback to individuals or small groups as needed
- individual differences viewed and handled by teachers and students as the norm rather than the exception
- immediate alternative instruction identified and provided before difficulties become learning problems
- students of all ability levels making steady, cumulative data-based progress
- students and teachers who look and act as if theirs is a mutually enjoyable and satisfying educational experience. (p. 21)

The feasibility of wide-scale replication of the ALEM, and evidence of the program's efficacy, have been reported in several studies (Wang & Birch, 1984b; Wang, Gennari, & Waxman, 1985; Wang, Peverly, & Randolph, 1984; Wang & Walberg, 1983).

Yet recent reviews of research involving the ALEM have challenged its efficacy based on research methodology grounds. According to Bryan and Bryan (1988), while the ideas in ALEM may be sound, the claims for it have not been established through careful analysis of the ALEM data.

The Resource Room Program

A key provision in PL 94–142 is an educational program for handicapped individuals in the least restrictive environment. Traditionally, students with LD were served primarily in self-contained classes. With the the mandate of a least restrictive environment, school systems throughout the nation have developed resource room programs in an attempt to bridge the gap between regular classrooms and special classes. Across the country, 75% of the 1,900,739 students with LD served in the 1986–1987 school year were served in regular classrooms, or in resource rooms with the balance of the day spent in regular classrooms (1988 Report to the U.S. Congress as cited by McCarthy, 1989). The resource room is described by Wiederholt, Hammill, and Brown (1983) as follows:

> Basically, a resource program is any school operation in which a person (usually the resource teacher) has the responsibility of providing supportive educationally related services to students and/or to their teachers. The resource teacher may provide the students with direct services in the form of analytic, remedial, developmental, or compensatory teaching and/or behavioral management. Such services may be conducted either in the regular classroom or in a room designated for that purpose, such as the resource room or center. The services offered to the regular or special teachers may include, but are not limited to, helping them either to adjust or to select curricula to meet the unique needs of some children and to manage the classroom behavior of disruptive students. In addition, the resource teacher also discusses with parents the problems evidenced by their students. (p. 3)

Wiederholt et al. (1983) described five different types of resource programs operating in schools. These include the categorical resource program, which serves handicapped students separately according to their designated areas of exceptionality; the cross-categorical resource program, which serves handicapped students from two or more disability categories; the noncategorical resource program, which serves students with mild to moderate learning and/behavioral problems and includes both handicapped and nonhandicapped students; the specific skill resource program, which provides basic skill training primarily to normal students; and the itinerant resource program, which "is literally a resource program on wheels" (p. 10) providing services in a variety of settings and which can employ any of the preceding formats.

While minor variations can be found in operational styles, the basic concept of the resource room is to provide instruction and services for individuals with exceptional needs who are assigned to regular classrooms for the majority of the school days, and consultation with regular classroom teachers.

Goals and Purposes

The goals and purposes of the resource room include the following:

1. To provide appropriate educational services in the least restrictive educational environment
2. To provide more adequate services to a greater number of handicapped children
3. To provide specialized instruction to individuals with special needs while they are enrolled in regular classrooms for the majority of the school day
4. To provide a remedial program including metacognitive-oriented strategic instruction that will enhance and strengthen the academic and social skills of individuals with exceptional needs so that they may function optimally in regular classrooms
5. To prevent serious learning problems through early identification and intervention
6. To increase the number of children maintained in the mainstream of education.

In addition, through the resource teacher, the program objectives are to provide parents and regular staff members with consultation, resource information, and materials regarding individuals with exceptional needs.

In the process of serving students with learning disabilities in the least restrictive environment, the majority of them are now being served in resource room programs.

traditional roles (Blankenship & Lilly, 1981). They need to collaborate to provide optimal learning to learning-disabled students in the least restrictive environment.

According to Wood and Carmen (1982), special education teachers consider regular classroom teachers successful in mainstreaming handicapped children if they possess the following characteristics:

1. They love children and are concerned about each individual's needs.
2. They understand special education and its goal to help students reach their full potential.
3. They have a positive attitude with respect to special education and mainstreaming.
4. They understand mildly handicapped children's capabilities.
5. They desire to help students learn to cope with everyday problems.
6. They enjoy teaching children regardless of their abilities or disabilities.
7. They interact with special education teachers to provide well-balanced programs.
8. They adjust to new situations and are receptive to new ideas.
9. They incorporate mainstreamed children into the activities of the regular classroom and make them feel comfortable.
10. They recognize the importance of social acceptance to handicapped children.
11. They view special students as more normal than different and accept them as such.
12. They can identify and motivate special students.
13. They can individualize instruction.
14. They are sensitive to handicapped children's feelings.
15. They have patience, flexibility, and organization.
16. They have a strong desire to help mildly handicapped children.

Hierarchy of Regular Teachers' Involvement

Both empirical and research evidence suggest that regular classroom teachers can and will work effectively with children who have special needs. Their attitudes and their willingness to be involved are directly related to (a) the principal's attitude toward handicapped individuals, (b) an exposure to special education through pre-service and in-service training, and (c) the availability of support services (Mayer, 1982). Though regular classroom teachers may be exposed to various aspects of successful mainstreaming, it is essential that they have the necessary skills and competencies to adapt the regular classroom environment for mainstreamed students. There is a basic progression of regular classroom teachers' involvement with individuals with exceptional needs. One cannot expect regular classroom teachers who have just entered the field to be fully committed to mainstreaming. More likely, it is a gradual process, suggesting a hierarchy of teacher involvement that encompasses the following:

1. Knowledge and awareness of individual differences of exceptional children

2. Awareness of special education services available at the school site and the district level
3. Specific knowledge about program intervention components, including the role and function of ancillary personnel such as the resource teacher, the DIS, and the school psychologist
4. Knowledge of the referral procedures and of support for regular classroom program modification
5. Knowledge and readiness to implement corrective procedures in the regular classroom
6. Willingness to share knowledge and acceptance of group responsibilities to help students in the mainstream
7. Willingness to collaborate with support personnel to provide an optimal mainstreaming environment for students with LD

Regular classroom teachers need to develop the ability to recognize behaviors associated with learning disabilities. They must know what to look for through the development of an observational framework that includes an understanding of individual differences and a familiarity with the characteristics of individual learning disabilities. Early recognition can assist in securing immediate help for students with LD. A regular classroom teacher observation checklist is provided in Appendix A. Its purpose is to assist regular classroom teachers in making the initial identification of students who may need additional help through program modification in the regular classroom and/or placement in special education programs.

Role of the LD Specialist in Mainstreaming

The role of the LD specialist is crucial to effective mainstreaming. Of particular importance is the resource teacher who is expected to function in a consulting role, providing remedial teaching suggestions and resource materials. When regular classroom teachers receive support from special education as well as from the administration, they are more likely to put forth the effort for optimal mainstreaming of exceptional individuals. Special education teachers who have been trained in specialized teaching approaches and intervention strategies can assist regular classroom teachers in modifying classrooms to meet the needs of mainstreamed students.

Loftus and Walter (1981) offer these suggestions for special education teachers in working with regular teachers:

1. Be accessible to teachers.
2. Show an interest in the work and opinions of teachers.
3. Make your role known to the teachers.
4. When a teacher has a problem or needs assistance in implementing a program, work with that teacher.
5. Establish an environment conducive to open communication.
6. Express your thoughts clearly and concisely.
7. Listen to views of others.
8. Clarify points.
9. Develop positive school relationships. (pp. 3–4)

Roles of the School Psychologist and the School Counselor in Mainstreaming

The school psychologist and the school counselor are in unique positions to contribute to the success of mainstreaming learning-disabled students by assuming leadership roles (Cochrane & Marini, 1977; Pryzwansky, 1981; B. Smith, 1973) and by creating climates in which handicapped and nonhandicapped children can appreciate, understand, and enjoy each other (Lombana, 1980).

School psychologists now assume a broader role that includes assessment and diagnoses; participation at IEP meetings; chairship of IEP meetings; and consultation with teachers, parents, and nonhandicapped students (Goldwasser & Meyers, 1983). School psychologists often fill a central role at IEP team meetings because they are usually more highly trained and experienced than other team members (Pryzwansky, 1981). They are expected to provide leadership in the diagnosis, identification, and programming of students with LD. Furthermore, school psychologists are perceived by many parents as having knowledge and skills related to the diagnoses and placement of their children.

Likewise, the school counselor can provide important contributions to the IEP process (Filer, 1981). Although role variations exist among elementary and secondary levels and among school districts, generally the counselor's role includes coordination of the activities of school personnel related to the referral and IEP process (Cochrane & Marini, 1977); assistance in the assessment process (Filer, 1981); participation at IEP planning conferences and IEP meetings (Filer, 1981; Humes, 1978); the monitoring of student progress; consultation with regular classroom teachers; and parent counseling (Humes, 1978). In addition, the counselor provides support for exceptional students and serves as a mediator between students with LD and their teachers (Cochrane & Marini, 1977; Perosa & Perosa, 1981).

The school psychologist's and the school counselor's training and experience in child development, psychology, interpersonal relationships, and socialization are valuable assets to the total collaborative efforts to provide optimal services to learning-disabled students in the least restrictive environment.

CONSULTATION WITH THE REGULAR CLASSROOM TEACHER

Defining Consultation

Consultation in education is a relatively new phenomenon. In trying to facilitate the success of their students in the LRE, learning disabilities specialists are involved in consultation with regular classroom teachers. Specialists who function as consulting teachers and resource teachers assist regular classroom teachers in understanding individuals with LD and in providing instructional modification in their classrooms. This consulting role is a natural outgrowth of the special education thrust to broaden the continuum of services for students with special needs in the LRE (Huefner, 1988).

Consultation concepts and frameworks in education have been borrowed from school counseling and various mental hygiene disciplines. Different definitions of consultation have been presented in the literature. West and Idol (1987) refer to consultation as "the process by which a consultant assists another professional, the consultee, in regard to a client for whom the consultee retains responsibility" (p. 389). The consulting process involves sharing information and ideas, coordinating, comparing, observing, providing a sounding board, and developing tentative hypotheses for action (Dinkmeyer, 1968). Generally, the consulting relationship is voluntary and is entered into primarily for the benefit of a third party (Brown, Blackburn, Wyne, & Powell, 1979), thus making it possible to maintain the relationship in an objective framework. The consultant attempts to assist the consultee to solve a problem of the consultee's client. The consultant is assumed to have the skills and knowledge to help find the solution of the problem.

Bindman (1964) defines consultation as "an interaction process of interpersonal relationships that takes place between two professional workers, the consultant and the consultee, in which one worker, the consultant, assists the other worker, the consultee, [to] solve . . . a problem of a client or clients, within the framework of the consultee's usual professional functioning." In addition, "the process of consultation depends upon the communication of knowledge, skills and attitudes through this relationship and, therefore, is dependent upon the degree of emotional and intellectual involvement of the two workers." Bindman further states that "a secondary goal of the process is one of education, so the consultee can learn to handle similar cases in the future in a more effective fashion, and thus enhance his professional skills" (p. 367).

According to Brown et al. (1979), consultation is usually a process that is based upon an equal relationship characterized by mutual trust and open communication. It is a shared responsibility involving joint approaches to problem identification, and the pooling of personal resources to identify and select strategies to solve the problem. The definition of consultation provided by Idol, Paolucci-Whitcomb, and Nevin (1986) describes the collaborative nature of the consultation process:

> Collaborative consultation is an interactive process that enables teams of people with diversified expertise to generate creative solutions to mutually defined problems. The outcome is enhanced, altered and produces solutions that are different from those that the individual team member would produce independently. The major outcome of collaborative consultation is to provide comprehensive and effective programs for students with special needs within the most appropriate context, thereby enabling them to achieve maximum constructive interaction with their nonhandicapped peers. (p. 1)

In the report of the National Task Force on School Consultation (Idol-Maestas, 1986), consultation is viewed as a process for providing special education and support services for students with special needs in the regular classroom.

> Consultation is (a) indirect in that the special education teacher does not provide the instructional service to the student(s); (b) collaborative in that

all individuals involved in the process are assumed to have expertise to contribute and to share responsibility for instructional outcomes; (c) voluntary in that all parties are willing participants in the process; and (d) problem-solving oriented in that the goal of consultation is to prevent or resolve student problems. (p. 2)

The consulting role for special education personnel has received a great deal of support within current literature (Cipani, 1985; Friend, 1984, 1985; Huefner, 1988; Idol-Maestas, 1981, 1983, 1986; Idol-Maestas & Ritter, 1985; Lilly & Givens-Ogle, 1981; Paolucci-Whitcomb & Nevin, 1985; West & Idol, 1987). The benefits of consultation services are enumerated by the National Task Force on School Consultation. In general, consultation is an effective means of increasing the academic and social skills of students with special needs in the regular classroom. It is cost-effective and allows for efficient use of both special education and classroom teachers' expertise. Through interaction and collaboration, it fosters mutual understanding and sharing of materials and instructional strategies, and enhances active involvement by all concerned, including parents.

The Collaborative Consultation Model

Collaborative consultation is based on a triadic consultation model (Figure 5–1), which is composed of three components: the target (T), the mediator (M), and the consultant (C) (Idol, et al., 1986). The model emphasizes the role of the consultee (the regular classroom teacher) as the mediator of change between the consultant (the special educator) and the target (student). The consultant and the consultee (mediator) share knowledge about appropriate content, process, and reinforcers that may be utilized to ameliorate the problem. The process is viewed as dynamic, involving creative solutions to mutually defined problems. Both direct (solid lines) and indirect (dotted lines) communication are keys to effective consultation. According to Idol et al. (1986), four principles form the basis for collaborative consul-

Figure 5–1 The Collaborative Consultation Model

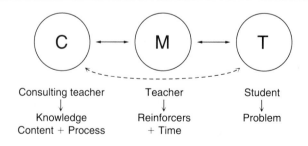

Source: From *Psychological Consultation in the Schools: Helping Teachers Meet Special Needs* (p. 137) by C. Parker (Ed.), 1975, Reston, VA: Council for Exceptional Children. Copyright 1975 by Council for Exceptional Children. Adapted by permission.

tation: (a) team ownership of the identified problem, (b) multiple levels of change for both teachers and administrators in the process of learning and adapting to new procedures, (c) the application of reinforcement principles and practices, and (d) decision making through data-based functional analysis of behaviors.

According to Idol et al. (1986), in collaborative consultation, the ownership of the problem is always shared and the consulting relationship is characterized by a sense of parity. Parity is demonstrated through two-way communication between the consultant and the consultee and through a sharing of knowledge and skills in solving the problem. A successful implementation of the triadic model entails progressive changes involving planning, learning new behaviors, and adapting to new routines. Collaborative consultation demands a commitment to assist the exceptional student and a firm belief that the student's learning and behavior can be affected. This requires the skills necessary to provide appropriate intervention through data-based instruction including functional assessment, specification of objectives, planning, implementation, and evaluation. In addition, an evaluation of the effects of the consultee and the consultant in solving the problem is critical to successful implementation of collaborative consultation.

Goals of Consultation

According to Brown et al. (1979), the goals of consultation include the following:

1. To develop a situation in which the educational and psychological development of the student is viewed as a high priority
2. To enlist and tap available resources to enhance the development of the student
3. To develop the skills of the consultee so that he or she may be able to handle similar situations in the future
4. To increase communication among the various professionals concerned with facilitating the educational and psychological development of the student
5. To enhance human relations in the school

The consulting process involves interpersonal relationships, the dissemination of information, demonstration and guidance, and management and decision making. To be effective in consultation, the resource teacher must demonstrate competency in (a) human interpersonal relationships, (b) clinical teaching skills, and (c) management and decision making.

The Consulting Process

Development of a Framework for Effective Consultation
In reviewing the role and functions of resource room teachers and the responses of regular classroom teachers to mainstreaming individuals with exceptional needs in their classrooms, one can conclude that consultation plays an important role in the mainstreaming process. Regular classroom teachers are more amenable to accom-

modating handicapped individuals in their classrooms if support services are provided. Resource teachers play a major role in providing these support services through direct instruction and consultation. For resource teachers to be effective in these areas, they must possess consulting skills/competencies. In addition, they must know the various aspects of regular classroom instruction and curriculum and the individual teacher's needs related to mainstreaming. A working framework is helpful in understanding the various aspects of the regular classroom environment. These include

- an awareness and identification of the teacher's needs related to the mainstreamed child
- the variables that enhance or hinder reaching these needs
- the process through which the special educator can respond to the teacher's needs, taking into account the preceding variables
- the specific content and information needed to facilitate the program
- the identification of the facilitator/provider and the delineation of responsibilities
- the means of evaluating the effectiveness of the program modifications in the regular classroom, including any monitoring devices for students and teachers

Procedures in the Consulting Process

The consulting process is viewed within the context of the total school environment. Resource teachers must be aware of the variables that affect the outcome of consultation in the school. Thus the first concern in consultation is the development of an atmosphere and a climate conducive to consultation. In addition, procedures for consultation and communication must be established. The following procedures may facilitate an effective consulting process:

1. Identify/delineate the consulting problem.
2. Determine the nature of the problem and assume team ownership of the identified problem.
3. Determine the consultant's ability to handle the problem.
4. Determine the consultee's ability to relate to the problem.
5. Establish collaborative procedures and the means of solving the problem.
6. Analyze the problem; gather additional information if needed.
7. Proceed with mutual, collaborative discourse to solve the problem.
8. Arrive at a consensus solution.
9. Clarify roles and responsibilities in providing a solution to the problem.
10. Provide reinforcements for the consultee.
11. Establish procedures for feedback, follow-up, and evaluation of efforts and procedures.
12. Keep anecdotal records and summations of consulting activities.

Effective Strategies for Consultation

The following section highlights effective strategies for consultation with regular classroom teachers, including the consulting environment, aspects related to effective interpersonal relationships and communication, consulting processes and styles, knowledge and application of sound principles of clinical teaching, and management and the decision-making process:

1. Consulting environment
   a. Organize the consulting physical setup so that it is conducive to the consulting relationship. It must be a comfortable place, free of distractions and with a relaxed atmosphere.
   b. If the consultee prefers, meet on her or his own territory.
   c. Provide for flexible scheduling of consulting time to meet the needs of the regular classroom teacher.
   d. Adhere to consulting steps and procedures, with specific attention to the appropriateness of the problem.
   e. Keep confidentiality in accordance with professional conduct.
2. Interpersonal relationships
   a. Develop personal rapport.
   b. Convey a positive and empathetic attitude.
   c. Develop a nonthreatening relationship.
   d. Provide consistency and credibility.
3. Communication
   a. Be aware of both verbal communication and body language.
   b. Speak in language easily understood by the consultee. Keep jargon to a minimum.
   c. Be an active listener. Don't assume that you have heard it before.
   d. Strive for a mutual dialogue. Don't take control of the situation.
   e. Maintain eye contact at all times. Be relaxed and calm.
   f. Keep the focus on the problem's solution.
   g. Make effective use of written communication.
4. Consulting process and style
   a. Be democratic in the consulting process.
   b. Establish a collaborative consultation effort so that the consultee and the consultant are viewed on an equal basis.
   c. Be deductive in your approach. Facilitate your problem solution through teacher suggestions and input.
   d. Use brainstorming techniques to arrive at a problem solution.
   e. Be a "doer" rather than a "stater" (don't claim that you know it all).
   f. Be supportive and follow through on the consulting situation.
5. Knowledge of clinical teaching and relevant resources
   a. Know about remedial teaching and approaches, including behavior management strategies.
   b. Be specific in recommendations. Provide handouts for easy understanding.
   c. Have knowledge of and access to resource material to support instructional goals.
   d. Know the regular classroom curriculum.

      e. Know what can and cannot be done within the restraints of the regular classroom environment.

      f. Know about innovative instructional approaches such as peer tutoring, cooperative learning, metacognition, and a strategy intervention model.

      g. Provide for demonstration teaching.

      h. Provide for modeling through itinerant teaching.

6. Management and decision making

      a. Develop and follow consistent consulting procedures, including a communication format and follow-up activities.

      b. Develop time management skills and realistic scheduling of activities.

      c. Develop a systematic record-keeping procedure and format.

      d. Be assertive in a nonthreatening manner. Guide the consultee to the solution of the problem.

      e. Draw on resources and materials available in the school and community.

REGULAR CLASSROOM PROGRAM MODIFICATION

The saying "It's easier said than done" has been expressed quite often by regular classroom teachers when modification suggestions are offered by student study teams, special educators, and/or other ancillary personnel. This section presents information and suggestions the LD specialist can use in working with regular classroom teachers.

In providing an optimal program for learning-disabled individuals in the mainstream, we must consider the totality of the educational environment and, within it, what is feasible to offer, what resources are available, and what support services are accessible. In addition, we must consider the general aspects of the students' ability to learn, learning styles, and general behavioral characteristics appropriate to age level and the demands they pose on individual students and the teachers.

Program modification suggestions must be adapted for age-appropriate and age-expected behavior, including developmental aspects. One must also adhere to the basic principles of learning, that is, readiness to learn, motivation, teaching to a student's level of functioning and preferred information-processing style, individualized instruction, and an effective feedback and reinforcement mode. Likewise, one must consider the utilization of resources and innovations to accommodate the needs of students in the learning process, including the use of paraprofessional volunteers, peer tutoring, cross-age tutoring, cooperative learning, and the use of media, teaching machines, and self-corrective materials.

At the primary level, teachers can provide careful adaptation of instructional methodology and materials through small increments of growth, continuous feedback, and nourishment of exploratory learning and creativity. More specifically, at this age, children are amenable to working with peers, paraprofessional volunteers, and aides. It is the teachers' role to train such individuals to provide appropriate instructional assistance to students, including the preparation and selection of material matched to the functional levels and age levels of the students.

Consideration must be given to developmental aspects of primary-age students, which include a short attention span, a need for immediate feedback, and reinforcement. Activities should be paced in short intervals to assure successful completion of tasks. Job packages, in which developmental, readiness, and other enrichment activities are compiled for students to complete during assigned periods, can be extremely helpful. Other effective resources are tape recorders to listen to books and tapes and some teaching machines.

At the elementary level, children with LD exhibit behavioral symptoms directly related to failure experienced during the first few years of schooling. To be successful, these students need a more structured learning environment, with clear indications of expectations and responsibilities relative to daily assignments. They respond well to program modifications with proper instruction and support services through the use of cross-age tutoring, paraprofessional volunteers, and aides, and through effective programming. These students are still eager to learn and master skills in school and are able to compete and play with peers.

At the secondary level, which includes both the junior and senior high levels, the modification of instructions follows a somewhat different pattern. The departmentalization of junior and senior high schools suddenly exposes learning-disabled individuals to numerous teachers with various styles of teaching and requirements. This exposure creates a tremendous burden on students as they attempt to adjust to the different teachers.

Regular secondary teachers are usually less nurturing and tend to be less supportive of individuals with learning disabilities, and they are often more resistant to program modifications, partly because of the general nature of secondary education. Yet with assistance from special educators, some secondary teachers are willing to modify programs and to offer the necessary support for students with LD in their classrooms, provided that they do not have to go to great lengths to make these modifications. Resistance to modification can also be attributed to students' self-perception and to the influence of the peer culture relative to those individuals who do not fit the mold. For example, a learning-disabled youngster at the secondary level who is functioning at approximately a third- or fourth-grade level would be ashamed of his performance and would consequently try to hide his deficiencies, resulting in a decrease in his ability to cope with the situation.

Suggestions for Program Modifications in the Mainstream

1. Modifications of the environment
   - Provide a flexible classroom arrangement that facilitates grouping and re-grouping of students.
   - Use natural settings to block off independent work areas.
   - Arrange preferential seating so students receive more individual attention.
   - Use elements such as music to filter out environmental distractions.
   - Use learning activity centers.
   - Provide peer tutoring.

- Arrange for cross-age tutoring.
- Use other ancillary personnel within the classroom.
- Use parent volunteers and paraprofessionals.
- Employ supplemental services in an adaptive education program.

2. Modifications of teaching approaches and modes of instruction
   - Utilize principles of corrective teaching in the classroom.
   - Match the teaching approach to the student's learning style.
   - Use concrete materials to facilitate learning.
   - Proceed from concrete through visualization to abstract learning.
   - Provide for practice and overlearning to facilitate recall and recognition.
   - Use a variety of compatible teaching approaches to reinforce learning and recall.
   - Simplify teaching presentations.
   - Present material using visual aids.
   - Break lessons down into smaller units with feedback intervals.

3. Modifications of instructional materials
   - Select materials appropriate for the functional and interest levels of students.
   - Follow a developmental learning sequence, that is, use materials that reflect the step-by-step development of concepts.
   - Provide a variety of instructional materials.

4. Modifications of student receptive modes
   - Allot students more time to copy notes/assignments from visual aids or the blackboard.
   - Allow students to use tape recorders if necessary.
   - Assist students in taking notes.

5. Modifications of student assignments and output
   - Check that assignments are within students' ability to complete.
   - Divide a major assignment, such as a term project, into smaller segments.
   - Simplify assignments when needed.
   - Pace assignments according to each student's ability, that is, allow more time for completion if necessary.
   - Provide visual cues to highlight the nature of an assignment, using color coding when appropriate.
   - Provide structure and direct student activities to complete assignments.
   - Provide intermittent feedback to assure successful completion of assignments.
   - Allow students to present assignments in forms other than written.
   - Allow students to demonstrate knowledge orally, that is, permit oral exams and oral presentation of assignments.

6. Modifications of behavior management approaches and intervention styles
   - Provide a structure within which students can respond.
   - Clarify behavior and performance expectations.
   - Organize daily assignments and utilize daily schedules.
   - Provide for the monitoring of behavior and performance.

- Provide immediate feedback and reinforcement modes.
- Administer individualized student contracts.
- Utilize contingency management.

Transitioning into Mainstream

Mainstreaming is based on the assumption that placing handicapped students in the mainstream will facilitate academic learning and individual social and emotional growth. However, too often students are indiscriminately placed in regular class-rooms or left there without support services (Salend & Lutz, 1984). Many school districts have interpreted the "least restrictive environment" of PL 94–142 to mean the mainstreaming of all handicapped individuals without due concern as to whether or not these students are ready for it (Gresham, 1982a). There has been little research dealing with the criteria to be used in determining the readiness of children with LD for mainstreaming (Wilks, Bireley, & Schultz, 1979). According to Salend, Brooks, and Salend (1987), 90% of the school districts surveyed had no such criteria for determining students' readiness. Salend and Lutz (1984) voiced their concern by stating that we "must develop guidelines that promote the development and success of mainstreaming by ensuring that mainstreaming students possess the skills necessary to perform successfully in the regular classroom milieu" (p. 27).

Salend and Lutz (1984) and Salend and Salend (1986) identified social skills competencies at the elementary and secondary levels. According to these authors, a competency-based approach to mainstreaming can provide placement teams with an objective means of assessing student readiness for entry into the regular classroom environment.

According to Salend and Lutz (1984), the following aspects of student behavior were considered critical by regular and special educators:

1. Follows directions.
2. Asks for help when it is appropriate.
3. Begins an assignment after teacher gives assignment to class.
4. Demonstrates adequate attention.
5. Obeys class rules.
6. Tries to complete task before giving up.
7. Doesn't speak when others are talking.
8. Works well with others.
9. Respects others' feelings.
10. Refrains from cursing and swearing.
11. Avoids getting into fights with other students.
12. Plays cooperatively with others.
13. Respects others' property.
14. Shares materials and property with others.
15. Refrains from stealing others' property.
16. Attends class regularly.
17. Tells the truth. (p. 28)

"Metacognitive Strategies for Problem Solving in Arithmetic." Then the students converted these statements to "I" statements, thereby making a transition from knowledge to action and emphasizing a shift in responsibility to implement and monitor the strategies. The teacher demonstrated how to use these strategies and coached the students as they rehearsed using them. Finally, the converted "I" statements were written on individual self-monitoring and recording sheets, as shown in Figure 6–1. These statements represent the metacognitive strategies for problem solving in arithmetic.

Students in this class are usually provided with a strategy guide to stimulate discussion regarding the nature of the task and the necessary strategies required to complete it successfully. As soon as they understand the nature of the task, emphasis is placed on strategy implementation. In subsequent activities, they are guided to implement strategies for problem solving in arithmetic.

In situations such as the preceding, students are engaged in metacognitive learning through exploratory learning and guided teaching. The teacher serves as a facilitator of learning, coaching and helping them to develop and use strategic behaviors. Whenever new strategies are introduced, the teacher models their effective use. Students' rehearsal is an integral part of the process as they attempt to become skillful in using strategies appropriately and effectively. The responsibility of monitoring and regulating their performance is gradually shifted to the students as they become capable in assuming responsibility for their own learning.

The metacognitive approach in teaching emphasizes the individual student's exploratory learning and problem-solving procedures in the acquisition of the metacognitive concepts. With reciprocal and interactive teaching, students are encouraged to explore methods of learning and problem solving, to observe how others learn and solve problems, and to exchange ideas with participating group members. Students are further encouraged to question themselves about their learning process. The metacognitive approach actively involves students in analysis of the learning situation and in the development and utilization of effective learning strategies in the various areas of curriculum as well as in general—in specific aspects of expected student behavior, study habits, study skills, and social interpersonal relationships. This approach is aimed at enhancing students' metacognitive awareness and providing systematic strategic approaches to learning and problem-solving in school and in life.

Defining Metacognition

Metacognition is generally referred to as one's knowledge of one's own cognition. It is a person's knowledge of and conscious control of his or her own cognitive processes (A. L. Brown, 1980b; Brown & Smiley, 1978). Wellman (1985) refers to metacognition as "a person's cognition about cognition, that is, the person's knowledge of cognitive processes and states such as memory, attention, knowledge, conjecture, illusion. . . . [The premise is that individuals]. . . form and hold conceptions about how the mind works, about which mental problems are hard, which easy, about their own mental states and processes" (p. 1). According to Flavell (1976),

Figure 6–1 Word Problems Strategy Implementation and Monitoring Sheet

COMMITMENT TO SUCCESS: STRATEGY USE

Set 9: Mathematics

Skills/Behaviors I Need to Learn:	How Will I Do It? (Strategies)	How Am I Doing? Key: √ −; √; √ +;					
		M	T	W	Th	F	Overall
Word Problems	I read and understand the problem.						
	I look for the question and recognize key words.						
	I select the appropriate operation.						
	I write the number sentence (equation) and solve it.						
	I check my answer.						
	I correct my errors.						
Individualized Goal							

Teacher's Comments:

Student's Comments: This Is the Way I See Myself

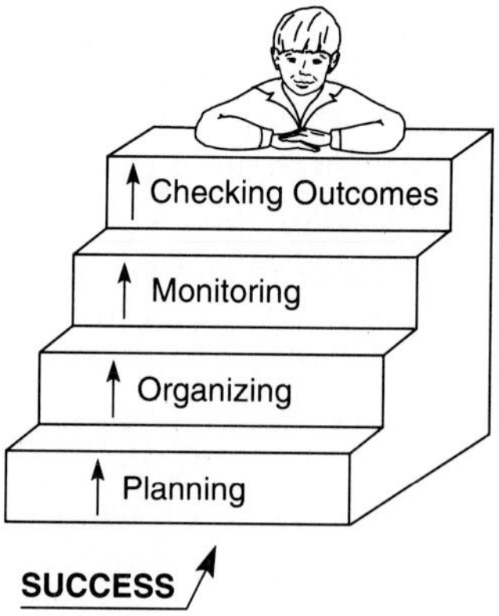

Checking Outcomes

Monitoring

Organizing

Planning

SUCCESS

From *Learning to Learn: Metacognition Student Handbook, Level II, Book 1* by A. Ariel, 1987a. Unpublished manuscript, California State University, Los Angeles. Reprinted by permission.

"Metacognition" refers to one's knowledge concerning one's own cognitive processes and products or anything related to them. . . . Metacognition refers, among other things, to the active monitoring and consequent regulation and orchestration of these processes in relation to the cognitive objects or data on which they bear, usually in the service of some concrete goal or objective. (p. 232)

Similarly, Baker (1982), Baker and Brown (1984a), and Brown and Palincsar (1982) distinguish between two types of metacognitive knowledge, namely, knowledge about cognition and regulation of cognition. Brown and Palincsar (1982) state that "knowledge about cognition involves conscious access to one's own cognitive operations and reflection about those of others. . . . Regulation of cognition [is] often referred to as executive control within information processing models" (pp. 1–2). Regulation usually involves planning, monitoring, and checking outcomes. Palincsar (1986) further recognizes the selection and utilization of effective strategies as aspects of metacognition.

Ariel (1986a) provides the following definition, which encompasses the various aspects of metacognition and their interrelationships:

> Metacognition is defined as knowledge about knowledge, knowledge of and conscious control of one's own cognitive enterprise, including strategic production and the regulation of such activities, usually using control executive functions. The nature of the individual's metacognition is affected by the individual's metacognitive base, i.e., the cognitive base, affective base, and knowledge base. Basic integrative and reciprocal relationships exist among the four dimensions of the metacognitive phenomenon, namely, the metacognitive process, the metacognitive base, the metacognitive variables, and the metacognitive control executive functions. (p. 14)

The metacognitive phenomenon can best be summarized in four areas:

1. Knowledge about knowledge; one's knowledge of and conscious control of one's own cognitive process
2. Knowledge/beliefs about variables affecting the cognitive enterprise, the learning process, and problem solving
3. Strategy acquisition and strategic productions
4. Regulations of cognition through the use of control executive mechanisms, that is, planning, organizing, monitoring, and checking outcomes

In order to fully understand the metacognitive phenomenon, one must acquire knowledge of the metacognitive process, the metacognitive variables, the metacognitive base, and the metacognitive control executive functions. These aspects directly affect an individual's metacognitive involvement and are discussed in the taxonomy of metacognition later in this chapter. Knowledge of such a taxonomy is essential to understanding the metacognitive phenomenon and to effectively implementing the metacognitive approach in applied settings.

Origin and Basic Assumptions

Tracing the development of metacognition leads to studies in cognitive psychology, information processing, metamemory, mediation theory, and cognitive behavior modification related to metacognition. However, metacognition received the most impetus from studies of metamemory (A. L. Brown, 1975, 1978, 1982; Flavell, 1976, 1979; Flavel & Wellman, 1977) and information-processing theories (Neisser, 1967). Although the term *metacognition* may be new, the type of knowledge to which it refers has long been recognized (A. L. Brown, 1981). Psychologists such as Dewey (1910), Huey (1908/1968), James (1890), and Thorndike (1917) addressed early on what can be identified today as aspects of metacognition, that is, the learning of how to learn a phenomenon and the learner's active role in learning, self-regulation, and self-control (A. L. Brown, 1982). The coming together of the behavioral and information-processing theories has led to the current work in metacognition and in learning strategy approaches (C. R. Smith, 1986).

Metacognition is based on the assumption that people are active in their own learning and can bring together all available resources to assure successful learning experiences. It is rooted in the assumptions that (a) individuals are active information processors (Bransford, 1979; Neisser, 1976) and are success oriented; (b) human learning is "servo regulated," that is, "pupils consistently readjust their learning activities on the basis of the feedback they received from their activities" (Mann & Sabatino, 1985, p. 156); and (c) "rather than portraying learners as passive participants who assimilate knowledge in a mechanical manner, this new conception characterizes learners as active information processors, interpreters and synthesizers" (Weinstein, 1982, p. 6).

Metacognition and Learning Disabilities

In a recent comprehensive study of the variables that are most important in enhancing children's learning in school (Reynolds, Wang, & Walberg, in press), metacognitive learning strategies were among the 20 most highly rated, in terms of both instruction and desired student characteristics. Metacognitive and learning strategy approaches have become topics of prime interest in the field of learning disabilities. Theory and research related to learning-disabled individuals both suggest that the remedial approach can be further strengthened when metacognitive training is included. The learner who does not spontaneously use a set of effective learning strategies can be trained to do so with time, effort, and appropriate approaches. The research evidence in metacognition points out that individuals with learning disabilities show significant improvement following training in the application of various appropriate strategies to the task at hand (Hallahan et al., 1983; Lloyd, Saltzman, & Kauffman, 1981; Palincsar, 1986; Palincsar & Brown, 1984; Paris & Oka, 1989; Pflaum & Pasarella, 1980; Schumaker, Deshler, Alley, Warner, & Denton, 1984; Stevens, 1988; P. Winograd, 1984). Research findings generally point to student improvements following metacognitive procedures and training (O'Sullivan & Pressley, 1984; Schunk & Rice, 1987; Short & Ryan, 1984; Stewart & Tei, 1983; Swanson, 1989). In general, recent developments in metacognition theory and research have led to greater success in designing instruction aimed at improving reading skills (Baker & Brown, 1984b).

In exploring the possible implications of metacognitive training for reading instruction, it is noted that "in contrast to skilled readers, less skilled readers lack knowledge about the purpose of reading, lack sensitivity to the need to behave strategically, fail to evaluate the appropriateness of chosen strategies, do not apply strategies spontaneously and rigidly apply chosen strategies" (Short & Ryan, 1984, p. 225). Moreover, poor adult readers are deficient in metacognitive awareness of the reading process (Gambrell & Heathington, 1981). Stewart and Tei (1983), in discussing the implications of metacognition training for reading instruction, noted that knowledge of the reading process gives readers control and facilitates their reading fluency. Moore (1983) pointed out that overall, high-ability readers are more metacognitively aware of many important parameters of reading than low-ability readers.

Individuals with LD are less aware than high-achieving students of modeled writing strategies and steps in the writing process (Englert et al., 1988). Metacognitively oriented approaches to written language result in improved performance following use of metacognitive strategies. "The writing of inefficient learners including adolescents and young adults with reading and language disorders can be improved by teaching them appropriate composition strategies and self-management routines that they can use independently. . . . [They can] be taught strategies for maintaining active task involvement and productivity, activating a search of appropriate memory stores for writing content, facilitating advance planning, and editing and revising texts" (Graham & Harris, 1987, p. 67). Learning-disabled individuals have also been shown to improve in their ability to monitor their activities as a result of metacognitive training (Rigney, 1980; Wong & Jones, 1982). The underlying characteristics of such research involve an increase of individuals' awareness of various aspects of the area treated, utilization of effective strategies to function successfully, and regulation of activities.

The application of metacognitive theory and its principles to intervention with learning-disabled individuals is viewed as a promising approach (Wong, 1985a; A. L. Brown, 1982). According to Wong (1982), the work on metacognition points out that metacognitive and elaboration skills are crucial for effective learning and that they are considered meaningful types of interactions. Thus intervention with children with learning disabilities should be directly aimed at improving their metacognitive skills. Metacognitive training of students with LD seems to enhance their use and generalization of strategies and to motivate many students to attribute success to their own efforts, increasing their feelings of self-efficacy and self-control (Paris & Oka, 1989).

Metacognition and the Characteristics of the Learning Disabled

The characteristics of individuals with learning disabilities have been extensively reviewed in chapters 1 and 3, and they suggest that in addition to having the classical symptoms of learning disabilities, those who struggle with learning problems and continue to experience failure for months or years become deficient in fundamental skills as well as in their approach to learning. In addition to feeling inadequate and worthless, they become unable to pursue learning appropriately and develop a sense of self-helplessness (Diener & Dweck 1978, 1980; Greer & Wethered

1984; Seligman 1975) quite often characterized by the "I cannot do" syndrome. As a result of negative interactions with learning experiences, those children become inactive learners (Torgesen, 1977, 1980; Wong, 1979), dependent upon others for regulating their learning. Furthermore, "the research evidence in cognitive psychology and the active role of information processor . . . strongly suggest that failure to take an active role in learning is a major source of performance problems for the learning disabled" (Wong, 1982b, p. 44). Individuals with LD experience difficulties with self-regulation, checking, planning, monitoring, testing, revising, and evaluating their learning and problem-solving efforts (Swanson, 1989), all of which are aspects of metacognition, and specifically of the control executive system.

In addition, recent research points to a production deficiency of learning-disabled individuals. They exhibit difficulties in using planful and organizational strategies in various activities and fail to engage spontaneously in strategic behavior. Learning-disabled individuals "do not engage readily in certain organized, goal directed strategies that aid performance on intellectual tasks" (Torgesen, 1982, p. 46). They do not perform well in school because they fail to adapt to tasks and fail to use efficient and organized strategies (Torgesen, 1980). In comparison with normal children, "learning disabled children have been characterized as lacking in spontaneous use of various types of attentional and mnemonic strategies . . . [and are] deficient in various metacognitive skills, such as planning, monitoring and checking" (A. L. Brown, 1982, p. 4). Similar findings reported by Hallahan and Reeve (1980) point to poor performance on tasks of selective attention as a result of deficiencies in the application of learning strategies. Torgesen (1980) states that "difficulties in the application of efficient task strategies may be a general characteristic of learning disabled children, even across groups that have different kinds of specific processing problems" (p. 366). These difficulties in the application of efficient task strategies have been attributed to information-processing disorders (Swanson, 1988). In fact, according to Swanson (1988, 1989), those with LD are more appropriately characterized as actively inefficient learners who exhibit faulty task performance. This inefficient learning is due to the failure of learning-disabled individuals to "integrate all cognitive planes into one complex act for successful task performance" (Swanson, 1988b, p. 73).

People with learning disabilities are not cognizant of the nature of their problem and consequently lack the ability to utilize existing faculties effectively. The production deficiencies, the self-helplessness syndrome, and the inactive characteristics of learning-disabled individuals all interact to produce learners who are passive, are incapacitated with feelings of self-defeat, and have a fear of learning. "The idea that many of the performance deficiencies of learning disabled children may be accounted for by their failure to employ efficient task strategies has received consistent support from the research" (Torgesen, 1980, pp. 367–368). Students with LD do not spontaneously use strategies, nor do they regulate and monitor their performance (Englert et al., 1988; Wong & Jones, 1982). Brown and Palincsar (1982) suggest "that children with learning problems are in desperate need of intervention aimed at improving their metacognitive skills, both declarative and self-regulatory" (p. 14).

A MODEL OF METACOGNITION

Adopting a framework and a model of metacognition is essential for understanding the metacognitive phenomenon and for developing and designing training programs and intervention research. The goals of the model are (a) to provide a framework of metacognition to facilitate the understanding of this phenomenon, (b) to provide a scientific paradigm with its heuristic value to guide future theory and research, (c) to facilitate the transition to an operational framework in which research on training in metacognition can be guided, and (d) to provide a framework for metacognition training for normal and exceptional individuals.

Consistent with both theory and research, a quadrivalent model of metacognition has been formulated. The model consists of the four interactive and reciprocating dimensions that comprise the metacognitive phenomenon. The concepts are not new and are easily recognizable in various writings on metacognition. The four dimensions are (a) the metacognitive process, (b) the metacognitive base, (c) the metacognitive variables, and (d) the metacognitive control executive functions. These dimensions are further analyzed into subcomponents. Together, they interact to provide the metacognitive phenomenon, as shown in Figure 6–2. The reader is cautioned that this model is not exhaustive and that it merely provides a guiding framework for metacognition in an attempt to generate cohesiveness to this concept.

To illustrate the interaction of the four dimensions of metacognition, a tetrahedron is used, as in Figure 6–3, with each of its dimensions corresponding to one of the four metacognitive dimensions of the taxonomy.

The Metacognitive Process

Although no clear delineation of the metacognitive process can be found in the literature, many researchers, such as Brown (1978), Flavell (1976), and Wellman (1985), have implied various processes in metacognition. Thus Flavell speaks of "numbers of metas . . . that a child may gradually acquire" (1976, p. 232), Flavell and Wellman (1977) of "sensitivity" to learning situations and to an awareness of "variables knowledge," A. L. Brown (1978) of an awareness of one's cognition, and

Figure 6–2   The Metacognitive Phenomenon

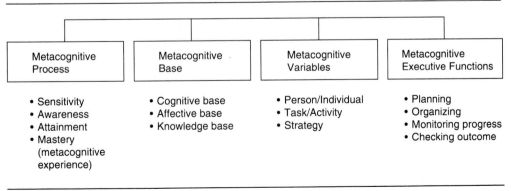

Figure 6–3   The Interactive Nature of the Metacognitive Phenomenon

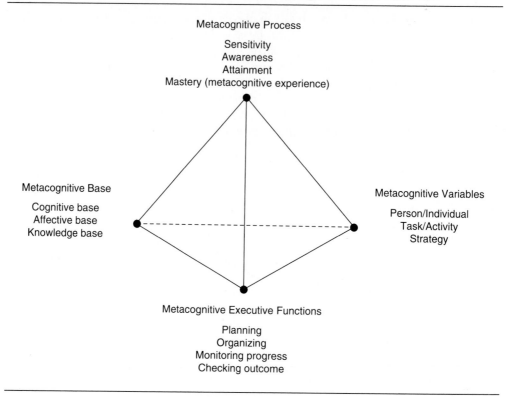

Flavell (1971) again of the "attainment" of different sorts of knowledge and the metacognitive experience (Flavell, 1979).

The metacognitive process is viewed as consisting of four phases: (a) sensitivity, (b) awareness, (c) attainment, and (d) mastery/the metacognitive experience.

The following account of Mike, a 16-year-old who exhibits severe difficulties in arithmetic, illustrates the metacognitive process. Although enrolled in 10th grade, Mike functions at about 2nd-grade level in arithmetic computation and responds almost fearfully to anything having to do with arithmetic. The first task of the teacher is to develop Mike's sensitivity to the learning situation, to arithmetic computation, and to the fact that the teacher and he are going to jointly explore the means of overcoming his difficulties. This initial sensitivity is essential for facilitating his involvement in the learning process. The next phase is to guide Mike in his development of an awareness of what is involved in the process of arithmetic computation, an awareness of his abilities and limitations, and an awareness that there are strategies that can facilitate the learning of arithmetic computation. Following this, the teacher helps Mike acquire the skills and strategies needed for the arithmetic computation. Most importantly, Mike must reach the mastery level. He must know how and when to effectively employ these skills and strategies and use the control executive mechanisms of planning, organizing, monitoring progress, and checking outcomes to regulate his learning. Mike is thus guided in the development of his sensitivity to the learning situation, in the development of his awareness of his cognitive repertoire vis-à-vis the task at hand, and in the acquisition of strategies and the utilization of control executive functions in order to successfully achieve the task.

The Phases of the Metacognitive Process

The first phase of the metacognitive process heightens students' *sensitivity* to learning situations and increases their role in the learning process. Individuals' subjective feelings about learning in general and about their chances to succeed directly affect their approach to learning. Thus "children who grow up in the face of failure tend to blame their [supposed] lack of ability, not their lack of effort, for their failure . . . [and] have learned to be passive and expect things to happen to them; they do not expect to make things happen for themselves" (Wiens, 1983, p. 147). Sensitivity to a learning situation and to a task at hand affects students' ability to perform the task. In fact, individuals' perception about their ability to perform a task may be more critical than their skill level (Brown, Bransford, Ferrara, & Campione, 1983).

In a practical situation, sensitivity implies involvement with a learning situation and acceptance of an active role in the learning process, including assuming responsibility for learning and formulating collaborative learning relationships. Through exploratory and self-discovery activities, students discover that they can in fact succeed in learning, can assume control over the learning process, and can be successful at the task at hand (Ariel, 1986a).

Awareness refers to individuals' knowledge about the learning environment and about the variables that might affect the outcome of learning, that is, individual, task, and strategy variables (Flavell, 1979). This awareness also involves knowledge about one's abilities and limitations, about one's strengths and weaknesses in relation to the learning experience. In more general terms, self-awareness emphasizes "the functional ability of knowledge of one's own actions, motives, and personality attributes" (Shrauger & Osberg, 1982, p. 267).

In metacognition, self-awareness is perceived to be a significant element in the process of change. Thus metacognition is, in part, aimed at heightening one's awareness of oneself in relation to the demands of the environment. According to A. L. Brown (1981), in order to be efficient learners, students must develop rudimentary knowledge of "1) available strategies for directing attention, 2) their own characteristics as learners including capacity, limitations and background knowledge, 3) text characteristics including important elements, structure features, etc. and 4) the value of the critical task or the test to which the learning must be put" (p. 524).

The manner by which students become aware of what it takes to perform well plays an important role in the extent to which they will succeed in learning. In a practical setting, activities such as "understanding metacognition," "understanding the way we learn," "understanding the way I learn best," "knowing your own individual factors," "knowing task activity factors," "knowing strategy factors," and "understanding the control executive system" contribute to students' awareness of the factors and variables that affect successful learning and problem solving (Ariel, 1986c, 1988).

Attainment refers to individuals' acquisition of skills and strategies appropriate to a situation, including use of the executive control mechanisms—planning, organizing, monitoring progress, and checking outcomes. Four main aspects encompass this phase: (a) increased emphasis on the learner's analysis of the learning situation and process, (b) strategy acquisition and utilization, (c) strategy generalization and transfer, and (d) effective use of control executive functions. Metacognition training provides learners with an organizational framework with which to evaluate their needs in accomplishing the task at hand and, accordingly, with which to select task-appropriate strategies. It thus involves one's ability to "stop and think" about what is needed to accomplish a task successfully, that is, the ability to analyze a learning situation in terms of the variables affecting learning and to acquire strategies to accomplish the task successfully, usually using control executive functions.

Mastery/metacognitive experience refers to individuals' effective interaction with learning situations and their knowledge of what they know, how they know it, and when and where to use what they know. Students reach metacognitive mastery when they spontaneously select appropriate strategies to solve problems and effectively use control executive mechanisms. Those who have mastered metacognition have conscious control over the cognitive processes involved in learning. According to Flavell (1979), "Metacognitive experiences have to do with where you are in an enterprise and what sort of progress you are making or are likely to make" (p. 908). Mastery is the overall summation of metacognitive functions; it involves strategy selection and strategic production: knowing what to do, knowing how and when to use skills and strategies, and effectively using control executive mechanisms (Ariel, 1986). Individuals at this level have a broad repertoire of strategic behaviors and are in control of their "cognitive enterprise."

Earlier in this section, you read about a 16-year-old with learning disabilities and how his training proceeded through the four phases of the metacognitive process. It seems obvious that the metacognitive processes and phases are not independent of each other, but are in complex interaction—hierarchical and interactive in nature. The reciprocal and interactive aspects of metacognitive training are noted by Borkowski, Johnson, and Reid (1987) and by Pressley, Borkowski, and O'Sullivan (1985). The metacognitive process is viewed as continuous: It begins with the development of sensitivity to a learning situation, moves to the heightening of awareness of those factors affecting learning, proceeds to the acquisition of skills and strategies and the knowledge of how and when to use them, and culminates with the metacognitive experience, which usually involves the use of control executive functions necessary for successful learning and problem solving.

The system is highly interrelated. The interactional aspect becomes clearer as one works with students to facilitate the metacognitive process. Classroom observations point to individual differences in the rate of progression and in the nature of the interaction. Some individuals move readily across the various phases of the metacognitive process, but others find the progression more laborious. To a degree, each phase can be seen as subordinate to the one above it in the hierarchy, requiring a set of skills to move to a higher level. This view is consistent with Flavell's (1981) belief that a sensitivity or awareness precedes and triggers the metacognitive experiences.

The Individual's Metacognitive Base

Metacognitive theory and research have been applied to a variety of situations and to heterogeneous groups, including preschoolers, intermediate school children, adolescents and young adults, the mentally retarded, the learning disabled, the behavior disordered, the gifted, and normal individuals. The wide range of applications suggests that individual differences in cognitive capacities, affective areas, and knowledge base determine the nature of the metacognitive training. All these areas—the cognitive base, the affective base, and the knowledge base—comprise the metacognitive base of an individual.

The *cognitive base* is defined as an individual's general cognitive and intellectual abilities that determine the capacity for cognitive processes. The *affective base* refers to an individual's emotional state and interaction patterns with the surrounding environment. The individual's state of mind, or "affective balance" (Heider, 1958), directly affects one's ability for, and approach to, learning, and how and what one perceives, remembers, or thinks. Also, it clearly affects motives and feelings and is indeed part of an individual (Mann & Sabatino, 1985). The *knowledge base* refers to an individual's acquired knowledge, which consists of declarative knowledge, or "knowing that"—factual knowledge about strategies; procedural knowledge, or "knowing how"—strategic knowledge (Chi, 1978, 1981; Gagne, 1985; Pressley et al., 1985; T. Winograd, 1975); and conditional knowledge, or "knowing when and why"—the conditions under which appropriate strategies can be optimally employed (Paris, Lipson, & Wixson, 1983). This knowledge base is acquired, updated, and modified throughout an individual's life span (G. Cohen, 1983). Though the preceding three aspects can be viewed separately, in reality they interact to comprise the metacognitive base. The functional level of an individual in these three areas dictates the approaches and levels of metacognitive involvement and training.

The Metacognitive Variables

Metacognitive variables are the factors/variables that affect the outcome of a learning experience. They are the factors that learners must be aware of in order to maximize their potential in a learning process. Three major categories of such factors or variables have been identified in metacognition and metamemory literature: person variables, task variables, and strategy variables (Flavell, 1981; Flavell & Wellman, 1977; Wellman, 1985). These variables are one of the sets of knowledge that form a person's metacognition (Wellman, 1985). According to Flavell (1981), most metacognitive knowledge implicitly or explicitly concerns interactions among the three categories. Addressing the interacting nature of these factors that affect learning, A. L. Brown (1982) states, "I would like to argue that this is exactly what efficient learners do. Before they can become expert, children also need to develop insights into the demands of the learning situation. They need to understand something about their own characteristics, the available learning strategies, the demand characteristics of various tasks and inherent nature of the material" (p. 97).

Person variables include knowledge about one's own capacities, limitations, and idiosyncrasies in relation to the learning environment. They include all temporary and enduring personal attributes, and all things one could come to know or believe about oneself (Flavell, 1981; Flavell & Wellman, 1977). Students who successfully perform a task are aware of the nature of the task and of their own strengths and weaknesses with regard to that task, and they thus adjust their behavior to accommodate these variables. This adjustment is necessary to successfully accomplish the task.

Task variables refer to the characteristics and attributes of a task. A learner must be aware of "task characteristics" and "task demands" (Flavell & Wellman, 1977), that is, what is required to complete a task successfully. The metacognitive process thus necessitates both an understanding of the characteristics and attributes of a task at hand and an identification of the specific learning processes that a task entails. The task demands or goals and their implications comprise another aspect of the task variable and make learning purposeful and goal-oriented. In this respect, metacognitive knowledge involves knowledge of what the task and goals call for in terms of the specific demands of the task, the effort, and the skills an individual must employ to complete the task successfully.

An individual has to be aware of the task variables across the metacognitive process. In this process, the first aspect related to sensitivity is the knowledge of what is involved in a specific area. For example, in reading comprehension, a student recognizes what reading comprehension is, recognizes its function, and recognizes the elements of the task. In short, this heightening of awareness of the learning process, as well as of knowledge of what skills are necessary for effective or successful task acquisition and completion, is the basic principle of the metacognitive process. In the attainment phase, an individual must know the specific skills and strategies that are needed for task mastery and the skills and strategies that promote the effective use of executive control functions. And last, for mastery related to the task variables, the individual must know what skills and strategies to use and how and where to use them effectively to successfully complete a task.

Strategy variables are another aspect of metacognitive knowledge. Strategy is defined as a set of skills, an "organized sequence of processing activities" that are necessary in order to successfully achieve a task (Brown & Palincsar, 1982; Torgesen, 1982). According to Rabinowitz and Chi (1987), "Strategies are often described as procedures that are used as an aid in a performance of a given task. . . . [T]he important characteristics of strategies are that they are goal-oriented processes" (p. 84). Strategies are enabling skills that promote successful learning and problem solving (Paris & Oka, 1989). The use of strategically oriented metacognitive skills results in successful outcomes and enhances individuals' feelings of self-efficacy and self-esteem (Borkowski, Estrada, Milstead, & Hale, 1989). As discussed previously, strategy knowledge is made up of three components: knowing that (declarative knowledge), knowing how (procedural knowledge), and knowing when and why (conditional knowledge). A strategy is only considered to be fully acquired when all components of this definition are present. Developmental differences in strategy employment have been reported in the literature, and strategy use usually increases with age (Andreassen & Waters, 1989).

Generally, three types of strategies have been recognized in metacognitive research: specific, general, and control executive (Brown & Palincsar, 1982; Newell, 1979; Torgesen, 1980). In the context of the present model and in an examination of the demands that are placed on individuals in school, at home, and in life in general, four main categories of strategies have been identified that are amenable to training: specific strategies, general/skill strategies, control executive strategies, and higher order control executive strategies.

Specific strategies are defined as strategies that can be used in one specific situation, for example, remembering that a *ck* combination makes a *k* sound in reading or how to convert a mixed number to an improper fraction. *General/skill strategies* apply across many areas of the curriculum and problem solving and include general study skills such as outlining skills, note-taking skills, and exam-taking skills. *Control executive strategies* involve the regulation and control of processes that apply across the board to an individual's learning and daily activities. More specifically, they involve planning, organizing, monitoring progress, and checking outcomes. Translated to daily activities, one can speak of planning one's weekly activities, organizing activities, monitoring how well one is doing, and checking the outcome of one's endeavor. *Higher order control executive strategies* apply to a higher level of functioning involving realistic evaluation, aspirations, and goal setting in line with an individual's abilities. This distinction among the types of strategic knowledge and their corresponding strategies is aimed at facilitating strategy generalization and strategy transfer in an effort to circumvent what A. L. Brown (1978) refers to as the "welding" of a strategy to a specific task. The acquisition of the various types of strategies is viewed as hierarchical and interactional in nature. While some prerequisite specific strategies are needed to attain skill strategies, it is possible to acquire various strategies of higher levels in a parallel fashion and to delegate to them the control executive functions. An individual's ultimate functioning as an independent learner and a successful individual is highly dependent on the functions of the control executive strategies and the higher order control executive strategies.

The Control Executive Functions

The fourth dimension identified in the metacognitive model is the control executive system, which involves four primary functions: planning, organizing, monitoring progress, and checking outcomes. This aspect of metacognition is well recognized and established in metacognitive theory and research (A. L. Brown, 1980b; Brown et al., 1983). The executive system initiates, regulates, modifies, and mediates the learning experience (Borkowski, 1985). It deals with executive decisions about planning, organizing, monitoring one's progress, and evaluating the outcome of one's learning efforts and endeavors and is viewed as a dynamic process (Justice, 1985).

Control executive functions are acquired skills. Individuals learn how to plan, organize, and monitor the success of various strategies and activities, and ultimately how to check the outcome of their endeavor. This self-regulatory mechanism can be understood best in terms of the principles of cybernetics (Wiener, 1948) and servomechanisms (Mann & Sabatino, 1985). Learning is "servo-regulated," that is, students constantly readjust their learning activities on the basis of the feedback they receive from these activities (Mann & Sabatino, 1985). The effectiveness and/or ineffectiveness of the self-regulatory mechanism is affected by children's previous learning experiences both at school and at home. In an environment that provides consistent routines with successful learning experiences, the progressive development of self-regulatory skills is likely to occur.

Planning refers to planning activities prior to undertaking an activity, a problem, or a project, and it involves complex, coordinated patterns of strategic activity (A. L. Brown, 1978; Brown & Palincsar, 1982). *Organizing* activities is another aspect of the control executive system, without which that system cannot function effectively. Organizational routines and strategies serve as organizational schemata within the control executive system and are crucial to an individual's overall metacognitive process. "Organization, goal directedness and use of feedback are basic characteristics of skilled performance" (Hall, 1980, p. 14). Individuals who lack these aspects tend to accomplish less and are less efficient.

Monitoring progress refers to the activities during learning—monitoring one's progress, revising, and rescheduling one's strategies for learning (Brown & Palincsar, 1982). Self-monitoring skills are necessary for successful task performance. Wagner and Sternberg (1984) point out that monitoring involves both looking ahead and looking back: "Looking ahead includes learning the structure of a sequence of operations, identifying areas where errors are likely, choosing a strategy that will reduce the possibility of errors and that will provide easy recovery. . . . [L]ooking back includes detecting errors previously made . . . and assessing the reasonableness of the present immediate outcome task performance" (p. 201).

Checking outcomes involves evaluation of the outcome of one's actions in terms of criteria of efficiency and effectiveness. Furthermore, individuals' ability to evaluate the outcome of their actions has a direct effect on their future behavior. Because checking outcomes provides the feedback loop across all control executive functions, students must be provided with corrective feedback regarding their success in executing learning strategies (Palincsar & Brown, 1987). The metacognitive orientation to the teaching process shifts the emphasis from a teacher's control of evaluation of instruction to an individual's own performance evaluation.

IMPLEMENTING A METACOGNITIVE TRAINING PROGRAM [1]

Objectives of a Metacognitive Training Program

The overall goal of a metacognitive training program is to maximize individuals' potential in school and in life. The objectives of the training program are consistent with metacognition goals and objectives:

---

[1]From *Metacognition Teacher's Guide* by A. Ariel, 1986a, 1991. Unpublished monograph, California State University, Los Angeles. Reprinted by permission.

1. To develop active learners who have a positive self-concept and realistic goals and aspirations, and who are active in their pursuit of knowledge
2. To facilitate the production of insightful and reflective processes in learners as a result of confrontation with both their abilities and the demands of the environment
3. To develop efficient learners through the development of their sensitivity to, and awareness of, the learning situation and through the utilization of effective strategies and control executive functions
4. To promote the acquisition of school-related academic skills by (a) developing an approach to learning, (b) developing an approach to

"They too can reach for the stars." Students with learning disabilities can maximize their potential as they learn to use metacognitive oriented strategies for learning and problem solving.

problem solving, (c) developing study patterns (study environment, study habits, study skills, and study methods), (d) developing individuals' ability to learn new strategies for learning, and (e) monitoring progress through the use of control executive functions

5. To promote the acquisition of social and life adjustment skills
6. To facilitate learners' generalization of metacognitive training to other aspects of school environment and life in general
7. To instill in individuals the belief in their capacity to learn, given appropriate utilization of strategies with which they can succeed
8. To produce self-directed learners who have the capacity to learn and to assume control over their learning
9. To produce self-directed learners who can guide themselves, ascertain the situation, and utilize strategic behaviors in order to succeed in school and life in general
10. To maximize individuals' power to succeed

Metacognitive Strategy Instruction

Strategic learning and the regulation of strategic behaviors are two of the main components of metacognitive training. The aim is to develop the individual's strategic repertoire and to teach a student to know when and how to use strategies effectively, and to know when and how to generalize this strategic knowledge to maximize the individual strategic productions. In addition, students are trained to use the control executive mechanism effectively, namely, to regulate and evaluate their strategic behaviors and output. This new emphasis on strategic training is due to the amalgamation of behavioristic, information-processing, and cognitive and metacognitive theories. This has resulted in (a) realistic analysis of a task at hand, (b) specific identification of the process for successful task completion, (c) the development of various strategy instruction models, and (d) the ability to design and execute research on strategy instruction (Pressley, Symons, Snyder, & Cariglia-Bull, 1989).

In essence, metacognitive-oriented learning strategy approaches utilize techniques common to good teaching practices. Good teachers are known to incorporate strategic learning in their teaching procedures, even though it is not referred to as such. The range of such strategies can be immense, covering all aspects of individual learning in school and in life. What makes the new metacognitive approach unique is the identification of specific areas of training and the formulation of instructional steps and procedures. Through the "learning process analysis" activity, the teacher, with students' input, develops metacognitive strategies specific to the task and commensurate with students' abilities. The learning process analysis becomes the vehicle to increase students' awareness of the task demands and the development of strategic behaviors. The learning process analysis is defined as an activity that involves the analysis of a learning task and/or problem and the development of strategies to ensure successful completion of that task. The teacher and students collaboratively discuss the nature of the task and possible means of achieving success through development and implementation of strategies. (See the section on learning process analysis in this chapter.) The teacher assumes the role of an interactive mediator. Through brainstorming and questioning techniques, the teacher leads students to an increased awareness of the task demands, vis-à-vis the students' strengths and weaknesses, and the strategies needed to achieve success in a particular area (Bartoli & Botel, 1988). The teacher thus encourages the students to develop strategies appropriate to the learning task and their individual needs and commensurate with their functional level.

Because the metacognitive approach attempts to develop students' sensitivity to the learning environment, increase their awareness of the factors affecting learning and problem solving, and develop strategic behaviors and the monitoring and regulating of such behaviors, it requires new teaching procedures. Since from a metacognitive perspective the teaching process is viewed as reciprocal and interactive, it requires the students' active participation in the learning process. In contrast to traditional teaching, this approach emphasizes exploratory and intuitive learning; teaching is more active and interactive. Students actively interact with their teacher and with other students, raise questions that make use of their prior knowledge, and develop their metacognitive awareness of learning how to learn (Bartoli & Botel, 1988). This teaching procedure adopts a step from similar procedures, such as reciprocal teaching developed by Palincsar and Brown (1984, 1986) and those developed in the Strategy Intervention Model (Schumaker, et al., 1986). (Also see chapters 7 and 13.)

A teacher who attempts to develop strategies for learning must have (a) knowledge of the principles of learning, (b) knowledge of the scope and sequence of the content to be learned, and (c) knowledge of task analysis. In addition, that teacher must consider the various levels of strategy acquisition. Consistent with the model of metacognition, strategies are developed in the four strategy categories—specific strategies, general/skill strategies, control executive strategies, and higher order control executive strategies. The premise of developing strategic learning is the heightening of one's awareness of the task, person, and strategy variables and the interaction among them. Strategic learning is also developed by understanding what is involved in a task, what it takes to complete a task successfully, and how to monitor progress. Although sequential training and acquisition are recommended for the mastery of strategic learning, one must be aware of the hierarchical and interactive aspects of strategic training and learning, and the generalization of them. The students and the teacher utilize the designed metacognitive strategy monitoring forms to highlight the strategies needed for mastery of a specific area, as well as to monitor the acquisition and generalization of the strategies. These forms are used on a daily basis until they are no longer needed.

Critical Components of a Metacognitive Training Program

Research over the past several years has demonstrated that the use of strategically oriented metacognitive training with individuals with LD results in successful outcomes (Ariel, 1987b, 1991; Borokowski et al., 1989). Though the literature is filled with theoretical information about metacognition, translation to instructional practices poses a serious challenge to educators. For that reason, most research with metacognitive training programs has limited itself to strategy training and the training of control executive functions. In line with our previous discussion about the nature of the metacognitive phenomena, a more comprehensive view of metacognition is taken here in accordance with the model illustrated in Figure 6–3. A metacognitive training program should develop students' sensitivity to the learning situation, as well as belief in their power to succeed, heighten awareness of factors that contribute to successful learning and problem solving, promote the development and utilization of strategies and the effective use of control executive functions, and lead ultimately to the metacognitive experience—knowing when, where, and how to use strategies effectively and how to monitor and evaluate strategic behaviors. The following is a list of key features that characterize the metacognitive training program:

1. The program is student centered and involves exploratory and discovery learning.
2. Students actively participate in the learning process through the analysis of the learning tasks, the processes involved in the acquisition of the task, and the development of learning strategies to ensure successful completion of the task.
3. Metacognitive instruction is interactive, reciprocal, and collaborative.
4. Students attribute successful completion of tasks to their own abilities to use strategies effectively.
5. Instruction is target oriented; strategies serve only as means to an end and are used only when necessary.
6. Strategies are developed through careful evaluation of the demands and the nature of the task, through the "learning process analysis."
7. The development of strategic behaviors involves student commitment, teacher's modeling, guided practice, and independent rehearsal of strategies.
8. Effective strategy utilization promotes transfer of strategies to other areas.
9. The training program maximizes student involvement and increases motivation and cooperation.
10. The program leads to the development of realistic evaluation and heightens the individual's level of goal aspiration.

The Nature of a Metacognitive Training Program

A metacognitive training program that corresponds to the model of metacognition is comprehensive in nature. It emphasizes the individual student's exploratory learning and problem-solving procedures in the acquisition of metacognitive concepts; students are encouraged to question themselves about their learning process. The program thus emphasizes the students' analysis of learning situations, self-verbalizations as means of guiding and controlling behavior, and regulation of behavior through the use of control executive functions. The approach is aimed at enhancing students' metacognitive awareness and thereby providing systematic strategic approaches to learning and problem solving.

As we have discussed, several distinctive phases are involved in a metacognitive training program. While leading students through these metacognitive phases, the program also introduces them to and trains them to use control executive functions. Students are encouraged to use self-monitoring strategies and to ask questions such as: What is it? What am I supposed to do? How shall I go about it? What procedures can I use? What strategies will work? What is the best way I can learn? Other questions related to effective use of the control executive functions include: Do I have a plan? How do I organize the material for solving the problem? How do I monitor my progress? How do I check the outcome?

Figure 6–4 illustrates the phases of the metacognitive process with its parallel training components.

A training program is hierarchical and interactive in nature. As individuals advance through the metacognitive phases, they acquire behaviors commensurate with the metacognitive level attained. They move from the simpler to the more complex, from the more undifferentiated and concrete to the more highly integrated and abstract, which usually involves effective utilization of control executive functions.

The program is holistic in nature and takes into account the individual factors that interact with learning situations, the individual's ability to utilize metacognitive processes effectively, and the individual's metacognitive base, cognitive base, affective base, and knowledge base. The metacognitive training level and complexity vary in accordance with a student's metacognitive base.

The importance of the learners assuming responsibility for their own learning is underscored by the metacognitive program. Students become more aware of how they learn and how they process information. They become aware of their strengths and weaknesses—what they can and cannot do. They take responsibility for their own learning, become active learners, and know that they are learning to succeed (Ariel, 1987b, 1989a, 1991). Throughout the training program, the emphasis is on assuming control over one's learning and developing belief in one's power to succeed. The main themes of the training program are "successful learning," "learning to learn," "stepping up to success," and "reach for the stars." The fundamental purpose of this metacognitive training program is to maximize the individual's power to succeed.

The application of the metacognitive approach to individuals with learning disabilities requires a change of attitude, first on the teacher's part and secondly on the students' part. This will necessitate a role change for both teacher and students. The teacher becomes the facilitator of learning, and the students assume an active role in their own learning through the nourishment of decision-making processes. The metacognitive approach is student centered rather than teacher centered.

The training program is not a new method of teaching but rather a procedure that can be used in conjunction with any method of instruction. It is an intervention mechanism that has as its major property the capacity to enhance an individual's power to succeed. Students who achieve success are motivated to attempt more

Figure 6–4 The Metacognitive Process and Parallel Activities

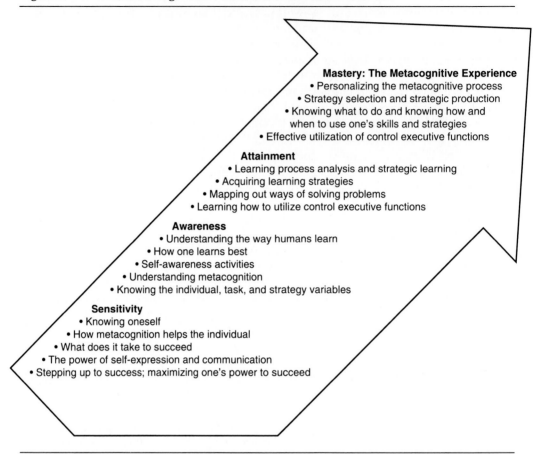

Mastery: The Metacognitive Experience
- Personalizing the metacognitive process
- Strategy selection and strategic production
- Knowing what to do and knowing how and
  when to use one's skills and strategies
- Effective utilization of control executive functions

Attainment
- Learning process analysis and strategic learning
- Acquiring learning strategies
- Mapping out ways of solving problems
- Learning how to utilize control executive functions

Awareness
- Understanding the way humans learn
- How one learns best
- Self-awareness activities
- Understanding metacognition
- Knowing the individual, task, and strategy variables

Sensitivity
- Knowing oneself
- How metacognition helps the individual
- What does it take to succeed
- The power of self-expression and communication
- Stepping up to success; maximizing one's power to succeed

From *Metacognition and Strategic Learning: Teacher's Guide* by A. Ariel, 1986a. Unpublished manuscript, California State University, Los Angeles. Reprinted by permission.

difficult tasks. Students with a pattern of successful achievement approach a new learning situation with confidence.

As with any other instructional method and approach, teachers must be trained in the metacognitive approach. Like their students, they must undergo the metacognitive experience in order to develop their sensitivity, awareness, and knowledge of this approach. Once teachers understand and internalize the concept of metacognition and develop the necessary skills and competencies, they are encouraged to use their creativity in teaching the metacognitive concepts.

The Training Program Format

Several aspects must be considered in preparing for the implementation of the metacognitive training program: (a) scheduling of the training component, (b) development of the metacognitive learning environment, (c) preparation of the students, and (d) instructional procedures.

For maximum effectiveness, the program should be scheduled for approximately 30 minutes each day as a separate training component in a resource room or a special class. Once students are introduced to strategic behaviors, they must be integrated and applied to the learning activities and the expected students' behavior throughout the day. This will facilitate the generalization of the training to the various learning activities and the production of strategic behaviors. The metacognitive training program can be scheduled for two or three times a week on alternate days, but this will reduce its intensity. The program can also be used effectively in regular classrooms in which an LD specialist is involved in collaborative consultation.

Developing the appropriate classroom environment for metacognitive teaching is critical to the success of the program. The classroom decor should reflect a success-oriented environment, for example, the use of posters to explain what success is and what it takes to succeed.

The metacognitive approach can and should be integrated into the existing classroom management routine. Although given the freedom to be involved in active learning, students need boundaries within which they can work. Therefore, the teacher should set up a classroom environment consisting of an established routine and a sound behavior management system. The teacher may incorporate a positive reinforcement system involving token economy cards, stamps, or merit awards, all of which reinforce appropriate student behavior.

Preparing students for the metacognitive training program involves getting them geared for success. They need to realize that they can contribute to the learning processes, have capabilities and talents, and can reach their potential. Students need to be encouraged to take an active role in the learning process and to express their thoughts and ideas.

In introducing metacognition to students, the teacher attempts to convey that each individual is a unique learner who can succeed in school. Individuals learn and solve problems in different ways. Despite one's learning disabilities, one can learn to use effective strategies in order to be successful in school and in life.

The metacognitive approach has built-in aspects of heightening individuals' awareness of what they need to learn, of establishing goals for learning, and of monitoring their progress in accomplishing these goals. The teacher must consider the different aspects of an optimal classroom environment and incorporate them into the metacognitive approach (see chapter 10). The emphasis of the training program is to develop students who are active in their pursuit of learning and who assume responsibility for their learning and the monitoring of their activities.

Metacognitive and Strategic Instruction Procedures

Activity Guidelines

Lessons are geared to develop students' sensitivity to learning and to enhance their awareness of factors affecting learning, which lead to the attainment of strategies and their application in real situations at school and at home. Students are introduced to the various aspects of metacognition through self-exploratory learning. Emphasis is placed on understanding how one learns and the way one learns best, on developing strategies for successful learning, and on developing one's own monitoring and self-regulation activities.

Each lesson begins with an activity that encourages exploratory and discovery learning. Activities are meaningful and relate directly to the students' experiences. The teacher facilitates student-generated discussion, encourages students to think creatively (all responses are recognized), and helps them discover that each of them learns in a different way and that there is more than one way to solve a problem. Each activity is followed by a discussion about the students' experiences. That discussion is followed by a summary and synthesis of the group input and the drawing of conclusions, which leads to (a) an understanding of the concept, (b) application of the concept through strategy utilization, and (c) independent practice and implementation. Activities are usually followed by the development of a strategy plan, rehearsal of the strategies, the carrying out of strategic behaviors, monitoring of strategy use, and evaluation of the outcomes of their efforts. The teacher models strategic behaviors and guides and monitors the students' rehearsal and their mastering and effective utilization of strategic behaviors.

Developing and Using Learning Strategies: The Learning Process Analysis

A primary feature of the metacognitive training program is the development of students' ability to use learning strategies effectively. This feature is common to both the metacognitive-oriented strategic instruction and the Strategy Intervention Model (Schumaker, Deshler, Alley, & Warner, 1983; Schumaker et al., 1986) (see also chapter 7). Both these approaches use specific instructional steps and procedures. The uniqueness of this metacognitive approach is its emphasis on interactive teaching through the learning process analysis.

The learning process analysis is an activity that involves the analysis of a learning task and/or problem, its characteristics, and the factors that contribute to successful completion of the task and/or problem solving. Through guided teaching, students discuss the nature of a task at hand, what the task involves, and the strategies necessary to complete the task successfully. This activity, which increases students' awareness, facilitates the learning and utilization of strategies. The students who develop sensitivity and awareness of the learning process develop their ability to analyze the process involved in each new learning and problem-solving situation. They learn to develop and effectively use appropriate strategies for successful task completion. The learning process analysis attempts to develop students' awareness of the task, person, and strategy variables and how these variables interact in facilitating successful task completion.

The learning process analysis activity involves (a) analysis of the task at hand, that is, the nature of the task, its characteristics and functions; (b) identification of the skills necessary to complete the task successfully; (c) identification and development of effective strategies; (d) delineation of the steps one must follow to ensure successful completion of the task; and (e) a de̶_____king process of how to go about implementing the strategies and ho̶_____ regulate one's attempt to complete the task successfully.

The learning process analysis ̶_____e analysis of academic learning, students' study patterns, a̶_____covers various areas of concern, such as students' expected ̶_____ion and selection of a study environment, students' study patt̶_____study skills), specific strategies in the three R's, strategies in the ̶_____s science and social studies), test preparation and test-taking stra̶_____social/interpersonal areas, and strategies in effectively utilizing the̶_____ system (planning, organizing, implementing, monitoring, and eval̶_____

The role of the teacher in such an activity is to ̶_____responses and to fully engage them in the process. It is like the role of a̶_____ding the support necessary through the metacognitive process (Palincsar ̶_____37). Initially, the teacher assumes responsibility in leading students in the ̶_____tion and development of the necessary strategies, in demonstrating strate̶_____in monitoring the rehearsal, mastery, and implementation of the strategies.̶_____dents develop their abilities to use strategies effectively, the teacher gradually t̶_____fers to them the responsibility for implementing the strategies and monitoring th̶__r progress, but provides continuous feedback and coaching throughout the process. ̶hroughout the instructional process, students are involved in setting their goals and in selecting appropriate strategies in order to complete the various tasks successfully. They can participate at the level of which they are capable. Furthermore, the selection of target areas and the development of strategies in these areas are geared to the individual functional level and learning pace. The teacher guides students to develop strategic behaviors that directly relate to successful task completion and takes into account individuals' strengths and weaknesses. Figure 6–5 is a sample activity guide for the development of strategies.

Strategies are developed and learned as they are needed, and they serve as a means to an end. Though strategic behaviors are initially specific (strategies) and welded to a specific task, students begin to recognize common elements among the various tasks and the various strategies acquired and applied. Eventually, they develop the ability to generate their own strategies and to generalize to other areas in school and in life. In addition, students are introduced to strategies, such as study skills strategies, that can be applied across many areas of the curriculum. Control executive and higher order executive strategies are slowly introduced. Throughout the process, the teacher remains an active facilitator in helping students become increasingly skillful at using strategies to achieve success. Gradually, responsibility for the development of strategies and the performance of the behaviors shifts from the teacher to the students. Converting strategy statements to "I" statements declares ownership of the strategy and facilitates the transfer of responsibility to the students.

The Learning Process Analysis: Steps and Procedures

As stated in the preceding section, the metacognitive approach uses specific instructional steps and procedures. Similar procedures are used in the Strategy Intervention

Figure 6–5 Learning Process Analysis (Activity Guide)

Area: Meta-_____
Elements of Successful Task Completion

1. Task variables:
   a. What is the nature of the task?

      _____

   b. What do I need to know in order to complete the task? (skills)

      _____

2. Individual variables:
   a. My strengths in this area:

      _____

   b. My weaknesses in this area:

      _____

   c. What skills do I need to learn in this area?

      _____

3. Strategy variables:
   a. What strategies can I use to complete the task successfully?

      _____

   b. What steps must I follow to assure successful task completion?

      _____

4. Decision making—commitment to succeed:
   a. How do I go about implementing the strategies?

      _____

   b. How do I monitor, regulate, and evaluate strategy implementation?

      _____

   c. Where and how can I use these strategies effectively?

      _____

Model (Schumaker, et al., 1983; Schumaker et al., 1986), reciprocal teaching (Palincsar & Brown, 1984) (see also chapter 13), and other metacognitive procedures. Several distinctive instructional steps are involved in the learning process analysis activity. These include the following:

1. Task identification and goal setting. This step involves the identification and delineation of a specific task or an area to be mastered and the setting of goals to be reached by students and teacher.
2. Identification of task characteristics and attributes. Students are provided with a challenging task. Through discovery learning, they

identify the characteristics of the task, that is, the nature of the task, what is involved in completing the task, and what skills are needed to complete the task.

3. Development of strategies for successful task completion. Students are engaged in identifying and developing strategies that facilitate task completion. These strategies take into account the task, person, and strategy variables. In the process of developing strategies, students are engaged in a discussion concerning the task that include questions such as: What is the nature of the task? What is needed in order to complete the task successfully? What are the specific strategies for successful task completion? A strategy guide is provided to students to stimulate the discussion and/or for adoption. Following the discussion, the teacher and the students reach a consensus on the most appropriate strategies. The strategies are then prioritized, listed on a poster, and displayed in a highly visible location for students' reference.

4. Strategy instruction. The teacher provides instruction on how to use the strategies appropriately and effectively.

5. Modeling. The teacher demonstrates to the students how to use the strategies.

6. Commitment to implement strategies. Students commit to implement strategies. During this step, strategy statements are converted to "I" statements to develop a sense of ownership and to facilitate a shift to personal responsibility in implementing the strategies.

7. Strategy rehearsal. Students rehearse the use of strategies. Rehearsal involves learning the various steps in the strategies. Self-verbalization is used to facilitate rehearsal and mastery of strategies. Rehearsals are of two types—teacher's guided rehearsal and independent self-rehearsal.

8. Development of a monitoring system. A monitoring and regulating system is developed.

9. Strategy implementation and monitoring. Students implement the strategies and monitor their performance. Though strategies are initially "welded" to specific tasks, students gradually learn how to select and use strategies most appropriate to the task at hand.

10. Evaluation of strategy implementation and the effect of strategy utilization and generalization. Both the teacher and the students evaluate strategy implementation and its effect on the learning outcome by evaluating student progress in the various areas of concern, including expected student behavior and academic performance.

These steps are outlined in Figure 6–6.

Utilizing Metacognitive Strategies for Learning

Strategic learning is a crucial and viable component of the metacognitive training program. Its purpose is to develop the individual strategic repertoire and to teach students to know when and how to use strategies effectively and when and how to

Figure 6–6 Metacognitive-Oriented Strategy Development and Implementation: The Learning Process Analysis: Steps and Procedures

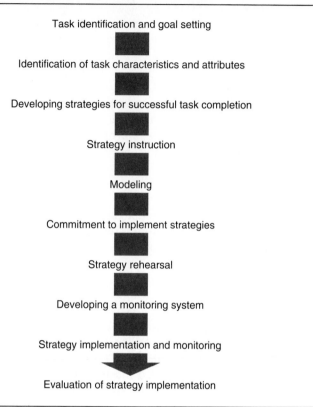

generalize this strategic knowledge to maximize individual strategic production. The range of such strategies can be immense, covering all aspects of learning in school and in life. As pointed out earlier, through the learning process analysis activity, the teacher, with the students' input, develops metacognitive strategies specific to a task and commensurate with students' abilities. The teacher thus encourages the students to develop strategies appropriate to the learning task and their functional level. (A sample of strategy guide and monitoring sheet in "Mastering Summarizing Skills" is presented in Figure 6–7 and Figure 6–8. Additional samples in various intervention areas can be found in chapters 12, 13, 14, and 15.)

Monitoring Student Progress

The importance of monitoring and regulating one's activities is emphasized throughout the training program. Students are provided with the means to monitor their activities and evaluate their progress through the use of self-monitoring and record-

Figure 6–7   Mastering Summarizing Skills: Strategy Implementation
and Monitoring Sheet

COMMITMENT TO SUCCESS: STRATEGY IMPLEMENTATION

Set 5: Mastering Summarizing Skills

Skills/Behaviors I Need to Learn:	How Will I Do It? (Strategies)	How Am I Doing? Key: √−; √; √+;					
		M	T	W	Th	F	Overall
Mastering Summarizing Skills	I read and understand the material.						
	I state the author's purpose, main idea, or thesis.						
	I support the thesis with the author's main ideas and supporting details.						
	I state the author's conclusion, if any.						
Individualized Goal							

Teacher's Comments:

Student's Comments: This Is the Way I See Myself

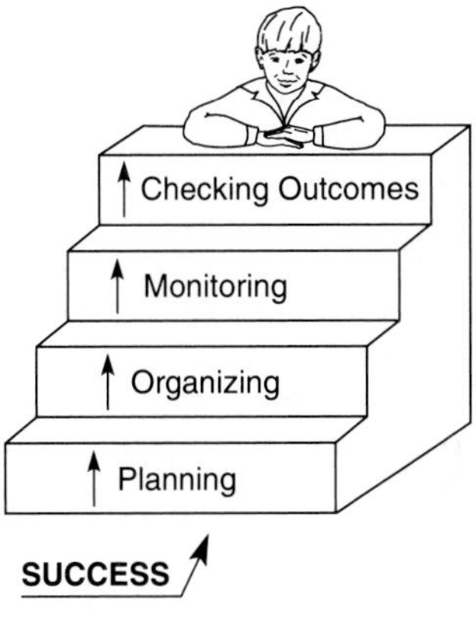

Checking Outcomes

Monitoring

Organizing

Planning

SUCCESS

Reprinted from Ariel (1989b), *Gateway to success: Metacognition college handbook.*

Figure 6–8   Mastering Summarizing Skills: Strategy Guide

Strategy Guide
   The purpose of summarizing material is to concisely state the main ideas and supporting details of the information read. In essence, it is another format to facilitate the processing and retrieval of information. In summarizing you become actively involved in processing the information in your own way. In the process of summarizing follow these steps:

Strategies for Mastering Summarizing Skills
Read and understand the material.
State the author's purpose, main idea, or thesis.
Support the thesis with the author's main ideas and supporting details.
State the author's conclusion, if any.

Implementing and Monitoring Summarizing Strategies
I read and understand the material.
I state the author's purpose, main idea, or thesis.
I support the thesis with the author's main ideas and supporting details.
I state the author's conclusion, if any.

Reprinted from Ariel (1989b), *Gateway to success: Metacognition college handbook.*

ing sheets. (See Figure 6–1, presented earlier in the chapter.) The teacher is fully involved with this activity during the initial phases of learning and implementing strategic behaviors, but responsibility is gradually shifted to the students, who assume full responsibility for their own actions. The monitoring and evaluation results can be effectively tied to a behavior management system or grading practices.

SUMMARY AND CONCLUSIONS

Metacognition theory and practice are presented in this chapter. The amalgamation of behavioristic, cognitive, and information-processing theories provides the foundation for the metacognitive approach. Its promise as an intervention approach for individuals with LD that received empirical support is emphasized. Through this approach, individuals with learning disabilities become active learners, continuously develop and use strategies for learning and problem solving, and monitor and evaluate their strategic behaviors. By employing strategic behaviors, learning-disabled individuals can increase their chances to succeed in school and in life and thus maximize their potential.

According to Gray (1981), the following are additional needs related to the young adult with LD: (a) the content of diagnostic and assessment devices and of educational services should be specific to life needs, (b) assessment and intervention should be directly related to adult life goals, (c) developmental and remedial instruction in basic skills should be made available for those who wish such training and for those for whom such programs are appropriate, and (d) views of appropriate content for adult services should be expanded beyond traditional literacy requirements and vocational training. Help must be readily available for the learning-disabled in dealing with life skills, including the attainment of a positive self-concept, effectiveness in family relationships, the ability to cope with social-sexual relationships, development of organizational skills, increased motivation and assertiveness, independence concerning financial matters, and effective use of leisure time and awareness of aesthetics—in short, those skills and interactions that enable satisfying, meaningful life functioning (Gray, 1981).

In considering the needs of young adults with LD, the National Joint Committee on Learning Disabilities (1985) makes the following recommendations:

1. Programs must be initiated to increase public and professional awareness and understanding of the manifestations and needs of adults with learning disabilities.
2. Selection of appropriate education and vocational training programs and employment for adults with learning disabilities is predicated on a clear understanding of how their condition influences their learning and performance.
3. Throughout the school years, individuals with learning disabilities must have access to a range of program and service options that will prepare them to make the transition from secondary to postsecondary or vocational training settings.
4. Alternative programs and services must be provided for adults with learning disabilities who have failed to obtain a high school diploma.
5. Adults with learning disabilities must have an active role in determining the course of their postsecondary or vocational efforts.
6. Consistent with the Rehabilitation Act of 1973 and regulations implementing Section 504 of that Act, appropriate federal, state, and local agencies as well as postsecondary and vocational training programs should continue the development and implementation of effective programs that will allow adults with learning disabilities the opportunity to attain career goals.
   a. Postsecondary Programs—Those persons responsible for planning postsecondary programs for individuals with learning disabilities should establish an interdisciplinary advisory council that will develop, implement, and monitor necessary procedures and services.
   b. Vocational Training—The Rehabilitation Act of 1973, including Section 504, mandates that vocational training programs be available to adults with learning disabilities.

    c. Employment Opportunities—Education and rehabilitation agencies should develop effective liaisons with business, industry, unions, and civil service employment agencies.

7. The development of systematic programs of research that will address the status and needs of adults with learning disabilities is essential for the provision of appropriate services.

8. Mental health professionals must be aware of the unique personal, social, and emotional difficulties that individuals with learning disabilities may experience throughout their lives. (pp. 164–167)

Delivery Service: Program Components for Adolescents and Young Adults With LD

The need to develop a comprehensive intervention program for adolescents and young adults with LD has received support from the literature. Deshler, Schumaker, and Lenz (1984) identified the following direct service components designed to meet the needs of learning-disabled adolescents: motivation, curriculum and content, generalization of skills, and transition. They also recommend indirect components designed primarily to facilitate the instructional and evaluation processes. These include a component detailing specific instructional practices that special education teachers could use to teach targeted academic and cognitive skills, a communication and coordination component, and an evaluation component. For the past several years, the Kansas Research Institute in Learning Disabilities has been developing the most progressive and comprehensive program currently proposed for adolescents with LD (see later section in this chapter).

While most school districts function within the "fit the system" rationale, schools can utilize their resources to provide program components for adolescents with LD. Many of these components can be served either through a special day class or through a resource room program with the support of ancillary personnel, such as school counselors, a school psychologist, vocational education coordinators, and/or other DIS personnel.

In chapter 4, we presented a service delivery framework for individuals with learning disabilities. The following suggested program components are consistent with that service delivery framework but emphasize meeting the needs of learning-disabled adolescents and young adults. While LD specialists at the secondary level should incorporate the core curriculum into their instruction, the intervention program must also include components that are not commonly identified as core curriculum. These suggested program components for adolescents and young adults with learning disabilities are as follows:

1. Intensive remediation of academic skills, that is, basic skills and core curriculum, with immediate application to survival skills including Community Based Instruction (CBI) (see later section in this chapter)
2. Training in the development and utilization of learning strategies
3. Training in metacognition and control executive functions

Figure 7–1 Service Delivery Components for Adolescents and Young Adults With Learning Disabilities

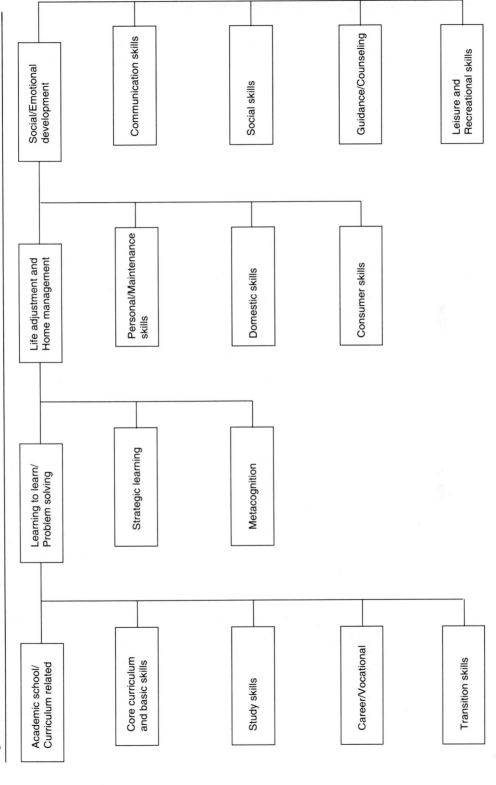

4. Training in study skills, study habits, and study patterns
5. Career/vocational preparation, including a training and work experience component
6. Counseling and guidance
7. Training in social skills, including leisure skills
8. Training in communication skills
9. Training in transition skills
10. Training in life-adjustment skills, including personal maintenance, domestic, consumer, leisure, and recreation skills, and preparation for marriage and home management skills for young adults.

The program components can be further grouped into the following primary service areas: academic school/curriculum, strategies for learning and problem solving, life adjustment and home management, and social/emotional development. These components and service areas are diagrammed in Figure 7–1.

Intervention and Teaching Approaches

In discussing the role of the LD specialist in chapter 4, we focused on the wide range of the specialist's responsibilities in assisting learning-disabled individuals. Adolescents with learning disabilities place a great demand on teachers in terms of both behavior management and the much broader spectrum of the curriculum that must address the needs of such adolescents (Knott & Fathum, 1984). The LD specialist who works with adolescents must go beyond the teaching of the basic skills to the delivery of a broader program in accordance with the components highlighted in the preceding section. Operating from a metacognitive perspective—namely, heightening individuals' awareness of their strengths and weaknesses and encouraging them to assume control over their learning through active participation and decision making related to their learning—will facilitate the transition from passive learners to active learners with established goals who are in control of their learning and who will ultimately pursue their goals.

The needs of adolescents with learning disabilities vary, and the LD specialist plays a major role in meeting those needs. The LD specialist at this level must be aware of, and knowledgeable about, developmental aspects of adolescents, as well as aspects of their learning disabilities vis-à-vis their needs, problems, and aspirations. Adolescents' needs must be considered in preparation of the classroom environment, the amount of curricular emphasis in the special day class and/or the resource room, instructional programming and instructional methodology, and behavioral management approaches. The LD specialist at this level must be skillful in utilizing appropriate teaching methods to effect immediate changes. Likewise, the selection of appropriate educational materials is crucial for optimal implementation of the program. Modifications are needed to meet the interests and needs of adolescents and young adults with LD. Wherever required, attention must be given to instructional procedures, teaching methods, and classroom management strategies that are most appropriate for this population.

The Strategies Intervention Model (SIM)

The University of Kansas Institute for Research in Learning Disabilities (KU-IRLD) was one of five research institutes funded by the U.S. Department of Education to conduct research in the field of learning disabilities. The main thrust of the KU-IRLD is to study adolescents with learning disabilities. Since its inception in 1977, its major mission has been the development of a validated intervention model for learning-disabled adolescents in school settings that meet both effectiveness and feasibility criteria (Deshler & Lenz, 1989; Schumaker, et al. 1983; Schumaker et al. 1986).

Learning strategies were initially defined by Alley and Deshler (1979) as "techniques, principles, or rules that will facilitate the acquisition, manipulation, integration, storage, and retrieval of information across situations and settings" (as cited by Schumaker, et al. 1983, p. 49). A more recent definition is offered by Schumaker et al. (1986):

> A strategy is a technique, principle, or rule which enables a person to function independently and solve problems in ways that will result in positive consequences for the person and others around him/her. Whereas strategy instruction is by no means a panacea to the problems encountered by LD adolescents, it is an approach that can increase the degree to which students can successfully cope with their environments. (p. 333)

The Strategies Intervention Model's philosophy rests on the following basic assumptions:

> Most students wish to complete high school with a standard, nonlimiting diploma.
> Students with learning disabilities have the intellectual ability to satisfactorily complete the secondary school requirements.
> Learning disabled students need as much social and academic contact with other adolescents as possible. (Deshler, Alley, & Carlson, 1980, p. 6)

It is not the objective of the learning strategies approach to teach specific content. Rather, the approach is designed to teach students how to learn and how to demonstrate strategic knowledge in the performance of academic tasks (Alley & Deshler, 1979; Deshler, Schumaker, Lenz, & Ellis, 1984). The learning strategies approach has been designed to enable students to cope effectively with secondary school demands and to teach them how to generalize these skills to a variety of settings, including mainstream classes and home and employment settings (Schumaker & Sheldon, 1985).

Deshler and Schumaker (1986) discussed the three major rationales underlying the learning strategies intervention approach for adolescents:

1. The development and application of learning strategies or metacognitive skills are significantly related to age; that is, older students consistently are more proficient in the use of such behaviors;

2. Adolescents who "learn how to learn" in secondary schools would be in a much better position to learn new skills and to respond to rapidly changing information and conditions in the future;
3. The learning strategies instruction approach requires students to accept major responsibility for their learning and progress . . . [s]uch a commitment must be made by students if they are to truly become independent. (p. 584)

For the past two decades, the Strategies Intervention Model has been influenced by the research findings of self-instruction in cognitive behavior modification approaches (Meichenbaum, 1977) and self-guided speech in mediation theory (Manning, 1984). In general, the SIM utilizes (a) principles of cognitive behavior modification and mediation theory, (b) sound principles of learning, and (c) sound principles of remedial education, specifically those of task analysis, sequential teaching, and the provision of a feedback mechanism.

In addition to the above principles, Deshler and Schumaker (1986) listed the following instructional principles that guide the implementation of the learning strategy interventions:

1. Match instruction with curriculum demands.
2. Use structured teaching methodology.
3. Deliberately promote generalization.
4. Apply "critical teaching behaviors."
5. Use scope and sequence in teaching.
6. Ensure that teaching decisions are governed by outcome goals.
7. Maximize student involvement.
8. Maintain a realistic point of view.

The learning strategies approach is intended for a specific learning-disabled population (Alley & Deshler, 1979). Students with LD who can benefit most from this approach need to have a reading level above third grade, the ability to deal with symbolic representation, and an IQ of 85 or above. Thus, according to Alley and Deshler (1979), the Strategies Intervention Model approach is not appropriate for the severely learning-disabled adolescent.

SIM Components

The Strategies Intervention Model consists of three major components, each of which has several subcomponents. These are illustrated in Figure 7–2.

The curriculum component consists primarily of the learning strategies curriculum, which specifies the areas of strategy learning. These areas include task-specific learning strategies, executive strategies, social skill strategies, motivation strategies, and transition strategies.

The second component of SIM is the instructional component, which specifies how specific strategies under the curriculum components will be taught to students

Figure 7–2   The Strategies Intervention Model, With Three Major Components and Their Subcomponents

Curriculum component	Instructional component	Organizational component
• Task-specific learning strategies	• Acquisition procedures	• Communication procedures
• Executive strategies	• Generalization procedures	• Management procedures
• Social skills strategies	• Maintenance procedures	• Evaluation procedures
• Motivation strategies	• Group instructional procedures	• Teacher training and adoption procedures
• Transition strategies	• Material and instruction modification procedures	

Source: From "Intervention Issues Related to the Education of LD Adolescents" by J. B. Schumaker, D. D. Deshler, and E. S. Ellis, in *Psychological and Educational Perspectives on Learning Disabilities* (p. 334) by J. Torgesen and B. Wong (Eds.), 1986, New York: Academic. Copyright 1982 by Academic Press. Reprinted by permission.

(Schumaker et al. 1986). Its subcomponents include acquisition procedures, generalization procedures, maintenance procedures, group instructional procedures, and material and instruction modification procedures.

The third major component of the SIM is the organizational component, which deals with system accommodation and adoption of the model procedures into ongoing instructional practices and traditions within a given school setting. Its subcomponents consist of communication procedures, management procedures, evaluation procedures, and teacher training and adoption procedures.

The learning strategies curriculum consists of three instructional strands: the acquisition strand, the storage strand, and the expression-and-demonstration-of-competence strand.

> Each strand consists of several task-specific learning strategies that have been designed to improve a student's ability to cope with specific curriculum demands. The strategies in the Acquisition Strand enable students to gain information from written material (e.g., textbooks, novels, technical manuals). The Storage Strand strategies are designed to enable students to organize, store, and retrieve information. Finally, the Expression and Demonstration of Competence Strand consists of strategies that enable students to complete assignments, to effectively express themselves in writing, and to take tests. (Schumaker & Sheldon, 1985, p. 1)

In each strand, various strategies were developed. For example, in the acquisition strand, word identification strategy, visual imagery strategy, self-questioning strategy, paraphrasing strategy, interpreting visual aids strategy, and SOS/multipass strategy (textbook surveying) were developed. In the expression-and-demonstration strand, sentence writing strategy, paragraph writing strategy, error monitoring strategy, theme-writing strategy, assignment strategy, and test-taking strategy were developed. In the storage strand, first-letter mnemonic strategy, paired associate strategy, and listening and note-taking strategy were developed.

The KU-IRLD recognized the absence of scope and sequence for skill development for the secondary level learning adolescent and recognized the need for a comprehensive master plan curriculum in order to ensure systematic introduction, practice, and review of skills for the secondary student with learning disabilities. Accordingly, the authors of the SIM have developed a sequential curriculum with strategies and skills to be taught in Grades 7 through 12.

SIM Training Procedures

The KU-IRLD developed elaborative procedures for effective instruction. Each of the strategies is taught through an eight-step instructional procedure that should be followed carefully by the teacher for successful acquisition of the strategies. These steps are as follows:

Step 1: Pretest and obtain commitment to learn. In this step, students are tested to determine their current level of performance. Feedback from pretests is provided to students as a means of obtaining a verbal commitment to learning the strategy.

Step 2: Describe the strategy. Here the teacher provides an overall picture of the strategy and the advantages of using it.

Step 3: Model the strategy. In this step, the teacher demonstrates the strategy by going through all the steps while thinking out loud.

Step 4: Use verbal rehearsal. In this step, students are asked to verbally rehearse the definition of important terms and the strategy steps.

Step 5: Include controlled practice and feedback. In this step, students use materials that are geared to the learning strategy. They are provided with individual feedback each time they practice a strategy.

Step 6: Use grade-appropriate practice/posttest and feedback. This step involves a test of students' mastery of a strategy and their ability to apply it to grade-appropriate assignments. It also provides students with ample opportunity to practice the strategy under the usual conditions.

Step 7: Obtain commitment to generalize. "This step involves encouraging an analysis of student progress and obtaining a student commitment to use the new strategy in a variety of settings" (Schumaker & Sheldon, 1985, p. 6).

Step 8: Use generalization. "Three distinct phases are addressed in generalization instruction. First, an Orientation Phase is designed to make students aware of situation and circumstances in which they can use their newly learned strategy and the way in which they may need to adjust the strategy to meet unique situations. Second, an Activation Phase allows students to practice using the strategy in a broad array of settings and situations . . . Finally, the Maintenance Phase is designed to periodically determine if students are continuing to use the strategy appropriately" (Schumaker & Sheldon, 1985, p. 6).

These steps are illustrated in Figure 7–3. A detailed description of this instructional methodology is provided in "An Instructional Model for Teaching Learning Strategies" (Ellis, Deshler, Lenz, Schumaker, & Clark, 1991).

Figure 7–3 SIM Instructional Steps

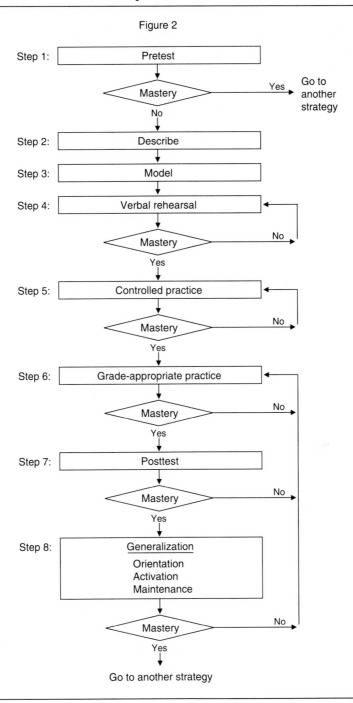

Figure 2

Source: From *The Test Taking Strategy* (p. 5) by C. A. Hughes, J. B. Schumaker, D. D. Deshler, and C. D. Mercer, 1988, Lawrence, KS: Edge Enterprises. Copyright 1988 by Edge Enterprises. Reprinted by permission.

The SIM training handbooks are elaborative. The authors have developed an intensive training program for the effective utilization of this approach, and the reader is referred to the training handbooks for further details.

TRANSITION FROM HIGH SCHOOL TO A POST-HIGH SCHOOL ENVIRONMENT

Transition refers to the process of movement from a high school environment to a post-high school environment, which includes postsecondary education, competitive employment, and the adult home and community environment. Thus transition is viewed as a purposeful, organized, outcome-oriented process designed to help students with learning disabilities move from high school to post-high school environments.

The transition from a secure high school environment to a post-high school environment is difficult enough for individuals who have no disabilities. Adolescents who have had a relatively secure home and school environment must embark on a new road leading to preparation for adult life. This process proves to be of great difficulty and, at times, causes turmoil for those with LD. Although the high school experience may have been tainted with failure experiences and frustration, this environment has still provided some security for learning-disabled students. The move from high school is fraught with uncertainty, anxiety, and fear, partially because of disability and partially because of the lack of preparation in our secondary schools for transition to post-high school environments. According to Cox, Frank, Hocutt, and Kuligowski (1984), transition programs to assist students' movement into postsecondary educational settings are virtually nonexistent. Services to assist youth with LD in the transition to postsecondary education and/or competitive employment are still a rarity rather than common practice. Benz and Halpern (1987) state that "the fundamental purpose of education is to prepare students to lead productive and rewarding lives. For high school students with disabilities, the achievement of this outcome is dependent upon the quality and the appropriateness of both the high school curriculum and the transition services that are provided to help the student accomplish his or her goals" (p. 513).

In general, transition programs have been designed to meet the needs of mentally retarded and severely handicapped youth. Despite recognition of the problem and increasing interest in transition programs across the country, few secondary school special education programs provide relevant services for adolescents with LD (Okolo & Sitlington, 1986).

The Office of Special Education and Rehabilitative Services (OSERS) defines transition as the following:

> The transition from school to working life is an outcome oriented process encompassing a broad array of services and experiences that lead to employment. Transition is a period that includes high school, the point of graduation, additional post secondary education or adult services, and the

initial years in employment. Transition is a bridge between the security and structure offered by the school and adult life. Any bridge requires both a solid span and a secure foundation at either end. The transition from school to work and adult life requires sound preparation in the secondary school, adequate support at the point of school leaving, and secure opportunities and services, if needed, in adult situation. (M. Will, 1984)

In 1983, Congress addressed itself to the transitional issue by passing Public Law 98–199. Section 626 of PL 98–199 is titled "Secondary Education and Transitional Services For Handicapped Youth." This law authorizes the Office of Special Education and Rehabilitative Services to initiate grant activity to develop transition programs for the handicapped that more specifically involve strengthening and coordinating education, training, and related services that assist handicapped youth in the transition to supported or competitive employment, postsecondary education, vocational training, continuing education, or adult services, and involve stimulating improvement and development of programs for secondary special education (D'Alonzo & Owen, 1985; Rusch & Phelps 1987).

According to Benz and Halpern (1987), "The transition into, through, and out of high school is a process that requires varying degrees of assistance from family, friends, and school personnel. . . . Many students with disabilities require additional support and assistance to negotiate this transition process successfully" (p. 507). Furthermore, the same authors state that "the achievement of satisfactory transition outcomes depends on the quality and appropriateness of both the high school curriculum and the transition services provided to help students achieve their goals" (p. 507).

Mithaug, Martin, and Agran (1987) believe that the transition process must begin with the instructional approach in the special education process at the high school level. Johnson, Bruininks, and Thurlow (1987) speak of the family's role in planning the transition. They assert that family participation in planning during children's adolescent years is essential for ensuring continuity between school and adult services. While the literature points to a lessening of parental involvement as youngsters get older (Lynch & Stein, 1982), such involvement is fundamental to effective transition planning for disabled adolescents (Benz & Halpern, 1987).

In discussing the role of special education in the transition of adolescents with LD from school to work, Okolo and Sitlington (1986) suggest that secondary special education programs should provide six vocational-relevant activities: (a) occupational awareness, exploration, and basic work experience; (b) in-depth career/vocational assessment; (c) instruction in job-related academic skills; (d) instruction in job-related interpersonal skills; (e) support services to other disciplines involved in vocational programming; and (f) postschool placement and follow-up.

The Role of the LD Specialist in Transition

Palmer (1985) asked the question, "What is transition?" and then answered it in this manner: "Basically it is a period in a young person's passive years of life after adolescence and before the assumptions of adult responsibility. Sometimes it is called youth" (p. 13). According to Palmer, young people who are disabled must learn the same skills as their nondisabled peers. They must prepare themselves for goals such as becoming economically independent; managing their own affairs; being wise consumers; relating to people of different ages, class, and cultural backgrounds; having others depend on them; operating within a group; and developing close interpersonal relationships. The fact remains that adolescents with LD are not ready to move into the postsecondary environment but are ready for a transition program. Several factors contribute to this: (a) lack of recognition on the part of the school system that a transition services program for individuals with LD must be provided, (b) the belief that most individuals with LD will continue with post-high school education, and (c) the lack of directiveness to the special education teacher and/or the resource teacher for including transitional elements within the curriculum.

While the responsibility for specific skill training should reside with appropriately trained personnel, such as career vocational specialists, the special education teacher can provide a variety of activities that can enhance access to, and success in, specific vocational skill training (Okolo & Sitlington, 1986). The LD specialist can also enhance the program by providing specific exposure to transitional elements from high school to post-high school.

It is essentially the responsibility of LD specialists to take the initiative and include elements of transition within their programs. Several curriculum emphases can be geared toward this transition, including (a) exploration of what is available after high school, (b) individual assessment of strengths and weaknesses in relationship to choices available after high school, (c) preparation of skills necessary for post-high school positions, and (d) preparation of life skills identified in Community Based Instruction. Depending on individuals' needs, the preparation of skills necessary for post-high school adjustment includes (a) specific remedial skills, (b) socialization and interpersonal communication skills, (c) career/vocational skills necessary for adaptation to the work environment, (d) skills necessary for adaptation to the junior college program, and (e) skills related to an individual's functional and leisure life activities.

Community Based Instruction

Community Based Instruction (CBI) is an instruction program for individuals with handicapping conditions that teaches functional academic and life skills in a community setting. The underlying philosophy of CBI is that students should be given maximum opportunities to learn and interact with nonhandicapped individuals and other peers in natural and real environments so that they can become independent as adults in their community (Falvey, 1989; Wehman, Kregel, & Baracus, 1985). This approach, developed primarily for severely handicapped students, is now being considered as an alternate approach for individuals with severe learning disabilities. The program is based on a life skills curriculum that includes the following areas: (a) domestic skills, (b) recreation/leisure skills, (c) community access skills, and (d) vocational skills. In addition, CBI also emphasizes personal maintenance skills,

Schools must broaden their curriculum to include program components that respond to the immediate and future needs of adolescents and young adults with learning disabilities.

socialization, and interpersonal communication skills. Training in these areas is designed to provide individuals with the skills necessary for successful transition to a "normalized" and productive life. This program involves actual hands-on experience at community sites such as restaurants, supermarkets, and laundromats, under teachers' supervision.

CAREER AND VOCATIONAL EDUCATION

The Learning Disabled in the Workplace

In order to determine the relevant career education needs of students with LD, employer expectations have been surveyed. Burton and Bero (1984) asked 25 employers of individuals with learning disabilities, "What skills are you looking for among handicapped students that you hire?" The most common responses included the following abilities:

1. To get along with people
2. To communicate with the public

3. To be on time/dependable
4. To stand on one's feet/have stamina
5. To cope with stress/work under pressure
6. To care about the job
7. To be willing to learn
8. To be neat and clean
9. To lead, stack, and/or stuff
10. To use common sense

Burton and Bero then asked, "What problems have you had with educationally handicapped employees?" The responses were predictable:

1. Lack of punctuality
2. Difficulty in communicating
3. Lack of transportation
4. Lack of respect for supervision
5. Inflexibility
6. Lack of endurance
7. No enthusiasm for the job
8. Social life interference
9. Inability to move quickly
10. Poor physical coordination and strength

Only two of the employers polled mentioned specific skill training or basic academics as critical needs.

A number of recent studies have focused on the vocational adjustment of adults with LD. Okolo and Sitlington (1986) found some consistent results among the follow-up studies. Unlike more severely handicapped groups, learning-disabled adults were found to have secured employment at nearly the same rate as their nonhandicapped age peers. However, the jobs held by these individuals had less social status, lower wages, and fewer regular hours than those of the nonhandicapped groups. Moreover, most of the adults with LD involved in the studies reported having received little vocational counseling in high school and having virtually no contact with vocational support agencies during or after high school. Family/friend networks were reported to be more helpful in location training and work than were public schools or agencies.

What are the reasons for unemployment or underemployment among youth with LD? In reviewing the research literature for the past 10 years, Okolo and Sitlington (1986) pointed out three main obstacles: (a) lack of interpersonal skills, such as work habits and attitudes and social communication skills; (b) lack of job-related academic skills; and (c) lack of specific vocational skills to perform more than entry-level personal service jobs.

Rosenthal (1985) named five major cognitive, affective, and motivational considerations related to the characteristics of those with LD. Each impacts the successful employability of such youth. The first consideration involves deficits in the areas of cognition and attention. Career education personnel and employers of learning-disabled workers must be made aware that instructions need to be concrete and tasks need to be broken down into small steps. Students with LD need encouragement to analyze and articulate attitudes and feelings and to discuss experiences. The second consideration is poor reality testing. Individuals with LD often lack insight and the ability to learn from prior experience. The third consideration is a poor sense of self, which often comes from years of failure in school. Resulting maladaptive defensive behaviors are unacceptable in the work environment. Next is poor visual imagery, which prevents many learning disabled from realistically imagining themselves as competent, self-sufficient working adults. The final consideration is learned helplessness, which manifests itself in passivity in learning and a crippling lack of independence at work.

In 1983, the Research and Demonstration Project on Improving Rehabilitation of Learning Disabled Adults conducted a survey of the attitudes of employers toward handicapped workers (Minskoff, Sautter, Hoffman, & Hawks, 1987). The employers responded positively about their willingness to make certain special allowances. The majority said that they would provide more support and encouragement, extra time for training, more detailed directions, and would suit a job to a particular person's abilities. Most would not, however, reduce work demands or become involved in the personal lives of workers. Employers surveyed were generally found to hold negative attitudes toward workers with LD because of prejudice and lack of experience supervising such workers. Only 51% of those surveyed said that they would hire a learning-disabled worker. Up to 9% stated that they would fire a worker for not telling them up front about a learning disability.

Many students with LD and their parents look eagerly toward the future and leaving behind the problems encountered in school. However, most find that the same deficits that caused problems in the school setting haunt them in the world of work. Obstacles related to self-concept, social interactions, academic skill levels, and cognitive processing abilities affect the vocational status of those with LD. From the job application, through the interview, and into the workplace, a learning-disabled worker without proper training can definitely be a handicapped worker.

Defining Career and Vocational Education

Career education is often confused with vocational or occupational education. But career education is a much broader concept. The U.S. Office of Education endorsed Donald Super's (1976) definition of career education:

> Career education must take into account the many theaters in which careers take place, the numerous roles which can constitute a career, and the nonoccupational roles which acquire prominence in society as that of occupation diminishes. Educators need to think of aptitudes, interests and values as traits which may be utilized, find outlets, and seek satisfaction in available occupations, avocational activities, in civic activities, and in family activities. (p. 42)

The Council for Exceptional Children's (1978) position statement echoed Super's philosophy by describing career education as the totality of experiences through which one learns to live a meaningful life . . . providing the opportunity for children to learn, in the least restrictive environment possible, the academic, daily living, personal-social and occupational knowledge and skills necessary for attaining their highest level of economic, personal and social fulfillment. The individual can obtain this fulfillment through work [both paid and unpaid] and in a variety of other societal roles and personal life styles. (p. 64)

Both definitions stress the range of options available to individuals manifesting various degrees of handicapping conditions, from mild to severe. The vast majority of adolescents and young adults with LD, however, have the potential to enter the work force and maintain successful employment. For them, vocational education is a vital component of any career education plan. Vocational education has been defined as "education designed to develop skills, abilities, understandings, attitudes, work habits and appreciations needed by workers to enter and make progress in employment on a useful and productive basis" (American Vocational Association, 1968, p. 12). Vocational education is one important facet of career education.

Career and Vocational Programs and Services

Modified vocational education programs have been available for certain groups of handicapped students for decades. Initially, enrollment was limited to seriously handicapped individuals. Programs for the blind, deaf, physically disabled, and mentally retarded were developed to meet the very specific training needs of each group (Marsh et al. 1978).

Students with LD have been excluded from participation in most modified vocational programs because of eligibility guidelines and overall inappropriateness of program designs. According to the Bureau of Education for the Handicapped (Technical Manual), there are some major weaknesses inherent in traditional vocational training programs for the handicapped: (a) training based on a low-achievement expectation; (b) lack of funds, good facilities, equipment, and materials; (c) too few effective instructors; (d) poor supervision and monitoring of progress; and (e) sexually stereotyped employment opportunities. Other problems and issues related to existing career education programs have included lack of interagency cooperation and agreements, inappropriate service delivery and program alternatives, incomplete program evaluation, inappropriate vocational assessment, and underutilization of the IEP process (Greenan, 1982).

Failure to provide modified vocational programs and services for the LD population has been based on the presumption that mainstreamed special education students can perform successfully in regular education courses of study. Unfortunately, this is often not the case. There are several obstacles facing students with LD who enroll in regular vocational programs. First, most courses require academic and interpersonal skills beyond the capabilities of many such students. Second, some vocational educators are reluctant to include students with LD in their classes, citing low academic ability and problem behaviors. Third, many regular education, career, and vocational programs do not begin until 11th grade and then fail to provide follow-up services. For learning-disabled students, a limited 2-year program is insufficient (Okolo & Sitlington, 1986). One additional problem facing adolescents with LD in the mainstream is programming. With new, more stringent graduation requirements being set, those students are finding fewer class periods available for vocational education.

Traditionally, career education models have been developed to address the needs of the mentally retarded, as well as those with more severe handicapping conditions. In this respect, the needs of the learning disabled have been largely neglected. This can be attributed to (a) the philosophical basis underlying treatment of individuals with LD, (b) the emphasis on the three R's curriculum in programs for learning-disabled individuals, (c) the pressure brought by parents to provide primary educational remediation to their children with LD, and (d) lack of professional skill and knowledge as to the career and vocational needs of the learning disabled.

The Life-Centered Career Education Model

Several models of career/vocational education have been addressed in the literature. Among these is the Life-Centered Career Education (LCCE) model (Brolin, 1973; Brolin, Malever, & Matyas, 1976; Brolin & Thomas, 1972), a competency-based curriculum for Grades K–12. Originally developed to meet the needs of mentally retarded students, the LCCE model has also proven effective for the LD population.

Three major curricular areas are included: (a) daily living, (b) personal/social skills, and (c) occupational skills. The daily living area contains nine competencies, all relating to skills needed to live independently and to raise a family. The personal/social area includes seven competencies that help students develop self-confidence and social skills. The occupational area contains six prevocational and vocational competencies.

The LCCE model takes into account the different settings in which the career competencies are experienced. These include school, family, and community. In each setting are individuals who share responsibility for the career education of handicapped individuals. The model requires close communication among all persons involved in that career education.

The third dimension of the LCCE model involves the four stages of career development: (a) awareness; (b) exploration; (c) preparation; and (d) placement, follow-up, and continuing education. Each stage begins at a particular phase within the educational time frame and ends late in life. This sequence of expanded stages reflects the LCCE philosophy of lifelong career education for handicapped persons.

Career Awareness

Career awareness should be emphasized during the elementary years. There are three major elements of this stage: attitude, information, and self-understanding. Good attitudes are developed when children learn that people work for a variety of reasons—economic, psychological, and societal. Young students need information about the many ways people earn a living and pursue avocational interests. Self-understanding helps students to visualize themselves as competent individuals moving toward adulthood.

Career Exploration

Career exploration should be emphasized during the junior high school years. The goal of this stage is for students to begin a careful self-examination of their unique abilities, interests, and needs. Daily living skills instruction should encourage exploration of methods utilized in managing a household, raising a family, and functioning in the community. Personal/social exploration, aided by testing, guidance, and counseling, should help students complete a realistic self-picture to develop understanding of other people. Occupation exploration allows students to examine carefully several career clusters. Whenever possible, students should experience vocations firsthand, trying out simulated situations, visiting work sites, and talking to employers and employees. During the exploration stage, students may begin to narrow the range of career choices under consideration.

Career Preparation

Career preparation generally takes place during the senior high school years but continues throughout a lifetime. While in high school, students should be offered a curriculum designed to help them reach competence in all the life career development competencies. They can receive daily life skills instruction in many regular education courses, including home economics, family studies, driver's education, and career match. Some students master all the personal/social skills before entering senior high school; others do not. Individualized programs of counseling, role playing, and/or values clarification can be implemented to remediate problem behaviors. Development of occupational skills should be directed toward a specific career cluster. Vocational courses and community work experiences should be provided, as well as instruction in skills needed to seek, secure, and maintain employment.

Career Placement, Follow-Up, and Continuing Education

Career placement can begin during the senior high school years. For students with LD, this stage should combine part-time paid work (ideally, within students' chosen career clusters) with classroom instruction. Real employment presents an opportunity to assess competency levels in all three major curricular areas. Problems in daily life, social/personal, and/or occupational skill areas become readily apparent and provide direction for follow-up remediation. The maintenance of support services during the transition period between high school and postgraduate situations may well be the key to successful vocational adjustment.

The LCCE approach differs from most vocational education programs in several important ways. Kokaska and Brolin (1985) described some of the features of their model:

> Career education interfaces education with work . . . Career education is a K–12 effort that involves all possible school personnel. Career education is an infusion concept . . . Career education does not replace traditional education or subject matter . . . Career education conceptualizes career development as a process that occurs in stages . . . Career education requires a substantial experiential component . . . Career education focuses

1. Staff development
2. Identification of instructional resources that can serve, or be adopted to serve, program participants, including
   - instructional centers or labs
   - media sources
   - specific courses that are more appropriate for some students with LD
3. Recruitment of trained LD specialists who have had experience working with adult college students with LD
4. Establishment of a core of peer tutors who can be trained for various needed functions, including
   - reviewing lecture content
   - assisting in note taking
   - discussing and answering questions
   - going over study guide questions
   - helping to prepare students for quizzes and exams
   - regularly reviewing materials
5. Establishment of assessment procedures
6. Provision of academic advisement
7. Provision of direct services in
   - developing study habits
   - improving written language skills
   - assisting with social/interpersonal skills

In consideration of program support for learning-disabled students at the college level, Vogel (1982) identified the following program components:

1. Remediation of basic skills
2. Course support
3. Use of compensatory strategies, such as strategic learning
4. Modification of academic requirements to include
   - extending time allowed to complete a program
   - adapting the method of instruction
   - substituting one course for another required course
   - modifying or waiving foreign language requirements
   - allowing for part-time rather than full-time study
   - providing modifications in examination procedures so as to measure achievement without contamination from the areas of deficit
5. Establishment of effective procedures for communication and coordination of efforts

Vogel (1982) suggested the following 12 methods of modifying evaluation procedures for college students with LD:

1. Allowing for untimed tests
2. Allowing a reader for students in objective exams
3. Providing essay instead of objective exams
4. Allowing students to take an exam in a separate room with a proctor
5. Allowing for oral, taped, or typed instead of written exams

6. Allowing students to clarify questions and rephrase them in their own words as a comprehension check before answering exam questions
7. Analyzing the process as well as the final solution
8. Allowing alternate methods of demonstrating mastery of course objectives
9. Allowing students to use a multiplication table, simple calculator, and/or secretary's desk reference in examinations
10. Avoiding double negatives, unduly complex sentence structure and questions embedded within a question in composing exam questions
11. Providing adequate scratch paper and lined paper to aid those students with overly large handwriting or poor handwriting
12. Providing an alternative to computer scored answer sheets (p. 527)

According to Mangrum and Strichart (1984), college advisors should assist students with LD in selecting courses taught by professors who are sensitive and sympathetic to their needs. More specifically, advisors should look for professors who

1. Support the goals of the LD program
2. Understand or are willing to learn about the nature of LD students
3. Are committed to meeting individual needs of students
4. Are willing to meet with students beyond class time
5. Have reasonable expectations
6. Exhibit patience when working with students
7. Clearly state all course requirements
8. Present material in an organized manner
9. Provide structure
10. Frequently review material
11. Present material at a reasonable pace
12. Are flexible regarding the format of examinations and time deadlines for assignments
13. Are interested in how students perform tasks as well as outcomes
14. Provide consistent feedback
15. Present information using techniques that enable the learning disabled student to learn through both auditory and visual modalities (p. 97)

Special Considerations in the Treatment of Incarcerated Youth

With the advent of PL 94–142, correctional education in the United States has been faced with the prospect of noncompliance in the provision of appropriate education to incarcerated handicapped individuals. We have discussed the prevalence of LD among juvenile delinquents. Clinical observations indicate that a large number of incarcerated youth have learning disabilities and general academic learning problems. In most states, the likelihood that an incarcerated population will meet special education eligibility criteria is quite high. In general, the quality of educational services in correctional institutions is unacceptable. Education usually receives a low priority in administrative decisions.

The following problems associated with the delivery of special education services to incarcerated youth have been cited in the literature: (a) inappropriate identification, assessment procedures, and assessment tools (Besag & Green, 1981); (b) staffing problems and the availability of qualified teachers (Gribben, 1983); (c) training of correctional special educators (Prout, 1981); (d) teaching loads and other nonteaching activity loads (Gribben, 1983); and (e) administration attitude toward education and teachers (Horvath, 1981).

According to Platt, Wienke, and Tunich (1982), the essential skills for the correctional teacher include knowledge of task analysis, knowledge of handicapping conditions, and orientation to functional compensatory education. To improve the quality of correctional education, Kriask and Ross (1981) suggested the inclusion of the following programming and intervention considerations:

1. Global diagnosis to measure students' general performance level
2. Specific diagnosis to measure students' functional level
3. Development of instructional objectives and selection of appropriate materials
4. Personalized instruction
5. Measurement of students' output and content mastery
6. Use of appropriate incentives and reinforcements

In programming learning-disabled incarcerated youth, special educators must address the nature of students' problems, the educational needs of students, instructional goals and objectives, intervention and instructional approaches, and evaluation of students' output and progress.

It is essential that special educators in correctional institutions know sound remedial teaching practices. Essentially, they have the primary responsibility of providing remedial education to incarcerated youth. Thus they must be able to provide learning environments conducive to positive educational growth. Classroom physical setups, intervention and instructional methodology, and the selection of appropriate material are just a few of the areas in which the special educator must be involved. Facing problems similar to those of learning disabilities specialists working with adolescents and young adults, correctional special educators must be aware of the specific needs of incarcerated youth in order to provide effective remedial programs.

SUMMARY AND CONCLUSIONS

Adolescents and young adults with learning disabilities continue to pose a challenge to LD professionals. Increased interest in, and concern for, these individuals has been evident in recent years. This has resulted in recommending comprehensive intervention programs that are geared toward developing the necessary skills for post-high school education and training, and toward functioning competently as adults in society. Innovative approaches have been developed in recent years, most notably metacognitive-oriented strategic instruction and specialized social skills training (see also chapter 12). The inclusion of these approaches into the training programs for adolescents and young adults with learning disabilities is critical to their academic growth, career development, and social/emotional adjustment.

PART 3

Identification, Assessment, and Instructional Planning

Part 3 presents material on identification, assessment, and instructional programming, including general principles and specific assessment and programming procedures. The role of the LD specialist in both formal and informal assessment is described. Special emphasis is placed on the function of informal assessment in relation to instruction. The Individualized Education Program and the IEP team, as well as instructional programming procedures to maximize the instructional process, are also discussed.

Assessment and Diagnosis of Individuals With Learning Disabilities

Questions to Consider

1. *What is the purpose of assessment?*

2. *Why is the team approach critical in the assessment process?*

3. *What is the role of the LD specialist in the assessment process?*

4. *Why does one need to develop an assessment framework?*

5. *Why are informal assessment procedures a key to effective instruction?*

PERSPECTIVES ON ASSESSMENT AND DIAGNOSTIC PROCEDURES

The Purpose and Importance of Assessment

Conceptual knowledge about learning disabilities and a service delivery framework were presented in previous chapters. Assessment is the first phase of the taxonomy for educational remediation. It is the first step toward consideration for placement and subsequently serves as the basis for program recommendations and for instructional programming. It provides guidelines for identification, eligibility for services, and appropriate placement, as well as for instructional planning and program evaluation for individuals with learning disabilities. Assessment directs the instructional approach and the selection of appropriate teaching methods and educational materials. From the educational, psychological, and special education perspectives, assessment must always be purposeful and functional. Purposeful assessment includes data collection procedures that yield information that is utilized for program placement and programming, whereas functional assessment denotes the utilization of assessment data for instructional purposes.

More specifically, assessment (a) identifies individuals who can benefit from programs specially designed for those with learning disabilities, (b) provides a remedial framework in which the process is more scientifically based than in a trial-and-error approach, (c) provides direction for program planning and program intervention, (d) identifies specific performance variables that have a bearing on instructional programming and on the nature of the educational instructional interventions, and (e) provides a means for evaluation and accountability of the educational process.

Assessment of Individuals With LD: Current State of Affairs

Although this chapter presents an assessment framework based on empirical findings and clinical experience, assessment remains an area of main concern in the literature. There are many problems associated with assessment procedures for the learning disabled (Adelman & Taylor, 1991; D. J. Johnson, 1988; Reynolds, 1984–1985; Swanson, 1991). An acceptable assessment framework is lacking, as are assessment instruments appropriate for diagnosing learning disabilities and assessing the concerned skill areas. Assessment procedures for learning disabilities have been under severe attack, and questions have been raised about some of the assumptions that are said to underlie the assessment process for students with LD.

For the most part, the assessment tools developed to identify learning disabilities lack validity and reliability and are based on poorly formulated constructs (Ysseldyke, 1979, 1983; Ysseldyke & Algozzine, 1982). In addition, these assessment procedures have been criticized for failing to appropriately identify individuals with LD and to discriminate between the learning-disabled, low achievers, and normal learners (Ysseldyke, 1983; Ysseldyke & Thurlow, 1983). The lack of clarity and consistency related to the implementation of the eligibility criteria set forth by federal regulations and guidelines, and the ineffectiveness of the assessment team decision-making processes further aggravate the situation (Ysseldyke & Thurlow, 1983). These conditions inadvertently result in the placement of low achievers, slow learners, mildly retarded students, culturally disadvantaged students, and students with behavior problems in learning disabilities programs (Mercer, 1987).

In reviewing assessment practices for learning-disabled individuals, Mercer (1987a) pointed out some of the obstacles impeding the search for better identification practices:

1. The lack of consensus regarding the definition of learning disabilities which makes it extremely difficult to establish criteria for identifying learning disabilities;
2. the difficulty to operationalize the discrepancy factor in identifying learning disabilities;
3. the lack of adequate assessment instruments; and
4. the heterogeneity of the learning disabled population makes it difficult to develop a unifying set of identification criteria. (p. 154)

While a state of uncertainty exists in the area of assessment for individuals with learning disabilities, LD professionals who are faced with making decisions in the identification and placement of such individuals must choose instruments and procedures that best meet their needs. Likewise, LD specialists must rely on assessment practices that have direct implications for instructional planning, programming, and evaluation.

Assessment Procedures as Currently Required by Law and Regulations

In the period prior to Public Law 94–142, many inequities existed in the process of assessment, identification, and placement of individuals in special programs. There were no regulations controlling the assessment of students and providing due-process procedures. Students referred for special education considerations were too often placed on waiting lists for 1 to 3 years. Many children were placed in special programs without parental consent and sometimes even without parental knowledge. Moreover, during that time, no careful considerations were given to linguistic and cultural differences in the assessment process. Consequently, many students were mistakenly identified and inappropriately placed in special education programs. There were serious flaws in monitoring and evaluating procedures. In most cases, once students were placed in special education, they remained there throughout their school years. Parents were not involved in the process and were denied access to their child's records, which were stamped "Confidential" by the district. On the other hand, students in need of services were often denied access to special programs.

The Education for Handicapped Children Act of 1975 (PL 94–142) clearly mandates procedures for the actual assessment process, selection, and administration of assessment tools; the utilization of assessment data; and due process to guarantee the rights of children and their parents. The purpose of these regulations is to ensure nondiscriminatory, appropriate assessment procedures that assure appropriate placement and adequate services for individuals with exceptional needs. Districts are accountable for, and required to follow, these procedures and guidelines.

More specifically, the following are Public Law 94–142 regulations pertinent to assessment of individuals with learning disabilities as cited in the Federal Register, volume 42, no. 163. They are classified under preplacement evaluation, evaluation procedures, and placement procedures.

Preplacement Evaluation

"Before any action is taken with respect to the initial placement of a handicapped child in a special education program, a full and individual evaluation of the child's educational needs must be conducted in accordance with the requirements of 121a532" (20 U.S.C. 1412[5][C]).

Evaluation Procedures

At a minimum, state and local educational agencies shall insure the following:

A. Tests and other evaluation materials:
   1. Are provided and administered in the child's native language or other mode of communication, unless it is clearly not feasible to do so;
   2. Have been validated for the specific purpose for which they are used; and
   3. Are administered by trained personnel in conformance with the instructions provided by their producer;
B. Tests and other evaluation materials include those tailored to assess specific areas of educational need and not merely those which are designed to provide a single general intelligence quotient;
C. Tests are selected and administered so as to best insure that when a test is administered to a child with impaired sensory, manual, or speaking skills, the test results accurately reflect the child's aptitude or achievement level or whatever other factors the test purports to measure, rather than reflecting

the child's impaired sensory, manual, or speaking skills (except where those skills are the factors which the test purports to measure);

D. No single procedure is used as the sole criterion for determining an appropriate educational program for a child;

E. The evaluation is made by a multidisciplinary team or group of persons, including at least one teacher or other specialist with knowledge in the area of suspected disability; and

F. The child is assessed in all areas related to the suspected disability, including, where appropriate, health, vision, hearing, social and emotional status, general intelligence, academic performance, communicative status, and motor abilities. (20 U.S.C. 1412[5][C])

In addition, "testing and evaluation materials and procedures used for the purposes of evaluation and placement of handicapped children must be selected and administered so as not to be racially or culturally discriminatory" (20 U.S.C. 1412[5][C]).

Placement Procedures

A. In interpreting evaluation data and in making placement decisions, each public agency shall:

1. Draw upon information from a variety of sources, including aptitude and achievement tests, teacher recommendations, physical condition, social or cultural background, and adaptive behavior;

2. Ensure that information obtained from all these sources is documented and carefully considered;

3. Ensure that the placement decision is made by a group of persons, including persons knowledgeable about the child, the meaning of the evaluation data, and the placement options; and

4. Ensure that the placement decision is made in conformity with the least restrictive environment rules in 121a.550–121a.554.

B. If a determination is made that the child is handicapped and needs special education and related services, an individualized education program must be developed for the child in accordance with 121a.340–121a.349 of Subpart C. (20 U.S.C. 1412[5][C]; 1414[a][5])

Determination of Eligibility

According to the Code of Federal Regulations, section 121a.5(b)(9), an individual with learning disabilities is eligible for special education services when he or she

does not achieve commensurate with his or her age and ability levels when provided with learning experiences appropriate to the individual's age and ability levels, and a severe discrepancy exists between the individual's intellectual ability and present level of academic functioning. (As cited by HOPE Project Handout)

Most definitions and eligibility criteria for learning disabilities include an ability-achievement discrepancy factor. While some states adhere to strict quantitative standards, others use test findings combined with clinical judgment to place students in LD programs (D. J. Johnson, 1988).

The Team Process in Assessment

As previously stated, PL 94–142 clearly mandates multidisciplinary approaches to placement decisions. In order to guarantee the provision of appropriate education to the handicapped, the law recognizes the strength of a team approach that includes, among others, parents of handicapped individuals. "The architects of PL 94–142 undoubtedly believed that group decisions would provide safeguards against individual errors in judgement, while recognizing that only a group of specialists from different professions could deal effectively with the increasing complex set of problems facing special education" (Pfeiffer, 1982a, p. 68). Thus if PL 94–142 is to work on behalf of handicapped children, school personnel and parents must work together and engender a spirit of cooperation, collaboration, and mutual respect. Support for the team approach has been provided by Vautour (1976) and Pfeiffer (1981b).

The team approach is intended to provide a systematic process for sharing information and expertise, appropriate input, and a deliberation platform in order to maximize the decision-making process. Its aim is the sharing of information and the achievement of a consensus as to the programmatic needs of children. It requires collaborative efforts that include the input of all individuals concerned. The practice of sharing knowledge and expertise in program planning offers the greatest likelihood of assuring optimal educational placement and instructional programming.

The sharing of responsibility by all IEP team members for implementation of the IEP accelerates the feedback loop of the taxonomy of educational remediation procedures discussed in chapter 4, increases expert input and monitoring of interventions, and provides for an exchange of expertise that can improve the individualized educational program process at all stages. The complex demands posed by individuals with learning disabilities on the educational system, the desire to provide the best appropriate education to those individuals, and the growing expertise and experience of parents, teachers, school psychologists, therapists, and administrators suggest the growing efficiency of the multidisciplinary team in the IEP/special education process.

The Role of the LD Specialist in Assessment and Diagnostic Procedures

The role of the LD specialist in assessment is central to the remedial process. The LD specialist serves as a member of the multidisciplinary assessment team. In addition, the LD specialist must be able to read and understand the assessment data and reports provided by the IEP team, and then translate this information into instructional terms and specific remedial and intervention approaches. This specialist must have sufficient knowledge to evaluate the adequacy of the IEP. Quite often, IEPs are written with insufficient and inappropriate goals for students, and they tend to lack clear direction for the remedial process. The LD specialist must know both formal and informal assessment procedures in order to obtain the necessary information for instructional programming. Finally, the LD specialist must be able to monitor students' progress and the effectiveness of the instructional process through an evaluative procedure.

More specifically, the role of the LD specialist in the assessment process includes the following:

1. Providing input to the IEP team through anecdotal records and observational data
2. Participating as a member of the assessment team in administering criterion- and norm-referenced tests
3. Supplementing the formal assessment procedures completed by the IEP team with informal assessment and/or criterion-referenced assessment tools for instructional planning and programming
4. Serving in a consulting capacity to regular classroom teachers in identifying students who may need to be referred to the school guidance team or the IEP team
5. Evaluating students' progress and the instructional process

Prereferral, Referral, Instructional Programming, and Implementation

In providing appropriate educational services for individuals with learning disabilities in the least restrictive environment, the LD specialist is involved at four different levels of assessment: assessment information for regular classroom program modification, additional assessment required for the IEP process, supplemental assessment for effective instructional programming in the resource room or the special classroom, and periodic evaluation of students' progress in special education services. The LD specialist usually participates in assessment at each of these levels and is involved in administering both formal and informal inventories related to direct services in special education, as well as consulting with regular classroom teachers. These levels are illustrated in Table 8–1.

In Level I—Prereferral, Referral Assessment—assessment is carried out in response to requests for assistance from regular classroom teachers to Students' Study Teams. The LD specialist's involvement is directed toward assisting regular classroom teachers in program modification, usually in a consulting capacity. The prereferral referral has been established as a vehicle for providing assistance to students who are having difficulties in the regular classroom as well as a screening process for formal referral. This process is referred to by different terms in different states, districts, and schools. The most common terms are Student Study Team (SST), School Guidance Team (SGT), Child Study Team (CST), Pupil Intervention Team (PIT), and Regular Classroom Program Modification Team (RCPMT). The procedures at this level are quite often referred to as "prereferral referral" to indicate that the primary functions are regular classroom program modification and advanced screening to the IEP referral process (Graden, Casey, & Christenson, 1985).

In Level II—Formal Referral Assessment, which follows a formal request for assessment for possible consideration of special services for the student—the LD spe-

Table 8–1 Assessment Procedures in Relation to Prereferral, Referral, Instructional Programming, and Implementation

Assessment Levels	Assessment Process	Resulting Outcomes
Level I Prereferral, referral assessment	Regular classroom teachers • Observations • Informal assessment Special educator • Observations • Informal assessment • Criterion-referenced assessment	Regular classroom program modification
Level II Formal referral assessment	School psychologist • Formal assessment (norm referenced) Special educator • Formal assessment (criterion referenced)	Placement and programming decision, development of IEP

Level III
Supplementary assessment in special class or resource room
	Special educator
	• Informal assessment
	  • Observations
	  • Informal inventories
	  • Student interviews
	• Formal assessment (criterion referenced)
		Instructional programming and implementation, development of IIP

Level IV Evaluation of students' progress	School psychologist • Formal assessment (Tri-annual review) Special educator • Formal assessment • Informal assessment	Placement and programming recommendations

cialist participates as a team member with the school psychologist and other school personnel in joint assessment efforts.

In Level III—Special Program Supplementary Assessment—the LD specialist is engaged in supplemental testing for the purpose of identifying students' programmatic needs in their classrooms and developing an Individualized Instructional Plan (IIP).

In Level IV—Special Program Evaluation and Assessment—the LD specialist is involved with ongoing, periodic evaluation of students' progress and the effectiveness of remedial programs.

The LD Specialist's Assessment Competencies

As we discussed in chapter 4, the LD specialist plays a significant role in assessment and evaluation and therefore must develop competencies in these areas. These competencies and skills vary with the LD specialist's involvement at the various levels of assessment presented in the previous section and with the particular characteristics of the student population. An LD specialist who works with learning-disabled children at the primary level is concerned with readiness skills and other assessment aspects related specifically to that age group; the teacher of adults with learning disabilities is concerned with career and vocational assessment as well as other assessment areas specifically related to that age group.

Generally, the LD specialist's assessment and evaluation competencies can be classified under the following headings:

I. Knowledge of assessment guidelines mandated by laws and regulations
II. Knowledge of assessment principles and procedures
III. Knowledge of assessment instruments on three levels: awareness, understanding and interpretation, and administration
   A. Awareness of assessment instruments used by the school district, including norm-referenced, criterion-referenced, and informal assessment instruments
   B. Ability to understand test results, including
      1. Knowledge of standard scores and what they mean
      2. Ability to interpret subtest performance
      3. Ability to interpret range of functioning as well as intratest and intertest variabilities, that is, the degree of consistency of student performance within the same test (intratest variability) and between two or more tests (intertest variability)
   C. Ability to administer both formal and informal assessment instruments and to carry out informal procedures such as observations, student interviews, and teacher-generated assessment inventories
IV. Ability to translate assessment data to instructional procedures, including
   A. Delineation of students' functional level, that is, what they know and do not know
   B. Students' cognitive learning style
   C. Students' strategic production strategy utilization
   D. Students' utilization of control executive functions
V. Knowledge of short- and long-term evaluation procedures
VI. Knowledge of how to relate and communicate assessment findings to students, parents, and other professionals

A major assessment process element identified by McNutt and Mandelbaum (1980) is the LD specialist's competency in synthesizing all the gathered assessment information to form a cohesive whole. This information then serves as the basis for instructional programming. According to McNutt and Mandelbaum (1980), the following are some of the skills that may be necessary to accomplish the task: "(a) Separating information that appears to be accurate from that which may need verifying. (b) Determining if conflicting assessment information is present; if so, deciding which information should be considered more accurate and finding why the discrepancy exists. (c) Eliminating information that is redundant or not useful for in-structural planning. (d) Comparing the information to draw up an order of importance for remedial action'' (p. 28).

THEORETICAL FOUNDATIONS OF DIAGNOSTIC PROCEDURES

Assessment Constructs and Approaches

Assessment procedures must be based on sound theory and empirical research. The theoretical foundations provide the basis for establishing an assessment framework and selecting assessment instruments for the various areas of concern. They reflect the assumptions regarding the nature of human learning and behavior, the type of data to be obtained, and the utility of such data. Knowledge of these various approaches enables the LD specialist to better understand the underlying parameters of assessment and the assessment process for individuals with learning disabilities.

Five basic assessment approaches have been identified in terms of their relevance to assessment of those with LD. Each of the assessment approaches places different emphases on the processes and outcomes of assessment. More specifically, they vary in terms of (a) the construct or theory underlying the approach, (b) the process of assessment, (c) the outcome of the data, and (d) the utilization and applicability of the data and information to educational practices. The five approaches are as follows:

1. Psychometric approach
2. Developmental approach
3. Behavioral approach
4. Ecological approach
5. Information-processing approach

The Psychometric Approach

In the psychometric approach, the goal of assessment is to document the characteristics of an individual with reference to chronological or mental-age peers (Simeonsson, 1986). The derived values are dependent on the comparison of the individual's performance and test scores with an explicit standard/norm for interpretation. These norms are derived from the performance of the reference group (the standardization sample) specified by variables, including demographic data. Thus the psychometric approach emphasizes norm-referenced assessment instruments yielding values such as standard scores, percentiles, and grade and age equivalents. This information is used primarily for group placement. This approach is exemplified by the work of Binet (1902), Guilford (1967), Terman (1916), and Wechsler (1974).

The Developmental Approach

This approach assesses the individual from a developmental point of view. It is drawn from developmental psychology, which views the onset of behavior through various stages of development. This developmental point of view has been emphasized by Gesell and Amatruda (1941), Bühler (1935), Erickson (1963), Werner (1957), and Piaget (1926, 1952, 1970). Assessment using this approach attempts to determine the individual's functioning in terms of stages of development, and age equivalents are usually used to report the results. The developmental approach has special relevance for the assessment of handicapped children whose functioning may be quite discrepant from chronological-age expectations. This approach stresses analyzing the nature of an individual's development within a developmental stage perspective, rather than comparing the individual's performance to that of a standardization group (Simeonsson, 1986). When the developmental assessments are applied to those with learning disabilities, assessment usually follows the evaluation of the individual's sensory-motor, perceptual, language, cognition, and social/emotional functioning (Frostig & Orpet, 1972).

The Behavioral Approach

The behavioral approach attempts to identify and describe behaviors and behavioral settings objectively and as scientifically as possible. It involves the analysis of behavioral and situational variables. Assessment using a behavioral approach yields data on the topology of an individual's behavior, a description of what the behavior looks like, generally described in terms of frequency, rates, and/or duration, and the relationship of behavior to antecedent and/or consequent stimuli (Simeonsson, 1986). The behavioral approach allows for a more precise and specific assessment based on empirical data and observations obtained directly from a student's performance. It is a "direct assessment" approach that attempts to pinpoint a specific student's performance (Dickinson, 1980). It facilitates the analysis of the task in terms of the skills and subskills needed to accomplish the task, its position in the sequence of skills acquisition, and its relevance to the curriculum. "The goal of this type of analysis is not only to identify the general academic area of difficulty, but to specify the skills that the individual has" (DeRuiter & Wansart, 1982, p. 110). These aspects are common to curriculum-based assessment and task analysis approaches discussed earlier in chapter 4. The behavioral approach uses task analysis and criterion-referenced and informal inventories to ascertain a student's specific functional level, that is, to pinpoint specifically what the student knows and does not know.

Task analysis focuses on an individual's levels of skills in relation to a particular task under defined conditions. It makes the assumption that learning occurs in a sequential fashion, and that certain skills must be acquired in order to facilitate the acquisition of higher order skills. Task analysis requires the LD specialist to pinpoint a student's skills and deficiencies, and to delineate the specific objectives of instruction by setting achievable goals that are observable and measurable. It involves direct, continuous, and precise measurement of behavior (Hallahan & Kauffman, 1976). The task analytic approach assumes a sequential teaching and step-by-step instructional procedures. While tasks may vary, they all have common elements, namely, the behavior, the conditions under which the behavior exists or is demonstrated, and the criterion measurements to determine students' skill knowledge (Mager, 1962). The common characteristics of this approach include the following:

1. It emphasizes direct assessment of skills related to content areas of the curriculum with direct implications for instruction.
2. It stresses target behaviors conducive to learning and student conduct.
3. It provides for a discreet description of what students know and do not know.
4. It emphasizes the LD specialist's role in assessment.
5. It encourages the use of criterion-referenced and informal assessment procedures.
6. It can be used to monitor and evaluate students' skill acquisition and progress.

Another assessment approach related to task analysis is curriculum-based assessment (CBA), discussed in chapter 4. This type of assessment differs from task analysis only in its use of the curriculum as the base from which to arrive at task analysis. It looks at the scope and sequence of the curriculum and determines what students know and do not know within that sequence. It provides the basis for a child's programming. Curriculum-based assessment is based on the assumption that the best way to assess children is in relationship to the curricular requirements of their schooling. Utilizing the curriculum material to be learned as the basis for assessing the degree to which students master skills is the fundamental concept of curriculum-based assessment and instruction. It involves the frequent measuring of a student's performance of sequentially arranged objectives derived from the curriculum used in the classroom (Blankenship & Lilly, 1981). In CBA, the essential measure of success in education is students' progress in the curriculum of the local school (Tucker, 1985). Furthermore, Tucker (1985) points out that each student's needs are best defined in terms of the context of that person's local educational program and the curriculum that a given student is expected to follow. Curriculum is defined as a course of study adopted by a given school system.

In describing the characteristics of curriculum-based assessment, Blankenship (1985) indicates the following:

1. Curriculum-based assessment links assessment to curriculum and instruction. Usually a student is given a pretest to determine the entry skill level and a posttest to measure the mastery of the skills.
2. Objective measures of performance are collected on classroom-relevant skills and are used as a basis in the making of instructional decisions.
3. Curriculum-based assessment is given over a period of a few days in order to provide students with multiple opportunities to respond to similar items on different occasions.
4. Curriculum-based assessment may be readministered immediately following instruction on a topic in order to assess skill mastery.
5. Curriculum-based assessment may be developed for any type of curriculum and instructional material.

In essence, the behavioral approach to assessment has directly influenced the task analysis and CBA approaches and has led to the development of criterion-referenced assessment tools that use the curriculum as the base from which to draw test items. This is the basis for teacher-developed informal assessment inventories, which are derived directly from the scope and sequence of the curriculum.

The Ecological Approach

The ecological approach attempts to assess an individual in various environmental contexts, as well as to address the tasks that exist in an individual's microecology. In this approach, the individual's behavior is viewed as an interdependent part of the total setting (Simeonsson, 1986). It focuses on observations of an individual's behavior in one's natural environment (Berkson, 1978). Its major objective is to define the environmental correlates of behavior, and its goal is to provide information about an individual's functioning within the natural environment. An analysis of an individual's environment involves both molecular and molar dimensions (Simeonsson, 1986). The molecular dimensions are those aspects of the environment that are easily recognizable, such as people and objects; the molar dimensions are broader in nature and include aspects of an individual's socioeconomic status and cultural indices. There are two general methods of assessment typical in this approach: the specimen record, which involves descriptions of behavior and speech in detail, a molecular level; and a chronology, which is a running narrative record of the individual's behavior at a molar level and usually involves a summarization of the situation (Simeonsson, 1986).

Using an ecological approach, the assessment process involves the following activities:

1. Defining a child's microecology
2. Completing a task inventory of each environment
3. Assessing a child's competency to perform the tasks
4. Assessing the characteristics judged deviant within each social setting
5. Assessing a child in each social setting
6. Assessing the tolerance of a child's interaction within his or her ecosystem
7. Analyzing data on a child's competency, deviance, and tolerance for differences (Thurman, 1977, as cited by Swanson & Watson, 1982)

According to Simeonsson (1986), there are several important implications of the ecological approach to the assessment of exceptional children. These include the minimal intrusive nature of the observations, the simplicity of data-gathering procedures, the ability to derive information regarding common behaviors and common environment, and the direct therapeutic implications of the data derived from an ecological perspective.

The Information-Processing Approach

The information-processing approach to assessment emphasizes assessment and observations that yield information and data on an individual's acquisition, storage, and utilization of information within a mediational model (Swanson & Watson, 1982). "The information processing framework assumes that a number of component operations or processing stages occur between a stimulus and a response. It is assumed that all behavior of a human information processing system is the result of combinations of these various processing stages" (Swanson, 1985, pp. 226–227). In the information-processing model, an individual's responses are influenced by one's information processing, that is, the way the individual mediates stimulation (Swanson & Watson, 1982). According to Swanson (1985), "Two theoretical components are postulated in information processing analysis: a structural component, which defines the constraints of a particular processing stage (e.g., sensory storage, short-term memory, long-term memory) and a functional component which describes the operations of the various stages" (p. 227). In applying the information-processing model to learning disabilities, an assumption is made that "the crux of the child's difficulty is a breakdown in the information processing component" (Swanson & Watson, 1982, p. 32). Thus the goal of assessment is to determine and identify information-processing deficiencies involving aspects of an individual's attention, modes of input, elaboration and integration of information, and output or response mode.

Swanson (1982, 1985, 1988c) has advocated the use of the information-processing model for assessing individuals with learning disabilities in order to "provide a more comprehensive and elaborate understanding of learning disabilities" (1988c, p. 76). The information-processing approach to assessment of learning-disabled individuals is based on the following assumptions: (a) learning disabilities reflect difficulties in information processing; (b) individuals with learning disabilities are viewed as actively inefficient learners; (c) individuals with learning disabilities fail to integrate all cognitive planes into one complex act for successful task performance; and (d) individuals with learning disabilities experience difficulties in selecting a relevant plan of action from a repertoire of strategies (Swanson, 1988c). Five major sources of information-processing activity are particularly relevant to learning disabilities assessment: knowledge base, executive function, strategy, strategy abstraction, and metacognition (Swanson, 1988c).

The information-processing perspective is an attempt to understand students' learning processes and the factors that affect the learning process. The human information-processing perspective includes the basic assumption that certain orderly mechanisms exist in processing information. This usually involves the input, elaboration, and output mechanisms. Information-processing models are useful in understanding learning disabilities (Farnham-Diggory, 1986; Senf, 1972; Swanson, 1982, 1985, 1988c). They emphasize how an individual comes to reduce the vast amount of external stimuli available at any given moment into manageable and meaningful units that can be easily stored and retrieved from the human information-processing system. Any dysfunction at any level may contribute to an individual's learning disabilities. According to Swanson (1982), "Information processing difficulties clearly differentiate learning disabled students from their normal counterparts" (p. 312). The literature points to deficient information-processing mechanisms among individuals with learning disabilities. They seem to exhibit difficulties in attention to the task (Hallahan & Reeve, 1980), in identification of incoming information (Hagen & Huntsman, 1971; Hallahan & Reeve, 1980), in short-

and long-term memory functions (Torgesen, 1977), in strategic productions (Torgesen, 1982), and in the automatization of skills and strategies (Kolligan & Sternberg, 1987). Strategic deficits are, in part, responsible for information-processing differences between learning-disabled and nondisabled individuals (Kolligan & Sternberg, 1987). Many studies have suggested that learning-disabled individuals' strategic learning is deficient and/or inefficient (Swanson, 1988c). In addition, those with LD experience difficulties in control processes such as self-regulation, checking, planning, monitoring, and the regulation of the flow of information (Brown & Palincsar, 1982; Hallahan, Lloyd, Kosiewicz, Kauffman, & Graves, 1979; Torgesen & Kail, 1980). These aspects of individuals with LD were discussed in depth in chapter 6.

Synthesizing Theories Into Practice

Assessment practices are closely aligned with educational philosophy and the conceptualization of the nature of learning disabilities. How one perceives the nature of learning disabilities directly affects the formulation of assessment procedures, and subsequently the remedial program. Assessment is directly related to the context in which individuals with learning disabilities are educated. Assessment, and the remediation process that follows, must respond to their needs. It must also be directly related to programmatic emphasis, curriculum considerations, and intervention approaches advocated for learning-disabled individuals.

Furthermore, how one views the nature of learning disabilities and what one considers to be the intervention and remedial approach both direct the assessment process, the formulation of assessment constructs, and the subsequent development of assessment instruments. The field of learning disabilities has drawn on the various preceding approaches and has integrated elements from each of them in an attempt to establish its own assessment framework. The use of norm-referenced tests embodies the psychometric approach, and task analysis represents the behavioral approach. Observing a child's home environment epitomizes the ecological approach, and examining an individual's functioning in various developmental areas typifies the developmental approach. Identifying an individual's information-processing deficiencies and inefficiencies embodies the information-processing approach.

The need for a systematic approach to assessment is critical for effective remedial programming based on sound principles of teaching and remedial education. Thus when deciding what to test and what instruments to use, the LD specialist must address two interrelated questions: "(1) What do I want the learner to know, to be able to do and to become? and (2) What do I want to know about the learner?" (Champion, 1979, p. 111).

DEVELOPING AN ASSESSMENT FRAMEWORK

The following profiles of Michael and Rachel represent two individuals with possible learning disabilities who exhibit marked variations in their performance, abilities, and disabilities. These variations in students' functional levels must be taken into account as one goes about the assessment process.

Michael is a 5½-year-old who is in kindergarten. He seems to have tremendous difficulties in attending to and staying on task, grasping a pencil, writing his name, and recognizing the letters of the alphabet. He gets frustrated easily and, at times, throws temper tantrums. The teacher says that Michael's language development seems to be delayed. In addition, he appears to have difficulties playing games involving gross motor coordination.

Rachel is a fourth grader who performs at the average range in reading but exhibits extreme difficulties in arithmetic and spelling. According to the teacher, Rachel does not exhibit any behavior problems, yet prefers to play alone. The teacher considers Rachel to be of normal intelligence and does not understand why she is experiencing arithmetic and spelling difficulties.

The main questions are

> What are the areas of concern?
> What are the areas of assessment?
> What type of assessment tools should be used?
> Who should be responsible for their administration?
> What are the assessment procedures appropriate to each of the situations?

In order to arrive at these decisions, the schools' personnel responsible for the assessment process must adopt an assessment framework, a road map, that includes knowledge of how to utilize the assessment data gathered. Learning disabilities specialists, whose role is critical in the assessment process, must have knowledge of such a framework in order to maximize their contribution to the assessment efforts. The ultimate purpose of an assessment framework is to guide the assessment efforts for placement and instructional planning.

A framework for assessment, diagnosis, and instructional programming for individuals with LD is offered in this section. This model considers the most effective means of assessment for the purpose of instructional planning, implementation, and evaluation. It is couched within behavioral and information-processing paradigms and emphasizes data collection from various sources and a decision-making process that directly affects the instructional process.

Description of Model Components

The model views overall assessment efforts as comprised of three dimensions: assessment phases, assessment measures, and assessment domains and areas (Figure 8–1). Knowledge of these dimensions facilitates an effective assessment process.

Assessment Phases

Assessment phases are distinct phases in the assessment process. To maximize students' response during assessment, the process must address students' sensitivity to, and awareness of, the assessment process and purpose.

Figure 8–1 Assessment Model

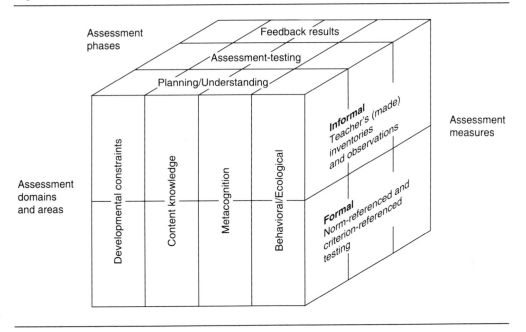

Consider the following account: A 15-year-old student was scheduled for assessment by the school psychologist. The psychologist routinely prepared the necessary assessment materials for the testing session. Upon entering the psychologist's office, the student asked, "Are you going to test me again?" signaling that in no way was he going to allow the psychologist to test him. Although caught by surprise, the school psychologist quickly realized with whom he was dealing, and replied, "No, not unless you want me to." As it turned out, this student had been tested by each of the five districts in which he had attended school. According to the student, no one had ever explained the purpose of assessment or what was wrong with him. Realizing the student's legitimate concerns, the school psychologist spent the first session explaining why the testing was necessary and what type of tests would be administered (prior to the continuation of assessment, the school district requested the student's previous testing data).

The purpose of assessment is to ascertain an individual's true level of functioning. To maximize a student's response in the assessment process, one must consider the following three phases of assessment: (a) planning and understanding, (b) assessment and testing, and (c) feedback and results.

In phase one—planning and understanding—two aspects are recognized. Planning involves consideration of the testing environment, the assessment plan (i.e., what to assess), and the assessment process. The understanding aspect of this phase implies that one must take time to explain to students the nature and type of activities employed in the assessment process. In addition, this phase serves to develop students' sensitivity to the situation and enables the school psychologist and the LD specialist to create a positive and collaborative atmosphere, so essential for optimal assessment.

The second phase of the process—assessment and testing—utilizes appropriate assessment procedures, including formal and informal measures. The assessment process is viewed as dynamic. It denotes the creation of a learning environment in which the testing situation involves test-teach-test procedures. It assesses students' performance in their natural learning environment, and the use of assessment procedures not otherwise available under standardized testing procedures. Measuring students' response to instruction as an assessment paradigm, often spoken of as dynamic referral, has been used in different ways for different purposes (Hamilton, 1983). Dynamic assessment, which usually uses test-teach-test procedures, provides information about children's performance as they learn—information about their responses to instructional approaches (Burns, Vye, Bransford, Deklos, & Ogan, 1987)—and as such, it is helpful in identifying effective instructional procedures (Burns et al., 1987; Feuerstein et al., 1979). Dynamic assessment usually provides the LD specialist with information about students' ability to perform tasks that was not predicted or available from standardized measures. "A substantial number of children in dynamic assessment complete tasks when static [standardized] measures suggest that they would not be capable of completing those particular tasks" (Burns et al., 1987, p. 60). Thus it is suggested that the LD specialist use dynamic assessment approaches in addition to the formal testing procedures indicated in the examiner's manual.

For example, Kevin, a 13-year-old, was administered the letter-word identification section of the Woodcock-Johnson Psychoeducational Battery (WJ-R), Test of Achievement, and obtained a reading grade equivalent score of 2.4. After completion of the standardized procedures of the test, the examiner then took the words that Kevin missed and color-coded them according to syllables and/or patterns. To Kevin's surprise, with the examiner's prompting, he was able to read many of the words missed earlier. During this process, the examiner asked Kevin whether reading the words in this manner was easier. Kevin confirmed the examiner's suspicion by responding in the affirmative. This information, which is of extreme value, provided input for the selection of the most appropriate reading approach for Kevin. Color-coded linguistics was one of the recommended approaches. (See also chapter 13.)

The third phase of the assessment process—feedback and results—involves the analysis and synthesis of assessment data and the communication of assessment results to parents and students. This phase culminates with the development of goals and objectives for the IEP. During this feedback/results phase, the examiner (usually the school psychologist) synthesizes and summarizes all information derived from various sources, and prepares to provide feedback to parents as well as to students. Providing assessment feedback to students is not a common practice in our public schools. The LD specialist must take the time to go over the essential information with students so they understand the nature of their difficulties. This process can begin as early as the primary grades. The language used and the degree of in-depth analysis varies, of course, with the intellectual and developmental level of children. Nevertheless, it is essential that students share the knowledge obtained through assessment. Such knowledge reduces their anxiety, heightens their awareness, and consequently directly affects their self-concept. The method in which the LD specialist provides the feedback is of crucial importance. The ultimate purpose of such feedback is to actively involve students in the instructional process by developing mutual understanding of their strengths and weaknesses and establishing realistic goals. It further helps to obtain students' commitment to the instructional process.

Assessment Measures

The second dimension of the assessment model is concerned with the type of assessment instruments and administration procedures employed. The various assessment measures include formal instruments, that is, norm-referenced and/or criterion-referenced tests, and informal measures, such as observations, student interviews, and teacher-generated inventories. A balanced assessment process includes both formal and informal measures.

Formal and Informal Assessment

A distinction is made between formal and informal measures. Standardized norm-referenced and criterion-referenced tests that require formal administration procedures comprise the category of formal assessment measures. Teacher-made inventories, observations, and student interviews, as well as criterion-referenced inventories that do not require formal administration procedures, are considered informal measures. In administering formal measures, examiners follow the testing conditions and procedures set forth in the examiner's manual. In addition, examiners follow the criteria specified for scoring. With informal measures, examiners are free to vary the procedures and are encouraged to develop a testing environment that resembles as closely as possible students' natural learning conditions. Informal measures are usually unrestricted, and the criteria for scoring is determined by individual examiners.

Norm-Referenced and Criterion-Referenced Testing

Norm-referenced tests use normative data as the basis for scoring and interpretation. They compare an individual's functions in relation to a normative group. These tests usually attempt to sample the area under consideration and establish normative scores, against which they ascertain an individual's level of functioning in a specific area. Norm-referenced tests emphasize interpersonal differences and thus report the results in terms of normative data such as scale scores, percentiles, and grade-equivalent scores. These scores are related to the distribution of scores of the population on which the test was standardized.

Criterion-referenced tests measure an individual's performance against absolute criteria for skill mastery. They attempt to bridge the gap between assessment and instruction by generating assessment information that can be easily translated into instructional programming and can assist in developing instructional goals and objectives (McLoughlin & Lewis, 1990). Criterion-referenced tests stress intraindividual differences. A criterion-referenced tool is not concerned with normative data, but with how an individual performs against a certain set of criteria for task completion. Some attempts have been made to combine aspects of norm-referenced and criterion-referenced testing (Champion, 1979). The Key Math Diagnostic Arithmetic Test-Revised attempts to provide both grade-equivalent scores and a set of instructional objectives relevant to each group of test items.

Assessment Domains and Areas

The third assessment model dimension is concerned with domains and areas, which vary with the developmental age of students and the severity of learning disabilities. For example, for a 5-year-old child, emphasis is placed on readiness skills and developmental areas, whereas for an adult, greater emphasis is placed on career/vocational skills and metacognitive functioning. The following assessment domains and areas have been identified as crucial to the remedial process. They are based on empirical findings in behavioral and information-processing paradigms and on clinical experience. The assessment domains and their respective areas include (a) developmental constraints—attentional processes, sensory-motor ability, perception, language, and cognitive functions; (b) knowledge base/content knowledge—academic achievement, conceptual knowledge, self-help and life-adjustment skills, and career vocational skills; (c) metacognition—strategic production, strategy utilization, and the use of control executive functions; and (d) behavioral/social-emotional development. The following sections describe these assessment areas in detail.

Developmental Constraints

Individuals' functioning in sensory-motor abilities, perceptual functioning (visual, auditory, and haptic), language development, and cognitive ability directly affects the way they interact with their environment. While research is equivocal, sensory-motor deficiencies, perceptual disorders, and language delay or dysfunction are commonly cited characteristics of those with learning disabilities (see chapter 1). One must examine individuals' functioning in various developmental areas, beginning with sensory-motor development which entails fine motor coordination, gross motor development, body awareness, body image, and development of laterality and directionality. The next area of concern is that of perceptual functioning—visual, auditory, and haptic—with attention to visual discrimination, spatial relationships, and auditory discrimination. In language, the concerns are with receptive and expressive language, especially the use of age-appropriate vocabulary and linguistic structures.

General cognitive and intellectual abilities involve the capacity for cognitive processes. People have different cognitive capacities, structures, aptitudes, abilities, and skills that create or otherwise make cognitive processes possible (Mann & Sabatino, 1985). Developmental aspects of cognitive capacities, documented in the literature, suggest that individuals' general cognitive and intellectual abilities have direct impact on their interaction with the environment and their ability to benefit from the remedial program.

Knowledge Base: Declarative/Content Knowledge

As described in chapter 6, knowledge base refers to an individual's acquired knowledge. One's knowledge base is affected by one's constitutional base and interaction with the environment. This knowledge base is acquired, updated, and modified throughout an individual's life span (G. Cohen, 1983). Knowledge base can be viewed as (a) general declarative knowledge—"knowing that," also referred to as content knowledge; (b) procedural knowledge—the knowledge "how to," which is usually contained within metacognition; and (c) conditional knowledge—knowledge of the conditions under which appropriate strategies can be optimally employed (Paris et al., 1983). The knowledge base is acquired through both incidental learning, which occurs fortuitously through an individual's interaction with the environment, and formal learning, which occurs through systematic learning in the classroom.

Assessment must provide information concerning an individual's content knowledge of the various areas of the curriculum, as well as conceptual knowledge and life-adjustment skills. The curricular areas include readiness skills, reading, math, written language, social studies, and science, as well as career awareness and prevocational skills. Assessment is also concerned with conceptual knowledge and self-help skills. Conceptual knowledge relates to concepts the learner usually attains that are not directly associated with any specific area of the curriculum. It is the learner's repertoire of concepts usually essential for commonsense judgments. Life-adjustment skills relate to a body of knowledge that facilitates an individual's functioning in life, such as money management and budgeting, and self-help skills relate to more rudimentary aspects of taking care of oneself.

Metacognition

Metacognition includes procedural knowledge, that is, the knowledge "how to" through strategic learning, and the knowledge of the conditions under which appropriate strategies can be optimally employed. As pointed out in chapter 6, metacognition involves students' sensitivity to self and the learning environment. The metacognitive process heightens individuals' awareness of the factors affecting learning, including the characteristics of a task and the strategies needed to complete that task successfully. Assessment of individuals' metacognitive functions is concerned with three main areas: individuals' strategic production, the employment of effective strategies appropriate to various types of learning, and individuals' utilization of control executive functions in monitoring and regulating strategic behaviors and outcomes.

Behavioral/Social-Emotional Development

Assessment of individuals' social/emotional development, often referred to as affective base, is concerned with their emotional state and interaction patterns with the environment. Four important aspects have been delineated in this component: (a) self-concept, (b) interpersonal relationships, (c) individuals' realistic evaluation of their behavior, and (d) individuals' realistic aspirations and goal setting.

Assessment Principles and Guidelines

The following principles should guide our assessment procedures for those with learning disabilities:

1. Assessment involves evaluation of the functional levels and interactions with the environment.
2. Assessment involves both formal and informal procedures.
3. Assessment is designed to provide information about students' level of mastery of academic skills, as well as daily living skills and problem-solving strategies.
4. Assessment provides useful information about the conditions that need remediation and about what students know and do not know in the various curriculum areas (Dwyer, 1987).
5. Assessment is relevant to individuals' needs in terms of school functioning and life skills.
6. Assessment provides useful information about how individuals learn best, that is, information-processing style/cognitive style.
7. Assessment provides useful information about individuals' utilization of effective learning strategies, including the use of control executive functions.
8. Assessment is functional and relevant to program planning and intervention approaches.

EARLY IDENTIFICATION OF AT-RISK CHILDREN

Purpose of Early Identification

A major growth area in education over recent years has been the early identification and intervention programs for "at-risk" children, which have received the support of both professionals across discipline lines and parents (Lindsay & Wedell, 1982; Mastropieri, 1988). Studies of the effect of early intervention with handicapped children (Kirk, 1958; Skeels, 1966) have provided the impetus for identifying children "at risk" early so that they can receive appropriate services. Early identification is defined as "the practice of screening infants and preschool children in an attempt to predict those likely to experience school problems" (Mercer, Algozzine, & Trifiletti, 1979, p. 52). Professionals agree that learning problems do not develop suddenly or capriciously and that many children with learning disabilities are reported to have had long and consistent histories of difficulties of various kinds (Keogh, 1969). Infants and preschool children who are likely to experience learning problems in school are referred to as "at-risk" or "high-risk" children. The belief is that many of the learning, social and emotional, and educational problems of at-risk children can be prevented and even remediated if identification and prevention are provided before children enter school (Keogh & Becker, 1973; Kirk, 1987). The enactment of PL 94–142 and specifically PL 99–457, the Education of the Handicapped Act Amendments of 1986, had a remarkable influence on early education and intervention programs in this country. PL 99–457 is landmark legislation which provides the basis of policy making for the early education and intervention programs for "at risk" handicapped children, from birth to 5 years of age, and their families (Raver, 1991).

The purposes of early identification and intervention are (a) to help children and their families to live fuller and happier lives from the outset, (b) to prevent and minimize the development of problems that have their roots in the first 3 or 4 years of life, and (c) to increase the chances for satisfactory future schooling and wholesome later-life patterns (Reynolds & Birch, 1982). Thus the major aims of early education programs are to provide resources, support, and information to parents in helping their children, and to provide early intervention programs. Proponents of early identification and intervention believe that young children are susceptible to positive change, that later progress will follow early intervention, and that early assistance to families will increase the chances of positive adjustment to their handicapped children (Mercer et al., 1979).

Procedures for Early Identification of At-Risk Children

The early identification of learning disabilities is a complex process due to the following factors: (a) learning disabilities are viewed primarily as an academic handicap, making it difficult to predict academic difficulty before kindergarten or first grade; (b) learning disabilities are more difficult to detect early than are severe handicaps; (c) differential developmental patterns make it difficult to distinguish between the existence of learning disabilities and a developmental lag; (d) the impreciseness of the definition of learning disabilities makes it difficult to establish widely accepted eligibility criteria; and (e) the use of labels permeates the identification of any of the "mildly handicapping conditions" (Mercer et al., 1979).

The importance of early recognition of children with potential learning problems places more responsibilities on nursery, kindergarten, and primary grades teachers. By and large, teachers were found to be good predictors of learning problems (Keogh & Becker, 1973). In order to increase the accuracy of early identification, it is recommended that we use an assessment procedure that utilizes the input of various assessment instruments and resources. A preliminary screening is recommended at the initial level of early identification to identify children who have a high probability of experiencing difficulties in school and/or demonstrating learning disabilities. Usually, this may involve a child's physician and/or teacher, a parent interview, observation techniques, screening instruments, and informal inventories. Following the preliminary screening, a decision is made for a more in-depth assessment when a child is suspected of having learning disabilities. At this level, the assessment procedures are in line with what has been discussed earlier in this chapter. This usually involves an evaluation of a child's sensory-motor, perceptual, language, and cognitive functions, as well as social and emotional development. In addition, school readiness skills are also assessed. The Denver Developmental Screening Test, the Development Indicators for the Assessment of Learning-Revised, the Rhode Island Pupil Identification Scale, the Evanston-Early Identification Scale, the First-Grade Screening Test, the Boehm Test of Basic Concepts, the Brigance Preschool

Early identification of learning disabilities and early intervention can prevent unnecessary failure experiences for the child and prepare the family to effectively deal with their child's problems.

Screen for Kindergarten and First Grade, the Metropolitan Reading Readiness Test (MRRT), the Lee Clark Reading Readiness Test, and the Stanford Early School Achievement Test are some of the instruments used for preliminary screening and early identification of children suspected of having learning disabilities.

Several problems have been noted in early identification. These include the question of the validity of identification techniques; the problems associated with the act of predicting learning problems, such as undue anxiety, which may generalize to affective and motivational aspects of development; and the fact that the use of labels and expectations evolving from self-fulfilling prophecy may result in differential treatment patterns (Keogh & Becker, 1973). The harmful effect of misdiagnosis and its influence on parents' and teachers' expectations have been discussed by professionals in the field (Mercer et al., 1979). In addition, the question still remains as to which aspects of development correlate with later learning difficulties and which are causally related (Lindsay & Wedell, 1982).

CROSS-CULTURAL AND BILINGUAL ASSESSMENT OF INDIVIDUALS WITH LD

Identifying monolingual children suspected of having learning disabilities is often a difficult task. When children's native language is other than English, the task is even more complex (Milne, 1982; Mowder, 1982). Students' test performance is mostly affected by their level of English proficiency, unfamiliarity with test content, and cultural values. In addition, the paucity of assessment tools with sound validity and reliability for minority students and examiner competency in bilingual assessment may also influence the assessment outcome.

For the most part, assessment instruments and procedure for children of different linguistic or cultural groups have not been adequate and culturally fair (Baca & Bransford, 1981; Rueda, 1989). Standardized tests are low in predictive validity when used with culturally different children (DeBlassie & Franco, 1983). Many of the tools are culturally biased, and translations of standardized tests into other languages may not eliminate those biases (Mowder, 1980). These factors were acknowledged when PL 94–142 and subsequent regulations were written for the selection of assessment tools and the administration of assessment procedures for culturally diverse children. (See section 1412(5)(C) of PL 94–142 presented earlier in this chapter.)

The assessment of bilingual students poses a challenge to school psychologists (Wilen & Sweeting, 1986). This problem is compounded by the diversity of cultures and the large number of combinations of bilingualism in America's schools (Mowder, 1979, 1980). The lack of trained personnel capable of assessing these children further aggravates the situation (Baca & Cervantes, 1984; Baca & Chinn, 1982; Rodriguez, Perieto, & Rueda, 1984). In general, bilingualism denotes the use of two languages and ranges from almost total use of one's native language to complete mastery in both languages. Furthermore, one's use of the two languages varies for specific purposes and functions and in different contexts (Mowder, 1979).

Procedures for Assessing Bilingual and Culturally Different Students

Current assessment practices for linguistically and culturally different students with special needs must incorporate the best and the most successful practices of special education and bilingual education (Baca, 1982; Baca & Cervantes, 1984). Information is needed regarding language dominance and proficiency. Then practitioners should use that information to determine the appropriate language for assessment and further instruction (Payan, 1984). "The term language proficiency refers to the degree to which the students exhibit control over the use of language" (Payan, 1984, p. 124). "Language dominance assessment refers to the measurement of the degree of bilingualism, which implies a comparison of the proficiencies in two or more languages. . . . This comparison provides an indication of the individual's bilingual abilities and identifies the stronger language" (Payan, 1984, p. 127). Cummins (1981) identifies two major dimensions of language proficiency—communicative language skills and academic language skills. The fact that Limited English Proficiency (LEP) students have acquired communicative proficiency in English does not necessarily imply the ability to handle tasks requiring academic language proficiency in English (Tempest, 1982). Measuring language proficiency is a complex task, and information from a number of sources, such as home surveys, teacher observations, and formal measures, should be used in assessing strengths and weaknesses in language skills. Students' proficiency in all language skills—speaking, listening, reading, and writing—should be measured.

Various methods of assessing bilingual and culturally different children for learning disabilities have been suggested in the literature. These include the use of developmental scales; linguistic translations of existing tests; pluralistic norms for existing tests such as a System of Multipluralistic Assessment (SOMPA); nonverbal assessment tests; the learning potential approach—an adaptation of the Feuerstein's Learning Potential Assessment Devise (Feuerstein, Rand, Hoffman, & Miller, 1979); criterion-referenced measures; teacher observations; and behavior rating scales (Duffey, Salvia, Tucker, & Ysseldyke, 1981; Mowder, 1979; Plata, 1982). According to Baca and Cervantes (1984), the assessment process for bilingual exceptional children must include the following areas:

1. Referral data
2. Primary language data
3. Observational and interview data
4. Other data available, including school records
5. Language proficiency
6. Educational assessment data
7. Perceptual-motor and/or psycholinguistic assessment data
8. Adaptive behavior data
9. Medical and/or developmental data
10. Intellectual assessment data (p. 173)

The following steps and procedures incorporate legal requirements and common practices in assessing linguistically and culturally different students suspected of having learning disabilities. They represent common sound practices and recommendations by the National Dissemination and Assessment Center (1980):

I. Selecting test instruments
   In choosing appropriate testing materials, the following criteria should be carefully considered.
   A. Test appropriateness
      1. Is the test designed only for placement purposes or does it reveal strengths and weaknesses in particular areas such as speaking and listening?

       2. Is the instrument suitable for local program needs? The test should fit the objectives and content of the local program or curriculum.

    B. Linguistic criteria

       1. What are the language skills that the instrument measures? All the language skills—speaking, listening, reading, and writing—should be measured.

       2. Does the instrument measure natural language usage? Testing should provide a true measure of communicative skills.

       3. Does the assessment tool measure language skills at appropriate developmental levels?

    C. Sociocultural criteria

       1. Is the instrument culturally appropriate for the individual being tested?

    D. Psychometric criteria

       1. Does the instrument provide a good measure of what it claims to measure? Is it valid?

       2. Is the instrument reliable? The measurement should be consistent every day, and it should be consistent from one form to another equivalent form.

    E. Other criteria

       1. Cost of the test

       2. Equipment required

       3. Need for bilingual trained test administrators

       4. Time required to administer and score tests

       5. Complexity of the scoring procedures

       6. Possibility of machine scoring (National Dissemination and Assessment Center, 1980)

 II. Designating an examiner who speaks the language of the student and is knowledgeable and sensitive to cultural diversity (Oakland & Matuzek, 1977; Plata, 1982)

III. Preparing the testing environment

IV. Measuring language proficiency

    A. Home survey

    B. Teacher's observations

    C. Formal assessment measures

 V. Assessing students

    A. Instruction given in the student's proficient language

    B. Use of formal measurements

    C. Use of criterion-referenced tests

    D. Use of informal inventories, teacher's observations, and work samples

VI. Compiling data, analysis, and synopsis

VII. Providing recommendations for placement and instructional programming

Many factors must be considered in assessing an LEP student. It is best to conduct a session bilingually, using the dominant language whenever possible. Assessment should focus on determining how the student functions in various areas discussed earlier in the assessment model in both English and the native tongue. The evaluations of the learning process should be conducted in both languages. If a consistent pattern of difficulty emerges in both languages, a student may have learning disabilities (Bozinou-Doukas, 1983). Several tests are now available in both English and Spanish, such as the Brigance Diagnostic Assessment of Basic Skills, Boehm Test of Basic Concepts, Peabody Picture Vocabulary Test (PPVT-R), and Woodcock-Johnson Psychoeducational Battery (WJ-R).

Tests Commonly Used With Individuals With LD

Many tests are currently being used in assessing the learning disabled. One local school district's guidelines for the administration of individual tests lists over 200 that can be utilized in the assessment process. Of the many hundreds of tests available, 40 to 50 are commonly used nationally. Their selection by various school districts and/or institutions is usually based on their educational philosophy, which dictates their views on the nature of learning disabilities and the educational program. Selection is also based on a school personnel's knowledge base and familiarity with assessment procedures and assessment instruments. Unfortunately, most assessment tools are selected on their face validity—what a test claims to measure— rather than on empirical data. The assessment battery for learning-disabled individuals varies from one geographical area to another, as well as from one district to another within the same geographical area.

A list of assessment instruments can be found in Appendix B. Its purpose is to familiarize the reader with the most commonly used tests within the field of learning disabilities. However, the reader must be cognizant that inclusion on the list is based on current practices in the field and not necessarily on the tests' objectively determined validities and reliabilities. For further information on validity and reliability data, refer to Salvia and Ysseldyke, 1985; Simeonsson, 1986; and Swanson and Watson, 1982.

The tests are classified in accordance with the assessment model described earlier in this chapter. Special attention must be paid to developmental and age variations, and necessary emphasis must be given to those in early childhood/preschool, adolescents, young adults, and learning-disabled individuals from cross-cultural backgrounds.

INFORMAL ASSESSMENT PROCEDURES: A KEY TO EFFECTIVE INSTRUCTION

Informal assessment and observation play critical roles in the LD specialist's decision making in the instructional process. Assessment data must be supplemented by the LD specialist's informal assessments and observations. These informal assessments and observations are carried out for instructional planning and programming, as well as for monitoring and evaluating student progress and instructional process.

They provide continuous information for identifying pupils' ongoing instructional needs. The assessment model discussed previously is presented as a framework for the LD specialist's informal assessment process.

Informal assessment is defined as the process of collecting data in an informal manner. It generally involves the collection of informal data in individuals' natural learning environment, usually their classroom (Sabatino, Miller, & Schmidt, 1981). Informal assessment procedures can be tailored to the needs of particular assessment situations (Bennett, 1982), used in classrooms for nearly any purpose, and constructed from materials widely available to teachers. These informal procedures allow the LD specialist to pinpoint what students know and do not know and to evaluate and draw conclusions regarding the effectiveness of the teaching process and approach. Quite often, informal assessment serves as means of validating students' performance under standardized testing procedures.

Informal assessments are effective when employed with specific purposes. The LD specialist must have a framework for informal assessment and must be cognizant of the areas to be assessed. In addition, the LD specialist must be familiar with the scope and sequence of the curriculum. This knowledge facilitates the development of informal teacher inventories, which in turn analyze students' skill mastery and deficiencies. More specifically, the purposes of the informal assessment process are as follows:

1. To obtain information not otherwise provided through formal assessment procedures
2. To obtain information about students' functioning under natural learning conditions
3. To validate the results of formal assessment
4. To permit direct teacher observations of students' activity during informal assessment
5. To permit immediate analysis of students' correct responses and errors

Various informal assessment procedures can be utilized by the LD specialist—observations, analyses of work samples, student interviews, and both commercial and teacher-generated inventories.

Informal Assessment Strategies

Teachers' Observations

Observation is the systematic watching and recording of behavior. Teachers' observations are of immense value and an important source of information. The use of observation techniques by teachers, specifically behavioral observations, is well recognized and documented in the literature. "Carefully identified observable behaviors are among the most objective measures available to the teacher" (Sabatino et al., 1981, p. 79). Behavioral observations that follow the behavioral approach achieve the following goals: (a) They describe the behavior in objective terms; (b) they include the condition under which it has occurred; and (c) they describe the behavior in measurable terms (Sabatino et al., 1981). Teachers' observations can be classified in terms of their approach and physical proximity. They are also categorized as purposeful/guided observations, incidental observations, and proximal or distal observations.

Purposeful or guided observations are directed by the observer's frame of reference. Quite often this type of observation is structured and conducted for the purpose of collecting data specific to an individual's performance on a particular parameter. Structured observations are also usually systematic and objective, involving the tabulation of behavioral frequencies recorded on observation checklists. Other types of observations are incidental or situational, consisting of observations of an activity without preset guidelines. The teacher records observations because they may prove helpful in understanding students' problems and provide useful information for instructional purposes.

An additional dimension of observations is the spatial or the physical proximity of the observer. Different data can be obtained by observing students in close proximity as the teacher works with them at their desks (proximal observations) and/or by observing students from a distance through a one-way glass window (distal observations). Proximal observations can provide information on how children approach and manage a task. Important information can also be gained by observing the interactions that occur among children, the teacher, and a task. Information derived from proximal observations is important in attempting to maximize students' interaction with the learning process. Data on aspects of attention to task, learning style, and utilization of learning strategies are best obtained through proximal observations. On the other hand, distal observation permits examination of students' interaction and performance within the classroom ecology. Students' interactions with each other, as well as their ability to regulate and monitor their own performance and behavior, provide important information related to their optimal functioning and the effectiveness of the remedial program.

Objectivity of Teachers' Observations

Observations must be objective. At times, teachers may be personally involved with their students; however, they must not allow personal biases to cloud or contaminate the record of the behavior observed. In order to be objective, LD specialists must have a criterion against which to compare their observations. This usually involves the use of baseline data and task analysis and/or curriculum-based assessment. Unrealistic reporting poses serious problems to the next teacher and to parents who attempt to monitor children's progress.

Observations must be domain specific. An LD specialist cannot observe all areas of behavior at once. If the teacher is concerned with students' language functions, then emphasis must be placed on their receptive or expressive language. However, care should be taken to consider students' overall functions as they are interrelated. Prior to conducting observations, the LD specialist must identify (a) the student to be observed, (b) a target area of observation, (c) the setting for observations and specific conditions, (d) measurable observable behaviors, and (e) guidelines and a recording format.

Students' Work Samples

Very similar to teacher observations are students' work samples. Work samples are examples or samples of students' performance under "normal" conditions in the classroom. Because of learning-disabled individuals' fear of failure, deficiency in test-taking skills, and generally high level of anxiety during testing, work samples prove to be an accurate reflection of student performance. They furnish a picture of students' performance under optimal conditions and provide an immense amount of information about students' capabilities, areas of strength, and areas of weakness. Work samples are also a helpful means of communicating students' present level of functioning and progress to their parents, giving the parents a more realistic picture of their children. In addition, work samples help to develop parents' realistic expectations of their children's performance.

Work samples can be structured or unstructured and are of various types. The intent of structured work samples is to evaluate students' mastery of a particular concept. This is accomplished by giving students a mixed practice or mixed review at the end of the week. The weekly mixed review includes practice exercises that incorporate the skills and concepts taught in class during the week. This mixed review is an excellent sample of students' work. It helps the teacher determine students' areas of strengths and weaknesses. A second type of work sample is unstructured. These can also demonstrate students' areas of strengths and weaknesses. For example, if on a specific day a child whose ability to produce a written product is generally doubted performs really well and produces an excellent paper, this paper can provide the teacher with helpful information. It reveals the extent of the student's performance potential under optimal conditions. The value of work samples can be heightened through teacher observations, providing additional information about the interaction between the student and the task (individual/task variable interaction), the way the student goes about completing the task and the strategies used (strategy variables), and the student's general feelings about the learning task.

The Interview

The next type of informal assessment is the interview. Three types of interviews are recognized in the literature: the traditional interview, the metacognitive interview, and the self-report. In the traditional interview format, the teacher attempts to gather more information about students by using a questioning approach. The metacognitive interview is an interactive process in which new information is obtained while other information is shared with students. The self-report is usually conducted with adolescents and adults in a modified interview format in which individuals are engaged in a self-description about their performance.

The validity of the interview and the self-report has been questioned (Loftus, 1975). Individuals with learning disabilities who continuously face failure experiences tend to underestimate or overestimate their abilities. The LD specialist must exercise careful judgment in evaluating the interview and self-report data. Despite their shortcomings, interview formats are important in the assessment process. They heighten individuals' awareness of their strengths and weaknesses and develop individuals' realistic evaluation and aspirations.

The individual teacher-student interview serves to

1. Develop positive interaction between the student and the teacher
2. Communicate genuine concern for the student and a feeling of acceptance and support
3. Develop open communication and procedures for request for assistance whenever the student encounters difficulties
4. Develop the student's sensitivity to the learning environment and instructional processes
5. Develop the student's awareness and knowledge of aspects related to the individual goals and objectives and the way in which they can be reached
6. Develop and/or modify the instructional plan to meet student needs

The interview technique can be used at various points of time during the school year. At the beginning of the year, the initial teacher-student interview provides the teacher with firsthand information on a student's present level of functioning, including social and emotional aspects. It helps to develop a sense of involvement and active participation, and to instill in the student a new ray of hope for a successful academic year. Using mixed reviews and informal inventories during the interview and incorporating an interview style of questioning during test-teach-test procedures can provide valuable information about a student's functional level and information-processing style.

The Metacognitive Interview

Like the traditional interview, the metacognitive interview is designed to involve students in the assessment of their functional levels and in the development of their educational plans. The involvement of the learner in a retrospective analysis of aspects dealing with the learning process makes the metacognitive interview unique. The literature reports the use of such procedures in numerous settings (Meichenbaum, Burland, Gruson, & Cameron, 1985). This interview is characterized by the subjects reporting their conscious awareness of aspects dealing with the cognitive processes. In the metacognitive interview process, the teacher faces the challenge of developing (a) an appropriate interview schedule that students can comprehend, (b) a way to motivate students to be involved in a productive manner in the interview, and (c) a way to facilitate students' ability to express themselves (Meichenbaum et al., 1985).

Problems associated with self-reporting in utilization of these procedures have been pointed out by Meichenbaum et al. (1985). The primary concern deals "with the extent to which metacognitions are accessible to the subject's conscious awareness, as well as to the extent to which the report represents veridical and complete account of private experience" (p. 7). As stated previously, despite the concerns expressed regarding the validity of self-reporting with techniques, the metacognitive interview can provide the teacher with important and viable information not otherwise attainable through the formal diagnostic procedures.

   2. Conceptual knowledge
   3. Life-management skills
   4. Career/vocational skills
  C. Metacognition
   1. Strategic production
   2. Utilization of strategies
   3. Utilization of control executive functions
  D. Behavioral/social-emotional development
   1. Self-concept
   2. Interpersonal relationships
   3. Goals and aspirations

Integration of Assessment Data to Determine Students' Performance Variables

A sample case study of a student classified as learning disabled by his school district is presented here. To facilitate the review of this case study, the following guidelines are provided:

1. Review essential information that facilitates understanding of the pupil case study.
   a. Review and study case study outlines discussed earlier in the chapter.
   b. Review material appropriate to interpretation of data.
   c. Review parameters of assessment and dynamic behavioral information-processing assessment model.
   d. Review common assessment instruments used with learning-disabled individuals.
2. Review the validity of assessment information.
   a. Do the assessment procedures utilized in the case study reflect a viable assessment framework?
   b. Is sufficient and adequate information provided?
   c. How relevant is the information to the case at hand?
   d. What additional information is needed?
   e. What are the areas that need further assessment?
   f. What should be the format of assessment (formal, informal)?
   g. What types of assessment instruments or inventories and recording forms are needed?
3. Develop a working knowledge about the case study and attempt to answer the following questions:
   a. What seem to be the student's primary problems?
   b. What are the concurrent problems, if any?
   c. What are some of the environmental contingencies that affect the individual's problems?
   d. How does the individual function across various areas? What are the individual's areas of strengths and weaknesses?

e. Does the individual use strategies for learning and control executive functions?

f. What is the student's information-processing style?

g. What are the individual's instructional needs in the various areas of the curriculum?

h. What are the individual's social-emotional needs?

i. What are the characteristics and elements of the intervention program?

j. What are the most appropriate teaching methods and intervention strategies?

k. What are the most appropriate instructional materials and resources?

l. What are the most appropriate behavior management strategies and reinforcement modes?

Sample Case Study—Dan
Presenting Referral Problem

Dan has been described as having difficulties in following routines, retaining mastered skills, and staying on tasks. He is uncooperative and exhibits aggressive behavior in the classroom, such as getting out of his seat, talking in a loud voice, making frequent negative comments to the teacher and peers, hitting, and refusing to do assigned work. His constant jittery behavior includes continually moving his fingers and tapping his desk.

Current intervention in the regular classroom includes cross-age tutoring and assistance from a volunteer aide and the school-based resource room. Other modifications include change of seating arrangement, loss of recess, and detention.

I. General background
   A. Identification data
      Age: 9 years, 5 months
      Sex: Male
      Grade: 4
      Primary language: English
   B. Health status
      The most recent report from Dan's physicians indicates that the child is in good health. There are no visual or hearing impairments. However, his behavior patterns indicate a degree of hyperactivity and lack of impulse control.
   C. Family background, including cross-cultural information
      Dan is the middle child of five and lives with both parents. Dan's father is a salesman, and his mother is a housewife. The family lives in a suburb of a metropolitan area.
II. Developmental history
   A. Birth history
      Prenatal history indicates difficulty during pregnancy, with the mother reporting some bleeding during the first trimester. This child was born full term weighing 6 lb, 3 oz after a brief labor. The mother was reported to be in good health.

B. Early development

Dan was a healthy-looking baby. Except for severe colic as an infant, for which he required medication, he had no serious illnesses, only the common childhood diseases. He had chicken pox at the age of 3 and mumps at the age of 7½. Dan was hospitalized overnight at the age of 4 when he fell off his bike and cut his forehead. He crawled at an early age and walked at 15 months. His language development was somewhat delayed; his first sentence was spoken between ages 2 and 2½. From age 2 through age 5, Dan exhibited behaviors that his mother considered more active than those of his siblings.

III. School history

A. Early school history—nursery school and kindergarten

Dan entered kindergarten at the normal age of 5 and was described by his teacher as having an extremely short attention span. He exhibited difficulties in group activities and did not make friends. He also had trouble following simple directions and in attaining readiness concepts, such as number readiness. Quite often, he seemed to be lost and was not even sure where some of his belongings were kept. In addition, he demonstrated poor eye-hand coordination.

B. Primary grades

In both the first and second grades, Dan had extreme difficulties attending to the teacher and staying on tasks. He was unable to perform in a group situation and at times refused to work even on a one-to-one basis with his teacher. He was avoided by other children because he would verbally abuse them and take their pencils. This behavior was also consistent during the third grade. He became more argumentative and easily frustrated when unable to complete tasks.

C. Recent school history

These behaviors continued during the fourth grade; however, Dan began to be more aggressive by actually using physical force against his classmates. His behavior is not tolerated by his present teacher, who requested a formal referral to the Student Study Team and subsequently to an IEP team meeting. The present teacher describes him as very active and easily distracted. According to the teacher, Dan cannot stay on tasks for more than 2 to 3 minutes at any one time, and he is distracted by the slightest noise or movement. Once distracted, he finds it hard to return to the task at hand. He has no real friends in class and only a couple in his neighborhood. Dan does not know how to keep friends. When he does make a new friend, the relationship does not usually last long because of his aggressive and antagonistic behavior.

On the referral form to the SST, the following items were indicated by the teacher:

- Exhibits short attention span.
- Is unable to stay on tasks for any length of time.
- Has difficulties following directions.

- Is easily frustrated and loses emotional control.
- Antagonizes and annoys other children.
- Demands excessive teacher attention.
- Has poor learning retention.

IV. Assessment of present functional level

Testing behavior observations: Dan was extremely restless during testing. He was unable to sit still and concentrate on the tasks for more than 5 or 10 minutes. However, he did become involved in test items when he understood the directions and met with some success. Dan responded very well to encouragement and positive reinforcement. The testing was carried out during several administering sessions with many breaks. Performance was very inconsistent, with some items completed successfully after failures on less difficult items.

A. Constitutional base

1. Developmental constraints

a. Sensory-motor-perceptual development

Dan is presently functioning at 6–10-year-old level in sensory-motor-perceptual activities as demonstrated by the Developmental Test of Visual Motor Integration (VMI). Dan demonstrated difficulties with orientation to figures, angulation, spatial relationships, and integration.

b. Language development and communication

Clinical Evaluation of Language Functions (CELF)

Language Processing Age:	8–3
Language Production Age:	8–1

Dan demonstrates deficiencies in his overall language expressive abilities. He seems to have trouble following directions and retaining material presented to him auditorily. In written language, Dan is able to write simple sentences but has a difficult time completing a story.

2. Cognitive capacity

On the Wechsler Intelligence Scale for Children-R (WISC-R), Dan obtained the following scores:

WISC-R:	Verbal Scale IQ:	88	Performance Scale IQ:	91
Subtests:	Information:	8	Picture completion:	9
	Similarities:	9	Picture arrangement:	8
	Arithmetic:	6	Block design:	8
	Vocabulary:	9	Object assembly:	10
	Comprehension:	9	Coding:	9
	Digit Span:	5		

Full-Scale IQ: 89

According to the scores obtained on the WISC-R, Dan is functioning in the low-average range of intellectual ability. Considering his short attention span and inconsistent test performance, it is conceivable that the scores are deflated and are not representative of his true functional level. Weaknesses were exhibited in tasks requiring concentration and attention to auditory stimuli, auditory memory, and mental manipulation.

B. Content knowledge base

1. Academic achievement

a. Woodcock Johnson Psychoeducational Battery (WJ-R) Test of Achievement

Grade Equivalent	
Reading cluster	2.1
Math cluster	2.0
Written language cluster	2.0

b. Wide Range Achievement Test-R

Grade Equivalent	
Reading	2E
Spelling	1E
Arithmetic	2E

c. Peabody Individualized Achievement Tests-Revised (PIAT-R)

Spelling	1.5
Reading recognition	1.6
Reading comprehension	2.1
Math	2.0

d. Brigance Inventory of Basic Skills

Word recognition	2.2
Oral reading	2.0
Reading comprehension	2.3
Math	2.2
Spelling	1.8

2. Teacher's Informal Assessment and Observations

a. Reading

(1) Word recognition

Dan's reading decoding patterns are characterized by slow word-by-word reading with guessing and substitution of words whenever he is unsure. Though he knows the consonant sounds in isolation (with the exception of soft and hard c and g) and the basic short and long vowel combinations of CVC and CVCV, he has trouble blending the sounds into whole words. Dan also demonstrates difficulties with consonant blends and digraphs such as *ch* and *ck*. His knowledge of diphthongs is completely deficient.

(2) Reading comprehension

Dan exhibits great difficulties in silent reading comprehension. However, when a passage is read to him, he is able to identify the main idea and usually remembers the sequence of events in the paragraph. Despite his difficulties in reading, Dan likes to listen to stories read to him.

b. Spelling

Dan's spelling ability is very minimal. He knows some simple words with CVC and CVCV patterns, such as cat and game. Generally, Dan does not spell or do activities related to spelling.

c. Oral and written language

Dan's oral expressive language abilities are more typical of an 8-year-old, although he seems to be able to carry on a conversation without much difficulty using proper grammatical structures. In contrast, his written output is minimal. Dan is unable to write one or two sentences without difficulty. Yet when asked to dictate a story related to a picture or an event in life, he is able to produce a story of one or two paragraphs, generally using proper grammatical structures.

d. Arithmetic

Dan is able to read and write whole numbers to the thousands. He can do simple addition and subtraction of whole numbers but has difficulties in carrying and borrowing. Dan understands the concepts of multiplication and division but does not know multiplication and division facts. Due to his reading difficulties, his arithmetic activities have been limited to computation, with little exposure to word problems. He is able to solve one-step-with-one-process arithmetic problems.

C. Metacognition (strategic production, strategy utilization, utilization of control executive functions)

Little evidence is seen of metacognitive abilities. Dan is very passive in his approach to learning and relies totally on others to direct his learning. Strategic learning is almost nonexistent, and there is very little evidence of the use of control executive functions (planning, organizing, monitoring, and checking outcomes). Study habits are haphazard. He seldom completes and returns homework assignments.

D. Affective base/behavioral ecological analysis (self-concept, interpersonal relationships, goals and aspirations)

Dan's social and emotional development is that of a younger child. He feels very insecure and is overly dependent on others. He has a low self-concept and demonstrates a low frustration tolerance. Dan has difficulties in getting along with others and is usually a loner.

1. Vineland Social Maturity Scale

Age equivalent   8.0

Social quotient   82

2. Devereux Elementary School Behavior Rating Scale
The Devereux indicates the following areas of concern as reported by his teacher:
   a. Classroom disturbance
      Dan teases or interferes with the work of peers, must be reprimanded by the teacher, or is quickly drawn into the talking or noisemaking of others.
   b. Impatience
      Dan starts work without understanding directions, does sloppy work, is unwilling to check work, or rushes through work.
   c. Disrespect-defiance
      Dan makes derogatory remarks, speaks disrespectfully, and refuses to follow rules or directions.
   d. External blame
      Dan is prone to blame others or external circumstances when things don't go well.
   e. Achievement anxiety
      Dan is sensitive to criticism, nervous during testing, or anxious about knowing the correct answers.
   f. External reliance
      Dan is easily swayed by others, reliant upon the teacher, and unable to follow directions, or has difficulty making decisions.
   g. Comprehension
      Dan does not understand what he reads or hears and is unable to apply what he has learned.
   h. Inattentiveness-withdrawnness
      Dan loses attention quickly, is oblivious to what is going on, or is difficult to reach.
   i. Irrelevancy-responsiveness
      Dan gives unrelated answers to questions, interrupts when others are talking, or exaggerates stories.

Information-Processing Capacity/Cognitive Learning Style

The following synopsis is based on the examination of the formal assessment instruments administered to Dan with consideration to intertest and intratest variability, as well as the teacher's observations through informal dynamic assessment. Dan's visual and spatial abilities are strong overall. He is more alert to visual materials. Dan's auditory processing difficulties are a major handicapping condition for him. He has extreme difficulties following all auditory directions. He must have something visually concrete with which to work. He benefits whenever visual and haptic modes are combined. His ability to complete tasks is also affected by distractibility factors, and he therefore requires presentation of material in a highly structured manner. In addition, because of his low frustration tolerance, materials must be presented to him in small units followed by immediate feedback and reinforcement.

Summary and Recommendations

Dan is currently a fourth grader who demonstrates an average intellectual potential overall, but learning delays are evident in academic areas because of attentional deficits and auditory processing difficulties. The IEP team recommended that Dan be placed in the resource specialist program for three periods a day for reading, spelling, language, and arithmetic.

SUMMARY AND CONCLUSIONS

In this chapter, we have discussed assessment procedures and practices with individuals with learning disabilities. The LD specialist assumes a critical role in assessment during the various phases of the assessment process and throughout the instructional process. The key element is to use assessment information to develop a sound and appropriate intervention program for learning-disabled individuals.

The IEP, Instructional Planning, and Programming

Questions to Consider	1. **What is the purpose of the IEP?**
	2. **What is the content of the IEP?**
	3. **What are the goals of effective instructional planning and programming?**
	4. **What are the variables and concerns in programming for individuals with LD?**
	5. **How does one develop an instructional program to maximize students' growth?**

Assessment and diagnostic procedures for individuals with learning disabilities are discussed in chapter 8. The ultimate purpose of assessment is to facilitate appropriate programming and intervention based on assessment data. The IEP becomes the vehicle for the implementation and monitoring of an effective intervention program. The purpose of this chapter is to assist the LD specialist in developing procedures and skills for understanding the IEP and instructional programming in order to provide an effective educational program for learning-disabled students. As discussed in previous chapters, effective remedial teaching presupposes a systematic approach usually involving assessment, programming, implementation, and evaluation. Both the IEP and teachers' instructional programming serve as means to reach that goal.

THE INDIVIDUALIZED EDUCATION PROGRAM (IEP)

The individualized education program is clearly defined in Public Law 94–142, along with procedures for implementations and due process guaranteed by the law:

> The term Individualized Education Program means a written statement for each handicapped child developed in any meeting by representatives of the local educational agency or intermediate educational unit who shall be qualified to provide, or supervise the provision of specially designed instruction to meet the unique needs of handicapped children, the teacher, the parents or guardians of such child, and whenever appropriate, such child, which statement shall include a) a statement of the present levels of educational performance of such, b) a statement of annual goals, including short-term instructional objectives, c) a statement of the specific educational services to be provided to such child, and the extent to which such child will be able to participate in regular educational programs, d) the projected date for initiation and anticipated duration of such services, an appropriate objective and criteria and evaluation procedures and schedules for determining, on at least an annual basis whether instructional objectives are being achieved. (20 U.S.C. section 140[19])

In interpreting the individualized education program concept, Abeson and Wein-traub (1979) stress that "individualized" represents the focus on the needs of a single child rather than on the needs of a class or group of children. "Education" refers to those elements of a child's education that are specifically special education and related services as defined by the act. The word "program" represents a statement of what is actually provided to a child in contrast to programs available in the school and/or school district.

The introduction of IEPs in our nation's schools was a step toward more adequate services to handicapped students. The embodiment of the elements of diagnostic prescriptive teaching principles in the individualized education program was actually a remedy for the intolerable conditions that existed prior to PL 94–142. "In general the IEP requirement has met with strong support. . . . [T]he IEP has given impetus to instructional planning and has helped define the instructional needs of handicapped students" (Meyen, 1982, p. 15). According to Turnbull, Strickland, and Hammer (1978), "The IEP has the potential of being the catalyst for more individualized and specified approach to education, increased accountability of educators, and shared decision-making between teachers and parents" (p. 46).

Purpose and Major Functions of the IEP

The IEP has both an administrative and an educational function. In its administrative role, the IEP specifies the educational program for a student and serves as a monitoring device to guarantee the provision of such services. In its educational role, the IEP specifies the instructional goals and procedures (Morgan, 1981b).

The United States Department of Education policy paper dated April 30, 1980, describes the functions and purposes of the IEP as follows:

1. The IEP meeting serves as the communication vehicle between parents and school personnel and enables them as equal participants to jointly decide upon what the child's needs are, what will be provided, and what the anticipated outcomes may be.
2. The IEP itself serves as the focal point for resolving any differences between the parents and the school; first through the meeting, and second, if necessary, through the due-process hearing procedures that are available to the parents.
3. The IEP sets forth in writing a commitment of resources necessary to enable a handicapped child to receive needed special education and related services.
4. The IEP is a management tool that is used to ensure that each handicapped child is provided special education and related services appropriate to his/her special learning needs. (Note: as a management tool, the IEP may be used to develop daily instructional plans for the child. However, this is not required for federal compliance purposes.)
5. The IEP is a compliance/monitoring document which may be used by monitoring personnel of each government level to determine whether a

handicapped child is actually receiving the services agreed to by the parents and the school.
6. The IEP serves as an evaluation device for use in determining the extent of the child's progress toward meeting the projected outcomes. (p. 16)

Fundamentally, the IEP guarantees appropriate education for handicapped individuals. It also ensures that the appropriate education be provided in a manner consistent with the best educational and remedial practices. The IEP serves as a comprehensive educational plan based upon thorough diagnostic assessment of a handicapped child's functioning. In addition, it serves as a guide to instruction, and contains guidelines and procedures for implementation of a total service plan (Walker, 1979).

Mayer (1982) summarizes the following positive aspects of the IEP as remarked by teachers and administrators:

- It extends full rights to the handicapped.
- It helps in planning and organizing instruction.
- It helps to establish curricular emphasis through specific goals and objectives.
- It helps teachers keep the instructional program on target.
- It provides a more efficient way of planning daily lessons.
- It provides a better approach to documenting student progress.
- It provides an accountability structure.
- It identifies who is responsible for what, including personnel other than teachers.
- It provides a way for teachers and parents to share information about a child, thus helps the communication process.
- It assures parents that teachers and other school personnel have their child's best interest at heart. (p. 291)

By definition, the individualized education program addresses two main aspects:

1. A written statement for each handicapped child, which refers to a written plan specifying program placement, annual goals, short-term objectives, and instructional procedures
2. The IEP meeting, which is the actual decision-making process determining the nature of the written IEP

Procedures and guidelines are set by federal and state regulations and are an integral part of the local educational agencies' policies and procedures.

The IEP as a Written Statement

Public Law 94–142, 20 U.S.C. section 140 (19), specifies the content of the individualized education program. The IEP for each child must include the following:

1. A statement of the child's present levels of educational performance, which involves a general assessment information summary in all appropriate areas including health, vision, hearing, cognitive general

ability, academic achievement, social/emotional status, speech and language, motor abilities, and other pertinent areas

2. A statement of annual goals, including short-term instructional objectives, which usually involves a description of the annual goals as determined by the IEP team and the specification of the interim/short-term objectives that are to lead to the attainment of the annual goals
3. A statement of the specific educational services to be provided to such child, which requires the specifications of the types of services the child will receive in the school and the names of the people responsible for providing these services
4. A statement of the extent to which such a child will be able to participate in regular educational programs, which requires a specification of the amount of time a child is participating in the regular classroom
5. The projected date for initiation and anticipated duration of such services
6. An appropriate objective, and criteria and evaluation procedures and schedules for determining, on at least an annual basis, whether instructional objectives are being achieved

Fiscus and Mandell (1983) discussed the IEP document from several perspectives: (a) From students' viewpoint, it is a personalized educational plan that acknowledges the special needs imposed on them by their disability and reflects the necessary provisions to assure appropriate educational environment/instruction; (b) from parents' viewpoint, it provides assurance of quality services for their children and a safeguard against improper referral and placement procedures. It provides parents with an opportunity to participate in the determination of their children's educational program. Furthermore, it guarantees special education and related services to be provided at no cost to parents; and (c) from teachers' viewpoint, "it is accessible and current data; it is a tool, direction, and link with supportive expertise. No longer isolated from the decision-making process which determines special education placement and services, the teacher is in the midst of sharing and analyzing the circumstances within which the student is ultimately faced on the educational frontlines. . . . The IEP is the basis for day-to-day lesson planning. It keeps student and teacher on target for the predicted outcome is in clear view to both" (p. 22). While the preceding perspectives are optimistic, the efficacy of the IEP, its usefulness to teachers, and its benefits to parents have been questioned in the literature (Dudley-Marling, 1985; Gerber, Banbury, & Miller, 1986). Studies generally point to less parent participation than expected (Gerber et al., 1986) and to relatively moderate use of the IEP by teachers. Teachers in general do not find the IEP useful in planning day-to-day instruction (Dudley-Marling, 1985).

According to Morgan (1981b), three elements determine the quality of the IEP: the assessment instruments and procedures employed to establish a student's current level of educational performance; the specificity of the short-term instructional objectives; and the extent to which the IEP is used by the teacher in planning a student's day-to-day instructional program. The IEP is not a legally binding document. It does not require that any teacher, agency, or other person be held accountable if a child does not achieve the growth projected in the IEP. Yet for some reason, "teachers frequently perceived the IEP as an accountability major that can be used against them if the student does not attain the specified annual goals and short-term objectives" (J. H. Cohen, 1982, p. 65).

The IEP Team

Goals of the IEP Team

Public Law 94–142 clearly mandates multidisciplinary approaches to placement decisions. The school must "ensure that the placement decision is made by a group of persons, including persons knowledgeable about the child, the meaning of the evaluation data and the placement options" (section 121a 533[a]). Furthermore, section 121a 532(e) of the law states that "the evaluation is made by a multidisciplinary team or group of persons, including at least one teacher, or other specialist, with knowledge in the area of suspected disability." Thus in order to guarantee the provision of appropriate education to handicapped individuals, the law recognizes the strength of a team approach that includes, among others, parents of handicapped individuals. "The architects of P.L. 94–142 undoubtedly believed that group decisions would provide safeguards against individual errors in judgement, while recognizing that only a group of specialists from different professions could deal effectively with the increasing complex set of problems facing special education" (Pfeiffer 1982a, p. 68). Thus if PL 94–142 is to work on behalf of handicapped children, school personnel and parents must work together and engender a spirit of cooperation, collaboration, and mutual respect. Support for the team approach has been provided by Vautour (1976) and Pfeiffer (1981a).

The team process is intended to provide a systematic method for sharing information and expertise, appropriate input, and a deliberation platform in order to maximize the decision-making process. Its aim is to share information and reach consensus as to the programmatic needs of children. It must include the input of all individuals concerned. The consistent practice of sharing knowledge and expertise in program planning offers the greatest likelihood of assuring optimal educational placement and instructional programming.

According to Fenton, Yoshida, Maxwell, and Kauffman (1979), the team members' awareness of the specific goals of the IEP team provides the basis for a rational decision-making process and facilitates the process of the IEP team. The authors suggested the following list of goals for the IEP team:

1. Determine eligibility.
   - Determine the student's eligibility for special education.
2. Determine adequacy of information.
   - Determine whether sufficient types of information about the student are available to the placement team before making decisions affecting the student's instructional program.
3. Interpret information.
   - Evaluate the educational significance of such data.
4. Determine placement.
   - Determine the student's placement.

5. Formulate long-term goals.
   - Formulate appropriate year-long educational goals and objectives for the student.
6. Develop short-term objectives.
   - Develop specific short-term instructional objectives for the student.
7. Communicate with parents.
   - Communicate with parents about changes in the student's educational program.
8. Determine criteria for review.
   - Plan information needed for future review of the student's program and progress.
9. Establish the specific date.
   - Establish the specific date for placement team review.
10. Review appropriateness of program.
    - Review the continued appropriateness of the student's educational program.
11. Review progress.
    - Review the student's educational progress.

Participating Members of the IEP Team Meeting

According to federal regulations, the IEP meeting shall include, but shall not be limited to, the following:

1. General. The public agency shall insure that each meeting includes the following participants:
   a. A representative of the public agency, other than the child's teacher, who is qualified to provide or supervise the provision of special education
   b. The child's teacher
   c. One or both of the child's parents subject to Sec. 121a345
   d. The child, when appropriate
   e. Other individuals at the discretion of the parent or agency
2. Evaluation personnel. For a handicapped child who has been evaluated for the first time, the public agency shall insure:
   a. That a member of the evaluation team participates in the meeting; or
   b. That the representative of the public agency, the child's teacher, or some other person who is knowledgeable about the evaluation procedures used with the child and is familiar with the results of the evaluation is present at the meeting. (Federal Register, 1977, Sec. 121a344)

Developing the IEP

IEP Components and Formats

The IEP has become the vehicle through which appropriate education is provided for handicapped children. The development of the IEP is a complex task and requires the knowledge and expertise of all members of the IEP team. The process of developing an IEP may be perceived as having two interrelated stages (Fiscus & Mandell, 1983). The first stage involves a comprehensive plan, usually referred to as the "total service plan" or the IEP. The second stage deals with the development of the implementation plan, sometimes referred to as the "individualized implementation plan" (IIP). The IEP usually includes the following components:

1. The individual's present level of performance, including a descriptive summary statement of the pupil's exceptionality
2. Eligibility as an individual with exceptional needs
3. Handicapping condition
4. Placement recommendation, including justification for type of placement and percentage of time in regular education
5. Statement of annual goals

The IIP usually includes the following components:

1. Elaboration of the annual goals and annual instructional objectives and of suggested strategies/materials
2. Short-term instructional objectives
3. Instructional strategies/techniques
4. Material/media
5. Methods of evaluation and measurement of student progress
6. The person or individual responsible for delivery of services to the handicapped individual

Though some districts distinguish between the total service plan and the implementation plan in their IEP forms, many others do not. Although PL 94–142 mandates that an IEP shall be written for each handicapped individual, no specific guidelines are given as to its format. The IEP can be written on a blank piece of paper provided it meets all the necessary requirements delineated in the law.

Writing Annual Goals and Short-Term Objectives

Annual goals are "statements which describe what a handicapped child can reasonably be expected to accomplish within one calendar year in his/her special education program" (U.S. Department of Education, Policy Paper, April 30, 1980, p. 27). Short-term objectives are defined as "measurable steps between the present level of performance and the annual goals" (U.S. Department of Education, Policy Paper, April 30, 1980, p. 22).

These statements of the annual goals and the short-term objectives—their selection, their description, and consequently their implementation—are crucial to the provision of adequate services for the handicapped. Once the IEP has been completed, the special education teacher and/or the designated instructional services personnel tend to abide by the goals and objectives to the letter of the recommendation of the IEP. Therefore, one cannot overstate the importance of proper designation and writing of both the annual goals and the short-term objectives.

Variables and Concerns in Programming the Learning Disabled

In reviewing a student's current IEP and in updating and/or developing a student's IIP and the day-to-day instructional plan, the LD specialist needs to be cognizant of the source and the nature of the diagnostic/assessment information. The specialist must be knowledgeable in the interpretation of the assessment data, understand the intervention decisions, and consider the monitoring and evaluation of a student's progress. The use of the "Teacher's Guide to Informal Assessment and Observations" (Appendix D) and other inventory profiles and checklists is essential to effectively program and monitor a student's progress. The LD specialist should utilize individual student profiles and inventories in the various instructional and intervention areas, and should organize the data in order to develop group profiles to facilitate the process of grouping of students in accordance with their functional level and abilities.

Programming Procedures

The primary goal of programming is to develop a comprehensive, integrated treatment plan that will effectively meet the needs of those with learning disabilities. However, it cannot be stressed too strongly that this comprehensive plan is designed to create an educational program commensurate with a student's abilities and to develop an active learner—one who can use strategic learning effectively and who can be engaged in strategic production, knowing when and how to use effective strategies appropriately, along with the remediation of academic and social skills.

The programming procedures discussed in this section may be used for the development of the IEP, the IIP, and the day-to-day instructional program, but they are presented primarily as steps that can guide LD specialists in developing an effective educational program for their students. The purpose of such procedures is to assist LD specialists in developing a comprehensive intervention program for learning-disabled individuals and to allow for monitoring of the instructional process and the evaluation of students' progress.

Figure 9–1 illustrates procedures in programming individuals with learning disabilities. Considerable resourcefulness on the part of the teacher is essential for effective programming.

The following are steps involved in effective programming:

Step 1. *Review of input from diagnostic information.* For a broad and complete picture of a student's functioning, review and analysis of assessment data are necessary in order to arrive at an optimal program. The assessment areas indicated in Figure 9–1 were discussed in depth in chapter 8. The components for this review and analysis are derived from three sources: (a) formal diagnostic information, which is available through a child's record and the school psychologist's report, as well as the additional formal testing conducted by teachers; (b) informal assessment conducted primarily by teachers, including assessment tools and informal observations; and (c) input from the student during the student interview. When receiving

Figure 9–1 Programming Procedures

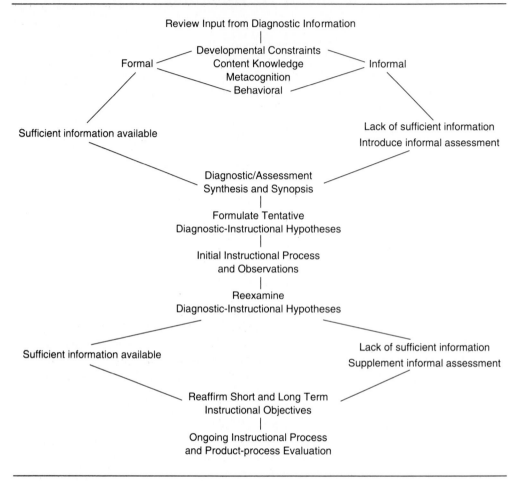

a new student, the LD specialist must examine all available information, which includes the student's past records and cumulative cards, the IEP document and the school psychologist's report, and work samples if available.

In reviewing the assessment information, the LD specialist must determine whether sufficient information is available in order to proceed and develop an educational program for the student, or if supplemental assessment is required. Whenever supplemental assessment is needed, the specialist can introduce various informal assessment procedures, as discussed in chapter 8.

In reviewing the available records, the LD specialist needs to pay special attention to the type of methods and techniques that were used with the student, which approaches were successful and which failed, and the instructional materials that were used. In addition, the LD specialist should ascertain the most appropriate reinforcers for a particular student and the techniques that will work for that student.

Step 2. Diagnostic/assessment synthesis and synopsis. The LD specialist must next synthesize the information derived from the assessment data, taking into account the individual's functional level and the variables affecting it. According to Cross and Goin (1977), the process of synthesis attempts to bring together the results of all the analyses so that they form an accurate picture of an individual's condition. The synthesis phase involves the interpretation of the assessment data along with the different variables enumerated in the assessment model discussed in chapter 8. The synthesis of information leads to a synopsis, which represents a summary of the findings. Again, the LD specialist may use the "Teacher's Guide to Informal Assessment and Observations" (Appendix D).

Step 3. Formulation of the tentative diagnostic instructional hypothesis. In this phase, the LD specialist must arrive at a diagnostic instructional hypothesis. Based on the assessment information, the specialist must now consider various aspects of the instructional process and ask "What methods and approaches will be most effective with this student?" and "What material will be most appropriate with the methodology chosen?" Once the diagnostic instructional hypothesis is completed, it translates itself to the selection of the teaching methods and strategies and the educational materials. The IIP form or a similar form may be used as a working document. This process delineates areas of needed services, the extent to which these areas are to be provided for by the special class or resource room teacher, and the extent of the student's participation in the mainstream of the school environment. The LD specialist must know exactly what skills the individual student needs to learn, as well as which devices to use to monitor the student's progress effectively. The specialist makes a decision as to the most appropriate intervention approaches and teaching methods, including the academic areas, social/emotional areas, metacognition, strategic learning, and the utilization of control executive functions. The LD specialist must be aware that this diagnostic instructional hypothesis is awaiting testing; To what degree and to what extent will the student respond to the selected instructional procedures?

Step 4. Formulation of short- and long-term objectives. With a diagnostic instructional hypothesis devised, the LD specialist proceeds to formulate the short- and long-term instructional objectives. These instructional objectives, which may constitute the content of the IEP and/or IIP, are directly translated to intervention in the classroom, and are directly related to skills acquisition and to the implementation of the diagnostic instructional hypothesis. Short-term objectives are normally objectives that the teacher will formulate for a period of a month or 6 weeks, whereas the long-term objectives are related to the entire term as well as to the academic year. In creating the short- and long-term objectives, the LD specialist must keep in mind the scope and sequence of the curriculum and the skill areas that require remediation.

Step 5. Start of initial instruction. Following the formulation of short-term and long-term objectives, initial instruction begins. The instructional process should follow the principles of learning and the principles of remedial education. In its simplest form, the instructional process must meet the needs of the student and ensure successful experiences. Both distal and proximal observations must be conducted to evaluate the student's responses to the learning process.

Step 6. Reexamination of the diagnostic instructional hypothesis and objectives. Following several weeks (usually 3–6) of instruction, the LD specialist should reexamine the diagnostic instructional hypothesis. If observations confirm that the student is moving along and shows steady progress, the specialist can continue with the short-term and long-term instructional objectives, as well as with an ongoing instructional process and product-process evaluation. On the other hand, if the reexamination of the diagnostic instructional hypothesis indicates that change or additional information is needed, the LD specialist may need to carry out additional informal assessment. After introducing such supplements, the specialist should again formulate short-term and long-term instructional objectives and reexamine the effect of the program after another 3 to 6 weeks. The cycle follows this pattern.

Step 7. Formulation of short- and long-term instructional objectives. The LD specialist can finalize the programming phase by reviewing and delineating the short- and long-term instructional objectives.

Step 8. Ongoing instructional process and product-process evaluation. The LD specialist continues with the remedial process consistent with the taxonomy of remedial teaching, monitoring the student's progress and conducting ongoing and periodic product-process evaluation. In order to maximize the remedial program and monitor the student's progress, the LD specialist should make use of assessment inventories and profiles. Such inventory profiles specify the sequence of skill acquisition and the individual's mastery of, or deficits in, the various skills.

Programming the Learning-Disabled Adolescent

The LD specialist who is planning to develop an intervention program for the individual with learning disabilities must be fully aware of the factors and variables affecting the learning-disabled adolescent.

In addition to the programming procedures and guidelines discussed earlier in this chapter, the following facets must be considered when programming the adolescent with learning disabilities:

1. The LD specialist must be cognizant of various variables and factors contributing to the present level of functioning of the adolescent.
2. Programming must stem from a utilitarian approach, mainly that which is practical to the immediate and future needs of the adolescent.
3. All components of the instructional program should be considered in programming the individual.
4. One must use an integrated approach in all aspects of remediation and move from the present needs and functional level of the adolescent to cover areas and gaps in the basic skills and the core curriculum.
5. Attention should be given to strategic learning and generalization to other situations.
6. The program must assure immediate success and significant progress.
7. The program must move from a metacognitive base, that is, it must promote the individual's self-control over learning situations and future learning.
8. The program should involve self-monitoring and self-evaluation.

In programming in the content areas, one must treat each area in totality while keeping in mind the basic day-by-day needs of the adolescent, as well as future considerations of vocational and post-high school educational needs. Usually, programming for the content areas should have a utilitarian approach, including elements that youngsters need and will use now or in the future.

Considerations for Midyear Evaluation and Programming

Although the IEP regulations and school policies do not require it, in order to maximize the benefits of the remedial program and its effectiveness, the LD specialist must conduct a midyear evaluation and programming at both the elementary and secondary levels. At the secondary level, a midyear evaluation is crucial, since students change their program at that point. The remedial program and objectives designed at the beginning of the year need reexamining.

Midyear evaluation and programming normally occur about the same time as the planning of parent conferences. The LD specialist should use the parent conference to assist both parent and student to view the student's progress realistically. If progress has been attained, both student and parent should be aware of it in order to facilitate a positive change in the student's self-concept.

The purposes of midyear evaluation are (a) to sum up the work accomplished since the beginning of the year; (b) to provide feedback to the student, the teacher and the parent; and (c) to provide for a new direction and establish new goals cooperatively.

In achieving these goals, the LD specialist must address the individual student program and examine the individual functional level, the educational methodologies and material, and the group functions and activities to the degree that a change of activities may be desired. In addition, the specialist should consider introducing new concepts and new projects. Midyear evaluation and programming basically follow the same guidelines indicated in the programming procedures. In addition, the teacher must consider both product and process evaluation. These activities culminate in a revised instructional plan for the remainder of the academic year.

Several factors must be recognized at midyear evaluation and programming:

1. The teacher's knowledge of students is much more solid. The children have been in the class for several months, and the teacher knows them well, is aware of their strengths and weaknesses. The students also know the teacher, and a sound relationship has developed during the course of the term.
2. Most students are now used to a routine schedule that includes daily activities. They know what is expected of them, both academically and in terms of student behavior. In other words, a steady flow of activities becomes evident.
3. Students are now active participants in the learning process. Their increased awareness of their strengths and weaknesses and the factors

that affect their learning can facilitate the midyear review process and provide an additional impetus to their active involvement in the learning process.

4. Because of the routine work, students may experience boredom, and as a result, the learning curve reaches a plateau. This plateau may change into a downtrend as a result of fatigue and a feeling of nonaccomplishment if students have not completed any work or projects.

The student with learning disabilities functions comfortably within a structure and within a frame of reference, so a complete or major change is unnecessary. However, consideration of inclusion of new elements in the instructional learning in order to accelerate learning progress is essential.

The midyear evaluation should follow the identical format of, and utilize the same procedures as, that from the initial part of the year, that is, identifying the primary problem; identifying the concurrent problem; examining the student's information-processing repertoire; examining the student's learning style; and making decisions in regard to the directions of remediation, including the prioritizing of areas of needed help, the most appropriate methodologies and approaches, the most appropriate feedback mode and reinforcers, and the monitoring of student progress, usually entailing both teacher and student participation.

The midyear programming provides an opportunity to emphasize new areas of training and to introduce new experiences. The introduction of new experiences can minimize the plateau effect and accelerate learning. Because of the relationship that has developed with the teacher, an opportunity exists for further development of social and interpersonal relationship skills.

Programming Considerations for Year-Round School Programs

Year-round programs have become a reality in many of our nation's schools, and with them, year-round programs for individuals with learning disabilities. This usually means that students attend school 4 quarters a year—each quarter lasting approximately 48 days—and are on vacation 21 days between quarters. While there is a lack of agreement on the effectiveness of a year-round program, the educational program can be developed to maximize learning for learning-disabled students.

Year-round programs can provide positive experiences when instructional procedures are designed to enhance students' motivation, learning, and retention. Teaching and learning can be viewed in a cyclical manner, involving four cycles, each of which is built upon students' learning in the previous cycle(s). This allows for programming that considers both previous program elements and new elements in order to develop students' motivation and enthusiasm to learn, and that develops a sense of accomplishment as one approaches the end of a cycle.

Though learning procedures must be consistent throughout the 4 quarters, there is also a need for new learning experiences. Thus it is suggested that the LD specialist design programmatic elements that are uniform throughout the year, such as behavior management systems, daily routines, and procedures for evaluating students' progress, and in addition, consider unique program components in each of the quarters that will increase students' motivation and enthusiasm to learn.

Planning of Activities for Critical Periods During the Year

During the academic year, many events have direct impact on the students and the teacher. These events include (a) holidays such as Thanksgiving, Christmas, Easter, and others; (b) short- and long-term vacations, such as the spring and winter breaks; (c) crises that occur in the community, such as natural disasters and/or major catastrophes; and (d) traumatic events that occur within the classroom.

Just preceding holiday seasons, children's attention and concentration are affected by the holiday mood and atmosphere. It is thus more effective for the teacher to gear studies to be seasonal. It is recommended that the LD specialist develop units commensurate with holidays and incorporate studies along these topics.

Prior to long-term vacations, students' attention and concentration are normally short, resulting from an expectation of the vacation and from the prior months of learning. Some fatigue may be observed in students, and consequently, lack of commitment to the educational program occurs. It is important for the LD specialist to develop short projects, normally of a week's duration. The specialist should combine the projects with classroom demonstrations and participation and guide students in planning the execution of activities for these projects.

Thus the LD specialist can serve as a major support system during a specific crisis within a classroom. The specialist's role, once again, is primarily that of providing emotional support, as well as facilitating the understanding of a crisis in relation to both an individual student and a large group of students.

Planning for Extended-Year Special Education Programs

Some school districts provide extended-year programs during the summer for students with learning disabilities. The summer program provides opportunities similar to those of the regular school year. The LD specialist must realize that students who attend the summer program have had a long year of remediation and are usually fatigued from the normal routine of the regular classroom structure. Therefore, in programming and planning for the summer, a complete shift of routine and approach to the remedial process must be made. Keeping in mind the specific goals and objectives of the summer program, the specialist can gear the activities to unit and project development and incorporate and integrate all skills into a project-oriented environment. The LD specialist should provide students with opportunities to create projects and to suggest projects in accordance with their needs, their strengths, and their desires, and should incorporate into the projects basic skill acquisitions that are needed as part of the remedial program. Projects should be short in nature and culminate in successful experiences. They can vary from projects in social studies and science to structured projects, gardening and other activities in the community, observations, interviewing individuals, and the development of a school journal. In this manner, the LD specialist can incorporate the acquisition of basic skills, study skills, social/interpersonal relationship skills, and metacognitive-oriented strategic learning.

SUMMARY AND CONCLUSIONS

Instructional planning and programming are the keys to effective implementation of an intervention program for those with learning disabilities. They provide a plan, a road map, by which to direct the remedial effort. They must, therefore, address the various needs and instructional components to provide a viable, comprehensive program for the learning disabled. The IEP documents and the LD specialist's instructional plan are critical elements for effective program implementation

PART
4

Program Implementation: Teaching Methods and Classroom Management Strategies

Program implementation is the subject of this section. It presents material on the development of an optimal classroom environment and the utilization of instructional approaches and technology. It also addresses meeting the social and emotional needs of students with learning disabilities through effective classroom management. A critical element in an intervention program is the development of necessary skills to meet both the academic demands of schooling and the challenges in adult life. This section emphasizes teaching students to become active learners and to acquire strategies for learning.

CHAPTER 10

Providing an Optimal
Classroom Environment

Questions to Consider

1. *What are the characteristics of an optimal classroom environment?*

2. *What are the correlates of an optimal learning environment?*

3. *How does one develop an optimal learning environment that maximizes an individual's performance and ensures successful experiences?*

4. *What are the various classroom designs, styles, and formats for a special class and a resource room?*

5. *What are effective classroom operation strategies?*

6. *What are the merits of having aides and volunteers in the classroom?*

DEVELOPING AN OPTIMAL LEARNING ENVIRONMENT

Assessment, instructional planning, and programming are critical elements of a remedial program. Equally important is the development of an environment that is conducive to learning and facilitates the implementation of an individualized education program. The effect of the classroom environment on learning and behavior merits much consideration, particularly for those with learning disabilities. Learning disabilities result in a discrepancy between children's capabilities to attend to, and benefit from, the educational environment provided in a standard classroom and the demands of such an environment. For many learning-disabled individuals, this discrepancy necessitates the development of a learning environment that takes into account their specific characteristics.

As stated elsewhere in this text, students with learning disabilities receive special education services in special classes and resource rooms. The majority of them are enrolled in regular classes, with support services from the resource programs.

The LD Specialist and the Learning Environment

Generally, LD specialists in special classes are responsible for providing the total educational program for their students. These students may receive additional services such as speech therapy when the needs for such are designated in their IEPs.

When appropriate, some students also participate in nonacademic activities at the elementary level and enroll in elective classes such as wood shop at the intermediate and/or secondary levels. On the other hand, LD specialists in resource rooms are responsible for providing instruction to their students in areas specified in each student's IEP. Students' participation in resource programs is determined by their needs and varies with the degree of the severity of their academic discrepancy. Some students may spend as much as three periods per day in a resource room (not to exceed 49% of the total school day), and others may average one period a day or less. Although the instructional goals of the two programs may differ, the educational environment in both settings should aim to meet the students' needs in accordance with their IEPs and foster a learning environment conducive to optimal learning.

The LD specialist plays a major role in the development of an effective learning environment. The specialist who has developed a comprehensive program for students in the classroom must now provide an educational environment consistent with the goals of the educational plan. Leitman and Churchill (1966) describe the teacher as a travel agent who helps children go wherever they want to go. The teacher counsels on the best way of getting there, and how to get along once children reach that destination. The teacher is a facilitator who is constantly watching the progression of children's learning, anticipating their needs, guiding them to proper learning, and encouraging them to discover answers for themselves.

Learning disabilities specialists must have a positive psychological attitude toward themselves and toward students, and the learning environment must reflect this. If a teacher has a negative feeling, then the learning environment will be negative and may suppress children's positive feelings toward learning (Hassett & Weisberg, 1973). The fundamental attitude should be the realization that every student with learning disabilities has the capacity to learn and should be treated as an individual in the classroom. Teachers must accept each student for what he or she is and aid in students' development of their maximum potential. The philosophy is that students develop better in a healthy and positive learning environment than in an unhealthy, negative, and rejective one.

The LD specialist must design and structure the educational environment in a manner that is conducive to remedial teaching and that facilitates progressive changes in student learning and behavior. This environment should provide many opportunities for successful experiences. Students who experience success are likely to attempt new tasks and to develop a positive feeling about themselves, whereas students who regard themselves as a loser or a failure will see themselves as incapable and develop a feeling of self-helplessness. The goal is to develop individuals' capacity to learn, with the ability to use strategic learning and to monitor their own activities, thus promoting independent learning and self-direction.

The Optimal Learning Environment Goals

The goal is to create an educational environment that will meet the needs of those with learning disabilities and provide them with an environment in which they feel comfortable and are free of failure experiences, an environment that provides optimal "classroom living." Moreover, the aim is to establish a climate that will maximize students' potential to succeed in learning and foster their active role in learning.

The basic goals are to develop an optimal learning environment that does the following:

1. Provides opportunities for appropriate behavior and successful experiences
2. Promotes the welfare of the whole student, that is, promotes academic skills development, social skills development, and strategic development, and fulfills general aspects of social/emotional needs
3. Provides physical conditions conducive to learning and a classroom design and organization geared to students' developmental and remedial needs
4. Provides individual students with work in accordance with their own level of functioning and pace and allows sufficient time for review, overlearning, and repetition
5. Is interactive, encouraging students to positively interact with their teachers and peers
6. Encourages students to assume an active role in their learning through the development of their sensitivity to the learning environment, their awareness of their capabilities and abilities, and their understanding of the relationship between the individual variables, the task variables, and the strategy variables
7. Facilitates the development of strategic learning and encourages students to engage in strategic production
8. Encourages students to assume responsibilities for their own learning through the development and use of control executive functions, that is, planning, organizing, monitoring, and checking outcomes
9. Provides opportunities for students to interact socially in a positive manner during the learning process and thus learn from each other
10. Provides immediate feedback and reinforcement modes, thereby making students aware of the result of their efforts so they can adjust their behavior accordingly

The resource program must also address elements that facilitate students' success in a mainstream environment. Thus it must provide a learning environment in which (a) support services (both direct and indirect) are geared to promote successful experiences in the resource room and the regular class; (b) academic learning, both remedial and core curriculum, is emphasized; (c) students' communication skills with the regular classroom teacher, self-advocacy, and knowledge of when and how to get help are stressed; and (d) self-monitoring of progress and realistic self-evaluation are developed.

Variables Affecting the Provision of an Optimal Classroom Environment

The manner in which an optimal learning environment can be achieved in any classroom depends upon numerous variables that exist in any given school and classroom. These variables include the following:

1. Existing conditions in the school and the availability of facilities and resources needed to develop an optimal learning environment
2. The teacher's philosophy, attitude, culture, educational background, and training
3. The developmental needs of those with learning disabilities
4. The curriculum emphasis for individuals with LD and the general intervention approaches advocated for such students
5. The teacher's teaching style
6. The extent of student participation in the learning process through increased awareness and acceptance of an active role in learning
7. The degree to which students are permitted to participate in decision making relevant to designing and conducting the learning environment
8. The extent to which students are enrolled in regular classes and participate in the mainstream activities of the school environment

The optimal classroom environment attempts to achieve a balance between the characteristics of learners and the learning environment in order to meet students' needs commensurate with their abilities.

Correlates of an Effective Learning Environment

One must consider several factors that are quite often referred to as correlates of an effective learning environment. These usually encompass the following:

1. Physical setup and classroom design
2. Daily and weekly schedules and activities
3. Students' individualized folders and job packages
4. Grouping and regrouping practices
5. Parameters for classroom operation
6. Classroom operation strategies
7. Effective utilization of teacher's aides, volunteers, and peer tutoring
8. Provision of feedback, monitoring of student performance, and record keeping

In addition, other factors that have a direct impact on the nature of the learning environment include (a) an appropriate individualized instruction plan, (b) effective utilization of sound principles of teaching and remedial education, (c) effective

An optimal learning environment takes into account the unique need of each individual student.

utilization of teaching methods and intervention approaches, (d) effective use of instructional technology and materials, and (e) effective implementation of a behavior management system. These aspects are addressed in detail in chapters 11, 12, 13, 14, and 15.

SETTING UP THE CLASSROOM

This Is My Classroom: An Example of an Effective Learning Environment

The following is a teacher's description of an optimal classroom environment.

My classroom is an upper-elementary learning disabilities special class located on a regular elementary school campus. It has 14 students, who are identified as learning disabled and who range from fourth- to sixth-grade level, a full-time aide, and a teacher. The room environment is pleasant. The walls, tables, and bookshelves contain a variety of visual stimuli. An orderly array of books, games, manipulative materials, and audiovisual equipment are within the students' reach. Lighting is adequate, and the windows are covered with venetian blinds.

There are four working stations in the classroom. Stations 1 and 2 are geared to small-group instruction. Activities are scheduled at 20- to 25-minute intervals, depending on their nature. I usually rotate between Station 1 and 2. I begin by leading an activity in one station. Then I leave these students to work independently on follow-up activities, and I rotate to Station 2 in order to work with that group of students on their follow-up activities. Each small group has a student leader for the week, who leads the group either at the beginning of the activities or during the follow-up activities, whenever I am with the opposite group. Usually Station 1 begins activities independently on Mondays and Wednesdays and continues the follow-up activities with me, and Station 2 begins with me on those days and continues independently with follow-up activities. Station 3 is a minilab run by the teacher's aide. It is designated to train students in specific skills, such as decoding skills in reading, specific arithmetic computations, or specific strategic learning. Usually there are at least two students in the minilab at one time. In Station 4, students work independently, and cross-level tutoring or peer tutoring is conducted.

In addition to the working stations, there are seven learning centers:

1. Listening and reviewing center. At this center, a variety of teaching machines can be found, in addition to a record player, a filmstrip projector, a tape recorder, a small viewing screen, earphones, and an organization box containing materials to be used (records, storybooks, and filmstrips).
2. Spelling center. Spelling-related activities conducted on an individual basis and usually supervised by the teacher's aide take place at this center. In addition to the spelling words of the week, students can find spelling games and crossword puzzles.
3. Oral and written language center. This center has a variety of activities related to both oral and written expressive language, including story cards, "stories you can finish," and activity worksheets. One may also find a typewriter and an Apple computer with appropriate software material, including typing lessons (see also chapter 11).
4. Reading center. A variety of reading materials—high-interest, low-vocabulary reading books, books on tapes, tape-recorded stories, and age-appropriate magazines and journals—can be found at this center. An area rug with pillows and plants make this center pleasant and relaxing.
5. Problem-solving and exploratory mathematics center. This center involves activities in higher thought processes, using materials such as brainteasers and Scholastic's *Dynamath*.
6. Science center. Scientific investigation materials and science teaching aids may be found at this center. Students engage in various activities, including gardening and raising animals.
7. Art center. Semistructured art activities are available at this center to encourage students to engage in creative art production.

Shelves can be found behind each station. Each shelf holds open trays that contain color-coded individual student folders. Each folder contains an individual and/or a group assignment and individual work packets. The folders are color coded to help students identify their own folder and the group to which they are assigned. (See Figure 10–1 for an illustration of this classroom design.)

Figure 10–1   Classroom Design of a Sample Effective Learning Environment

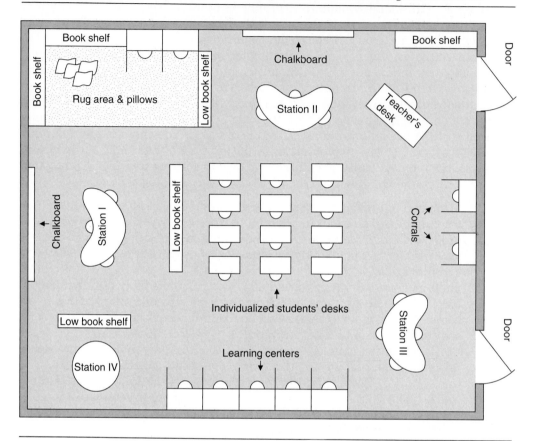

Classroom procedures and routine are designed to maximize students' assumption of responsibility for their own conduct and the development of ability to work independently when independent activities are assigned. They also are aimed at minimizing distractions and interference with the learning process. For example, upon entering the room, students take their own working folder from the shelf, go to their desk, open the folder, and read the given assignments. Both a given assignment and the material necessary to complete it are contained in each packet. In addition, the daily schedule of activities is displayed and easily accessible to students; the various activity components list the name of each student for that period and the activities and centers at which each student will work. Students usually receive help in rotation, between working with me or the aide and working independently. Completed work is self-checked or checked immediately by me or my aide. Students who complete their work early may spend time at the different activity centers, where various job packages and activity packages, prepared earlier for each student, are available.

I utilize assignment sheets and a behavior management system to reward students for on-task behavior as well as for task completion. Two carrels are used for students who require reduced environmental stimulation. Points are given for attempted academic work, for the quality of performance, for student efforts, and for expected student behavior. Backup reinforcers, such as prizes, are available to the students and may be purchased on Fridays with their earned tokens. In addition, other exciting responsibilities and rewards can be bought by the student with their earned tokens, such as being the monitor of the week or collecting the money for milk.

The preceding setting is an example of an optimal learning environment beneficial to both students and the teacher. This optimal classroom environment provides students with opportunities for productive learning and successful experiences, and the teacher with an instructional climate conducive to creative instruction and positive individual mental health. In such an environment, students actively engage in classwork, become much more alert, and demonstrate greater independence, originality, and initiative. They acquire habits of resourcefulness and self-help, listen more attentively, follow directions more independently, and contribute to classroom discussions. Since they focus on their tasks, the accuracy and the quality of their work increase. Moreover, with feelings of success and self-respect, they develop the ability to accept responsibility and to be thoughtful of the rights and feelings of others.

In such optimal settings, teachers also assume a new role; they become facilitators of learning rather than controllers of behavior. They are no longer disciplinarians and dispensers of facts, but specialized educators trained in clinical teaching procedures whose aim is the development of children—their self-concepts, their ability to learn and to be self-directed, and their concern for others. The classroom environment is viewed as a laboratory that is geared to self-development and in which teachers are sensitive to feelings and values, and encourage students to examine their strengths and weaknesses, ideas, thoughts, and feelings.

In such an interactive and collaborative environment, both teachers and students constantly work toward the basic goals of developing well-adjusted, responsible, self-directed active learners and self-actualizing individuals with a healthy image of themselves.

Students Design Their Classroom—An Experiment

The classroom represents the learning environment most conducive to, and desired for, students' learning. It must represent the students' "living skills" in a classroom atmosphere according to their developmental stages and needs. In an experiment, in a special class of senior high school learning-disabled students attending a private school, the director and the teacher decided to allow the students to create their own classroom environment with the teacher's guidance. The students were provided with an empty classroom and were asked to provide a wish list of resources and furniture. In choosing the resources, the students included the following environmental components: (a) individualized and group working stations; (b) an informal studying station, which included a couch and pillows; (c) learning centers such as a computer center and a listening post to facilitate the learning process; and (d) rec-

Figure 10–2   A Classroom Design by Secondary Students

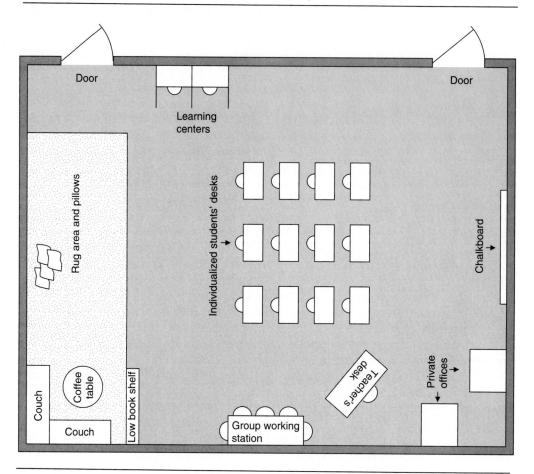

reation and leisure activity stations. In addition, the students made room for two private offices, that is, study areas secluded from distractions and unnecessary noise levels.

Figure 10–2 illustrates such a student-designed classroom.

The students designed their classroom to meet their needs, specifically, (a) individual and group formal learning needs, (b) individual and group exploratory and informal learning needs, (c) social-interpersonal relationship and communication needs, (d) leisure and recreation needs, and (e) individual needs for study and retreat in a private, quiet area. The nature of a learning environment varies in accordance with the developmental needs of students, the needs of students attributed to learning disability factors, and the general needs attributed to life-styles quite often impacted by socioeconomic level. Failure to meet these needs may lead to maladaptive behavior, low self-concept, and behavioral crisis. It may result in failure experiences, which in turn may lead to more inability to handle schoolwork and other aspects and activities of life. Such a cyclical effect can be set in motion by an environment that does not meet the needs of those with learning disabilities, for it involves academic failure and poor mental hygiene.

Design and Physical Setup Considerations

There is a growing awareness among professionals working with exceptional children that the physical environment plays an important role in meeting the needs of these individuals. According to Preiser and Taylor (1983), the physical setting facilitates, mediates, or distracts from desired behaviors. The classroom environment must be designed to facilitate students' learning and provide for a comfortable classroom living environment. It must meet individual as well as group needs. It must be attractive and flexible enough to meet the varying needs of students. The classroom environment must be carefully constructed to include individualized working stations, group working stations, activity and learning centers, informal studying stations that may include comfortable furniture such as couches and/or pillows, and leisure and recreation activity centers. The creation of personal space through alteration of physical environment could be a means of reducing individual students' classroom anxiety, thereby allowing students to achieve positive interpersonal relationships in the classroom setting and reducing behaviors associated with anxiety (Hood-Smith & Leffingwell, 1983).

Generally, there is a glaring omission of empirical research data on the effect of classroom design modifications upon student behavior (Evans & Lovell, 1979). This omission is a result of the complexity of the many variables affecting the person-environment interaction, otherwise referred to as ATI, Aptitude Treatment Interaction (Hunt, 1975). Attempts have been made to study single design variables such as the effect of seating arrangement on behavior (Hood-Smith & Leffingwell, 1983) and the relationship of teacher-pupil interaction and seating position in a traditional classroom (Eastman & Harper, 1971; Jackson & Lahderne, 1967). These studies point to the failure of the traditional classroom seating arrangement to facilitate interaction between the teacher and students on an equal basis. Usually, the students sitting in the front center rows are apt to engage in as much as 70% of the classroom action. The remainder of the students' participation is divided between the sides of the class, leaving virtually no direct interaction between the teacher and those students sitting in the central rear portion of the classroom.

The traditional classroom arrangement is not effective with individuals with learning disabilities inasmuch as they require continuous teacher attention. Positive classroom behavior is more likely to occur when teachers and students are in close proximity. Students are more likely to respond to both verbal and nonverbal cues, such as smiles, eye contact, and head nods, which increase the probability of positive classroom behaviors when the teacher is accessible. Therefore, a classroom design must facilitate the teacher's personal contact with each student in the classroom (Jackson & Lahderne, 1967). Alternate seating arrangements for acting-out students must take into consideration both individual students' needs and the needs and interaction patterns of group activities.

The learning environment for individuals with learning disabilities should support the various curricular activities aimed to meet their needs, such as academic remediation, study skill development, strategic learning, problem-solving and self-help skills, social skills development, conceptual knowledge and life-coping skills, career/vocational preparation, and effective utilization of control executive functions. The classroom structure and design should enhance students' ability to benefit from the program and to develop independent learning skills. Furthermore, it should develop students' ability to participate responsibly in the learning process and to develop the ability to use control executive functions. In designing the classroom environment, the LD specialist must consider the following elements:

1. A classroom environment that reflects a positive atmosphere, develops a trusting relationship, and encourages independent study habits and self-evaluation.

2. An optimal learning environment in which the instructional process and the format of classroom operation and activities are understood by the students and the teacher.

3. A classroom environment that fosters active learning, the use of strategies for learning, and the regulation and monitoring of such activities through effective utilization of control executive functions.

4. A classroom setting that increases learning-disabled children's personal contact with the teacher, increases the proximity of students to the teacher, and provides students with equal opportunity to receive the teacher's attention. Making it easier for the teacher to exert control and for students to receive both verbal and nonverbal cues and reinforcements is essential.

5. Conditions of the physical facility—the source of light, the location of windows and doors, the source of distractions, the availability of furniture and the degree to which this furniture is comfortable for students, and the availability of essential items for classroom design, such as working tables and chairs, bulletin boards, chalkboards, bookshelves, file cabinets, pillows, and couches.

6. A classroom arrangement that provides for easy and safe access to all study and activity areas.

7. Provision of adequate work space for students so that each individual has a desk, as well as the availability of a quiet study area. This provision may include the use of study carrels or partitions to minimize students' visual distractions and to aid in achieving a sense of privacy for students who need reduced environmental stimulation.

8. General classroom space and availability of areas needed for group activity, which includes the availability of areas for learning centers, activity centers, and minilabs.

9. Organization of instructional materials in a manner that makes them accessible to students, as well as the provision of self-corrective instructional materials that allow for immediate feedback and immediate reinforcements.

10. General classroom operations, such as the location of individual student folders, activity guides, and schedules.
11. Utilization of visual communication methods through effective incorporation of bulletin boards and display charts.
12. A seating arrangement that takes into account behavioral characteristics and specific patterns of individual students such as the acting-out student, the excessively active child, and the withdrawn student.
13. Implementation of a behavior management system within which students can exercise a degree of freedom.
14. Provision of both alternative and enrichment activities upon completion of individual student work.
15. Provision of immediate feedback and easy access to students' records of progress.

Considerations for Secondary Students

The classroom environment for adolescents with learning disabilities must meet their specific needs and characteristics. It must meet the structural needs of learning-disabled adolescents, specifically of those individuals who have attention deficits, who tend to be hyperactive, and who have acting-out behaviors. It must also meet the

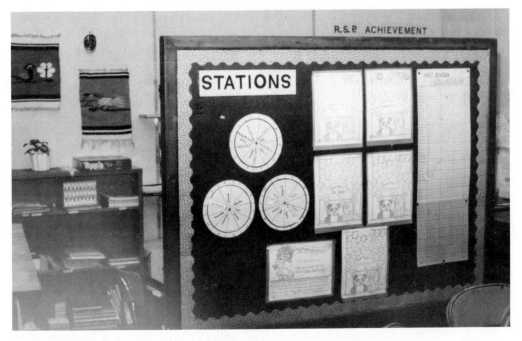

Learning centers and stations motivate students and make the classroom environment more lively.

socialization needs of such adolescents. The classroom environment should be structured to provide for both small and large group activities and individualized activities.

One of the developmental characteristics of the adolescent period is the need to be involved in the decision-making process. It is thus recommended that although classroom teachers have a preset plan for the design of a classroom, they should involve students in planning the room layout. The typical classroom for adolescents with LD should include learning centers, independent study areas, media centers, and areas for informal study activities and relaxation, usually served by an area with homelike furnishings, such as an area rug and a couch. When secondary learning-disabled students were given an empty classroom and were allowed to design it, their setup reflected the activity needs as perceived by them, namely individualized and group academic activity areas including informal studying areas, learning media centers, and recreation and leisure activity stations.

Classroom Designs, Styles, and Formats

Numerous classroom arrangement designs have been presented in the literature. The designs discussed here represent sample classroom arrangements that attempt to take into consideration the physical facilities, the teacher's style of teaching, and student characteristics, as well as the availability of resources. These elements must be congruent for a special class or resource room environment to be comfortable for both the students and the teacher.

The classroom arrangement design will vary in accordance with (a) the nature of the physical facility and the availability of resources, such as individual and group desks, and bookcases and file cabinets that can serve as natural barriers and room dividers; (b) the developmental level and characteristics of the students, that is, primary, elementary, or secondary; (c) the characteristics associated with the learning disabilities, including the degree of severity of disabilities and/or behavioral patterns; (d) the availability of support personnel, such as teachers' aides and other paraprofessional volunteers; (e) the degree to which the teacher utilizes cross-age tutoring and peer tutoring; and (f) the teaching style and whether the classroom is child centered or teacher centered.

Basic Classroom Setup Designs

Some classroom setups attempt to maximize students' interaction and provide a balance between individual and group activities. However, when working with students with behavior problems, one may need to minimize students' interaction. Generally, classroom designs can be classified as follows:

1. A modified traditional room arrangement. Desks are arranged in rows in the center of the room or in a specific area of the room, with small group working stations and learning and activity centers available (Figure 10–3).
2. A U-shape arrangement. Individual desks are arranged in a U shape, with a small group activity working space at the center of the U and various learning centers at the perimeters of the U shape. Students can face the

Bookcases are ideal natural classroom dividers that can be used to block off learning and activity centers.

center or the perimeter depending on the degree of student behavior patterns and the degree to which the minimization of peer contact is necessary (Figure 10–4).

3. Desk grouping. Three or four desks are grouped as a common working area, with a general group activity area and learning and activity centers (Figure 10–5).

4. Individual desks with small activity groupings. Individual desks are provided, with emphasis on small activity grouping and various interest and activity centers (Figure 10–6).

Sample Classroom Designs

A plethora of possible designs exist from which teachers can choose a specific design for their classroom. Teachers must keep in mind the principles of classroom design discussed earlier in this chapter. Variations of designs exist because a design must correspond to the developmental needs of students, to the general characteristics of

Figure 10–3   Basic Classroom Setup Design/Modified Traditional

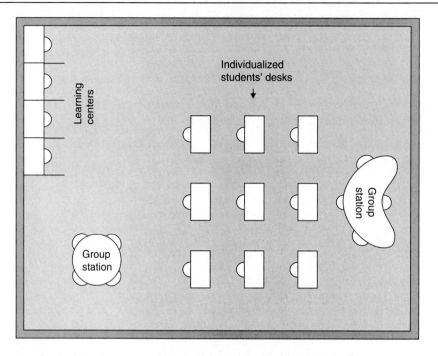

Figure 10–4   Basic Classroom Setup Design/U-Shape Arrangement

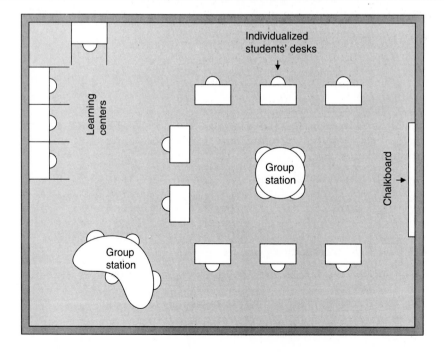

Figure 10–5 Basic Classroom Setup Design/Desk Grouping

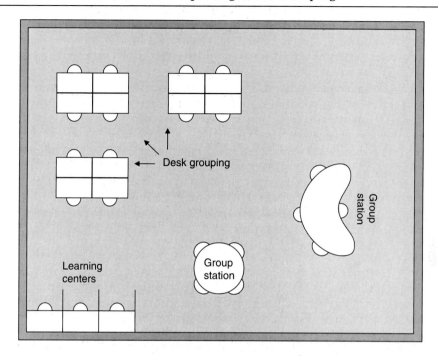

Figure 10–6 Basic Classroom Setup Design/Individual and Small Group Clustering

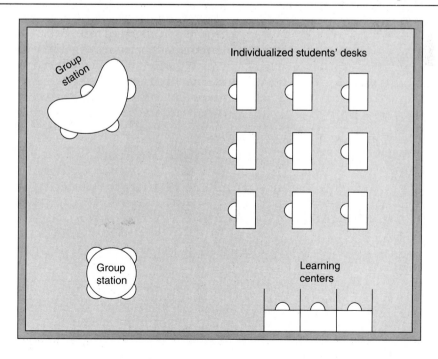

Figure 10–7   Primary Classroom Design

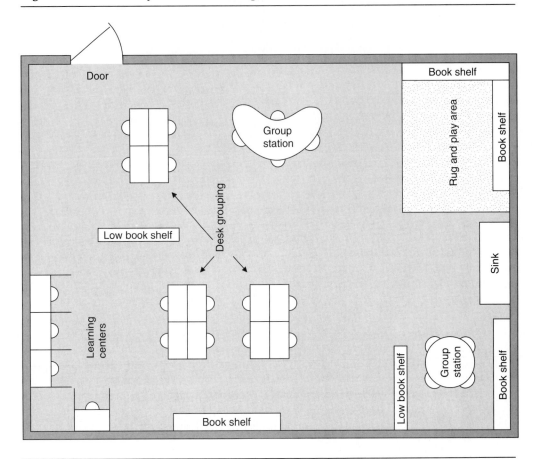

each student, and to the characteristics of a group as a whole, and must be congruent with the philosophy of a school and the approaches of the teacher. The following sample classroom designs (Figures 10–7 through 10–10) have been selected randomly across age and grade levels.

Design Considerations for Resource Programs

In designing the classroom environment in a resource program, one should keep in mind the goal of the program—to facilitate full-time mainstreaming. The physical setup should reflect a continuum of arrangements from more restrictive setups, such as individualized working stations, to the least restrictive setup that approximates the regular classroom environment. The students' assumptions of responsibility for their own learning and actions are emphasized. In addition, classroom routines and procedures resemble the regular class in course demands, behavior management,

Figure 10–8   Intermediate Classroom Design

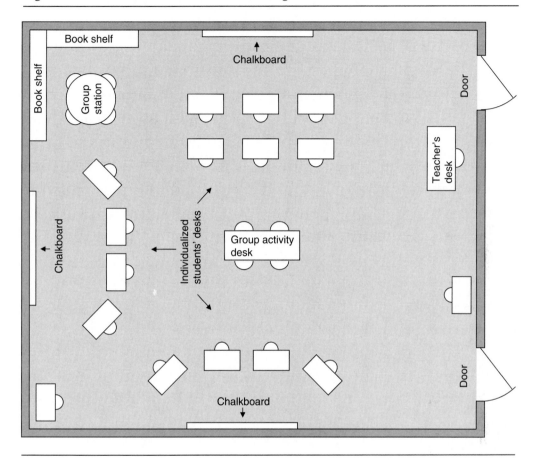

and modes of evaluation of students' progress. Because of the diversity of students' functional levels and the age span involved, the classroom design should allow for changes to meet students' needs with easy transition from small to large group functions. As a function of the mainstream program, resource rooms should be centrally located on the school campus.

One must also consider the role of the resource teacher in indirect services such as testing students, providing consultation to regular teachers, coordinating services, and providing guidance and resource information to parents of resource students. A quiet area must be set aside for testing whenever the room conditions allow it. A mini-instructional resource material center should be available, with professional materials on serving students with learning disabilities in the mainstream, including suggestions for program modification. Resources for parents, which include information about the resource program, learning disabilities, and home intervention strategies, should also be placed at this center. Figure 10–11 is a sample resource room design for the upper elementary level.

Figure 10–9   Secondary Classroom Design (see also Figure 10–2)

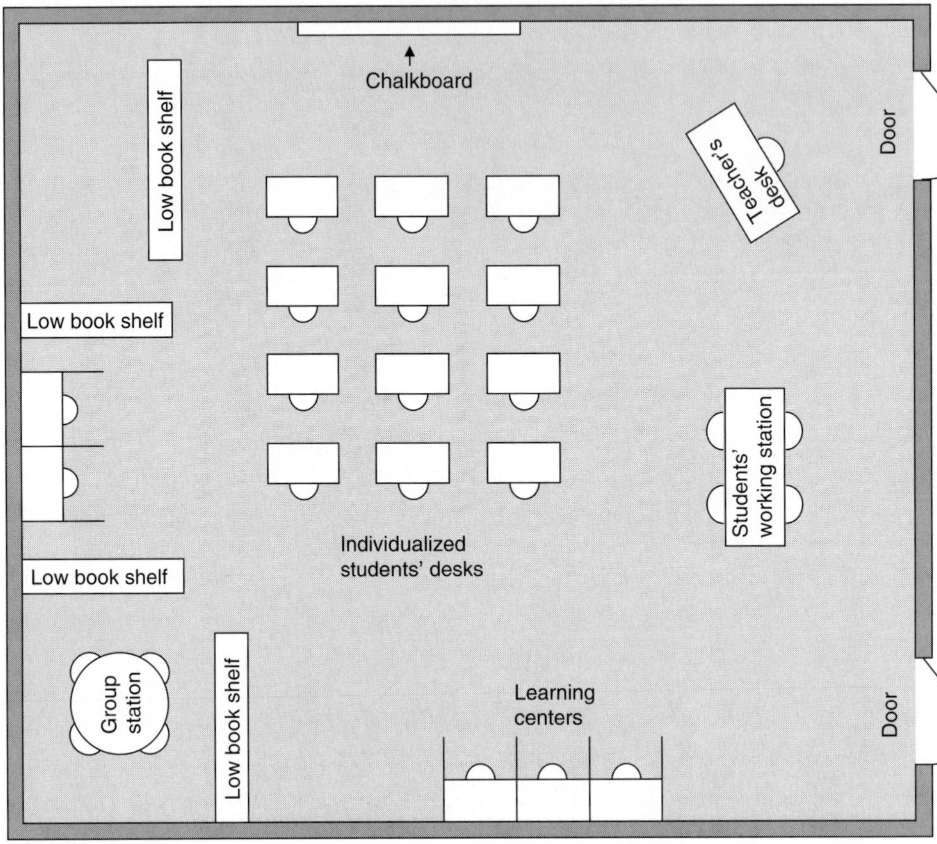

Checklist for Classroom Design

In developing an optimal learning environment and in designing the classroom, one can distinguish between procedural elements and objectives that are quite often under the control of teachers, and elements associated with the acquisition of needed equipment and materials. Teachers have very little control over the latter elements and are highly dependent on the district and school policies and budgets. However, teachers can recruit assistance from parents and the community in procuring what is needed for the classroom. The following checklist, which consists of procedural items, as well as equipment, instructional materials, and media items, can assist teachers in designing an optimal classroom environment and can serve as a monitoring device.

I. Procedural items
   A. Design the physical setup of the classroom.
   B. Procure available necessary furniture, equipment, and educational materials.

Figure 10–10 Young Adults Classroom Design

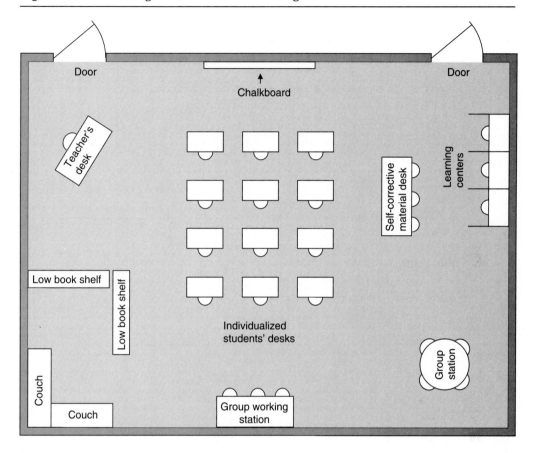

C. Determine classroom routines and management systems.
D. Establish the daily and weekly schedules and activities.
E. Prepare students' individualized folders and assignment sheets.
F. Decide how to utilize teacher aides and other available paraprofessional volunteers effectively.
G. Decide how to utilize peer and cross-age tutoring.
H. Determine the nature of students' grouping and regrouping corresponding to the daily and weekly activities.
 I. Select appropriate instructional materials for individual and group activities.
 J. Develop the format for feedback mechanisms, reinforcement modes, and general classroom management procedures.
K. Determine procedures for the monitoring of student progress and product-process evaluation.

Figure 10–11 Elementary Resource Room Design

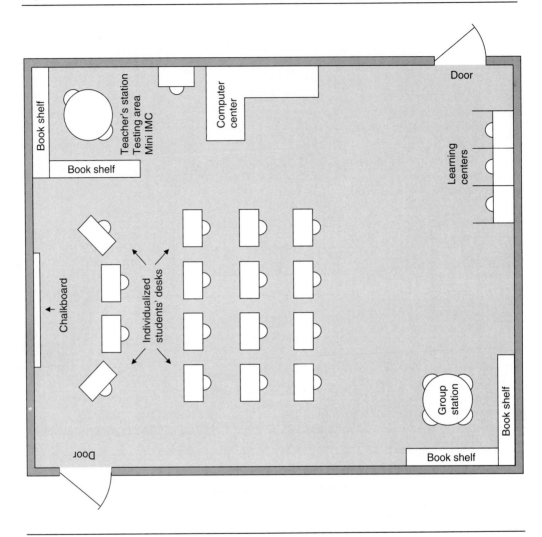

II. Equipment, instructional materials, and media
   A. Furniture
      1. Desk and chair for each student
      2. Small group activity desks (having a circular, oval, and/or trapezoid shape)
      3. Learning centers desks (having a circular, oval, and/or trapezoid shape)
      4. Cubicle or carrel tables (at least two)
      5. Carpet, toss-away pillows, and/or couch
      6. Life science accessory equipment, such as animal cages
      7. Interior decorating accessory items, such as an aquarium and plants

B. Equipment
   1. Tape recorder and earphones
   2. Projector and screen
   3. Typewriter
   4. Computer
   5. Teaching machines
   6. Radio, television, and VCR
   7. Pencil sharpener
C. Instructional media
   1. Globe/maps
   2. Appropriate 3-D materials
   3. Instructional tapes, records, and talking books
D. Supplies
   1. Writing paper (several kinds, including graph paper)
   2. Pencils and erasers
   3. Manila folders and envelopes of all sizes
   4. Colored pencils, crayons, and markers
   5. Tape and glue
   6. Stapler and staples
   7. Stickers, adhesive stars, and other reinforcing supplies and materials
   8. Flash cards and index cards
E. Instructional games
   The teacher should obtain various instructional/educational individualized and group games commensurate with the developmental and functional levels of individuals and the group.
F. Student instructional material
   The teacher must have sufficient educational materials appropriate to the functional and interest levels of the students in the various areas of the curriculum. The teacher should attempt to acquire both self-corrective and programmed instruction materials. In addition, enrichment materials and materials related to current events, (e.g., weekly readers, weekly magazines, and specialized activity magazines such as Scholastic's *DynaMath*) should be made available to students for formal and incidental learning.
G. Teacher's instructional resource materials
   1. Criterion-referenced tests
   2. Informal tests in the various academic areas
   3. District procedural handbook
   4. Professional books and instructional guides

Daily and Weekly Schedules and Activities

Children and adults in general, and specifically children and adults with learning disabilities, can work much more efficiently once learning routines and activity schedules have been established. The establishment of a routine and an activity schedule reduces anticipatory anxiety of the unknown. Children with learning disabilities work more effectively once they are familiar with the daily and weekly routines and know what is expected of them as well as what to anticipate in terms of the nature and type of activities. Thus it is important for the LD specialist to develop both daily and weekly schedules.

In scheduling activities, the teacher must take into account a number of factors:

1. The structural nature of the learning environment, namely, the degree of structure necessary in order for students to work optimally.
2. The developmental needs of the students in the classroom and their ability to benefit from the learning situation, taking into consideration attention span and concentration ability.
3. The specific nature and characteristics of the students in the classroom, both individually and as a group. Some LD classrooms may have a higher proportion of acting-out children. In these situations, a more highly structured learning environment is desired.
4. The curriculum and intervention components for the individual with learning disabilities at various levels, including training in metacognition and strategic learning, social skills development, conceptual knowledge and life-coping skills, and career/vocational preparation.
5. The characteristics inherent in the activity or task.
6. The degree to which activities are designed for individualized and/or group instruction.
7. The teacher's style of teaching and classroom management strategies.
8. The weekly and daily academic diet and other program intervention components, namely, the optimal time allocation in each subject area, such as reading, math, spelling, and creative writing, and time allocation for other activities, such as strategic learning/training, social skills development, and other intervention components. These considerations will vary based on the age level of the students and the degree of severity of their learning disabilities.
9. The preparation of daily and weekly assignment folders, assignment sheets, and job packets.
10. The availability of aides and paraprofessionals, and effective utilization of peer and cross-age tutoring.

In preparing the daily activities, the teacher must also take into account the other daily activities of the week. It is extremely essential to vary activities throughout the week so they will not be monotonous, and at the same time to provide consistency and carryover from one activity to another throughout the week.

In a more practical sense, the teacher must provide for continuous activities from Monday to Friday to reinforce any concepts introduced on Mondays, thus chaining in order to facilitate retention of materials. In addition, the teacher must take into account the time of day as a factor in the learning process. Some subjects are easily learned and retained in the morning, and others can be tolerated by fatigued students in the afternoon. Moreover, activities must be assigned in consideration of previous ones. When a teacher plans to give students a creative writing activity based on the spelling vocabulary of the week, the spelling lesson should precede the language and creative writing activity. Activities less structured in nature, such as recess and lunch, must be considered in planning the daily activities. To facilitate the learning process, following activities such as recess, lunch, or assembly, the teacher should begin with tasks that have a built-in structure, such as arithmetic computation. When arithmetic computation is programmed at individuals' functional level, students coming directly from recess or lunch can begin working on their materials. Furthermore, the teacher may select various types of calming activities immediately following recess or lunch, such as reading a story or a book over a period of time. As a general rule, upon completion of their activity, students should be allowed to become involved in activities of their own choice, which were prepared in advance by the teacher and were established as contingency reinforcers.

Styles of Daily Schedules

Four styles of daily schedules are discussed in this section. They are the highly structured schedule, the choice-within guided schedule, the contracting schedule, and the contingency schedule. In all situations, individualized instruction, grouping, and regrouping practices must be considered and incorporated.

The Highly Structured Daily Schedule and Activities

In this type of schedule, each segment of the day is carefully scheduled and planned for students, and they thus have very few choices. This highly structured style must take into account the developmental age, particularly in relation to an individual's attention and concentration abilities.

Table 10–1 contains examples of daily schedules and activities in a highly structured learning environment for the primary, intermediate, and secondary levels. These examples of daily schedules take into account the developmental level of students, their attention span and concentration abilities, and the nature of the task. All these must be congruent with the teacher's style of teaching and the students' abilities.

As illustrated in the schedules in Table 10–1, the length and the order of the activities vary. The teacher may consider variations in the order of the instructional activities based on teaching style and students' needs.

The Choice-Within Guided Schedule

In this style, the daily schedule is divided into various blocks, for example, A.M. prior to recess, or prior to lunch, and another block of time following lunch. Each block of time normally consists of about 2 hours. During each time period, students are required to complete the task assignments in areas allotted to that block of time. However, they may select the order in which to work on each area.

Table 10–1 Daily Schedule and Activities for a Special Class

Primary Level

Time	Activity
8:00– 8:05	Children line up, enter class
8:05– 8:10	Greetings
8:10– 8:25	Reading readiness, story telling
8:25– 8:55	Reading groups
8:55– 9:25	Language
9:25– 9:55	Developmental readiness activities
9:55–10:10	Recess
10:10–10:25	Math readiness/games
10:25–10:45	Math groups
10:45–10:55	Watching "Sesame Street"
10:55–11:30	Exploratory science, social studies
11:30–12:00	My book/story writing
12:00–12:45	Lunch
12:45– 1:15	Music/art
1:15– 1:35	Games/activity packets
1:35– 1:50	Magic circle

Intermediate Level

Time	Activity
8:00– 8:15	Opening exercises, flag salute/calendar, checking homework
8:15– 8:50	Reading
8:50– 9:00	Nutrition
9:00– 9:05	Relaxation exercises
9:05– 9:45	Math
9:45–10:30	Language/spelling/writing
10:30–10:40	Break
10:40–11:20	Social studies (M,W,F), science (T,TH)
11:20–12:05	Training in metacognitive-oriented strategic learning
12:05–12:45	Lunch
12:45– 1:20	Physical education
1:20– 1:45	Music/art
1:45– 1:55	Break
1:55– 2:30	Individualized tutoring, activity packets
2:30– 2:40	Closing homework assignment

Table 10–1 Continued

Secondary Level	
Time	**Activity**
8:00– 8:15	Class business, homework assignment
8:15– 8:55	Reading
8:55– 9:50	Language arts/spelling, written expression
9:50–10:20	Nutrition
10:20–11:05	Math
11:05–11:45	Social studies (M,W,F), science (T,Th)
11:45–12:15	Training in metacognitive-oriented strategic learning
12:15– 1:05	Lunch
1:05– 1:40	Current events (M,W,F), social relationship seminar (T,Th)
1:40– 2:05	Individualized projects, activity packets
2:05– 2:35	Relaxation/yoga
2:35– 2:50	Closing/clean up, homework

The Contracting Schedule

In this style, the teacher provides each individual with the assignments of the day, and the students are free to choose which activity they want to do throughout the day as long as the assignment is completed that day. This form of contracting is completely individualized, and the teacher must work with each student.

The Contingency Schedule

In this style, students are given the assignments for a whole week, and they may elect when to do each assignment, aiming to complete all assignments by the end of the week. When the assignments are completed within the first 4 days of the week, the 5th day becomes a contingency activity day. Contingency activity days must be planned ahead, for the teacher must receive the approval of both parents and principal. Contingency activities may include taking a field trip, working in the school library or school cafeteria, and doing other activities within the availability of the school's resources.

Scheduling Considerations for Resource Room Programs

A major challenge for resource teachers is scheduling students and resource room activities. The nature of the program calls for collaboration between the regular education program and the resource room support services in both direct and indirect services. Many factors influence the scheduling of students in the resource program: (a) the general education school program and its specific scheduling of activities and classes, (b) teacher preferences for when students should be pulled out or when collaborative teaching can occur, and (c) students' need for support and their developmental level. The resource teacher must juggle the external constraints of the regular program and the scheduling of activities within the resource room to promote optimal learning. The following guidelines should assist resource teachers in scheduling students and developing their direct and indirect services schedule:

1. Scheduling should be carried out in collaboration with regular class teachers and include school counselors at the intermediate and high school levels.
2. The schedule must be consistent and predictable, including activities such as library research and computer skills development.
3. At the outset, scheduling and the nature of the support services should be established with clear guidelines regarding the students' responsibility to complete the regular class work and the grading procedures to be used.
4. When parallel activities are preferred at the elementary level, the program in the resource room should be consistent with regular classroom activity.
5. At the intermediate and high school levels, parallel scheduling is recommended. Resource students can be mainstreamed easily once they reach a skill level that allows them to function successfully in the regular classroom.
6. At the intermediate and high school levels where more than one resource teacher is available, departmentalizing the resource program can be effective in providing optimal learning and a smooth transition to the mainstream.
7. Collaborative team teaching should be scheduled parallel to regular classroom activities and should meet the remedial needs of resource room students.
8. The resource teacher can maximize the services of the resource room by increasing the number of students who can be grouped for a given teaching area in accordance with their functional level and age (but it is not advisable to group primary students with upper elementary students, even though they may be functioning at the same level).
9. Resource students who can benefit from regular classroom activities in weak areas should remain in the regular classroom and be pulled out for resource help during a period that is least distracting to them.
10. Generally, when students are so far behind the regular classroom work that they cannot benefit from the regular program, they should be scheduled for resource help.
11. Their ability to concentrate during the various instructional periods must be taken into account in scheduling students for resource help and in selecting the area of remediation. Students, particularly those in the primary grades, are more productive in the morning hours than later on in the day and should be scheduled for resource help during those hours.

12. Students should not be pulled out of regular classroom activities in areas they enjoy or like best or in which they excel, including activities such as P.E. or art. In addition, when special events, such as school assemblies, conflict with resource time, the special events take precedence.

Table 10–2 contains a sample schedule for an elementary school resource program.

Students' Individualized Folders, Assignment Sheets, and Job Packages

Individual Student Folders

It is important to design an individual folder for each child in which assigned work is kept. In general, the folder contains an assignment sheet, which also contains a monitoring and a feedback section, and the material assigned to the student.

Students like to know what their assignments are and to see the results of their efforts. Individual activity folders heighten students' awareness of the various areas of learning and facilitate their assumption of responsibility for the assigned work. In addition, a folder serves as an organizational and monitoring device for both a student and the teacher. Styles of student folders vary from a simple manila folder to a decorative one that contains a specific message for the child on the cover, such as "Catch the power to succeed" or "Fun with success." The folder may contain the assignment sheet on the left side and the actual assigned material on the right side. The student's folder can also be designed as a threefold file that includes sections for "doing," "completed work," and "teacher-checked work."

Table 10–2 Daily Schedule and Activities for an Elementary Resource Program

Time	Activity
7:30– 8:20	Consultation with teachers, SST and IEP meetings
8:20– 9:05	Primary grades students—individualized and small group instruction in language arts
9:05– 9:35	Collaborative team teaching in the regular classroom (alternate schedule, M,W,F, & T,Th)
9:35–10:15	Classroom and student observations, preparation and distribution of materials for individual students and teachers in the mainstream
10:15–10:30	Recess
10:30–11:20	Upper elementary students—arithmetic
11:20–12:10	Upper elementary students—language arts and study skills
12:10– 1:00	Lunch
1:00– 1:35	Primary grades students return—arithmetic
1:35– 2:15	Assessment, observations of students in the regular classroom, collaborative consultation
2:15– 3:00	Classroom preparation, IEP meeting, on-site staff meetings

Daily/Weekly Assignment Sheets

Assignment sheets are extremely helpful. They provide students with the assignments to be completed, and they facilitate the monitoring of students' work output and progress. They offer immediate feedback on student performance. Styles of daily assignment sheets vary in accordance with the developmental age of a student and the teacher's style of teaching. Assignment sheets reflect the general operation routine of a classroom and the daily schedule of activities. In addition, they reflect the teacher's general classroom management format, system of feedback, monitoring of student progress, and evaluation of student output. The examples shown in Figures 10–12 to 10–14 are daily and weekly assignment sheets at various educational levels.

In addition to the daily assignment sheet, the teacher should have activities and assignments listed on the blackboard or on bulletin boards. These additional lists will guide students as to the various activities in which they may engage throughout the day. At the primary and elementary level, an activity wheel is very useful. Activities for nonreaders at the primary level could be color coded, but at the secondary level, a clearer designation of activities is preferred.

Preparing Students' Assignments and Job Packages

The assignments given to students must take into account the general activities of the classroom, in terms of both individualized work and group work. In general, assignments should be geared to the functional level of students and should ensure success. In an independent study activity, assignments should be geared toward mastery level. Material at students' instructional level must be supplemented with support from either the teacher or the teacher's aide. The assignments must also take into account the developmental aspects of students in terms of attention span, concentration, and interest. One cannot expect primary children to perform the same amount of work as secondary children. In preparing assignments for students, one must keep in mind the approximation of these assignments to regular classroom functioning. For students with LD who are being considered for mainstreaming or for those who are partially mainstreamed in regular classrooms, assignments should approximate as much as possible the assignments and routine in regular classrooms.

Principles and Guidelines for Preparing Students' Assignments

In preparing assignments, the LD specialist may need to modify the instructional material presented to students. Material must be easily readable and uncluttered. For example, in arithmetic, the teacher may choose to present computation exercises on a 4" by 3" grid on a page. The students are then faced with only 12 problems on a page, which are easily manageable, and thus the students get a feeling of success upon completion. Likewise, the teacher may modify reading assignments by shortening them or by providing reading material appropriate to the functional level of students, along with a short follow-up assignment. The same principles can be applied to all areas of the curriculum. At the secondary level, higher level conceptual material in social studies and/or science can be rewritten at a simplified level to match students' functional level.

Figure 10–12 Daily Assignment Sheet

Name _____

Date _____

Subject Area	Assignments	Evaluation and Teacher's Comments		
Completed Homework		Poor	Fair	Good
Math:				
Reading:				
Language:				
Social studies/Science:				
Other areas:				
Homework assignment:				

Figure 10–13 Daily Assignment Sheet

Name _____

Date _____

Assignment	Completed
Reading:	
Language and writing:	
Spelling:	
Math:	
Social studies/science:	
Other activity:	
Homework assignment:	

Job packages are individualized activities that may consist of academic work and/or other supplementary and enrichment activities. Job packages are made available to students upon completion of the assigned work. Students are usually given a choice as to which activity to work on first. There are primarily five types of activity job packages:

1. Follow-up independent assignments stemming directly from the academic work assignment of the day, week, or month. Such assignments may include a simple follow-up assignment or a more elaborate project in social studies.

Figure 10–14 Weekly Assignment Sheet

Subject area _____
Name _____
Week of _____

	Assignments	**Evaluation and Teacher's Comments**
Monday		Poor Fair Good
Tuesday		
Wednesday		
Thursday		
Friday		

2. Supplementary skill development packages that include supplementary work related to specific skill acquisition in the various academic areas, such as word searches, math facts flash cards, math operations and vocabulary decoding and enrichment, bingo, and activities to enhance the development of study skills.
3. Activity job packages that guide students in working with teaching machines and/or a computer.
4. Problem-solving job packages related to students' general ability to function in school and in life. They include problem-solving activities such as brainteasers, various learning games, puzzles, mazes, and other problem-solving and manipulative activities.
5. Fun activity packages, which include various games and/or listening material, such as songs and stories.

A teacher may decide to implement job packages as a part of the daily assignment and thus design a package that includes activities and materials that have to be completed for each segment of the daily schedule.

Grouping and Regrouping Practices

The LD specialist should attempt to provide a learning environment conducive to independent learning and both small and large group instruction. Principles of individualized instruction and group instruction should be practiced as appropriate for the various learning activities.

Grouping and regrouping practices refer to the grouping of students to maximize the learning process. Because of the variability of the learning-disabled functioning, it is quite common for a student with learning disabilities to function at one level in one area and at another level in another area. Thus students must be grouped according to their functional level across pertinent variables.

It should be the continuous practice to group and regroup students according to their social-emotional and academic needs. Choices made in determining grouping may be critical because they affect the total climate of the classroom. Ideally, students should be grouped according to their overall abilities in both social-emotional and academic areas. In practice, however, such grouping is not always possible, and where a choice has to be made, the social-emotional needs must be regarded as the most important variable. If students are at the academic level of a particular grouping, but are immature in social interaction, it might be possible to integrate them into the group by gradually increasing the time spent with the group.

Grouping and Regrouping and the Daily Schedule and Activities

Grouping is an integral part of the daily schedule and activities and, subsequently, of the teaching process. Grouping and regrouping practices facilitate the individualization of the teaching process and promote group activities and social interaction. In developing the daily schedule and activities, the teacher should consider the various possibilities of student grouping and the support resources available, including teacher aides, volunteers and paraprofessionals, and peer tutoring. The LD specialist must develop a sound management system to maximize the effectiveness of the grouping process. This system may include the use of a variety of devices, such as activity wheels and bulletin board signs. The teacher may also involve the students by assigning them leadership responsibilities on a rotating basis.

Here is an example of grouping in a junior high school LD classroom. The LD specialist makes use of an activity wheel to designate the group that works with the teacher, the aide, or independently. As a routine, four groups are involved in reading comprehension activities, rotating between working with the teacher or the aide and working independently. Thus Group A works with the teacher on Mondays and Wednesdays and follows up with independent activities assigned by the teacher and guided by a designated student for that week. During the time that the teacher is working with Group A, Group B is engaged in independent activities. The teacher then rotates and works with Group B while Group A is engaged in independent activities. This schedule alternates on Tuesdays and Thursdays, when the teacher begins working with Group B while Group A is engaged in independent activities. The same format is applied to Group C and Group D, who are assigned to the teacher aide. (At the primary level, the groups can be identified by various colors; for example, the reading groups may be called the red, yellow, and blue groups.)

The success of the grouping and regrouping process lies in the degree of the teacher's and the aide's continuous monitoring and supervision of students' activities. Also, advanced preparation of students' assignments and the necessary instructional materials is critical to optimal grouping practices. Generally, a group consists of two to five students, thereby allowing each student to receive individualized instruction and causing the students to develop stronger and more positive relationships among themselves. Grouping also enables the teacher and the aide to closely monitor the students' progress. Moreover, the monitoring and the daily recording of the students' progress assist the teacher in the grouping and regrouping practices.

The Highly Structured Learning Environment for the Learning-Disabled

Clinical data and empirical research indicate that excessive external environmental stimuli contribute to the poor performance of individuals with learning disabilities, specifically of hyperactive children. According to Cruickshank and Hallahan (1975), an individual's inability to respond selectively to stimuli and to differentiate figure and ground in visual or auditory environments has a significant impact on a child's learning and results in a succession of failure experiences. "If the child cannot ignore stimuli, and if the environmental stimuli interfere with the child's learning activities, it goes without saying that the teacher or other adult must reduce the stimuli factor in the environment to such a level that it is within the tolerance level of the child" (p. 230).

Consideration must be given to the inclusion of elements of the highly structured classroom environment when necessary. These elements of a highly structured environment advocated by Cruickshank (1967) should be included: (a) a reduction of environmental stimuli, (b) a reduction in space, (c) a structured school program and life plan, and (d) an increase in the stimulus value of the teaching material. Individual carrels will reduce unnecessary environmental stimuli. The effectiveness of these carrels can be maximized when the teacher takes into consideration all aspects related to the reduction of environmental stimuli. A total reduction of environmental stimuli in the classroom is not advocated, but the classroom design must allow for highly structured components in the learning environment for those individuals who have a short attention span, who have difficulty concentrating, who are hyperactive, and/or who need reduced environmental stimuli and reduction of space. As space increases, so do the number of stimuli in the space. If space is limited, hyperactive children will be able to attend to essential stimuli for a longer period of time without interruption and thus achieve more successfully.

An increase in the stimulus value of teaching material will help students to focus on the task at hand. The goal is to provide learning tasks so that the learning material is highly accentuated in order to draw students' attention to a task.

A structured school program and life-style should also include the structuring of the daily schedule and activities, thus allowing greater opportunity for successful experiences. A highly structured classroom environment is one in which clear directions, firm expectations, and consistent follow-through are paramount (Haring & Phillips, 1962). In organizing the classroom, the teacher needs to take into account (a) the physical setup of the classroom; (b) organization factors affecting direct instruction (i.e., individual student folders, individual student assignments, and individual student packages); and (c) general and basic routines in the classroom, such as where to place self-correcting materials, where students should pick up their materials, where they should place their materials when they finish work, where they should place their homework when they come in, and where and how they should get their homework when they leave. These factors are extremely important in facilitating the process of instruction during the day. Once students are used to a basic routine, they will direct their energy primarily to the learning process.

CLASSROOM OPERATION STRATEGIES: ESTABLISHING PARAMETERS

Setting the Limits and Monitoring Students' Self-Control

Students with learning disabilities, like normal students, are inclined to test the limits during the first few days of the school year. If certain parameters (limits) are not established, testing of the limits will continue throughout the year.

The question of setting limits is basically a philosophical one and ultimately relates to the issue of free will. However, all human beings implicitly or explicitly live within a definite set of parameters. Likewise in a classroom, the teacher must set parameters within which students can function and exercise a degree of freedom. In order for students to function optimally in the classroom, it is extremely important that they and the teacher mutually set the limits.

Consider the following situation: A class of 14 upper elementary students with LD was assigned to a teacher and a teacher's aide. The majority of the students were generally cooperative. However, three students were a challenge to the teacher and the teacher's aide, acting in defiance of authority. When the teachers could no longer tolerate the situation, they raised their voices at the three students in front of the entire class. In essence, they lost their control. The three students still continued to manipulate the situation and occasionally succeeded in appearing to have the upper hand.

Many students with learning disabilities lack self-control. They may act without carefully considering the consequences of their actions. Setting limits in the classroom is one way of providing external guidance for children who lack self-control. The rationale for setting limits should be explained to students. In addition, much consideration should be given to the feelings of the students toward those limits. The limits set should help generate an optimal classroom environment, protect the rights of every individual student in the classroom, and reflect common sense.

External guidance is needed to proceed in the direction of self-control. An individual's self-awareness and self-control can be heightened through (a) participation in setting the limits; (b) participation in the control and maintenance of behavior, including self-evaluation; and (c) establishment of behavioral goals that are directed toward self-control.

The heterogeneity of those with learning disabilities and the fact that they function at various levels will dictate the amount of external control the teacher may want to exercise. External control should be exercised only to the extent necessary for individuals to function optimally. The external control should be geared toward self-control and using control executive functions, that is, planning, organizing, monitoring, and checking outcomes.

Some teachers may find themselves in a situation in which they really lack control of the classroom. Several factors may contribute to such a situation: (a) There are deficits in the total classroom environment (see correlates of classroom environment); (b) teachers most likely have not set limits, either alone or through mutual agreement with the students; and (c) in some cases, teachers will use external control to control the classroom, including raising their voice, sending students to the principal's office, and making contact with students' parents. While these last actions may prove a temporary relief, the ultimate goal is to develop a set of limits mutually agreed upon by both the teacher and the students, thereby establishing parameters and a framework that make sense for an optimal classroom environment.

Now return to the situation described earlier in this section involving the three defiant students. The teacher's inability to tolerate the behavior of those students increased, but he did not act decisively. Hesitant and fearful of the impression on the principal, the teacher decided to handle the situation on his own without involving the principal. As revealed in their cumulative records, those three students had had extreme behavior problems in previous years. However, the principal had not notified the teacher of this, and therefore the teacher viewed his inability to cope with these three students as his own failure. He did not realize that even the most experienced teacher would have had difficulty in dealing with these particular students. A recommendation followed that decisive action must be taken with these three, not as a group, but rather as individual students. Moreover, the consequences for the students' behavior had to be jointly established with the principal. The principal was extremely supportive and agreed to take a strict approach with these students. Subsequently, each of these students received only one warning prior to being sent to the principal's office. At the same time, positive reinforcers were also selected. All three students were notified of these new procedures and behavior contingencies.

It is important that teachers feel confident in whatever course of action is decided upon from the first day of the school year. Teachers should allow for some degree of elasticity, but a frame of reference should be established in order to provide students with a comfortable environment in which to function. Children like to know their limits. They like to know how far they can go and how far they can exercise their free will. It is therefore extremely important for the LD specialist to set the limits at the outset of instruction.

Establishing Classroom Rules

For a stable and secure classroom atmosphere, classroom rules and expectations must be consistently applied to, and observed by, all students. Thus it is important to be certain that students understand the expectations that are placed upon them through discussions and explanations of classroom rules that help to guide their behavior. Classroom rules should be explained clearly and posted in the room. They should be stated in positive terms as much as possible, followed by positive consequences/reinforcements. On the other hand, students must also be made aware of possible consequences for unacceptable behavior. The consequences should be objectively specified and continuously applied (see chapter 12).

The following are samples of classroom rules:

1. Upon entering the classroom, go to your desk and sit down.
2. Follow the teacher's direction and pay attention at all times.
3. Get your assignment folder and begin working.
4. Raise your hand when you need help or when you have completed your work.
5. Be courteous and polite to others.
6. Respect the property of other people.
7. Work quietly.

Involving Students in Classroom Decisions

The need of individuals with LD to learn how to manage their own life suggests that they be encouraged to participate in decision making relative to classroom operations and the classroom setup. Although a classroom teacher expresses a feeling of cooperation and willingness to have students participate in the formulation of a decision, at the same time, students should know who is in charge of the classroom operation. The LD specialist should delineate the roles and responsibilities of students by establishing behavior parameters, including consequences for both positive and negative behavior, usually through group participation and consensus; establishing behavior management procedures involving student monitoring and evaluation; and deciding on various roles that students can assume in order to facilitate an optimal classroom environment. In addition, the LD specialist should establish a daily schedule and an activity-planning format that will facilitate the monitoring of student output, by the students and the teacher.

Receiving Classroom Assignments and New Students at the Start of the Year

Most teachers, but primarily new ones, experience anxiety in anticipation of new classroom assignments. This is a normal phenomenon—individuals usually tend to experience a mild level of anxiety prior to taking on a new task or exploring a new environment. Receiving new students at the beginning of the year poses challenges to both experienced and new LD specialists. One can view the initial encounter between teachers and new classroom assignments in three phases: (a) getting familiar with the students by reading their records and cumulative cards, (b) meeting the students and initiating interpersonal relationships with them, and (c) establishing steady relationships with all the students in the classroom.

The LD specialist's first exposure to new students is through written information in their files and cumulative records. Though most of that material is objective, some will be subjective in nature, contaminated with the biases of previous teachers. The teacher-student interaction variable plays a major part in student behavior in the classroom. As teachers review students' files, they must do so with an open mind and try to be objective and not biased by the presumptions of former teachers.

The second phase involves meeting students on a one-to-one basis and/or in a group situation. To facilitate the adjustment of the learning disabled to a new teacher and classroom, they should be introduced to the teacher gradually, which fosters the development of a positive relationship. This allows students to learn more about the teacher and the classroom routine, and the teacher to learn the new students' aspirations and goals. The teacher may share with the students highlights of the program in general and the specific instructional program to be used. An interview format, traditional or metacognitive (as discussed in chapter 8), may be used at this phase to allow more in-depth interchange of ideas; the development of student sensitivity to, and awareness of, the instructional program; the development and modification of the instructional program; and the obtainment of a student's commitment to learn. This phase provides the opportunity to both resource room students and resource teachers to review students' programs in the regular classroom and to examine elements that can increase their chances to succeed in those classes.

The third phase involves the gradual development of teacher-student relationships and the provision of an optimal learning environment. Teachers should formulate general classroom management strategies and identify basic factors that will contribute to an optimal classroom environment. Once teachers have formulated these goals, they can introduce them to the students and encourage input as to how they feel about the goals. Teachers must know the goals, have a firm idea of what they want to accomplish in the classroom, guide students to participate fully in the process, and arrive with students at a mutual decision concerning the classroom operation. In preparation for new assignments, teachers must consider the correlates of an optimal classroom environment, discussed earlier in this chapter.

Preparing for the First Week of Instruction

The first few weeks of the school year set the tone and direction for the remainder of the year. Learning disabilities specialists should formulate in their mind, as well as on paper, the standard by which they want the classroom to be conducted. They should also resolve any questions related to specific intervention approaches, general classroom atmosphere, and routine.

Quite often new teachers do not realize the extreme significance of the general atmosphere and classroom practice during the first or second week of class. Establishment of a positive classroom atmosphere is prerequisite to an optimal classroom environment. The degree of students' cooperation and participation in the learning process is dependent upon the degree to which the classroom environment meets their needs.

In preparation for the first week of instruction, teachers should do the following:

1. Design and complete the physical arrangement of the classroom.
2. Secure needed educational materials.
3. Develop specialized activity packets that include mixed practices for review and updates of information concerning students' functional level.
4. Decide on general classroom routine, including styles and formats of students' folders and students' assignment sheets.
5. Decide on general classroom parameters and a specific management approach.

Teachers must also be prepared to alter initial plans to accommodate the needs of individual students and the group at large.

Receiving a New Student in Midyear

Several times a year, teachers are likely to receive new students. The introduction and integration of these new students into the classroom require considerable thought. Under normal conditions, it is extremely difficult for a student to be transferred in midyear, and for someone with learning disabilities, it can prove overwhelming. Teachers can facilitate the introduction and adaptation of a student to a new room assignment by preparing the classroom for the new student and involving the total group in the integration of the student into the class. In addition, teachers can use a buddy system to assist the student both academically and socially, and should provide additional attention during the first few weeks.

Teachers should follow the programming and planning procedures discussed in chapter 9 and develop an educational plan in accordance with a new student's abilities and needs.

Structuring the Lunch Period

For students with learning disabilities, lunchtime needs to be guided, planned, and structured. If lunchtime is unstructured and unsupervised, a pleasant experience can become an unpleasant one. For example, in one situation, an LD specialist maintained that it was almost impossible to grant students a lunch period because they fought continuously with each other. In analyzing the lunch period, it was observed that it lasted for about 40 minutes and that very little supervision was provided. In addition, no activities were planned for the students during this time. Because the lunch period was too long and had no structured activities, it was difficult for the students to interact positively. The recommendation was to break the 40-minute lunch period into segments—the eating of lunch, planned activities, and calming activities prior to entering the classroom. Supervision must be provided at all times.

Assigning Homework and Home Activities

The purpose of assigning homework is to facilitate the development of independent study habits. For that reason, homework assignments should be geared to students' mastery level, or in other words, students should be able to complete an assignment independently (without the assistance of others) with at least 95% accuracy. The parents' role in students' completion of homework assignments should be minimal and informative in nature, that is, parents can observe what their children are doing and become aware of their children's learning and activities. Parents can assist in monitoring their children and establishing a homework study time routine. Students may not depend on receiving assistance from their parents or from other tutors to complete their homework assignments. Thus every effort must be made to provide homework assignments that can be handled by students at their independent level. Homework assignments generally consist of a review of material covered in class, a generalization of material learned in class through projects in social studies or science, and independent projects and activities.

On the other hand, parents can provide home enrichment activities for individuals with learning disabilities. Teachers can supply guidelines and resources for enrichment activities that can facilitate both incidental learning and exposure to new concepts and reinforce material learned in the classroom. Generally, home activities should be activity oriented and enjoyable in nature, for example, cooking, gardening, and/or variations of games that parents can play with their children to develop basic skills and increase children's attention, concentration, and general problem-solving strategies.

Working With Aides

Teacher aides and paraprofessional volunteers are an integral part of special education programs throughout the nation. In many LD classrooms, there is at least one paid teacher aide. In addition, LD specialists can effectively utilize paraprofessional aides. Training aides and integrating them into a total program can produce many benefits and have positive effects on the program. Instructional aides can provide instructionally related and noninstructional assistance to teachers, more individualized attention to students, and better communication with the community.

Many school districts now have job descriptions for paid aides. Usually, the aide's function can be classified under two main headings: noninstructional activities and instructional-related activities.

Noninstructional Functions

The aide provides assistance in planning and preparing for the ongoing activities of the classroom, including preparing material, typing and duplicating necessary materials for students, and assisting the teacher in the various tasks related to the operation of the classroom. These tasks include maintaining student folders and student assignment sheets, preparing bulletin boards, maintaining an orderly classroom arrangement, managing instructional material, and finding resource materials for various teaching units. The aide can also assist in preparing special learning materials, taping reading assignments, simplifying reading material for students, and developing general supportive instructional material.

Instructional-Related Functions

The teacher's aide can provide support to the instructional process by performing activities directly related to it, such as correcting students' homework and class work. The aide may also be directly involved in the instructional process by listening to students, reading to them, helping pupils who were absent to get caught up with the rest of the class, working with individual students in support of learning and instruction, and reinforcing the rehearsal of learning activities.

In addition, the aide can facilitate the instructional process in a more formalized setting: (a) by working in a minilab within the classroom, which could be a basic skills development lab in arithmetic, reading decoding skills, spelling, or basic elements in creative writing. This lab is centered around structural materials developed by the master teacher and the teacher's aide. The tasks in the lab must be structured, and students will usually spend 5 to 7 minutes on a specific task in a certain lab and then return to their desk. The aide must be taught to monitor students' progress and mastery of those specific skills; (b) by working with a small group of students, assisting them in their activities in various aspects of the curriculum, for example, to begin reading a story in a small group and then assist each student in the follow-up activities; (c) by assisting individual students in developing individual projects, including locating and finding resource materials to support the projects; and (d) by contributing to the general classroom functions in personal areas of talent and strength.

The majority of teacher's aides begin working without adequate training (McManama, 1972). Studies have pointed out that aides can produce positive changes in academic achievement and reduce student self-defeating behavior (Wyskoff, 1977).

The importance of training teacher's aides cannot be overstated. Although some school districts provide training, the primary responsibility too often falls on teachers.

Teachers can facilitate the process by providing training in the following areas: (a) general knowledge and characteristics of individuals with learning disabilities; (b) general classroom operations and routine; (c) approaches to teaching, including specific teaching methods as deemed appropriate; (d) general classroom management techniques; and (e) effective use of educational materials and resources.

In addition, it is suggested that teachers develop a handbook for teacher's aides consisting of material related to

1. The philosophy of the program
2. The role and responsibilities of the aide
3. A code of ethics and professional conduct
4. The monitoring of students' progress and evaluation of students' output

The instructional aide must be knowledgeable about classroom operation procedures and must maintain a consistent approach with students. Following training and the demonstration of skills and competencies, an instructional aide can be integrated into the instructional and management process. Teachers should give careful consideration to the supervision and monitoring of an aide's work, including the establishment of communication procedures and format. Teachers should be fully involved in all aspects of an aide's activities and assume full responsibility for the aide's actions.

Working With Volunteers

Many of the principles of working effectively with aides also apply to working effectively with paraprofessionals. Paraprofessionals and/or volunteers must project a sense of responsibility in what they are doing. Teachers should be aware of volunteers' background in order to maximally utilize their talents and abilities to support both instructional and noninstructional functions. Unlike teacher aides, volunteers are restricted in both time and commitment in their involvement. It is important to provide training for volunteers that includes (a) acquainting them with the general classroom operation procedures, (b) acquainting them with the nature (characteristics) of learning disabilities, (c) acquainting them with specific methodologies and intervention strategies to be used in working with the learning disabled, and (d) acquainting them with specific managerial procedures in the classroom and with expected student behavior. It is suggested that volunteers begin first with noninstructional duties so that teachers can become acquainted with them and volunteers can evaluate and test whether they would like to become more involved in working with those with learning disabilities.

Providing Feedback and Monitoring Student Performance

The performance of each student should be systematically monitored relative to the instructional objectives and the IEP goals. The teacher should monitor student progress on an ongoing and periodic basis. Weekly and monthly tests and review practices should include the material for that specific period. The teacher must have an efficient and organized record-keeping system. The organization of student folders, student assignment sheets, and behavior management recording sheets facilitates the monitoring of student progress. In addition to descriptive information, the teacher's utilization of individual profiles and inventories can facilitate the monitoring of students' progress and the evaluation of performance.

Providing feedback to students and monitoring their progress serve to reduce their anxiety. These actions also assist the teacher to be on target in the remedial process. Immediate feedback reinforces students' output and prevents unnecessary failure experiences. As the teacher monitors students' work, the altering of assignments is sometimes necessary. Students with learning disabilities who have a continuous history of failure should not be given assignments too high for their level of functioning because of the increased likelihood of failure. Whenever a student's assignment proves to be too difficult, even though the student might have been previously exposed to the material and/or might have forgotten it immediately, assistance should be provided in terms of reduction and/or modification of the assignment. Students' mistakes must be carefully noted. The teacher may elect to note only the mistakes relevant to the assigned task and the ability of students to address themselves to those mistakes. Records of students' performance are essential in order to evaluate progress. Completion of assignments and mastery of skills should be recorded by the teacher and that record should be made available to students. Progress charts should be simply designed and readily available for students' review. Progress records can be kept in students' individual folders, as well as in the teacher's record book.

Student self-monitoring should be incorporated into the daily assignment sheets by providing columns for students' evaluation. The teacher may select specific metacognitive strategic learning self-monitoring sheets (see also chapter 6). Students are thus more involved in the monitoring of their own progress and can provide input to the teacher when changes in the program are necessary.

To ensure objectivity and realistic evaluation, the teacher must refer to the scope and sequence of the curriculum and the expected student outcome at the corresponding grade level. Such monitoring of student performance provides the teacher with information necessary to make decisions relative to students' skill mastery and the appropriateness of the teaching procedures and methods.

In monitoring student performance, the teacher must keep in mind product/process analysis, as well as aspects of programming procedures. In other words, the teacher must be aware of clear indications of students' progress, the effectiveness of the intervention method, and the approach used. If there are signs that students are not making optimal progress, the teacher should refer back to the programming procedure chart and alter procedures accordingly.

Keeping a Planning Book and Records

The discussion of programming for individuals with learning disabilities (chapter 9) emphasized the importance for the teacher of specific programming and the monitoring of student progress. It is thus in LD specialists' best interest to keep a planning book and clinical records. Teachers' planning books are available commercially. Because of the individualized characteristics of the clinical teaching approach, teachers may need to modify a planning book to accommodate both individual and group program planning and monitoring. Teachers may utilize students' assignment sheets and metacognitive task cues as part of the recording system. The teacher's planning book and record keeping can facilitate the evaluation of the teaching-learning process. In addition, the planning book can serve as a source of information for parent conferences and the annual IEP review.

SUMMARY AND CONCLUSIONS

The classroom environment must be designed to be conducive to learning and personal growth. The goal is to create a classroom environment that meets the needs of individuals with learning disabilities and provides them with opportunities for successful experiences. That environment should encourage students to assume an active role in learning—to participate in decision making and take responsibility for their own actions.

CHAPTER
11

Instructional Approaches and Instructional Technology

Questions to Consider | 1. **What is cooperative learning?**

2. **What are the merits of peer and cross-age tutoring?**

3. **How can one maximize the teaching of cross-level concepts?**

4. **How does one select appropriate educational material and media?**

5. **How does one utilize effective computer technology in the classroom?**

In the preceding chapters, we have discussed factors that contribute to an effective remedial program and the development of an optimal learning environment for individuals with learning disabilities. The remedial program can be further enhanced through the use of instructional procedures that make sense, such as cooperative learning, peer tutoring, and cross-level and cyclical teaching. In addition, the effective use of instructional technology, instructional materials and media, computers, and teaching machines can contribute immensely to the remedial program for those with LD. These procedures not only enhance the remedial program but also prepare students to function more effectively in the mainstream.

INSTRUCTIONAL APPROACHES: TEACHING PRACTICES THAT MAKE SENSE

Cooperative Learning

Cooperative learning is defined as a group learning experience in which the outcome results from common effort, the goal is shared by all its members, and each member's success is dependent on each other's (Kohn, 1986). Cooperative learning is based on the assumption that cooperation promotes higher achievement than competition and that it provides a more positive cross-handicap relationship than do competitive, individualistic, or traditional learning experiences (Johnson, Johnson, & Maruyama, 1983; Madden & Slavin, 1983).

According to Johnson and Johnson (1986), there are four elements of cooperative learning: positive interdependence, individual accountability, collaborative skills, and group processing. Positive interdependence refers to the group perception that "one cannot succeed unless the others do" (p. 555). It includes the recognition of group responsibility for learning, a reward based on the group's overall achievement, the distribution of resources and coordination of efforts, and the group members' assignment and responsibilities. Individual accountability refers to the recognition of individual performance and responsibilities so that the group can be successful. Collaborative skills "include leadership, decision-making, trust-building, communication, and conflict-management skills" (p. 555). Group processing refers to the group monitoring and maintenance activities, including provision of feedback to all group members and the development of collaborative skills.

Schniedewind and Salend (1987) describe three basic formats of cooperative learning: peer teaching, in which one student tutors and assists another in learning a new skill; the group project format, in which students pool their knowledge and skills to create a project or complete an assignment; and the jigsaw format, in which each group member is assigned a task that must be completed for the group to reach its goal. The type of format teachers choose for their classes depends upon the unique needs and characteristics of their students and classrooms, as well as their experiences in working cooperatively (Schniedewind & Salend, 1987).

Promoting cooperative learning requires a set of practical strategies that regular and special education teachers can use to structure cooperative learning activities in the classroom (Johnson & Johnson, 1980). The following procedures were adapted from Johnson and Johnson (1980) and Schniedewind and Salend (1987):

1. Establish guidelines for working.
   a. Explain the general principles of cooperative learning and the responsibility of each group and each group member.
   b. Explain the task and the cooperative goal.
2. Form cooperative groups.
   a. Select the group size most appropriate for the activity.
   b. Assign students to groups to maximize the heterogeneity of students in each group.
3. Arrange the classroom.
   a. Arrange seating so that group members are close together and facing each other.
   b. Provide a group activity area.
   c. Provide appropriate support materials.
4. Develop cooperative skills.
   a. Provide opportunities for students to practice specific cooperative skills.
   b. Observe student-student interaction and act as a facilitator when needed.
   c. Assign group members specific roles and train them.
   d. Provide feedback to students concerning their effectiveness in cooperative learning.
5. Evaluate cooperative learning.
   a. Develop evaluation and grading procedures.
   b. Evaluate groups for their product as well as their ability to work together.
   c. Gather both individual and group data so groups know when to give help and assistance to individual members.

Cooperative learning can be used effectively in special classes, resource rooms, and regular classrooms. The implementation of metacognitive procedures in a classroom naturally leads to cooperative learning. In general, social acceptance of academically handicapped students is enhanced by cooperative learning (Madden & Slavin, 1983). Furthermore, during cooperative learning activities in the classroom, positive relationships are formed among peers, including handicapped and nonhandicapped students, and are generalized to other school situations (Johnson, Johnson, Warring, & Maruyama, 1986).

Peer and Cross-Age Tutoring

Peer tutoring, also referred to as student-assisted learning and pupil-mediated instruction (Young, 1981), is defined as the instruction of one student by another student under the supervision of a classroom teacher.

Children have been teaching other children throughout history. Older, more advanced students teach younger, less advanced ones. Likewise, students who are more advanced in their skills assist friends of the same age. In a one-room schoolhouse in rural America, such practices were common. Currently in America's schools, there are two general aspects of peer tutoring: tutoring of handicapped students by nonhandicapped students, and peer tutoring, or handicapped students helping other handicapped students.

Within these major aspects, two general styles of tutoring exist: cross-age tutoring and peer tutoring. Cross-age tutoring involves older, more advanced students teaching younger ones. Peer tutoring, or peer-assisted learning, involves students of the same age and of the same class assisting each other in the learning process.

The benefits of a tutoring program along these two dimensions have been well documented in the literature, both in terms of nonhandicapped students tutoring handicapped students and handicapped students assisting other handicapped students. Peer tutoring that uses students with LD to help other students with LD can be extremely effective (Scruggs & Osguthorpe, 1985). It can be considered another component in the remedial education process (Humphrey, Hoffman, & Crosby, 1984). Peer tutoring does the following:

1. Increases the amount of individual instruction students can receive
2. Heightens the understanding of individual differences
3. Promotes understanding of the handicapped by the nonhandicapped
4. Facilitates the instructional process
5. Heightens the understanding of the tutor's own abilities, strengths, and weaknesses
6. Produces both academic and social/emotional gains

Peer tutoring occurs both on a one-to-one basis and in small groups. Peer tutors are especially useful when paired with students who present a challenge to educators (Canning, 1983). For example, Mary, a 14-year-old with learning disabilities whose functional reading level was about the third grade and who exhibited behavior disorders, was defiant and resisted her teacher's attempts to help her. Mary openly stated that she did not want to learn to read, and she showed no progress in reading over a 3-year period.

In another classroom, Tony, a 10-year-old who had learning disabilities and was basically a nonreader, was also resistant to his teacher's instruction and had given up learning how to read. He cooperated only in activities that he liked to do.

A decision was made to pair Mary with Tony in a cross-age tutoring situation. Tony was described to Mary as a student who presented a challenge to his teachers because of his reading difficulties and his general attitude toward learning how to read. Mary was asked whether she could help tutor Tony in reading. It was explained that she would need to meet with Tony's teacher each day in order to develop Tony's reading program. It was stated that the teacher would actually instruct Mary on how to teach Tony by providing her with the material that Tony needed and suggesting the approach to be used in teaching.

Upon Mary's acceptance of this assignment, Tony's teacher met with her and developed both the program and the monitoring approach in general, as well as the specific learning tasks for each of the tutoring sessions on a daily basis. Tony's teacher was aware of Mary's own difficulties and functional reading level and thus worked closely with Mary's teacher.

Mary was extremely eager to take up the challenge. She met with Tony's teacher daily, and thoroughly studied the material that would be taught at each session. It was fascinating to observe how this child, who exhibited the same basic character-istics as Tony relative to reading, was able to motivate Tony to read, as well as to make a shift in her own approach to learning how to read by reflecting upon her own difficulties in learning to read and the resulting behavior. After working with Tony for 3 weeks, Mary explained to her teacher that she understood why Tony wouldn't read because she herself had the same difficulties. Mary continued tutoring Tony effectively, meeting with his teacher daily and, for the first time, asking her teacher for assistance in improving her own reading skills. During the course of that year, both Mary and Tony made significant progress in reading.

This experience exemplifies the effectiveness of students tutoring other students. Both the tutee and the tutor benefit from the tutorial program. The child who is being tutored does not feel threatened by the process of instruction. A greater closeness exists between the tutee and the tutor than between an adult teacher and a child, and a strong element of cooperative learning is thus evident. This type of tutoring neu-tralizes the no-win/lose relationship that sometimes exists between adult teachers and students with LD.

Designing a Peer Tutorial Program

The purpose of this section is to assist teachers in the development of a peer-tutoring program in the classroom. Two formats of peer-tutoring programs can be initiated by the special day-class teacher or the resource room teacher:

1. The development of a core of nonhandicapped student tutors selected by their teachers for outstanding performance and in recognition of their achievement. The students undergo special training culminating in

certification as student assistants and recognition by the school principal and teachers. This core of student aides can be utilized in both peer tutoring and cross-age tutoring.

2. The training of individuals with learning disabilities to function as peer tutors and in cross-age tutoring. Students are selected by their teachers in recognition of their efforts and performance, and they also undergo specialized training.

Generally, peer tutoring should follow sound principles of teaching. In designing a peer-tutoring program, give special considerations to the selection of participating students, the training procedures for the students, and the monitoring of the program.

Tutors should learn about the instructional goal in general and students' individual needs in particular. Tutors have to be trained in appropriate instructional procedures and interpersonal behaviors that will result in a comfortable, effective, and satisfying experience for both them and the tutees. Tutors must know the content to be taught and the material and methods to be used. They must be taught how to plan for the tutoring session and how to organize the materials. In addition, tutors must learn how to check for mastery of concepts and how to use continuous reinforcements and feedback. In the training of tutors, both role playing and practice tutoring sessions are important (Lundell & Brown, 1979). Paired learning is recommended as a prerequisite to cross-wide tutoring in the classroom. In paired learning, each child is both the teacher and the learner (Ginot, 1975).

In order for a tutoring program to be successful, teachers must provide full support to students in planning the tutorial station, as well as in preparing the material for the tutors. Material must be organized in a hierarchy of tasks to facilitate the step-by-step acquisition of skills.

For peer tutoring to be effective, teachers must work carefully with tutors in developing a plan for the entire week and in monitoring the tutees' progress and the tutors' work. Teachers must select and relay to tutors (a) the academic target behaviors and skills, (b) the material to be used, (c) the method of the student-assisted instruction, and (d) the tutor/tutee monitoring of progress and the delivery of reinforcements.

Teachers have to carefully monitor the first few tutoring sessions and conduct posttutoring debriefing sessions (Jenkins & Jenkins, 1985). In addition, tutors, as well as tutees, should be reinforced for appropriate expected behavior, efforts, and good progress. Both teachers and tutors should keep a daily tutoring journal, recording the time, activities, and achievements of tutees. One must remember that though students are tutoring to assist in instruction, the primary purpose is to maximize the potential of both tutors and tutees. Teachers must therefore assume the primary responsibility for the peer-tutoring process by preparing the material and monitoring it.

Under no circumstances should punishment be used by tutors. They have no authority over tutees. They act as facilitators to the instruction and as additional mediators in the instructional process. Tutors and tutees should be equally involved in the tutoring process to promote cooperative learning and interpersonal relationships.

In general, peer tutoring produces tangible gains in academic areas (Roach, Paolucci-Whitcomb, Meyers, & Duncan, 1983; Scruggs & Osguthorpe, 1985) and social/emotional areas, and attitudinal improvements in motivation and self-esteem (Osguthorpe, 1984), which in turn increase on-task behavior and self-esteem and develop a more positive feeling toward learning (Allen, 1976; Strain & Odum, 1986). Furthermore, peer tutoring promotes cooperative learning, assists in the development of social/interpersonal relationship skills, and when organized properly, provides every child in the class with the opportunity to receive 10 to 15 minutes of direct practice time with key learning skills (Delquadri, Greenwood, Whorton, Carta, & Hall, 1986).

Cross-Level Teaching

Through the educational process, students are introduced to concepts in a sequential and cyclical manner, in which more advanced levels are built on former ones. For example, the acquisition of arithmetic skills requires an operational level of arithmetic skills, that is, knowing the basic operations of +, −, ×, and ÷ with whole numbers, fractions, decimals, and percents. Students are exposed to whole number operations in the primary grades and move on to fractions at the intermediate elementary level and to decimals and percents at the upper elementary level. The integration of these concepts is required at the junior high level prior to the acquisition of basic algebraic concepts. Thus as students progress from first grade onward, they are exposed to various concepts in a linear, sequential fashion. The repetition of conceptual knowledge in various cycles at different levels can be observed. This is meant to reinforce prior learning and to prepare learners for subsequent higher level skills.

Children with learning disabilities exhibit academic gaps and deficiencies. They do not acquire the concepts taught at the various grade levels in a normal fashion. They are more apt to miss concepts and skills, thereby accumulating a general pattern of academic deficits. These academic gaps may be exaggerated if one uses only the scope and sequence of the school curriculum as a point of reference. In reality, as one examines the sequential skills acquisition throughout the first 6 years of school, one can easily detect the cyclical structure of the curriculum and identify common elements throughout the preceding four conceptual levels of arithmetic. Children who apparently have not fully mastered the basic operations of +, −, ×, and ÷ with whole numbers can continue to strengthen their skills while working on decimals. They are gradually introduced to the subsequent levels of arithmetic and work on more than one level. This is represented by the horizontal and vertical dimensions in the diagram of cross-level teaching shown in Figure 11−1. The horizontal dimension specifies the sequential acquisition of skills within a level such as whole numbers. The vertical dimension illustrates the movement from one conceptual level to the next successive one.

In developing the educational plan in the area of arithmetic, teachers must take into account both the operational level and the conceptual level of students. Students can easily be introduced to the concepts of money equivalents, which is an

Figure 11–1 Cross-Level Teaching in Arithmetic

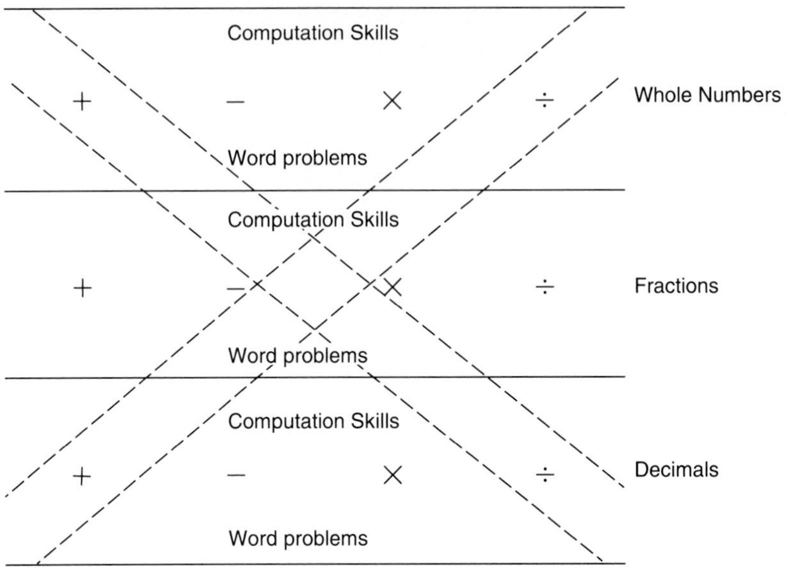

introduction to the decimal system using basic whole number operations. In other words, LD specialists are working with students on two levels, assisting them to master basic arithmetic facts and exposing them to the decimal system. The clustering of such concepts and the teaching across levels is referred to as "cross-level teaching."

Cross-level teaching is thus defined as a clustering of concepts across levels and an introduction of these concepts to students in accordance with their level of functioning. Cross-level teaching brings into a more realistic perspective the academic gaps of those with learning disabilities within the domain of the school curriculum. The use of cross-level teaching helps bridge the gap between students' functional level and the demands of the core curriculum. It makes the remedial process more sensible and time efficient, and assists learners in dealing with concepts covered by their peers in the regular classroom.

The Spiral Curriculum Approach to Learning

As discussed in the preceding section, the teaching and acquisition of academic skills and concepts throughout the school years can be viewed as cyclical. Usually, concepts are introduced at one level and then expanded at a subsequent, higher level of learning. This practice is consistent with sound principles of teaching and with the scope and sequence of the curriculum. The various levels of acquisition of concepts and skills can be viewed as a spiral, in which the teaching and acquisition of higher skills are built on lower levels of learning. In reading, for example, primary level students are introduced to monosyllabic words prior to multisyllabic words, compound words, and words containing prefixes and suffixes.

The purpose of the cyclical approach is to introduce concepts at various levels as cycles and to provide closure for both the teacher and the students. Teaching concepts in a cyclical manner heightens students' awareness of the learning process and increases their feeling of success. Many learning-disabled students who are nonreaders have been introduced numerous times to the same concepts and often at the same level without any closure. Quite often, a teacher introduces a nonreader to letters and sounds of the alphabet and phonic rules without completing a meaningful cycle or providing closure. When repeated over the years, this pattern results in minimal progress in reading.

The LD specialist should attempt to have a closure on a cycle at least in each term and should develop instructional objectives accordingly. It is recommended that a decoding cycle involving meaningful reading with nonreaders be completed within one term. This does not mean that students are expected to master all the decoding skills during one term. However, the skills necessary for mastery of a cycle, such as learning CVC and CVCV word patterns in a meaningful text, can be attained by students, and this develops a true sense of accomplishment and success for both students and teacher. One can practice cyclical teaching in all the curriculum areas and can integrate it with cross-level teaching, discussed in the previous section. Cyclical teaching makes sense to both the teacher and students, who can observe definite progress in the learning cycle.

INSTRUCTIONAL TECHNOLOGY: EFFECTIVE USE OF INSTRUCTIONAL MATERIALS AND MEDIA

Guidelines for Selecting Instructional Materials

While much material has been developed for those with learning disabilities during the last 20 years, there is still a paucity of adequate instructional material for the learning-disabled in general and for intermediate and secondary level students specifically. In selecting and developing instructional materials, teachers must keep in mind the scope and sequence of the curriculum, the instructional level of students, and the interest and developmental age of students. In addition, the instructional materials must provide students with practice, rehearsal, and immediate feedback.

More specifically, the selection of appropriate instructional materials must include the following considerations:

1. Appropriateness of the educational material
   a. Does it appear to cover the scope and sequence of the curriculum it claims to teach?
   b. Does it represent or approximate a step-by-step progression of the skills to be learned?

      c. Are the assignments short enough to allow for successful completion of a unit within a set time?

      d. Does it allow for modification to meet the needs of each student?

  2. Relevancy of the educational material to the teaching process

      a. Is the instructional material commensurate with the learning objectives designed for the students?

      b. Are there specific objectives for the students?

      c. Is the level appropriate to the functional level of the students?

  3. Modes of presentation

      a. Is the material presented with clarity—not overly crowded but rather very well spaced out?

      b. Are the directions for the assignment clear? Does it come with a teacher's manual?

      c. Does the material provide for follow-up activities in accordance with the desired skills to be developed?

      d. Does the material provide for immediate correction and feedback?

      e. Does the material have a built-in system for evaluating students' progress?

  4. Motivational aspects of the material

      a. Is the material stimulating to students? Does it seem to appeal to students?

      b. Is the material presented in accordance with the developmental and interest levels of students?

  5. Cost of material

      a. What is the initial cost of the material? Is it within a reasonable range?

      b. Is the cost of the material within the teacher's budget?

Instructional Materials Concerns for Adolescents With LD

Because most instructional material is written at a seventh- to ninth-grade level and the reading level of adolescents with learning disabilities is usually between the third- and fifth-grade level, the sciences and social studies have proven to be very difficult for youths with LD. However, there are other ways to introduce these adolescents to the same concepts covered in those higher level reading materials. Teachers must be aware that some elements of the curriculum are repeated at the higher level. For instance, United States Government is a topic normally introduced in the fifth grade. The same subject area material is also taught at about the ninth- to tenth-grade level, which means that there is material available at about the fourth-grade level that covers basically the same topics. In addition, there is some material, both in the sciences and social studies, that has been adjusted specifically for adolescents and that has been written at about a fourth- to fifth-grade reading level. If such materials are unavailable, it is suggested that the LD specialist make use of paraprofessionals and parents to simplify existing materials.

Programmed Instruction, Self-Corrective Materials, and Teaching Machines

Programmed instruction is a method of introducing concepts to students by presenting information to be learned in a series of small steps. It usually includes a logical sequence of small learning steps that directly involve students in active responding and provide them with immediate feedback and reinforcement. In addition, programmed instruction is geared toward individual rates of learning and self-pacing. The utilization of programmed instruction, self-corrective materials, and teaching machines, in the classroom facilitates the general teaching process by providing activities for individual students, thereby freeing the teacher to devote time to other students. Programmed instruction provides self-instruction and step-by-step instruction at students' functional level, and it serves as a motivational factor for students.

Self-corrective materials provide students with immediate feedback on their work. Such material should follow the sequence of the curriculum, and, like programmed instruction, it should provide for small increments of mastery.

Teachers should use various media in support of instruction, such as tape recorders, language masters, typewriters, teaching machines, and computers. When using such machines, teachers must review and certify that the program material is consistent with the principles of remediation and good learning. Generally, teaching machines can be strong motivators for youngsters who have had difficulty in developing interpersonal relationships. They can be used in conjunction with other instructional material and can reinforce the teacher's instructions.

Utilization of Three-Dimensional Materials

The LD specialist must use three-dimensional (3-D) and illustrative materials with students with learning disabilities in order to facilitate understanding of the learned material, the acquisition of knowledge, and the development of concepts. Experience with 3-D materials involves students in exploratory learning and enables them to manipulate aspects of their environment in the process of learning. It also aids the development of imagery and memory processes. Likewise, the use of illustrations—pictures, designs, and diagrams—in the absence of concrete objects helps students to understand and acquire new information.

The use of 3-D and illustrative materials as instructional aids is consistent with developmental and cognitive theory and research. According to Bruner (1964), individuals interact with their environment through three modes of representation: enactive, iconic, and symbolic. Accordingly, the development of children's thinking and memory is directly related to their individual modes of interaction with the environment. At the enactive, concrete level, children form concepts and attempt to arrive at solutions by manipulating objects in their environment. In addition, they form images that correspond to concrete experiences. At the iconic, figural level, children's interaction with their surroundings is through visual images; thus this level is intermediate between the concrete and symbolic levels. Illustrations can

Teaching can be further enhanced when instructional technology is effectively utilized to provide students with the opportunity to learn and to reinforce previously attained concepts.

further assist children to understand the content learned and to develop visual imagery and memory processes. At the symbolic level, children think abstractly, using symbols as a means of interaction and communication with their environment.

Interaction with the environment through these three modes is both hierarchical and interactive, and is necessary for the formation of concepts and the development of memory processes. According to Dunlap and Brennan (1979), "Prior to abstract (symbolic) experiences, instruction must proceed from concrete (enactive) experiences to semi-concrete (iconic) experiences" (p. 90). Learning proceeds through concrete experiences to the development of imageries and abstract thinking. Conversely, abstract thinking rests on visualization and concrete experiences. Thus 3-D and illustrative materials are essential aids to the learning process.

COMPUTER TECHNOLOGY IN OUR SCHOOLS

The Use of Microcomputers in Education

Generally, two major functions of microcomputers in education are recognized. The first is the direct use of computers in assisting student instruction. This function is referred to as computer-assisted instruction (CAI). Burke (1982) defined CAI as "any method of learning in which a computer is the primary delivery system . . . [found as a] direct interactive instruction in which the student is on line to a computer" (p. 118). The other use of microcomputers in education is in management. Burke (1982) defined computer-managed instruction (CMI) as "a systematic control of instruction by the computer. It is characterized by testing, diagnosis, learning prescription and thorough record keeping" (p. 188).

Currently, many claims are being made about the positive benefits of microcomputer use in education. Microcomputers are being proclaimed as the teaching tool that will help children think and learn more effectively and efficiently than ever before. According to Neufeld (1982), computers provide a failure-free mastery of new knowledge because they reinforce and support prior attainment in a nonthreatening environment. They provide a supportive atmosphere that promotes an increase in students' self-concept (Budoff & Hutton, 1982). Generally, computers have been found to highly motivate students (Codsen, Gerber, Semmel, Goldman, & Semmel, 1987; Rappaport & Savard, 1980).

After studying the effect of the use of microcomputers in schools, Schiffman, Tobin, and Buchanan (1982), concluded that computer-assisted instruction was viewed favorably by all involved. The computers gave students undivided attention and allowed them to work at their own pace. Drill and practice, often seen as necessary but tedious procedures, became more exciting. Parents reported positive attitude changes in their children. Furthermore, computers proved to be a powerful aid to teachers in presenting individualized instruction to students (Hannaford & Taber, 1982). They also extend a teacher's area of expertise in the teaching process. Particularly beneficial to special educators are the data collection, storage, and retrieval aspects of computers, which are simplified with the use of memory disks (Levin & Doyle, 1983). The use of computers has also been shown to improve students' skills of attending and following directions (Siegel & Clapp, 1981).

Questions have been raised as to whether these benefits are worth the expenditure on the equipment and whether the gains are maintained over time (Hofmeister, 1982). In response to criticism of computer-assisted instruction, Gleason (1981) reported that for the overall population of students, research has shown that the use of CAI leads to savings in student time in learning tasks and to an improvement in achievement. In addition, in a meta-analysis of 51 separate research studies, Kulik, Bangert, and Williams (1983) reported that students who received CAI scored better on objective tests than students with only traditional instruction. Computer-assisted instruction also improved retention when students were tested sometime after the CAI program ended. Some studies even reported that CAI can improve the speed at which students learn a given amount of material (Hofmeister, 1982; Kulik et al., 1983; Taber, 1981).

With the current interest in the use of microcomputers in schools, it is becoming increasingly important for learning disability specialists to address aspects related to the use of this technology in their classroom. The benefits of computer technology have been gradually and impressively applied in special education (Yin & Moore, 1987). The utilization of computers with individuals with learning disabilities is one of the most exciting and promising developments of the last decade. While studies comparing computer-assisted instruction and traditional teaching show no significant differences in student outcome (Blaschke, 1986), the benefits of CAI cannot be ignored. The use of microcomputers with those with LD has been shown to be effective across a wide range of skill areas (Hagen, 1984; Jones, Torgesen, & Sexton, 1987; Morocco & Neuman, 1986). Microcomputer instruction with learning-disabled students is a highly motivating vehicle for imparting information (Codsen et al., 1987). In addition, having students work on microcomputers permits the LD specialist to provide more individualized instruction (Fitzgerald, Fick, & Milich, 1986).

Computer-Assisted Instruction With the Learning Disabled

The questions about appropriate use of microcomputers in the education of students with learning disabilities require close examination. Computer-assisted instruction achieves educational outcomes by causing an interaction between students and the computer system to help them learn new material or improve their knowledge of material previously studied (Taber, 1981). Buckley and Johnson (1983) have identified the following as major contributors to CAI effectiveness:

1. It is individualized, and students move at their own pace.
2. It provides up-to-the-minute diagnoses of students' strengths and weaknesses, thus helping teachers perform their tasks more thoroughly and efficiently.
3. It can be structured to allow students a limited amount of time to respond to questions presented.
4. It provides students with feedback on their progress.
5. It utilizes a reporting system that provides students with a clear picture of their progress.
6. It has a positive impact on cognitive growth when used properly.
7. Students who use CAI are more likely to perceive themselves as capable learners.
8. Students who use CAI become increasingly self-directed in their learning style.

Computer assisted instruction can be an asset to teaching, helping students to think and learn more effectively and efficiently.

9. Students who use CAI are able to identify for themselves specific skill areas in which they have improved, as well as areas in which they need to improve.
10. Students who use CAI can watch their own scores and are able to see general progress.
11. Among CAI users, effective growth results in more rewarding learning experiences and helps to account for improved cognitive growth and more regular attendance.
12. As adult students using CAI cease to perceive it as being experimental and gamelike, it becomes a much more effective learning tool.

For those with learning disabilities, the use of microcomputers can be a positive break from the routine of failure experiences. It can be established as a positive source of education and new learning experiences. Boettcher (1983) pointed out that for learning-disabled students, CAI can provide:

- a secure one-on-one learning environment
- responsibility to students for their own learning
- truly individualized programs of learning
- a demand for responses and, therefore, increased decision-making abilities in students
- prompt, immediate feedback
- the requirement of type-in responses, which appear to be ideal for students with learning disabilities
- decision points, giving students control and a sense of self-esteem
- mathematical and linguistic modeling
- multisensory learning experiences, given by a dynamically responsive visual learning pattern, with the possibility of auditory clues. (Cited by Schmidt, Weinstein, Niemic, & Walberg, 1985–86, p. 494)

According to McDermott and Watkins (1983), "Combinations of computerized and conventional remedial instruction may work as well with problem learners in that success will vary as a function of the severity of the learning disorders and differential styles of learning" (p. 86). Pupils can be assigned to CAI programs to increase motivation and reduce the resistance often detected among problem learners. Microcomputer programs can be easily incorporated into students' daily schedules. Students interact with programs in several ways, depending upon the format in which a program is presented. Computer-assisted instruction can take the following forms: drill and practice, tutorial programs, simulations, and adventure games.

Drill and Practice

Drill and practice reinforces previously learned material (Taber, 1981). Using a microcomputer in a drill-and-practice mode is much like using electronic flash cards. In drill-and-practice programs, the computer presents students with questions, which the students answer. Depending on the answers, the computer may modify its next function. Optimally, drill and practice on a computer is interactive and response sensitive (Budoff & Hutton, 1982). The microcomputer makes repetition manageable and provides frequent feedback (Mason, 1983). Students are immediately reinforced if their answers are correct. If answers are incorrect, students are not allowed to continue, thus avoiding the practice of errors. In addition, drill and practice allow students to work at their own pace. Students are less embarrassed to make errors on a computer because they do not have to turn to their teacher for help but can immediately make corrections themselves.

Drill and practice can be presented in two forms: straight format and game format. In a straight format, the material to be practiced is presented directly and specific responses are expected, very much as in a workbook. On the other hand, in a game format, drill programs are very much like any other computer game, and various techniques are used to elicit a student's response before a timer runs out. Game format drills utilize graphics and simulate competition between students and their past performance. Thus the features of video arcade games are easily adaptable to educational drill-and-practice games, and include instant feedback, clear-cut goals, fast pacing, and variable levels of challenge.

Tutorial Programs

Tutorial programs are designed to teach students a given skill without the teacher's assistance. According to Budoff and Hutton (1982), tutorial instruction programs assume the role of teacher and present material in a program learning format. As students move from one step to the next by answering questions, they may be directed to remedial or review segments and/or a more advanced skill level. Tutorial programs are very effective for, and beneficial to, students with learning disabilities. The students can move through tutorials at their own pace and in a nonthreatening manner. Thus tutorial programs are more motivating than traditional instruction and can ensure children's failure-free mastery of new skills. A good tutorial program should be designed and written to incorporate various levels of instruction. Instruction is presented in small segments, and students are branched to the appropriate sequence depending on their performance level. Learning takes place in an individually tailored, nonjudgmental manner in which students assume full control of their learning (Hannaford, 1983; Hannaford & Taber, 1982).

Simulations

Simulations are programs designed to emulate real-life situations and utilize principles of discovery learning (Behrmann, 1984). In simulations, true-life situations are presented, and students must decide how to continue. A computer simulation enhances the development of high-level cognitive skills and involves students in various problem-solving approaches. Most simulations developed for the general educational population can be used by the learning disabled. However, the LD specialist must screen out those simulations that involve too many rules, are too distracting, or require skills that are too high for students. It is thus imperative for the LD specialist to review simulation games to determine their appropriateness and level before presenting them to students.

Adventure Games

Like simulations, adventure games promote problem-solving skills and concise expression (Mason, 1983). Some adventure games allow students to role-play a fictional character, and their reaction in a given situation can then alter the plot line. As in simulations, in adventure games players must master some aspects of the environment. Typically, players are placed in a prelude situation with a specific mission to be accomplished. Again like simulations, adventure games require decisions on the part of students as to what the next step should be. In addition to promoting reading skills, adventure games branch to other skills, such as map reading and logical thinking.

If students with learning disabilities are to use computers in their learning process, the LD specialist must be familiar with computer technology and be able to select an appropriate approach and software that will meet students' needs. Hoge (1985) suggested that in order for teachers to become well adjusted to, and successful with, their microcomputers, they must be provided with the opportunities to become expert users of whatever computer system their school possesses. The use of microcomputers in the classroom is directly related to the degree to which the LD specialist is informed and knowledgeable about the use of microcomputers and programs.

Computer-Managed Instruction

Computers can also be useful for planning and managing classroom instruction. For teachers and administrators, CMI includes using the computer to construct, score, and analyze tests, and to keep track of records, grades, attendance, and budget. Kolich (1985) recognized the various benefits in using CMI. It keeps student records efficiently, organizes curriculum information, and assists administrators in managing the vast amounts of information related to the laws and regulations for handicapped students. It also facilitates the management of IEPs and assists in tracking students from referral and placing them in special education programs.

Computer-managed instruction allows the LD specialist to use the computer to manage, organize, and monitor prescriptive, diagnostic, and evaluative information. Making a successful instructional decision requires the specialist to know, for each individual student, when and in what direction an instructional plan should be changed. Research shows that graphing student progress and developing a set of decision rules to apply to that data dictate when an instructional program should be changed and what kind of change should be made. Hasselbring and Hamlett (1984) created a program for Apple II microcomputers titled Aimstar. Through Aimstar, teachers are able to enter and store daily data on each instructional program for each student in a class and then carry out formal decision making on each program in a matter of minutes. Computers can be utilized for the assessment of exceptional children, providing required information for educational decisions concerning service eligibility, diagnostic classification, educational programming and placement, and progress review (Maher & Bennett, 1982). Moreover, computers have been found to be extremely useful in generating individualized education programs. N. P. Brown

(1982) suggested that to be truly effective and useful, any computerized IEP system should be flexible enough to address individual students' needs and complete enough to make the IEP process more efficient. Examining the relative efficiency of computer-assisted IEPs, Enell and Barrick (1983) determined that parents and teachers responded favorably to them. With computer assistance, IEPs were found to be more legible and easier to understand.

Microcomputers can also aid in the management of special educational instruction by providing the following:

1. Lists of incomplete information on student records
2. Data-based reports for compliance with state and federal mandates
3. Child counts cross-referenced by age, program, and handicapping condition
4. Counts of students screened, assessed, placed, and reviewed
5. Budget and program projections
6. Audit trails for program placement and review
7. Equipment and material reports
8. Transportation scheduling

Computers can also be programmed to provide qualitative and evaluative information, such as the relationship between student progress and type of placement, type of intervention, length of intervention, handicapping condition, and the severity of a handicapping condition (Ragghianti & Miller, 1982).

Software Selection

The primary criticism of the use of microcomputers in education stems from the inadequacy of software programs currently available. All software programs should be evaluated before they are used with learning-disabled individuals. Hannaford (1983) and Hannaford and Taber (1982) listed three dimensions by which software should be evaluated: educational compatibility, instructional design, and technical adequacy. For a software program to be considered educationally compatible, use of the microcomputer must be appropriate for a particular educational task. The software must address individual learners' needs and ability levels. The software must also be compatible with the curriculum and should meet the needs of the teacher. An adequately designed instructional software program must do the job it is intended to do. Software should be developed with specific objectives and audiences in mind, and this information should be stated on the package. Also, program content, organization, and language must be correct. The manner in which students are required to respond and the way the software handles those responses are important.

In order for software to be used effectively with those with learning disabilities, it must have the following characteristics:

1. Software material must be designed with specific goals and objectives in mind.
2. Software material must be consistent with the scope and sequence of the curriculum.
3. The presentation of material must be consistent with sequential acquisition of skills.

4. The presentation of material must be clear, with adequate spacing.
5. The program must allow students to learn at their own pace.
6. The program must be "user friendly."
7. The program should provide for sufficient drill and practice.
8. The program should provide continuous feedback and reinforcement to students.

Lee (1987) identified the following additional essential components that must be included if courseware is to be of optimal benefit to students with learning disabilities:

1. Directions students read should be simple enough as not to interfere with the students' comprehension.
2. The courseware must provide alternate means of presenting the same concept if students do not comprehend the first presentation (recasting).
3. The screen must be uncluttered.
4. Students should be able to operate the program with minimal keyboard skills.
5. The program must provide praise/feedback regarding the correctness or incorrectness of responses.
6. The courseware must provide adequate opportunities for students to review concepts.
7. The software must teach very basic skills that nonhandicapped students would learn incidentally. (p. 437)

Technically, adequate software utilizes the computer's capability to produce color, graphics, and sound. It is flexible and easily adapted to the individual user's needs. The program must be "kid proof," yet the source and the amount of control must be appropriately assigned to both teachers and students. For a list of recommended software for students with LD in Grades K to 8, the reader is referred to a catalog of special computer software available from Cambridge Development Laboratory, Inc., 214 3rd Avenue, Waltham, MA 02154. Over 250 titles in all subject areas from over 40 software publishers are listed and reviewed by LD specialists. The reader may also find Dolores Hagen's *Microcomputer Resource Book for Special Education,* published by Reston, helpful in implementing microcomputer aids in the classroom.

The use of microcomputers in classrooms of learning-disabled students, while still in its infancy stage, can be advantageous. It maximizes the process of individualized instruction, eliminates unnecessary hours of drill preparation by the teacher, and allows the teacher to act as a facilitator in the learning process. (For information on using word processors in the classroom, please refer to chapter 14.)

SUMMARY AND CONCLUSIONS

The LD specialist must utilize instructional procedures that maximize the effect of the remedial program. Effective use of instructional materials, media, and computer technology can enhance the nature of the remedial program. Though software for the field of learning disabilities is still limited, we must make use of what appropriate software is available. Furthermore, we must extend computer use to those who formerly would not have had access to computers and related technology.

Classroom Management: Meeting Social and Emotional Needs

Questions to Consider

1. **What is the role of the LD specialist in assisting individuals with learning disabilities to meet their social and emotional needs?**

2. **What are correlates of classroom management?**

3. **What is classroom management?**

4. **How does one select appropriate strategies for classroom management?**

5. **How does one utilize effective classroom management strategies?**

EMOTIONAL AND SOCIAL NEEDS OF INDIVIDUALS WITH LD

As emphasized throughout this text, the remedial program must be viewed as comprehensive, providing students with learning disabilities with the necessary skills and strategies to function both within and out of school. Equally important is providing a classroom environment that enhances their social and emotional development. Throughout their life experience, the learning disabled face challenges both at school and at home. More often than not, they encounter failure experiences. Individuals who are continually exposed to failure experiences develop feelings of inadequacy and low self-concept, and become internally frustrated and passive in their approach to learning. These people are apt to develop an external locus of control, that is, blame themselves for their failures and attribute their successes to luck. This is detrimental to their development as healthy human beings in control of their destinies. In addition, they exhibit inappropriate behavior patterns and often have difficulties in interpersonal relationships. Yet their behavior is not severe enough for them to be considered emotionally disturbed. More often, their social and emotional problems may be considered as adjustment reactions to learning disabilities. At times, though, these individuals exhibit behaviors that reflect more severe emotional disturbances and approximate behavior patterns characteristic of behavior disorders.

The characteristics of those with LD are discussed in chapters 1 and 3. Their behaviors must be understood within the context of their adjustment reaction to learning disabilities. The characteristics range from a fear of learning exhibited by the learned-helplessness syndrome, to frequent excessive disruptive behavior, to withdrawal and depression. However, the general behavior characteristics of learning-disabled individuals do not distinguish them from their peers. It is the frequency, magnitude, and duration of the disturbances that may indicate the existence of a behavior disorder.

Paul (1987) distinguished between behaviors that are transient or episodic ("He'll grow out of it"), and behavior patterns that denote the existence of chronic behavior disorders (usually lasting 6 months or longer) and interfere with expected age-appropriate functioning. He indicated that it is the quality, duration, or intensity of children's behavior that distinguishes a behavioral disorder from a transient developmental disturbance, that is, chronic rather than episodic.

The secondary characteristics of those with LD also include adjustment reactions to learning disabilities. One can recognize various levels of these, from mild to severe. The levels represent a continuum, ranging from adjustment reactions to the development of maladjusted behavioral characteristics:

1. A general fear of learning. Individuals approach a new learning task hesitantly and quite often say, "I can't do it," or "I don't know it." Usually, these students exhibit no behavior problems other than what is characterized by their learned-helplessness syndrome and low frustration.
2. Extreme low frustration tolerance. When encountering a learning situation, individuals are likely to exhibit temper flare-ups and tantrums. These students are marginal in their behavioral characteristics and may exhibit some acting-out behaviors.
3. Resistance to learning exhibited by passive-aggressive behavioral patterns. Such individuals may exhibit extreme passivity or aggressive behavior.
4. Behaviors that approximate behavioral pattern characteristics of behavior disorders.

To generate an understanding of the relationship between social-emotional adjustment and learning disabilities, Schloss (1984) provided us with the model shown in Figure 12–1.

Failure in school and the loss of social reinforcements produce social-emotional maladjustments that further diminish academic performance and positive social-emotional interactions.

The delineation of behavior disorders of students with learning disabilities has been problematic, inasmuch as there is no clear differentiation between behavior difficulties and behavior disorders resulting from their interaction with their environment and behavior disorders of another origin. One may ask the question, "Are the social-emotional difficulties of individuals with learning disabilities related to their interaction and inability to cope with their environment, or are they symptoms of behavior disorders?"

Defining Behavior Disorders

Although the behavior difficulties of those with learning disabilities are primarily considered as adjustment reactions to the disabilities, the severity of their behavior may be indicative of existing behavior disorders. Knowledge of what constitutes behavior disorders is essential for LD specialists so they can refer students for ad-

Figure 12–1   Learning Disabilities and Social-Emotional Maladjustment

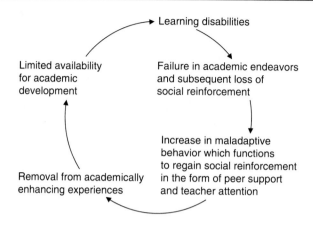

Source: From *Social Development of Handicapped Children and Adolescents* by P. J. Schloss (1984), p. 47. Copyright by PRO-ED, Inc. By permission.

ditional professional help when deemed necessary. The terms *behavior disorders* and *emotional disturbances* are used interchangeably in the literature (Kauffman, 1985). However, "behavior disorders" is preferred by many educators and is more acceptable than "emotional disturbances." The Council for Children with Behavioral Disorders prefers the term *behavior disorders* because it is more objective, divorced from any causation, and less stigmatizing (Morgan & Jenson, 1988; Shea & Bauer, 1987).

According to Bower and Lambert (1976), the emotionally handicapped child is defined as "having moderate to marked reductions in behavioral freedom, which in turn reduces his ability to function effectively in learning or working with others" (p. 95). They noted that these losses of freedom affect a child's educative and social experiences and result in noticeable susceptivity to the following behavioral patterns:

1. An inability to learn, which cannot be adequately explained by intellectual, sensory, neurophysiological, or general health factors
2. An inability to build or maintain satisfactory interpersonal relationships with peers and teachers
3. Inappropriate or immature types of behavior or feelings under normal conditions
4. A general pervasive mood of unhappiness or frustration
5. A tendency to develop physical symptoms such as speech problems, pains, or fears associated with personal or school problems

From Bower's (1981) perspective, "Emotional handicaps may be displayed in transient, temporary, pervasive, or intensive types of behavior" (p. 119). Thus Bower recognizes behavior disorders as consisting of a continuum ranging from mild adjustment to more pervasive and recurring emotional difficulties, which help us understand the contrast between adjustment reactions to learning disabilities and emotional disturbances. According to Bower (1981),

> One could begin such a continuum with (1) children who experience and demonstrate the normal problems of everyday living, growing, exploration, and reality testing. There are some, however, who can be observed as (2) children who develop a greater number and degree of symptoms of emotional problems as a result of normal crises or stressful experiences, such as death of father, birth of sibling, divorce of parents, brain or body injury, school entrance, junior high school entrance, or puberty. Some children move beyond this level of adjustment and may be described as (3) children in whom moderate symptoms of emotional maladjustment persist to some extent beyond normal expectations but who are able to manage an adequate school adjustment. The next group would include (4) children with fixed and recurring symptoms of emotional maladjustment who can with help profit by school attendance and maintain some positive relationships in the school setting. Beyond this are (5) children with fixed and recurring symptoms of emotional difficulties who are perhaps best educated in a residential school setting or temporarily in a home setting. (p. 119)

In PL 94–142, the term *seriously emotionally disturbed* is defined as

> (i) a condition exhibiting one or more of the following characteristics over a long period of time and to a marked degree, which adversely affects educational performance.
>
> a) An inability to learn which cannot be explained by intellectual, sensory, and health factors;
>
> b) An ability to build or maintain satisfactory interpersonal relationships with peers and teachers;
>
> c) Inappropriate types of behaviors or feelings under normal circumstances;
>
> d) A general, pervasive mood of unhappiness or depression; or
>
> e) A tendency to develop physical symptoms or fears associated with personal or school problems.
>
> (ii) The term includes children who are schizophrenic or autistic. The term does not include children who are socially maladjusted unless it is determined that they are seriously emotionally disturbed. (Federal Register, 42 (163), August 23, 1977, 42,478)

The LD specialist must recognize the similarities and differences between individuals with learning disabilities and those with behavior disorders. As pointed out earlier and elsewhere in the literature, at times there are more similarities than differences between the learning disabled and mildly or moderately disturbed children (Kauffman, 1985). The difference is more with respect to the intensity and duration of the behavioral disorder than the kind of behavior.

The Role of the LD Specialist in Providing Social-Emotional Support

Although many school administrators view the role of the LD specialist as providing only academic remediation, meeting the social and emotional needs of students with learning disabilities becomes an integral function of the specialist. The LD specialist is confronted daily with students who exhibit emotional and behavioral problems ranging from low frustration tolerance, to resistance to any interventions, to defiance. Understanding the emotional difficulties and incompetencies in the affective and social skills of the learning disabled is essential to clinical teaching. For many students with LD with behavior problems, the school provides the only consistent and predictable environment. Many of them come from homes in which, even in the best situations, their parents do not fully understand their plight, why they cannot learn, and why they are "lazy."

Often the LD specialist is involved in providing the climate that will foster the social-emotional needs of these individuals. More specifically, the role of the LD specialist in providing social and emotional support includes the promotion of (a) a positive self-concept, (b) success identity through successful experiences, (c) self-growth and development through the use of control executive functions, (d) general emotional well-being so individuals feel secure and self-confident and have the hope that they too can succeed, (e) social skills to facilitate interaction with peers and adults in the environment, and (f) skills for problems and conflict resolutions.

THEORETICAL CONSIDERATIONS OF CLASSROOM MANAGEMENT: UNDERSTANDING THE DYNAMICS OF BEHAVIOR

Theoretical Foundations for Classroom Management Approaches

Approaches to classroom management are in general allied to basic theories in psychology and related fields. They are founded on sociophilosophical convictions that permeate the theoretical assumptions and constructs on the nature of human behavior, how it is acquired, and the role of the environment in its development. They reflect an educational-ideological orientation based on a value or belief system accepted by society. They provide the framework for understanding, analyzing, and explaining both normal and maladaptive behavior, and the treatment and management approaches they advocate. From these perspectives, the various theories underlying classroom management have attempted to (a) explain the phenomena of human behavior and factors contributing to its development and occurrence, (b) prescribe what is accepted as normal and what is considered maladaptive behavior, (c) prescribe measures to identify maladaptive behavior, and (d) provide treatment and intervention approaches.

Consider Robert, a 10-year-old student with learning disabilities, who attends a resource room for two periods a day. In both the regular classroom and the resource room, he exhibits behavioral problems characterized by disruptions, refusal to follow teachers' directions, difficulty staying on task, and generally abrasive behaviors toward peers. These inappropriate behavioral patterns result in his removal from the regular classroom and suspension on almost a daily basis.

Psychodynamic theories may attempt to attribute Robert's behavior to a conflict in his personality system, and/or unresolved conflicts, and/or fixation at various stages of psychosexual development. The biophysical model may attribute his behavior to metabolic imbalances or neurophysiological abnormalities. The behavioristic model attributes Robert's behavior problems to environmental contingencies that maintain or reinforce these behaviors, and it thus examines stimuli in the environment that can alter this student's behavior. The ecological approach views Robert's behavior as a result of disequilibrium between him and his environment and is concerned with examining his ecosystems to determine what environmental contingencies contribute to his current behavior. These theoretical positions and their approaches to classroom management are discussed in depth later in this chapter.

In the preceding example, behavioral problems are attributed to various variables depending on the assumptions one makes about the nature and causes of human behavior, the constructs attempting to explain the origin, and the development of human behavior. Although the diverse approaches may be initially viewed as markedly different, the distinction among the models is a matter of relative emphasis placed on the origin of behavior as emanating from the individual, and/or from the interaction of the individual with the environment, and the type of interaction that occurs.

The different views of the nature of social and emotional development, and what contributes to normal development and/or to maladjustment, evolve from different theoretical formulations and perspectives. Each approach makes assumptions about the nature of human behavior, the origin of maladaptive behavior, and the intervention needed to cause behavioral changes. The language utilized to describe the dynamics of behavior reflects the constructs of the approach. Thus the psychodynamic approach uses the terms *dynamics, ego mechanism,* and *fixation.* The biophysical model employs terms such as *nutritional deficiencies, neurological dysfunctions,* and *megavitamin dosage,* and the ecological approach uses expressions such as *ecosystem* and *equilibrium.* The behavioral model employs terms such as *reinforcement, tokens,* and *contingency contracting,* and the cognitive behavior modification approach uses expressions such as *self-control* and *self-regulation.* Knowledge of the different perspectives provides the LD specialist with an understanding of the nature of an individual's behavior and social and emotional development, and with information that enables the development of a sound classroom behavior management approach.

Too frequently, teachers take a very simplistic view of classroom management. They believe that using one approach or another will solve behavior problems in the classroom. This is a fallacy, for an effective classroom environment must first and foremost meet the overall needs of students and address itself to the various correlates of an effective learning environment. In a classroom with an effective management system, students function comfortably within acceptable parameters. The classroom represents a comfortable learning environment with clear expectations and recognition of what is considered appropriate and inappropriate behavior. The behavioral repertoire of each student and the group at large represents a conglomeration of positive classroom behaviors. Certain behaviors are considered prerequisites to other behaviors. In designing a behavior management system, the LD specialist must identify and delineate areas of emphasis to promote changes in students' behavior.

Understanding Classroom Management

What Is Classroom Management?

Many teachers equate classroom management with preserving order, maintaining control, or disciplining. Teachers are frequently judged to be effective managers if their pupils are quiet, attentive, industrious, and respectful (Froyen, 1988). Even though the observance of classroom work routine and orderly conduct in general are important outcomes of effective management practices, viewing classroom management in that narrow perspective is not particularly useful in clinical teaching. Classroom management can be better described as organizing and coordinating the learning environment and fostering students' efforts to achieve their own educational objectives in the classroom and in school in general. Classroom management is defined as "a distinct pattern of activities by which teachers establish and maintain conditions whereby individuals in the classroom can apply all their rational creative talents to the challenge of educational tasks. It is the development of an effective classroom organization, and a predictable system of relationships" (Johnson & Bany, 1970, p. 9). Classroom management involves handling the problems that affect instruction "by using processes that increase group unity and cooperation, and, in addition, strengthen each child's feeling of dignity, worth, and his satisfaction with classroom conditions" (Johnson & Bany, 1970, p. 3).

Classroom Management Functions

Classroom management is intrinsically related to the correlates of an effective learning environment. The two go hand in hand. Management activities are directed toward creating the best learning conditions for individual students and the group as a whole. Thus classroom management must be viewed from a broad perspective of providing an optimal learning environment in which students are engaged in active learning and which promotes their social and emotional development. It is an environment that develops behaviors that are personally fulfilling, productive, and socially acceptable (Walker & Shea, 1988). Froyen (1988) distinguishes between various management functions, content management, conduct management, and context management. The management functions for a classroom for students with learning disabilities include physical setup, content/instruction, atmosphere/context, and behavior/conduct (Figure 12–2).

Management of the physical environment involves the classroom physical setup, the classroom appearance, and the schedule of activities. Content management refers to the

Figure 12–2   Classroom Management Functions

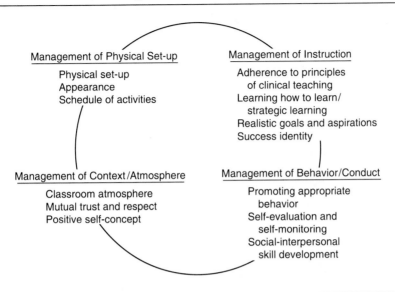

Management of Physical Set-up
- Physical set-up
- Appearance
- Schedule of activities

Management of Instruction
- Adherence to principles of clinical teaching
- Learning how to learn/ strategic learning
- Realistic goals and aspirations
- Success identity

Management of Context/Atmosphere
- Classroom atmosphere
- Mutual trust and respect
- Positive self-concept

Management of Behavior/Conduct
- Promoting appropriate behavior
- Self-evaluation and self-monitoring
- Social-interpersonal skill development

effective delivery of instruction through the application of principles of clinical teaching. Students with learning disabilities, like any other students, seek and respond well to an enriched learning environment in which the teachers and students are involved in active learning, with interesting materials and projects. Engaging students in meaningful learning activities at functional and interest levels that meet their needs is the best hedge against student discipline problems. Students who are successfully engaged in learning activities are likely to develop a positive attitude toward learning and a commitment to succeed. Classroom atmosphere/context management refers to the development of a classroom climate and atmosphere that promote the social and emotional growth of students. The development of a quality relationship between teachers and students based on mutual trust and respect is paramount to the development of such a positive classroom atmosphere. Behavior or conduct management relates to the development of an orderly classroom environment in which students are engaged in acceptable conduct. In a classroom for the learning disabled, the LD specialist should design a behavioral management system that helps to maintain a sound learning environment. Generally, behavior management involves management of expected student behavior, strategies for crisis and conflict resolution, and the development of affective behaviors and social skills.

Purposes and Goals of Effective Classroom Management
The purposes and goals of effective classroom management include the following:

1. To create a learning climate based on mutual trust and respect between the teacher and the students and among the students themselves

2. To develop active participation and commitment, and to establish a workable, pleasant social climate in the classroom
3. To cultivate a positive self-concept and success identity
4. To assist students in developing appropriate expected behavior in school with generalization to other settings in the community
5. To develop social skills and role identity as a function of the classroom as a social organization
6. To develop independent learners who can monitor and regulate their activities
7. To develop and nurture positive self-initiative
8. To develop and nurture leadership capabilities
9. To provide immediate feedback on appropriate expected student behavior and appropriate academic product
10. To develop self-control and reliance on intrinsic rather than extrinsic controls

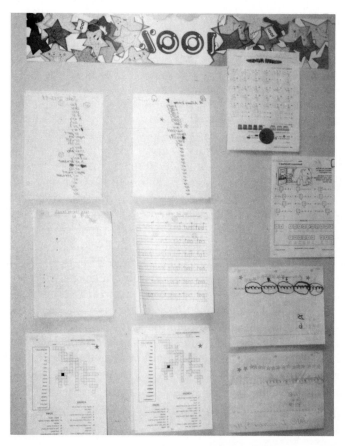

Reinforcing students for their positive performance by displaying their work and recognizing their efforts cultivates a positive self-concept and success identity.

Principles of Classroom Management

Classroom management is viewed as the provision of an appropriate educational environment conducive to learning that promotes the social and emotional well-being of students. The manager of a classroom environment promotes academic learning, social growth, and development. To ensure success, it is imperative to provide a learning environment and activities commensurate with the functional and interest levels of students. It is also essential to promote the development of self-regulation and self-control through student participation and effective utilization of executive control functions. The following principles represent the basis for a comprehensive classroom management plan for those with learning disabilities:

1. Teachers draw from each of the theoretical positions and management approaches that which is congruent with their educational philosophy and personality.
2. No matter how well designed and executed classroom management procedures may be, their effectiveness will be limited unless they relate to the individual child's needs and desires (Walker & Shea, 1988).
3. No single management approach and/or technique is effective under all conditions for all students.
4. Effective classroom management involves the deliberate teaching of classroom rules, procedures, routines, and contingencies that are consistently enforced throughout the daily activities (Jenson & Morgan, 1988).
5. The development of classroom rules must be based on mutually beneficial and reasonable guidelines designed primarily to develop a classroom environment in which both teachers and students maintain a high level of respect for each other (Froyen, 1988).
6. Students need to participate in setting and establishing classroom rules to accept the teacher's management system.
7. Students are encouraged to learn and apply democratic principles within the classroom and the school under teacher supervision and direction (Walker & Shea, 1988).
8. The classroom environment must be conducive to self-exploratory, intuitive, and self-directed learning.
9. The classroom environment provides freedom to explore, investigate, and implement age-appropriate social behaviors without adult interference within the social classroom organization.
10. Teachers must bestow affection and acceptance on all students. Students must feel that they are worthwhile individuals whose teacher cares for them.

Assessment of Behavior and Social-Emotional Difficulties

Assessment of student behavior and emotional difficulties is multifaceted and in-fluenced by the theoretical constructs underlying the nature of human behavior. Though emphasis varies with the behavior management approaches, the ultimate goal of behavior assessment is to aid the LD specialist in identifying student behaviors that interfere with the learning process and that manifest social-emotional difficulties. The psychodynamic approach employs projective techniques utilizing assessment tools specifically designed for that purpose, such as the Children Apperception Test (CAT), sentence completion, and human figure drawing. From the psychodynamic perspective, emphasis is placed on developing a case study through intensive interviews with an individual's "significant others." Through this intake interviewing, the clinician collects data relative to (a) the individual's development and significant events during each stage of development, (b) the major impact of traumatic events in the individual's past history, and (c) the individual's interpersonal relationships with children and adults in the environment. Thus psychoeducational, psychoneurological, and personality assessments are aspects of psychodynamic assessment. The behavioral and ecological approaches, which also include an in-depth case study, place more emphasis on direct measurement of the individual behavior in various settings through direct observations, employment of behavioral inventories, and rating scales.

Direct and systematic observations of a student's behavior in various settings provide the best source of information for the LD specialist. The teacher is concerned with an individual's behaviors that interfere with the learning process and general social-emotional adjustment. Assessment can employ both formal and informal measures—the use of behavioral inventories and checklists, direct and systematic observations of behavior, and student interviews. Attention to behavioral excesses and deficits as well as assets may be helpful in ascertaining an individual's behavioral repertoire and in developing a program for behavioral changes. (Also see chapter 8.) Typical assessment procedures for the LD specialist involve the use of behavior checklists and rating scales, and direct and systematic observations in both academic and nonacademic settings. Observation procedures must involve direct observation of behavior, analysis of antecedent conditions, and contingencies involved in various settings. More specifically, the teacher should determine what behavior is inappropriate; what environmental contingencies, including the setting demands, serve to maintain or reinforce that behavior; and what environmental changes, including the use of reinforcers, are needed to alter a student's behavior. (The reader is referred to the discussion of behavioral inventories, observational techniques, and the interview format in chapter 8.)

CLASSROOM MANAGEMENT APPROACHES AND STRATEGIES

Developing a Knowledge Base

The LD specialist confronted with a group of learning-disabled students is faced with practical problems of how to conduct the classroom effectively, develop an appropriate educational environment conducive to learning, and implement a classroom management approach to regulate, monitor, and control students' behavior.

Synthesizing the various approaches into one cohesive classroom management approach is essential for effective classroom management (Evans & Levine, 1982). Learning disabilities specialists are likely to choose classroom management systems that are congruent with their educational philosophy, with which they feel most comfortable, and that are most appropriate for their educational setting. Moreover, the selection of classroom management systems is influenced by the LD specialist's knowledge base of management approaches and practical knowledge of behavior management techniques. The theoretical perspectives most relevant to classroom management are psychodynamic theories, biophysical theories, behavioral theories, cognitive behavioral theories, and ecological theories.

The Psychodynamic Approach

The word *psychodynamic* is a combination of *psycho* meaning "mind" and *dynamic* meaning "energies." The psychodynamic approach derives many of its major concepts of personality development and behavior dynamics from Freudian psychoanalytic theory. Central to the pychodynamic theory is its emphasis on intrapsychic functioning and the internal dynamics of personality evolving from the personality system of the individual. Thus it views mental life and overt behavior as a result of (a) unconscious impulses whose basic configurations are set by an inherent biological disposition; (b) the interaction of the ego, the superego, and libidinal forces within the personality system of the individual; and (c) the events of the environment from birth on. From a Freudian perspective, the personality of an individual is molded by that individual's personality system, which is based on a closed energy system. This energy system—the libido or id—draws its energy from eros—the instinct of self-preservation and love opposed to self-punishing and self-destroying behavior. The personality system is made up of three major subsystems: the id, which is the energy-driven instinct; the ego, which seeks to procure objects in the real world for the gratification of the id while attempting to follow the reality principles; and the superego, which represents the norms and values of society and is at times referred to as the individual conscience (Rezmierski & Kotre, 1972). In a mentally healthy child, these three subsystems work in relative harmony with one another, meeting an individual's basic needs and desires. If, on the other hand, these subsystems are in conflict with one another, a child is said to be maladjusted (Reinert, 1980).

The psychodynamic approach emphasizes an individual's past history and experiences with the environment, and the development of personality and its disorders as a result of interaction with significant people and events in that individual's life. It further stresses observations of behavior and an understanding of the dynamics of these behaviors. Thus behavioral observations lead to interpretations of factors contributing to individual behavior patterns. The psychodynamic theory proposes a sequence of developmental stages through which children pass from birth through adulthood. Each of the stages is characterized by the interaction of the individual personality system with the demands of the environment in an attempt to gratify the individual's own needs. Freud and his contemporaries posited a sequence of psychosexual development beginning with the oral stage at the earliest period of life, continuing to an anal phase in early childhood, to the phallic stage of the preschooler, the latency period of the 6-year-old, and the genital stage beginning with the onset of puberty. Normal progression through these stages involves the gratification of the individual's desires within a reality principle. Abnormal progression, or maladjustment, is viewed in terms of the fixation of libidinal energy, the degree of gratification or deprivation of the individual's desires, and the existence of conflicts and their resolutions during the various stages of development (Rezmierski & Kotre, 1972).

The concept of development as an orderly progression from stage to stage is expanded by Erikson's (1950, 1963) model. Erikson's work incorporates all the constructs of the Freudian theory with a shift of emphasis from the id to the ego, from centering on the psychic process as totally internal to the individual interaction and adaptation to one's environment at each stage of psychosexual development. From his perspectives, the psychic processes are constantly being restructured, and restructuring depends in large measure upon the environment (Rezmierski & Kotre, 1972). Erikson posits eight distinct stages of psychosocial development through which we all progressively pass as we mature. Each stage is characterized by the emergence of crisis and its resolution and culminates in the assumption of new functions and responsibilities essential to normal development and adjustment in life (Rezmierski, Knoblock, & Bloom, 1982). The contributions of Erikson's theories to the understanding of the dynamics of personality development and disorders are significant for the LD specialist. His psychosocial model identifies the distinct stages of development, gives a sequence of development through which each person may potentially pass, speaks directly to the aspects of struggle that the environment affects, and indicates ways in which environmental resources might assist in the successful resolutions of conflict at each stage (Rezmierski et al., 1982).

The eight stages that Erikson delineates appear in his classic work *Childhood and Society* (1950, 1963):

1. Basic trust versus basic mistrust
2. Autonomy versus change and doubt
3. Initiative versus guilt
4. Industry versus inferiority
5. Identity versus identity diffusion
6. Intimacy versus isolation
7. Generativity versus stagnation
8. Ego integrity versus despair

Erikson's theory, which is basically a social interaction theory based on psychoanalytic principles, became attractive to many educators due to the commonsense description of the various stages of development from birth through death. Erikson combines the dynamics of personality development with the individual's interaction with the environment at various stages of development. Thus from this point of view, maladaptive behavior can be seen as an interaction between the individual personality system and events in the environment during various stages of development. It is through the analysis of the patterns of an individual's interaction with the environment that one comes to understand that individual's behavior.

The following constructs are critical to psychodynamic theories:

1. The individual's self-pattern evolves around significant biological predispositions (Cheney & Morse, 1972).
2. A predetermined developmental sequence of personality growth exists.
3. Frustration, anxiety, and psychological crisis play an important part in energizing growth.
4. Unconscious forces determine behavior.
5. All behavior is meaningful and purposeful.
6. Primary interpersonal relationships are of major significance in fostering or deterring growth of personality (Rezmierski & Kotre, 1972).
7. Previous life experience persists by becoming structurally integrated with present experience (Rezmierski et al., 1982).

The Application of Psychodynamic Theories to Education

The psychodynamic intervention procedures emphasize an individual's environment and life milieu and the role of the teacher as a therapeutic agent. The attention of the teacher is channeled toward an understanding of an individual's behavior with regard to that person's past history and experiences and the present elements in the environment that continue to foster this behavior. In order to understand each individual's development, from a psychodynamic point of view the LD specialist needs to realize that each person is a unique entity, that growth reflects a continuity of experience, that developmental stages are crucial, and that part of the growth process is the emergence of new goals and interests. The role of the LD specialist is to provide guidance and emotional support to students.

The educational environment facilitates the emotional development of the individual through the provision of a comfortable setting and conditions that meet that individual's needs, including the expression of emotions and the provision of successful experiences. A person's healthy development is characterized by (a) an attitude toward self that includes realistic self-awareness and the development of positive self-esteem; (b) the development of acceptable crisis coping mechanisms; (c) an ability to regulate one's own behavior; (d) meaningful interpersonal relationships; (e) curiosity, creativity, and expressiveness to cultivate individual resources and potential; and (f) an understanding of the world through effective utilization of cognitive and language skills (Cheney & Morse, 1972).

From a psychodynamic viewpoint, the LD specialist is engaged in the development of an educational environment that facilitates the total emotional growth of the individual. Emphasis is placed on case histories and an understanding of the dynamics of personality development. Psychodynamic types of interventions usually include the development of a learning environment that maximizes success, crisis intervention, the use of the life space interview, individual and group counseling, and family counseling and therapy.

Behavior Management Strategies
From Psychodynamic Perspectives

From a psychodynamic point of view, the synthesis of educational and therapeutic processes is essential for mental health development. The LD specialist is a significant therapeutic agent in promoting social-emotional growth, and the classroom environment is a therapeutic environment that fosters social and emotional development. Intervention in the classroom should provide a low-pressure, high-reward structure for learning and the elimination of crisis or stressful situations. Educational intervention facilitates the individual's expression in the form of catharsis, play therapy and/or art therapy, and other creative art media. Learning disabilities specialists are expected to be trained in the personality development of children, abnormal psychology, and therapeutic intervention strategies; to engage in various counseling roles; to provide play and art therapy; and to be skillful in crisis intervention and the life space interview.

Milieu Therapy

The concept of milieu therapy implies total involvement of the environment in which an individual lives. It is everything that is done to, with, for, or by a child in the overall educational environment (Redl, 1959b). Essentially, this approach attempts to utilize all the patient's daily experiences for therapeutic purposes. Thus all those who interact with a child throughout daily activities assume a therapeutic role. Milieu therapy procedures are usually associated with residential settings in which the service provider has control over a child's environment and is able to provide an environmental arrangement that has a therapeutic relevance.

Crisis Intervention

Crisis intervention provides emotional support to children in crisis. By and large, students are able to control and regulate their behavior. For some, though, coping with certain areas of the academic curriculum and social interaction becomes so intense that they tend to lose control over their own behavior, which may lead to temper tantrums. In such cases, children who have lost self-control become disruptive and present a serious problem beyond the teacher's ability to control and/or to manage. Usually, these children are removed from the classroom and sent to the principal's office or they may be suspended for an entire day. The teacher, through the process of crisis intervention, provides such students with the emotional support necessary to resume normal functioning. In settings that follow a psychodynamic approach, a crisis teacher is available on the school site and is called upon to provide crisis intervention to students whenever deemed necessary. Usually a crisis room, specially designed and equipped with necessary educational and therapeutic material, is set aside for crisis intervention. Students are taken to this room until they "cool down" or until they come to terms with the situation eliciting their uncontrolled behavior. Generally, a crisis room provides an environment in which students can relax and/or be structured to regain control over their behavior while receiving emotional support and a means of therapeutic release. Crisis rooms are supplied with rocking chairs, TVs, toys, sandboxes, and other items that help create a comfortable, nonthreatening environment for the release of anger, hostility, and frustration. Crisis teachers are trained in various crisis intervention approaches, including life space interviewing and play and art therapy.

Life Space Interview

Life space interviewing is an approach developed by Redl (1959a) as a method of handling children's life conflicts in a therapeutic way in proximity to their time and place and occurrence. Originally designed to be used in a residential setting with teachers trained for these procedures, the process can also be utilized effectively by the LD specialist. Although Redl (1959a) describes life space interviewing as a complex process involving various functions, its strength and utility lie within the concept. Students who appear in the classroom upset and unable to function due to some precipitating event are in need of immediate intervention that can provide them with needed emotional support. Likewise, students in crisis in and/or out of the classroom because of their inability to cope with the stressful demands of their environment or to resolve conflicts in an acceptable manner are equally in need of the LD specialist's emotional support. In simple terms, when students are emotionally so engulfed with stressful events in life that they cannot manage well on their own, the teacher must respond by providing emotional support to alleviate the stress caused by the situation. Redl (1959a) identifies two major goals of life space interviewing: emotional first aid on the spot and clinical exploitation of life events.

The teacher serves as a mediating agent between children and what life holds for them. A life space interview takes place in the natural setting and can be conducted by the LD specialist. The purpose of on-the-spot emotional first aid is to provide emotional support until children "cool off." Throughout the process, the teacher provides avenues to "drain off" students' frustration and provides support for the management of panic, fury, and guilt by helping children sort things out, decide between "good" and "bad" judgments, and return to normal functioning. In addition, the teacher helps students regulate their behavior by the consistent application of commonsense rules given on the spot. The goal is to maintain communication that expresses empathy and support with students throughout the process.

According to Redl (1959a), the second goal of life space interviewing is the clinical exploitation of life events for long-term therapeutic benefits. This is usually done when the situation is receptive to therapeutic changes. The process is aimed at helping students realize that inappropriate behaviors are not necessary to achieve a goal. It also helps them develop appropriate behaviors and coping mechanisms in line with society's values and norms. Other functions include helping children to remove preconceived notions and rationalizations that distort what really happened and to develop appropriate defense mechanisms. In order to maximize the effect of such procedures, according to Redl (1959a), a relevant central theme must be decided and agreed upon before the interview. These exploitation techniques must be used when time is available and the situation is amenable to therapeutic change. Not all events can or should be exploited. At the time of an occurrence, the teacher must make the decision if and how the event can be used (Reinert, 1980).

Life space interviewing is essentially an intervention strategy for students in a time of crisis or potential crisis who need emotional support. It is on-the-scene, impromptu talks about specific troublesome incidents (Clarizio & McCoy, 1983). The purpose of life space interviewing is to give individuals who face momentary difficulties appropriate support to help them return to their normal selves. The teacher may also attempt to work through some long-range goals with children. Sometimes it is difficult to know which of the two broad objectives of life space interviewing is to be addressed, and thus in most instances, the two are combined (Clarizio & McCoy, 1983). The primary function of life space interviewing is to provide emotional support: developing a positive self-concept and feelings of worthiness and pride while keeping an individual's perspectives within reality. Although the procedures have been designed for use in clinical settings, the LD specialist can effectively utilize life space interviewing as a means of providing emotional first aid to students and developing a life-long appropriate and acceptable behavioral repertoire. At times, the utilization of life space interviewing may be problematic for the LD specialist because of environmental constraints and lack of resources. Conducting life space interviewing requires a quiet area and the full attention of the teacher, which is not always possible in our schools.

Physical Restraints

The LD specialist is to be aware that sometimes some students, specifically those with more severe behavior problems, may lose control, exhibit aggressive, threatening behavior toward others and/or themselves, and/or exhibit behavior tantrums. On such occasions, physical restraints are necessary in order to preserve the welfare of the individual and the group. Losing one's control can be very frightening to a person. A supportive and empathetic physical restraint, with encouragement and verbal communication from the teacher in a calm voice, can reassure the student. The teacher may communicate to the student, "You are safe, I will protect you, I will not let you harm yourself" (Walker & Shea, 1988, p. 179). A discussion of the incidence using elements of life space interviewing should follow when the child regains control.

The Biophysical/Psychogenic Approach

The biophysical model is a disease model that presupposes that the problem of pathology lies within the individual. It assumes that emotional difficulties arise directly from constitutional factors resulting from genetic influences, developmental irregularities, neurological damage, and biochemical irregularities. Included in this perspective is the concept of an "inherited predisposition" and a "biogenetic triggering system" that predetermine and affect an individual's emotional well-being and disorders. From a biophysical perspective, a positive relationship exists between children's physical health and their emotional well-being. It is therefore essential to conduct a comprehensive medical evaluation that includes vision, hearing, body chemistry, and neurology (Reinert & Huang, 1987).

The Application of the Biophysical/ Psychogenic Approach to Education

The biophysical/psychogenic model has been mostly applied in medically oriented settings. The major purpose of interventions in this model is to decrease the frequencies of inappropriate behavior or to change behavior that interferes with learning through medically related interventions, such as drug therapy, nutritional therapy, and megavitamin therapy. The role of the LD specialist, from a biophysical perspective, is somewhat limited. The primary role is the support of medical interventions by monitoring the effect of drug therapy, megavitamin therapy, and nutritional interventions through careful observations of students' behavior. In addition, the LD specialist can play a significant role in identifying health problems, including loss of hearing, nearsightedness, and even some metabolic disorders such as hypoglycemia that may manifest themselves in behavioral changes.

The Behavioral Approach

The basic tenets of the behavioral approach are not new; their roots can be traced to ideas incorporated in the hedonistic philosophy and to the empiricists who developed laws and/or principles that provided the basic ideas for early behavior theories. Definitive experimental evidence for the principles of the behavioral approach have been produced by Thorndike (1911, 1913), J. B. Watson (1913, 1919, 1928), Watson and Rayner (1920), Jones (1924), Hull (1951), Tolman (1933), and Skinner (1938, 1953, 1961, 1966, 1968). The terms *behavior modification, behavior therapy,* and *applied behavior analysis* have been used to refer to behavioral procedures.

The behavior modification approach employs different kinds of positive and negative reinforcers in a variety of tasks and situations. This is an attempt to determine how reinforcement variables may be most efficiently utilized to influence the behavior of the individual toward more effective functioning, and to initiate and strengthen desired academic and social behaviors through behavior modification techniques based on the operant conditioning paradigm.

The behavior modification strategies focus on overt subject responses and stimuli that control these responses. According to Hewett (1967), rather than viewing an emotionally disturbed child as a victim of psychic conflicts, the behavioral approach "concentrates on bringing the overt behavior of the child into line with minimum standards for learning [by] [l]engthening attention span, promoting successful accomplishment of carefully graded tasks, and providing a learning environment with gratification and structure for the child" (p. 459). The behavior modifier has three main concerns:

1. What behavior patterns are maladaptive and require change?
2. What environmental contingencies currently support the subject's behavior?
3. What environmental changes, usually reinforcing stimuli, may be employed to alter the subject's behavior? (Franks, 1969; Ullmann & Krasner, 1965)

Applied Behavioral Analysis

In recent years, the term *applied behavioral analysis* has been preferred to the early term *behavior modification*. Although earlier behavior modification applications were typically directed toward individuals' inappropriate and incompetent behaviors, recently principles of behavior modification have been used with a wide range of behaviors in institutions, educational settings, communities, homes, and many other situations. These approaches to behavior change procedures are now addressed under the term *applied behavioral analysis* (Cullinan, Epstein, & Kauffman, 1982). Applied behavioral analysis generally involves human efforts to modify specific human behavior.

The Application of the Behavioral Approach in the Classroom

The application of behavioral approaches in classroom settings has been extensively reviewed in the literature, and research supports the employment of behavioral approaches in classroom management for students with learning and behavioral disorders (Kazdin, 1982; Lysakowski & Walberg, 1981; Nelson & Rutherford, 1985; O'Leary & Drabman, 1971). From a behavioristic point of view, such application of behavioral theory seems logical. The behavioristic model represents a coherent and pragmatic way to explain behavioral disorders and the basis for successful intervention and treatment approaches. The assumptions underlying the behavioristic approach in the classroom can be summarized as follows:

1. Most human behaviors are not automatically elicited but rather are omitted by the individual in response to circumstances. These behaviors, called "operants," are controlled by the environmental events that follow them, that is, reinforcers/consequences (Cullinan et al., 1982).
2. All behaviors (maladaptive as well as normal) are learned and therefore can be changed through appropriate learning experiences (Basualdo & Basualdo, 1980).
3. Normal, healthy, or desirable behavior may be acquired to replace or supplement undesirable behavior by consistently applying established principles of learning (Swanson & Reinert, 1984).
4. Behavior modification is an attempt to change a certain type of behavior using various procedures that either strengthen or weaken the operant behavior (Glavin, 1974).
5. In applied behavioral analysis/behavior modification, "the unit of analysis is almost always molecular; the behavior of an individual is defined and measured in small, discrete units of observable behavior" (Rogers-Warren, 1984, p. 287).

The behavioristic approaches emphasize arranging environmental stimuli, often reinforcing events or contingencies that serve to strengthen or weaken the future likelihood of operant behaviors. They usually employ behavior management approaches that include contingency contracting, token economy, and modeling. Though research indicates that punishment may be as powerful a change agent as positive reinforcement, punishment is poorly understood, and its effect may be harmful to students.

Behavior Management Strategies
From Behavioristic Perspectives

From a behavioristic point of view, the teacher is a behavior analyst whose task is to identify student behaviors that require change, the environmental contingencies that currently support these behaviors, and the selection of management procedures, usually involving the use of reinforcers to produce the desired behavioral changes. Teachers are expected to be trained in applied behavioral analysis, including behavioral assessment and shaping procedures. They are expected to use behavioral procedures such as contingency contracting, token economy, time-out, and response cost procedures.

Basic Concepts

The following are concepts critical to behavioristic approaches:

Reinforcement. An event or a stimulus that alters the future probability of occurrence of the behavior that immediately precedes it.

Primary reinforcers. Stimuli or events that satisfy the individual's primary (biological) needs, and serve as consequence to increase the probability of behaviors immediately preceding them, such as food and water (Cooper, Heron, & Heward, 1987).

Secondary reinforcers (or second order reinforcers). Those initially neutral stimuli that are associated with primary reinforcers and acquire reinforcing properties of their own, for example, tokens (Kameya, 1972).

Positive reinforcement. A stimulus or an event that increases the probability of occurrence of the behavior that immediately precedes its presentation.

Negative reinforcement. An aversive stimulus that increases the future probability of occurrence of a behavior that immediately precedes its termination.

Punishment. The presentation of an aversive stimuli and/or the withdrawal of positive reinforcement following the behavior. The future probability of occurrence of the behavior will decrease with the termination of a positive reinforcer as well as with the application of a negative reinforcer (punishment) (Kameya, 1972).

Extinction. The process of removing the contingent stimuli that maintain the behaviors, hence reducing the frequency of those behaviors.

Shaping. "The reinforcement of successive approximation of a desired behavior" (Sabatino, Sabatino, & Lester, 1983, P. 60).

Reinforcement schedules. The patterns of timing of the delivery of reinforcers following emission of desired responses. When reinforcers are delivered on a continuous basis, that is, upon the emission of each desired response, it is referred to as continuous reinforcement schedule (CRF). Reinforcements that follow some but not all desired responses are called intermittent reinforcement schedule (Alberto & Troutman, 1986).

Intermittent reinforcement schedules are of two types: ratio schedules, in which reinforcement is dispensed upon a number of responses emitted, and interval schedules, in which reinforcers are dispensed upon the occurrence of appropriate response and the passage of time. These schedules can be either fixed (after a set number of responses or a specific time lapse), or variable (desired behaviors are reinforced on the average of specific responses and/or the average length of time).

Shaping Procedures

The teacher's knowledge of shaping procedures is crucial to implementation of a sound behavioral approach in the classroom. Shaping procedures are based on the method of successive approximation, that is, successive, gradual progression of desired behavior leading to the ultimate target behavior. In shaping procedures, the teacher uses reinforcements of successive behaviors that approximate the target behavior. The process involves the following: (a) identification of the target behavior, (b) the breaking down of the target behavior to a chain of successive behaviors and the steps toward the terminal behavior usually involving task analysis procedures, (c) identification and selection of effective reinforcers, (d) selection of reinforcement schedules and a recording format, (e) selection of backup reinforcers and a reinforcement menu, and (f) implementation of shaping of behaviors that approximate the terminal behavior. As with any other reinforcing procedures, the teacher should consider varying reinforcement schedules in order to develop behaviors that are more resistive to extinction and less dependent on extrinsic reinforcers.

Contingency Contracting

Contingency contracting grew out of Premack's (1965) principle that a high-probability response can be used to reinforce a low-probability response. Homme (1974) translated the Premack principle to what he called "Granma's Law": "First you finish your dinner and then you get your dessert"; or more applicable to the classroom, "First you complete three pages of arithmetic and then you may have 10 minutes of free time." A contracting procedure involves a contract negotiated between the students and the teacher—a mutually advantageous agreement. In contingency contracting, "the target is improvement in the student's behavior, and the strategy involves making explicit the conditions under which improved behavior would be recognized and reinforced. Contracting, then, is a covenant that makes high-probability behavior contingent on the performance of low-probability behavior" (Ninness & Glenn, 1988, pp. 59–60).

Contingency Contracting Procedures

Contingency contracting can be an effective strategy in promoting classroom management. Developing and carrying out an effective behavioral contract requires a great deal of teacher's effort and a considerable sensitivity to students' needs (Ninness & Glenn, 1988). In a contingency contracting, the student is viewed as an equal partner in developing the contract, in monitoring and regulating goal attainment, and ultimately in carrying out commitments. Thus, contracting procedures involve the student's participation in analyzing the factors that will contribute to the improvement of behavior and/or task completion and in establishing the goals. Contracting agreement nourishes the assumption of the student's responsibilities for appropriate behavior, the regulations of such behaviors, and the evaluation of the outcome of such efforts.

Behavioral contracting adheres to principles of applied behavioral analysis and behavior modification. The LD specialist has to be skillful in designing the contract and developing environmental contingencies that will ensure successful completion of the contract. The contract should include only those behaviors which are within the student's range of success. In addition, the language used in the contract should be simple and concise (Figure 12–3). Contracting procedures can be carried out with students of all ages, from primary school through young adulthood, but care should be given to the format and age appropriateness.

Although a contracting procedure is most often a contract between student and teacher, it can also serve as a form of communication between school and home. Thus the teacher who wants to make parents aware of a student's activities in school

Figure 12–3   Sample Student Contract

Contract

I, Student's name , do hereby agree to do the following: (List in specific terms the behavior to be performed and specify completion date and the performance criteria.)

_____

_____

_____

_____

In exchange, I will receive the following:
(State the reinforcement in precise terms.)

_____

_____

_____

_____

Signed, sealed, and witnessed this _____ day of _____ , 19 ___ .

_____
(Student's signature)

_____
(Teacher's signature)

Source: From © 1988, Abraham Ariel, Ph.D.

may, with the student's agreement, ask a parent to sign the contract upon its completion. Guidelines for contingency contracting are as follows:

1. Determine how contracting procedures are to be utilized with students and how to incorporate them into the classroom management procedures and grading practices.
2. Introduce the concept of contingency contracting to students, including how it will be used (incorporated into grading practices and report cards).
3. Establish the necessary conditions for contracting arrangements/ interviews to include physical setting, contract form, and monitoring procedures.
4. Determine the general goal and outcome of the contact. Delineate desired behaviors and outcomes.
5. Specify the contingencies (reward and reinforcement).
6. Establish time lines for contract completion and monitoring of ongoing progress.
7. Provide prompts and encouragement throughout the course of the contract.

Token Economy Systems

Generally, teachers use reinforcers in the classroom, that is, they present pleasurable consequences as rewards for desired academic and social performance and aversive consequences following inappropriate behavior they wish to decrease (Ariel, 1971). To induce desirable behaviors, these reinforcers must be made contingent upon desired behaviors, but in a classroom situation, this is not always possible. Therefore, the LD specialist must use reinforcement procedures that temporarily supplement the natural contingencies, employing conditioned reinforcers (tokens) backed up by reinforcing objects and events.

The classroom might be viewed as a microeconomy in which objects or events reinforce desirable classroom behaviors (Ninness & Glenn, 1988). In a token economy system, students earn tokens following the emission of desired responses. Stars, check marks, points, happy faces, and credit slips may be used as tokens. They effectively bridge the time gap between desired responses and the delivery of reinforcements. Tokens facilitate the reinforcement of desired responses at any time and without delay (Kameya, 1972). According to Ninness and Glenn (1988), "The use of a token economy in a classroom can teach children some extremely important concepts as well as provide behavioral procedures that effectively increase the rate of productive and personally satisfying behavior and decrease the rate of destructive and inherently unproductive behavior" (p. 200). The effect of the token system is directly related to the nature of backup reinforcers. Backup reinforcers can be considered as tangible reinforcers, such as candy or gum, and nontangible reinforcers, such as field trips, projects, and activities.

Implementing a Token Economy

The following are suggested steps and procedures for developing and implementing a token economy system:

1. Ascertain general classroom conditions and general characteristics of students.
2. Determine procedures to implement: (a) management of the environmental setting, (b) management of instructional elements, and (c) context management.
3. Determine behavior management procedures to be implemented in the classroom and consider how to integrate these procedures with environmental, instructional, and context management.
4. Prepare all necessary materials connected with token economy, such as assignment sheets, charts, stars, tokens, behavior management recording sheets, and backup reinforcer menus.
5. Determine the behaviors to be reinforced, as well as the consequences for inappropriate behaviors.
6. Clarify the conditions under which positive reinforcers and negative consequences/reinforcers are to be dispensed for appropriate and inappropriate behaviors.
7. Determine the value of reinforcers/tokens per activity and/or specific students' behavior (follow the rule of thumb discussed later in this chapter).
8. Determine a schedule of reinforcement.
9. Determine when students will exchange reinforcers/tokens for backup reinforcers.
10. Determine how to individualize management systems by incorporating contingency contracting and varying the schedule of reinforcement to meet individual students' needs.
11. Decide how to incorporate the token economy system with the daily schedule and activities of the students.
12. Determine how to record the tokens and how to keep an ongoing ledger of the tokens earned by each student.
13. Determine monitoring and regulation procedures, including how to dispense reinforcers, use checklists or tokens, and record the reinforcers.
14. Determine how to involve the students in recording and monitoring the reinforcers.
15. Determine how to introduce management systems to the students, keeping in mind active student participation related to classroom rules, routines, and establishment of management system.
16. Begin implementing management systems.
17. Monitor and regulate the effect of the management systems.

Graduated Reinforcement System: Token Economy in a Continuum

A behavioral reinforcement system can be utilized with individuals with various levels of behavioral competencies. At a lower level of performance, Level 1, the behavior of an individual is typified by a single response to environmental stimuli (Ariel, 1971, 1972), characteristic of students with severe behavior difficulties who do not respond to appropriate stimuli as defined by the teacher. These students have a difficult time attending to a task and demand almost complete attention from the teacher. They are unable to work in group situations and have not yet established the relationship between cause and effect. At this level of a token economy management, referred to as the "response" level (Ariel, 1971, 1972), the student is given a contingent reinforcement for each response in the academic as well as social areas (continuous reinforcement schedule). The reinforcement is given in the form of a token (check marks) or a tangible reinforcer such as candy. At the end of each session, the student and the teacher tally the check marks, and the teacher inserts a written comment in the space provided on the work record sheet. The student is provided with a daily work record sheet (Figure 12–4).

At a higher level of behavior management system, Level 2, also referred to as "response chaining," students are reinforced for a sequence of responses. At this level, students emit a set of individual S-R's in a sequence to form more complex responses. These students are able to attend to a task and to work in small groups. They are also able to complete given assignments and shift from one activity to another. The students are provided with a daily work schedule sheet (Figure 12–5) corresponding to the daily work record (Figure 12–6). The daily work schedule indicates what is expected of the students. It describes the daily classroom activities and the weight of reinforcers for each activity. The daily work record is the actual recording and tabulating sheet that students keep in their folder or on their desk. Each student is given contingent reinforcements upon completion of the task in the form of tokens (points or credit slips). Total effort, in any area, carries the maximum amount of points allowed for that area. For example, if students complete all the daily math assignments and work to the best of their ability, they receive the maximum amount of points for math, even though they made some mistakes. Students are also reinforced intermittently using fixed or variable ratio or interval schedules

Figure 12–4 Daily Work Record Card

Student's name _____	Date _____	
		Teacher's comments
_____		_____
_____		_____
_____		_____
_____		_____
_____		_____
	Total _____	

Source: From © 1988, Abraham Ariel, Ph.D.

Figure 12–5   Daily/Weekly Work Schedule

Column number and activity	Maximum points
1. Reading skills and comprehension	5
2. Spelling	5
3. Language	5
4. Math	5
5. Social studies and/or science	5
6. Effort	5
7. Student evaluation	5
8. Expected student behavior	
a. Cooperation	5
b. Listens attentively	5
c. Follows instructions independently	5
d. Is thoughtful of the rights and feeling of others	5
e. Returns to seat and gets back to work	5
9. Special projects completed on time	5
10. Group activity	5
11. Individual goal	10

Source: From © 1988, Abraham Ariel, Ph.D.

of reinforcement for appropriate behavior, effort, and other behavior areas indicated on the students' daily work schedule. At a higher level of functioning, the teacher may dispense tokens contingent on accuracy of work, neatness, or other elements considered important. All earned tokens are recorded by the teacher on the students' daily work record sheet immediately upon completion of the activity. In addition, students are reinforced by the teacher's approval expressed orally and/or in writing. For example, the teacher may say to a student, "That was excellent, Jim!" and may also write, "Good work, Jim!" in the space provided for teacher's comments. At the end of each day, students tally their points and credit slips. At a still higher level, students are asked to evaluate their total daily work and are reinforced for realistic self-evaluation.

Establishing Backup Reinforcers and Developing Reinforcement Menus
Although the principles of establishing a token economy are the same for all age levels, variations in its implementation are necessary in order to meet the needs of students at various stages of development. The success or failure of a token system lies in the values of the tokens assumed and the nature of the backup reinforcers. The LD specialist should be careful in determining the weight of reinforcement, that is,

Figure 12-6 Daily/Weekly Coded Work Record

Date	1	2	3	4	5	6	7	8	9	10	11	TOTAL	Poor	Fair	Good
													Poor	Fair	Good
													Poor	Fair	Good
													Poor	Fair	Good
													Poor	Fair	Good

Student's name _____   Week _____

Evaluation

Source: From © 1988, Abraham Ariel, Ph.D.

Figure 12–8   Daily/Weekly Coded Work Record

Student's name _____							Week _____		
Date	**1**	**2**	**3**	**. . . .**	**10**	**Total**	**Evaluation**		
Accuracy							Poor	Fair	Good
Neatness									
Completion									
Effort and ind. tasks									
Evaluation									
Accuracy							Poor	Fair	Good
Neatness									
Completion									
Effort and ind. tasks									
Evaluation									
Accuracy							Poor	Fair	Good
Neatness									
Completion									
Effort and ind. tasks									
Evaluation									
Accuracy							Poor	Fair	Good
Neatness									
Completion									
Effort and ind. tasks									
Evaluation									
Accuracy							Poor	Fair	Good
Neatness									
Completion									
Effort and ind. tasks									
Evaluation									

Source: From © 1988, Abraham Ariel, Ph.D.

Figure 12–9 Daily/Weekly Coded Work Record

Student's name _____							Week _____		
Date	**1**	**2**	**3**	**4**	**. . . .**	**Total**	**Evaluation**		
Accuracy							Poor	Fair	Good
Neatness									
Completion									
Effort and ind. tasks									
Evaluation									
Self-reinforcement									
Accuracy							Poor	Fair	Good
Neatness									
Completion									
Effort and ind. tasks									
Evaluation									
Self-reinforcement									
Accuracy							Poor	Fair	Good
Neatness									
Completion									
Effort and ind. tasks									
Evaluation									
Self-reinforcement									
Accuracy							Poor	Fair	Good
Neatness									
Completion									
Effort and ind. tasks									
Evaluation									
Self-reinforcement									
Accuracy							Poor	Fair	Good
Neatness									
Completion									
Effort and ind. tasks									
Evaluation									
Self-reinforcement									

Source: From © 1988. Abraham Ariel, Ph.D.

teacher reinforces students for matched self-reinforcement and matched self-evaluation using both tokens and verbal expressions. Subsequently, students are advanced to a higher level of management in which they are provided with assignments in conventional ways and reinforced with conventional reinforcements.

The application of self-regulation and self-reinforcement techniques can be very effective, particularly with adolescents. Both theory and experience in the classroom suggest that students at this level differ from primary grade students in their response to the application of operant techniques. The effect of a token reinforcement system is less intense and less lasting (Ariel, 1971, 1972). This could possibly be explained by the fact that the operation of intelligence of adolescents is markedly different from that of primary school children. The thinking of the latter is closely tied to the concrete situation present in their immediate experience; they are primarily concerned with tangible objects that can be manipulated and are subject to real action (Piaget, 1966, 1967). In contrast, adolescents have become capable of reflective thinking and self-evaluation, and are able to abandon the concrete in favor of the abstract (Piaget, 1966). Adolescents can look at themselves with some objectivity and evaluate themselves with respect to personality, intelligence, and appearance (Elkind, 1970). It is this important change in adolescents' cognitive functioning that must be taken into account in the application of classroom management techniques at this level.

The teaching of behavioral self-control is aimed at developing self-control in gradual, progressive procedures involving self-regulation and self-reinforcement. Students are taught to evaluate their performance in terms of school demands. This is done by developing and operating a hierarchical reinforcement system in which the reinforcement methodology is shifted according to students' behavioral functional level (Ariel, 1971, 1972). By means of a continuous self-evaluation and feedback mechanism, individuals move from total dependency upon extrinsic reinforcers, originally required to motivate the desired academic and social behavior, to self-direction and intrinsic motivation.

Metacognitive Behavior Management Strategies

The metacognitive approach to classroom management is a natural outcome of the integration of cognitive behavior modification and mediation learning within an information-processing paradigm. The metacognitive approach makes the basic assumption that individuals want to exhibit behavior patterns that are commensurate with expectations and their abilities, and that, in fact, they want to be and can be in control of their own behavior and can be active participants in the course of developing intervention procedures.

The purpose of a metacognitive approach to classroom management is to

1. Develop students' sensitivity to acceptable behaviors and coping strategies
2. Develop students' awareness of the factors contributing to their behavior and the consequences of various behaviors
3. Develop individual awareness that different behaviors are appropriate for different situations

4. Develop behavioral strategies for successful behavior management in school and in life
5. Develop individuals' self-regulation, monitoring, and self-evaluation of behavioral output through the use of the control executive system

From a metacognitive perspective, individuals are guided (a) to develop their sensitivity to what constitutes acceptable and appropriate behaviors and the need to exhibit behaviors in line with societal expectations and norms; (b) to increase their awareness of specific aspects of behaviors, what behaviors are appropriate for what situations, and how these behaviors are related to their own social validity; (c) to attain strategies for behavioral coping and conflict resolutions, and effective behavioral strategies appropriate to various situations; and (d) to utilize the control executive functions in the execution, regulation, and evaluation of their behavioral outcomes.

Applying the metacognitive approach to classroom management requires students' participation in all aspects of that management. It includes development of group management procedures through classroom rules, consequences, and feedback modes, and identification of the expected student behavior patterns conducive to an effective learning environment. The learning process analysis, which was discussed in depth in chapter 6, serves as the vehicle through which aspects of classroom management are discussed, analyzed, delineated, and ultimately translated to what is necessary in terms of individuals' behavior or strategies in order to function as students in the classroom. This process highlights the factors needed for a classroom environment in which all students can live and participate in a positive and happy manner. Students may bring factors directly related to the development of an optimal classroom environment, including the physical setup, the seating arrangement, the availability of self-corrected material, the ability to follow assignments, the need for clarity in the daily schedule, the daily assignments for each student, and the need for monitoring and use of a feedback mechanism by the teacher. In addition, students may suggest basic rules that can facilitate their daily living within the classroom setting.

Similarly, through learning (behavioral) process analysis, students are guided to analyze behaviors that interfere with individual functioning in school and in life, to examine antecedents to these behaviors, and to realistically evaluate their consequences. Through this process, the students and the teacher can analyze as follows:

- What does it take to be a good student?
- What student behavior is expected in the classroom?
- What student behavior is expected outside the classroom?
- What student behavior is expected in terms of facilitating a group interaction in the classroom?

For example, in a small group discussion in an upper elementary classroom, the teacher and the students mutually selected and prioritized the following target behaviors as required expected student behavior in the classroom:

Attend school regularly.
Be on time to all your classes.

Have all your materials ready for all your classes.
Follow the teacher's instructions.
Ask for help when you do not understand.

These statements are converted to "I" statements, which represent the students' metacognitive strategies for expected student behavior:

I attend school regularly.
I am on time to all my classes.
I have all my materials ready for all my classes.
I follow the teacher's instructions.
I ask for help when I do not understand.

Following these steps, self-regulating, monitoring, and evaluative procedures and format are established. A token economy, contingency contracting, or other reinforcing procedures can be effectively incorporated with this approach. Figure 12–10 shows a sample strategy implementation and monitoring sheet for metacognitive strategies for expected student behavior.

The therapeutic effect of the learning process analysis is evident as it assists the individual to examine the environmental factors that contribute to, maintain, or interfere with appropriate desired behaviors and individual selection of target behaviors for change. Thus a metacognitive approach considers an individual's behavior repertoire from various perspectives. It recognizes the dynamics of behavior— that it can be learned or unlearned and that it in fact involves behavioral task analysis and cognitive restructuring.

The Ecological Approach

The ecological approach attempts to integrate concepts from various perspectives of psychodynamic, biophysical, and behavioristic theories. The ecological model emphasizes the ecology—the study of the structure and function of nature, the description of the composition of living and non-living things, and the range of conditions under which the population lives. The organism and the environment represent structural components, and their interaction represents functional components (Feagans, 1972). Furthermore, the environmental patterns are defined as ecological niches and represent the objective match between individuals and their environment. A concept central to ecological theory is the "ecosystem," which is defined as the "interaction system comprised of living things together with their non-living habitat. . . . In its fundamental aspects, an ecosystem invokes the cumulation, transformation, and accumulation of energy and matter through the medium of living things and their activities" (Evans, 1956 as cited by Feagans, 1972, p. 330).

The ecological theory views individuals' behavior within the context of their ecosystem. People are said to live within a set of ecosystems that are linked with one another, influencing the formulation of individual interactive behaviors. From an ecological point of view, individual disturbances are viewed as disturbances within

Figure 12–10   Strategy Implementation and Monitoring Sheet for Expected Student Behavior

PLEDGE FOR SUCCESS: STRATEGY USE

Set 1: Expected Student Behaviors

Skills/Behaviors I Need to Learn:	How Will I Do It? (Strategies)	How Am I Doing? Key: √−; √; √+;					
		M	T	W	Th	F	Overall
Basic Elements of Success in School	I attend school regularly.						
	I am on time to all my classes.						
	I have all my materials ready for all my classes.						
	I follow teacher instructions.						
	I ask for help when I don't understand.						
Individualized Goal							

Teacher's Comments:

Student's Comments: This Is the Way I See Myself

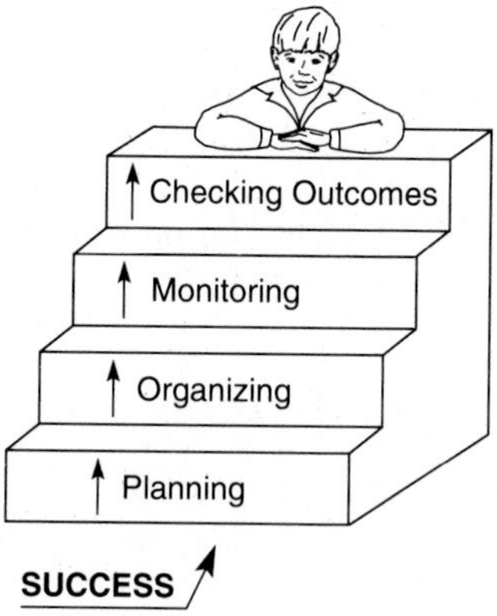

Checking Outcomes

Monitoring

Organizing

Planning

SUCCESS

Source: From *Learning to Learn: Metacognition Student Handbook, Level II, Book 1* by A. Ariel, 1987. Unpublished manuscript, California State University, Los Angeles. Reprinted by permission.

the ecosystem that reflect a mismatch between circumstances and individuals, or a lack of "goodness of fit." Disturbances are not centered within individuals. It is, rather, the interaction between idiosyncratic individuals and their unique environment that produces the disturbance (Feagans, 1972). The interaction among the many variables within the environment and individuals is seen as the most important factor in behavioral disturbances. From an ecological perspective, the goal is to develop an ecosystem with a state of equilibrium in which there is a balance of forces. However, when there is "a rapid change or an unbalance of forces caused by a catastrophe or any other intrusion into the system the result is often disequilibrium" (Feagans, 1972, p. 336).

The ecological model assumes that an individual child's disturbance is attributed to an interaction between the child and her or his environment, that interventions must alter the ecological system, that ecological interventions are eclectic, that interventions in a complex system may have anticipated consequences, and that each interaction between child and setting is unique (Swap, Prieto, & Harth, 1982).

The Application of the Ecological Approach in the Classroom

Although the basic theoretical assumptions in the ecological perspective make a great deal of sense, the ecological model nevertheless lacks a methodological and systematic approach to explore the fit or match between an individual child and a given setting. Thus the ecological model has turned to the behavioral approach to learn and study individuals' behavior and maladjustment from an ecological perspective, and as a result, the ecobehavioral approach has emerged (Rogers-Warren, 1984). The ecological and the behavioral approaches are aligned and share the assumption that behavior is determined by its environmental context. The "ecobehavioral analyst is a hybrid form of behavioral analyst resulting from the incorporation of the broader definitions of behavior and environment found in ecological psychology within the functional analysis of behavior for therapeutic purposes characteristic of applied behavior analysis" (Rogers-Warren, 1984, p. 287). Ecological psychologists emphasize studying the educational environment and its effect on children's behavior, observing children's behavior in natural settings and in meaningful ways, and measuring effects of the environment on behavior (Swap et al., 1982).

Behavior Management Strategies From Ecological Perspectives

The primary goal of ecological interventions is to restore the "functionality and vitality to the ecosystem" (Paul, 1987, p. 20) of which a child is a part. Thus the purpose of the intervention approach is to deal with the child and the setting in order to promote harmony or equilibrium, "a better fit between the child and the social setting" (Paul, 1987, p. 20).

The emphasis in the intervention approaches from an ecological perspective is on altering the system in which the behaviors occur. Assessment must view the total system—the characteristics of the child and the setting and the points of discord (discourse) between the two. Assessments from an ecological perspective involve assessment of behavior in various settings. Wallace and Larsen (1978) stated that in the classroom ecosystem, the role of the teacher is to assess "those situational factors that may, in fact, have initiated or, at least, maintained the behavioral patterns that are of concern to the teacher" (p. 101). They suggested that "at a minimal level the teacher should be prepared to assess pupil-teacher interaction, pupil-curriculum 'match', peer relationships, school and classroom climate, and extraneous variables existing outside the school setting" (p. 102). In the classroom, the application of an ecological approach is exemplified by the ecobehavioral approach. According to

Rogers-Warren (1977), ecobehavioral-based intervention includes (a) a comprehensive definition of the behavioral and its environmental contingencies, leading to the identification of the target behavior; (b) assessment of the various elements of the physical setting and the role they play in relation to the target behavior; (c) identification of environmental contingencies and consequences for behavior; (d) identification of the program constraints, which include the people available to help carry out the program and the resources available; and (e) delineation of necessary environmental rearrangements that might facilitate the behavioral interventions.

In the process of behavioral change, the teacher must bear in mind individuals' behavioral patterns that have developed over the years. Although the patterns may be unacceptable to others, they have been and continue to be more or less successful for the survival of the children. Thus children cannot and should not be forced to immediately relinquish their coping mechanism or survival behaviors and begin adapting to new and more productive ways of coping (Walker & Shea, 1988). Behavioral changes and their adoption by children require time and energy, and the teacher must be patient and must focus on children's progress in small segments rather than on the end goal (Walker & Shea, 1988). "Miracles and instant cures are few in number and difficult to observe when they do occur" (Walker & Shea, 1988, p. 9).

Social Skills Training (SST)

Understanding the competences involved in affective and social skill development is essential for functioning in a complex social context. In addition, affective and social functioning have been shown to have a major impact on both school adjustment and academic achievement (Forman, 1987). Problems in social skills are more debilitating than academic problems and hinder the ability to succeed in life (Alley & Deshler, 1979; Carter & Sugai, 1988; Kronick, 1978; Vaughn, 1987; Vaughn & McIntosh, 1989). Schumaker and Hazel (1988) defined social skills "as any cognitive function or overt behavior in which an individual engages while interacting with another person or persons" (p. 112). The learning disabled are often characterized as exhibiting social skills deficits (McKinney, 1989; Schumaker & Ellis, 1982): They usually experience difficulties with perception and expression of language in social situations (Bryan, 1979; Cicourel, 1981; Donahue, Pearl, & Bryan, 1983; Sisterhen & Gerber, 1989); they exhibit poorly organized communication skills in social situations (Bryan & Pflaum, 1978; Gibbs & Cooper, 1989; Kronick, 1976); and they are unable to interpret social cues associated with nonverbal behavior (Siperstein & Goding, 1983). Generally, those with learning disabilities participate less in school activities (Deshler & Schumaker, 1983). They were consistently reported as being less popular than nondisabled children and incur a lower social status (Bryan, 1974a; Bryan & Bryan, 1983; Perlmutter, Crocker, Cordray, & Garstecki, 1983; Siperstein, Bopp, & Bak, 1978). Furthermore, Gresham (1982b) and Vaughn (1985) asserted that lack of social skills is a major factor in handicapped individuals' failure in the mainstream. According to Minskoff (1982), in order to function effectively in the mainstream and in life, those with LD must possess adequate social skills.

Research findings underscore the importance of social competence for present and future adjustment of individuals with learning disabilities. They further recognize the need to include affective and social skills as a distinctive training area for the learning disabled and that they must be specifically and directly taught (Bryan & Bryan, 1981; Foster, Delawyer, & Guevremont, 1985; LaGreca & Mesibov, 1981; Vaughn, 1988; West, 1985). The primary objective of SST is to teach socially valid behaviors that would improve social interaction and peer acceptance (Foster et al., 1985). Although SST has been moderately effective in improving social skills, the area has many issues to address and improvements to make. According to Foster et al. (1985), the primary issue is the selection of target behaviors for intervention programs and the social validity (the degree to which they have empirically demonstrated their importance to social competence) of such programs.

In reviewing the intervention targets of 53 studies employing SST with children and adolescents, Foster et al. (1985) reveal a plethora of target behaviors chosen for training: initiating contact with peers and adults, making friends, greeting others, asking for information, giving information, joining peer activities, joining an ongoing social activity, utilizing appropriate verbal and nonverbal communication, providing socially accepted feedback through smiles and positive physical contact, demonstrating conversational skills, giving verbal compliments, standing up for one's rights, using appropriate assertion, resisting peer pressure, doing problem solving in social situations, attending to physical appearance, practicing grooming, and maintaining eye contact. Although considerations have been given to age-appropriate target behaviors, one cannot help but remain bewildered as to what constitutes social competence.

Viewing social competence as consisting of various skills led Sheldon, Sherman, Schumaker, and Hazel (1983) and their colleagues at the Kansas Institute for Research in Learning Disabilities to develop a social skills curriculum designed to improve the social competence of mildly handicapped adolescents and young adults. They identified 30 social skills that are essential for social competence. These social skills were identified through a literature review process and a survey of mildly handicapped persons and their parents, teachers, and experts in the fields of social skills and the mildly handicapped (Schumaker, Pederson, Hazel, & Meyen, 1983). These 30 skills are as follows:

Accepting Compliments	Body Basics
Accepting Criticism	Conversation
Accepting "No"	Following Instructions
Accepting Thanks	Giving Compliments
Active Listening	Giving Criticism
Answering Questions	Giving Help
Apologizing	Giving Rationales
Asking for Feedback	Goodbye Skills
Asking Questions	Greeting

Interrupting Correctly	Problem Solving
Introducing Yourself	Responding to Teasing
Joining Group Activities	Resisting Peer Pressure
Making Friends	Saying Thanks
Negotiation	Starting Activities with Others
Persuasion	(Sheldon et al., 1983, p. 110)

The social skills curriculum was designed to include effective instructional methods to facilitate social skills learning and generalization to real-life situations. The instructional approach included three kinds of sequenced activities: awareness, practice, and application activities. In the awareness phase, learners are introduced to social problem situations through written materials that consist of illustrated booklets and workbooks. In the practice phase, students are involved in role-playing practice. Activities to facilitate generalization of newly acquired skills are employed in the application phase (Sheldon et al., 1983).

Approaches to social skills training programs usually include contingency reinforcement, modeling, role playing, coaching, and counseling (Carter & Sugai, 1988; Foster et al., 1985; LaGreca & Mesibov, 1979; M. C. Nelson, 1988; Oden & Asher, 1977; Siperstein & Goding, 1983). Social skills training must provide opportunities for practice at school, at home, and in the community (Keefe, 1988; Schulze, Rule, & Innocent, 1989; Vaughn, 1985). It also must involve training of metacognitive strategies. Like any other curriculum area, social skills training should involve assessment and planning. Prior to beginning SST, students' strengths and weaknesses should be assessed. This usually involves the use of informal inventories and checklists of social skills (Figure 12-11). It is suggested that social skills development should be geared to the classroom setting, utilizing a predetermined, structured SST program and supplemented with other activities such as games, "magic circles," discussion groups, and practices in particular strategies through simulations and real-life situations.

Social Skills Training Programs

Although a variety of social skills training procedures have been developed in recent years, their social validity remains in question (Foster et al., 1985). In addition, the many programs differ in their emphasis on critical behavior and skills needed for social competence. In selecting a social skills curriculum, Schumaker, et al. (1983) suggest that the curriculum be simple and easy to understand, with low readability levels and a minimum of required writing; provide students with practice in the discrimination of significant social cues and the acquisition of problem-solving skills; and provide students with strategies for acquiring the skills, as well as opportunities for generalization of learned skills to real-life situations.

The following list represents a sample of commercial social skills training programs:

Figure 12-11   Skill Checklist

	Has Mastery	Has Some Competence	Needs Instruction	Comments
Greeting Others				
Listening to Others				
Initiating a Conversation				
Contributing to Discussion				
Positive Self-Statements				
Positive Statements to Others				
Expressing Feelings				
Speaking Assertively				
Speaking Kindly and Using Courtesy Words				
Labeling Emotions				
Emotions in Self				
Emotions in Others				
Sending Messages				
Participation in a Group Activity				
Mediating Group Rules				
Sharing Materials				
Offering and Giving Assistance				
Respecting Others' Property				
Game Social Skills				
Motor Game Social Skills				
Following Game Rules				
Winning and Losing				
Putting Away Materials				
Ignoring				
Leaving the Situation				
Responding Defensively				
Negotiating Conflict				

Source: From "Teaching Social Communication Skills to Elementary School Children With Handicaps" by G. Cartledge and J. Kleefeld, 1989, *Teaching Exceptional Children, 22*(1), p. 16. Copyright 1989. Reprinted by permission.

1. Program: Developing Understanding of Self and Others: Revised (DUSO-R)
   Skills emphasized: Beginning of social skills, making choices and decisions
   Level: Primary
   Publisher: American Guidance Service

2. Program: A Curriculum for Children's Effective Peer and Teacher Skills
       (ACCEPTS)
   Skills emphasized: Basic classroom interaction skills; social interpersonal
       relationships skills with peers and adults
   Level: Primary and elementary
   Publisher: PRO-ED

3. Program: Human Development Program
   Skills emphasized: Self-control, interpersonal communication, and
       relationships.
   Level: Preschool through elementary
   Publisher: Human Development Training Institute

4. Program: Toward Affective Development (TAD)
   Skills emphasized: Self-awareness, relationship with others
   Level: Elementary
   Publisher: American Guidance Service

5. Program: Skillstreaming the Elementary School Child
   Skills emphasized: Basic classroom survival skills, social/interpersonal
       relationships skills, and skill alternatives for dealing
       with aggression and stress
   Level: Elementary
   Publisher: Research Press

6. Program: A Social Skills Program for Adolescents (ASSET)
   Skills emphasized: Social-interpersonal and communication skills
   Level: Intermediate and secondary
   Publisher: Research Press

7. Program: Skillstreaming the Adolescent
   Skills emphasized: Basic and advanced social skills, skill alternatives for
       dealing with feelings, stress and planning skills
   Level: Secondary
   Publisher: Research Press

8. Program: Social Skills for Daily Living
   Skills emphasized: Communication, interpersonal relationship, and
       problem-solving skills
   Level: Secondary and young adults
   Publisher: American Guidance Service

SUMMARY AND CONCLUSIONS

In a classroom with an effective management system, students function comfortably within acceptable parameters. The classroom represents a comfortable learning environment with clear expectations and recognition of what is considered appropriate and inappropriate behavior. The behavioral repertoire of each student and the group at large represents a variety of positive classroom behaviors. Certain behaviors are considered to be prerequisites to other behaviors. In designing a behavior management system for a classroom, the LD specialist must identify and delineate areas of emphasis to promote changes in students' behavior. Effective utilization of classroom management strategies facilitates students' function within established parameters. In a special day classroom or a resource room, the LD specialist applies management strategies and techniques derived from various approaches. This usually includes the application of behavioristic and cognitive behavioristic approaches, such as token economy, contingency management, self-regulation, and self-reinforcement procedures, as well as crisis intervention and life space interviews derived from psychodynamic approaches. In addition, consideration is given to the effect of various settings/ecosystems on students' behavior.

Teaching Individuals With Learning Disabilities to Read

Questions to Consider

1. *How does one develop a learning environment conducive to the teaching of reading?*

2. *How does one develop a comprehensive remedial reading program that maximizes individuals' successful experiences?*

3. *How are word recognition skills taught?*

4. *How are reading comprehension skills taught?*

5. *How does one individualize the remedial reading program to maximize students' growth?*

6. *How does one monitor students' progress and evaluate the success of remedial reading instruction?*

This chapter presents the reader with an explanation of the reading process and the steps needed to assess, plan, and implement a remedial reading program. It provides guidelines for creating a comprehensive reading program aimed at developing students' basic skills in reading and their appreciation of reading as a means of communication, a practical tool, and a vehicle for enjoyment of the literary world. Emphasis is on an integrated approach to reading and language arts, with attention to the use of specialized teaching approaches in reading, including the use of instructional materials.

UNDERSTANDING THE READING PROCESS AND READING PROBLEMS: THEORY AND CONCEPTS

Reading is a complex process in which the recognition and comprehension of written symbols are influenced by the reader's linguistic repertoire, cognitive skills, reasoning abilities, mind-set, and experiential and cultural background (Bartoli & Botel, 1988). It requires an active involvement in which the reader uses prior knowledge, or schemata, to facilitate understanding of the text. It is the meaningful interpretation of printed or written verbal symbols. Reading serves as both a communication tool and an information-gathering tool. As a communication tool, it provides for the immediate communication of a writer's intentions and ideas, and it opens the door to the sharing of experiences. Reading facilitates effective daily living. It is the royal road to learning (Harris & Sipay, 1985). It is the key to learning and personal enjoyment (Strang, 1978). At a conference of reading experts (Carnegie Corporation, 1962), the following statement was made: "Reading is the most important subject to be learned by children; a child will learn little else in today's world if he does not first learn how to read properly" (p. 1). Most children who are classified as learning disabled exhibit difficulties in reading, spelling, and writing. The reported prevalence figures vary from 85% to as high as 90% (Kaluger & Kolson, 1978). These reading difficulties adversely affect those with LD as they progress through school. They are not only cut off from intellectual enrichment, but likely to experience failure and be deprived of occupational opportunities later in their lives.

The following profiles portray individuals with learning disabilities who exhibit difficulties in reading.

Bill is a 13-year-old student who reads at about the second-grade level. He avoids reading because it is a very hard task for him. Except for glancing through sports or automotive magazines, he does not attempt to read on his own. Bill exhibits difficulties in auditory reception and auditory discrimination. His verbal expression, while age appropriate, is characterized by timidity and low intonation level. He lacks self-confidence and feels that he can never learn to read. However, Bill has an adequate attention span and exhibits no behavioral problems in school or at home.

Matt is a 9-year-old fourth grader enrolled in a special day class. He demonstrates severe delay in the development of reading and writing skills. His reading is at about first-grade level. Matt is limited in his ability to decode words and has limited sight vocabulary. His current IEP states that Matt is of normal intelligence with strengths in the visual performance areas. He demonstrates moderate to severe delay in receptive and expressive language. His teacher indicates that Matt's visual channel is stronger than his auditory channel and that he prefers to read sight words.

At the beginning of each academic year as well as throughout the year, the LD specialist is faced with the challenge of developing an effective remedial reading program for students like Bill and Matt. The LD specialist must have (a) an understanding of the reading process and reading difficulties; (b) knowledge of the core curriculum, with specific attention given to core literature; (c) the ability to assess reading skills; (d) the ability to develop an appropriate reading program for students, including the selection of appropriate teaching methods and instructional materials; and (e) the ability to monitor and evaluate students' progress. The LD specialist who is oriented toward tailoring the remedial instructional program to individual students' needs must consider the process of individualization of the remedial reading program. The main concerns are: How should the teacher go about it? What variables should be considered? What decisions have to be made?

The Nature of Reading

The essential skills in reading involve the ability to decode and derive meaning from written symbols (J. B. Carroll, 1978). Beyond these abilities, reading involves comprehension of the material read and the relating of it to the reader's background and experience. The reading process is a function of the individual ecological system, including cognitive, linguistic, and cultural background (Bartoli & Botel, 1988). Research in metacognition and reading has pointed out that the reading process is influenced by an individual's prior schemata and experience. Schemata are organized structures of knowledge based on individual experience and provide a framework for processing and integrating information (Schank & Abelson, 1977). Readers activate their own schemata (prior knowledge and personal experience) as they attempt to understand the information read and draw inferences from it. In addition, metacognition theory and its application to reading have made us aware of reading as an interactive process that can be heightened through the individual awareness of the reading process, the skills necessary for various types of reading, and the individual use of strategies (Bartoli & Botel, 1988; A. L. Brown, 1982).

The reading process is viewed as an interactive one—it goes from bottom-up (from letters, to words, to phrases and sentences) and from top-down (from linguistic meaning to coding) simultaneously or alternatively (Spiro & Myers, 1984). It is an interaction between reading decoding skills and the linguistic components of reading. Reading is also viewed as a whole made up of highly interrelated subskills, usually involving word recognition (decoding) and reading comprehension, and integrated with oral and written language, reasoning, and strategic skills.

The Relationship of Reading to Language

Reading is an extension of oral language and the ability to decode written language. It is considered part of an individual's language repertoire and is directly affected by one's language background and linguistic abilities. In Myklebust's (1960) hierarchical model of language development (Figure 13–1), reading is second to written language at the top of the hierarchy. These two aspects of language follow the development of inner language evidenced by children's formation of concepts, early communication and play activities, auditory receptive language (understanding spoken language), and auditory expressive language (speaking).

Reading depends upon an individual's ability to associate sounds (phonemes) with written symbols (graphemes) for meaningful words in one's environment. Deriving meaning from written symbols is linked to one's oral language repertoire. In its early stages, reading is "parasitic on language" (Kavanagh, 1968), and continues to be influenced by an individual's language background and linguistic skills (V. A. Mann, 1986). Beginning readers seem to be more dependent upon graphic information for reading decoding, but as they become more proficient, usually about fourth-grade level, their reading comprehension appears to more closely approximate oral language comprehension (Glass & Perna, 1986). At this level, reading seems to depend upon knowledge of structural (syntactic) rules and word selectional (semantic) rules of the native language (Wiig & Semel, 1984). The ability to draw meaning from reading is also influenced by prior knowledge and experience (schemata), which guide and structure reading material into a meaningful set or structure. Proficient readers use their prior schemata to match printed phrases, clauses, and sentences with their previously learned and stored meaning counterparts. They anticipate what may come next and form tentative hypotheses about possible structures and

Figure 13–1   Language Development Systems

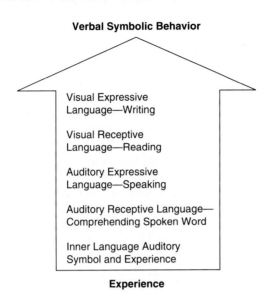

Verbal Symbolic Behavior

Visual Expressive
Language—Writing

Visual Receptive
Language—Reading

Auditory Expressive
Language—Speaking

Auditory Receptive Language—
Comprehending Spoken Word

Inner Language Auditory
Symbol and Experience

Experience

Source: *The Psychology of Deafness* (p. 232) by H. R. Myklebust, 1960, New York: Grune & Stratton. Copyright 1960 by The Psychological Corporation. Adapted by permission.

meanings (Wiig & Semel, 1984). "The efficient reader also uses three types of information simultaneously: the graphic input, syntactic structure, and the semantic interpretation" (Wiig & Semel, 1984, p. 594).

Understanding Reading Problems

The majority of students who are labeled "learning disabled" experience difficulties in learning to read. Reading problems are often referred to as "dyslexia." Dyslexia is generally defined as "a disorder manifested by difficulty in learning to read despite conventional instruction, adequate intelligence and social cultural opportunity" (World Federation of Neurology, 1968, cited by Snowling, 1985, p. 2). Because of the high incidence of reading failures in individuals with learning disabilities, the term *dyslexia* is quite often misused to describe those with LD.

D. J. Johnson (1988) cites several studies that point out that primary problems in reading are related to linguistic deficits. Phonological processing deficiencies, short-term memory, and/or lexical access are considered the main sources of reading problems (D. J. Johnson, 1988; Mann, Cowin, & Schoenheimer, 1990). Many poor readers have difficulties with listening comprehension—with understanding spoken vocabulary, sentences, and discourse (D. J. Johnson, 1988). Early difficulties in learning to read have been associated with language impairment. Furthermore, the co-occurrence of developmental language disorders and reading problems in the same children at various ages has been established through research (V. A. Mann, 1986; Tallal, 1988). Difficulties in short-memory have also been linked to reading problems. Deficits in short-term memory limit one's ability to hold linguistic material in working memory, causing phonological processing problems (Mann et al., 1990). The primary cause of reading problems is attributed to linguistic factors rather than visual-motor or visual-perceptual factors (Robinson & Schwartz, 1973; Stanovich, 1986; Vellutino, 1977, 1986; Vellutino & Scanlon, 1985). Visual skills such as visual discrimination and visual perception are needed to differentiate and remember the various letters and words in the reading process, but they are weakly related to reading acquisition (Stanovich, 1986).

Individuals with reading problems (a) have a short attention span, poor discrimination abilities, poor memory, and difficulty with sequencing and associating print with sound (Bateman, 1964); (b) perform significantly less well on vigilance tasks than good readers (Noland & Schuldt, 1971); (c) perform significantly less well on tasks requiring the use of rapid information-processing skills (Torgesen, 1978–79); (d) have poor decoding skills, read word by word, and put all their energy into trying to decode the words (Samuels, 1987); (e) have difficulties in applying contextual cues in identifying unknown words (D. J. Johnson, 1988); (f) have difficulties in reading comprehension (Samuels, 1987; Stanovich, 1980); (g) do not enjoy reading and do not initiate reading on their own; and (h) have metacognitive deficits—in contrast to skilled readers, they lack knowledge about the purpose of reading, do not utilize strategic learning, and fail to monitor their progress and check their outcomes (Bransford, Shelton, Stein, & Owings, 1980; Brown & Smiley, 1978; Canney & Winograd, 1980; Markman, 1979; Paris & Myers, 1981; Pearson, Hansen, & Gordon, 1979; Smiley, Oakley, Worthen, Campione, & Brown, 1977).

Organization of Reading Skills

Teachers' overall conceptualization of reading and the processes involved in it strongly influence their approach to the diagnosis and treatment of reading difficulties (May, 1986; Strang, 1978). Though reading should be viewed as an integrated process, two primary skill areas of reading—reading decoding and comprehension—are recognized. Reading decoding involves word recognition through phonic analysis, structural analysis, contextual analysis, and sight vocabulary. Reading comprehension is viewed in terms of numerous functions such as literal, interpretive, critical, and applied reading.

Decoding

The act of decoding, that is, "the act of translating written symbols into sounds" (Forrest-Pressley & Waller, 1984), entails three main functions: phonic analysis, structural analysis, and contextual analysis. Phonic analysis, also referred to as word analysis, involves a systematic analysis of words by sound units, with a primary task of associating the units of sounds, or phonemes, with the corresponding written symbols, or graphemes. Structural analysis includes the ability to break a word into its component parts—root words, affixes, syllables, compound words, contractions, consonant blends, diphthongs, and digraphs (Gallant, 1977). Contextual analysis involves the recognition of words from the meaning of the phrase or sentence containing the words (Zintz, 1981). It involves the use of semantic and syntactic clues to identify unknown words.

In addition to these three main functions, the individual repertoire of sight vocabulary, also referred to as basic word vocabulary, facilitates recognition of sight words at the automatic level. It includes the recognition of words that usually do not follow the general phonetic and orthographic rules of the English language. From a metacognitive perspective, decoding involves students' knowledge that there are different ways to figure out what a word says and that some decoding strategies are more efficient and appropriate than others (Forrest-Pressley & Waller, 1984).

Reading Comprehension

Reading comprehension is considered a "secondary language skill" that has phonetic, syntactic, semantic, and memory components (Wiig & Semel, 1984). It is the process that enables individuals to extract and remember specific information and that facilitates an understanding of a text's material by making inferences and drawing conclusions. It involves many skills, including memory, association, and reflective thinking, and is highly affected by one's language facility. Some students who can decode and pronounce words but have difficulties in reading comprehension usually experience language difficulties and demonstrate metacognitive deficiencies. Reading involves more than just decoding symbols that the mature reader is able to decipher "automatically," and cognitive efforts are focused on extracting information that is meaningful within the context of the purpose of reading the material (Forrest-Pressley & Waller, 1984). From a metacognitive perspective, reading comprehension involves the use of one's prior knowledge and experience (schemata) to structure the reading material into a meaningful set and to facilitate anticipation of text material. Comprehension involves a reader's knowledge of the text's content, the utilization of comprehension strategies, and the ability to monitor one's understanding of the text (Palincsar & Brown, 1984).

According to Wilson (1972), children need direction, encouragement, and specific instruction on how to apply their thinking skills to reading. Often, comprehension exercises involve simply the asking of one or more questions at the end of a story. For children who have difficulties in reading comprehension, this is not enough. They need to be actively engaged in understanding how texts are constructed and to be taught explicit strategies, that is, how to read for purpose, information, and direction. Furthermore, they need to be taught how to select, deploy, and monitor appropriate strategies and to regulate the quality of their understanding of the text (Paris & Oka, 1989).

Four main levels of reading comprehension are usually recognized in the literature, namely, literal comprehension, interpretive reading, critical reading, and applied reading. A further distinction of reading comprehension is made in terms of the condition under which reading comprehension occurs—listening comprehension, silent reading comprehension, and oral reading comprehension.

Literal comprehension produces knowledge of what the author says (Kaluger & Kolson, 1978; N. B. Smith, 1969; Wilson & Hall, 1972; Zintz, 1981). It involves understanding the meaning of words and the meanings and interrelations of increasingly larger units, that is, phrases, sentences, paragraphs, and whole selections (Harris & Sipay, 1985). This level "requires the student to derive literal meaning from sequential words and their grammatical relations to each other (the syntax) in sentences, paragraphs, and chapters" (Strang, 1978, pp. 68–69). Thus it involves the ability to weave words together and give each its proper weight and to understand the accumulation of significance in successive sentence structures (Strang, 1978).

Interpretive/inferential reading emphasizes the understanding and recalling of inferred information—finding relationships among statements in the material read and being able to relate them to one's own experience (Harris & Sipay, 1985; Kaluger & Kolson, 1978; N. B. Smith, 1969; Wilson & Hall, 1972; Zintz, 1981). This level of reading comprehension requires readers to distinguish between facts and opinions, to separate their own ideas from those of the author, and to evaluate a passage read in terms of its literary value and authority (Strang, 1978).

Critical reading involves the ability to pass judgment on the material read by analyzing and evaluating it (Lanier & Davis, 1972; N. B. Smith, 1969). Applied reading involves the ability to apply the information to new situations and to solve problems. "On this level the reader may arrange the author's ideas into new patterns, extend their scope, or fuse them with ideas that he himself has gained from reading or from experience. By means of both analysis and synthesis, the reader gains a new insight for a higher level of understanding and [that] enables him to reflect on the significance of the ideas" (Strang, 1978, p. 69). This level is also referred to as problem solving and creative-level reading (Lanier & Davis, 1972; Wilson & Hall, 1972; Zintz, 1981).

Several basic reading comprehension skills make up the literal, interpretive, critical, and applied levels of reading comprehension. Table 13–1 is a taxonomy by Lanier and Davis (1972) of reading comprehension with corresponding specific comprehension skills.

Most teachers' guides to various reading programs provide the teacher with a sequence of reading comprehension skills that are sometimes arranged according to their difficulty. These usually include finding the main ideas; noting details; distinguishing important from unimportant information; determining cause-and-effect relationships; comparing and contrasting; and making inferences, drawing conclusions, and making judgments (Wilkins & Miller, 1983).

While the ability to decode words and perform various reading comprehension activities is essential for getting the most out of reading, overreliance on subskill training carried out of the student cognitive linguistic and cultural context has quite often deprived students with learning disabilities of literacy experience. Reading may become a task rather than a tool for enriched knowledge and exposure to the world of prose. Thus reading instruction requires the integration of subskill knowledge, reading fluency, and comprehension of meaningful and relevant material that promotes students' exposure to the literary world.

Table 13–1   Lanier and Davis' Model of Reading Comprehension Skills

Level 1 Literal	Level 2 Interpretive	Level 3 Critical	Level 4 Creative
Recall of facts (details)	Inferring:	Judging	Applying information to new situation
sequence	sequence	Detecting	Responding
main idea	main idea	propaganda	emotionally
directions	cause-and-effect	Analyzing	
organization	comparison	Checking validity	
cause-and-effect	contrast	Checking author's	
comparison	purpose	reputation, biases,	
contrast	details	purposes	
character traits	character traits		
Recognition of	Drawing conclusions		
facts	Generalizing		
sequence	Deriving meaning		
main idea	from figurative		
directions	language		
organization	Speculating		
cause-and-effect	Predicting		
comparison	Anticipating		
contrast	Summarizing		
character traits			

Source: From "Developing Comprehension Through Teacher-Made Questions" by R. J. Lanier and A. P. Davis, 1972, *Reading Teacher, 26* (2), pp. 153–157. Reprinted with permission of Ruby J. Lanier and the International Reading Association.

THE REMEDIAL READING PROGRAM

The primary goal of remedial reading instruction is to develop students' decoding and comprehension reading skills within a meaningful context. The ultimate purpose is to expose students to the world of reading, which involves both reading for enjoyment through literature and appreciation of reading as a communication tool. Remedial reading instruction is viewed as a comprehensive program integrating the various components of reading, with emphasis on the meaningfulness and purposefulness of reading stemming from, and integrated with, one's language and prior experience. It is also integrated with the language arts curriculum, including oral and written language and spelling.

Program Development and Instructional Considerations

Principles of Remedial Reading Instruction

The remedial reading program must be carefully planned to meet the needs of learning-disabled students with reading difficulties. It must take into account students' developmental level, including language, cognition, and affective aspects associated with reading failures and reading difficulties. The following guidelines for developing a remedial reading program are suggested:

1. The program should be based on analysis of the assessment data and should address itself to (a) students' strengths and weaknesses, (b) students' information processing/learning style, and (c) students' interest level.
2. The program should be balanced and comprehensive, including various reading components and skills, and integrated with individuals' language, cognitive, and experiential background.
3. The program should include diverse reading materials and media, such as literature, plays, and puppetry, in order to develop an appreciation for reading as well as enhance reading skills.
4. The program should be success oriented, attempting to build self-confidence, and should facilitate students' overcoming of inhibiting behaviors in reading.
5. The program should attempt to utilize teaching methods that are compatible with each other in order to develop reading decoding, fluency, and comprehension skills.
6. The program must develop students' sensitivity to reading, their enjoyment of reading, and their utilization of reading as a communication skill.
7. The program should heighten students' awareness of the reading process and of what is necessary to develop strong reading skills.
8. The program should utilize strategic learning in the acquisition of the various reading skills. It should use diverse mnemonic devices whenever necessary.
9. The program must involve practice and overlearning, which bring reading to the mastery and automatic levels.
10. The program should be integrated with other areas of the curriculum, such as social studies and science, using various activity projects appropriate to the interest level of students.

Developing a Comprehensive Reading Program

The LD specialist must develop a comprehensive reading program. The key element in the remedial process is the integration of word recognition skills with reading comprehension and with meaningful activities in which students read, write, speak, and listen (Gove, 1983). For example, using a selected passage from literature and incorporating concepts and vocabulary into a student's own story using a language experience approach (LEA) (refer to section on LEA later in this chapter) can help show that reading is meaningful and relevant. An integrated approach to remedial reading instruction, in which attention is given to reading skills within a meaningful context, is recommended. The exposure of students to literary experiences through the integration of a core literature curriculum with reading skills development is viewed as an integral component of the remedial reading program. Incorporating literature into the instructional process increases student motivation and overcomes problems inherent in a strict phonic approach (McClure, 1985). Reading materials should be diverse and include informational reading, fiction and nonfiction literature, poetry, and drama. In addition, the LD specialist must consider the integration of the reading program, including the appropriate selection of an approach, with other areas of the language arts, such as spelling and writing, and with other curricular areas. In this context, reading skills development is integrated with students' prior schemata and includes the development of strategies for learning to read within a meaningful context (Bartoli & Botel, 1988).

Reading decoding and comprehension skills should involve a variety of reading materials and activities encompassing all aspects of reading. Taking into account students' decoding and comprehension levels, the teacher must consider activities such as independent silent reading, group reading and discussion, and listening to literary selections. Reading activities may include the reading of, and follow-up activities for, material at various levels:

1. One or more paragraphs. The emphasis in this type of reading should be on understanding main ideas and remembering details.
2. Short stories consisting of five or more paragraphs. This approach is especially important because those with learning disabilities have difficulty remembering a whole story in a sequential manner.
3. Longer stories of two or more pages. These are more complicated and more difficult to comprehend and remember.
4. Literature reading, novels, and plays.
5. Material related to current events, such as newspapers and magazines.
6. Reading for fun. Material is selected by children purely on the basis of their own enjoyment.

In addition, word recognition activities should include phonic analysis, structural analysis, and contextual analysis reinforced with reading aids and media, such as flash cards, reading instruments, and computer programs.

Creating a Reading Learning Environment

Teachers must create an environment conducive to reading. Despite students' past history of failure with reading, teachers can create a supportive and stimulating reading learning environment. They can provide an atmosphere of trust and comfort in which students are exposed to successful experiences and are no longer fearful of learning. This can be achieved through the development of an attractive physical environment, one in which meaningful posters are displayed and a rich selection of reading materials appropriate to students' interest and functional levels are accessible. In addition, fun reading materials such as magazines and comic books should be available. Students should also be encouraged to engage in fun reading and reading games. Displaying "easy reader" books strategically and attractively and creating a relaxing reading corner in which students can sit on a couch and/or throw pillows can make reading more captivating to students.

An integrated and comprehensive reading program which develops reading skills within a meaningful context makes reading relevant and significant for the student.

Assessment of Reading

The purpose of assessing reading skills is to ascertain students' level of functioning in the various aspects of the skills and to provide direction and guidelines for programming. The selection of assessment procedures and inventories must be based on the utility of the information they provide. This assessment data should provide the LD specialist with the following:

1. Students' specific skill mastery in reading decoding and reading comprehension

2. Students' grade reading decoding and reading comprehension (silent and listening) levels
3. Students' response to reading approaches and reading materials in the past
4. Students' information-processing style
5. Students' affective reaction to reading
6. Students' interest areas
7. Students' language development level
8. Students' functional level in other language arts areas, such as spelling and written expression
9. Students' metacognitive awareness of the reading process
10. Students' repertoire of strategic learning in reading, including the use of control executive functions throughout reading activities.

The use of both formal and informal assessment procedures in reading, including the teacher's observations and informal inventories, can assist in the development of an appropriate and optimal reading program for students.

Formal Reading Measures

There are many norm-referenced achievement tests in reading, some of which can be administered to groups of students and others that must be administered individually. Some emphasize silent reading, and others stress oral reading or a combination of the two forms. Generally, reading achievement tests are classified as general/survey reading tests and diagnostic reading tests. The general/survey tests provide the teacher with students' overall functioning in the major areas of reading, such as reading recognition and reading comprehension. They are the tests given most frequently in schools. General/survey reading achievement tests are silent reading tests. The primary purpose of using them is to determine students' achievement level (Miller, 1978).

Diagnostic reading tests are designed to evaluate the level of students' knowledge of various subskills involved in word recognition and reading comprehension. They can provide information about students' reading strengths and weaknesses and serve as the basis for a sound remedial reading program.

Criterion-referenced reading tests are also available to the LD specialist. They systematically evaluate students' strengths and weaknesses in reading. They are usually based on task analysis of reading skills and help to determine whether students have achieved mastery of specific reading skills, both in reading recognition and reading comprehension (Miller, 1978).

Tests of Reading

Following are examples of the most commonly used reading tests. They are organized in terms of their utility.

Reading Readiness Tests

Boehm Test of Reading Skills
Gates-MacGinitie Reading Readiness Test
Metropolitan Readiness Test

General/Survey Reading Achievement Tests

California Achievement Tests
Comprehension Tests of Basic Skills
Iowa Tests of Basic Skills
Kaufman Test of Educational Achievement
Metropolitan Achievement Tests
Slosson Oral Reading Tests
Stanford Achievement Tests
Woodcock-Johnson Psycho-Educational Battery (WJ-R) Test of Achievement

Diagnostic Reading Tests

Botel Reading Inventory
Doren Diagnostic Reading Test of Word Recognition Skills
Gilmore Oral Reading Test
Gray Oral Reading Test
Spache Diagnostic Reading Scales
Stanford Diagnostic Reading Test
Woodcock Reading Mastery Test

Criterion-Referenced Reading Tests

Brigance-Diagnostic Inventory of Basic Skills
Systematic Approach to Reading Improvement
Wisconsin Tests of Reading Skill Development

Informal Reading Measures

Students' performance on formal reading tests provides general information about their performance level. However, too often the information is insufficient and does not tell us very much about students' reading abilities and difficulties. Information from formal tests must be supplemented with criterion-referenced tests and with informal testing procedures, which include teachers' observations, informal inventories, and anecdotal records.

Informal reading inventories (IRI) are of two types: reading decoding and reading comprehension. Although commercial inventories are available, many teachers still prefer to compose their own informal reading inventories (Gillete & Temple, 1982). Informal reading inventories are based on the scope and sequence of the various reading skills and can assist the LD specialist in identifying students' particular strengths and weaknesses in reading decoding and reading comprehension. In addition, they provide the teacher with an understanding of students' personal interests, enabling the teacher to gear the program and the instructional materials to students' functional and interest levels. The information derived should assist the teacher in developing an appropriate reading program and should provide a means of monitoring students' progress. The use of IRI profiles can help the teacher pinpoint students' skill level and facilitate the monitoring and evaluation of their progress.

Informal Reading Decoding Inventories

Many teachers find it very difficult to rely on formal test results to create a well-designed and specific reading decoding instructional program for their students. Though various reading formats, such as word lists and words in context, can be used to assess students' decoding skills, a structured IRI can prove to be more helpful in identifying students' specific strengths and weaknesses. Informal reading decoding inventories usually include several skill areas, such as knowing the alphabet, consonant sounds, consonant digraphs, consonant blends, short vowel sounds, long vowel sounds, and diphthongs.

Steps in Administering an Informal Reading Decoding Inventory

In order to maximize the benefits of an informal reading decoding inventory, the LD specialist must follow basic procedures. In general, an IRI should be administered individually, with careful recording of the student's performance. The child reads one copy of the inventory while the teacher follows the reading on another copy. As the child reads, the teacher marks any errors, omissions, substitutions, or unique behaviors the child exhibits. When a child starts giving few correct responses and making many errors, the reading may be stopped and the next subtest presented.

In general, the teacher should follow these steps when administering an informal reading inventory:

1. Approximate the reading level of the child.
2. Select the appropriate inventory level, allowing for variation in the child's performance. The child may perform at higher levels in some reading skills than in others. However, it is better to start at the lower level with the child and work up, rather than start at a higher level at the beginning of the test itself.
3. Observe and record the child's reading behavior; note substitutions above the letters; underline repetitions; circle any omissions.
4. Transfer test results to the IRI profile. The same form can be used for monitoring and evaluating the child's progress.
5. Use the inventory results as a basis for a very discrete and specified remedial reading program.

Informal Reading Comprehension Inventories

Students' performance on reading comprehension tests is usually affected by the various aspects of reading comprehension and the testing format. Some students perform better in oral reading comprehension than silent reading comprehension. Therefore, the use of informal inventories in reading comprehension is extremely important in tapping students' reading comprehension skills.

Informal reading inventories for reading comprehension consist of a set of passages for both oral and silent reading selected from basal readers or other school texts. These passages are followed by a balanced set of comprehension questions that can assess both oral and silent reading, keeping in mind the various comprehension skills appropriate to the specific age level (Gillete & Temple, 1982). Some commercial informal inventories are also available. They usually accompany a basal reading series, and the reading selections are made up of packages from that series.

The following guidelines for constructing an IRI were provided by Gillete and Temple (1982):

1. Select passages for oral and silent reading for each grade level of the basal series, beginning with the preprimer level. It is suggested that a teacher prepare two or more different passages for each grade level. The passages should be complete in themselves to facilitate reading comprehension. Passages should be roughly from 100 to 200 words long. At the preprimer level, passages should be approximately 50 words long. Beyond the sixth- or seventh-grade level, the authors suggest that the passages be around 250 to 300 words in order to provide enough text to adequately prompt the reader's comprehension.

2. The teacher then develops comprehension questions for each passage. Five questions are usually sufficient for the preprimer, primer, and first-grade levels, and about 10 questions are needed for the grades thereafter. The questions should sample the various comprehension skills appropriate to the grade levels, including main ideas, supporting details, sequence, inferences, cause-and-effect relationships, and understanding of vocabulary.

   Each reading passage should be clearly presented; it should be typed double or triple spaced in order to allow the examiner to record the student's patterns of reading. The percent of correctly read words should be recorded. In addition, the teacher should identify the various skills covered by each of the comprehension questions, such as main ideas, vocabulary, or contextual cues.

The teacher's knowledge of the various reading comprehension skills is essential to assess students' specific skills in reading comprehension. Most teacher's guides to reading programs provide a summary of the reading comprehension skills covered in the series. The teacher should use scoring and recording sheets. These should provide information essential to instructional programming and planning as well as record students' progress.

Steps in Administering an Informal Reading Comprehension Inventory

The following steps have been suggested in administering an informal reading inventory (Gillete & Temple, 1982):

1. Begin the IRI two or three levels below present grade or at a level at which you think the student can read comfortably.
2. Administer the first oral reading passage and code the miscues. Tape record oral reading, if you wish, for greater accuracy. Ask comprehension questions and record the gist of the answers.
3. Administer the first silent reading passage. Ask comprehension questions and record the gist of the answers.

4. When silent and oral comprehension scores drop to 60 percent or less, read one of the next level passages aloud and ask questions as before.
5. When listening comprehension drops lower than 60 percent, stop the IRI. (p. 98)

Using Cloze Procedure

Cloze procedure requires the ability to supply missing words in a passage based on contextual information, word knowledge, and text structure. Cloze procedure may be used in informal assessment of student's ability to use semantic and syntactic clues. A student is presented with a reading passage of approximately 250 words in which every fifth word throughout the text, with the exception of the first sentence, is omitted. The student's task is to supply the missing words while reading the passage. Ranking and Culhane (1969) provided the following criteria to determine the functional reading level of the student:

- 61% or more correct responses—independent reading level
- 41%–60% correct responses—instructional reading level
- 40% or less correct responses—frustration reading level

Determining Reading Ability Levels

Locating the individual reading ability level is essential for the selection of appropriate reading materials. Generally, three levels have been identified and recognized in the literature. As shown in Figure 13–2, these include independent, instructional, and frustration levels.

The independent reading level is the reading level at which readers feel most comfortable. At this level, reading is executed automatically. Generally, readers can decode almost all the words without difficulties, and reading comprehension is good. "At this level of difficulty the student can read text easily, without help. Comprehension of what is read is generally excellent, and silent reading at this level is rapid because almost all the words are recognized and understood at sight" (Gillete & Temple, 1982, p. 85).

The instructional reading level is the difficulty level of reading materials at which reading instruction is most effective (Fry, 1968). Students can read the material but

Figure 13–2 Reading Ability Levels

Reading Level	Accepted Criteria for Reading and Listening Comprehension	Oral Reading
1. Independent reading level	90–95% or higher	97% or higher
2. Instructional reading level	70–89%	90–96%
3. Frustration reading level	Below 70%	Below 90%

exhibit some difficulty with word recognition and reading comprehension. At this level, readers need instructional support in order to fully grasp information from a reading passage. The instructional level would involve activities related to structural word analysis and to the acquisition of reading comprehension skills. One important concept is the balance between the percentage of vocabulary students can decode and the percentage they cannot decode. An instructional level should be considered when individuals can, without difficulties, decode about 80% of the material. This is an arbitrary limit, but the principal point is that one would not want to provide students with material too high above their functional level and thus cause frustration and anxiety related to the reading process. Also, one would not want to provide readers with material that involves a high percentage of reading vocabulary they are unable to decode and thus force them to use all their energy on decoding skills, which will hinder their comprehension.

The frustration level is the level at which students feel frustrated and are unable to cope with the reading material. At this level, "the material is too difficult in vocabulary or concepts to be read successfully. Comprehension is poor with major ideas forgotten or misunderstood. Both oral and silent reading are usually slow and labored, with frequent stops to analyze unknown words. . . . Because of this difficulty, it is frustrating for students to attempt to read such material for sustained periods of time, and their efforts often fail" (Gillete & Temple, 1982, p. 86). When we give children a passage that they have tremendous difficulty decoding, it is almost impossible for them to derive meaning from it.

To evaluate the grade level of reading material presented to students, Fry (1968) developed a formula for estimating readability level (Figure 13–3). The procedures evaluate the average number of syllables and sentences per 100 words to determine the grade level of the material.

Following are the directions for using Fry's formula:

> Randomly select three 100-word passages from a book or an article. Plot the average number of syllables and the average number of sentences per 100 words on the graph to determine the grade level of the material. Choose more passages per book if great variability is observed and conclude that the book has uneven readability. Few books will fall in the gray area, but when they do, grade level scores are invalid. (p. 16)

Teacher Observations: Key Points in Observing Reading Patterns

Trained LD specialists who have sound knowledge of clinical teaching, including assessment and programming of learning-disabled students, and who have a broad knowledge of diagnostic procedures can successfully develop an observational framework, which is immensely important. The teacher's role in observations is often overlooked. A teacher who is aware of what to look for, and who has developed a diagnostic and an observational framework, can be very effective in observing students' performance and in analyzing the observational data. This process usually involves the use of informal reading inventories, students' performance profiles, and anecdotal records. Teachers' observations in reading provide additional data related

Figure 13–3 Fry's Graph for Estimating Readability

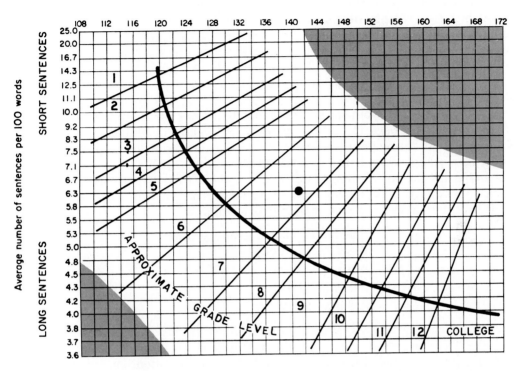

Average number of syllables per 100 words

SHORT WORDS   LONG WORDS

DIRECTIONS: Randomly select three 100-word passages from a book or an article. Plot the average number of syllables and the average number of sentences per 100 words on the graph to determine the grade level of the material. Choose more passages per book if great variability is observed, and conclude that the book has uneven readability. Few books will fall in the gray area, but when they do, grade level scores are invalid.

	SYLLABLES	SENTENCES
EXAMPLE: 1st Hundred Words	124	6.6
2nd Hundred Words	141	5.5
3rd Hundred Words	158	6.8
AVERAGE	141	6.3

READABILITY 7th GRADE (see dot plotted on graph)

For further information and validity data, see the April, 1968 Journal of Reading and the March, 1969 Reading Teacher.

Source: From "A Readability Formula That Saves Time" by E. Fry, 1968, _Journal of Reading, II_, p. 16, and the International Reading Association.

to students' functional level of reading, their reading habits, and their affective response to reading. Quite often, these observations provide information not otherwise obtainable. Teachers can observe students and determine their reading patterns and habits. For example, do students read word by word? Do they read in a monotone voice or with expression? Do they use their fingers as a pointer? Do they omit or add sounds to the words? Do they read in a fluent manner or are they stutter readers?

The following are a teacher's observations and anecdotal records of a student named Nelson.

Nelson is a 12½-year-old sixth-grade student who is enrolled in a resource room for reading and language. His functional reading level is at about the fourth grade. He fits in well with the rest of his peers in the regular classroom and enjoys all aspects of the curriculum except language arts, namely, reading, spelling, and creative writing. In the past, Nelson has successfully used avoidance behaviors to get out of these subject areas. Nelson is at grade level in mathematics.

Nelson's formal test results in reading are as follows:

Spache Diagnostic Reading Skills

Word Recognition	2.4
Instructional level	2.5
Individual level	2.5
Potential level	4.5

Observations by Nelson's teacher are summarized in these key points:

General student behavior patterns. Despite Nelson's difficulties in the language arts, his general attitude toward work is still positive. His attention and concentration abilities are good. Nelson relates well to his peers and exhibits no behavioral problems.

Behaviors significant to the reading process. His sitting behavior is awkward. Sometimes he slides down in his chair until his head is near the table. Nelson also holds his books or papers close to his eyes. He prefers to read aloud and finds it easier than reading silently. His oral expressive abilities are excellent. He expresses himself very well and uses complete sentences appropriate to his age level.

Observations of student's reading patterns and word analysis and comprehension skills. Nelson knows individual letter sounds in isolation but often fails to recognize soft c and g in words.

He knows most consonant blends in isolation but seems to encounter difficulties in decoding words, especially with consonant blends that appear in the middle or at the end of the words. He also has difficulties with three-letter consonant blends, such as *str* and *spr*.

He knows long and short vowel sounds when heard and asks for them orally, but does not always recognize them in written words, for example, words with a final *e* and a long vowel sound.

Nelson can also read syllables in isolation but experiences difficulties in blending them together. Moreover, he can blend orally from sounds given by the teacher but not well from the written word.

Nelson reads slowly word by word. While reading, he points to each word. He tends to mumble at times and to guess at words, usually using the first letter or blend as a cue. His use of word attack skills is inconsistent. In areas of mastery, he uses phonic knowledge effectively, but as soon as he sees a complex word, he tends to freeze and shows signs of helplessness, guessing rather than applying word attack knowledge. Occasionally, he still reverses and rotates words, for example, reading *was* as *saw*.

His oral reading comprehension is excellent. He usually has a strong memory for details and main ideas. Given the same reading passage, Nelson has difficulties in silent reading comprehension.

What can we learn from the teacher's observations relative to Nelson's problems in reading? What is his primary problem? What factors are impeding his progress in reading? What factors can assist him in the acquisition of reading skills? What approach(es) should be utilized with this student? What material should be used? How can this student be taught to read, to assume control over his reading, and to utilize strategic learning in reading?

From the teacher's observation notes, we can draw the following conclusions:

1. Nelson is extremely anxious about the process of reading.
2. He has tremendous difficulties in sequencing.
3. He needs auditory feedback.
4. He has difficulties synthesizing parts into a whole when material is presented visually.
5. He is very cooperative and is still motivated to learn.
6. Nelson is a bright student.

We can also conclude that the following elements and characteristics are essential to Nelson's reading program:

1. The program must be success oriented.
2. The program should integrate Nelson's verbal expressive abilities with the teaching of reading decoding and comprehension skills; the use of a language experience approach seems very appropriate here.
3. To take advantage of his visualization strengths, the program should employ color coding.
4. The program should provide material at a level comfortable to him to reduce the anxiety related to reading.
5. Reading approaches that are compatible to each other should be used, namely, for structural reading, use of a linguistic approach supplemented with analysis and synthesis of words using link letters, flash cards, or word wheels.
6. To force automaticity of reading, the use of a tachistoscope can be beneficial.
7. The program may use a language experience approach to bridge the gap between oral-verbal and written-verbal expressive abilities.

8. For reading fluency, the program may use a neurological impress method with high-interest low-vocabulary level material. Selected literary passages on tapes should also be used to increase his exposure to prose.

Variables and Concerns in Reading Programming

In programming in reading, the LD specialist should follow the programming steps and procedures discussed in chapter 9, with specific attention to the annual goals and short-term objectives of a student's IEP in reading and other language arts areas.

As stated earlier in this chapter, the remedial reading program must be comprehensive in nature, encompassing reading decoding and comprehension skills and leading students to reading meaningful material at their interest level. All too often, LD specialists and remedial reading teachers begin remedial reading instruction with letter-sound correspondence. They usually start with consonant sounds, consonant blends, and short and long vowels in teaching students reading. In reality, many students with learning disabilities repeat this cycle year after year without acquiring reading competency. The primary goal in programming in reading is to provide students with successful reading experiences. Students must be able to read meaningful material in context within a relatively short period of time. To achieve this goal, we must address ourselves to the cyclical teaching approach described in chapter 11. The reading program must be designed to facilitate the completion of a cycle at a certain skill mastery level that will encompass both reading decoding and reading comprehension in accordance with students' functional and interest levels. This calls for the integration of both the analytic approach to reading (from letters to words to phrases) and the synthetic approach to reading (from linguistic meaning to coding) in the remedial reading program. The use of approaches that are compatible with each other can further heighten students' phonological awareness and subsequently lead to reading fluency. For example, as we teach letter-sound correspondence, we can also introduce students to sight vocabulary and word patterns using linguistic patterning. These word patterns can be color coded in accordance with linguistic patterning rules, reinforcing the letter-sound correspondence and increasing ability in reading decoding. Furthermore, in order to promote the acquisition of reading skills and to develop an appreciation of reading as an extension of oral expressive language and as a communication tool, reading activities must be integrated with both oral and written language, including spelling. The incorporation of the language experience approach or its modification in conjunction with other reading approaches increases students' mastery level in reading. This is true for elementary school students, but it becomes critical for secondary students who have had a long history of failure in reading. The essence of the remedial reading program is to teach students how to read meaningful material at their functional and interest levels.

The following procedures can assist LD specialists in developing an optimal remedial reading program:

1. Determining the functional level of students and their affective reaction to reading

2. Ascertaining students' past experience with reading, including reading approaches and instructional materials utilized
3. Deciding and prioritizing the areas of emphasis in the reading program
4. Developing a comprehensive reading program, and integrating the reading program with other language arts areas, such as written expressive language and spelling
5. Developing the weekly and daily "diet" of the students' reading program by combining reading decoding and comprehension and using a variety of reading materials, including selected passages from literature
6. Determining the most appropriate teaching approaches
7. Deciding on instructional materials in the various areas of reading, including reading decoding and reading comprehension, for both individualized and group activities and for oral and written activities
8. Selecting appropriate motivators, elicitors, and reinforcement modes
9. Facilitating students' active involvement in the reading process through metacognitive awareness, strategic learning, and effective utilization of control executive functions
10. Establishing monitoring and evaluation procedures, including product-process evaluation

METHODS AND STRATEGIES FOR TEACHING READING

The Need for Specialized Approaches

Helping learning-disabled students with reading difficulties is challenging. The development of students' word recognition skills (decoding skills), reading fluency, reading comprehension skills, and appreciation for reading is among the major objectives of remedial reading instruction.

The LD specialist is faced with making decisions on approaches and instructional materials that will maximize students' response to the remedial reading program. Not all students have the same patterns of abilities and disabilities, nor do they all learn in the same way and at the same pace. No particular approach or material is appropriate for all students. The analysis of each student's cognitive/learning style, strengths, and weaknesses indicates the specific methods and approaches that should be used. Some students respond better to methods that emphasize auditory processing, others respond better to reading approaches that emphasize visual processing, and still others respond better to kinesthetic approaches. Empirical findings of matching reading method to sensory modalities are equivocal. Rather than spending energy on a quest for the best methods of teaching reading, Harris and Sipay (1985) suggest that "for most children a balanced eclectic approach that uses varied sensory clues in combination and that gives balanced attention to word recognition and comprehension seems advisable. When a child continues to fail in a particular reading program, consideration should be given to employing a program that utilizes a different methodology and makes different demands on the learner" (p. 81).

The following section provides some basic information about the most prevalent remedial teaching approaches that have proven to be helpful with those with learning disabilities. No attempt has been made to cover all reading methods or programs. An elaboration of the language experience approach has been provided in view of its prevalent and effective use with all age-level students with appropriate modifications.

Word Recognition Approaches and Strategies

Word recognition approaches are classified as (a) code emphasis approaches and (b) meaning emphasis approaches. Code emphasis approaches stress decoding and primarily teach symbol-sound associations and blending skills; meaning emphasis approaches teach phonics along with other decoding strategies, with less emphasis on sounding and blending techniques (Harris & Sipay, 1985).

The code emphasis approaches consist of letter-sound relationships, for example, the word *cat* is sounded out as *kkk-aa-tt* and pronounced *cat*. Phonic and linguistic approaches are classified as code emphasis programs. Some major code emphasis programs include Lippincott Basic Reading Program, Distar, Merrill Linguistics Reading Program, Miami Linguistic Program, Eye and Ear Fun, and Modern Curriculum Press Phonic Program.

The meaning emphasis approaches begin with words that appear frequently, are familiar to students, and consequently are easier to learn. These approaches emphasize the whole word method and follow a controlled vocabulary sequence. Teachers are not restricted to any specific methods of decoding techniques. Some meaning emphasis programs include Ginn Series (Ginn & Company), Houghton Mifflin Reading Series (Houghton Mifflin), and the New Open Highways and Reading Unlimited (Scott, Foresman). The language experience and the Fernald approaches are classified as meaning emphasis approaches.

Code Emphasis Approaches and Strategies
The Phonics Approach

The phonics approach to reading is a code emphasis approach based on phonetics, that is, classification, description, and articulation of sounds in relation to printed representation of those sounds. The task of readers is to learn the letters of the alphabet and their sounds, and use the proper phonetic rules to employ them in the decoding process.

There are generally two basic approaches to the teaching of phonics, the synthetic method and the analytic method. In the synthetic method, students learn that letters represent certain sounds (e.g., $B = buh$) and then find out how to synthesize the sounds to form words. It usually begins by introducing students to pictures of an apple, elephant, Indian, ostrich, and umbrella so they can become familiar with the short vowel sounds. These pictures carry phonic clues that provide information about the beginning letter sounds. Likewise, students are introduced to other key pictures that provide clues to illustrate the common sounds of the consonants. The students begin with generalizations about the sounds of letters, which are then applied to pronunciations of specific syllables and words. This process tends to be synthetic inasmuch as it initially concentrates on parts of words that are later combined into whole words (Goodacre, 1978).

The analytic method teaches letter sounds as integrated parts of words (e.g., "B as in baby"). In the analytic approach, the teacher first introduces readers to a limited sight word vocabulary, which is usually meaningful, and then the students begin to compare these words for similarities and thus to construct valid phonic generalizations from the experience. This particular approach to phonics is analytic because specific words are used to generalize the sounds of the letters in whole words and are analyzed to identify recurring letters and their associated sounds. Reading of interesting material is delayed until students have achieved a high degree of mastery of the sounds and are competent at word building (Goodacre, 1978).

According to Kaluger and Kolson (1978), most experts in the field of reading consider that phonics (a) is an essential and important part of the reading program; (b) is essential for students to unlock words; (c) should be used in conjunction with other word attack skills; (d) is a sequential reading teaching and acquisition process; (e) is most effective when taught in a meaningful situation; (f) must be taught so as to emphasize its usability; and (g) must be taught in a manner that prevents distortion and confusion.

The basic procedures in a phonics approach include the following:

1. Students learn the shapes of the letters, their names, and their sounds.
2. After learning the alphabet and the sounds of the vowels, consonants, and blends, students learn to articulate words by combining sounds and blending them into words.
3. Students drill and practice on words in isolation, in sentences, and in paragraphs.
4. Students learn to decipher words that have not been previously learned as sight words by associating speech sounds with their written representations, namely, with letters or groups of letters.
5. Students read phonetic stories.

The Linguistic Approach

The linguistic approach to teaching reading is a code emphasis approach based on a linguistic framework. This approach assumes that children coming to school have already mastered oral language. Their main task is learning to break the coded relationship between sounds and symbols (Lamb & Arnold, 1972). The English language is viewed as consisting of regular linguistic patterns, and the task of readers is to learn the relationship of sounds (phonemes) to symbols (graphemes), which form the structure for the linguistic method of teaching reading (Kaluger & Kolson, 1978). The whole word approach is used in linguistic readers. Words are taught in word families, which correspond to linguistic patterns. Reading is introduced by carefully selecting only those words having a consistent and regular spelling pattern. Words that use consonant-vowel-consonant (CVC pattern) are presented as whole words, and children are expected to learn the code by making generalizations through minimal contrasts of sounds in the words selected. For example, children are to make generalizations concerning the short *a* sound by learning words such as *can*, *pan*, *man*, and *ran*. These carefully selected, regularly spelled words are then strung together to make sentences, for example, "Dan can pan fast." Thus in a linguistic approach, consistent visual patterns are presented. Students are taught to spell and read as a whole unit, and an association of reading with students' natural knowledge of their language is developed. The linguistic approach differs from the phonics approach in that the letter and sound equivalents are not presented in isolation to be blended into a whole word, but the letters are embedded in words with regular spelling patterns so that learners can make generalizations about minimal contrast elements.

In a linguistic reading approach, "1) children should learn the alphabet before reading instruction is begun. 2) a one-sound-one-symbol correspondence is employed initially. 3) regularly spelled words are introduced first (e.g., cat, hat, sat) before irregular words are introduced. 4) words are always read as wholes, sounds are never isolated. 5) oral reading is stressed in the beginning stages of instruction" (Bloomfield & Barnhart, 1961, p. 198).

The use of linguistic reading as a remedial approach has many advantages. Lessons can be arranged in a sequential and developmental manner, with simple patterns of reading and spelling. Students follow the patterning and within a short period of time develop a feeling that they can read and decode words. Following is a sample from the Merrill Linguistic Readers (Fries, Wilson, & Rudolph, 1980, p. 10):

> **Fat Nat**
> A cat sat on a mat.
> Pat the cat.
> Is the cat Nat?
> The cat is fat Nat.
> Pat Nat on the mat.

In preparation for a linguistic reading lesson, the teacher must provide the appropriate readiness skills, which should involve exploration of, and exposure to, the vocabulary students will encounter in the story. Some linguistic readers provide pictures and illustrations that serve as cues. Follow-up activities involve analysis and synthesis of patterns, including grouping of words according to family patterns and color coding. Furthermore, a linguistic approach can be reinforced with a language experience approach, in which students learn to group words according to family patterns. It can also be reinforced by either a neurological impress approach or shadow reading. The use of linguistic patterning with color coding can further facilitate the acquisition of reading. The Catherine Stern Structural Reading uses color coding at all levels of instruction.

In his book *Linguistics and Reading*, Fries (1963) outlines the sequence of common linguistic patterns of the English language. These include

1. The first pattern—one-syllable words with the consonant-vowel-consonant pattern (CVC), such as *mad* and *hat,* in which the middle vowel is a short phoneme.
2. The second pattern—words built with a consonant-vowel-consonant plus a final silent *e,* such as *made* and *game.* These are the one-syllable words in which the middle vowel is long.
3. The third pattern—many subpatterns in which a vowel digraph is substituted for the short vowel in the CVC pattern, such as *meat* for *met.*

According to Fries, students should not be asked to identify words in the second pattern until they have mastered those in the first pattern. Until all the regular patterns have been mastered, no irregular words should be presented to children. The basic premise for the linguistic approach of teaching word recognition rests on the ability of students to develop rapid recognition of word patterns by identifying contrasts within patterns (*mad-met*) and graphic contrasts between patterns (*mad-made*) (Harris & Smith, 1976).

In recent years, linguistic programs have placed more emphasis on meaning and sentence structure. For example, the Miami linguistic readers and the Modern Curriculum Press linguistic readers stress meaningful reading in very carefully selected linguistic patterns. The material is supplemented with pictures that depict the story. Throughout these programs, the acquisition of meaningful linguistic patterns is emphasized. Some linguistic programs consist of relatively short booklets on specific linguistic patterns. These provide students with an immediate feeling of success, inasmuch as it takes a relatively short period of time to complete a booklet of 5 or 10 pages. The Modern Curriculum Press program is an example of such a program. Joe Stanchfield's Appreciate Your Country Reading Series (Century Schoolbook Press) is appropriate for the intermediate level. At the secondary level, linguistic programs are scarce. The Score and the Hip Reader series have attempted to include linguistic patterns in their reading.

The Color-Coding Approach

Color coding can be helpful in learning to read and can be used with a variety of teaching approaches. It can be used with a matching approach in a variety of ways. If the teacher's intent is to introduce students to initial sounds, only initial sounds are color coded. On the other hand, if the intent is to emphasize middle sounds, such as the short vowel *a,* then the short vowel sounds in words such as *cat, hat,* and *nap* are color coded. Color coding can also be used to stress sounds, blends, and other aspects of reading instruction. In a linguistic pattern, color coding is used to heighten the various linguistic patterns introduced to students.

A color-coding approach can be utilized with any reading method. Its purpose is to highlight sounds or patterns that are being emphasized during the teaching of reading. It provides students with color cues that facilitate word recognition skills and the student acquisition of reading skills. The Psycholinguistic Color System developed by Bannatyne (1971) is a phonetic system in which children learn each individual letter as a phoneme, with the color names serving as cues to the sounds that the colors represent. This color-coding system uses 17 vowel phonemes that are color coded. Color-coded wall charts, flash cards, workbooks, and colored pencils are presented as part of the program. Another color-coding system is Words in Color (Gattegno, 1962), which is a linguistic-phonetic system. "Initially, the children learn the short vowel sounds, such as the white a, the e in end (yellow) and the i in ill (red). Then they are introduced to consonant sounds so they can begin to spell words. . . . As their skill increases, they gradually learn to identify words in black and white and the use of color is discontinued" (Kaluger & Kolson, 1978, p. 335).

Learning disabilities specialists can devise their own color-coding system, keeping in mind the phonetic rules and linguistic patterns of the English language. Generally, the following guidelines for a color-coding system can be used by teachers:

1. Color coding of initial, medial, and final sounds
2. Color coding of consonants and consonant blends
3. Color coding of short vowels in CVC patterns
4. Color coding of long vowels in CVCV patterns, with silent e being stippled
5. Color coding of digraphs and diphthongs
6. Color coding of syllables
7. Color coding of root words, prefixes, and suffixes

Teachers must be consistent in using colors in coding: all consonant sounds coded with one color; short vowels coded with pastel colors, each color representing a specific short vowel sound; and long vowel sounds coded with strongly hued colors such as strong red, blue, green, yellow, or orange, each of them representing a long vowel sound.

The Word Identification Strategy

The word identification strategy was developed and validated by Deshler and his colleagues (Lenz, Schumaker, Deshler, & Beals, 1984) at the University of Kansas. It is based on the Strategies Intervention Model discussed in chapter 7 and is part of the acquisition strand. The word identification strategy is designed to help students quickly attack and identify unknown words in their reading material.

The word identification strategy teaches students a problem-solving procedure that uses seven steps to decode a word. Using the acronym DISSECT, students learn to read multisyllable words. DISSECT stands for

D Discover the context.
I Isolate the prefix.
S Separate the suffix.
S Say the stem.
E Examine the stem.
C Check with someone.
T Try the dictionary.

Using prefix, suffix, and stem identification, and the mastery of three short syllabication rules, students quickly solve unknown words. They are given pretests to determine their oral reading and comprehension levels. Those students interested in developing this strategy write a goal indicating their commitment. Students are given advance organizers in which they monitor their progress. Over a 30- to 45-day period, and with the use of cue cards, students are taught the meaning of context, prefix and suffix lists, and stem identification. Those students still not able to pronounce a word learn how to ask for help and use the dictionary. This strategy is mastered by students using controlled practice and instructor feedback. Students use their textbooks from their regular classes to generalize this strategy. Their progress is monitored using a word identification progress chart and posttesting. An instructor's manual provides specific guidelines and procedures for the implementation of the strategy.

Meaning Emphasis Approaches and Strategies
The Whole Word Method

The whole word approach is based on the assumption that children have a natural ability to learn to read as they develop verbal expressive abilities and the basic necessary perceptual skills. Normally, children learn to read as they develop their verbal expressive abilities and are able to relate to signs in the environment as a means of communication. In their attempt to decode signs, children associate words that are heard with their corresponding visual equivalents. As they learn a word, children begin to isolate letters and sounds and are engaged in analysis and synthesis of the word. Thus a child who is familiar with a stop sign will say, "This is S-T-O-P," which reads "STOP." In a very natural way, children learn to read sight words (whole word approach); they also use structural analysis (linguistics and/or phonics). In addition, they learn to read while playing with puzzles by matching letters to pictures and by putting together letters to make words.

The whole word method is a teaching procedure that attempts to associate whole printed words with their oral equivalents and the concepts represented by the words:

> The rationale for using the whole-word method includes: 1) most children can learn to read by it; 2) words can be taught quickly and then used to construct meaningful context—children read for meaning sooner than if a phonic method is employed; 3) some young children find it difficult to learn through a phonic method, especially one that depends on phonemic analysis and synthesis; and 4) a number of high-utility words are phonemically irregular (e.g., said, of), and therefore must be learned as wholes. (Harris & Sipay, 1985, p. 385)

The success of a whole word method depends on the degree to which the words introduced are meaningful, the degree to which the proper associations using various cues are developed, and the degree to which the words are incorporated in meaningful reading passages. Words can be introduced initially in isolation and then presented in a printed phrase or sentence, and they can be introduced in association with objects and pictures in the environment.

The Matching Approach

The use of a matching approach facilitates the whole word method, in which a word is initially presented in association with a pictorial representation. With this approach, children learn how to recognize words in isolation and/or in context. In using the matching approach, teachers usually follows these steps:

1. *Picture-word associative learning.* At this step, the word is presented simultaneously with a picture on the same flash card.

The teacher introduces the word by stating, "This is a car."

2. *Paired and multiple picture-word discrimination.* At this step, more than one word-picture card is presented to students.

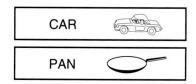

3. *Paired- and multiple-word discrimination.* Though this step is similar to Step 2, the pictures are not presented with the words. The teacher introduces the activity by stating, "Which is the car? Which is the pan?"

4. *Reading of single- or multiple-word lists.* At this step, the teacher asks students to read the word presented. The teacher introduces the activity by stating, "What is this word?"

   At each of the preceding levels, the teacher may provide students with printed cards of the introduced vocabulary. The students can use them to form sentences or stories (Figure 13–4).

5. *Reading of words in phrases or in sentences.* At this step, the teacher asks students to read phrases and/or sentences. The students may now create sentences or stories. There are two considerations involved in presenting contextually potent sentences: using language structures that are within children's repertoire, and embedding new words in the middle or end of the sentences in order to provide more semantic and syntactic information (Harris & Sipay, 1985). In addition, the learning of the new words can be aided by using a color-coding system. Words can be color coded as whole words, as parts of words, or as desired sounds, such as initial consonant sounds and various vowel sound combinations.

The Peabody Rebus Program

According to Woodcock, Clark, and Davies (1979), the term *rebus* is derived from a Latin word that means "thing." Linguistically, a rebus is a symbol or a picture that

Figure 13–4   Sample Sentences and Story Writing

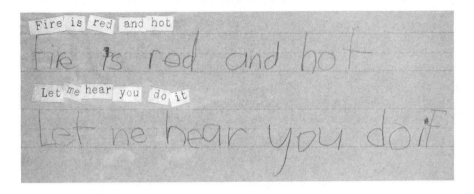

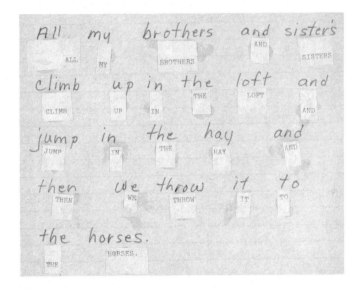

represents an entire word or a part of a word, in contrast to letters, which generally represent sounds. The rebus approach may be viewed as a transition between the spoken and the written word. In the rebus approach, symbols are usually substituted for words, usually pictures that represent words. According to Zintz (1981), "With the rebus, the child can: 1) give more attention to the meaning of the passage; 2) avoid some of the frustrations of the abstract symbols in lines of print; 3) by-pass part of the traditional readiness programs; 4) give more attention to left and right direction and visual motor perceptual training which may be helpful" (p. 227). According to Woodcock et al. (1979), after learning the basic skills of the reading process using a rebus approach, students proceed through a controlled transition program in which spelled words are substituted for the rebuses and structural and phonetic analysis skills are acquired. In the remedial reading program, the rebus method can be best used in conjunction with the language experience approach, in which a rebus can be inserted in lieu of a word.

The Language Experience Approach

The language experience approach integrates the development of reading skills with the development of listening, speaking, and writing skills (Johnson, Vickers, & Norman, 1984). This approach is based on the premise that reading development approximates individuals' oral expressive language. Vocabulary derived from individuals' oral expressive language for reading is more meaningful and directly related to students' environment. The language experience approach directly relates to students' experiences and interests. It reinforces students' sight vocabulary and develops an appreciation and understanding of what reading is all about, namely, "Just talk written down" (Van Allen, 1968).

Van Allen (1968) describes the language experience approach in the following way:

> What I can think about, I can talk about.
> What I can say, I can write or someone can write for me.
> What I can write, I can read.
> I can read what I write, and what other people can write for me to read.
> (p. 263)

The following basic assumptions underlie the language experience approach:

1. Oral expressive language is a precursor or prerequisite to reading and written expressive language.
2. Reading decoding and comprehension skills can be built on individuals' verbal-oral expressive language abilities.
3. Verbal-oral expressive language can assist in reading comprehension and written expressive language.
4. The material for reading instruction is derived from students' natural environment and experiences.
5. The instructional procedure is based on students' active involvement with reading material taken from their environment and experiences.

The language experience approach is based on a psycholinguistic emphasis: The main focus of reading is to make sense of what is read, and therefore students should learn to read only for meaning and be allowed to skip or guess at words they do not know (Spitzer, 1975). In a language experience approach, students read their own dictated stories. Reading becomes easier inasmuch as they possess previous information about the text. This approach is designed to help students develop basic sight vocabulary and see the relationship between language and print (Rude & Oehlkers, 1984). The language experience approach has a major role in remedial teaching approaches. "Some poor readers confront the teacher with a dilemma: they reject material easy enough for them to read on the grounds that it is 'baby stuff' and the books they are willing to try to read are all too difficult for them" (Harris & Sipay, 1985, p. 334). The advantage of using the language experience approach becomes more evident as one learns its various aspects.

Because of its unique characteristics—its approximation to the individual oral expressive language and its appealing nature (the reading of whole words and sentences immediately)—the language experience approach is attractive to students at all age levels, particularly adolescents and young adults with learning disabilities. These latter students have experienced a long history of failure in trying to decode words, usually by using the analytic approach, that is, breaking words into sounds. The language experience approach provides a change to a routine of failure experiences in reading. It brings about a change in perspectives about the individual ability to learn to read. Used appropriately, the language experience approach and its variations can become a powerful tool both for teaching students with LD to read and for improving their oral and written expressive language repertoire.

The language experience approach can take different forms. It can be presented to students on an individual or a group basis. The teacher or the students choose a theme, and the students make up a story about it, using their own words and experiential information. The teacher writes down the children's stories somewhere they can be easily seen, usually using charts often called language experience charts. After a story has been written, students are asked to read it back to the teacher. The teacher may then select a variety of follow-up activities to reinforce students' learning of the vocabulary in the story. Students may also copy the story from the language experience chart into a personal storybook.

The basic principles of the language experience approach can be used with variations with learning-disabled individuals at all age levels. While the use of charts may be more appropriate for primary school children, the use of individual storybooks becomes more appropriate for intermediate- and secondary-level students.

The question is quite often raised concerning how much guidance and control the teacher should have in the language experience approach. Virtually all school-age students can speak in sentences, and they should be allowed to express their thoughts in meaningful sentences. However, when a student's usage is incorrect, the teacher should rephrase a sentence in the proper manner and ask the student to restate the phrase before putting it on the charts or in the student's storybook. Furthermore, the teacher may guide students to dictate material that can be easily recalled. When dictation is completed, the student provides a title for the story. Then the teacher reads the story back to the student. The read-back serves two purposes: "1) it allows the student to revise any portions which are unclear or contain improper usage; 2) the students hear the account as a whole, thereby assisting their recollection of the story on subsequent days" (Rude & Oehlkers, 1984, p. 118).

Teacher's Preparation. The teacher's knowledge of language experience instructional procedures is essential for optimal implementation. The teacher must decide on the nature of the language experience activity, the necessary elicitors, and the instructional aids. More specifically, the LD specialist must address the following:

1. The selection of elicitors for the language experience activity such as
   a. An immediate event in students' environment
   b. A past and/or future event in students' life
   c. An event in the community or state, or at the national level
   d. Elicitors in areas of students' interest
   e. At the advanced levels, materials for plays, debates, and/or speeches
2. The selection of an appropriate style of presentation
   a. Teacher/individual presentation of topic
   b. Teacher/student group discussion
   c. Film or media
3. The selection of instructional aids and materials such as
   a. Pictures
   b. Newspaper and magazine articles
   c. Other media (slides, audiotapes, videocassettes, and/or films)

Styles of Activities. The styles of the language experience activities vary in accordance with students' developmental and functional levels and areas of interest:

1. Group activities
   a. A traditional language experience activity, perhaps using language charts
   b. A "story go-around"—a group activity centering around story development as students take turns adding to a story in a sequential manner
2. Individualized activities
   a. Individualized storybook
   b. Individualized story unit

Readiness Activities. The purpose of the readiness activities is to prepare students to attend to the group activities, to elicit background information relative to the story, and to foster language and vocabulary development. During this segment of the language experience approach, an attempt is made to expose students to all the vocabulary that will be used in the subsequent activities. Activities can be for a group or individuals:

1. Group activities
   a. Group discussion
   b. Vocabulary development and enrichment
2. Individualized activities
   a. Topic discussion
   b. Vocabulary development and enrichment

The readiness activities precede both the group and the individual language experience lessons and are directed toward the development of students' thought processes. Vocabulary readiness activities are meant to introduce students to a story's vocabulary.

Instructional Levels. The level of the language experience approach should be in accordance with students' developmental and functional levels as well as interest areas. An attempt should be made to approximate students' language experience output to their reading decoding and comprehension ability. For beginning reading students, an initial language experience output may involve a single sentence, usually a description of a picture or a situation, followed by a short paragraph consisting of three to five short sentences, which is followed by more extensive written material such as a short story. At the intermediate level, story writing can begin at the paragraph level and extend to several paragraphs and even a full story. At the more advanced level, the language experience approach may begin with an extended story in line with students' functional level.

Four instructional levels are distinguished in a language experience approach:

Level 1: Students dictates material to the teacher.
   a. Picture captions: Students are presented with a picture for which they provide a brief description. The students' verbal expressive output is dictated to the teacher, who in turn writes it down for the students.
   b. Story elaboration: Students dictate to the teacher several sentences describing the picture. The teacher writes them down for the students.
   c. Story dictation: Students dictate to the teacher several sentences or a short story in their area of interest. (Figures 13–5 and 13–6.)

Figure 13–5   Sample Color Coded Dictated Story

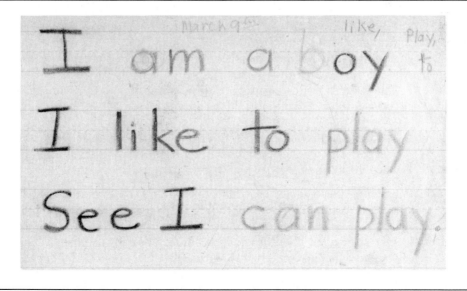

Figure 13−6   Sample Color Coded Dictated Story

Level 2: Students dictate material to the teacher. The teacher writes it down, and the students copy what the teacher has written (Figure 13−7).

Level 3: Both the teacher and students are involved in the writing process. The teacher writes a sentence, which is followed by a sentence written by a student, and/or the student completes the sentence (Figure 13−8, p. 399).

Level 4: Students write the story on their own with assistance from the teacher. The teacher provides any words with which students may have difficulties (Figure 13−9, p. 400).

In all the language experience levels, the teacher must keep in mind the following principles: (a) Sentence and story lengths should be in line with students' ability to read back the story; (b) a degree of vocabulary control should be maintained through guided teaching—the teacher should use a vocabulary box for each story; (c) repetition of words should be encouraged through guided teaching; (d) language experience output should be typed and returned to students as soon as possible; and (e) language experience output should be followed with activities in vocabulary development and reading comprehension. In addition, the language experience ap-

Figure 13–7   Sample Students' Stories

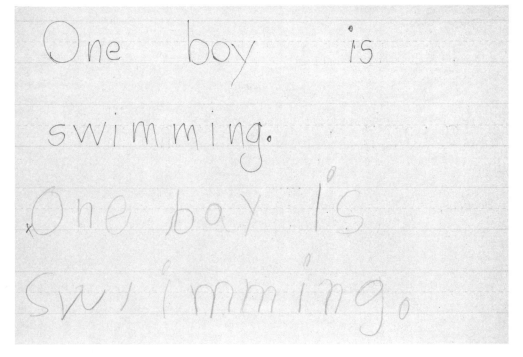

proach can be enhanced at all levels by using word processors. The use of computer technology makes generating written material and correcting errors easy and provides immediate feedback to students (see also chapter 14).

Integration With Other Teaching Procedures. The language experience approach should be integrated with other reading methods and with other language arts areas,

Figure 13–7   Continued

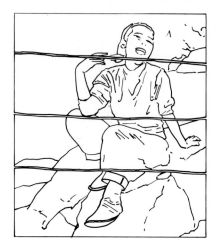

A girl is sitting
on a rock near the lake.
She is happy.

A girl is sitting
on a rock near the lake.
She is happy.

specifically spelling and reading. The teacher may include selected vocabulary from the language experience output in the spelling unit for the week. Appropriate selection of reading materials can further expose students to vocabulary in a similar area of interest and/or content. In addition, the teacher should integrate other reading approaches within the language experience approach, such as the phonic and/or

Figure 13–8   Sample Sentence Completion Stories

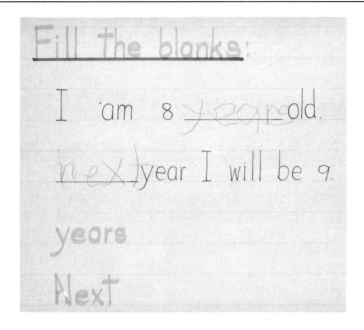

linguistic approach, color coding, and the use of a rebus (a symbol) in lieu of a word when it is necessary (Figures 13–10, p. 401 and 13–11, p. 402).

The Fernald (VAKT) Approach

The Fernald approach is a whole word multisensory approach. It is somewhat of a modification of the basic language experience approach in which the emphasis is on individual student storybooks. Generally, the day begins with story writing. The teacher presents a discussion topic to motivate students to write. Students are then given the choice of writing on this topic or on one of their own choosing. As they begin to write the story, they may raise their hand when needing help in writing a new word. Such words are written for the students with crayon on 3" × 11" sheets of newsprint in plain blackboard-size script or print. Students trace the words with their finger while saying each part of the words. Students write the words first on scrap paper and then in their story. The words are filed in a word file under the proper initial letters. After a story has been written, it is typed and read by the students the next day.

Four stages are involved in the Fernald approach (Fernald, 1943):

Stage 1. Children learn by tracing words.
          a. Words are written for children with crayon on paper in plain blackboard-size script (or print).

Figure 13–9 Sample Students' Stories

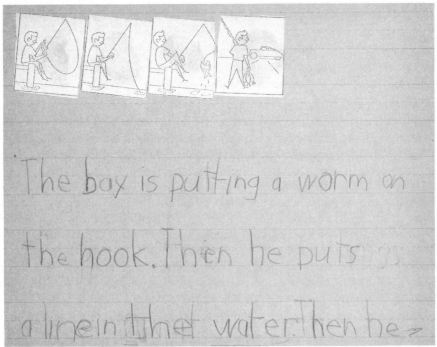

Figure 13–10   Sample Science Language Experience Story

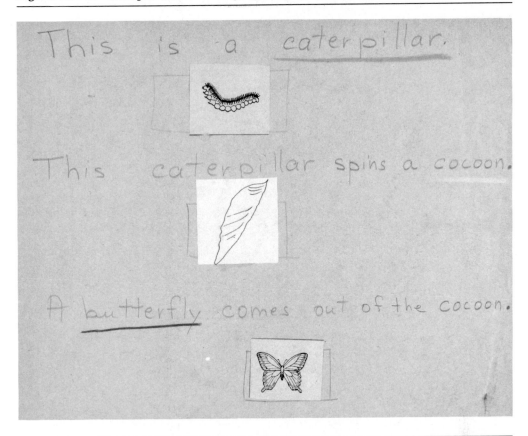

b. Children trace words with finger contact while saying each part of the words.
c. Children repeat the process as many times as needed to write the words without looking at the copy.
d. Children write words once on scrap paper and then in their story.
e. After a story has been written, it is typed for them, and they read it in print.
f. Children file words under their proper letters in a word file.

Stage 2. Same as Stage 1, except tracing is no longer needed.

Stage 3. Like Stage 2 except children are able to learn from the printed word by merely looking at it and saying it to themselves before writing it.

Stage 4. Children have the ability to recognize new words from their similarity to words or parts of words already learned.

The Fernald approach is a modified language experience approach in which reading, writing, and spelling are integrated. The stories are printed with the new words

Figure 13-11 Sample Language Experience Coding Stories

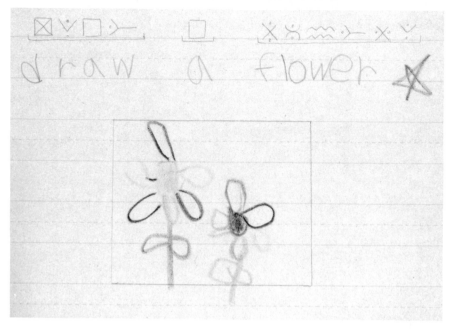

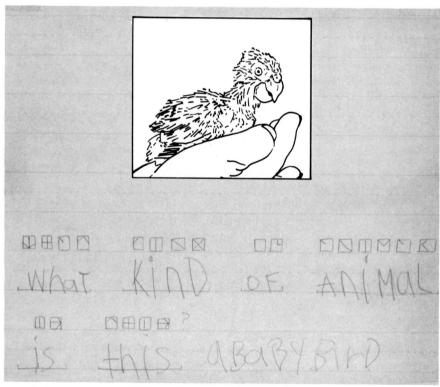

listed at the bottom, and children usually review these words for 3 consecutive days until mastery occurs. In addition, children review the words in the file box weekly. Words that children recognize are normally put away in a different file or destroyed.

The Neurological Impress and Shadow Reading Methods

The neurological impress and shadow reading approaches are based on the natural approach to reading. They are similar to the reading activities parents and grandparents do with young children, namely, reading to them and reading along with them as soon as they acquire some word recognition skills. Children acquire reading skills naturally through imitation. The format of these activities underlies the neurological impress and shadow reading approaches.

The neurological impress method in reading is a remedial reading approach developed and used first by Heckelman in 1966 in the Merced/Sonoma county schools. The general feature of this approach is that students and the teacher read orally in unison at a rapid pace. Generally, the teacher sits slightly behind a student and directs his or her voice into the student's ear at close range. The author recommends that this approach be used consistently for at least 15 minutes per day. The following procedures are usually involved in the neurological impress method:

1. A student sits slightly in front of the teacher.
2. The teacher and the student hold the book jointly.
3. Material is read in unison. The teacher directs her or his voice into the ear of the student at close range.
4. The teacher uses the index finger as a locator, sliding it along to follow the words that are being read.
5. At a later stage, students are instructed to use one finger as a locator, sliding it along to follow words being read.
6. The major goal is to cover as many pages of reading material as possible in the time available (Kaluger & Kolson, 1978).

The shadow reading approach is similar to the neurological impress approach in that the students and the teacher read in unison. Usually the student reads ahead of the teacher. The teacher reads the appropriate word whenever the student stumbles. The student repeats the missed word and continues reading. No attempt is made to analyze the words or to pause for structural analysis. As students gradually achieve mastery level in reading, the teacher's voice fades away, allowing students to read on their own. The use of the neurological impress and shadow reading approaches in remedial reading is very helpful in developing an appreciation for reading.

Oral Reading Strategies

Various opinions exist as to the benefit of oral reading in the process of reading instruction. According to Strang (1978), "Oral reading through intonation, stress, and rhythm, gives additional clues to meaning that silent reading does not give" (p. 70). Others admit some possible interference with silent reading from overemphasis on oral reading (Spache, 1963).

In the remedial reading process, oral reading may have a facilitating and/or an inhibiting effect, depending on the situation in which it is applied. Some learning-disabled individuals who are shy and have low self-confidence reluctantly agree to oral reading. The level of anxiety in oral reading does not justify its use for these individuals. On the other hand, some learning-disabled students benefit from oral reading inasmuch as they need auditory feedback to facilitate reading comprehension. As a matter of fact, their reading comprehension is heightened through oral reading.

According to Strang (1978), if oral reading is to take its rightful place in the total reading program, it must be properly taught. Because oral reading interferes with reading comprehension for some individuals, students should be given time to read the text silently before reading aloud.

Heideman, as cited by Smith and Johnson (1980), notes 10 good reasons why reading instruction should also involve reading aloud:

1. All language has oral beginnings. Story telling is probably the first and most ancient of language arts experiences.
2. Reading aloud is a way of reaching nonreaders in a special way.
3. Reading aloud is a way of expanding even good readers' horizons.
4. Many people are impoverished in their language experiences, and reading out loud can enrich students' language background.
5. Reading aloud can significantly improve children's writing ability.
6. Reading aloud is the only way to teach and appreciate poetry.
7. Oral reading is a wonderful way to help children step outside themselves, to visit another culture, to experience what someone else may be feeling, to go back in time to a period in which ways of thinking and expression may have been quite different from our own.
8. Reading aloud is the best way in the world of taking a break in the middle of a frantic school day, thus bringing a sense of relaxation and enjoyment.
9. Reading aloud is a wonderful way to get close to people.
10. Reading aloud develops careful critical listening, which lays the groundwork for critical thinking in the children we teach.

Oral reading can be used in different formats: taking turns in small groups; having individuals read to the teacher; finding and reading answers to questions; doing audience reading; doing choral reading; reading parts in radio or TV scripts or plays; and reading with varied intonation patterns (Harris & Sipay, 1985).

Bringing Reading Skills to an Automatic Level

At any level of reading instruction, the teacher should attempt to have students reach a mastery level. The mastery level is that level at which students demonstrate mastery in the decoding skills appropriate to the level of instruction. Automaticity is a process that facilitates the mastery level. The extent to which students have reached a mastery level is determined by the degree of automaticity of this level, namely, that students should be able to read these word patterns at an automatic level without any hesitation. The automatic level of reading is the goal of reading instruction—that students read materials at the automatic level that corresponds to their verbal expressive level. This type of reading is important if we are to develop students' reading fluency. Skillful readers are able to read at the automatic level. Freed from the burdens of decoding, they can thus focus on higher order processes and reading related to deriving meaning from the material read. Two criteria apply to the mastery of reading: accuracy and automaticity. Accuracy requires learners' attention and involves responding to stimuli correctly, and automaticity involves producing the correct response rapidly (LaBerge & Samuels, 1974). In other words, students know how to decode CVCV words and generally read them rapidly.

Reading Comprehension Approaches and Strategies

Developing Reading Comprehension Skills

Reading comprehension involves a complex system of processing written information, requiring both general and specific skills, and it is directly related to one's background, including language and cognitive domains, social experience, and emotional development. Among the factors that influence the ability to comprehend are language development and competence, cognitive abilities, subjective feelings toward reading, the ability to relate to reading content in a positive way, the general developmental and interest levels, the decoding skills level, and the level of the material read.

Readers must possess various abilities that facilitate the reading comprehension process:

1. *Ability to locate answers.* To become proficient at this task, readers must be able to distinguish relevant information from irrelevant information, and to skim to find pertinent paragraphs.
2. *Ability to follow a sequence.* Cause-effect relationships must be understood if readers are to reproduce a story or events in order.
3. *Ability to grasp the main idea.* Basic to many other comprehension skills is the ability to skim material in order to glean a total impression. Grasping the main idea gives readers the scope and tone of material to be read.
4. *Ability to note details.* In-depth studies require the use of this skill. Until readers have mastered this skill, they are unable to see the relationship of details to the main idea.
5. *Ability to determine organization.* To fully comprehend factual material, readers must recognize elements such as introduction, body, conclusion, headings, subheadings, paragraph organization, and topic sentences.
6. *Ability to follow direction.* This skill is the amalgamation of three skills: noting details, determining organization, and grasping sequence.
7. *Ability to read critically.* Readers must engage material in a dialogue, comparing this printed material with other material or with the total conceptual background possessed. They must be able to recognize and

resist subtle persuasions and propaganda. It is an investigation calling for reason.

8. *Ability to organize and summarize.* This highest skill involves all other skills (Kaluger & Kolson, 1978).

Reading comprehension skills development can be achieved through the following teaching procedures:

1. *Oral/listening reading comprehension.* Stories are read by the teacher and/or by students individually or in a group, and the material is discussed across the various levels of reading comprehension, involving as many reading comprehension skills as possible.

2. *Silent reading comprehension.* Stories are read by students and are usually followed by reading comprehension exercises. These involve a variety of reading comprehension materials and follow-up activities, encompassing various types of reading comprehension skills. They include reading fiction material, facts and information, newspapers and magazines, and other current events materials. These materials may vary with their complexity and difficulty levels, and may include a single paragraph, ministories (about 4–5 paragraphs), short stories (about 10–12 paragraphs), selected passages from literature, and books.

3. *Dramatization and plays.* The integration of reading comprehension with oral language and active participation is achieved through students' involvement in play production.

4. *Media presentation and discussion.* Viewing films and/or television shows and listening to stories from tapes or radio followed by a discussion promote understanding of story episodes, development of sequential thought processes, and critical thinking.

5. *Critical thinking activities.* Critical thinking activities such as determining analogous relationships, understanding multiple meanings, inferring from context, organizing and sequencing ideas, and finding cause-and-effect relationships are among the various logical thinking activities that promote reading comprehension. One may also use various games that promote logical thinking and sequencing, such as Treasure Hunt, Charades, and others.

Cognitive and Metacognitive Approaches and Strategies

The characteristics of the learning disabled and poor readers have been discussed earlier in the text. Generally, learning-disabled students fail to become actively involved in their own learning process (Torgesen, 1982); they approach cognitive tasks in an inefficient manner (Wiens, 1983); and they do not use active learning strategies. Unlike skilled readers, poor readers lack knowledge about the purpose of reading and do not apply strategies spontaneously. They also fail to monitor their progress (Bransford et al., 1980; Brown & Smiley, 1978; Canney & Winograd, 1979; Markman, 1979; Paris & Myers, 1981; Pearson et al., 1979; Short & Ryan, 1984; Smiley et al., 1977).

The metacognitive approach takes the position that students can be taught to become more aware of the reading processes and factors that impede or facilitate their progress in reading. They can be taught various strategies to master the skills of reading, including the monitoring of their reading activities.

Recent developments in theory and research on metacognition have led to greater success in designing instruction aimed at improving reading skills (Baker & Brown, 1984). The application of metacognitive theory to various aspects of reading has been extensively investigated. The findings point to a significant improvement in students' reading behavior following metacognitive training. After metacomprehension training, students tend to use strategies more effectively and to monitor their reading behavior, which results in general improvement in their reading comprehension (Babbs & Moe, 1983; Brailsford, Snart, & Das, 1984; Brown & Palincsar, 1982; Canney & Winograd, 1979; Chan & Cole, 1986; Heller, 1986; Sanacore, 1984; Short & Ryan, 1984; Wagoner, 1983; Wong & Jones, 1982). Training children to segment and blend words increases their word recognition skills (Lloyd & Kniedler, 1979). Knowledge of the reading process and strategies gives readers control and facilitates their reading fluency (Stewart & Tei, 1983). The underlying characteristics of metacognitive approaches to reading involve an increase in individuals' awareness of various aspects of reading, the utilization of effective strategies, and the regulation of activities.

In applying metacognitive principles to reading instruction, the LD specialist must know the reading process and the functions involved in reading, including the specific skills necessary in reading recognition and comprehension. Because of students' past failure experiences and difficulties in reading, the teacher must carefully create an environment that is conducive to reading instruction. The following represent the features of successful metacognitive instruction (Palincsar & Brown, 1987): "1) careful analysis of the task at hand, 2) the identification of strategies which will promote successful task completion, 3) the explicit instruction of these strategies accompanied by metacognitive information regarding their application, 4) the provision of feedback regarding the usefulness of the strategies and the success with which they are being acquired, and 5) instruction regarding the generalized use of the strategies" (p. 73).

Development and Utilization of Metacognitive-Oriented Strategies
There are several distinctive phases in utilizing a metacognitive approach to reading instruction: (a) the development of students' sensitivity to reading (the purpose and function of reading, students' sensitivity to their own capacity to succeed in learning how to read); (b) the development of students' awareness of what is involved in the reading process and what skills are necessary for successful word recognition and comprehension; (c) the development of selected sets of strategies for specific areas of reading; and (d) the monitoring of strategy acquisition, strategy implementation, and progress.

Through the learning process analysis activity (discussed previously in chapter 6), the teacher and students discuss the goals and the purpose of reading, the functions involved in reading, and the specific skills necessary to complete the tasks successfully. Students increase their metacognitive knowledge of the reading process, including the demands imposed by different types of reading tasks and materials. The teacher and students plan how to go about succeeding in specific tasks and jointly develop metacognitive-oriented strategies. The learning process analysis activity involves (a) analysis of the task at hand, its characteristics and functions; (b) identification of the skills necessary to complete the task successfully; (c) identification of effective strategies needed, taking into account individuals' strengths and weaknesses and learning styles; (d) the steps to be followed to ensure successful completion of the task—students are encouraged to discuss and rehearse the steps in order to assure that they understand the process; and (e) a decision-making process of how to go about implementing the strategies and how to monitor and regulate one's attempt in completing the task successfully (Ariel, 1991). Through interactive teaching, students discuss the nature of the task, its characteristics, and the requirements for its successful completion. They identify and develop appropriate strategies and reach consensus on the most effective ones, prioritizing them in order of their implementation. To facilitate discussion, students are provided with a strategy guide. Figure 13–12 is a sample strategy guide for reading comprehension.

The role of the teacher in such activity is to elicit student responses and to engage students in the process. It is like the role of an "expert" providing the support necessary through the metacognitive process (Palincsar & Brown, 1987). Initially, the teacher assumes responsibility in leading students in the identification and modeling of the necessary strategies. Responsibility is gradually shifted to students, who take control of their own learning in implementing the strategies and monitoring their progress. Throughout the instructional process, students must be involved in setting their goals and in the selection of appropriate reading tasks and materials. In addition, the teacher should share with students the rationale for the selections of the reading teaching approaches.

The learning process analysis procedures can be applied to any area of reading, including sounding out words, developing vocabulary, finding the main idea, comprehending selected passages, and reading and analyzing literature. For example, following a discussion of the skills necessary to find the main idea of a paragraph effectively, these strategies were identified and suggested:

1. Know what you are asked to do.
2. Read the story and identify the key words (when, where, who, what, why) and phrases.
3. Use clues to help you (title of story and pictures).
4. Identify the topic sentence.
5. Identify the character or supporting details associated with the main idea.
6. Complete the follow-up activities and check your answers.

The students use a metacognitive checklist for finding the main idea to help them monitor their strategy application. The responsibility for monitoring is given to the students, and therefore the checklists are written in the first person form ("I" statements). Figure 13–13 is a sample strategy implementation and self-monitoring sheet for finding the main idea. Similarly, Figure 13–14, p. 411, is a sample strategy imple-

Figure 13–12   Strategy Guide for Reading Comprehension

Read, Think, Strategize:

ON THE ROAD TO SUCCESS

Strategies For Processing Information

Reading Comprehension: Understanding What We Read

Challenge Guide
   Reading comprehension involves many skills. All of these skills will help you understand and remember what you read. Reading comprehension will help you do better in all of the subjects. The use of strategies will help you to improve your reading comprehension.
Super Skills
   Identify the main idea and pertinent details
   Discriminate essential from nonessential material
   Sequence information in the proper order
   Determine cause and effect relationships
   Make inference and draw conclusions
   Predict outcomes
Pledge for Success
   I identify the main idea and pertinent details
   I discriminate essential from nonessential material
   I sequence information in the proper order
   I determine cause and effect relationships
   I make inference and draw conclusions
   I predict outcomes

Source: From *Stepping Up to Success: Metacognition Elementary Student Handbook* by A. Ariel, 1989. Unpublished manuscript, California State University, Los Angeles. Reprinted by permission.

mentation and self-monitoring sheet for reading comprehension. These forms are used daily to monitor students' implementation and success in using the strategies. They can be easily integrated with the teacher's grading and evaluation system as well as classroom management procedures.

Self-Questioning Instruction

Self-questioning instruction is a procedure that utilizes self-questioning technique in an attempt to guide students to draw meaningful information from a text and to monitor comprehension of text material. These questions activate relevant prior knowledge or schemata to aid and/or enrich students' prose processing (Wong, 1985). According to Wong (1985), this self-questioning instruction is based on the assumption that "active comprehenders and independent thinkers" generate questions that shape and guide their thinking in reading. In order to generate self-questioning that promotes thorough comprehension, the reader must possess "a) an

Figure 13–13 Finding the Main Idea: Strategy Implementation and Monitoring Sheet

COMMITMENT TO SUCCESS: STRATEGY USE

Set 6: Power Reading

Skills/Behaviors I Need to Learn:	How Will I Do It? (Strategies)	How Am I Doing? Key: √−; √; √+;					
		M	T	W	Th	F	Overall
Finding the Main Idea	I know what I am asked to do.						
	I read the story and identify the key words (when, where, who, what, why) and phrases.						
	I use clues to help me - title of story and pictures.						
	I identify the topic sentence.						
	I identify the character or supporting details associated with the main idea.						
	I do the followup and check my answer.						
Individualized Goal							

Teacher's Comments:

Student's Comments: This Is the Way I See Myself

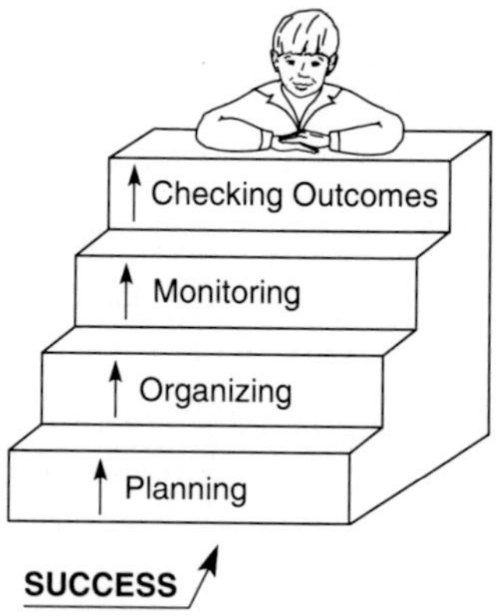

Checking Outcomes

Monitoring

Organizing

Planning

SUCCESS

Source: From *Successful Learning: Metacognition Secondary Student Handbook, Level III, Book 1* by A. Ariel, 1987. Unpublished manuscript, California State University, Los Angeles. Reprinted by permission.

awareness of the functional importance of clarifying and comprehension-monitoring questions and other useful self-questions (e.g., critical evaluative ones), and b) an awareness of the task demands (i.e., the purpose in one's reading)" (p. 240).

Students are encouraged to generate questions about the important parts of the text, such as: What is the main idea in the paragraph? and What are the supporting

Figure 13–14 Reading Comprehension: Strategy Implementation and Monitoring Sheet

COMMITMENT TO SUCCESS: STRATEGY USE

Set 6: Power Reading

Skills/Behaviors I Need to Learn:	How Will I Do It? (Strategies)	How Am I Doing? Key: ✓−; ✓; ✓+;					
		M	T	W	Th	F	Overall
Reading Comprehension	I identify the main idea and pertinent details.						
	I sequence information in the proper order.						
	I determine cause and effect relationships.						
	I make inference and draw conclusions.						
	I can predict outcomes.						
	I can discriminate essential from nonessential material.						
Individualized Goal							

Teacher's Comments:

Student's Comments: This Is the Way I See Myself

↑ Checking Outcomes

↑ Monitoring

↑ Organizing

↑ Planning

SUCCESS ↗

Source: From *Successful Learning: Metacognition Secondary Student Handbook, Level III, Book 1* by A. Ariel, 1987. Unpublished manuscript, California State University, Los Angeles. Reprinted by permission.

details? In addition, the students also generate questions that help them monitor their comprehension of the text: Do I understand the material read? Do I know the main idea? Is there anything I do not understand in this paragraph?

Similar to self-questioning instruction, story structure training (Griffey, Zigmond, & Leinhardt, 1988) guides students as they read to ask questions pertaining to story structure elements: Who are the main characters in the story? What is the aim of the story? Is there a problem and how do the characters solve the problem?

Both self-questioning and story structure strategies are effective in enhancing reading comprehension skills of individuals with learning disabilities (Griffey et al., 1988; Wong, 1985).

Developing Reading Comprehension Using a Paraphrasing Strategy

The paraphrasing strategy was designed to help increase students' reading comprehension. It was developed and validated by Deshler and his colleagues (Schumaker, Denton, & Deshler, 1984) at the University of Kansas, and it is a part of the acquisition strand of the Strategies Intervention Model. This strategy uses the acronym RAP as a mnemonic system to help students improve their ability to recall the main idea and specific details of a reading passage by putting them into their own words.

The acronym RAP stands for

R Read a paragraph.
A Ask yourself, "What were the main idea and details in this paragraph?"
P Put the main idea and details into your own words.

Students are given a pretest using a reading passage comparable in difficulty to those used in regular classroom textbooks. This pretest determines whether or not students have mastered the procedure of paraphrasing. Those students requiring the strategy write a goal indicating their commitment to learn, and receive an advance organizer to monitor their progress. Over a period of 4 to 6 weeks, students learn to define the main idea and details of a paragraph and to locate them. Cue cards are used to help students find the main idea by asking questions—What is this paragraph about? What does it tell me about?—and telling them where to look—Look in the first sentence of the paragraph; look for repetition of the same word or words in the whole paragraph. Requirements as to what constitutes a good paraphrase are also outlined on the cue cards. Through controlled practice and feedback, students soon master the procedure of paraphrasing. Deshler and his colleagues cite this strategy as being useful "when students have to read something and then have to take a test over the information, have to answer oral teacher questions or written homework questions in their own words, or have to write a report using their own words about something they have read" (Schumaker et al., 1984, p. 3). Teaching the strategy involves adherence to the instructional procedures using the eight steps that were highlighted in chapter 7.

Reciprocal Teaching Strategy

In reciprocal teaching, Palincsar and Brown (1984) train students in critical strategies to enhance comprehension of a text. Reciprocal teaching is "a dialogue between teachers and students for the purpose of jointly constructing the meaning of a text" (Palincsar, 1986, p. 119). In reciprocal teaching, teachers and students are engaged in a dialogue about the content of the text as well as the value of strategy utilization. Students are encouraged to act as discussion leaders and coach each other in applying the strategies. They are asked to assume the role of teachers at times in order to generate questions, summaries, predictions, and clarifications (Paris, Cross, & Lipson, 1984).

Four activities or strategies structure the dialogue:

1. Summarizing—Identifying and paraphrasing the main idea in the text.
2. Question Generating—Self-questioning about the type of information that is generally tapped on tests of comprehension and recall.
3. Clarifying—Discerning when there has been a breakdown in comprehension and taking the necessary action to restore meaning (e.g., reading ahead, rereading, asking for assistance).
4. Predicting—Hypothesizing what the structure and content of the text suggest will be presented next. (Palincsar, 1986, p. 119)

Reciprocal teaching is based on the principle of expert scaffolding in which the expert guides the learner. As the learner becomes more experienced and capable of performing more complex tasks, the expert gradually allows the learner to take over the major responsibilities for strategy utilization. The strategy attempts to develop students' understanding of both the explicit and implicit purposes of reading and to activate students' background knowledge. It is aimed at engaging students in a more meaningful way to facilitate an awareness of the text. The purpose of reciprocal teaching is to teach students strategies to enhance comprehension, to apply strategies independently, and to monitor text comprehension (Brown, Palincsar, & Armbruster, 1984; Palincsar, 1986).

Six functions critical to successful comprehension of a text were identified by Brown et al. (1984):

1. Clarifying the purposes of reading (i.e., understanding the task demands, both explicit and implicit)
2. Activating relevant background knowledge
3. Allocating attention so that concentration can be focused on the major content at the expense of trivia
4. Critical evaluation of content for internal consistency and compatibility with prior knowledge and common sense
5. Monitoring ongoing activities to see if comprehension is occurring, by engaging in such activities as periodic review and self-interrogation
6. Drawing and testing inferences of many kinds, including interpretations, predictions, and conclusions (p. 263)

The following are procedural steps in using the reciprocal teaching approach:

1. Students are encouraged to make use of background information regarding the topic at hand, to make predictions of what they will learn in the text, and to indicate what they would like to learn regarding the topic.

2. The teacher and students read the segment silently or orally.
3. The teacher or the students ask questions about the text.
4. The teacher summarizes and invites elaborations on the summary from others in the group.

According to Palincsar (1986), during the initial phases of reciprocal teaching, the adult teacher assumes responsibility for initiating and sustaining the dialogue, and models and provides instruction regarding the four strategies. As students learn the strategies, the teacher transfers increased responsibilities to them while providing feedback and coaching them through the dialogue. An example of a dialogue from a reciprocal teaching session is provided in Figure 13–15.

Use of Graphic Organizers

Story mapping, semantic mapping, and the story frame use graphic organizers to improve students' ability to recall and comprehend information within the text (Fowler & Davis, 1985; Idol, 1987; Pearson & Johnson, 1978; Sinatra, Berg, & Dunn, 1985). These approaches use visual means to develop strategies for organizing verbal material, concepts, and important vocabulary to be learned.

Story Mapping

Story mapping increases students' awareness of the text structure and their sequential thought processes. In story mapping, story parts can be thought of as a type of story schema for organizing important story components. In addition, students learn to distinguish between important and unimportant information. In story mapping, story parts can be organized into components such as the setting, the problem, the goal, action events and episodes, and the outcome (Idol, 1987).

Idol (1987) used a three-phase design to gradually develop students' behavior toward a mastered and independent level of learning. In the first phase, the teacher models the desired comprehension responses. In the second phase, students follow the teacher's lead receiving assistance when necessary. In the third phase, students are required to apply the story-mapping strategy independently without teacher assistance. A story map and a set of questions are used to teach story mapping. The questions are as follows:

1. Where did this story take place?
2. When did this story take place?
3. Who were the main characters in the story?
4. Were there any other important characters in the story? Who?
5. What was the problem in the story?
6. How did _____ try to solve the problem?
7. Was it hard to solve the problem? Explain.
8. Was the problem solved? Explain.
9. What did you learn from reading this story? Explain.
10. Can you think of a different ending? (Idol, 1987, p. 197)

Students are also provided with a story-mapping chart (Figure 13–16).

Figure 13–15 Sample Reciprocal Teaching Dialogue

Text from which students are working:

Crows have another gift. They are great mimics. They can learn to talk and imitate animal sounds. Some have been known to learn 100 words, and even whole phrases. They can imitate the squeak of a chicken, the whine of a dog, or the meow of a cat.

Games have a certain fascination to crows. In a game of hide-and-seek, a crow hides in the hollow of a tree and then sounds a distress caw. The others rush to the spot, look around, then flap away. This may be done over and over, after which the young crow pops out of its hiding place and caws gleefully. Far from being annoyed at this, the flock bursts into loud cawing themselves. They seem to like the trick that has been played on them.

T: Chantel, you're our teacher, right? Why don't you summarize first? Remember, just tell me the most important parts.

S1   Crows have a hundred words they can learn by imitation. They can imitate chickens, the whine of a dog, and cats.

T   Okay. We can shorten that summary a bit.

S2   You could say they can imitate other animals.

T   Oh! Good one! There's a list there, Chantel, did you notice that? It says they can imitate the squawk of a chicken, the whine of a dog or the meow of a cat; and you could call that "animal sounds." Can you ask us a question?

S1   Ain't no questions here.

S3   The words (sic.) that need to be clarified are (sic.) "mimics."

S4   That means imitate, right?

T   Right. How did you figure that out, Shirley?

S4   The paragraph.

T   Show us how somebody could figure out what "mimic" means.

S5   They are great mimics. They can learn to talk and imitate animal sounds.

T   Yes, so the next sentence tells you what it means. Very good. Anything else need to be clarified?

All No.

T   What about that question we need to ask? (pause) What is the second paragraph about, Chantel?

S1   The games they play.

S3   They do things like people do.

S4   What kinds of games do crows play?

S3   Hide and seek. Over and over again.

T   You know what, Larry? That was a real good comparison. One excellent question could be, "How are crows like people?"

S4   They play hide and seek.

T   Good. Any other questions there?

S2   How come the crows don't get annoyed?

S5   What does annoyed mean?

T   Irritated, bothered.

S5   Because they like it, they have fun. If I had a crow, I'd tell him he was it and see what he'd do.

T   Let's summarize now and have some predictions.

S1   This was about how they play around in games.

T   Good for you. That's it. Predictions anyone?

S2   Maybe more tricks they play.

S4   Other games.

T   Maybe. So far, they have told us several ways that crows are very smart; they can communicate with one another, they can imitate many sounds, and they play games. Maybe we will read about another way in which they are smart. Who will be the next teacher?

Source: From "Metacognitive Strategy Instruction" by A. S. Palincsar, 1986, _Exceptional Children, 53_(2), p. 120. Copyright 1986 by Exceptional Children. Reprinted by permission.

Figure 13–16 Story-Mapping Chart

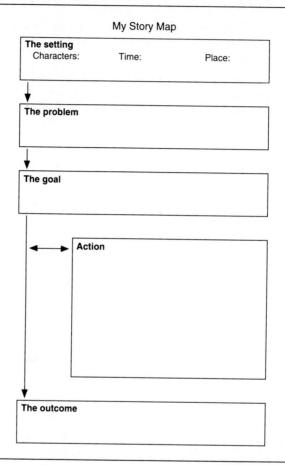

Source: From "Group Story Mapping: A Comprehension Strategy for Both Skilled and Unskilled Readers" by L. Idol, 1987, *Journal of Learning Disabilities, 20,* p. 199. Copyright 1987 by Journal of Learning Disabilities. Reprinted by permission.

Semantic Mapping

Similarly, semantic mapping or a semantic network (Sinatra et al., 1985) uses a visuospatial graphing strategy to organize verbal material in a meaningful way. The semantic mapping approach is based on classification of relationships that exist among concepts and utilizes the individual's prior schema in the process of organizing the new material (Pearson & Johnson, 1978; Stein & Glenn, 1978). Semantic mapping attempts to develop students' schemata so that they may activate them as they read. Semantic mapping is a network that has both verbal and nonverbal components in which concepts are displayed within nodes and links are drawn between nodes to represent association between concepts. In a semantic mapping procedure, meaningful connections are developed between vocabulary, concepts, and different story parts. It provides a framework for the organization of information and develops a mind-set for exploration of new material. The map is used both in the readiness stage, when new vocabulary and concepts are introduced, and during a group discussion during the reading activity. The map helps students in associating present learning with previously acquired learning and in enhancing comprehension of a text. A sample semantic mapping for the selection "Mickey Mouse Becomes a Star" is presented in Figure 13−17. In this graphic organizer, one can easily identify the four major episodes in the story along with the subevents and details related to each one. Semantic mapping helps students relate story episodes to each other and to their own life experience, thus strengthening comprehension of a text (Sinatra et al., 1985).

Story Frame

In the story frame approach (Fowler & Davis, 1985), the teacher constructs frames that become the focus of students' discussions and written assignments. A story frame is used to guide students in follow-up activities and replaces the traditional comprehension questions following reading assignments. The story frame is an activity prompt that guides students to pay attention to specific elements in a story. It provides a meaningful structure for organizing the text information (Fowler & Davis, 1985). A typical story frame for identifying problems/main ideas is presented in Figure 13−18.

Figure 13−17   Semantic Map Based on Story Episodes Within "Mickey Mouse Becomes a Star"

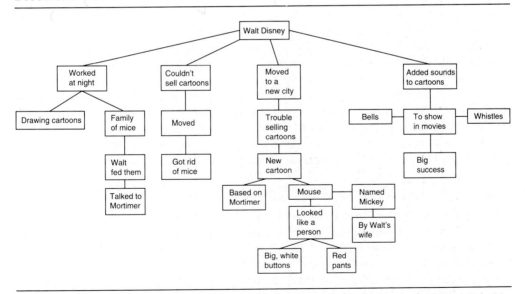

Source: From "Semantic Mapping Improves Reading Comprehension of Learning Disabled Students" by R. C. Sinatra, D. Berg, and R. Dunn, 1985, *Teaching Exceptional Children*, 17(4), p. 313. Copyright 1985 by Teaching Exceptional Children. Reprinted by permission.

Figure 13-18   Story Frame: Identifying Problem/Main Ideas

The problem in this story was _____

It started when _____

After that _____

Then _____

The problem is solved when _____

The story ends _____

Source: From "The Story Frame Approach: A Tool for Improving Reading Comprehension of EMR Children" by G. L. Fowler and M. Davis, 1985, *Teaching Exceptional Children, 18*(3), p. 297. Copyright 1985 by Teaching Exceptional Children. Reprinted by permission.

Story-Retelling Strategy

This is probably the most simplistic and yet very effective approach to teaching individual readers to understand what reading comprehension involves and to heighten reading comprehension skills. Depending on the level of each individual and the nature of the material, students are asked to pretend that they are the author and to relate the story in their own words to the teacher or to a group of listeners. Through this process, students realize that they have to (a) attempt to retain the information read in a sequential manner, (b) sift unimportant from important information, (c) attempt to distinguish between detailed information and general information, (d) be able to understand the sequence of events, and (e) lead the listener to the aims of the author in terms of the primary intentions of the story.

Remedial Reading Instructional Materials and Aids

Strategies for Selecting Instructional Materials

As pointed out previously, the objectives of the remedial program are to develop students' overall reading skills and an appreciation for reading. One of the best ways to reach these goals is to give students opportunities to be exposed to reading materials that are at their functional and interest levels, which increase their success. If reading materials are too high for their abilities, as is quite often the case, feelings of success and adequacy are supplanted by feelings of helplessness and frustration. In general, teachers tend to ignore students in the selection of reading materials.

Through properly structured interviews, a teacher can elicit student input as to the types of materials they like to read.

Reading instructional materials must be evaluated in terms of their appropriateness in meeting the major goals of reading decoding and/or reading comprehension. The materials must cover the various necessary subskills. They must have an age-appropriate style and an easily presentable format. Students' functional and interest levels must always guide the teacher in the selection of appropriate reading materials.

Reading Instructional Materials
The list in Table 13–2 is a sample of reading instructional materials and/or programs and their age appropriateness and/or instructional level.

Using Reading Instruments
The purpose of reading instruments is to provide students with drill and practice in word recognition skills and reading fluency. They provide an additional avenue for individualized instruction. The most common reading instruments are tachisto-scopes and accelerating devices. The tachistoscope exposes letters or words for a short period of time, usually ranging from $\frac{1}{100}$ to $1\frac{1}{2}$ seconds, and assists students in developing their word recognition skills to the automatic level. Accelerating devices such as the control reader present material in the left-to-right direction at a predetermined rate. A moving slot travels across the screen in a left-to-right direction, covering and uncovering the materials as it moves along. This activity is par-

Table 13–2 Reading Instructional Materials

Program	Reading Level	Interest Level	Publisher
Action Reading System and Double Action	2–6	Intermediate/Secondary	Scholastic Book Services
Advanced Reading Skills	4–8	Intermediate/Secondary	Readers Digest
Breakthrough Series	1–8	Intermediate/Secondary	Allyn and Bacon
Cowboy Sam Series	PP–3	Primary/Elementary	Allyn and Bacon
Distar Reading	1–3	Elementary/Intermediate/Secondary	Science Research Associates
Encyclopedia Brown Series	1–4	Elementary	Bantam Books
Eye and Ear Fun	P–5	Primary/Elementary/Intermediate/Secondary	Webster
Miami Linguistic Readers	P–2	Primary/Elementary	Heath
Merrill Linguistic Readers	1–5	Elementary	Merrill Publishers
New Diagnostic Reading Workbook Series	1–6	Elementary/Intermediate	Merrill

Table 13–2   Continued

Program	Reading Level	Interest Level	Publisher
Pal Paperback Series	1–5	Elementary/Intermediate/Secondary	Xerox Education Publication
Phonics Skill Builders	1–6	Primary/Elementary	McCormick-Mathers
Primary Readers	P–2	Primary	Modern Curriculum Press
Readers Digest Skill Builders	1–4	Elementary	Readers Digest
Reading Developmental Kits	P–10	Elementary/Intermediate/Secondary	Addison-Wesley
Reading for Concepts	3–8	Elementary/Intermediate/Secondary	McGraw-Hill
Reading for Meaning	4–10	Intermediate/Secondary/Adults	Lippincott
Sailor Jack Series	P–3	Elementary	Benefic Press
Specific Skill Series	2–8	Elementary/Intermediate/Secondary	Barnell Loft
SRA Reading Laboratory	1–12	Elementary/Intermediate/Secondary	Science Research Associates
Structural Reading Series	P–5	Primary/Elementary	Singer
Study Skills Library	2–8	Elementary/Intermediate	Educational Development Laboratory
Trouble Shooter I & II	2–6	Intermediate/High school	Houghton Mifflin

ticularly helpful for slow readers and for readers having difficulties with eye movement patterns.

SUMMARY AND CONCLUSIONS

The LD specialist must know about remedial reading teaching approaches in order to select the appropriate method for students. While no one specific remedial reading approach is appropriate for all students, the LD specialist must select such approaches in accordance with students' level of functioning, information-processing style, age, and interest level. The LD specialist must select remedial reading methods that are compatible with each other and include strategy teaching in achieving the goals of the remedial reading instruction discussed in this chapter. In addition, the teacher should incorporate students' oral expressive language abilities and literary experiences in the remedial process to enhance both reading decoding and comprehension and to develop an appreciation for reading.

Teaching Written Language: Written Expression, Spelling, and Handwriting

Questions to Consider

1. **What are the principles of remediation of written expressive language? What are the problems?**

2. **How does one develop a remedial writing program to maximize successful experiences?**

3. **What are some of the concerns in teaching spelling and in the remediation of spelling problems?**

4. **How does one develop an effective spelling program?**

5. **What are the techniques for teaching handwriting skills?**

This chapter is organized into three sections: written language, spelling, and handwriting. Emphasis is on the relationship of these areas to each other and to reading. The text explains the processes involved in the teaching and learning of these language arts areas, with attention given to specific teaching and learning strategies in an integrated, oriented approach to teaching and remediation of language arts deficits.

UNDERSTANDING WRITTEN LANGUAGE AND WRITTEN LANGUAGE PROBLEMS

Writing is often one of the most difficult areas for those with learning disabilities. These students encounter problems in both reading and spelling. They have a hard time acquiring the basic skills for writing, and generally do not understand the basic grammatical rules underlying the written expression process. Inasmuch as writing activities involve spelling and the understanding of grammatical structure, many of the learning-disabled shy away from these activities and usually prefer not to write unless it is an absolute requirement. The written language of students with LD, compared to that of the normal population, has been shown to be significantly lower in syntax, ideation, word usage, and the mechanics of language (Myklebust, 1973; Nodine, Barenbaum, & Newcomer, 1985; Poplin, Gray, Larsen, Banikowski, & Mehring, 1980; Poteet, 1978). For many students with learning disabilities, the source of the problem can be found within the dimension of cognitive processing. In spite of normal intelligence, learning-disabled students have difficulty processing various aspects of linguistic information and hence usually have problems in understanding or producing language (Wren, 1983).

In comparison to good writers, poor writers have difficulties in generating ideas, in understanding cause-and-effect relationships, and in using sequential thought processes. Poor writers are incapacitated by their experience of failure to produce good written output. They are fearful of making mistakes in the various aspects of written language, including syntax, grammar, and spelling. They are fearful of being criticized or ridiculed. They generally have poor verbal expressive abilities, usually do not like to read, and avoid writing as much as possible. More specifically, according to Englert and Raphael (1988), poor writers (a) have difficulty categorizing ideas into sets of related ideas and providing conceptual or superordinate labels for their categorized ideas; (b) have difficulty organizing the presentation of their ideas in the text; (c) lack an understanding of story schemata that is essential not only to writing stories but also to comprehending them; (d) have problems in retrieval and use of relevant schemata from memory that might sustain their thinking and writing in a creative way; (e) reach writing limits far below that of their relevant stored knowledge and lack strategies to guide them in activating new or more complete knowledge searchers; and (f) "exhibit less control of the writing process and are clearly more dependent on external criteria and resources (e.g., teachers) than on their own internal resources to help them monitor the completeness and accuracy of their text" (p. 516).

The Nature of Written Expressive Language

Although it is beyond the intent and scope of this chapter to describe language development fully, an understanding of the nature of language and of its relationship to reading and written expressive language can be helpful to the LD specialist. Language is defined as "a rule-governed symbol system that is capable of representing or coding one's understanding of the world . . . [Furthermore] linguistic knowledge includes learning the tacit rules that govern the meaning of language (semantics), the linguistic structures that encode or represent the semantic intent (syntax), and the rules governing the delivery system of language—either spoken language (phonemic system), signing, or written language (graphic system)" (Bryen, 1981, pp. 27–29). Moreover, language involves "the ability to attach meaning to words and to employ words as symbols for thought. In that respect, written language may be considered as the element of the process that uses symbols for thought so that the result is a visual, readable representation" (Major, 1983, p. 297). Written language involves the complex task of integrating oral language ability with the use of written symbols to produce written expression. It is usually developed after oral language has been nearly mastered and the written symbol system used in reading has been introduced. It is a semantic type of learning in which the auditory symbol system basic to oral language is translated to visual symbols in the form of written language. In addition, written language involves the superimposition of the visual process of the auditory verbal symbol, which results in a complex language process that is extremely difficult for many students with learning disabilities to master (Major, 1983).

Research suggests that the following elements contribute to the development of written expressive language: (a) students' experiential background—those with limited opportunities have fewer expressive abilities and more difficulty in understanding and learning relationships between verbal symbols and the relevant experiences; (b) students' oral expressive language abilities; (c) students' auditory and oral systems, which must be functioning efficiently before writing can be learned; (d) the development of basic visual processing skills that are prerequisite to written language (Major, 1983); and (e) cognitive processing.

Written Language Framework

A framework of language can provide a useful structure in understanding, diagnosing, and remediating language learning disabilities. The LD specialist's understanding of the different forms and components of language is essential to the remedial process. Generally, two forms of language are identified: spoken and written. Spoken language includes speaking and listening. Written or printed language encompasses writing and reading (Harris & Sipay, 1985). Each form has two modes: expressive and receptive. The basic components related to both spoken and written language are phonology, the study of sounds; morphology, the study of the smallest meaningful unit of language; syntax, the arrangement of words in a meaningful order to communicate ideas; and the semantics or vocabulary used and understood (Creaghead, 1986).

Wren (1983) provided us with a multidimensional model of language learning. The model identifies four dimensions of language learning: forms of language, modes of language, modalities of language processing, and a hierarchical order of language experiences.

The first dimension of the model describes the forms of language in terms of verbal and nonverbal. According to Wren, not all language experiences are verbal: There are those that are nonverbal and can interfere with normal communication. Receptive and expressive languages are identified as the second dimension in the model. Students with LD may exhibit different patterns of receptive and expressive learning disabilities. The processing of language through the sensory modalities is identified as the third dimension. The fourth dimension of the model relates to the hierarchy of language experiences—attention, perception, short-term memory, symbolization, conceptualization, and metacognition. Wren (1983) emphasized the interrelationship existing among the four dimensions. An attempt to explain the language difficulties of individuals with learning disabilities based on only one dimension may lead to wrong conclusions. Figure 14–1, based on Johnson and Myklebust's (1967) model of language development and Wren's (1983) multidimensional model of language learning, illustrates the various facets of language and their interrelationship.

The Relationship of Written Language to Reading

Reading is characterized as a language-based activity (Gerber, 1981). In the early stages of the process of learning to read, reading is parasitic on language (Mattingly, 1972), and in the later stages, additional language learning becomes parasitic on reading (H. E. Nelson, 1980). Based on their review of the literature, Kavale et al., (1987) suggest that nearly half the children referred to reading clinics have a history

Figure 14–1   Written Language Framework

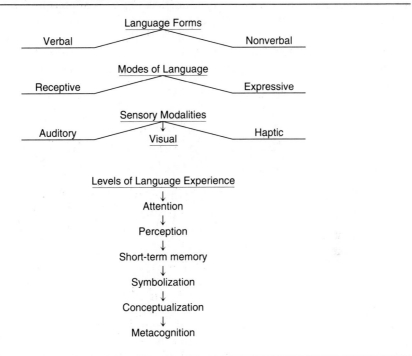

of language and speech difficulties and that their reading difficulties are due to subtle disorders in language.

Reading and writing should be taught together, and the skills of both areas enhance each other's growth (Durkin, 1966; Graves, 1979; Loban, 1976; May, 1986). When children start to write, they are beginning to grasp the vital connection between writing and reading as two interrelated communication systems. In the remedial approach, the language experience approach can be used in teaching reading, which further provides a positive vehicle to reach students who have been turned off from reading (Dionisio, 1983; Graves & Murray, 1980).

THE REMEDIAL WRITTEN EXPRESSIVE LANGUAGE PROGRAM

Program Development and Instructional Considerations

Learning disabilities specialists must be skillful in creating an environment conducive to the development of written expressive language skills. They must be creative in using various motivational elicitors to promote students' written expressive abilities. Written expression is best produced when it is related and relevant to individuals' immediate environment and background. Enrichment activities, such as field trips and art projects, can provide additional experiential background from which students can draw information.

The following are more specific principles of remedial written expressive language instruction:

1. Written expressive language activities should be related to individuals' background, experiences, and interests.
2. Written expressive language activities should utilize individuals' verbal expressive repertoire, and thus must also develop students' oral language necessary for written output. This usually involves topic discussion and listings of words and/or ideas on the blackboard that will help students express themselves well.
3. The LD specialist must also develop essential written expressive language skills. At the preliminary phases of the writing, students should be provided with written output structure to facilitate their written expression. This may include activities such as sentence completion, expository questions, and sequencing exercises involving written outputs.
4. The LD specialist must provide students with guided instruction and assistance in their writings through various procedures, including the development of metacognitive written expressive language strategies.
5. A strong written expressive language training program develops students' sensitivity to writing—specifically to the communicative function of writing—develops their awareness of the writing process, and trains them to use strategies to facilitate their writing.
6. A strong written expressive language program should involve modeling of good writing through sharing of students' writings and, if necessary, the teacher's modeling for the students.
7. The LD specialist must stress development of ideas and fluency of writing, rather than language mechanics and spelling, and must provide students with easy access to correct spelling through availability of resources, including the teacher.
8. The LD specialist must provide encouragement and positive reinforcement.
9. A strong written expressive language program involves teaching students editing skills and involving them in the editing of the written output of other students.
10. A strong written expressive language program must also teach specific aspects of structural grammar followed by writing activities tailored to reinforce the specific skills, without inhibiting the writing fluency of students through unnecessary corrections of concepts not previously taught.

Graham and Harris (1988) provide the following recommendations for teaching writing:

1. Allocate time for daily writing instruction.
2. Expose students to a broad range of writing tasks to meet social, recreational, and occupational needs.
3. Create a climate conducive to writing development in which teachers are accepting and encouraging.
4. Integrate writing with other academic subjects.
5. Assist students in developing the process central to effective writing with discrete writing stages such as prewrite, write, and rewrite stages.
6. Automatize skills for getting language onto paper by minimizing interference from production and mechanical factors.
7. Help students develop explicit knowledge about the characteristics of good writing.
8. Help students develop skills and abilities to carry out more sophisticated composing processes.
9. Assist students in the development of goals for improving their writing products.
10. Avoid instructional practices that do not improve students' writing performance.

Development of a Comprehensive Written Language Program

The goals of written expressive language development and remediation are to develop individuals' ability to express themselves in writing and to develop standards of language usage that promote individuals' growth and development in written expression. "The purpose of fostering creative writing in the classroom is to make a contribution to each child's academic and personal growth. Growth is best fostered in an atmosphere of freedom, respect, approval, and trust" (Cramer, 1978, p. 1). Students are initially encouraged and are provided with ample opportunity to write creatively and freely without concern for spelling and/or correct grammar. The idea is to develop their written expressive repertoire. Once the initial writing task is completed, students can clarify their thoughts through organization, refinement, and expansion in the postwriting activity (Cramer, 1978), during which they can transform their written expression into proper language. This provides them with sufficient opportunities to learn the appropriate standards and conventions of writing. The LD specialist should establish an environment in which students write frequently and the communicative functions of writing are clear (Englert, Raphael, Anderson, Anthony, Fear, & Gregg, 1988).

In developing a written expressive language program, one must consider the various environmental influences of language acquisition, which include imitation, expansion, and meaning. Imitation or modeling refers to the acquisition of language through imitation of adult language. Expansion relates to the elaboration and/or expanded forms of statements, and meaning involves the understanding of language (Cramer, 1978). In addition, students must be engaged in sustained writing and have opportunities to share their writing with an appropriate audience, including peers (Englert et al., 1988).

The written language program should be viewed as a comprehensive one, interrelated with some areas of the curriculum and incorporated into others. A comprehensive written language program should include the following:

1. *Integration of written language skills with reading skills.* As discussed earlier, written language development is parallel to the development of reading skills, both decoding and reading comprehension. The benefits of the language experience approach for increasing individuals' reading decoding skills, as well as vocabulary enrichment and reading comprehension skills, have been discussed. At higher levels, writing activities can be directly derived from reading materials by requiring expository writing, based on elements of what has been read. At the advanced levels, assignments involve critical reviews of selected passages from literature.

2. *Integration of written language with aspects of study skills development.* Written language skills can be further enhanced by incorporating aspects of study skills, including summarizing skills, outlining skills, and inferential skills such as finding main ideas and inferences. Students can be exposed to more structural materials in this area, developing both their vocabulary and their feeling of the structure of language. In a way, summarizing reading material provides a model of written language for students. This approach can be further enhanced by incorporating written language activities in areas such as social studies projects.

3. *Incorporation of written language skills with logical thinking, sequential thought process, and inferential skills.* Much of written language involves the ability to put together a sequence of events in a logical manner. Thus logical thinking activities, along with reading thinking skills, can further help students to develop language writing skills. For example, putting material read in a sequential order, anticipating future events, and utilizing inferential skills related to the material read can enhance the development of written language skills.

4. *Involvement of students in the production of various types of written output.* Written language can be classified under these categories:
(a) creative writing, referred to by Halliday (1975) and Creaghead (1986) as personal, imaginative, and biographical writing;
(b) instrumental/practical writing involving letters of communication and requests for information, referred to by Halliday (1975) and Creaghead (1986) as interactional and heuristic writing; (c) descriptive informational writing involving descriptions of events, writing about issues and events in life in general, and writing for the purpose of providing factual information; and (d) poetry writing.

5. *Integration of written and oral expressive language.* The integration of written expressive language with oral expressive language can facilitate

the development of language writing skills. The use of diversified media such as tape recordings and the editing of sequential story production and plays help to bridge the gap between oral and written language abilities.

Graves (1985) discussed the essential components of a writing program:

1. Write daily, at the same time if possible, for a minimum of 30 minutes.
2. Work to establish each child's topical turf, an area of expertise for each writer.
3. Collect writing in folders so that writers can see the accumulation of what they know. Papers do not go home; rather the collected work is present in class for student, teacher, parent, and administrator to examine. Some writing is published in hardcover or some more durable form.
4. Provide a predictable pattern of teacher participation by sharing your own writing, moving in the midst of students during writing time, and responding in predictable structure to your students' writing.
5. End each writing time with children responding to each other's writing in a predictable format: receiving, questioning.
6. Set up classroom routines in which you examine the entire day to see which responsibilities can be delegated to the children. Solve room problems in discussion. The group learns to negotiate, whether in working with a draft or solving a classroom problem.
7. Continually point to the responsibilities assumed by the group, as well as the specifics of what they know. (p. 41)

Development of Written Language Skills

In order to facilitate the development of written language skills in learning-disabled students, the LD specialist must always keep in mind the objectives of written language programs whatever the approach adopted. In selecting and developing writing activities, the specialist must choose activities (a) that are interesting, (b) that can activate the cognitive processes necessary for good writing, (c) that can accelerate the acquisition of skills essential to the successful completion of school assignments, and (d) that can make students use writing to meet social, recreational, and occupational needs (Graham & Harris, 1988).

Englert et al. (1988) suggest the inclusion of daily writing, sustained writing, and information status and peer collaboration into the writing program. They further state that students with learning disabilities should be given the opportunity to write daily and given ample time to develop their ideas. Though some students may complete their writing assignment in a single period, others may wish to research their topic and work on it for several days. In addition, students should be encouraged and given opportunities to share their writing with others. This will help to develop a sense of the "communicative function of writing." Sharing their writing, publishing a classroom newsletter, and contributing to the school newspaper achieve this sense of the communicative function of writing.

Assessment of Written Language

Although tests of written language are available commercially, informal assessment procedures using students' written work samples can prove very helpful. The use of language composition and language mechanics checklists can further assist the LD specialist in identifying students' strengths and weaknesses in written language.

Tests of Written Language

The following is a selection of written language tests:

> Comprehensive Written Language Test
> Picture Story Language Test (PSLT)
> Test of Written Language (TOWL)-Revised
> Test of Adolescent Language (TOAL)
> Woodcock-Johnson Psycho-Educational Battery (WJ-R) Test of Achievement

METHODS AND STRATEGIES FOR TEACHING WRITTEN LANGUAGE

While the ultimate goal is to develop individuals' written expressive language skills and abilities, by no means should output be restricted to a single mode, such as writing down students' thoughts. Inasmuch as written language closely correlates with oral expressive language, the teacher can utilize approaches that provide a vehicle for transition of students' oral expressive language skills and abilities to a written format.

The literature identifies four major approaches to the development of written language skills:

1. An experiential/language experience approach, in which students are encouraged to develop a sense of correct language usage through the transformation of oral expressive language into written language. This approach usually also involves the development and enrichment of oral expressive language.
2. A structural approach, emphasizing structural linguistics, language mechanics, and grammar rules to develop written expressive skills.
3. A process-oriented approach, in which emphasis is placed on teaching students the various stages involved in the writing process, such as prewrite, write, and rewrite.
4. Cognitive and metacognitive approaches, in which emphasis is placed on increasing students' awareness of the process and the skills necessary for writing. These approaches usually employ learning strategies and procedures such as story mapping and story frames.

Experiential/Language Experience Approach

This approach emphasizes deriving written language output from students' immediate background. Students are encouraged to write about events and experiences in their own life. Emphasis is placed on automatizing the writing process without undue concern for spelling and language mechanics at the initial stages of writing. Students are taught to generate ideas in a sequential manner and to support them throughout their writing. Bridging the oral expressive abilities with written language is stressed. In addition, this approach suggests the integration of all aspects of the language arts curriculum—reading, writing, and spelling. (The language experience approach is discussed in detail in chapter 13).

Structural Approach

The structural approach to writing is based on the assumption that students must develop knowledge of linguistics in order to be competent writers. Students are taught sentence structure, paragraph and story organization, and the rules of language mechanics. Once students are exposed to various levels of sentence and paragraph structure, they are encouraged to apply the rules learned to what they write.

Process-Oriented Writing

The process-oriented approach to writing (Bos, 1988; D'Aoust, 1986; Englert & Raphael, 1988) involves specific writing stages such as planning, drafting, revising and editing, sharing, and publication. The essential features of this approach include daily writing, the use of student-selected topics, group sharing and peer editing, opportunities to revise and rework writing, and publication of student papers (Englert & Raphael, 1988).

According to Bos (1988), six instructional features are necessary for implementation of the process-oriented approach with the learning disabled:

1. Creating an environment that provides opportunities for sustained writing—allowing time to think, reflect, and write
2. Establishing a writing community that provides an atmosphere in which students share their writings with each other
3. Allowing students to choose their own topics for writing
4. Modeling by the teacher and peers
5. Developing reflective thinking and a sense of audience through talking about their work with peers and listening to their questions and comments
6. Assuming responsibility for controlling their writing progress and using strategies.

According to Englert and Raphael (1988), the process-oriented writing approach encourages reluctant writers to write. Students directly experience the writing process as they plan and revise their papers. Peer sharing and collaboration prompt students to activate related background knowledge and enhance their realization of the communicative function and purpose of writing.

The Prewrite, Write, and Rewrite Model

Use of the prewrite, write, and rewrite process model to facilitate the development of students' essential skills for writing has been suggested by Bartoli and Botel (1988) and Graham and Harris (1988). A written expressive language unit can be viewed as composed of three instructional components:

1. *The prewriting phase.* Activities in this phase usually involve the development of students' oral language repertoire on a given topic, including the development of vocabulary, theme, and supporting ideas. This can usually be accomplished through (a) eliciting activities, normally followed by group discussion; (b) development of key vocabulary appropriate to the topic; (c) development of key points for main ideas; and (d) development of supporting ideas.
2. *The writing phase.* In this process, students are engaged in (a) organizing the materials in a sequential and meaningful manner, (b) writing it in an acceptable format, and (c) expanding on previous ideas.
3. *The postwriting and editing phase (rewriting phase).* This phase involves (a) reading the written output to check whether it makes sense and whether it is consistent with the theme development and the sequential development of the supportive ideas, (b) analyzing sentence and paragraph structures, (c) analyzing punctuation, and (d) correcting spelling errors.

Cognitive and Metacognitive Approaches and Strategies

Metacognition and Written Expressive Language

Skillful writing requires the ability to use task specific strategies and to monitor and regulate the composing process (Englert & Raphael, 1988; Graham & Harris, 1987). Furthermore, it requires goal setting, organizing, reflecting, revising, and reworking to achieve the goals (Scardamalia & Bereiter, 1985). In contrast, poor writers have problems accessing ideas from background knowledge (idea generation), developing an organizational plan that structures their ideas both into topic grouping and categories (text organization), and regulating their writing activities, all of which affect their ability to reread and revise the text (Englert & Raphael, 1988). Learning-disabled students exhibit difficulties in using organizational and planning strategies in writing. As in other areas of the curriculum, they fail to engage spontaneously in strategic behavior. Evidence from research has pointed out their difficulties in producing multiple statements about familiar topics; generally, they seem able to produce far more information about the topic than is reflected in their written compositions. The factors associated with writing difficulties were discussed earlier in this chapter. Due to a lack of basic writing skills, including language mechanics and spelling, and having difficulties in oral language (Olsen, Wong, & Marx, 1983), students with LD are inhibited in their writing output. They "reach" writing limits far short of their experience and knowledge. They lack strategies to guide them in achieving new or more complete knowledge searches (Englert & Raphael, 1988).

Recent developments in metacognition and its approach to written language indicate that performance can be improved by utilizing metacognitive strategies. "The writing of inefficient learners including adolescents and young adults with reading and language disorders, can be improved by teaching them appropriate composition strategies and self-management routines that they can use independently . . . [They can] be taught strategies for maintaining active task involvement and productivity, activating a search of appropriate memory stores for writing content, facilitating advance planning, and editing and revising tests" (Graham & Harris, 1987, p. 67).

Metacognitive-Oriented Strategies for Writing

The first step in the development of written language through metacognition involves the development of students' sensitivity to, and heightened interest in, the purpose and communicative functions of writing. The second step involves the development of students' awareness of the skills necessary for different kinds of writing. This also involves knowledge of the expository writing process, text structure, and writing strategies (Raphael, Kirschner & Englert, 1989). The third step involves the development of strategies appropriate to the writing task, the identification of specific steps in the strategy, and strategy implementation. And the last step involves the regulation of individuals' effective use of strategies for writing during the writing process.

Through the learning process analysis discussed previously, students can develop metacognitive learning strategies for creative writing. They discuss the purpose, goals, and functions of creative writing, the structure of such an output, and what it takes to produce a creative output successfully. With the teacher's guidance, students develop strategies for writing and identify the specific steps to follow. Through this process, they learn to attack writing skills in an orderly fashion. Figures 14−2 and 14−3 are samples of a strategy guide and an implementation and monitoring sheet for metacognitive strategies for creative writing.

As noted earlier, these metacognitive strategies are written in the first person form, which emphasizes the assumption of responsibility for implementation and monitoring of the strategies by students.

Cognitive Strategy Instruction for Writing

The program called Cognitive Strategy Instruction for Writing (CSIW) was designed by Englert et al. (1988) to teach cognitive and metacognitive strategies in writing expository texts to students with LD. Two main aspects in the development of expository writing are considered: the social context in which students write, which highlights the importance of the audience in planning, composing, and editing compositions; and the role of text structure in planning, organizing, drafting, and revising papers.

To facilitate the writing process, Englert et al. (1988) recommend the use of "think sheets," which are intended to prompt the writer to consider certain strategies to improve the quality of writing. In essence, the think sheets are cognitive maps that provide guidance to the writer during each writing stage. They include planning, organizing, writing, editing, and revising sections for students' drafting of the writing assignment. Each think sheet poses questions that guide the writer in writing each of the sections of the text.

Figure 14–2   Metacognitive Creative Writing Strategies: Strategy Guide

---

Read, Think, Strategize:

ON THE ROAD TO SUCCESS

Strategies For Processing Information

Developing Your Writing Skills: Creative Writing Strategies

Challenge Guide

Writing serves to communicate your thoughts and ideas on paper. Writing involves many language skills. Using these skills effectively will make you a better writer. Strategies will help you develop these skills.

Effective Strategies

Figure out what you have to do
Choose your topic and then write down your ideas
Organize your ideas in sequence
Check your grammar and punctuation
Check your spelling
Read your story and decide if it makes sense

Commitment to Success

I figure out what I have to do
I choose my topic and then write down my ideas
I organize my ideas in sequence
I check my grammar and punctuation
I check my spelling
I read my story and decide if it makes sense

Source: From *Stepping Up to Success: Metacognition Elementary Student Handbook* by A. Ariel, 1989. Unpublished manuscript, California State University, Los Angeles. Reprinted by permission.

The planning section helps the writer to focus on the audience, the purpose, and background knowledge, and prompts consideration of the following questions: "Who will read my paper? Why am I writing this? What do I know about the topic? How can I group/label my facts?" During the organizing stage, students use graphic organizers (organizing think sheets) that contain questions and key words associated with a specific text structure. The organizing think sheet contains questions such as "What happens first? What happens second? What happens third? . . . What happens last?" Students "complete the organizing think sheet by filling in the pattern guide with information from their background knowledge and from their brainstormed ideas on the planning form" (Englert et al., 1988, p. 108).

During the writing stage, students write their first draft, and are told not to be concerned with spelling or other language mechanics. In a think-aloud procedure, the teacher models how to transfer knowledge from the planning and organizing

Figure 14–3   Creative Writing Strategies: Strategy Implementation and Monitoring Sheet

COMMITMENT TO SUCCESS: STRATEGY USE

Set: Strategies For Processing Information

Skills/Behaviors I Need to Learn:	How Will I Do It? (Strategies)	How Am I Doing? Key: $\sqrt{-}$; $\sqrt{}$; $\sqrt{+}$;					
		M	T	W	Th	F	Overall
Developing Your Writing Skills: Creative Writing Strategies	I figure out what I have to do.						
	I choose my topic and then write down my ideas.						
	I organize my ideas in sequence.						
	I check my grammar and punctuation.						
	I check my spelling.						
	I read my story and it makes sense.						
Individualized Goal							

Teacher's Comments:

Student's Comments: This Is the Way I See Myself

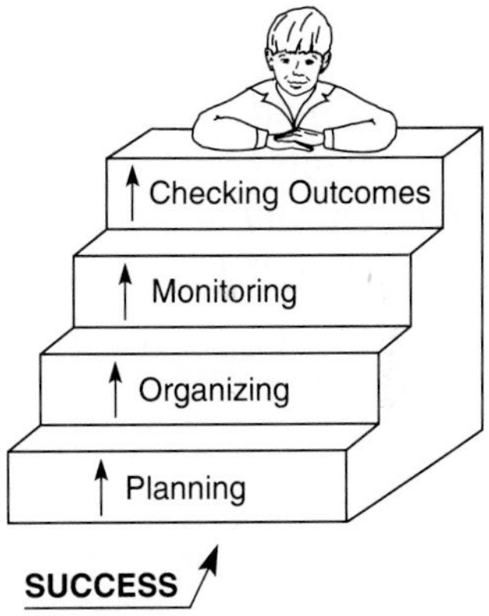

↑ Checking Outcomes

↑ Monitoring

↑ Organizing

↑ Planning

SUCCESS

Source: From *Stepping Up to Success: Metacognition Elementary Student Handbook* by A. Ariel, 1989. Unpublished manuscript, California State University, Los Angeles. Reprinted by permission.

think sheets to the first writing draft. During the editing stage, students are taught to edit their papers by referring back to their planning and organizing think sheets, thereby monitoring and evaluating their own writing. In addition, all students act as peer editors for each other. Finally, during the revision stage, students incorporate the suggestions provided by the peer editor and consider their writing by referring back to the think sheets. At this stage, spelling and language mechanics are given attention. After students make their revision, they recopy the paper in a final draft for presentation to their audience or for submission for publication.

Sentence-Writing Strategy

The sentence-writing strategy developed by Schumaker and Sheldon (1985) at the University of Kansas helps students develop their writing ability. It instructs them on ways to recognize and write four different types of sentences using a set of steps and formulas. (This strategy comes under the expression and demonstration of competence strand of the learning strategies curriculum of the Strategies Intervention Model discussed in chapters 7 and 13.)

The sentence-writing strategy teaches students how to recognize and generate sentences in four areas: simple, compound, complex, and compound-complex. Students learn how to identify the number of subjects (S) and verbs (V) in a sentence by using formulas such as S V and SS V.

Students are given a pretest to determine the types of sentences they are currently using in their writing. If they are in need of the strategy, they write a goal indicating their commitment to learn a strategy for writing complete and interesting sentences. They are given an advance organizer to monitor their progress. Over a period of 5 to 10 days, students learn how to write four kinds of simple sentences, and after about 50 days, they can be writing up to 14 different kinds of sentences. Cue cards are used to help define such terms as *simple sentence, independent and dependent clauses, subject, predicate, compound sentence, coordinating and subordinating conjunctions, complex sentence,* and *compound-complex sentence.* Students are instructed in the steps for writing sentences using the acronym PENS.

PENS stands for

P   Pick a formula.
E   Explore words to fit the formula.
N   Note the words.
S   Subject-verb identification.

As in other strategies in the SIM, instruction follows rigorous steps, outlined in the instructor's manual and highlighted in chapter 7. Through modeling, verbal rehearsal, controlled practice and feedback, and grade-appropriate practice, students learn how to formulate sentence types. Students monitor their progress using charts for each sentence type and generalization. Posttests and sentence checklists are used to maintain generalization. This particular strategy can be used at, and adapted to, the elementary levels with some excellent results in terms of developing students' writing ability.

Graphic Organizers

The use of story mapping, semantic mapping, and story frame procedures to enhance reading comprehension is discussed in chapter 13. The use of semantic mapping can facilitate idea generation and thought structuring during the writing process. Through brainstorming technique and discussion, students are taught first to generate ideas about the topic and then to connect and organize the ideas into meaningful clusters to develop the topic. Later on, they are taught to identify the topic sentence and supporting details and to sequence their ideas.

Similarly, story frames can provide a framework for developing students' ideas in each of the writing segments, such as topic sentence, supporting details, and concluding sentence. Process-oriented writing procedures are used in conjunction with story-mapping procedures. Students focus on each of the writing stages. For example, during the prewriting phase, students are encouraged to pose the following questions: What do I know about the topic? Can I rely on my own thoughts or do I need to look at other sources? In the writing stage, students are encouraged to pose the following questions: What do I want to communicate/What is my topic sentence? How do I support my topic sentence? What is the climax in my story/Do I have a conclusion? In the editing and rewriting stages, students are encouraged to pose the following questions: Did I communicate what I wanted to communicate? Does my story make sense? Are the thoughts presented sequentially?

Self-Instructional Strategy Training

Graham and Harris (1987, 1988) developed self-instructional strategy training for teaching composition skills to individuals with LD. This approach is based on Meichenbaum's (1977) model of self-instructional training. In this approach, students are taught strategies to facilitate the generation, framing, and planning of text. Specifically, they are taught to use self-directed prompts that require them to "(a) consider their audience and reasons for writing, (b) develop a plan for what they intended to say using knowledge-of-discourse schemas or frames to generate and organize writing notes, (c) evaluate possible content by considering its impact on the reader, and (d) continue the process of content generation and planning during the actual act of writing" (Graham & Harris, 1989, p. 202).

Self-instructional strategy training involves scaffolding teaching procedures, in which the teacher initially provides external support to students, then gradually shifts the responsibility for applying and monitoring the strategies to the students. Four basic steps are followed in self-instructional strategy training: teacher's modeling of strategies, students' implementation of strategies using overt guidance and verbalization, fading of self-verbalization, and independent implementation of strategies guided by "covert (internal) self-instructions" (Graham & Harris, 1987).

Word Processing and Writing Skills

The use of computer technology with the learning disabled is discussed in depth in chapter 11. In this section, we will discuss the impact of word processing on the writing skills of those with LD. Computers provide a wide range of opportunities for improving the writing skills of such individuals. The use of simple word processors in writing allows students to express themselves without concern for undue corrections and erasures. Word processors allow flexible editing of text. They create possibilities for teacher-student interaction throughout the writing process by providing prompts and assistance in a nonthreatening writing environment and give the teacher direct access to students' writing process (Morocco & Neuman, 1986).

Word processors change the physical aspects of producing a text, replacing handwriting with typing. They help students learn strategies for planning, writing, and revising (MacArthur, 1988). The use of word processing improves the quantity and quality of students' writings (Vacc, 1987). It increases students' confidence in writing, which results in increased story length (Outhred, 1989). To a degree, word processors facilitate a kind of "self-brainstorming" in which ideas are initially generated, followed by an organizing activity that sorts the information, arranges it in proper sequence, and deletes nonessential information. All these processes can be performed right on the screen without students' fear that someone may be looking over their shoulder.

Kistinger and Kerchner (1984) used a process approach to written expression using the Bank Street Writer word-processing program to teach students with learning disabilities composition skills. The writing activity following their approach involves eight steps:

1. Having a prewriting conference in which students and the teacher meet to discuss students' choice of topic and to generate ideas regarding the topic.
2. Composing at the keyboard during which students are encouraged to record their thoughts without regard for errors in spelling and other aspects of writing that can be corrected later.
3. Printing a draft for easy reading.
4. Having an editing conference during which students and teacher or students and peers collaboratively provide input for improvement of the text, including spelling, sentence structure, punctuation, and content.
5. Editing at the keyboard to effect appropriate alterations to text.
6. Printing final copy with designated margins and spaces between lines.
7. Illustrating the composition to enhance the overall appeal of the work.
8. Providing an audience, which is accomplished by sharing material with other students, contributing to a class journal, and participating in the "Writer's Club."

The use of word processors in teaching writing to students should not be confused with the task of introducing students to computers nor with training on the keyboard. These are prerequisites skills to using word processors. Although students should not be expected to demonstrate mastery of the keyboard, minimal proficiency and basic knowledge of how the computer operates are essential in order to avoid failure and frustration. Furthermore, Collins and Price (1986) caution us that when we attempt to develop students' "friendliness" with the computer, we must be cognizant of some of the problems that computers pose to students. These problems include inappropriate software, lack of clear directions, and intricate modes of display on the screen. In addition, many instructional manuals are complex, fail to repeat key concepts, or introduce terms and then use them in different contexts later in the manual. Despite these shortcomings, the use of word processors with individuals with learning disabilities remains a promising and an enriching teaching tool. The LD specialist becomes the facilitator of learning by using the computer as an aid to instruction.

Teaching Language Mechanics

Individuals' written expressive skills are affected by the following three main factors: (a) written expressive abilities; (b) repertoire of English composition skills, namely, structural grammar and language mechanics; and (c) spelling ability.

While many learning-disabled individuals have difficulty expressing themselves in writing, they experience greater difficulties in the areas of grammar and language mechanics. Many students simply do not understand the mechanics of language necessary to produce acceptable writing. The goal is to help the learning disabled develop appropriate writing skills and learn to use proper grammar and correct spelling to facilitate meaningful communication. However, it is not always possible to achieve all this at once. The emphasis on language mechanics often interferes with students' production of written output by inhibiting fluency (Graham & Harris, 1988). According to Graham and Harris (1988), the development of language mechanics should not be undertaken at the expense of composition time, but rather should be taught at a separate time. Students can even be directed not to pay attention to mechanics and sentence structure during writing and/or oral dictation. Learning-disabled students in upper elementary grades composed better stories when the requirements of language mechanics were removed (MacArthur & Graham, 1987). It is recommended that the written expressive language instructional process emphasize (a) written expressive language output that approximates as much as possible proper grammatical usage and sentence structure; (b) the inclusion of language mechanics activities apart from written expressive language activities, usually following a structural approach and using a variety of resources (exemplified by the Corrective English Series, which were developed for the purpose of building students' skills and language mechanics); (c) the integration of language mechanics with creative writing activities as long as it does not interfere with the written output; and (d) that spelling and the correction of spelling errors should be done according to students' functional level in spelling and to the extent that is absolutely necessary.

Specific Instructional Activities and Strategies

The following activities and strategies are suggested by Cramer (1978) to stimulate and encourage written expression:

1. Use students' experiences. Written expressive language can directly evolve out of students' own experience. The classroom teacher is further encouraged to provide a host of rich and varied experiences for the students.
2. Encourage pupils to write about things that are relevant to their interests and needs. The teacher must take time to develop interest, enthusiasm, and background knowledge.

3. Develop in students an appreciation of good writing by reading poetry, stories, and other literature to them to provide models for language usage, style, and story format.
4. Value what children have written by praising and reinforcing their written work.
5. Guide the writing personally by providing students with guidance and direction while they write and by providing them with whatever resources are needed. This may include correct spelling and vocabulary enrichment.
6. Provide a number of writing ideas for students who may have trouble getting started on their own.
7. Share with students your own stories and poetry, thereby motivating them.
8. Relate written expressive language to the entire curriculum, thus integrating the teaching of written language skills with the study of other subject areas.
9. Have pupils make books.
10. Make certain that students' writing results in outcomes or products.
11. Develop a writing center in the classroom.

The reader is referred to Cramer (1978) for additional writing activities. They are classified under the following categories: beginning writing, writing techniques, encouraging creative thinking, feelings and values, poetry, story writing, books to motivate writing, letter writing, television, holidays, music, book reports, social studies, science, practical writing, editing, and ideas for advanced or older children.

Sample Written Expressive Activities

Story-Go-Round

In this activity, a small group of students jointly develop a story to which each student contributes a segment. Each student takes part in the development of the story by taking turns in contributing ideas for the plot. This activity involves three to six students, usually using a tape recorder. The recorded story is typed with minor corrections and distributed to the students. The teacher may elect to use the story for further elaboration by providing the students with additional elicitors. The story can also be used for reading fluency and reading comprehension by developing the appropriate exercises.

Stories You Can Finish

In this activity, elicitors are provided to help students complete a story. Various formats can be used in this activity: (a) an open-ended story, which begins with one or two paragraphs followed by an open-end question asking students to complete the story; or (b) a guided story, which begins with one or two paragraphs followed by several lead questions. The following represent a sample of activities for this story type:

Activity 1: A journey into the future

Write a story about a trip you are planning to take, or would like to take. Use the following questions to aid you in writing your story:

1. Where are you going?
2. Why are you going to your selected destination?
3. When will you leave?
4. What will you do there?
5. How will you get there?
6. Will the trip be an adventure?
7. What kind of food will you eat?
8. Who is going with you?

Here are some of the words you may use in writing your story:

Vocabulary Bank

airline	stewardess	train	automobile	road
turnpike	ocean	sky	highway	boat

Activity 2: A trip to the beach

One day Sam and Cathy decided to go to the beach. It was very hot, and the weather report said that the water temperature would be excellent for swimming. They obtained their parents' permission to go to the beach, but they were told to return by 6:00 P.M. With this news, they hurriedly packed their lunches and . . .

Here are some questions that might help you complete this story:

1. How did Sam and Cathy get to the beach?
2. What beach did they go to?
3. Were there many people at the beach?
4. What did they do while at the beach?
5. Did they meet any friends?

Here are some words you can use in your story:

Vocabulary Bank

sand	glasses	driver	shower	walk
suntan lotion	swimming	burn	hot	surf
sleep	sun	blanket	bus	waves

Activity 3: On a tropical island

Think of yourself trapped on a deserted island with a friend. You have no tools, and there is no store or place to buy anything. This is a tropical island with many fruit trees and waterfalls. Describe your adventure on the island.

Here are some questions that might help you write your story:

1. What did you find in your surroundings?
2. Where did you sleep?
3. What did you eat?
4. How did you protect yourself from any dangerous animals?

5. What were your activities during the day?
6. What was the most exciting thing that happened to you?
7. How did you finally return to civilization?

Here are some words you can use in your story:

Vocabulary Bank

solitude	communication	natives
weather	aborigines	canoe

Activity 4: Sensory grid
Complete the following thoughts:

I lie on the grass,	I lie on the grass,
seeing	watching
hearing	wondering
smelling	wishing
feeling	feeling
tasting	

Written Language Instructional Materials

Here is a sample list of written language instructional programs:

Program	Level	Publisher
For Those Who Wonder	Elementary	Ginn & Company
Imagine & Write	Elementary/Intermediate	American Educational Publication
Making It Strange	Secondary	Harper & Row
Stories You Can Finish	Intermediate/Secondary	American Educational Publication

UNDERSTANDING THE SPELLING PROCESS AND SPELLING PROBLEMS

It can probably be said that spelling is the area in which most individuals with learning disabilities experience the greatest difficulty. The spelling orthography of the English language, the limitation of appropriate remedial spelling approaches, and the lack of appropriate instructional materials make it very difficult for individuals with LD to have a command and mastery of spelling. The spelling process requires a high level of integration, both within and across modalities. Students must be able to relate the sounds of letters and words to visual symbolic systems and to execute them motorically. Unlike reading, which is primarily an interpretative task, spelling is an expressive task involving the auditory, visual, and haptic channels, thereby increasing the chances for greater difficulties. For most individuals with LD, spelling is a much more difficult activity than reading (Bradley & Bryant, 1979). The competent speller must possess abilities in (a) auditory discrimination, (b) visual discrimination, (c) motoric expression, (d) cross-modal integration, (e) short- and long-term memory, and (f) imagery across modalities (auditorization, visualization, and kinesthetic imagery) (see Glossary). Students with difficulties in any of the above areas are likely to exhibit problems in spelling. Generally, students with spelling disabilities have trouble associating phonemes (units of speech sound) with graphemes (letter forms), and graphemes with morphemes (words or parts of words).

Many spelling programs in our schools involve the traditional basal spelling series, in which students are given a list of about 20 words to learn throughout the course of a week. In addition, average children are gradually introduced to conceptual vocabulary and word units that relate to life experiences in a meaningful way. This approach is often unsuccessful with the learning disabled (Wallace, Cohen, & Polloway, 1987). Those with learning disabilities who experience difficulties with spelling have not been able to retain spelling words learned in this manner, and thus they exhibit a gap in structural spelling and sight vocabulary. They generally lack knowledge and understanding of spelling patterns and rules. Many of the words they encounter do not fall within any commonsense pattern and must be learned visually, usually within a short period of time. This puts undue demand on the learning disabled.

What Is Spelling?

Spelling is an essential tool of written language. From a linguistic point of view, spelling is considered to be the bridge between the speaking and reading vocabularies, and it is on this basis that spelling relates to the language arts as a whole (Hanna, Hodges, & Hanna, 1971). Students are quite often required to write down words or sentences to communicate ideas or concepts. They participate in written expressive language activities and are expected to spell correctly.

The spelling process, which is complex, requires individuals to function at a high level of integration, both within and across modalities. In spelling, which is an encoding process, students recall the symbols for various sounds or groups of sounds in order to spell a word. In reading, the process is reversed; it is a decoding process in which students associate a printed symbol with the sound of a word and its associated meaning (Snowling, 1985). Furthermore, reading is a recognition process, and spelling is a retrieval process (Frith & Frith, 1980). Individuals usually spell in two ways: by matching letters for sounds in the words they want to spell (matching phonemes to graphemes), and by retrieving words they already know from their memory (H. E. Nelson, 1980). According to Major (1983), spelling requires that the auditory-visual correspondence be recognized, recalled, and then transformed into a visual-motor product.

Reflecting on the complexity of the spelling process, Hodges (1966) states:

> The act of spelling may also be described as one kind of information processing. Words to be spelled are assimilated through the sensory

modes of hearing and vision, while the writing of them (the behavior which is sought) represents the results of many complex cognitive processes in which what the ears hear and the eyes see is reinforced by the haptical senses of touch and kinesthetics. Clearly, sensory and motor processes are a part of the act of spelling, but the intervening cognitive processes lie at the heart of effective spelling ability. (p. 38)

Personke and Yee (1971) gave us a theoretical model presenting a systematic description of a spelling behavior. The model, which is based primarily on information-processing systems, identifies the following phases: "1) initial input processing—sensing and analyzing problems and needs, 2) processing information before deciding what course of action to consider and take, 3) decision making as to what information is available and acting through chosen channels, 4) execution of selected behavior, 5) feedback of information through self-evaluation or from other persons to modify or reinforce processing of information and decisions" (p. 16).

THE REMEDIAL SPELLING PROGRAM

Program Development and Instructional Considerations

The objectives of the remedial spelling program are (a) to help students become more proficient spellers, and to maintain and promote spelling growth; (b) to help students develop effective methods of studying new words; (c) to develop students' use of the dictionary, and (d) to promote a desire to spell words correctly (Graham & Miller, 1979).

The following principles and guidelines should direct the remedial spelling program:

1. The teaching of spelling to individuals with learning disabilities must be considered within the context of a comprehensive language arts program. It should be made meaningful and interesting and should be integrated with rich and varied language activities. An excellent writing program is the key to a strong spelling program (Cramer, 1978).
2. Spelling instruction must be direct, not incidental (Allen & Ager, 1965; Graham & Miller, 1979).
3. The spelling program must be an integrated one, including structural spelling instruction, acquisition of concept and survival words, word usage exercises (Rose, 1982), and essential words for written expressive language and creative writing.
4. The spelling program should be based on individuals' functional level. In evaluating students' learning difficulties, the teacher needs to look at each student's performance level and determine where the breakdown occurs through error analysis.

5. The teacher should select a teaching method that works best with each student.
6. The spelling process should be an active one, utilizing metacognitive strategies.
7. Students should be encouraged to discover the way they learn best and to adopt a learning method that works best for them.
8. The teaching of spelling must follow a utilitarian approach, emphasizing essential spelling skills.
9. The number of words per week should be geared to individuals' ability level (5 to 10 words per week) (Bryant, Drabin, & Gellinger, 1981).
10. The spelling program should involve continuous evaluation and monitoring of students' progress (Graham & Miller, 1979).

Developing the Remedial Spelling Program

In the process of remediating learning-disabled students' spelling difficulties, the LD specialist must be concerned with the following:

1. Determination of individuals' functioning level in spelling
2. Development of a comprehensive spelling program fully integrated with language arts and the content areas of the curriculum
3. Selection of appropriate teaching methods suited to each student's learning style
4. Placement of students at the appropriate instructional level and selection of appropriate spelling materials and workbooks
5. Selection of appropriate spelling words/units for individual students in line with their functional level and areas of interest
6. Establishment of monitoring of progress and evaluating procedures.

The way a person learns how to spell can provide us with some direction in the development of a remedial program. Generally, an individual's spelling vocabulary includes (a) words learned incidentally, which include concept words and words associated with general experiences and events in life, such as holidays, vacations, and current events; (b) words learned through formal spelling instruction using phonological rules and word patterning; (c) words learned through reading and writing; and (d) words learned through vocabulary and word games, such as Scrabble and Boggle.

The spelling program for learning-disabled students should include the following components:

1. *Structural spelling.* This approach follows a systematic approach to spelling, teaching spelling in a structural manner.
2. *Development of sight vocabulary.* This approach develops students' sight vocabulary for essential spelling words and concept (unit) words.
3. *Word usage exercises* (Rose, 1982). This approach usually involves the use of state-mandated spelling texts that include various follow-up activities, such as sentence writing, word meanings, and dictionary skills.

4. *Integration of spelling with writing.* This approach involves the utilization of words learned during the week in various writing activities.
5. *Word usage activities involving various spelling games.* Throughout the week, the spelling program includes gamelike activities involving (a) word meanings and comprehension, including dictionary work, synonyms, and antonyms; (b) word analysis exercises, including syllabication, reinforced by activities such as color coding, cut-up words, link letters, and rainbow tracing; (c) the integration of spelling with written expressive language and the development of appropriate writing skills; and (d) word games.

Strategies for a Personalized Spelling Program

Personalized spelling lists should be prepared weekly for each child or group of children. The number of words to be included in students' weekly spelling list should vary according to their ability to learn and retain the words (Cramer, 1978). Each student's weekly spelling list should include (a) words with structural patterns—phonetically and/or linguistically patterned words; (b) concept or unit words; (c) essential words for writing; and (d) selected survival words, spelling demons, and selected vocabulary from lists such as the Doltch Word List. The teacher may also consider the selection of the weekly spelling lists from students' language experience output when this approach is used in teaching reading, as well as from social studies or science topics. It is usually recommended that the weekly spelling word list for the learning disabled not exceed 10 words.

Spelling cannot be learned in isolation. Spelling lists do not promote optimal learning because they are not associated with meaningful aspects of students' life. Structural patterns and sight words should be introduced in context and integrated with various activities, such as group discussions, film presentations, research topics, and meaningful creative writing.

In addition, students must be taught a method of study and practice suitable to their own level of functioning and their own learning style. Students are encouraged to be actively engaged in activities that promote and reinforce retention of newly acquired words through their direct use in academic areas, communication activities, and spelling and vocabulary enrichment games.

The Weekly Spelling Activities Schedule

Most spelling programs follow procedures for teaching and practicing spelling during the week. In a traditional spelling program that utilizes a spelling workbook as its primary source, the teacher introduces one unit each week. In these units, a selected list of words is usually presented on Monday. These words are read in a story that serves as the material for various follow-up activities. On the second day, a pretest is administered to determine the words students know. Students are asked to alphabetize the words and to use them in sentences. The third and fourth days of the week usually involve the completion of follow-up activities and exercises and the studying of words with which students are unfamiliar. Activities may involve spelling games and other reinforcement activities. In addition, students engage in creative writing activities using the words of the week. On the fifth day, a test is administered on the weekly words. Misspelled words are added to the students' list for the following week. Although similar procedures are practiced in programs for learning-disabled individuals, more attention has to be given to the selection of the weekly words and to the specific instructional spelling methods appropriate to each student, pacing students' rate of learning, overlearning, and practice.

The LD specialist must develop procedures for the studying and the mastering of spelling. These procedures provide an organizational framework and a study routine for students. During a typical week, the spelling activities may be distributed as follows: On the first day of the week, all the words are presented to the students. Students are paired and take a pretest. They are given appropriate testing directions—to say the word, to use the word in a sentence, and to repeat the word. Partners correct each other's spelling words. Once a study list is made up, it is divided into three groups according to word patterns and/or spelling rules. The first group of words is studied, using appropriate learning approaches and word analysis techniques. On the second day of the week, students review the first group of words and study the second group. On the third day, students review word groups one and two and study group three. On the fourth day, students review all three word groups and take a preliminary test. They then study any misspelled words. On the fifth day of the week, the students take a spelling test.

Assessment of Spelling

The LD specialist needs to evaluate (a) students' overall functional spelling level, (b) students' specific skills mastery and skills deficits in spelling, and (c) students' spelling error patterns.

To evaluate students' level of functioning, a variety of both standardized and informal procedures should be used. Formal assessment tests are primarily of two types: general/survey tests and diagnostic spelling tests. General/survey tests assess the overall functioning level of students, such as the spelling section of the Stanford Achievement Test. These survey-type tests sample general or global areas of functioning and provide grade equivalent scores. Survey tests are of two types: the recall type, in which students must recall and write a word after hearing it in isolation and/or in a sentence, and the recognition type, in which students select the correctly spelled word from several choices. The advantage of a recall type of test is that it provides the teacher with information as to the nature of the difficulty through analysis of spelling errors.

Diagnostic spelling tests—the other type of formal assessment test—provide more diagnostic information about the nature of students' spelling errors and are sometimes referred to as standardized diagnostic tests, such as the Gates-Russell Spelling Diagnostic Test. These tests supply information about students' strengths and weaknesses in spelling and quite often provide an analysis of students' spelling errors.

Spelling Tests

The following are samples of spelling tests:

General/Survey Spelling Tests
Iowa Tests of Basic Skills
Peabody Individual Achievement Tests-Revised
Wide Range Achievement Tests-Revised

Diagnostic Spelling Tests
Gates-Russell Spelling Diagnostic Test
Test of Written Spelling

Criterion-Referenced Spelling Tests
Brigance Diagnostic Inventory of Basic Skills
Kottmeyer's Diagnostic Spelling Test

Watson's Informal Tests of Spelling Ability

As early as 1935, A. E. Watson suggested informal diagnostic spelling procedures that a teacher can use with an entire class. The list that follows is a summary of those suggested procedures:

1. Select a list of 30 to 50 words based on any graded list at the grade level of the child or the class.
2. Administer the spelling test.
3. Score the test and tabulate the results. If used with a class, note the lowest 20%.
4. Have the pupils define the words they misspelled. Omit unfamiliar words since they are not in the children's vocabulary.
5. Have the pupils spell any remaining words orally. Keep a record of the spelling, noting the syllabification, phonic use, and speech or hearing difficulties.
6. Compare the original spelling to note differences in oral and written responses.
7. Ask the children to study words missed (for about 10 minutes), and observe their methods of study.
8. Analyze errors and incorporate information from the data obtained from other sources.
9. Draw conclusions as to the nature of the spelling problem. Plan educational strategies to overcome the difficulties.
10. Discuss the analysis and teaching plan with the pupil. Provide for pupils to see progress.

Analyzing Spelling Errors

Error analysis provides the LD specialist with information about the nature of students' spelling difficulties. The following are typical student spelling errors (Brueckner & Bond, 1955; DeHaven, 1983):

I. Omission errors
  A. Omission of a pronounced letter, such as "say" for "stay"
  B. Omission of a silent letter, such as "ofen" for "often"
  C. Omission of double letters, such as "super" for "supper"
II. Substitution errors
  A. Consonant sound confusion
    1. Substitution of *t* for *d, f* for *v, sh* for *ch, s* for *z*
  B. Vowel sound confusion
    1. Use of wrong vowels, such as "pet" for "pat"
    2. Substitution of one vowel for another, such as "injoy" for "enjoy"
  C. Phonetic substitution for a word, such as "obay" for "obey"
  D. Word substitution, such as "gals" for "girls"
III. Addition/insertion errors
  A. Addition of unnecessary sounds and letters
  B. Addition by doubling, such as "suppervision" for "supervision"
  C. Addition of *ed* when unnecessary
  D. Addition of unnecessary suffixes
IV. Confusion of digraphs, such as "wead" for "weed"
V. Application of phonetic spelling to nonphonetic words, such as "sum" for "some"
VI. Confusion between words with similar pronunciation (homonyms), such as "except" for "accept"
VII. Sequencing errors, with one letter out of sequence, such as "barn" for "bran"
VIII. Sound letter reversals, such as "form" for "from"

METHODS AND STRATEGIES FOR TEACHING SPELLING

There is a paucity of research supporting spelling strategy procedures for those with learning disabilities (Bain, 1982). While research findings on the matching of teaching approaches to individuals' strongest sensory modalities are equivocal, clinical observations suggest that some students respond better to some approaches than to others. The complex process of spelling and the involvement of the auditory, visual, and kinesthetic modalities in spelling suggest the inclusion of active learning utilizing all these modalities in the process of spelling instruction. According to Donoghue (1985), the best approach for aiding learning-disabled spellers depends on matching a spelling method to students' information-processing style. Students' learning style and information-processing style guide us in the selection of appropriate remedial spelling teaching approaches. Quite often students are exposed to a method that is not compatible with their information-processing style, such as using a phonics method with a student who exhibits auditory-processing difficulties, resulting in continuous failure. Students "whose auditory competencies are reasonably intact but who suffer from poor visual memory can at least be expected to spell phonetically and to develop a visual memory bank for some of the phonologically irregular words. . . . [P]upils whose spatial and visual skills are fairly intact may learn to spell through these strengths, recalling many sight words readily . . . [For] pupils [who have] neither visual nor auditory competencies . . . haptic methods are suggested" (Donoghue, 1985, p. 228). Some individuals do better when they are taught to visualize a word pattern and structure. They are able to remember a word through visualization. For them, color coding reinforces the visual imagery. Some students have to learn a word and a pattern in an auditory manner. They must hear the sound of each letter and each syllable. These students do better with a phonics approach to spelling. Finally, there are those students who seem to learn best when they simply write words over and over again, saying the words as they write them. These students seem to utilize their kinesthetic memory in conjunction with auditory and/or visual memory.

The complexity of the spelling process requires examination of students' behavior during it. The following is an account of a teacher who has helped a fourth-grade learning-disabled student to become an efficient speller. This student, whose primary difficulties were in spelling and written expressive language, attended the regular classroom with support from the resource room in the language arts. His reading level was at about grade level. However, he had great difficulty memorizing the 20 assigned spelling words per week. Though various approaches had been used to help him learn to spell, including rote practice and color coding, the student performed very poorly on his weekly spelling tests. The teacher observed him attempting to vocalize the words as he wrote them. The teacher suggested that the student sound out the words as he wrote them—say a word as it sounds and say a word as it is written. For example, in spelling the word *knowledge,* the student would say "knowledge" and spell it in syllables—"k-n-o-w/l-e-d-g-e." To the surprise of both student and teacher, he performed very well on his weekly spelling tests, receiving *B*'s.

Approaches to spelling instruction should be consistent with those of reading. Reading is a decoding process and spelling is an encoding process, but both processes require analysis and synthesis of words and word patterns. They can reinforce each other in the remedial process. In general, spelling approaches follow reading approaches, with the added dimension of the reproduction of words in a written format. The most commonly cited approaches to the teaching of spelling that are directly derived from reading methods include (a) a phonics approach that emphasizes phonetics and spelling rules (Hanna & Moore, 1953). Advocates of this approach contend that 49% of 17,000 words could be spelled using phoneme-grapheme correspondence and another 37% could be spelled with only a single error (Hanna, Hanna, Hodges, & Rudorf, 1966); (b) a linguistic approach that stresses the teaching of phonology (speech sounds), morphology (meaningful units of speech), and syntax (rules that govern word order in a sentence), (Hammill, Larsen, & McNutt, 1977); (c) a synthetic approach—a whole word approach that attempts to teach spelling through a visualization approach; and (d) a multisensory whole word approach (Fernald, 1943) that emphasizes a kinesthetic approach to learning. (The reader is referred to the reading methods section in chapter 13 for elaboration of these and other methods for teaching reading.)

Due to the complexity of the spelling process, students should be taught spelling using more than one approach by integrating elements that reinforce visualization and motoric imprint in the spelling process, such as color coding and tracing. For example, when using a linguistic or phonetic approach, color coding is recommended; this facilitates students' awareness of analysis and synthesis of patterns and reinforces visualization. When using a kinesthetic approach, it is very helpful to utilize auditory and/or visual cues.

In general, all spelling methods must involve the following:

1. Analysis and synthesis of patterns
2. Auditory memory—auditory imagery
3. Visual memory—visual imagery
4. Motoric memory—motoric imagery
5. Meaningful association
6. Commonsense patterns and phonological rules
7. Mnemonic devices to facilitate memory
8. Overlearning and chaining

The following procedures were found to be relevant to remedial spelling instruction and are supported by empirical research:

1. The test-study-test method was found superior to the study-test method.
2. Learning spelling words by a synthetic approach is better than learning words by syllables.
3. Presenting words for study in lists in column form is better than in sentence or paragraph form.
4. Students' self-correction of spelling tests under the teacher's direction is the single most important factor in learning to spell.
5. The use of spelling games stimulates student interest (Graham & Miller, 1979).

Introducing a Spelling Unit

In introducing a spelling unit to a class, the teacher must consider the appropriate teaching methods and techniques for each student. Students should be taught to organize their weekly spelling activities, utilizing their best learning styles.

The following steps describe how a teacher might introduce a spelling unit to students:

1. Introduce spelling words as meaningful words through spelling readiness activities appropriate to students' level of functioning. This usually involves (a) a topic discussion in which the spelling words are utilized in a meaningful context; (b) word-meaning readiness activities, such as picture-word association, the finding of meanings, synonyms, antonyms,

and classifications; and (c) word-analysis readiness activities, such as picture-sound association, the grouping of words according to sound pattern, identification of prefixes and suffixes, compound words, and syllabication.

2. Provide students with weekly spelling learning-plan activities. This involves a weekly spelling routine and activities so students know what to do on each day of the week. It is helpful to develop a weekly spelling contract with each student, delineating the activities for each day of the week, with monitoring and evaluation procedures.

3. Provide students with learning strategies for spelling tailored to each student's needs and information-processing style. This activity should involve (a) the utilization of specific learning strategies for spelling, (b) memory prompts, and (c) development of students' monitoring and evaluation skills so they can evaluate their progress throughout the week.

4. Provide students with appropriate follow-up activities, such as structural analysis, the finding of word meanings, vocabulary usage and enrichment, and written expressive language.

5. Provide students with activities to reinforce mastery and automaticity of spelling words, such as writing words in a student dictionary, using link letters and/or letter tiles, creating crossword puzzles with the weekly words, and utilizing games, such as Spill & Spell, Scrabble, and Boggle.

Cognitive and Metacognitive Strategies for Spelling

Like any other academic skill, spelling requires declarative, procedural, and conditional knowledge. Spelling is acquired in a repeated fashion using generalized problem-solving processes that result in an increased awareness of structural patterns (Gerber & Hall, 1989). Thus it requires students' knowledge of words, letter/sound association, structural analysis, and the orthography of the English language (Wong, 1986). The goals of a metacognitive-oriented approach are to develop students' sensitivity to the purpose and functions of spelling and to increase students' awareness of how words are constructed and the relationship of word structure to the English orthography, including an awareness of skills necessary for spelling and spelling strategies. In addition, it involves the development of spelling strategies, the identification of specific steps in the strategy, and strategy implementation. The last element includes the regulation of effective use of strategies for spelling during spelling and writing activities.

Cognitive Strategy Instruction for Spelling

Wong (1986) recommends the use of two main procedures in teaching spelling: domain specific knowledge that employs phonics and/or linguistic analysis of word structure and knowledge of spelling strategies. She uses the spelling grid in Table 14–1 to guide students in structural analysis of words. In addition, Wong uses self-questioning strategy to guide students in learning how to spell. Students are encouraged to ask the following questions:

Table 14−1 Spelling Grid in Exploratory Study

Word	No. of syllables	Syllables in word	Base word	Addition	Suffix	Change in spelling
information	4	in-form-a-tion	inform	+ tion	ation	
education	4	e-du-ca-tion	educate	+ tion	tion	*e* in
vacation		va-ca-tion	vacate	+ tion	tion	base word
location			locate	+ tion		dropped
relation			relate	+ tion		
direction			direct	+ tion		
formation			form + a	+ tion		
election			elect	+ tion		
correction			correct	+ tion		
action			act	+ tion		
inflation			inflate	+ tion		

Source: From "A Cognitive Approach to Teaching Spelling" by B. Y. L. Wong, 1986, *Exceptional Children*, 53(2), p. 171. Copyright 1986 by Exceptional Children. Reprinted by permission.

1. Do I know this word?
2. How many syllables do I hear in this word? (Write down the number.)
3. I'll spell out the word.
4. Do I have the right number of syllables down?
5. If yes, is there any part of the word I'm not sure of the spelling? I'll underline that part and try spelling the word again.
6. Now, does it look right to me? If it does, I'll leave it alone. If it still doesn't look right, I'll underline the part I'm not sure of the spelling and try again. (If the word I spelled does not have the right number of syllables, let me hear the word in my head again, and find the missing syllable. Then I'll go back to steps 5 and 6.
7. When I finish spelling, I tell myself I'm a good worker. I've tried hard at spelling. (p. 172)

Metacognitive-Oriented Strategies for Spelling

Through the learning process analysis discussed previously, students can develop metacognitive learning strategies for spelling. Students discuss the purpose, goals, and functions of spelling, the nature of spelling patterns and irregularities, and what it takes to spell. With the teacher's guidance, they develop strategies for spelling and identify the specific steps to follow. Through this process, students learn to attack writing skills in an orderly fashion. Steps and procedures in the learning process analysis (described in chapter 6) should be followed. Figures 14−4 and 14−5 are a sample strategy guide and a self-monitoring sheet for metacognitive learning strategies for spelling.

Figure 14–4   Metacognitive Spelling Strategies: Strategy Guide

---

Read, Think, Strategize:

LEARNING MY SPELLING WORDS

Challenge Guide
   Spelling is an important tool for writing. You are often asked to write words or sentences to communicate your ideas. Spelling is the bridge between oral and written language. In order to write effectively we need to know how to spell correctly. Words are spelled according to certain patterns, rules, and common usage. Strategies can be developed to help us learn these patterns and rules to become better spellers.

Super Spelling Strategies
   Say the word, know what it means
   Write the word down, say the letters as you write them
   Analyze the word (sounds, syllables, patterns)
   Practice spelling the word using your best way of learning
   Test yourself. Do you know the words?

Pledge for Success
   I say the word, I know what it means
   I write the word down, I say the letters as I write them
   I analyze the word (sounds, syllables, patterns)
   I practice spelling the word using my best way of learning
   I test myself. Do I know the words?

Source: From *Successful Learning: Metacognition Secondary Student Handbook, Level III, Book 1* by A. Ariel, 1987. Unpublished manuscript, California State University, Los Angeles. Reprinted by permission.

Specific Strategies for Spelling

Integrating Spelling With Creative Writing

This is a complete integrative spelling approach that uses writing as a medium to learn and reinforce weekly spelling words. Both a group language experience and the student's own book are utilized for the written product. The common characteristic of this approach is that the words being learned are to be used every day. Students' written output is displayed on the bulletin board, and a weekly classroom magazine is issued each week with entries from each student. This involves an editorial staff consisting of students working collaboratively to produce the magazine. In addition to the weekly topic writing, students are encouraged to take part in various writing activities, including poetry, riddles, coding activities, and the creation of crossword puzzles.

Using Spelling Workbooks

Spelling workbooks are designed to develop students' spelling skills gradually and sequentially. Most of them attempt to follow the scope and sequence of the spelling

Figure 14–5   Metacognitive Spelling Strategies: Implementation and Self-Monitoring Sheet

PLEDGE FOR SUCCESS: STRATEGY USE

Set: Spelling

Skills/Behaviors I Need to Learn:	How Will I Do It? (Strategies)	How Am I Doing? Key: √−; √; √+;					
		M	T	W	Th	F	Overall
Learning How to Spell	I say the word, I know what it means.						
	I write the word down, I say the letters as I write them.						
	I analyze the word (sounds, syllables, patterns).						
	I practice spelling the word using my best way of learning.						
	I test myself. Do I know the words?						
Individualized Goal							

Teacher's Comments:

Student's Comments: This Is the Way I See Myself

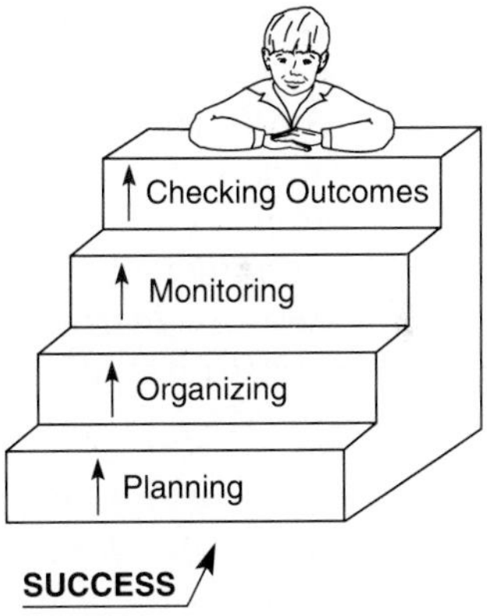

↑ Checking Outcomes

↑ Monitoring

↑ Organizing

↑ Planning

SUCCESS

Source: From *Successful Learning: Metacognition Secondary Student Handbook, Level III, Book 1* by A. Ariel, 1987. Unpublished manuscript, California State University, Los Angeles. Reprinted by permission.

curriculum. Most spellers are highly organized and systematic. In addition to spelling vocabulary units, they provide students with drill-and-practice follow-up activities essential to spelling and students' general language development. Many teachers resort to word lists to remedy the problem of poor spellers. However, teaching and learning words in isolation is not effective (Henderson, 1985). What is important is the integration of words from spelling lists into the weekly diet of the spelling program. Spelling workbooks usually provide exercises in word analysis, vocabulary development and enrichment, and proper usage in written expressive language and/or reading.

For average schoolchildren introduced to weekly spelling units, spelling workbooks meet the objectives of the spelling curriculum. Most teachers attempt to integrate the weekly spelling units with other language arts activities. On the other hand, for learning-disabled students, spelling workbooks have limited use, inasmuch as it is almost impossible to assign a spelling workbook that meets their needs. Too often teachers assume that if students score 4.1 on a spelling achievement test, they can be assigned to a fourth-grade speller. This does not take into account students' range of functioning, which is uneven, with skills extending across a wide range and gaps in many areas. In line with previous discussion in this chapter, the teacher should consider the use of workbooks as a supplemental component to the spelling program. Although spelling workbooks may not fully meet the needs of the learning disabled, their inclusion as a part of the comprehensive spelling program is important. Spellers provide a structure with appropriate drill, practice, and follow-up activities. They also develop a sense of involvement with the spelling program similar to that of peers, and a sense of closure and satisfaction through the completion of an assignment.

The following guidelines are suggested for the selection of spelling workbooks:

1. Approximate the range of optimal functioning of students.
2. Select a speller that is compatible with the teaching approach; for example, use a linguistic speller if a linguistic approach is utilized.
3. Evaluate the mode of presentation to determine if it is compatible with students.
4. Determine if word usage exercises are comprehensive and reinforce the vocabulary learned.
5. Ascertain if it allows for easy checking and monitoring of students' skill mastery.

Furthermore, spelling exercises must be evaluated in terms of (a) their focus on word meanings, (b) their focus on inductive learning and spelling generalization, (c) their incorporation of word games and puzzles, and (d) their clarity and illustration (Cramer, 1978).

Morphographic Spelling

Morphographic Spelling (Dixon & Englemann, 1979), published by Science Research Associates (SRA), is a program of corrective spelling that utilizes the analysis of words according to units of meaning. A morphograph is the smallest part of a word that has meaning, for example, *re* in *recycle*. The program is based on the knowledge that all morphographs have meaning that can be affixed to root words either at the beginning of a word or at the end. These morphographs then change, refine, or clarify the meanings of the root word according to usage.

The program requires active participation by students in a large group setting. Students are prompted to respond orally to questions, to spell aloud, and to write words in specific areas of worksheets, as delineated in the instructor's manual. A means of monitoring success as well as correcting mistakes is an integral part of the program.

The teacher follows a set pattern of instruction, as outlined in the instructor's manual, in order to introduce each lesson in a methodical and consistent manner. The teacher may introduce additional activities to enhance the successful learning of each student. The lessons utilize all modes of learning—auditory, visual, and haptic. Students listen to the teacher spell words, repeat spellings aloud as a group, write the words on command, analyze the meanings of the different morphographs, and participate in activities such as finding and circling correct spellings from groups of letters in a row.

In addition to increasing competency in spelling, morphographic analysis is a useful tool in assisting learning-disabled students to decode new words they might encounter in their reading. Students begin to recognize the morphographic composition of words and to attach meaning to them. Thus this approach to spelling enhances the reading program in addition to building successful spelling strategies.

Monitoring and Evaluating Spelling Progress

The spelling program must be geared to students' functional level and spelling needs. Following the functional assessment and the development of the spelling program, monitoring students' progress and evaluating their mastery level are essential for an effective personalized weekly spelling program. In developing the spelling program for each student, the teacher should devise a format that will enable the monitoring of students' progress. This can be done through the use of spelling skills sequence charts, found in most spelling workbooks, and through the development of word mastery lists. In addition, students should be encouraged to monitor their own progress by keeping a spelling vocabulary book and a record of their weekly word lists and weekly spelling test scores. Individualized and/or group charts can be used for this purpose.

Using Spelling Games

Students like to play games. Games provide a means of relaxation, are fun activities, are usually highly motivating, and have a positive effect on students. They serve as a natural medium to reinforce learning and to bring about the integration of spelling words with students' language repertoire. Games are free of anxiety and tend to produce the best outcome from individual students. In teaching spelling, games serve several purposes. They help to reinforce the weekly spelling words and bring spelling to an automatic level. They also enhance students' active vocabulary. They generally help students to utilize the spelling words in a manner that is meaningful to them. Games also serve as disguised drill and practice for students.

The following guidelines for spelling games are provided by Manning and Manning (1986):

1. Keep games simple. Often spelling games become so complicated that students lose sight of why they are playing the game.
2. All students in a small group should be actively involved in the game.
3. Students should work on spelling activities or games in pairs or small groups so they can capitalize on each other's spelling knowledge.
4. Students should write spelling words rather than spell the words orally. Writing helps students develop the correct visual image.
5. Competitive games should only be played with students of similar abilities. Only in children's stories should rabbits and turtles compete.
6. Checking for the correctness of the spelling should be a natural part of any spelling activity.
7. Spelling activities should always be success-oriented. (p. 30)

Playing spelling games should follow the same procedures and principles as all other games. The teacher must make sure that the games selected are appropriate for students' level of functioning. Spelling games should not only utilize the spelling unit of the week but also encourage individual and group participation and creativity.

Using spelling games enhances students' active learning in spelling.

Spelling Instructional Materials

Table 14–2 is a sample list of instructional materials for remedial spelling.

UNDERSTANDING HANDWRITING AND HANDWRITING PROBLEMS

Handwriting is widely thought of as a tool for written communication and as a means of personal expression (T. L. Harris, 1960). As a written communication tool, it permits individuals to extract information from written outputs, to take notes, and to record activities and experiences in life. It also provides people with means of self-expression through prose and literature. Children are usually introduced to prewriting and handwriting skills by their parents as soon as they demonstrate their ability to recognize, manipulate, and copy forms of letters. These prewriting skills are reinforced in nursery school and kindergarten through various activities such as coloring, painting, tracing, and copying. Children are introduced to manuscript writing in the first grade and transitioned to cursive writing in about the second half of the third grade.

Many individuals with learning disabilities exhibit poor handwriting skills. They tend to write illegibly, causing written messages to be misinterpreted and/or misunderstood. As students grow older, the impact of illegible handwriting upon their functioning in school and the quality of their lives becomes more significant. They are unable to take notes legibly, have tremendous difficulties in reading what they have written, and tend to avoid written communication in any form. Among the variety of handwriting difficulties identified in the literature are slowness, incorrect directionality, mirror writing, too much or too little slant, spacing difficulties, inability to stay on line, too much or too little pencil pressure, illegible letters, and general messiness (Mercer & Mercer, 1985).

Causes of Handwriting Difficulties

As early as 1936, Hildreth identified two primary sets of factors that contribute to handwriting difficulties: factors that are inherent to an individual, and factors that result from the inadequacies of an instructional program.

Table 14–2 Remedial Spelling Instructional Materials

Program	Level	Publisher
A Perspective Spelling Program	Elementary/Intermediate/Secondary	Barnell Loft
Spell Correctly	Elementary/Intermediate	Silver Burdett
Spelling Your Way to Success	Secondary/Adult	Barron's Educational Series
Target Spelling	Intermediate/Secondary	Steck-Vaughn Co.

Among the factors that are inherent to an individual, visual perception difficulties and motor deficiencies are recognized by most authorities (Major, 1983). In addition, attention deficits have also been observed as contributing factors to handwriting difficulties (G. Smith, 1983). Disorders of visual perception include visual discrimination, visual-spatial relationships, directionality (Kirk & Chalfant, 1984), and deficit in revisualization (the individual cannot revisualize letters or words and cannot write them spontaneously). Disorders of motor control include eye-hand coordination. Disorders in visual-motor integration are known as dysgraphia (Johnson & Myklebust, 1967). In this condition, an individual can speak and read but cannot execute the motor patterns for writing letters, numbers, or words, and can spell orally but cannot write. Kirk and Chalfant (1984) further describe this condition: "The child knows the word he wishes to write. He knows what it sounds like, can say it and can identify it when he sees it; yet, he is not able to organize and produce the necessary motor movements in copying or writing the word from memory" (p. 198).

Other factors of inadequate teaching—teaching too early, forced instruction, inappropriate writing materials, incorrect paper position, poor transition from manuscript to cursive writing, and practice of errors—were recognized as early as 1936 by Hildreth (Otto, McMenemy, & Smith, 1973). These factors make the learning of handwriting skills even more difficult for learning-disabled individuals.

THE REMEDIAL HANDWRITING PROGRAM

Program Development and Instructional Considerations

Principles of remedial handwriting instruction are as follows:

1. Handwriting instruction should be based on analysis of students' handwriting difficulties.
2. Handwriting instruction should be geared to students' chronological age and their ability to profit from manuscript or cursive writing.
3. Remedial handwriting instruction should be systematic and sequential and follow appropriate instructional procedures and teaching approaches.
4. A strong remedial handwriting program should include a carefully devised sequence of handwriting skills based on analysis of students' difficulties and diagnosis of handwriting defects revealed in daily work (Otto, et al., 1983).
5. The remedial handwriting program should consist of lessons 15 minutes in duration and scheduled daily at the same time (Bachor & Crealock, 1986).
6. The teaching of handwriting skills to learning-disabled individuals should be made as simple as possible by grouping letters of similar shapes requiring similar formation movements.

7. Handwriting instruction should be integrated with the language arts curriculum.
8. Remedial handwriting instruction should provide many opportunities for practice (Kaminsky & Powers, 1981).
9. Remedial handwriting instruction should provide immediate feedback and prevent error practice.
10. The remedial handwriting program should involve students in self-evaluation by teaching them to become more proficient in identifying general and specific handwriting inaccuracies such as letter forms, slants, size, and adequate spacing (Kaminsky & Powers, 1981; Otto et al., 1973).

Assessment and Diagnosis of Handwriting Skills

Attempts have been made to identify the most common errors in the formation of cursive and manuscript letters, the most notable being those of Lewis and Lewis (1965) and Newland (1932). Newland (1932) examined the cursive handwriting of 2,381 individuals ranging from elementary-school age to adults. He sought to identify (a) "what letters are most frequently illegible"? (b) "in what way or ways do these illegibilities occur?" and (c) "do the answers to these questions suggest any remedial or preventive measures?" (pp. 240–241). A very small number of frequent error patterns account for approximately 50% of the illegibilities. The analysis of letter malformations is presented in Table 14–3.

Similarly, Lewis and Lewis (1965) investigated errors in the formation of manuscript letters by 354 first-grade children. The identification of students' errors can provide the LD specialist with diagnostic information that can serve as the basis for the remedial program. The most common errors included the following:

1. The most frequent type of error was incorrect size. While the error was distributed among all letters, it was more frequent with the descenders p, g, y, q, and j, than with other forms.
2. The letter forms most frequently reversed were N, d, q, and y.
3. Partial omission occurred most frequently in m, U, and I.
4. Additions were most frequent in m, U, and I.
5. Incorrect relationship of parts was generally common, occurring most frequently with k, R, M, and m.
6. Incorrect placement relative to line was a common error with descenders and a less frequent error with other letters.
7. The letter forms most frequently misshaped were j, G, and J.
8. In general, errors were most frequent in letter forms in which curves and vertical lines merge—J, U, f, j, m, n, r, u; errors were least frequent in letter forms constructed of vertical lines or horizontal and vertical lines—E, F, H, I, L, T, i, l, t (as cited by Otto, et al., 1973).

Formal handwriting tests are available—such as the handwriting subtest of the Basic School Skills Inventory (Hammill & Leigh, 1983), the Zaner-Bloser Evaluation Skills (1979), and the handwriting subtest of the Test of Written Language (Hammill

Table 14–3 Analysis of Letter Malformations

Type	Percentages Contributed			
	Elementary	**High School**	**Adult**	**Total**
1. Failure to close letters (*a, b, f, g, j, k, o, p, q, s, y, z*)	24	20	16	18
2. Top loops closed (*l* like *t, e* like *i*)	13	14	20	18
3. Looping nonlooped strokes (*i* like *e*)	12	27	12	16
4. Using straight up-strokes rather than rounded strokes (*n* like *u, c* like *i, h* like *li*)	11	10	15	13
5. End stroke difficulty (not brought up, not brought down, not left horizontal)	11	6	9	9
6. Difficulty crossing *t*	5	5	9	7
7. Difficulty dotting *i*	3	5	5	5
8. Top short (*b, d, f, h, k, l, t*)	6	7	3	5
9. Letters too small	4	5	4	4
10. Closing *c, h, r, u, v, w, y*	4	3	3	3
11. Part of letter omitted	4	4	3	3
12. Up-stroke too long	2	3	1	2
13. Letters too large	2	1	—*	1
14. Beginning stroke off line	—	3	1	1
15. Bottom short (*f, g, j, q, y, z*)	2	1	—	1
16. Using rounded up-strokes instead of straight ones (*i* like *e, u* like *ee*)	—	1	2	1
17. Down-loop turned incorrectly	1	1	1	1
18. Excessive flourishes	—	1	1	1
19. Part added to letter	—	—	1	1
20. Down-stroke too long	1	1	—	—
21. Up-loop turned incorrectly	—	—	—	—
22. Down-loop closed	—	—	—	—
23. Printing	—	—	—	—
24. Palmer *r*	2	1	—	—
25. Unrecognizably recorded	2	1	3	3
26. Unclassified	10	9	9	9

*The dashes represent frequencies which accounted for less than one-half of one percent of the total.

& Larsen, 1983)—but informal handwriting procedures using students' writing samples are the most efficient tools in diagnosing handwriting difficulties. The unique qualities of handwriting make it possible to pinpoint the nature of writing errors. The remedial process can then be directed toward developing students' writing skills (Otto et al., 1973).

When selecting writing samples, the teacher should select samples under three different conditions: students' usual handwriting, students' best handwriting, and students' fastest handwriting (Mann, Suiter, & McClung, 1979; Towle, 1978).

In observing students' handwriting samples, the LD specialist should pay specific attention to the following areas:

1. Does the student maintain appropriate position and posture?
2. Does the student grip the pencil correctly?
3. Does the student stay on the lines when writing?
4. Does the student consistently use the same hand for writing?
5. Does the student use excessive crossing out and erasing?
6. Does the student mix manuscript and cursive writing?
7. Is the student's writing consistent or is there an erratic variation within the student's writing sample?
8. Are there malfunctions of specific letters?
9. Does the student have spacing difficulties between letters or words?
10. Does the student fail to close letters or to close the top loops in letters? (Bachor & Crealock, 1986; Mercer, 1987a; Newland, 1932)

Informal surveys such as the Bain Handwriting Survey (Bain, 1980) (Figure 14–6) can guide the teacher's observations and can facilitate the recording and monitoring of students' handwriting output.

METHODS AND STRATEGIES FOR TEACHING HANDWRITING

Teaching Handwriting Skills to Individuals With LD

In teaching the learning disabled handwriting skills, the traditional emphasis on form and quality of handwriting must give way to the major goal of legible writing. The LD specialist must know the sequence of handwriting skills, and must be able to apply it appropriately to various age groups and to various individuals within an age group.

Generally, instruction begins with a prewriting and readiness stage, followed by a manuscript (printing) stage and a cursive writing stage. Though this sequence may be appropriate for primary school children, modifications are necessary for elementary and secondary school children. There is some difference of opinion as to whether writing instruction for children with learning disabilities should begin with manuscript or cursive writing. The arguments for beginning with manuscript writing

Figure 14–6 Bain's Handwriting Survey

Student: Observer:
Age: Date:
Grade:

Handwriting skills should be compared on the following activities to determine the type of problem and the extent of difficulty.

1. Write the lowercase alphabet
2. Write upper- and lowercase letters from dictation
3. Write single words from dictation
4. Near Point Copy
5. Far Point Copy
6. Creative Writing
7. Note Taking

Assessment of Component Skills:

Organization of Paper	Word Spacing
Handedness	Word Slant
Pencil Grip	Omissions
Pencil Pressure	Substitutions
Position of Paper	Additions
Anchor Hand Position	Reversals
	Mixed (Cursive/Manuscript)
Letter Formation	Mixed (Lower/Upper Case)
Letter Size	Erasing
Letter Slant	Speed
Letter Spacing	Fluency
Letter Alignment	

Additional Comments:
On Task?

Student's Attitude Towards Handwriting:

Source: From *Handwriting Survey,* (p. 76) by A. M. Bain, 1980. Unpublished paper, Loyola College, Baltimore MD. Reprinted by permission.

are that it is simpler, requires fewer movements, and is more consistent in appearance, and the letters are more similar to those printed in books (Johnson & Myklebust, 1967; Wallace & Kauffman, 1986). Some researchers suggest that many of the handwriting problems of the learning disabled can be minimized by teaching cursive writing directly, as it is more continuous and rhythmic and provides additional kinesthetic feedback (Banas & Wills, 1970; Fernald, 1943; Gillingham & Stillman, 1960; Orton, 1937; Strauss & Lehtinen, 1947). The evidence as to the relative effectiveness of teaching manuscript or cursive writing to learning-disabled individuals is inconclusive (Graham & Miller, 1980). Further studies are needed to provide us with a profile of a child most likely to succeed with manuscript or cursive writing (Bain, 1988).

The LD specialist must be well versed in the characteristics of manuscript and cursive writing in order to be able to make an adequate decision. In manuscript writing, or printing, letters are made separately with straight lines and circles, and the lowercase and capital letters are similar. In cursive writing, the letters are joined and upstrokes, ovals, and connecting strokes are used; the writing is slanted toward the right; and lowercase and capital letters may differ (Rose, 1982). An important consideration for the LD specialist is the simplicity of manuscript letters—they are easier to form than those of cursive writing (Rose, 1982). According to Bain (1988), compensatory strategies should be encouraged for students with persistent handwriting difficulties. These may include the use of tape recorders, typewriters, or word processors in lieu of handwritten output.

Principles of Teaching Handwriting Skills

The teaching of handwriting skills, whether manuscript or cursive, requires a systematic and sequential approach built upon individuals' abilities and the necessary prerequisite skills for handwriting. From the beginning, handwriting is a visual-motor skill. It requires visual perception, muscular (motor) control, and visual-motor integration through eye-hand coordination. Handwriting is a complex process requiring basic skills and abilities across modalities. Although emphasis is on the visual motoric mode, it is quite obvious that the auditory mode, by way of associating the grapheme with the morpheme, is also essential. Handwriting instruction should be viewed as an integral part of the language arts curriculum and should be integrated with students' daily activities in written expressive language and spelling as well as in the content areas. The following principles should serve as guidelines in teaching and remediating handwriting skills:

1. Always include readiness activities appropriate to students' functional level.
2. Group letters based on similar movement pattern and structure in order to facilitate the generalization of movement patterns to letter formation.
3. Teach letters in isolation and as parts of words.
4. Provide an initial model, followed by a fading model, to facilitate the imitation of movement patterns.
5. Provide clear directions for movement patterns with visual and verbal cues.
6. Use various media to develop smooth and fluent letter formation movement patterns.
7. Provide practice experience in isolation and as part of words.
8. Integrate handwriting throughout the language arts activities.

Stages of Teaching Handwriting Skills

The following suggested handwriting teaching stages represent common practice and are based on Rose's (1982) stages of writing growth.

Readiness Stage

Readiness activities should be geared to students' chronological and developmental age. For primary school students, readiness activities are more general in nature, usually involving activities across many areas, such as painting, coloring, sorting, working with clay, cutting out shapes, and fitting puzzles together (Rose, 1982). For older students, these activities must be directed to the essential readiness elements of handwriting. These include the following:

1. Grasping the pencil appropriately
2. Developing finger dexterity
3. Developing right-to-left, up-down, and cursive movement patterns
4. Being able to write different forms and shapes
5. Being able to manipulate spatial relationships
6. Mastering directionality

Prewriting Stage

This stage involves the teaching of the essential handwriting movements using paper-and-pencil activities, such as copying geometric designs and preletter forms that approximate the components of written letters, both manuscript and cursive. It includes horizontal, vertical, and angular lines, circles, squares, triangles, half-circles rotated in different directions, and intersecting lines and hooks (Johnson & Myklebust, 1967). These straight and curved movements are geared to approximate letter formation movements.

Geometric templates can help students to develop control over the pencil. The movements developed through the use of templates can be reinforced by the use of shaded and/or stippled letter forms. In addition, the teacher can use a fading model, in which models of the letters are presented with gradual fading. During the readiness stage, the teacher must also introduce students to the vocabulary needed to teach handwriting, such as *up, down, in, out, above,* and *below.*

Model Stage

In this stage, students are provided with model letters, either manuscript or cursive. The students' primary function is to copy the letter and/or word approximating the model using appropriate movements. This stage also involves the actual modeling of writing by the teacher and guided movements, in which the teacher holds a student's hand and guides it with the appropriate movement. Copying involves copying from a page and copying from the chalkboard, gradually moving from forming large-size letters to forming actual-size letters, with the same form grid used in the prewriting phase. All letters should be grouped according to movement patterns required to form the letters. In addition, single letter practice should be followed immediately with meaningful word and sentence writing. This facilitates the development of handwriting skills and generalization, and usually expedites the instructional process.

Memory Stage

In this stage, students are able to write their own name and other words without looking at the model. This is considered to be the mastery stage, at which attention should be given to the appropriate formation of letters and words and automaticity. Emphasis is placed on legibility of handwriting rather than perfect letter formation.

Strategies for Teaching Manuscript Writing

Rose (1982) suggests the following techniques and principles for teaching manuscript writing:

1. Models and copies are always provided for children's use.
2. All letters and numbers are made with straight lines and circles.
3. All straight letters begin from the top.
4. All circle letters begin at the 2 o'clock position.
5. Move from left to right in writing letters.
6. Space circular letters close together.
7. Space straight letters farther apart.
8. Space words one finger apart when using ruled paper.
9. Write on the line.
10. Capital and tall letters are initially made two spaces high, small letters one space.
11. Group letters and numbers with similar structure for instruction. (pp. 419–420)

A sample of manuscript handwriting using the rainbow tracing technique is presented in Figure 14–7.

Strategies for Teaching Cursive Writing

The transition from manuscript to cursive writing can be done once students show a readiness for it. According to Rose (1982), this includes (a) students' ability to write manuscript letters with ease and without using a model, (b) students' ability to read cursive writing, and (c) students' expressed desires to write in cursive.

The following techniques and principles are suggested for teaching cursive handwriting:

1. Develop students' readiness for cursive writing through sequential movement patterns that approximate the movements of letter formations. These patterns are illustrated in Figure 14–8. Figure 14–9 (p. 470) shows samples of a student's readiness activity for cursive writing.

Figure 14–7   Manuscript Handwriting Using Rainbow Tracing

2. Provide a model of cursive letters in isolation and as parts of words.
3. Provide clear directions of movement patterns (Figure 14–10, p. 471).
4. Group letters of similar movement patterns and structure (Figure 14–11, p. 472) The most common letter groupings for cursive writing are as *follows: a o c d; i u t; m n; l b e; v w x; j g y z; f h k; p q;* and *r s.*
5. Transition from manuscript to cursive writing through the joining of manuscript letters.
6. Teach cursive letters in isolation and as parts of words (Figure 14–12, p. 472).
7. Teach size reductions.
8. Utilize various media to develop smooth and fluent letter formation movements, such as a fading model and rainbow tracing (Figures 14–13, p. 473, and 14–14, p. 474).
9. Integrate cursive handwriting throughout language arts activities.

The Use of Verbal Mediation

Verbalization of movements by the teacher followed by students' self-verbalization provides students with language reinforcement to the kinesthetic mode. It heightens and clarifies the movement directions and develops associations of movement patterns with familiar objects and/or the auditory image of movement patterns. Providing students with appropriate guidelines in the process of forming letters is extremely important. The LD specialist should verbalize the movement patterns during

Figure 14–8   Sequential Movement Patterns

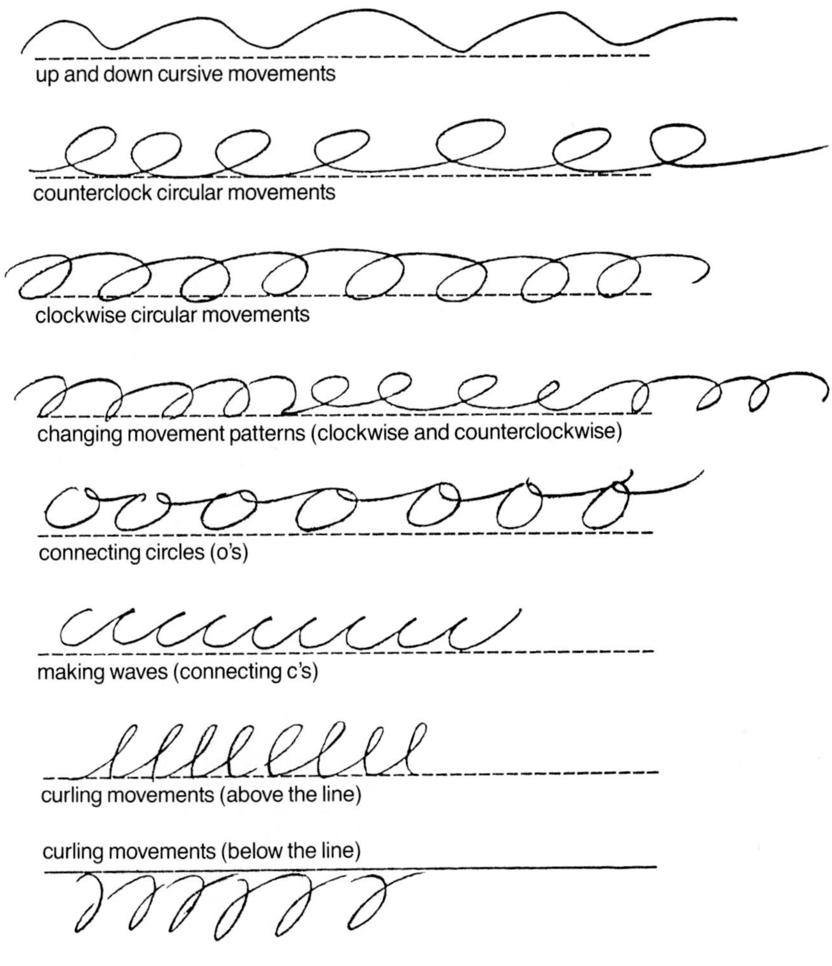

up and down cursive movements

counterclock circular movements

clockwise circular movements

changing movement patterns (clockwise and counterclockwise)

connecting circles (o's)

making waves (connecting c's)

curling movements (above the line)

curling movements (below the line)

the instructional process and encourage students to do so. Labeling letters' patterns by using mnemonics can also be very helpful.

Handwriting Instructional Material

Table 14–4 (p. 474) is a list of commercially available handwriting programs appropriate for individuals with learning disabilities.

Figure 14–9 Cursive Writing Readiness Activity

Figure 14-10   Directions for Movement Patterns

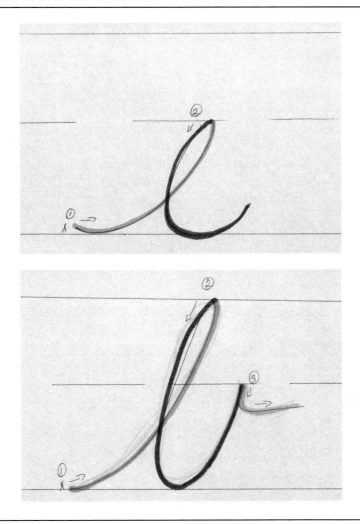

Figure 14–11 Letter Grouping of Similar Patterns

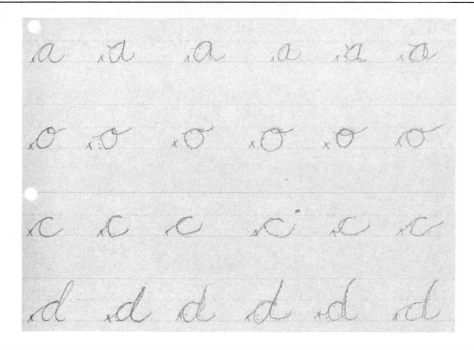

Figure 14–12 Letters as Parts of Words

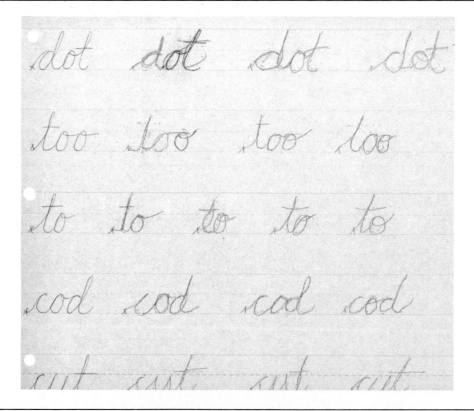

Mathematics disabilities are often referred to as *dyscalculia.* Kosc (1974) defines dyscalculia as "a disorder of the maturation of mathematical abilities" (p. 48). In general, dyscalculia means the inability to calculate. The term *developmental dyscalculia* is used to distinguish the children with mathematics problems from young adults who may have the same difficulties as a result of trauma or injury (Hallahan et al., 1985).

The two profiles that follow are of individuals with LD who exhibit difficulties in mathematics.

Mary is a 16½-year-old learning-disabled student attending the eleventh grade; she is assigned to the resource room for assistance in mathematics. Mary is functioning at about eighth-grade level in reading and spelling. She is doing okay in her other classes, including history and science. When it comes to mathematics, according to her teacher, Mary cannot grasp concepts or apply knowledge from one area to another. Her thinking is scattered, and she is unable to focus. She is having difficulties learning arithmetic concepts because she is unable to integrate new concepts with those already learned. Mary still lacks the basic skills and remembers the multiplication tables only at times. She does not know what to do with the various numerical values in word problems and generally feels lost with them. She has difficulties shifting from one operation to another and performing basic operations with fractions.

Michael is a 12-year-old fifth grader attending a special day class for individuals with learning disabilities. His arithmetic functional level is at about second grade. He also has difficulties in reading and spelling, in which he is functioning at about the third-grade level. The teacher reported that Michael has difficulties in the following areas: He cannot follow directions and has difficulties understanding mathematical operations unless the process is presented with 3-D material. Moreover, Michael does not really understand what he is doing, inasmuch as mathematics in general is meaningless to him. He seems to have auditory receptive difficulties and is disorganized.

Various factors contribute to mathematics disabilities. These include (a) problems of attention and concentration (Kirk & Chalfant, 1984; Siegel & Gold, 1982); (b) disorders of imagery, memory, and abstraction including mental manipulation (Siegel & Gold, 1982); (c) difficulties in symbol substitutions and processing of graphic symbols; (d) difficulties in visual-spatial relationships (Kirk & Chalfant, 1984; Siegal & Gold, 1982); and (e) difficulties in analysis, synthesis, and reproduction of patterns, in seeing whole-versus-part relationships, and in visualization. Difficulties in mathematics can often be attributed to faulty teaching approaches and faulty learning experiences in the early grades (Russell & Ginsburg, 1984). Faulty learning experiences in early grades may be due to (a) unreadiness to learn, (b) teaching approaches that place too much emphasis on abstract teaching and rote memory—individuals being taught without understanding mathematical operations, and (c) anxiety and emotional blocks developed as a result of early negative experiences.

What Is Mathematics?

Mathematics is a quantitative representation of objects and elements in the universe. It is the logical study of shape, arrangement, and quantity. (Baur & George, 1976). It devotes itself to exploration in number, form, abstract structures, and order relationships (Freitag & Freitag, 1962). It involves the formulation and testing of hypotheses of the various quantitative phenomena in the universe, attempting to establish relationships and laws of mathematics presented in a symbolic, abstract manner. The science of mathematics follows the logical rules of order in the universe. Mathematical operations involve aspects of quantification that have corresponding concrete representation in the universe and are usually presented in an abstract mode using mathematical symbols. This concrete representation can be as simple as dividing one pie into two halves, with each half representing one half of the pie, and as complex as developing Einstein's ultimate formula, $E = mc^2$.

The characteristics of mathematics are numerous, and knowing them facilitates our understanding of the mathematical phenomenon. Mathematics may be described as the following:

1. The use of symbols to represent objects, elements, and phenomena in the universe
2. A structured body of knowledge
3. A way of thinking and doing
4. Objective
5. Exact and consistent
6. Logical, reflecting orderly and systematic patterns
7. Multidimensional
8. Predictable
9. Universal
10. A communication tool that uses mathematical symbols to describe quantified relationships in the universe

Mathematics is an essential tool, encompassing various levels of skill attainment, which serves the needs of a wide variety of people. It is needed by people in all walks of life to manage their money, make change, figure cost, figure real estate interest, and deal with a host of other daily problems. The field of mathematics includes arithmetic, which is the science of numbers, symbolization, relationships, concepts, and counting. Beyond the simple knowledge of arithmetic, there are the higher levels of geometry, trigonometry, algebra, and calculus, which serve as basic tools of thought in the physical, biological, and medical sciences and increasingly in the social sciences.

THEORETICAL FOUNDATION OF TEACHING MATHEMATICS

Understanding the Learning Process in Mathematics

The teacher's view of mathematics is extremely important and directly affects the process of instruction (Baur & George, 1976). In addition, students' knowledge and understanding of the processes involved in mathematics affect their performance.

The nature of the mathematical experience is highly influenced by the mode of interaction of learners with the mathematical experience and by the way they learn this information. This is illustrated by the following account of Nelson and Mike.

Nelson, a junior high student with learning disabilities, was given a problem: He was asked to change a mixed number, $4\frac{5}{7}$, into an improper fraction. He solved the problem this way: $4\frac{5}{7} = \frac{27}{7}$. When asked to explain how he arrived at the answer, Nelson first indicated that he did not remember. He then stated that his teacher showed him to solve the problem in this way: to multiply 4 times 5 and add 7 to it. Most likely, Nelson was taught mechanically how to change a mixed number to an improper fraction without understanding the process involved.

Mike, also a junior high student with learning disabilities, was given the same problem. He did not initially remember how to solve the problem. However, because Mike was taught to achieve understanding of the process involved, he could easily check his process and his answers by resorting to a figural representation of the problem. Namely, given 4 wholes and $\frac{5}{7}$, Mike drew 4 pies and divided each of them into seven sevenths and another incomplete pie consisting of $\frac{5}{7}$ (Figure 15–1). The various fractions were counted by Mike to arrive at the correct answer. Using this process, Mike could verify that he needed to multiply 4 by 7 since there are seven parts within each of the pies, and add to that the remaining $\frac{5}{7}$. Thus Mike who was taught using concrete and figural representations has a backup system with which to check his own processes and operations.

Understanding the way an individual interacts with the environment may facilitate our understanding of the acquisition process in mathematics. From Bruner's (1964) perspectives, three modes of representation depict the way in which experiences are represented in children's thoughts. The first type of representation is enactive; that is, it results from both kinesthetic and muscular motor activity. The second type is iconic, that is, the images of what is perceived visually, haptically, and auditorily. The final type of representation is symbolic, in which the events of an experience are represented in symbolic language. Similarly, Inhelder and Piaget (1958) identified this sequence as concrete, figural/perceptual, and abstract. Figure 15–2 illustrates these modes of representation.

Usually, learners proceed in this sequence: They first act upon and manipulate objects in the environment (concrete experience, enactive representation), then de-

Figure 15–1 Figural/Visual Representation of Arithmetic Problem Involving Mixed Numbers

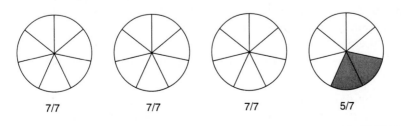

Figure 15–2 Modes of Representation

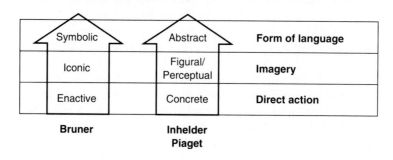

Symbolic		Abstract	**Form of language**
Iconic		Figural/Perceptual	**Imagery**
Enactive		Concrete	**Direct action**
Bruner		**Inhelder Piaget**	

velop mental imagery (figural, iconic), and later associate labels (names) with the objects (symbolic, form of language). Individuals not only act upon the environment through these means, but they have an appropriate internal counterpart in the central nervous system for representing sensory-motor acts, percepts, and thoughts. With growth and with the development of language, people increasingly deal with their environment at a symbolic level. Yet they continue to interact with the environment through actions and imagery throughout life.

The preceding accounts of Nelson and Mike illustrate the importance of teaching mathematics to students with learning disabilities by presenting material through both the enactive and figural modes. Since so many of the problems of mathematics learning disabilities are associated with students' lack of understanding of the process, the use of 3-D, concrete materials, and figural/pictorial aides enhances the acquisition and maintenance of mathematical skills in a meaningful way.

An important feature of the physical operations is that they provide learners with immediate feedback for all applications. This feedback often takes the form of contingencies that occur if an operation is not being performed correctly (Carnine, 1983). Suggested teaching procedures, therefore, involve moving from a concrete manipulative experience, to the development of figural representation and imageries, to the symbolic level (Peterson, Mercer, & O'Shea, 1988).

In discussing suggestions for the teaching of mathematics, Beilin and Gotkin (1964) state the following:

> Take the learner where you find him but be prepared through the preparation of adequate materials and techniques to move as rapidly as possible to learning mathematics on a symbolic level. The stress in the early materials should be on sensory-motor manipulation. Later materials can be pictorial and still later, materials can be abstract and symbolic. The presentation of materials may be either simultaneous or sequential depending on the learning status of the child. (pp. 22–23)

In the day-by-day teaching process, the teacher must provide students with manipulative materials in order to explore the various aspects of mathematical opera-

The teacher can help the student understand mathematical concepts by using manipulative materials, graphs, charts, and tables.

tions. This process can be further facilitated by advancing to a second level of figural representation, in which pictorial representation of a mathematical operation can be offered, and finally culminating in a mathematical sentence at the symbolic level. Related to the arithmetic problem of converting mixed numbers to improper fractions, this would involve (a) the actual activities with fractions and whole numbers, (b) the drawing of pictorial representations of the pies and the fractions of the pies, and finally (c) writing the mathematical sentence. The understanding of mathematical operations by students is increased by this process, which allows the attainment of concepts at the enactive, iconic, and symbolic levels and facilitates feedback across modes of presentation, which permits students to fall back to lower levels when needed (Figure 15–3).

Levels of Arithmetic Concept Development

The principal task of the teacher is to organize learners' activities to facilitate meaningful experiences through exploratory activities, through transitioning to the iconic mode, and finally into symbolic representation. Children progressively move to the point of being able to deal with symbolic representation while understanding relationships and meanings.

Figure 15–3 Modes of Representation and Feedback Mechanism

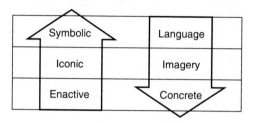

Arithmetic teaching should follow these levels:

1. Exploratory learning that allows children to experience the various aspects of mathematics through manipulation and visualization
2. Discovery learning involving didactic and guided teaching (Van Hiele, 1986)
3. Attainment/acquisition of concepts at a symbolic level in which activities involve primarily convergent productions
4. Automaticity of learning
5. Mastery of concepts, when students are comfortable with the concepts attained and are able to create new mathematic problems and thus engage in divergent production

Table 15–1 illustrates the levels of arithmetic concept development.

The Mathematics Continuum and the Remedial Process

The teaching of mathematics follows a sequential development in which higher skill levels are built upon lower skill levels. In addition, there is an inherent relationship between the various levels of mathematics. According to Heimer and Trueblood (1977), "This situation is a mixed blessing for the teacher of mathematics . . . The virtue of the structure rests in the fact that mathematical ideas are interrelated, a quality which should help make the subject easier to understand and remember provided it is taught meaningfully. Yet this same feature is the cause of serious teaching/learning problems which occur when one or more of the links in the structure are missing" (p. 13).

One can visualize the areas of mathematics, its concepts and subconcepts, as building blocks of mathematics (Figure 15–4).More specifically, one can visualize each brick as representing a concept or a group of concepts in the mathematical continuum. Higher level bricks are built upon lower ones. It is important for the LD

Present Level of Functioning in Other Academic Areas
Michael functions in reading at a 2.8 level and in spelling at a 2.1 level. In creative writing, he can write a simple paragraph using appropriate punctuation.

Nature of the Primary Problem
Michael has low academic achievement in all areas of the curriculum and general auditory-processing difficulties.

Intellectual Functioning
Performance on the WISC-R places Michael in the low-average range of intelligence.

Specific Learning Disabilities
Michael has general difficulties in auditory reception, short-term auditory and visual memory, and poor motor coordination. He seems to have a delay in laterality and motor sequencing.

Strengths and Weaknesses
Michael is cooperative, likes school, tries hard to please, and works hard. He is popular with other students and responds well to positive reinforcements. His weaknesses include general difficulties with auditory processing and low academic achievement.

Information-Processing/Learning Style
Michael is primarily a visual learner. He does well when three-dimensional materials are used. Reception is best when visualizing and listening at the same time.

Factors Impeding Learning
Michael seems to have difficulties in receptive processes, primarily information received through the auditory channel. He has difficulties in following directions. He does not always "get in" (understand) what is taught.

Factors That Can Facilitate Learning
Michael is strongly motivated and wants to learn. He likes to work for concrete rewards. His cognitive abilities are within the normal range. He is a visual learner and likes to use manipulatives. He does not show any behavior problems that might interfere with his learning.

Characteristics and Elements of the Remedial Program
Using manipulatives and inductive and deductive reasoning, Michael should be introduced to new concepts in mathematics. A metacognitive approach to mathematics that includes active participation in planning his new program is suggested. In addition, the instructional routine should include positive reinforcement.

Program Recommendations

Michael's peers in the regular sixth-grade classroom are working on decimals (addition, subtraction, and multiplication), fractions (addition, subtraction, multiplication, and division), whole numbers (addition and subtraction of five-digit numbers, multiplication of four-digit numbers times three-digit numbers, and long division of two-digit numbers into four-digit numbers, two- and three-step word problems, place values to millions, and liquid measurements.

Michael's general knowledge of the basic operations of addition and subtraction makes him ready to move on and to learn concepts parallel to those being taught in the regular classroom:

1. Decimals through the use of money and money equivalents, including reading and writing and addition and subtraction of money equivalents, reading menus, and using change
2. Place values and numerical analysis to millions
3. Addition and subtraction of decimals
4. Mathematical concepts, such as liquid measurements
5. Word problems, using menus, making change, and simple fraction problems using one step/one process initially, moving on to two steps/one process, and then to two steps/two processes

Upon completion of the previous units, Michael may be introduced to fractions using manipulative materials (see section on teaching fractions).

Teaching Approaches, Instructional Materials, and Teaching Aids

With the appropriate techniques, Michael's learning in mathematics should involve all three representational levels—concrete (manipulative), figural (figures and pictures) and abstract (mathematical symbols). Materials must be clearly presented in short units to ensure successful completion.

Daily Arithmetic Program

Michael should be engaged in arithmetic learning for a period of 50 minutes a day. This should include 20 minutes of fundamental operations, 15 minutes of word-problem activities, including practical mathematics, 10 minutes of hands-on experience using arithmetic concepts such as liquid measurements, and 5 minutes a day of drill and practice of already-learned concepts.

Feedback and Reinforcement Procedures

Immediate error correction should be provided to Michael to avoid unnecessary failure experiences. The teacher should also use positive reinforcement congruent with classroom management practices.

Ongoing Evaluation and Monitoring of the Student's Progress

Procedures for daily/weekly monitoring of Michael's progress should be established. Percent of correct responses and degree of task completion can be used as criteria. Michael should be involved in monitoring his own progress.

METHODS AND STRATEGIES
FOR TEACHING ARITHMETIC

Arithmetic Teaching Strategies

The remediation of mathematics difficulties is possible through effective mathematics teaching. The LD specialist must take into consideration (a) basic principles of arithmetic teaching, (b) the application of sound principles of learning and remedial education, and (c) considerations of students' specific learning disabilities.

Consider the following: Students in a junior high learning disability classroom had difficulties understanding the concept of fractions. The teacher was frustrated with the students' lack of understanding and asked for assistance from her consulting supervisor. To the teacher's surprise, the consulting supervisor asked the teacher to order three pizza pies, two pounds of apples, two pounds of pears, and about half a pound of candies. The pizza pies were used to introduce the students to fractions. The teacher began by asking students to cut a pizza into various fractions, first to halves, then to fourths, eighths, and so forth. The same process was followed with the apples, the pears, and the candies (fraction of a group). Following the students' grasp of the concept of fractions, they were introduced to fraction equivalents by demonstrating that two quarters of a pizza equals one half of a pizza. Addition and subtraction of fractions with like denominators were then introduced and practiced. Concrete, manipulative materials (pizza pies, apples, pears, and candies), as well as pictorial and figural representations, were used throughout the process. All students had to draw and cut out circles and fractions of circles as they proceeded with addition and subtraction of fractions with like denominators. In addition, each student was encouraged to use other three-dimensional materials, such as the Fraction Learner and pies cut out of cardboard, which the teacher had prepared ahead of time in preparation for the lesson. Thus when the students were asked to add one half plus one half, they had to either draw the two halves or use the Fraction Learner, visualizing such processes as

$$\frac{1}{2} + \frac{1}{2} = \frac{2}{2} = 1 \text{ or } \frac{2}{2} - \frac{1}{2} = \frac{1}{2}$$
$$\frac{1}{4} + \frac{1}{4} = \frac{1}{2} \text{ or } \frac{3}{4} - \frac{1}{4} = \frac{2}{4} = \frac{1}{2}$$

Within one lesson, the students were able to understand the concept of fractions, the concept of fraction equivalents, and the basic concepts of addition and subtraction of fractions with like denominators. They were reinforced by food and by praise. Not only did they learn the concept of fractions, but they also realized that the learning of mathematics could be fun. If nothing else, they associated math with a good time—eating pizza, apples, pears, and candies.

This example illustrates how the teaching of mathematics should be approached with individuals with learning disabilities. There is no need to rush students through the acquisition of concepts. One must give them ample time to discover mathematical relationships and to understand the meaningful aspects of mathematics through inductive and deductive reasoning. As indicated in the example, one must use cross-level teaching to bring students' level of arithmetic functioning as close as possible to their peer group. The teaching process must also consider chaining aspects and overlearning—the sequential acquisition of skills—and the ratio between new skills and review skills. Overlearning can be further strengthened through traditional practice and, if necessary, through rote learning. However, rote learning should not be encouraged in mathematics unless students understand the mathematical concepts involved.

Strategies for Specific Arithmetic Content Areas

Essential Number Readiness Concepts

Mathematical readiness or the lack of it directly affects the performance of children at any level of arithmetic functioning (Hammill & Bartel, 1979). The following aspects of readiness must be considered in the development of a mathematics program for learning-disabled individuals: (a) general developmental readiness, (b) conceptual number readiness, and (c) readiness for a higher level of skill acquisition.

Developmental readiness includes attention span, concentration abilities, perception skills, and motor development. Children who have short attention spans and poor perception often have trouble seeing objects in groups or sets and have difficulty discriminating specific objects or attributes from others. A poor sense of direction and spatial orientation can lead to reversal of numbers, difficulty in understanding reversibility, and problems with geometric concepts and measurements.

Readiness abilities essential for mathematics learning include classification, one-to-one correspondence, seriation, conservation, flexibility, and reversibility. These basic readiness concepts are learned by children throughout their daily experiences at home and at school. Thus a child is able to relate to words such as *more, big,* and *small.* Play activities further provide experiences with essential readiness concepts. Building a tower with blocks of different sizes by putting a smaller block on top of a bigger one represents an activity in seriation. Sorting blocks according to colors or shapes represents an activity in classification.

The ability to count, to understand one-to-one correspondence, to match, to sort, and to compare are all dependent upon individuals' experience in the manipulation of objects. A child with a short attention span, with poor perception, or with poor motor development may not have had appropriate readiness experiences for mathematical learning (Johnson & Myklebust, 1967). A child with arithmetic learning disabilities may miss basic essential concepts and develop difficulties with numerical relationships quite early in life. Many children experience difficulties in mathematics because their instruction has been at a developmental level for which they were not ready.

Strategies for Teaching Whole Numbers

Prior to formal instruction in addition and subtraction, the LD specialist must make sure that students have adequate number concepts. It is important to develop in students a sense of, and friendliness with, numbers. Number games such as odd and even, partial counting, and counting by 2s, 5s, and 10s should help students develop a good sense of numerical values. This initial friendliness with numbers (or the opposite, fear of numbers) will set the tone for higher levels of mathematical learning.

The teaching of whole numbers should be done within a mathematics frame of reference. In order to understand mathematical relationships, students must be able to develop a sense of numerical relationships and quantification, seriation and ordering, and the mathematical continuum. Students should be exposed to numerical values from small to large, and to numerical relationships of values such as that between 10, 100, and 1,000.

Basic operation of whole numbers should follow a sequential teaching-learning of mathematical operations of addition and subtraction. The sequence of teaching whole numbers should be as follows:

1. To the sum of 10
2. To the sum of 20
3. To the sum of 100
4. To the sum of 1,000
5. To the sum of 10,000
6. To the sum of 100,000
7. To the sum of 1,000,000

Representing the same problem in concrete, figural, and symbolic modes must be done at all levels of instruction. Students must have access to concrete materials, such as Cuisenaire rods, Montessori rods, Unifix material, and Catherine Stern material; the traditional abacus can also be helpful. Thornton and Toohey (1985) suggest teaching easy addition facts and then easy subtraction facts, followed by other addition facts, and then other subtraction facts. Our experience in teaching arithmetic to students with LD using concrete objects suggests that addition and subtraction be taught at the same time, and the reversibility of the processes should be stressed. Students should also be exposed to simultaneous horizontal and vertical presentation of addition and subtraction problems:

$$34 + 5 = 39 \qquad 39 - 5 = 34$$

$$
\begin{array}{r}
34 \\
+5 \\
\hline
39
\end{array}
\qquad
\begin{array}{r}
39 \\
-5 \\
\hline
34
\end{array}
$$

It should be noted that children without cognitive reversibility do not understand the subtraction process as a reverse operation of addition. Consequently, those children may be better served if such instruction is delayed.

Using the Cuisenaire, Montessori, or Catherine Stern rods, students can see how numerical values are related, such as

$$3 + 5 = 8$$
$$5 + 3 = 8$$
$$8 - 3 = 5$$
$$8 - 5 = 3$$

These relationships are referred to in mathematics as "inverse operations" or "number families." These number family relationships should be taught to students at the very early stages of learning, facilitating their understanding of various numerical relationships.

Inverse operations also apply to multiplication and division:

$$8 \times 4 = 32$$
$$4 \times 8 = 32$$
$$32 \div 8 = 4$$
$$32 \div 4 = 8$$

When students are taught numerical operations to the sum of 10, they should be encouraged to use concrete aids to discover for themselves the various numerical combinations to the sum of 10, and to proceed from concrete to figural and then to writing mathematical sentences (symbolic) (Figure 15–6).

Likewise in teaching to the sum of 100 or 1,000, students must be able to manipulate and understand the various numerical relationships. To facilitate the acquisition of these concepts, concrete and visual aids should be used. The Unifix math materials, which consist of 100-block trays, are ideal for this purpose. Partial counting can help develop a sense of quantities from 0 to 10, to 100, to 1,000, to 10,000, and so forth. In addition, the teacher can develop number charts to correspond to the Unifix math materials.

Students can practice partial counting by color coding a chart to correspond to the appropriate partial counting. To develop a sense of 1,000, 10 of these charts can be

Figure 15–6   Numerical Operations to the Sum of 10

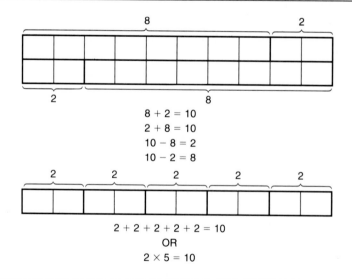

used. The teacher can further use classroom posters corresponding to the charts provided to each student.

In addition to helping students develop a sense of numerical relationships, partial counting serves as preparation for the grasp of multiplication and division facts (Figure 15–7).

Most math curricula separate and isolate mathematical operations into the four distinct elements of addition, subtraction, multiplication, and division. Such a separation is artificial and does not correspond to mathematical functions in the real world. With appropriate exploratory activities, students can discover for themselves the relationships between these four aspects of numerical operations. When given a problem such as 7 × 8, a student who does not remember this multiplication fact can solve the problem by using the distributive property of multiplication by performing the following operations:

$$7 \times 8 = (3 \times 8) + (4 \times 8) = 24 + 32 = 56$$

Both multiplication and division should be taught to students at the same time. It is important that students understand the relationship between the two concepts: Division is the inverse of multiplication, or in simpler terms, division undoes multiplication.

The basic commutative and associative laws in addition and multiplication must be discovered in the process of learning whole numbers.

The commutative law:

$$A + B = B + A; 8 + 7 = 7 + 8$$

Figure 15–7   Partial Counting in Arithmetic

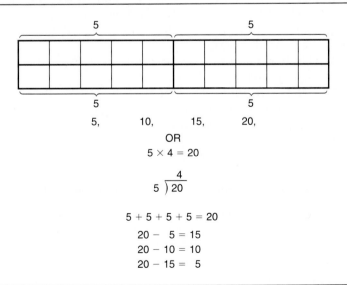

$$A \times B = B \times A; 6 \times 3 = 3 \times 6$$

The associative law:

$$A + (B + C) = (A + B) + C$$
$$A \times (B \times C) = (A \times B) \times C$$

The teaching of whole numbers must be applied to word problems, simulations, and real-life situations. Students should also be exposed to mathematical concepts such as weights and measurements in accordance with curriculum guidelines.

Strategies for Teaching Fractions

To many learning-disabled individuals, the concept of fractions and the way they are written seem a mystery. To develop an understanding of the relationships between fractions and wholes, fractions should first be explored in the environment. The teacher should bring into the classroom materials that can represent the various fraction equivalents, including both real-life and three-dimensional teaching aides. For example, the teacher may use a pizza, with corresponding pictures of pizza and/or circles made of cardboard, to introduce the concept of fractions. Students should be encouraged to experience fractions by cutting wholes into fractions. The matching of concrete, figural, and symbolic representations in the process is extremely important. As the students and the teacher cut a pie into a half, the teacher may say, "Here we have one-half," and the symbol of ½ should be put on the board and on each student's page. One half and one half give two halves, or one whole; ½ + ½ = ²⁄₂ = 1. The concepts are taught without using unnecessary terms, such as *numerators* and *denominators*. As students cut their materials into fourths, the teacher may ask, "How many fourths make one half?" "How much is one fourth plus one fourth?" or "If I have three fourths and I give Michael one fourth, how many fourths do I have left?" The answer will be two fourths, which equals one half; ¾ − ¼ = ²⁄₄ = ½. The students can see that two fourths form one half by overlapping the two fourths with one half using the fraction learners. Students may also be introduced to the concept of fraction equivalents through manipulative activities, such as grab bag activities and shading parts of figures. From the very beginning, students should be exposed to addition and subtraction of mixed numbers—1¼ + 2¼, or 3¾ − 1¼—written both horizontally and vertically. When introduced in this manner, such learning becomes an integral part of learning addition and subtraction of fractions and does not represent a new level.

Consistent with the principles of the teaching of mathematics, the teaching of fractions should begin with the exploration of fractions through concrete manipulation of materials, reinforced with the figural representation level (pictures, figures, and charts). The following sequence may be used in the teaching of fractions:

1. Exploration with fractions, using concrete and visual aids
2. Recognition of fractions as parts of wholes, using shading of figures
3. Addition and subtraction of fractions with like denominators
4. Addition and subtraction of mixed numbers with like denominators

5. Fraction equivalents
6. Reduction of fractions to their simplest forms
7. Addition and subtraction of fractions with unlike denominators when a common denominator is present
8. Addition and subtraction of mixed numbers with unlike denominators when a common denominator is present
9. Addition and subtraction of fractions and mixed numbers with unlike denominators when a common denominator is not present
10. Addition and subtraction of fractions and mixed numbers with three or more elements
11. Multiplication of fractions
12. Multiplication of mixed numbers (horizontally)
13. Multiplication of mixed numbers (vertically)
14. Division of fractions
15. Division of mixed fractions

Strategies for Teaching Decimals

For all practical purposes in the United States, decimals are extensions of whole numbers using money equivalents, and teaching students to read and write them is the first step in teaching decimals. Students are introduced to addition and subtraction of money concepts as early as third grade; third-grade texts include activities and exercises in addition and subtraction of money equivalents, usually using dollar signs. Thus the LD specialist should begin teaching decimals using money equivalents (Carraher & Schlieman, 1988). Consistent with the principles of mathematics teaching, the teacher must proceed from the concrete level, using money and/or play money, to the figural and symbolic levels.

To actualize the process of operations with decimals, the teacher should display a dollar bill and ask students its value. Students will most likely respond by saying "One dollar." The teacher can then ask students to write the symbol that represents $1. Generally, students will write 1 or $1. The teacher can then ask, "What is another way of writing $1?" If no answer is given, the teacher can ask, "How many pennies are in $1?" Through manipulation and/or prior knowledge, students should be able to say that there are 100 pennies in $1. The teacher can then ask students to write $1 in a way that indicates the number of pennies in it. Through guided teaching, the concept of one dollar written as $1.00, or one dollar and 25 cents written as $1.25, becomes clear.

Following this step, the teacher introduces the concept of addition and subtraction of decimals, with special attention to place values. Practicing writing place values in columns helps students understand the concept. For example,

1.00	15.00
.50	2.50
.25	11.25
.15	7.15

Addition and subtraction follow this activity:

$$
\begin{array}{ll}
1.00 + 1.25 & 10.00 + 20.25 \\
1.25 + 1.00 & 20.25 + 10.00 \\
2.25 - 1.00 & 30.25 - 10.00 \\
2.25 - 1.25 & 30.25 - 20.25
\end{array}
$$

Addition and subtraction problems written horizontally and vertically should be presented at the same time.

The teaching of multiplication and division of decimals should be done simultaneously. Here again the teacher should use concrete and three-dimensional materials to illustrate that $2.00 \times 2 = 4.00$ and that $4.00 / 2 = 2.00$. Throughout the instructional process, the teacher should use concrete and visual aids to facilitate students' understanding of decimals. The sequence of teaching decimals is very similar to the sequence teaching of whole numbers, with the added dimension of the decimal points.

Strategies for Teaching Percent

The concept of percent should be directly related to the use of percentages in real-life situations. Moreover, students should understand the concept of percent in relationship to whole numbers, fractions, and decimals. An understanding of the concept of 100% as an arbitrary concept to indicate a wholeness should be achieved. Percent can be introduced through the use of money: $1 is the same as 100 pennies. Therefore, one half of a dollar is 50 cents, and 50% of a dollar is equivalent to one half. The concept of percent as hundredths can be further reinforced through the use of hundredths charts involving cutting and shading activities. The relationship of percent to decimals and fractions must be understood at this level. Thus,

$$
\begin{array}{lll}
1 & 1.00 & 100\% \\
\frac{1}{2} & .50 & 50\% \\
\frac{1}{4} & .25 & 25\% \\
\frac{1}{10} & .10 & 10\%
\end{array}
$$

The various operations with percentages, such as finding a percent of a number, should follow this activity.

Problem Solving in Arithmetic

What are arithmetic story problems? Arithmetic story problems represent situations involving mathematical operations. Word problems, often called "story problems" or "thought problems," provide practice in which students apply the skills learned in basic operations to real-life situations.

Successful problem solving requires mental manipulation, reasoning, and inductive and deductive thinking, whereas procedural knowledge usually involves effective utilization of strategies, the monitoring of progress, and the checking of outcomes. Students need to learn a systematic approach to problem solving. To accomplish this, they must be able to do the following:

1. Receive the information presented either orally or in writing
2. Comprehend and understand the situation
3. Analyze the components of word problems
4. Retain the information specifically when a word problem is given orally
5. Mentally manipulate the various mathematical components involved in a problem
6. Employ logical thinking and inductive and deductive reasoning
7. Determine what numerical operations are necessary
8. Formulate mathematical sentences that will lead to the solution of a problem
9. Know the skills necessary to complete a mathematical sentence
10. Solve a mathematical sentence and check the outcome

Strategies for Teaching Story Problems

Story problems may be presented orally or in writing, and they may be simple or complex. They can be analyzed in terms of the steps, processes, and operations involved and the basic fundamental skills required in order to solve them.

Many children with LD fail to use organized and systematic strategies for problem solving (Parrill-Burnstein, 1981). Learning-disabled children, like younger children or children with lower mental ages, tend to use more stereotyped, perseverative, and trial-and-error approaches to solving problems (Bruner, 1973). While learning problem-solving skills, students must be introduced to a systematic approach to problem solving, including the utilization of strategies, the monitoring of progress throughout the process, and evaluation of the outcome. The teacher must guide students through the process, using modeling and visual and verbal cues. Furthermore, the teaching of problem-solving skills should proceed from the concrete to the pictorial and the symbolic levels (Souviney, 1984). Cawley et al. (1987) suggest that LD teachers do the following:

1. Begin problem solving the day a child enters school.
2. Make problem solving the reason for computation.
3. Develop long-term programs of problem solving.
4. Conduct problem solving as a multimodal activity.
5. Partial out the effects of one variable on another. If the child cannot read the problem, rewrite it. If the computation is too complex, make it simpler.
6. Have children prepare or modify problems.
7. Differentiate between process and knowledge.
8. Prepare problems in such a way that children must act upon the information. Prepare a set of problems in which all problems have the same question.
9. Present problems dealing with familiar subject matter.

10. Constantly monitor progress and modify problems to fit the child's weaknesses and progress. (pp. 91–92)

Shuard (1984) suggests the following heuristic processes in teaching word problems in mathematics:

1. Making a graphical or diagrammatic representation of a situation, or representing it by concrete objects
2. Noticing patterns of numbers
3. Using verbal mediation through discussion and oral explanations, and exploring ideas in conversations

Teachers should create a classroom environment in which problem solving can flourish, an environment in which students are encouraged to question, experiment, estimate, explore, and suggest explanations (Shuard, 1984). Students should be encouraged to solve problems through simulations and applied activities. In addition, the teacher and students should create their own problems, which increase their awareness of the steps and processes necessary to solve problems.

In teaching problem solving, the following aspects should be considered:

1. Problem solving should be directly derived from individuals' learning environment and be directly related to their experience.
2. Problem solving should reflect activities that can be easily understood by students.
3. The level of verbal language in mathematical problems should be appropriate to students' functional level in verbal receptive and expressive abilities, and special terms should be used only if they are necessary for an understanding of the concepts or required knowledge.
4. Story problems should be presented in oral form, in written form, or in both.
5. The teacher should assist students with reading difficulties so they can understand story problems.
6. The teacher should teach logical thinking processes in analyzing story problems into components. Consider, for example, the following story problem: "Last month, Dan earned $60.00 from his paper route. This month, he earned $69.00. On his friend's birthday, Dan spent $25.00 for a gift. What percent of his money did Dan spend on his friend's gift?" (Ariel, 1983, Level IV-B, #1) Students should be assisted in breaking down this story problem into the following components, usually written in a logical analysis format:

> Last month, Dan earned $60.00.
> This month, he earned $69.00.
> Total earning = $129.00
> Dan spent $25.00 for a birthday gift.
> Percent of money spent on gift?

7. The teacher should provide students with appropriate manipulative materials to assist in the solution of problems.

8. The teacher should provide students with pictorial representation of the elements in story problems, using photographs, drawings, and diagrams.
9. The teacher should assist students in the development of metacognitive problem-solving strategies.
10. The teacher should assist students in the development of systematic procedures to evaluate the answers/outcomes of story problems.

The Sequential Teaching of Arithmetic Story Problems

Like any other aspect of mathematical operations, the acquisition of arithmetic story problem skills follows a logical and pedagogical sequence. The following represents the sequence of arithmetic story problem teaching:

1. One step-one process
2. Two steps involved:
   a. Two steps-one process
   b. Two steps-two processes
3. Three steps involved:
   a. Three steps-one process
   b. Three steps-two processes
   c. Three steps-more than two processes
4. Four steps-one to four processes

This acquisition sequence for arithmetic story problems should be attained at three representational levels: Students may acquire story problem skills at the concrete level, the figural level, and the abstract level. In all cases, story problem materials should be closely related to students' experience and environment in order to heighten the meaningfulness of the problems.

The Use of Metacognitive Strategies in Problem Solving

The use of the metacognitive approach assists learning-disabled individuals to develop their sensitivity to the processes involved in arithmetic computation and word problems. It increases their awareness of the factors that contribute to effective problem solving and helps them invent their own strategies to solve problems in mathematics. In addition, the metacognitive approach is aimed at developing students' control executive functions so that they will be able to monitor and evaluate their problem-solving activities (Cawley & Miller, 1986). The central role of the metacognitive approach is to make students more active in the problem-solving process. Unlike the traditional approach in which the teacher assumes control for students' activity, in a metacognitive-supported learning environment, students are charged with the responsibility of actively engaging in effective problem-solving strategies.

The metacognitive approach to problem solving involves general strategies of problem solving related to general situations in the environment, and specific strategies for arithmetic problem solving in school. The approach begins with the development of students' sensitivity and awareness to problem solving in general. They are made aware of the processes involved in problem solving and the factors that directly affect the outcome of problem-solving behavior. Figure 15–8 is a sample critical-thinking and problem-solving strategy guide. Throughout these activities, students are introduced to a systematic way of solving problems, utilizing effective problem-solving strategies, monitoring progress, and evaluating solutions.

Following the development of students' general problem-solving strategies, they are introduced to problem solving in mathematics. Through the learning process analysis activity, they analyze the processes involved in problem solving and the factors affecting effective problem solving. A strategy guide is provided to elicit students' responses (Figure 15–9). Students are made aware of the steps necessary to solve problems effectively. For example, following a discussion of the strategies necessary to solve math problems effectively, these strategies were identified and suggested:

1. Read and understand the problem.
2. Look for the key question and recognize key words.

Figure 15–8   Strategy Guide to Critical Thinking and Problem Solving

CRITICAL THINKING AND PROBLEM SOLVING

In daily life, individuals constantly encounter problems which they perceive to be inconvenient barriers. These problems, which are an integral part of life, can be viewed in a positive sense. Problems can be viewed as opportunities to actively participate in life by engaging in problem solving activities. Problems stimulate the individual, who, in the process of solving the problem, experiences individual growth and moves forward in the attainment of his goals. As the individual is engaged in problem solving, he develops a repertoire of problem solving strategies in various areas which ultimately lead to successful problem solving.

Metacognitive Critical Thinking and Problem Solving Strategies
Recognize the problem cues, aspects of the problem that are important.
Determine the processes involved, listening, visualizing, taking action.
Select the most effective strategy/ies.
Develop a plan of action, steps involved in solving the problem.
Monitor your progress, checking how you are doing.
Check your outcomes, evaluating your success in solving the problem.

Monitoring Critical Thinking and Problem Solving Skills
I recognize the problem cues.
I determine the processes involved.
I select the most effective strategy/ies.
I develop a plan of action.
I monitor my progress.
I check my outcomes.

Source: From *Learning to Learn: Metacognition Student Handbook, Level II, Book 1* by A. Ariel, 1987. Unpublished manuscript, California State University, Los Angeles. Reprinted by permission.

Figure 15−9   Using Problem-Solving Strategies in Math: Strategy Guide

---

Read, Think, Strategize:

USING PROBLEM SOLVING STRATEGIES IN MATH

Challenge Guide:
   Like critical thinking and problem solving strategies used in daily living, developing a systematic approach to problem solving in mathematics can facilitate success in math courses. Mathematics is defined as the quantitative representation of objects and elements in the universe. The science of mathematics and mathematical processes follows the logical rules of order in the universe. Successful problem solving in mathematics requires abilities in understanding mathematical information, mental manipulations, and basic mathematical skills. Successful math students utilize a systematic approach and effective strategies in solving math problems.

Super Strategies
Read and understand the problem.
Look for the question and recognize key words (how much, difference, total, product, sum).
Select the appropriate mathematical operation/s.
Write the equation and solve it.
Check your answer.

Pledge for Success: Monitoring Problem Solving
I read and understand the problem.
I look for the question and recognize key words.
I select the appropriate mathematical operation/s.
I write the equation and solve it.
I check my answer.

Source: From *Learning to Learn: Metacognition Student Handbook, Level III, Book 1* by A. Ariel, 1987. Unpublished manuscript, California State University, Los Angeles. Reprinted by permission.

   3. Select the appropriate operation.
   4. Write the number sentence (equation) and solve it.
   5. Check your answer.
   6. Correct your errors.

   Students use a metacognitive problem-solving strategies implementation sheet to help them monitor their use of strategies. The responsibility for monitoring is given to the students, and therefore the checklists are written in the first person ("I" statements). Figures 15−10 and 15−11 are samples of strategy implementation and monitoring sheets for metacognitive strategies for arithmetic word problems and arithmetic computation. Students are encouraged to verbalize their steps, to monitor their activities, and to evaluate the problem solutions. Through continuous use of these metacognitive strategies validated by their successful approach in problem solving, these metacognitive queries become internalized.

Figure 15–10   Arithmetic Word Problems: Strategy Implementation and Monitoring Sheet

PLEDGE FOR SUCCESS: STRATEGY USE

Set 6: Mathematics

Skills/Behaviors I Need to Learn:	How Will I Do It? (Strategies)	How Am I Doing? Key: √−; √; √+;					
		M	T	W	Th	F	Overall
Word Problems	I read and understand the problem.						
	I look for the question and recognize key words.						
	I select the appropriate operation.						
	I write the number sentence (equation) and solve it.						
	I check my answer.						
	I correct my errors.						
Individualized Goal							

Teacher's Comments:

Student's Comments: This Is the Way I See Myself

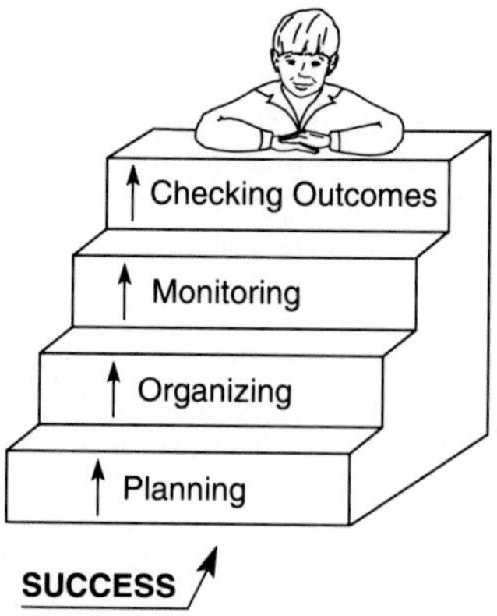

Checking Outcomes

Monitoring

Organizing

Planning

SUCCESS

Source: From *Learning to Learn: Metacognition Student Handbook, Level II, Book 1* by A. Ariel, 1987. Unpublished manuscript, California State University, Los Angeles. Reprinted by permission.

The Use of Verbal Mediation to Solve Arithmetic Problems

Verbal mediation can be utilized to systematically affect arithmetic performance. This approach uses verbal mediation as a means of assisting students with problem solving by encouraging them to ask themselves questions relative to how to go about

Figure 15–11   Arithmetic Computation: Strategy Implementation and Monitoring Sheet

PLEDGE FOR SUCCESS: STRATEGY USE

Set 2: Strategic Learning Readiness in the Content Areas

Skills/Behaviors I Need to Learn:	How Will I Do It? (Strategies)	How Am I Doing?					
		Key: √−; √; √+;					
		M	T	W	Th	F	Overall
Arithmetic Computation	I read my directions and understand the assignment.						
	I look at what I have to do: add, subtract, multiply, or divide.						
	I use the correct process to complete the problem.						
	I check my answer.						
	I redo my problem if it is wrong.						
Individualized Goal							

Teacher's Comments:

Student's Comments: This Is the Way I See Myself

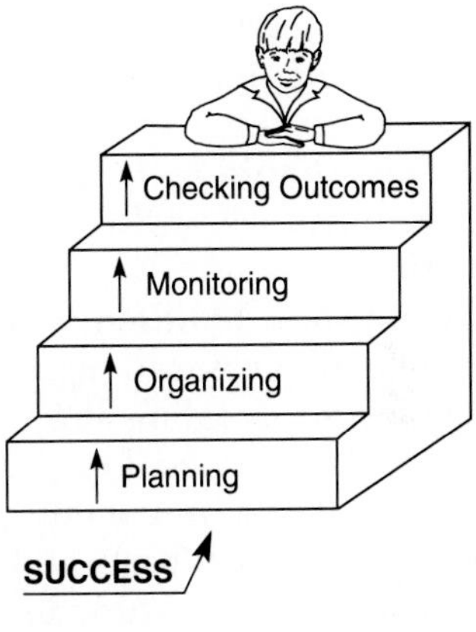

↑ Checking Outcomes

↑ Monitoring

↑ Organizing

↑ Planning

SUCCESS ↗

Source: From *Learning to Learn: Metacognition Student Handbook, Level II, Book 1* by A. Ariel, 1987. Unpublished manuscript, California State University, Los Angeles. Reprinted by permission.

solving problems. Thus students recite and rehearse a series of steps to facilitate the solution of problems. Verbal mediation results in increased accuracy; the oral recitation serves as a second input channel to the visual presentation (Lovitt & Curtis, 1968). Furthermore, it helps students become more deliberate, slows down the pace through verbalization, and focuses on the task, resulting in improved arithmetic performance.

Age- and Developmental-Level Considerations

In developing the remedial mathematical program for those with learning disabilities at various levels of education, one must consider (a) students' developmental level, (b) mathematical concepts needs of students commensurate with the functioning of the peer group at their age level, (c) the utilitarian and functional aspects of arithmetic, (d) teaching approaches and variations of teaching methodologies appropriate to age level, and (e) the daily life needs of students for mathematical concepts and mathematical skills.

The teacher of learning-disabled primary children, through appropriate teaching methodology, has the opportunity to develop sound mathematics skills with these youngsters. They have not had a prolonged history of failure in mathematics. In addition, the skills to be taught are somewhat more narrow, and thus it is possible to bridge the mathematical gap within a relatively short period of time. The teacher must emphasize the development of a positive attitude toward mathematics and numerical relationships. The establishment of an understanding of mathematical concepts at this level is crucial and serves as a foundation for higher levels of mathematics. Primary children who are at the preoperational level are attached to concrete elements in the environment and must be introduced to arithmetic concepts through the use of concrete manipulative materials involving inductive and deductive learning. Because of their learning disabilities, these individuals may require more time to understand and attain basic concepts in arithmetic. In addition to the basic skills of addition, subtraction, and multiplication, other mathematical concepts should be taught through the creation of an active mathematics learning environment, as well as problem-solving skills applied to students' immediate experiences.

While some children with LD at the elementary level have already experienced failure and developed negative attitudes toward arithmetic, it is still possible to desensitize the situation and to help them develop a more positive attitude toward the subject. This can be done by simplifying the arithmetic program through the use of appropriate teaching methods leading to a full understanding of mathematical numerical relationships. In addition to the basic skills, the teacher must attempt to teach elementary school students age-appropriate mathematical skills, such as utilizing change, handling money equivalents, and knowing basic concepts of weights and measurements. As discussed earlier, one does not necessarily have to follow the sequence of whole numbers to fractions, to decimals, and then to percents. It is quite feasible for the teacher to introduce students to new math concepts, such as fractions and decimals, while reinforcing the basic fundamental skills, thus bridging the gap between the conceptual understanding of learning-disabled students and their peers in the regular classroom. The use of cross-level teaching is a viable approach at this level.

The learning disabled at the junior and high school levels, have had a prolonged history of failure and frustration with mathematical concepts. Many of them are fearful of math and have developed a negative attitude toward it. It is thus important for the learning disabilities specialist to develop a mathematical program that will be appealing to students. This is done through the introduction of new concepts to students in a very meaningful way. It is important to develop mathematical social competencies for students at the secondary level so that when they encounter a real-life situation involving mathematical concepts, they are able to relate to it in a meaningful way. Thus managing money, doing comparative shopping, maintaining a checking account and a savings account, understanding interest earning and income earning, buying and financing a car, and reading tables and schedules are among the necessary skills for mathematics competence in daily living. Furthermore, the use of cross-level teaching is essential in order to bridge the gap between students' conceptual understanding and their operational levels in mathematics.

Learning-disabled young adults are in need of mathematical skills that will enable them to function optimally and independently in their environment. At this level, math applications take on new importance. These learners are on their own in an adult world in which application skills are required for survival. A simple trip to the grocery store presents dozens of challenges in math applications. The shopper must choose the best buys by computing the price per unit, keep an estimated running total of expenses, write out a check, and figure the new balance. As for adolescents, skills for mathematics competency are equally essential; the only difference is in the urgency of acquiring these skills for daily living. An understanding and mastery of household budgeting, fee paying, and banking is vitally important for young adults. A utilitarian approach in which students are taught mathematical concepts that are directly applicable to everyday living is the most appropriate one for this level. This approach can address the following questions: What are the skills that individuals need in order to survive in life? What are the immediate skills needed? Using the interview approach with young adults, the teacher can prioritize, keeping in mind cross-level teaching, overlearning, and chaining in the process of developing a mathematical program for students. In addition, the teacher must integrate conceptual knowledge in mathematics and individual ability and skills in problem solving in mathematics.

Specific Arithmetic Teaching Strategies

The Role of Drill and Practice

Following the understanding of arithmetic operations, fundamentals, and concepts, drill and practice can bring students' knowledge to an automatic level. At the automatic level, students perform without hesitation and demonstrate a full mastery of skills.

Mathematical practice should be geared to reinforcing concepts already learned; conceptual understanding must precede practice in order to increase retention (Siegel & Gold, 1982). Practice must be spaced in order to avoid fatigue and maintain interest. It should invoke a variety of strategies. Practice should also be supervised to ensure use of correct methods and responses.

Acceleration of Learning Through Cross-Level Teaching

The concept of cross-level teaching is discussed in depth in chapter 4. Its application to remedial teaching in mathematics is of extreme importance. Clustering concepts

Once students gain an understanding of arithmetic concepts, drill and practice can be used to help bring their knowledge to an automatic level.

into units and taking into account the scope and sequence of the curriculum can facilitate students' acquisition of arithmetic skills and thus bridge the knowledge gap in this area.

The Use of Color Coding in Mathematics

Students with learning disabilities tend to make what seem to be careless errors in simple arithmetic computation; for example, they may add rather than subtract or misplace digits not in accordance with their place value. The use of color coding to accentuate a process will heighten students' attention to the problem at hand.

The Teaching of Number Families

To further understand mathematical relationships, reversibility, and other characteristics of mathematical operations, students should be exposed to the concept of number families using concrete, figural, and abstract representations:

$$10 + 30 = 40 \qquad 3 \times 4 = 12$$
$$30 + 10 = 40 \qquad 4 \times 3 = 12$$
$$40 - 10 = 30 \qquad 12 \div 3 = 4$$
$$40 - 30 = 10 \qquad 12 \div 4 = 3$$

The Use of Matrix Paper

Many arithmetic worksheets present mathematical problems to students in a crowded and overwhelming fashion, with as many as 50 to 100 computational problems printed on one page. For many students with learning disabilities, this is particularly frustrating and discouraging. These students need to experience success in mathematics. To achieve this objective, the material presented to them must (a) be in a format easily read and understood by students; (b) be at 95% success level; (c) be geared toward immediate feedback and error correction by oneself, peers, or the teacher; and (d) enable students to complete assignments within a given time.

The use of matrix grid paper, on which a smaller number of problems are spaced throughout an entire page, is helpful to the learning disabled. This format of presentation is easier for both the students and the teacher, who needs to correct students' work and monitor their progress. In addition, when students complete a few of these pages, they develop a feeling of accomplishment and success.

Figure 15–12 shows samples of students' arithmetic work and demonstrates the positive effect of using matrix paper.

Correction of Students' Work

The purpose of error correction is to provide immediate feedback to students and to facilitate the teacher's monitoring of their progress. Too often, learning-disabled students are engaged in mathematics activities for long periods of time without receiving any feedback from the teacher, resulting in assignments with many errors.

The analysis of children's output in mathematics should involve both product and process analysis (what students know and how they arrive at a solution). Furthermore, it should involve analysis of students' modes of operation (concrete, figural, or abstract level). In other words, the teacher should see what process students use to arrive at a solution.

Teachers should encourage students to write neatly and produce products that are clean and readable. This basic principle should be followed when the teacher corrects students' work. Scribbling on students' papers and/or correcting them so that the errors are accentuated rather than the successful attempts serve only to heighten students' failures rather than their successes. When students make too many errors on one page, the teacher should examine their levels of functioning and instructional processes by providing assignments appropriate to their level of understanding and their ability to complete assignments. Figure 15–13, p. 516, contains samples of effective and ineffective teacher error-correction styles.

The Use of Mathematical Games

In any classroom, games are an important part of the curriculum. In a learning disability classroom, they are especially important and should be an integral part of the mathematics curriculum and instruction. Games add to a well-rounded and well-balanced program of learning activities and experiences in mathematics; they make the mathematical activities exciting, practical, and satisfying. Furthermore, due to the characteristics of games, they assist students to bring the mastery level to automaticity, enabling them to solve problems rapidly.

Figure 15–12   Students' Arithmetic Work With and Without Matrix Paper

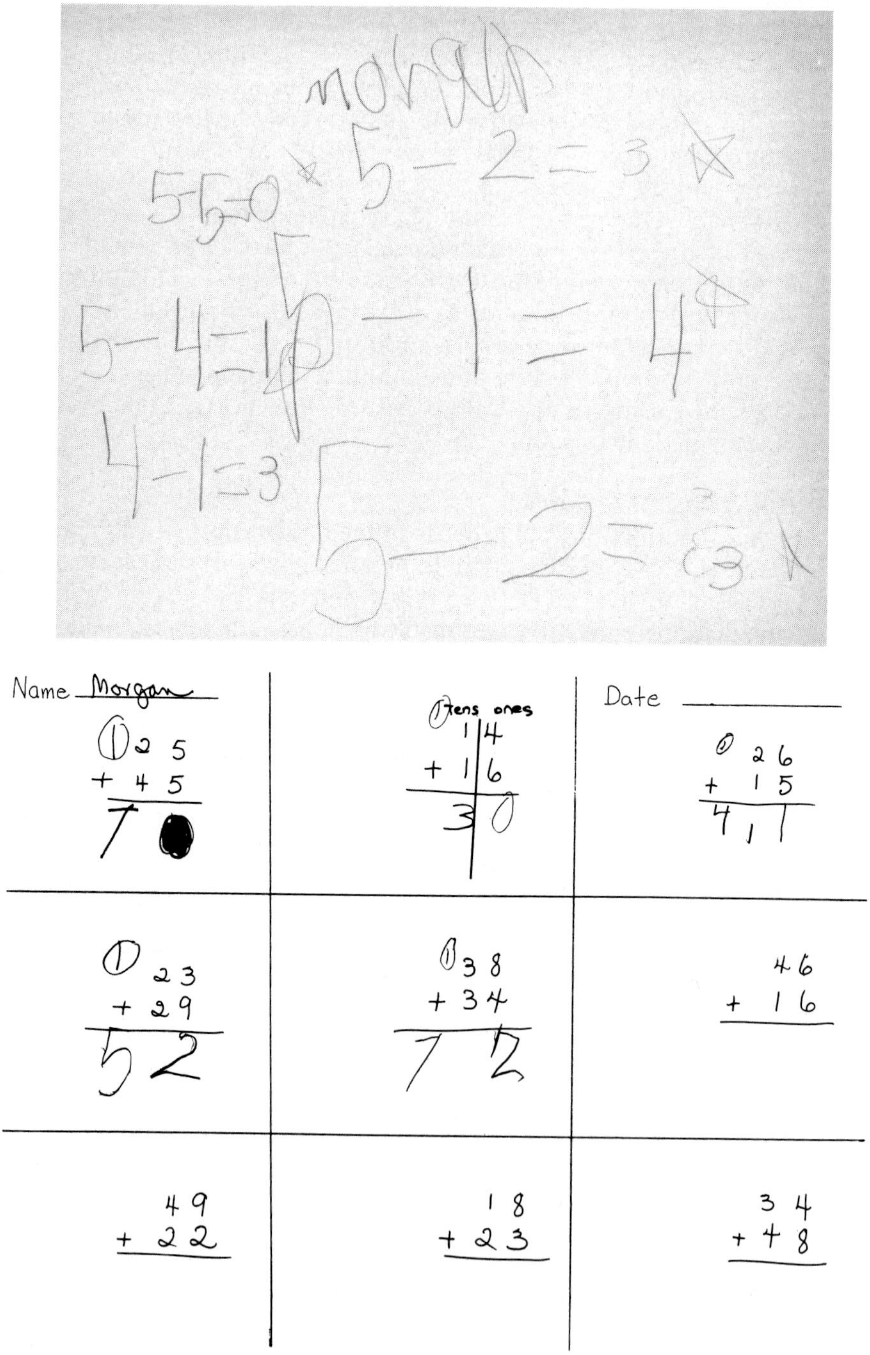

Figure 15-12   Continued

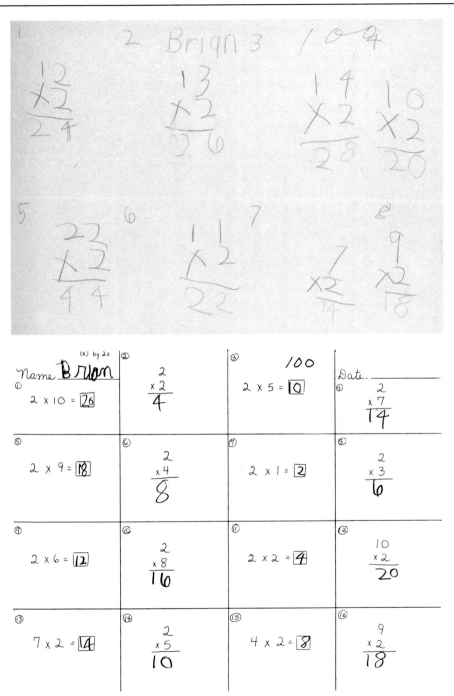

Figure 15–13 Samples of Effective and Ineffective Teacher Error-Correction Styles

Name _Irene_ | ✗ 25 | ✗ 16 ÷ 2 = 8 | Date _12-10-71_
① ✗ 2 ÷ 2 = 1 | −20 / 05 | | ④ ✗ 8 + 9 = 7

⑤ ✗ 5̶/10 / −45 / 15 | ⑥ ✗ 4 ÷ 2 = 2 | ⑦ ✗ 6̶/10 / −39 / 31 | ⑧ ✗ 14 ÷ 2 = 7

⑨ ✗ 10 ÷ 2 = 5 | ⑩ ✗ 5̶0̶0̶ / −192 / 308 | ⑪ ✗ 6 ÷ 2 = 3 | ⑫ ✗ 17 / − 8 / 9

⑬ ✗ 5 × 5 = 25 | ⑭ ✗ 12 ÷ 2 = 6 | ⑮ ✗ 3 × 5 = 15 | ⑯ ✗ 8 ÷ 2 = 4

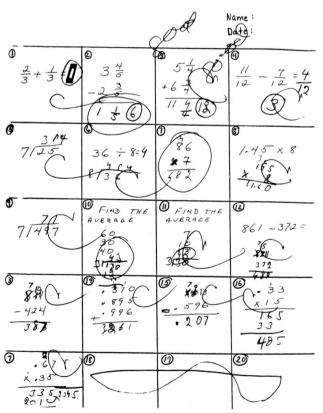

The motivational aspects of games cannot be ignored. Motivation is usually high in activities involving games. Games are a break from the regular routine of mathematical instruction. They provide drill that has built-in motivation, reinforce learned skills, are fun, and help develop an appreciation for the usefulness of numbers. In addition, they allow students to interact with one another positively, cooperatively as well as competitively, and promote the use of problem-solving strategies. Mathematical games can generally be classified under the following divisions:

1. Exploratory games for arithmetic readiness, mathematical concepts, and numerical relationship readiness that usually involve activities such as seriation, conservation, the matching of objects to figures, numerical equivalence, and numerical relationships
2. Exploratory games for the acquisition of new concepts
3. Practice games used to reinforce acquired skills, such as math operation bingo
4. Problem-solving games geared toward developing problem-solving strategies
5. Comprehensive mathematical games that include all the preceding elements

Reflecting on the importance of games in the mathematics program, Heimer and Trueblood (1977) list the following reasons why they should be incorporated into the mathematics curriculum:

1. If appropriately designed, games can be used successfully with children who have several types of learning problems, such as some forms of language deficiency (reading or verbal skills).
2. Games can be used to help students who exhibit discipline problems which are the results of being bored with the regular classroom routine.
3. Games fit well into classrooms where the laboratory or learning center approach is used. This feature is made possible when the game is made to operate independent of direct teacher control.
4. Games provide students with the opportunity to exert control and influence over their social environment by enabling them to switch from being passive consumers of information to being active decision makers.
5. Games can promote desirable social interactions among children by encouraging cooperation and discussion with each other.
6. Games can provide teachers with diagnostic information which they can use to help individual children correct misconceptions or to fill gaps in their learning instruction.
7. Games can be used to integrate mathematics with other subjects, and they also can be geared to conform to a particular interest of students. (p. 34)

Teachers can use commercial mathematics games or develop mathematics games of their own. They must make sure to select games that are within students' mastery level. Mathematical games are designed for reinforcement of skills and for fun activities, not necessarily to teach concepts. The teacher must be familiar with games in order to introduce students to them.

In designing their own games, teachers should adhere to the following steps, as outlined by Trueblood and Szabo:

1. Establish specific outcomes.
2. Make simple materials.
3. Write simple rules and procedures.
4. Make provisions for immediate feedback.
5. Build in some suspense.
6. Create the material so as to allow variations.
7. Evaluate the game (as cited in Heimer & Trueblood, 1977).

REMEDIAL ARITHMETIC INSTRUCTIONAL MATERIALS

Strategies for Selecting Instructional Materials

The process of selecting instructional materials in math is somewhat easier than in any other area of the curriculum. Knowledge of the scope and sequence of the mathematics curriculum is essential for the selection of the instructional materials. The following guidelines can assist the teacher in the selection of instructional materials in mathematics:

1. Materials must be consistent with the principles of mathematics teaching, that is, they must allow various modes of presentation and inductive and deductive reasoning.
2. Materials must be presented in a format amenable to remedial teaching, which means content must be visually spacious with a small number of problems on each page.
3. Materials must follow step-by-step progression of skills.
4. Materials must include activities in arithmetic fundamentals, concepts, and word problems.
5. Materials must be attractive and age appropriate.
6. Materials must be presented in a format that facilitates error correction and the monitoring of student progress.

Three-Dimensional Materials in Mathematics

Operations in math should always portray an action and/or an event. Work with numbers should not be based merely on work in two-dimensional space, such as pictures, drawings, diagrams, lines, or symbols. Arithmetic operations should always be combined with action and should be accompanied by manipulation of three-dimensional materials. This should assist students in developing awareness

Assessment Area	Assessment Instrument	Range	Publisher
	Illinois Test of Psycholinguistic Abilities	2–10 yrs	University of Illinois Press
	Peabody Picture Vocabulary Test Revised (PPVT-R)	2.5 yrs–adult	American Guidance Service
	McCarthy Scales of Children's Abilities	2–8 yrs	Psychological Corporation
	Language Assessment Battery	K–12	Riverside Publishing Co.
	Clinical Evaluation of Language Functions (CELF)	All grades	Charles E. Merrill
Language/Bilingual			
	Language Assessment Scales	All grades	Linguametrics Group
	Del Rio Language Screening	3–7 yrs	National Educational Laboratory Publishers
	Bilingual Syntax Measure	Grades K–12	Harcourt, Brace
	Dos Amigos Verbal Language Scales	5–12 yrs	Academic Therapy
	Spanish/English Language Proficiency Survey (S/ELPS)	Grades K–2	CTB/McGraw Hill
Cognitive Ability			
	Wechsler Preschool and Primary Scale of Intelligence (WPPSI)	4–6 1/2 yrs	Psychological Corporation
	Wechsler Intelligence Scale for Children—Revised (WISC-R)	6–17 yrs	Psychological Corporation
	Wechsler Adult Intelligence Scale Revised (WAIS-R)	Over 16 yrs	Psychological Corporation
	Woodcock-Johnson Psycho-Educational Battery (WJ-R)	3–80+ yrs	DLM/Teaching Resources
	Kaufman Assessment Battery for Children (K-ABC)	2 yrs, 6 mos–12 yrs, 6 mos	American Guidance Service
	Leiter International Performance Scale	2–18 yrs	Stoelting Company

Assessment Area	Assessment Instrument	Range	Publisher
	Detroit Tests of Learning Aptitude Revised II	6–17 yrs	PRO-ED
	McCarthy Scales of Children's Abilities	2 yrs, 6 mos–8 yrs, 6 mos	The Psychological Corp.
	Peabody Picture Vocabulary Test Revised (PPVT-R)	2.5 yrs–adult	American Guidance Service
	Columbia Mental Maturity Test	3.5–10 yrs	Psychological Corporation
Knowledge Base: Content Knowledge			
For test listings in the various content areas, see chapters 13, 14, and 15.			
Metacognition			
	Ariel Individualized Metacognitive Scales (AIMS)	Elementary/Secondary/ Adult	Unpublished, California State Univ., L.A.
Behavorial/social-emotional			
	Piers-Harris Children's Self-Concept Scale	Grades 3–12	Counselor Recordings and Tests
	Vineland Social Maturity Scale-Revised	Ages birth–25 yrs	American Guidance Service
	AAMD Adaptative Behavior Scale Public School Version	Ages 7–13	American Assoc. on Mental Deficiency
	Adaptative Behavior Inventory for Children (ABIC)	Ages 5–12	Psychological Corporation
	Walker Problem Behavior Identification Checklist (WPBIC)	Grades 4–6	Western Psychological Services
	Burks Behavior Rating Scales	Preschool–high school	Arden Press
	Devereux Adolescent Behavior Rating Scale	Ages 13–18	The Devereux Foundation
	Devereux Child Behavior Rating Scale	Ages 8–12	The Devereux Foundation
	Devereux Elementary School Behavior Rating Scale	Kindergarten through grade 6	The Devereux Foundation
	Scale of Independent Behavior		DLM/Teaching Resources

APPENDIX
C

Interview Format and Elicitors for the Metacognitive Interview

Metacognitive Interview

(Interview Format and Elicitors)

Student _____ Date _____

Interviewer _____

Below is a set of questions/elicitors you may want to use in the process of conducting a metacognitive interview with your student. (Student would have already been introduced to metacognitive process and procedures.)

Breaking the Ice/What's Happening

_____

_____

_____

Review of Current Schedule/Program

1. What classes are you taking? _____

2. What subject/activity do you like best? _____

3. What subject/activity do you like least? _____

How Am I Doing?

1. Given best areas (#2 above), how do you feel about how you are doing in school?

_____

_____

_____

2. Why do you think you are doing better in these areas?

_____

_____

3. Given least areas (#3 above), how do you feel about how you are doing in these?

_____

_____

4. What are some of the difficulties you're having?

_____

_____

5. What specific behavior/activities keep(s) you from doing well in these (least) areas?

_____

Use Student Self Evaluation Checklist to determine areas of strengths and weaknesses. Proceed to fill out Learning Plan. Learning Plan components include areas the student needs to work on, the specific strategies to be utilized, monitoring and feedback procedures.

Source: From *Metacognition Student Handbook, Secondary Level* (p. 101) by A. Ariel, 1986b.

Read, Think, Write:

SELF-AWARENESS WORKSHEET
My Activities

Activities in which I do well:

_____

_____

Why?

_____

I succeed in these activities because

_____

_____

Activities that are hard for me:

_____

_____

Why?

_____

In order to succeed in these activities, I need to

_____

_____

Consider and list your **personal attributes** that contribute to your success and challenges in your activities.

Personal attributes that relate to success:

_____

_____

Personal attributes that relate to activities' difficulties:

_____

_____

Source: From *Target Success: Metacognition Student Handbook* by A. Ariel, 1990. Reprinted by permission.

Read, Think, Write:

SELF-AWARENESS WORKSHEET
My School Work

Subjects in which I do well: Subjects that are hard for me:

_____   _____

_____   _____

Why?   Why?

_____   _____

_____   _____

I succeed in these areas because   In order to do well in these subjects I need to

_____   _____

_____   _____

Consider and list your **personal attributes** that contribute to your success and challenges in school.

Personal attributes that relate to academic success:

_____

_____

Personal attributes that relate to academic difficulties:

_____

_____

Source: From *Target Success: Metacognition Student Handbook* by A. Ariel, 1990 Reprinted by permission.

SELF-AWARENESS

MY STRENGTHS:

1. _____
2. _____
3. _____
4. _____
5. _____
6. _____
7. _____
8. _____
9. _____
10. _____

MY WEAKNESSES:

1. _____
2. _____
3. _____
4. _____
5. _____
6. _____
7. _____
8. _____
9. _____
10. _____

AREAS OF NEEDED ATTENTION:

_____
_____
_____
_____
_____

Source: From *Metacognition Student Handbook: Elementary Level* by A. Ariel, 1986a.

Developing Your Learning Plan

You need to consider:

Your Goals:

_____

_____

_____

_____

_____

How to Meet Your Goals (Use of Effective Strategies):

_____

_____

_____

_____

_____

How Do You Ensure Success?

_____

_____

_____

SUCCESS

Source: From *Metacognition Student Handbook: Secondary Handbook* by A. Ariel 1986b.

My Learning Plan			
I Need to Learn **(Areas of concern)**	**How?** **Strategies**	**How Am I Doing?**	
		Student	Teacher

APPENDIX D

Teacher's Guide to Informal Assessment and Observations

Student _____   Date _____

Indicate areas of strengths (+) and deficits (-).

Provide anecdotal records wherever deemed necessary.

Assessment Domain: Developmental constraints

Assessment Areas:

Sensory-motor

Points of Observations:

The individual functioning in sensory-motor areas can be tapped through behavioral observations of the student's activities, both in and out of the classroom. Observe the student in and out of the classroom in such activities as holding a pencil, writing, painting, cutting, walking, running, hopping, playing ball, and using playground equipment for indications of areas of competencies and difficulties.

Sensory-motor

- Fine motor coordination _____

- Gross motor coordination _____

- Laterality _____

- Directionality _____

- Additional observations _____

Perceptual Functions

Points of Observations:

The individual functioning in sensory-motor-perceptual areas can be tapped through behavioral observations of the student's activities, both in and out of the classroom. Observe the student's ability to follow directions, copy letters and forms, write and draw, and manipulate tools and objects (manual dexterity), as well as analyze the student's work samples for indications of areas of competencies and difficulties.

Perceptual functions

- Visual _____

- Auditory _____

- Haptic (kinesthetic, tactile) _____

- Additional observations _____

Language Development and Communication

Points of Observations:

The individual's functioning in language development and communication can be tapped through observation of the student's behavior in various language and communication settings. Observations of the individual student's difficulties in understanding spoken language and simple directions as well as drawing meanings from visually presented materials, such as pictures, may indicate difficulties in receptive language. Observations of the student's difficulty in speaking in complete sentences with proper grammar, and using age-appropriate/proper vocabulary, may indicate difficulties in expressive language. Written language samples provide material for analysis of the student's written expressive language abilities (see also chapter 14).

Receptive language

- Auditory reception _____

- Visual reception _____

Expressive language

- Oral expression _____

- Written expression _____

- Additional observations _____

Cognitive Capacity

Points of Observations:
The individual's functioning in cognitive areas can be tapped through observations of student's performance in academic areas that demand thinking logically, drawing inferences, understanding cause-and-effect relationships, and understanding, attaining, and retaining concepts at various levels of instruction. Attention should also be given to problem solving in mathematics and daily living.

Concept formation
Thinking generally is at the

- Concrete level _____

- Figural level _____

- Abstract level _____

Cause and effect

- Commonsense judgment _____

- Comprehension/understanding situations _____

Problem solving

- Logical thinking _____

- Creative thinking _____

- Additional observations _____

Attention and Concentration

Points of Observations:
The individual's attention and concentration functioning can be tapped through behavioral observations of the student in various settings involving academic and nonacademic activ-

ities. This can be best achieved through the use of both proximal and distal observations and the use of behavioral inventories.

Coming to attention

- Coming to attention _____
- Task organization _____
- Selective attention _____

Vigilance

- Attention span _____
- Sustaining on task _____
- Task completion _____
- Working independently _____
- Ability to work (one-to-one, small and large groups) _____

Decision making

- Selective attention _____
- Following directions _____
- Impulsivity _____
- Deliberate planning _____

Attentional shifts

- Flexibility to shift tasks _____
- Perseveration _____

DEVELOPMENTAL CONSTRAINTS: INFORMATION-PROCESSING SYNOPSIS
Summary Statement

_____

_____

_____

_____

_____

Assessment Domain: Knowledge Base-Content Knowledge

Assessment Areas-Academic Achievement

Points of Observations:

The individual's academic functioning can be tapped through effective use of teacher's informal inventories, analysis of work samples, and observations of the student's output. (For specific areas of the curriculum, see chapters 13, 14, and 15.)

Language arts-reading

- Reading decoding skills _____
- Reading comprehension skills _____

Language arts-language

- Oral expression/communication _____
- Written expression/communication and grammatical skills _____

_____

Language arts-spelling/handwriting

- Structural analysis _____
- Sight vocabulary (concept spelling) _____
- Handwriting _____

Mathematics

- Arithmetic computation _____
- Arithmetic concepts _____
- Arithmetic application _____

Social studies/science

- History _____
- Science _____

ACADEMIC ACHIEVEMENT SYNOPSIS

Summary Statement

_____

_____

_____

_____

_____

Assessment Domain: Metacognition

Assessment Areas-Metacognition

Points of Observations:

The individual's metacognitive functions can be tapped through observing the individual's sensitivity and awareness to the learning situation and the manner in which the individual approaches the learning process and problem solving. Observations of the student's abilities to develop and implement strategies for learning are important in this area. In addition, the individual's ability to effectively utilize control executive functions—specifically, planning, organizing, and monitoring one's progress—is also essential.

Strategic production

- Sensitivity to self and the learning environment _____

- Awareness of self and the learning environment _____

- Student's development of strategies for learning _____

Strategy utilization

- Ability to choose, change, and invent new strategies _____
- Ability to know when to use skills and strategies appropriate to the situation _____
- Ability to effectively utilize strategies _____

Control executive functions

- Planning _____
- Organizing activities _____
- Monitoring and using self-regulation _____
- Checking outcomes and using self-evaluation _____

METACOGNITION SYNOPSIS
Summary Statement

_____
_____
_____
_____
_____

Assessment Domain: Behaviorial Social/Emotional
Assessment Area-Social/Emotional
Points of Observations:
The individual's functioning in the affective areas can be tapped through behaviorial obser-
vations of the student's interaction in the various facets of the school environment. These
include interaction with the learning task, peers, and adults. Behavioral observations check-
lists can be very helpful in this process.
Self-concept

- Feelings about oneself _____
- Maximization of output/motivation _____
- Frustration tolerance _____
- Attempts at new learning _____
- Initiation of activities _____
- Assumption of responsibility/attribution _____
- Acceptance of criticism/praise _____

Interpersonal relationships

- Self-control _____
- Relationships with peers _____
- Relationships with adults _____
- Relationships with significant others _____

Goals and aspirations

- Self-evaluation _____
- Realistic goals _____
- Realistic aspirations _____

BEHAVIORAL SOCIAL/EMOTIONAL SYNOPSIS

Summary Statement

Source: From Teachers' Resource Assessment Kit (TRAK) by A. Ariel, 1983.

Ariel, A. (1974). Piaget, behavior modification, and the adolescent with learning disabilities. In G. I. Lubin, J. F. Magary, & M. K. Poulsen (Eds.), *Piagetian theory and the helping professions* (277–280). Proceedings of the Fourth Interdisciplinary Seminar. Los Angeles: University of Southern California.

Ariel, A. (1975). *Parents perceptions of learning disabilities and the helping professionals* (Tech. Rep. A14). Los Angeles: University of California, Graduate School of Education.

Ariel, A. (1978). *Perspectives on the resource specialist program.* Publication of the California State Department of Education.

Ariel, A. (1983). Teacher Resource Assessment Kit (TRAK) (1983). Curriculum Based Assessment. Unpublished manuscript. California State University, Los Angeles.

Ariel, A. (1985). *Parents perception of learning disabilities and the helping professionals—ten years later.* CEC 63rd annual convention, Anaheim, CA.

Ariel, A. (1986a). *Metacognition and strategic learning: Teacher's guide.* Unpublished manuscript, California State University, Los Angeles.

Ariel, A. (1986b). *Metacognition student handbook: Secondary level.* Unpublished manuscript, California State University, Los Angeles.

Ariel, A. (1986c). *Metacognition student handbook: Elementary level.* Unpublished manuscript, California State University, Los Angeles.

Ariel, A. (1987a). *Learning to learn: Metacognition student handbook, Level II, Book 1.* Unpublished manuscript, California State University, Los Angeles.

Ariel, A. (1987b). *Metacognition and the learning disabled individual.* Paper presented at the CEC 65th annual convention, Chicago, IL.

Ariel, A. (1987c). *Successful learning: Metacognition secondary student handbook, Level III, Book 1.* Unpublished manuscript, California State University, Los Angeles.

Ariel, A. (1988, October). *Metacognition and its application to reading.* Paper presented at the meeting of Harvard Dyslexic group, Harvard University, Cambridge, MA.

Ariel, A. (1989a). *Stepping up to success: Metacognition elementary student handbook.* Unpublished manuscript, California State University, Los Angeles.

Ariel, A. (1989b). *Gateway to success: Metacognition college handbook.* Unpublished manuscript, California State University, Los Angeles.

Ariel, A. (1990). *Target success: Metacognition student handbook.* Unpublished manuscript, California State University, Los Angeles.

Ariel, A. (1991). *Making sense of metacognition: A framework and a comprehensive training program for individuals with learning disabilities.* CEC 69th annual convention. Atlanta, GA.

Ariel, A. (in press). Metacognition: A promising approach for individuals with learning disabilities. In G. M. Robson & R. M. Maxwell (Eds.), *Marianne Frostig, teacher and humanitarian.* Ann Arbor, MI: University of Michigan Press.

Ariel, A. & Mayer, L. C. (1974). *A training program for the resource specialist in special education.* Unpublished monograph, Division of Special Education, California State University, Los Angeles.

Ashlock, P., & Stephen, A. (1966). *Educational therapy in the elementary school.* Springfield, IL: Charles C. Thomas.

Association for Children with Learning Disabilities. (1967). *Proceedings of ACLD Annual Conference.* New York City.

Association for Children with Learning Disabilities. (1986). ACLD Description: Specific learning disabilities. *ACLD Newsbriefs,* pp. 15–16.

Ayres, A.J. (1965). Patterns of perceptual motor dysfunction in children. *Perceptual and Motor Skills, 20,* 335–368.

Ayres, A. J. (1968). Sensory integrative processes and neuropsychological learning disabilities. In J. Hellmuth (Ed.), *Learning disorders* (Vol. 3, pp. 43–58), Seattle, WA: Special Child Publications.

Ayres, A. J. (1972). *Southern California Sensory Integration Tests.* Los Angeles: Western Psychological Services.

Babbs, P. J., & Moe, A. J. (1983). Metacognition: A key for independent learning from text. *The Reading Teacher, 38,* 422–426.

Baca, L. (1982). The exceptional child: A new challenge for exceptional people. In A. M. Ochoa & J. Hurtado (Eds.), *Special education and the bilingual child* (pp. 1–8). San Diego State University: National Origin Desegregation Law Center.

Baca, L., & Bransford, J. (1981). Meeting the needs of bilingual handicapped children. *Momentum, 12,* 26–29.

Baca, L. M., & Cervantes, H. (1984). *The bilingual special education interface.* St. Louis, MO: Mosby.

Baca, L., & Chinn, P. (1982). Coming to grips with cultural diversity. *Exceptional Education Quarterly, 2*(4), 33–45.

Bachor, D. G., & Crealock, C. (1986). *Instructional strategies for students with special needs.* Canada: Prentice-Hall.

Bain, A. M. (1980). *Handwriting survey.* Unpublished paper, Loyola College, Baltimore, MD.

Bain, A. M. (1982). Written expression: Assessment and remediation for learning disabled students. *Learning Disabilities, 1*(5), 49–61.

Bain, A. M. (1988). Written expression. In K. A. Kavale, S. R. Forness, & M. Bender (Eds.), *Handbook of learning disabilities: Vol. 2. Methods and interventions* (pp. 73–88). Boston, MA: Little, Brown.

Baker, L. (1982). An evaluation of the role of metacognitive deficits in learning disabilities. *Topics in Learning and Learning Disabilities, 2,* 27–35.

Baker, L., & Brown, A. L. (1984a). Cognitive monitoring in reading. In J. Flood (Ed.), *Understanding reading comprehension* (pp. 21–44). Newark, DE: International Reading Association.

Baker, L., & Brown, A. L. (1984b). Metacognitive skills and reading. In P. D. Pearson (Ed.), *Handbook of reading research* (pp. 353–394). New York: Longman.

Banas, N., & Wills, I. H. (1970). Child and cursive writing. In J. Arena (Ed.), *Building handwriting skills in dyslexic children* (pp. 23–25). San Rafael, CA: Academic Therapy.

Bandura, A. (1965). A case of no-trial learning. In L. Berkowitz (Ed.), *Advances in experimental social psychology* (Vol. 2, pp. 3–55). New York: Academic Press.

Bandura, A. (1969). *Principles of behavior modification.* New York: Holt.

Bannatyne, A. D. (1971). *Language, reading and learning disabilities.* Springfield, IL: Charles C. Thomas.

Barsch, R. (1965). *A movigenic curriculum.* Madison, WI: State Department of Public Instruction.

Barsch, R. (1967). *Achieving perceptual motor efficiency* (Vol. 1). Seattle: Special Child Publications.

Barsch, R. (1968). *Enriching perception and cognition* (Vol. 2). Seattle: Special Child Publications.

Bartoli, J., & Botel, M. (1988). *Reading/learning disability: An Ecological Approach.* New York: Teachers College Press.

Basualdo, S. M., & Basualdo, E. A. (1980). *Models to prevent and deal with disruptive behavior(s) in the classroom: A review of literature.* (ERIC Document Reproduction Service No. ED 202 812).

Bateman, B. (1964). Learning disabilities: Yersterday, today and tomorrow. *Exceptional Children, 31,* 139–146.

Bauer, R. H. (1979). Memory, acquisition, and category clustering in learning disabled children. *Journal of Experimental Child Psychology, 27,* 365–383.

Bauer, R. H. (1982). Information processing as a way of understanding and diagnosing learning disabilities. *Topics in Learning and Learning Disabilities, 2,* 33–45.

Baur, G. R., & George, L. O. (1976). *Helping children learn mathematics.* Menlo Park, CA: Cummings.

Behrmann, M. (1984). *Handbook of microcomputers in special education.* San Diego, CA: College-Hill Press.

Beilin, H., & Gotkin, L. G. (1964, April). Psychological issues in the development of mathematics curricula for socially disadvantaged children. *Proceedings of the Conference on Mathematics Education for Below Average Achievers.*

Bender, W. N., & Golden, L. B. (1990). Subtypes of students with learning disabilities as derived from cognitive, academic, behavioral, and self-concept measures. *Learning Disability Quarterly, 13*(3), 183–194.

Bennett, R. E. (1982). Cautions for the use of informal measures in the educational assessment of exceptional children. *Journal of Learning Disabilities, 15,* 337–339.

Benson, B., Reiss, S., Smith, D. S., & Laman, D. S. (1985). Psychosocial correlates of depression in mentally retarded adults: II. Poor social skills. *American Journal of Mental Deficiency, 89,* 657–659.

Benton, A. L. (1975). Developmental dyslexia: Neurological aspects. In W. J. Friedlander (Ed.), *Advances in neurology* (pp. 1–47). New York: Raven Press.

Benz, M. R., & Halpern, A. S. (1987). Transition services for secondary students with mild disabilities. A statewide perspective. *Exceptional Children, 53*(6), 507–514.

Berkson, G. (1978). Social ecology and ethology of mental retardation. In G. P. Sackett (Ed.), *Observing behavior, Vol. 1: Theory and applications in mental retardation* (pp. 403–409). Baltimore, MD: University Park Press.

Berman, A. (1974). Delinquents are disabled. In B. L. Kratoville (Ed.), *Youth in trouble* (pp. 39–43). San Rafael, CA: Academic Therapy.

Berman, A. (1975). *Incidence of learning disabilities in juvenile delinquents and non delinquents: Implications for etiology and treatment.* Ann Arbor, MI: ERIC Clearinghouse. (ERIC Document Reproduction Service No. ED 112 620)

Bersoff, D. N., Kabler, M., Fiscus, E., & Ankney, N. (1972). Effectiveness of special class placement for children labeled neurologically handicapped. *Journal of School Psychology, 10*, 157–163.

Besag, F., & Green, J. (1981). Reply to the incidence of suspected exceptional education needs among youth in juvenile correction facilities by H. Thomas Prout. *Journal of Correctional Education, 33*(1), 19–20.

Bindman, A. J. (1964). The psychologist as a mental health consultant. *Journal of Psychiatric Nursing, 2*, 367–380.

Binet, A. (1902). *L'Etude experimentale de L'intelligence.* Paris: Ancienne Librairie Schleicher.

Birch, J. W. (1978). Mainstreaming: Definition, development and characteristics. In C. Hawkins-Shepard (Ed.), *Making it work: Practical ideas for integrating exceptional children in the regular classes* (pp. 5–12). Reston, VA: Council for Exceptional Children.

Blalock, J. W. (1981). Persistent problems and concerns of young adults with learning disabilities. In W. Cruickshank & A. Silver (Eds.), *The best of ACLD: Vol. 2. Bridges to tomorrow* (pp. 35–56). Syracuse, NY: Syracuse University Press.

Blalock, J. W. (1982). Persistent auditory language deficits in adults with learning disabilities. *Journal of Learning Disabilities, 15*(10), 604–609.

Blankenship, C. S. (1985). Using curriculum-based assessment data to make instructional decisions. *Exceptional Children, 52*(3), 233–238.

Blankenship, C., & Lilly, M. S. (1981). *Mainstreaming students with learning and behavior problems: Techniques for the classroom teacher.* New York: Holt, Rinehart & Winston.

Blanton, G. H. (1984). Social and emotional development of learning disabled children. In W. M. Cruickshank & J. M. Kliebahn (Eds.), *The best of ACLD: Vol. 5: Early adolescence to early adulthood* (pp. 25–36). Syracuse, NY: Syracuse University Press.

Blaschke, C. (1986). Technology for special education: A rational strategy. *T.H.E. Journal, 13*(6), 77–82.

Bloomfield, L., & Barnhart, C. L. (1961). *Let's read—A linguistic approach.* Detroit: Wayne State University Press.

Boettcher, J. V. (1983). Computer-based education: Classroom application and benefits for learning disabled students. *Annals of Dyslexia, 33*, 203–219.

Borkowski, J. G. (1985). Signs of intelligence: Strategy generalization and metacognition. In S. R. Yussen (Ed.), *The growth of reflection in children* (pp. 105–144). New York: Academic Press.

Borkowski, J. G., Estrada, M. T., Milstead, M., & Hale, C. A. (1989). General problem-solving skills: Relations between metacognitive and strategic processing. *Learning Disability Quarterly, 12*(1), 57–70.

Borkowski, J. G., Johnson, M. B., & Reid, M. K. (1987). Metacognition, motivation, and the transfer of control processes. In S. J. Ceci (Ed.), *Handbook of cognition, social, and neuropsychological aspects of learning disabilities* (Vol. 2, pp. 147–174). Hillsdale, NJ: Erlbaum.

Borkowski, J. G., Peck, V. A., & Damberg, P. R. (1983). Attention, memory and cognition. In J. L. Matson & J. A. Mulick (Eds.), *Handbook of mental retardation* (pp. 479–497). New York: Pergamon.

Borkowski, J. G., Weyhing, R. S., & Carr, M. (1988). Effects of attributional retraining on strategy-based reading comprehension in learning-disabled students. *Journal of Educational Psychology, 80,* 46–53.

Bos, C. S. (1988). Process-oriented writing: Instructional implications for mildly handicapped students. *Exceptional Children, 54*(6), 521–527.

Bower, E. M. (1981). *Early identification of emotionally handicapped children in school* (3rd ed.). Springfield, IL: Charles C. Thomas.

Bower, E. M., & Lambert, N. M. (1976). In-school screening of children with emotional handicaps. In N. J. Long, W. C. Morse, & R. G. Newman (Eds.), *Conflict in the classroom* (4th ed., pp. 95–100). Belmont, CA: Wadsworth.

Bozinou-Doukas, E. (1983). Learning disability: The case of the bilingual child. In D. R. Omark and J. G. Erickson (Eds.), *The bilingual exceptional child* (pp. 213–232). San Diego, CA: College-Hill Press.

Brackbill, Y., McManus, K., & Woodward, L. (1985). Medication in maternity: Infant exposure and maternal information. *Monograph Series No. 2.* Ann Arbor: University of Michigan International Academy for Research in Learning Disabilities.

Bradley, L., & Bryant, P. (1979). Independence of reading and spelling in backward and normal readers. *Developmental Medicine and Child Neurology, 21,* 504–514.

Brailsford, A., Snart, F., & Das, J. P. (1984). Strategy training and reading comprehension. *Journal of Learning Disabilities, 17*(4), 287–290.

Bransford, J. D. (1979). *Human cognition: Learning, understanding and remembering.* Belmont, CA: Wadsworth.

Bransford, J. D., Shelton, T. S., Stein, B. S., & Owings, R. A. (1980). Cognition and adaptation: The importance of learning to learn. In J. Harvey (Ed.), *Cognition, social behavior and the environment* (pp. 93–110). Hillsdale, NJ: Erlbaum.

Breiter, C., & Englemann, S. (1966). *Teaching disadvantaged children in the preschool.* Englewood Cliffs, NJ: Prentice-Hall.

Breitmayer, B., & Ramey, C. (1986). Biological non-optimality and quality of postnatal environment as codeterminants of intellectual development. *Child Development, 57,* 1151–1165.

Broder, P. K., Dunivant, N., Smith, E. C., & Sutton, L. P. (1981). Further observations on the link between learning disabilities and juvenile delinquency. *Journal of Educational Psychology, 73,* 838–850.

Brolin, D. (1973). Career education needs of secondary educable students. *Exceptional Children, 39,* 619–624.

Brolin, D. E., Malever, M., & Matyas, G. (1976). *PRICE needs assessment study* (Project PRICE, Working paper 7). Columbia, MO: University of Missouri-Columbia.

Brolin, D. E., & Thomas, B. (Eds.). (1972). *Preparing teachers of secondary level educable mentally retarded: Proposal for a new model.* Final Report, University of Wisconsin-Stout, Menomonie.

Brown, A. L. (1975). The development of memory: Knowing, knowing about knowing, and knowing how to know. In H. W. Reese (Ed.), *Advances in child development and behavior* (Vol. 10, pp. 103–152). New York: Academic Press.

Brown, A. L. (1978). Knowing when, where, and how to remember: A problem of metacognition. In R. Glaser (Ed.), *Advances in instructional psychology* (Vol. 1, pp. 77–165). Hillsdale, NJ: Erlbaum.

Brown, A. L. (1980a). *Learning and development: The problems of compatibility and access*. (Technical Report 165) Champaign: University of Illinois, Center for the Study of Reading.

Brown, A. L. (1980b). Metacognitive development and reading. In R. J. Spiro, B. B. Bruce, and W. F. Brewer (Eds.), *Theoretical issues in reading comprehension: Perspectives from cognitive psychology, linguistics, artificial intelligence, and education* (pp. 453–481). Hillsdale, NJ: Erlbaum.

Brown, A. L. (1981). Metacognition: The development of selective attention strategies for learning from tests. In M. L. Kamil (Ed.), *Directions in reading: Research and instruction* (pp. 501–526). Washington, DC: The National Reading Conference.

Brown, A. L. (1982). Learning and development: The problem of compatibility, access and induction. *Human Development, 25,* 1–17.

Brown, A. L. (1987). Metacognition, executive control, self-regulation, and other more mysterious mechanisms. In F. E. Weinert & R. H. Kluwe (Eds.), *Metacognition, motivation and understanding* (pp. 65–116). Hillsdale, NJ: Erlbaum.

Brown, A. L., Bransford, J. D., Ferrara, R. A., & Campione, J. C. (1983). Learning, remembering and understanding. In J. H. Flavell & E. M. Markman (Eds.), *Handbook of child psychology: Cognitive development* (Vol. 3, pp. 77–166). New York: Wiley.

Brown, A. L., & Palincsar, A. S. (1982). Inducing strategic learning from texts by means of informed, self-control training. *Topics in Learning and Learning Disabilities, 2,* 1–18.

Brown, A. L., Palincsar, A. S., & Armbruster, B. B. (1984). Instructing comprehension-fostering activities in interactive learning situations. In H. Mandl, N. Stein, & T. Trabasso (Eds.), *Learning and comprehension of text* (pp. 255–286). Hillsdale, NJ: Erlbaum.

Brown, A. L., & Smiley, S. S. (1978). The development of strategies for studying texts. *Child Development, 49,* 1076–1088.

Brown, A. L., Smiley, S. S., & Lawton, S. C. (1978). The effects of experience on the selection of suitable retrieval cues for studying texts. *Child Development, 49,* 829–835.

Brown, D., Blackburn, J. E., Wyne, M. D., & Powell, W. C. (1979). *Consultation.* Boston: Allyn & Bacon.

Brown, N. P. (1982). CAMEO: Computer-assisted management of educational objectives. *Exceptional Children, 49,* 151–153.

Brueckner, L. J., & Bond, G. L. (1955). *The diagnosis and treatment of learning difficulties.* New York: Appleton-Century-Crofts.

Bruininks, V. L. (1978). Peer status and personality characteristics of learning disabled and nondisabled students. *Journal of Learning Disabilities, 11,* 484–489.

Bruner, J. (1964). The course of cognitive growth. *American Psychologist, 19,* 1–15.

Bruner, J. S. (1966). *Toward a theory of instruction.* New York: Norton.

Bruner, J. S. (1973). *Beyond the information given: Studies in the psychology of knowing.* New York: Norton.

Bryan, J. H., & Bryan, T. H. (1983). The social life of the learning disabled youngster. In J. D. McKinney & L. Feagans (Eds.), *Current topics in learning disabilities* (Vol. 1, pp. 57–85). Norwood, NJ: Ablex.

Bryan, J. H., & Bryan, T. H. (1988). Where's the beef? A review of published research on the adaptive learning environment model. *Learning Disabilities Focus, 4*(1), 9–14.

Bryan, J. H., & Pflaum, S. (1978). Social interactions of LD children: A linguistic social and cognitive analysis. *Learning Disability Quarterly, 1*(3), 70–79.

Bryan, J. H., Sonnefeld, L. J., & Grabowski, B. (1980). The relationship between fear of failure and learning disabilities. *Learning Disability Quarterly, 6*(2), 217–222.

Bryan, T. H. (1974a). An observational analysis of classroom behaviors of children with learning disabilities. *Journal of Learning Disabilities, 7*, 26–34.

Bryan, T. H. (1974b). Peer popularity of learning disabled children. *Journal of Learning Disabilities, 7*, 621–625.

Bryan, T. H. (1977). Learning disabled children's comprehension of nonverbal communication. *Journal of Learning Disabilities, 10*, 501–506.

Bryan, T. H. (1979). Communicative competence in reading and learning disabilities. *Bulletin of the Orton Society, 29*, 172–188.

Bryan, T. H., Bay, M., & Donahue, M. (1988). Implications of the learning disabilities definition for the regular education initiative. *Journal of Learning Disabilities, 21*(1), 23–28.

Bryan, T. H., & Bryan, J. H. (1975). *Understanding learning disabilities.* New York: Alfred.

Bryan, T. H., & Bryan, J. H. (1978). Social interactions of learning disabled children. *Learning Disability Quarterly, 1*(1), 33–38.

Bryan, T. H., & Bryan, J. (1981). Some personal and social experiences of learning disabled children. In B. Keogh (Ed.), *Advances in special education* (Vol. 3, pp. 147–186). Greenwich, CT: JAI Press.

Bryan, T. H., & Bryan, J. H. (1990). Social factors in learning disabilities: An Overview. In H. L. Swanson & B. Keogh (Eds.), *Learning disabilities: Theoretical and research issues* (pp. 131–138). Hillsdale, NJ: Erlbaum.

Bryant, N. D., Drabin, I. R., & Gellinger, M. (1981). Effects of varying unit size on spelling achievement in learning disabled children. *Journal of Learning Disabilities, 14*(4), 200–203.

Bryen, D. N. (1981). Language and language problems. In A. Gerber & D. Bryen (Eds.), *Language and learning disabilities.* Baltimore, MD: University Park Press.

Buchanan, M., & Wolf, J. S. (1986). A comprehensive study of learning disabled adults. *Journal of Learning Disabilities, 19*(1), 34–38.

Buckley, E., & Johnson, E. (1983). *Pilot project on computer assisted instruction for adult basic education centers.* Great Neck, NY. (ERIC documentation reproduction Service No. ED 230 758)

Budoff, M., & Hutton, L. R. (1982). Microcomputers in special education: Promises and pitfalls. *Exceptional Children, 49*, 42–48.

Bühler, C. (1935). *Testing children's development from birth to schoolage.* New York: Ferrar & Reinhart.

Bullock, L. M., & Reilly, T. F. (1979). A descriptive profile of the adjudicated adolescent: A status report. In R. B. Rutherford and A. G. Prieto (Eds.), *Monograph in behavioral disorders* (Vol. 2, pp. 153–161). Reston, VA: Council for Children with Behavioral Disorders.

Bureau of Education for the Handicapped [Technical manual]. Washington, DC: Author.

Burham, W. H. (1924). *The normal mind.* New York: Appleton.

Burke, R. L. (1982). *CAI sourcebook.* Englewood Cliffs, NJ: Prentice-Hall.

Burns, M. S., Vye, N. J., Bransford, J. D., Deklos, V., & Ogan, T. (1987). Static and dynamic measures of learning in young handicapped children. *Diagnostic, 12*(2), 59–73.

Burton, L., & Bero, F. (1984). Is career education really being taught? A second look. *Academic Therapy, 4,* 389–395.

Canney, G., & Winograd, P. (1979). *Schemata for reading and reading comprehension performance* (Tech. Rep. No. 120). Urbana: University of Illinois, Center for the Study of Reading.

Canning, J. (1983). Peer facilitator projects for elementary and middle schools. *Elementary School Guidance and Counseling,* December, 124–129.

Caparulo, B., & Ziegler, E. (1983). The effects of mainstreaming on success expectancy and imitation in mildly retarded students. *Peabody Journal of Education, 60,* 85–98.

Carnegie Corporation of New York Quarterly. (1962). 10.

Carnine, D. (1983). Direct instruction: In search of instructional solutions for educational problems. In D. Carnine, D. Elkind, A. D. Hendrickson, D. Meichenbaum, R. L. Sieben, & F. Smith (Eds.), *Interdisciplinary voices in learning disabilities and remedial education* (pp. 1–66). Austin, TX: PRO-ED.

Carraher, T. N., & Schliemann, A. (1988). Mathematical concepts in everyday life. *New Directions in Child Development, 41,* 71–87.

Carroll, A. W. (1974). The classroom as an ecosystem. *Focus on Exceptional Children, 4,* 1–12.

Carroll, J. B. (1978). The nature of the reading process. In J. Chapman & P. Czerniewska (Eds.), *Reading from process to practice* (pp. 95–105). London: Routledge & Kegan in association with Open University Press.

Carter, J., & Sugai, G. (1988). Teaching social skills. *Teaching Exceptional Children, 20*(3), 68–71.

Cartledge, G., & Kleefeld, J. (1989). Teaching social communication skills to elementary school children with handicaps. *Teaching Exceptional Children, 22*(1), 14–17.

Caster, J. (1975). Share our specialty: What is mainstreaming? *Exceptional Children, 42,* 174.

Cawley, J. F. (1978). An instructional design in mathematics. In L. Mann, L. Goodman, & J. L. Wiederholt (Eds.), *Teaching the learning-disabled adolescent* (pp. 201–234). Boston: Houghton Mifflin.

Cawley, J. F., & Miller, J. H. (1986). Selected views on metacognition, arithmetic problem solving, and learning disabilities. *Learning Disabilities Focus, 2*(1), 36–48.

Cawley, J. F., Miller, J. H., & School, B. A. (1987). A brief inquiry of arithmetic word-problem-solving among learning disabled secondary students. *Learning Disabilities Focus, 2*(2), 87–93.

Ceci, S. (Ed.). (1986). *Handbook of cognitive, social and neuropsychological aspects of learning disabilities.* Hillsdale, NJ: Erlbaum.

Cellini, H. R., & Snowman, J. (1982). Learning disabilities and juvenile delinquents. *Federal Probation, 3,* 26–32.

Chalfant, J. C. (1985). Identifying learning disabled students: A summary of the National Task Force report. *Learning Disabilities Focus, 1*(1), 9–20.

Champion, B. W. (1979). Educational assessment, diagnosis, and evaluation. In W. C. Adamson & K. K. Adamson (Eds.), *A handbook for specific learning disabilities* (pp. 107–143). New York: Gardner.

Chan, L. K. S., & Cole, P. G. (1986). The effects of comprehension monitoring training on the reading competence of learning disabled and regular class students. *Remedial and Special Education, 7*(4), 33–40.

Cheney, C., & Morse, W. C. (1972). Psychodynamic interventions in emotional disturbance. In W. C. Rhodes & M. L. Tracy (Eds.), *A study of child variance: Vol. 2. Interventions* (pp. 253–393). Ann Arbor: University of Michigan Press.

Chi, M. T. H. (1978). Knowledge of structures and development. In R. S. Siegler (Ed.), *Children's thinking: What develops?* (pp. 73–96). Hillsdale, NJ: Erlbaum.

Chi, M. T. H. (1981). Knowledge development and memory performance. In M. P. Friedman, J. P. Das, & N. O'connor (Eds), *Intelligence and learning* (pp. 221–229). New York: Plenum.

Cicourel, A. U. (1981). Cognitive and linguistic aspects of socialization. *Annual Review of Sociology, 7,* 87–106.

Cipani, E. (1985). The three phases of behavioral consultation: Objectives, intervention, and quality assurance. *Teacher Education and Special Education, 8*(3), 144–152.

Clarizio, H. F., & McCoy, G. F. (1983). *Behavior disorders in children.* Cambridge, MA: Harper & Row.

Clements, S. D. (1966). *Minimal brain dysfunction in children: Terminology and identification* (NINDS Monograph No. 3. U.S. Public Health Service Publication No. 1415). Washington, DC: U.S. Department of Health, Education and Welfare.

Clements, J. (1987). *Severe learning disability and psychological handicap.* New York: Wiley.

Cochrane, P. V., & Marini, B. (1977). Mainstreaming exceptional children: The counselor's role. *The School Counselor, 25*(1), 17–21.

Codsen, M. A., Gerber, M. M., Semmel, D. S., Goldman, S. R., & Semmel, M. I. (1987). Microcomputer use within micra-educational environment. *Exceptional Children, 53,*(5), 399–409.

Cohen, J. H. (1982). *Handbook of resource room teaching.* Rockville, MD: Aspen.

Cohen, G. (1983). *The psychology of cognition.* New York: Academic Press.

Cohen, R. L. (1983). Reading disabled children are aware of their cognitive deficits. *Journal of Learning Disabilities, 16*(5), 286–289.

Cohen, S. (1983). Low birthweight. In C. C. Brown (Ed.), *Childhood learning disabilities a prenatal risk: An interdisciplinary data review for health care professionals and parents* (pp. 70–78). Skillman, NJ: Johnson & Johnson.

Collins, T. G., & Price, L. (1986). Micros for LD college writers: Rewriting documentation for word processing program. *Learning Disabilities Focus, 2*(1), 49–54.

Compton, R. C. (1974). Diagnostic evaluation of committed delinquents. In B. Kratoville (Ed.), an address to the symposium, *Youth in trouble: The learning disabled adolescent.* San Rafael, CA: Academic Therapy.

Comptroller General of the United States. (1977). *Learning disabilities: The link to delinquency should be determined, but should do more now.* Washington, DC: General Accounting Office.

Conger, J. J., & Peterson, A. C. (1984). *Adolescence and youth: Psychological development in a changing world.* New York: Harper & Row.

Cooper, J. O., Heron, T. E., & Heward, W. L. (1987). *Applied behavior analysis.* Columbus, OH: Merrill/Macmillan.

Cotman, C. W., & Lynch, G. S. (1988). The neurology of learning and memory. In J. E. Kavanagh & T. J. Truss (Eds.), *Learning disabilities: Proceedings of the national conference* (pp. 1–69). Maryland: York Press.

Cott, A., (1972). Megavitamins: The orthomolecular approach to behavioral disorders and learning disabilities. *Academic Therapy, 7* (3), 245–258.

Cotungo, J. A. (1987). Cognitive control functioning in hyperactive and nonhyperactive learning disabled children. *Journal of Learning Disabilities, 20,* 563–567.

Council for Exceptional Children. (1976). Official actions of the delegate assembly at the 54th annual international convention. *Exceptional Children, 43,* 41–47.

Council for Exceptional Children. (1978). Position paper on career education. Reston, VA: CEC.

Cox, J. L., Frank, N. L., Hocutt, A. M., & Kuligowski, B. A. (1984). *An exploration of issues regarding transition services for handicapped students in secondary school.* Research Triangle Park, NC: Center for Educational Studies. Research Triangle Institute.

Cramer, R. L. (1978). *Writing, reading and language growth.* Columbus, OH: Merrill/Macmillan.

Creaghead, N. A. (1986). Meaning in written language. *Topics in Language Disorders, 6*(4), 73–82.

Critchley, E. M. R. (1968). Reading retardation, dyslexia, and delinquency. *British Journal of Psychiatry, 115,* 1537–1547.

Critchley, M. (1970). *The dyslexic child* (2nd. ed.). London: Wm. Heinemann Medical Books.

Cross, L. & Goin, K. W. (1977). *Identifying handicapped children.* New York: Walker & Co.

Cruickshank, W. M. (1953). The multiple handicapped cerebral palsied child. *Exceptional Children, 20,* 16–22.

Cruickshank, W. M. (1958). Realistic educational programs for most cerebral palsy children. *The Crippled Child, 37,* 6–7, 22.

Cruickshank, W. M. (Ed.). (1966). *The teacher of brain-injured children: A discussion of the bases for competency.* Syracuse, NY: Syracuse University Press.

Cruickshank, W. M. (1967). *The brain-injured child in home, school, and community.* Syracuse, NY: Syracuse University Press.

Cruickshank, W. M. (1976). Foundations and significant people. In J. M. Kauffman & D. P. Hallahan (Eds.), *Teaching children with learning disabilities personal perspectives* (pp. 94–127). Columbus, OH: Merrill/Macmillan.

Cruickshank, W. M., & Hallahan, D. P. (1975). *Perceptual and learning disabilities in children.* Syracuse, NY: Syracuse University Press.

Cullinan, D., Epstein, M. H., & Kauffman, J. M. (1982). The behavioral model and children's behavior disorders: Foundations and evaluations. In R. L. McDowll, G. W. Adamson, & F. H. Wood (Eds.), *Teaching emotionally disturbed children* (pp. 15–46). Boston, MA: Little, Brown.

Cummins, J. (1981). The role of primary language development in promoting educational success for language minority students. In *Schooling and language minority students: A theoretical framework* (pp. 3–49). Los Angeles: California State University, Evaluation, Dissemination and Assessment Center.

Dalke, C., & Schmitt, S. (1987). Meeting the transition needs of college bound students with learning disabilities. *Journal of Learning Disabilities, 20*(3), 176–180.

D'Alonzo, B. J., & Owen, S. D. (1985). *Transition services for the disabled: A national survey.* Tempe: Arizona State University.

D'Aoust, C. (1986). Teaching writing as a process. In C. B. Olson (Ed.), *Practical ideas for teaching writing as a process* (pp. 7–16). California: California State Department of Education.

Davis, W. E. (1983). Competencies and skills required to be an effective resource teacher. *Journal of Learning Disabilities, 16*, 596–598.

Davis, W. E. (1989). The regular education initiative debate: Its promises and problems. *Exceptional Children, 55*(5), 440–446.

deBettencourt, L. V. (1987). Strategy training: A need for clarification. *Exceptional Children, 54*, 24–30.

DeBlassie, R. R., & Franco, J. N. (1983). Psychological and educational assessment of bilingual child. In D. R. Omark & J. G. Erickson (Eds.), *The bilingual exceptional child* (pp. 55–68). San Diego: College-Hill.

DeCecco, J. P. (1968). *The psychology of learning and instruction.* Englewood Cliffs, NJ: Prentice-Hall.

Decroly, O. (1937). *L'initiation a l'activite intellectuelle et matrice par les jeux educatifs; contribution a la pedagogie des jeunes enfants et des irreguliers.* Neuchatel, Delachaux & Niestle.

DeFries, J. (1985). Colorado reading project. In D. B. Gray & J. F. Kavanagh (Eds.), *Biobehavioral measures of dyslexia* (pp. 107–122). Parkton, MD: York.

DeFries, J. C., & Decker, S. N. (1982). Genetic aspects of reading disability: A family study. In R. N. Malatesha & P. G. Aaron (Eds.), *Reading disorders: Varieties and treatments* (pp. 255–279). New York: Academic Press.

DeHaven, E. (1983). *Teaching and learning the language arts* (2nd ed.). Boston: Little, Brown.

Delquadri, J., Greenwood, C., Whorton, D., Carta, J., & Hall, R. (1986). Classwide peer tutoring. *Exceptional Children, 52*(6), 535–541.

DeRuiter, J. A., & Wansart, W. L. (1982). *Psychology of learning disabilities*. Rockville, MD: Aspen.

Deshler, D. D. (1978). Psychoeducational aspects of learning disabled adolescents. In L. Mann, L. Goodman, & J. L. Wiederholt (Eds.), *Teaching the learning disabled adolescent* (pp. 47–99). Boston: Houghton Mifflin.

Deshler, D. D., Alley, G. R., & Carlson, S. A. (1980). Learning strategies: An approach to mainstreaming secondary students with learning disabilities. *Education Unlimited, 2*(4), 6–11.

Deshler, D. D., & Lenz, B. K. (1989). *The strategies instructional approach*. Lawrence, KS: University of Kansas.

Deshler, D. D., Lowrey, N., & Alley, G. R. (1979). Programming alternatives for LD adolescents: A national survey. *Academic Therapy, 14*(4), 389–397.

Deshler, D. D., & Schumaker, J. B. (1983). Social skills of learning disabled adolescents: Characteristics and intervention. *Topics in Learning and Learning Disabilities, 3*(2), 15–23.

Deshler, D. D., & Schumaker, J. B. (1986). Learning strategies: An instructional alternative for low-achieving adolescents. *Exceptional Children, 52*(6), 483–590.

Deshler, D. D., Schumaker, J. B., Alley, G. R., Warner, M. M., & Clark, F. L. (1982). Learning disabilities in adolescent and young adult populations: Research implications. *Focus on Exceptional Children, 15*(1), 1–12.

Deshler, D. D., Schumaker, J. B., & Lenz, B. K. (1984). Academic and cognitive interventions for LD adolescents: Part I. *Journal of Learning Disabilities, 17*(2), 108–117.

Deshler, D. D., Schumaker, J. B., Lenz, K., & Ellis, E. (1984). Academic and cognitive interventions for LD adolescents: Part II. *Journal of Learning Disabilities, 17*(3), 170–179.

Dewey, J. (1910). *How we think*. Boston: Heath.

Dickinson, D. J. (1980). The direct assessment: An alternative to psychometric testing. *Journal of Learning Disabilities, 13*, 472–476.

Diener, C. I., & Dweck, C. S. (1978). An analysis of learned helplessness: Continuous changes in performance, strategy, and achievement cognition following failure. *Journal of Personality and Social Psychology, 36*, 451–452.

Diener, C. I., & Dweck, C. S. (1980). An analysis of learned helplessness: II. The processing of success. *Journal of Personality and Social Psychology, 39*, 940–952.

Dinkmeyer, D. C. (Ed.). (1968). *Guidance and counseling in the elementary school: Readings in theory and practice*. New York: Holt, Rinehart, & Winston.

Dionisio, M. (1983). Write? Isn't this reading class? *Reading Teacher, 36*, 746–750.

Dixon, R., & Engelmann, S. (1979). *Corrective spelling through morphographs*. Chicago, IL: Science Research Associates.

Donahue, M., Pearl, R., & Bryan, J. (1983). Communicative competence in learning disabled children. In K. Gadow & I. Bialer (Eds.), *Advances in learning and behavioral disabilities* (Vol. 2, pp. 49–84). Greenwich, CT: JAI Press.

Donoghue, M. R. (1985). *The child and the English language arts*. Dubuque, IA: Wm. C. Brown.

Duane, D. D., & Leong, C. K. (1985). *Understanding learning disabilities: International and multidisciplinary views*. New York: Plenum Press.

Dudley-Marling, C. (1985). Perceptions of the usefulness of the IEP by teachers of learning disabled and emotionally disturbed children. *Psychology in the Schools, 22,* 65–67.

Duffey, J. B., Salvia, J., Tucker, J., & Ysseldyke, J. (1981). Nonbiased assessment: A need for operationalism. *Exceptional Children, 47*(6), 427–434.

Duling, F., Eddy, S., & Risko, V. (1970). *Learning disabilities of juvenile delinquents.* Morgantown, WV: Department of Educational Services, Robert F. Kennedy Youth Center.

Dunlap, W. P., & Brennan, A. H. (1979). Developing mental images of mathematical processes. *Learning Disability Quarterly, 2*(2), 89–96.

Durkin, D. (1966). *Children who read early: Two longitudinal studies.* New York: Teachers College Press.

Dwyer, K. P. (1987). School psychology assessment. In K. A. Kavale, S. R. Forness, & M. Bender, (Eds.), *Handbook of learning disabilities: Vol. 1. Dimensions and diagnosis* (pp. 325–348). Boston, MA: College-Hill.

Eastman, E. M., & Harper, J. (1971). A study of prexemic behavior—toward a predictive model. *Environment and Behavior, 3,* 418–437.

Elkind, D. (1970). *Children and adolescents.* London: Oxford University Press.

Elkind, D. (1972). *A sympathetic understanding of the child six to sixteen.* Boston: Allyn & Bacon.

Ellis, E. S., & Lenz, B. K. (1987). A component analysis of effective strategies for LD students. *Learning Disabilities Focus, 2*(2), 94–107.

Ellis, E. S., Deshler, D. D., Lenz, B. K., Schumaker, J. B., & Clark, F. L. (1991). An instructional model for teaching learning strategies. *Focus on Exceptional Children, 23*(6), 1–24.

Ellis, N. R. (1963). The stimulus trace and behavioral inadequacy. In N. R. Ellis (Ed.), *Handbook of mental deficiency, psychological theory and research* (pp. 134–158). New York: McGraw-Hill.

Ellis, N. R. (1970). Memory processes in retardates and normals. In N. R. Ellis (Ed.), *International review of research in mental retardation* (Vol. 4, pp. 1–32). New York: Academic Press.

Enell, N. C., & Barrick, S. W. (1983). *An examination of the relative efficiency and usefulness of computer-assisted individualized education programs.* Office of Special Education, LA State Department of Education (Grant No. 34-3651-67447-01-82).

Englert, C. S., & Raphael, T. E. (1988). Constructing well-formed prose: Process, structure, and metacognitive knowledge. *Exceptional Children, 54*(6), 513–520.

Englert, C. S., Raphael, T. E., Anderson, L. M., Anthony, H., Fear, K., & Gregg, S. (1988). A case for writing intervention: Strategies for writing informational text. *Learning Disabilities Focus, 3*(2), 98–113.

Englert, C. S., Raphael, T. E., Fear, K. L., & Anderson, L. M. (1988). Students metacognitive knowledge about writing informational texts. *Learning Disability Quarterly, 11,* 18–46.

Erikson, E. (1950). *Childhood and society.* New York: Norton.

Erikson, E. (1963). *Childhood and society* (2nd ed.). New York: Norton.

Evans, S. (1980). The consultant role of the resource teacher. *Exceptional Children, 46,* 402–403.

Evans, M., & LeVine, E. (1982). The humanistic, behavioral and cognitive-developmental approaches to education: A call for a synthesis. *Contemporary Education, 53*(4), 202–205.

Evans, G. W., & Lovell, B. (1979). Design modification in an open plan school. *Journal of Educational Psychology, 71*(1), 41–49.

Fafard, M. B., & Haubrich, P. A. (1981). Vocational and social adjustment of learning disabled young adults: A follow-up study. *Learning Disability Quarterly, 4,* 122–130.

Falvey, M. A. (1989). *Community-based curriculum.* Baltimore: Brooks.

Farnham-Diggory, S. (1978). *Learning disabilities: A psychological perspective.* Cambridge, MA: Harvard University Press.

Farnham-Diggory, S. (1986). Time, now, for a little serious complexity. In S. J. Ceci (Ed.), *Handbook of cognitive, social, and neuropsychological aspects of learning disabilities* (pp. 123–158). Hillsdale, NJ: Erlbaum.

Feagans, L. (1972). Ecological theory as a model for constructing a theory of emotional disturbance. In W. Rhodes & M. Tracy (Eds.), *A study of child variance* (pp. 323–389). Ann Arbor: University of Michigan Press.

Federal Register, 42 (163) 8-23-1977. Washington, DC: United States Government Printing Office.

Federal Register, Sec. 121a344, 1977. Washington, DC: United States Government Printing Office.

Fenton, K. S., Yoshida, R. K., Maxwell, J. P., & Kauffman, M. J. (1979). Recognition of team goals: An essential step toward rational decision making. *Exceptional Children, 5,* 640.

Fernald, G. M. (1943). *Remedial techniques in basic school subjects.* New York: McGraw-Hill.

Feuerstein, R., Rand, Y., Hoffman, M. D., & Miller, R. (1979). *Instrumental enrichment.* Baltimore, MD: University Park Press.

Filer, P. (1981). Preparing for IEP. *The School Counselor, 29*(1), 100–103.

Fine, E., & Zeitlin, S. (1984). Coping means survival for learning disabled adolescents. In W. M. Cruickshank & J. M. Kliebhan (Eds.), *The best of ACLD: Vol. 5. Early adolescence to early adulthood* (pp. 39–48). Syracuse, NY: Syracuse University Press.

Fiscus, E. D., & Mandell, C. J. (1983). *Developing individualized education programs.* New York: West Publishing.

Fisk, J. L., & Rourke, B. P. (1984). Neuropsychological subtyping of learning-disabled children: History, methods, implications. In J. K. Torgesen & G. M. Senf (Eds.). *Annual review of learning disabilities* (Vol. 2, pp. 46–48). New York: Professional Press.

Fitzgerald, G., Fick, L., & Milich, R. (1986). Computer-assisted instruction for students with attentional difficulties. *Journal of Learning Disabilities, 19*(6), 376–379.

Flavell, J. H. (1971). First discussant's comments: What is memory development the development of? *Human Development, 14,* 272–278.

Flavell, J. H. (1976). Metacognitive aspects of problem solving. In L. B. Resnick & R. Glaser (Eds.), *Nature of intelligence* (pp. 231–235). Hillsdale, NJ: Erlbaum.

Flavell, J. H. (1979). Metacognition and cognitive monitoring: A new area of cognitive-developmental inquiry. *American Psychologist, 34,* 906–911.

Flavell, J. H. (1981). Cognitive monitoring. In W. P. Dickson (Ed.), *Children's oral communication skills* (pp. 35–60). New York: Academic Press.

Flavell, J. H., & Wellman, H. M. (1977). Metamemory. In R. V. Kail & J. W. Hagen (Eds.), *Perspectives on the development of memory and cognition* (pp. 3–33). Hillsdale, NJ: Erlbaum.

Fleischner, J. E., & Garnett, K. (1987). Arithmetic difficulties. In K. A. Kavale, S. R. Forness, & M. Bender (Eds.), *Handbook of learning disabilities: Vol. I. Dimensions and diagnosis* (pp. 189–209). Boston: Little, Brown.

Florida, Department of Education. (1979). State Board of Education Rule 6A-6.3016. Tallahasse, FL.

Forman, S. G. (1987). Affective and social education. In C. A. Maher & S. G. Forman (Eds.), *A behavioral approach to education of children and youth* (pp. 75–108). Hillsdale, NJ: Erlbaum.

Forness, S., & Esveldt, K. (1975). Prediction of high-risk kindergarten children through classroom observations. *Journal of Special Education, 9,* 375–388.

Forrest-Pressley, D. L., & Waller, T. G. (1984). *Cognition, metacognition, and reading.* New York: Springer-Verlag.

Foster, S. L., Delawyer, D. D., & Guevremont, D. C. (1985). Selecting targets for social skills training with children and adolescents. In K. Gadow (Ed.), *Advances in learning and behavioral disabilities* (Vol. 4, pp. 77–132). Greenwich, CT: JAI Press.

Fowler, G. L., & Davis, M. (1985). The story frame approach: A tool for improving reading comprehension of EMR children. *Teaching Exceptional Children, 18*(3), 296–300.

Franks, C. M. (Ed.). (1969). *Behavior therapy appraisal and status.* New York: McGraw-Hill.

Freitag, H. T., & Freitag, A. H. (1962). *The number story.* Washington, DC: National Council of Teachers of Mathematics.

Frey-Mason, P. (1985). Teaching basic mathematics and survival skills. *Mathematics Teacher, 78,* 668–671.

Friend, M. (1984). Consultation skills for resource teachers. *Learning Disability Quarterly, 1,* 246–250.

Friend, M. (1985). Training special educators to be consultants. *Teacher Education and Special Education, 8*(3), 115–120.

Friend, M., & McNutt, G. (1984). Resource room programs: Where are we now? *Exceptional Children, 51*(2), 150–155.

Fries, C. C. (1963). *Linguistics and reading.* New York: Holt, Rinehart & Winston.

Fries, C. C., Wilson, R. G., & Rudolph, M. K. (1980). *Merrill linguistic readers.* Columbus, OH: Merrill/Macmillan.

Frith, U., & Frith, C. (1980). Relationships between reading and spelling. In J. F. Kavanagh & R. L. Venezky (Eds.), *Orthography, reading and dyslexia* (pp. 287–295). Baltimore, MD: University Park Press.

Frostig, M. (1961). *Frostig developmental test of visual perception* (3rd ed.). Palo Alto, CA: Consulting Psychologists Press.

Frostig, M. (1963). Visual perception in the brain-injury child. *American Journal of Orthopsychiatry, 33*, 665–671.

Frostig, M. (1966). The needs of teachers for specialized information on reading. In W. Cruickshank (Ed.), *The teacher of brain injured children* (pp. 387–398). Syracuse, NY: Syracuse University Press.

Frostig, M. (1967). Testing as a basis for educational therapy. *Journal of Special Education, 2*, 13–14.

Frostig, M. (1968). Education of children with learning disabilities. In H. Myklebust (Ed.), *Progress in learning disorders* (Vol. 1, pp. 234–266). New York: Grune & Stratton.

Frostig, M. (1972). Visual perception, integrative functions, and academic learning. *Journal of Learning Disabilities, 5*, 1–15.

Frostig, M., & Horne, D. (1964). *The Frostig program for the development of visual-perception.* Chicago: Follett.

Frostig, M., & Maslow, P. (1968). Language training—a form of ability training. *Journal of Learning Disabilities, 1* (2), 15–25.

Frostig, M., & Orpet, R. E. (1972). Cognitive theories and diagnostic procedures for children with learning difficulties. In B. Wolman (Ed.), *Manual of child psychopathology* (pp. 820–843). New York: McGraw-Hill.

Froyen, L. A. (1988). *Classroom management.* Columbus, OH: Merrill/Macmillan.

Fry, E. (1968). A readability formula that saves time. *Journal of Reading, II.*

Gaddes, W. (1985). *Learning disabilities and brain function* (2nd ed.). New York: Springer-Verlag.

Gagne, E. D. (1985). *The cognitive psychology of school learning.* Boston: Little, Brown.

Gallagher, J. (1984). Learning disabilities and the near future. *Journal of Learning Disabilities, 9*, 571–572.

Gallant, R. (1977). *Handbook in corrective reading: Basic tasks* (2nd ed.). Columbus, OH: Merrill/Macmillan.

Gambrell, L. B., & Heathington, B. S. (1981). Adult disabled readers' metacognitive awareness about reading task and strategies. *Journal of Reading Behavior, 13*(3), 215–222.

Garnett, K., & Fleischner, J. E. (1983). Automatization and basic fact performance of normal and learning disabled children. *Learning Disability Quarterly, 6*(2), 223–230.

Gattegno, C. (1962). *Words in color—a new method of teaching the reading and writing of English.* New York: Xerox Corporation.

Gerber, A. (1981). Problems in the processing and use of language in education. In A. Gerber & D. N. Bryen (Eds.), *Language and learning disabilities* (pp. 75–112). Baltimore, MD: University Park Press.

Gerber, M. M., & Hall, R. J. (1989). Cognitive-behavioral training in spelling for learning handicapped students. *Learning Disability Quarterly, 22*, 159–171.

Gerber, P. J., Banbury, M. M., & Miller, J. H. (1986). Special educators' perceptions of parental participation in the individual educational plan process. *Psychology in the Schools, 23*, 158–162.

Gersten, R., Woodward, J., & Darch, C. (1986). Direct instruction: A research-based approach to curriculum design and teaching. *Exceptional Children, 53*(1), 17–31.

Gesell, A., & Amatruda, C. (1941). *Developmental diagnosis: Normal and abnormal child development.* New York: Hoeber.

Getman, G. N., & Kane, E. R. (1964). *The physiology of readiness: An action program for the development of perception in children.* Minneapolis, MN: Programs to Accelerate School Success.

Gibbs, D. P., & Cooper, E. B. (1989). Prevalence of communication disorders in students with learning disabilities. *Journal of Learning Disabilities, 22,* 60–63.

Gillete, J., & Temple, C. (1982). *Understanding reading problems: Assessment and instruction.* Boston, MA: Little, Brown.

Gillingham, A., & Stillman, B. W. (1936). *Remedial work for reading, spelling, and penmanship.* New York: Sachett & Wilhelms.

Gillingham, A., & Stillman, B. W. (1960). *Remedial training for children with specific disability in reading, spelling, and penmanship.* Cambridge, MA: Educators Publishing Service.

Ginot, H. (1975). *Teacher and child.* New York: Macmillan.

Glass, A. L., & Perna, J. (1986). The role of syntax in reading disability. *Journal of Learning Disabilities, 19*(6), 354–359.

Glavin, J. P. (1974). *Behavioral strategies for classroom management.* Columbus, OH: Merrill/Macmillan.

Gleason, G. (1981). Microcomputers in education: The state of the art. *Educational Technology, 21,* 7–18.

Goldberg, H. K., & Schiffman, G. B. (1972). *Dyslexia: Problems of reading disabilities.* New York: Grune & Stratton.

Goldstein, K. (1942). *Aftereffects of brain-injuries in war.* New York: Grune & Stratton.

Goldwasser, E., & Meyers, J. (1983). The impact of PL 94–142 on the practice of school psychology: A national survey. *Psychology in the School, 20,* 153–165.

Goodacre, E. J. (1978). Methods of teaching reading. In J. Chapman & P. Czerniewska (Eds.), *Reading from process to practice* (pp. 169–183). London: Routledge & Kegan in association with Open University Press.

Goodman, L. (1973). *Efficacy of visual motor training for orthopedically handicapped children.* Unpublished doctoral dissertation, Temple University, Philadelphia.

Goodman, L., & Mann, L. (1976). *Learning disabilities in the secondary school: Issues and practices.* New York: Grune & Stratton.

Gottlieb, J. (1981). Mainstreaming: Fulfilling the promise? *American Journal of Mental Deficiency, 86,* 115–126.

Gove, M. K. (1983). Clarifying teachers' beliefs about reading. *Reading Teacher, 37,* 216–268.

Graden, J. L., Casey, A., & Christenson, S. L. (1985). Implementing a prereferral intervention system: Part I, The model. *Exceptional Children, 51,* 377–387.

Graham, S., & Harris, K. R. (1987). Improving composition skills of inefficient learners with self-instructional strategy training. *Topics in Language Disorders, 7*(4), 66–77.

Graham, S., & Harris, K. R. (1988). Instructional recommendations for teaching writing to exceptional students. *Exceptional Children, 54*(6), 506–512.

Graham, S., & Harris, K. R. (1989). Improving learning disabled students' skills at composing essays: Self-instructional strategy training. *Exceptional Children, 56*(3), 201–214.

Graham, S., & Miller, L. (1979). Spelling research and practice: A unified approach. *Focus on Exceptional Children, 12*, 1–13.

Graham, S., & Miller, L. (1980). Handwriting research and practice: A unified approach. *Focus on Exceptional Children, 13*(2), 1–16.

Graves, D. H. (1979). Research update: What children show us about revision. *Language Arts, 56*, 312–319.

Graves, D. H. (1985). All children can write. *Learning Disabilities Focus, 1*(1), 36–43.

Graves, D. H., & Murray, D. H. (1980). Revision in the writer's workshop and in the classroom. *Journal of Education, 162*, 38–56.

Gray, D. B., & Yaffe, S. J. (1983). Prenatal drugs. In C. C. Brown (Ed.), *Childhood learning disabilities and prenatal risk: An interdisciplinary data review for health care professionals and parents* (pp. 45–49). Skillman, NJ: Johnson & Johnson.

Gray, R. A. (1981). Services for LD adult: A working paper. *Learning Disability Quarterly, 4*, 426–434.

Greenan, J. P. (1982). Problems and issues in delivering vocational education instruction and support services to students with learning disabilities. *Journal of Learning Disabilities, 15*(4), 231–235.

Greer, J. G., & Wethered, C. E. (1984). Learned helplessness: A piece of the burnout puzzle. *Exceptional Children, 50*, 524–530.

Gresham, F. M. (1982a). Misguided mainstreaming: The case for social skills training with handicapped children. *Exceptional Children, 48*(5), 422–433.

Gresham, F. M. (1982b). Social interactions as predictors of children's likeability and friendship patterns: A multiple regression analysis. *Journal of Behavioral Assessment, 4*, 39–54.

Gribben, B. (1983). Prison education in Michigan City, Indiana. *Phi Delta Kappan, 64*, 656–658.

Griffey, Q. L., Jr., Zigmond, N., & Leinhardt, G. (1988). The effect of self-questioning and story structure training on the reading comprehension of poor reader. *Learning Disabilities Research, 4*(1), 45–51.

Guerin, G. R., & Maier, A. S. (1983). *Informal assessment in education.* Palo Alto, CA: Mayfield.

Guilford, J. (1967). *The nature of human intelligence.* New York: McGraw-Hill.

Gullota, T. P. (1983). Early adolescence, alienation, and education. *Theory Into Practice, 22*, 152–154.

Hagen, D. (1984). *Microcomputer resource book for special education.* Reston, VA: Reston Publishing.

Hagen, J. W., & Huntsman, N. J. (1971). Selective attention in mental retardes. *Developmental Psychology, 5*, 151–160.

Hall, R. J. (1980). An information-processing approach to the study of exceptional children. In B. K. Keogh (Ed.), *Advances in special education* (Vol. 2, pp. 9–14). Greenwich, CT: JAI Press.

Hallahan, D. P., & Cruickshank, W. M. (1973). *Psychoeducational foundations of learning disabilities.* Englewood, NJ: Prentice-Hall.

Hallahan, D. P., Hall, R. J., Ianna, S. O., Kneedler, R. D., Lloyd, J. W., Loper, A. B., & Reeve, R. E. (1983). Summary of research findings at the University of Virginia Learning Disability Research Institute. *Exceptional Education Quarterly, 4*(1), 95–114.

Hallahan, D. P., & Kauffman, J. M. (1976). *Introduction to learning disabilities: A psychobehavioral approach.* Englewood Cliffs, NJ: Prentice-Hall.

Hallahan, D. P., Kauffman, J. M., & Lloyd, J. W. (1985). *Introduction to learning disabilities* (2nd ed.). Englewood Cliffs, NJ: Prentice-Hall.

Hallahan, D. P., Keller, C. E., McKinney, J. D., Lloyd, J. W., & Bryan T. (1988). Examining the research base of the regular education initiative: Efficacy studies and the adaptive learning environment model. *Journal of Learning Disabilities, 21,* 23–28.

Hallahan, D. P., Lloyd, J., Kosiewicz, M. M., Kauffman, J. M., & Graves, A. W. (1979). Self-monitoring of attention as a treatment for a learning-disabled boy's off-task behavior. *Learning Disability Quarterly, 2,* 24–34.

Hallahan, D. P., & Reeve, R. E. (1980). Selective attention and destractibility. In B. K. Keogh (Ed.), *Advances in special education* (Vol. 1, pp. 141–181). Greenwich, CT: JAI Press.

Hallgren, B. (1950). Specific dyslexia (congenital word-blindness): A clinical and genetic study. *Acta Psychiatrica et Neurologica* (Suppl. 65), 1–287.

Halliday, M. A. K. (1975). *Learning how to mean.* London: Elsevier/North Holland.

Hamilton, J. L. (1983). Measuring response to instruction as an assessment paradigm. In K. D. Gadow & I. Bialer (Eds.), *Advances in learning and behavioral disabilities* (Vol. 2, pp. 111–133). Greenwich, CT: JAI Press.

Hammill, D. D. (1972). Training visual perceptual processes. *Journal of Learning Disabilities, 5*(10), 552–559.

Hammill, D. D. (1990). Defining learning disabilities: The emerging concensus. *Journal of Learning Disabilities, 23,* 74–84.

Hammill, D. D., & Bartel, N. R. (1979). *Teaching students with learning and behavioral problems.* Boston: Allyn & Bacon.

Hammill, D. D., Goodman, L., & Weiderholt, J. L. (1974). Visual-motor processes: What success have we had in training them? *The Reading Teacher, 27*(7), 469–480.

Hammill, D. D., & Larsen, S. C. (1974). The effectiveness of psycholinguistic training. *Exceptional Children, 41*(1), 5–14.

Hammill, D. D., & Larsen, S. C. (1978). The effectiveness of psycholinguistic training: A reaffirmation of position. *Exceptional Children, 6,* 402–417.

Hammill, D. D., & Larsen, S. C. (1983). *Test of written language* (rev. ed.). Austin, TX: PRO-ED.

Hammill, D. D., Larsen, S. C., & McNutt, G. (1977). The effects of spelling instruction: A preliminary study. *The Elementary School Journal, 78,* 67–72.

Hammill, D. D., & Leigh, J. E. (1983). *Basic school skill inventory—diagnostic.* Austin, TX: PRO-ED.

Hammill, D. D., Leigh, J. E., McNutt, G., & Larsen, S. C. (1981). A new definition of learning disabilities. *Learning Disability Quarterly, 4*(4), 336–342.

Hampton, B. R., & Fernandez, M. C. (1985). *Parental involvement in the special education process* (Contract No. 300-83-0272). Washington, DC: Offices of Special Education and Rehabilitative Services.

Hanna, P. R., Hanna, J. S., Hodges, R. E., & Rudorf, E. H. (1966). *Phoneme-grapheme correspondences as cues to spelling improvement.* Washington, DC: Department of Health, Education, and Welfare.

Hanna, P. R., Hodges, R. E., & Hanna, J. S. (1971). *Spelling: Structures and strategies.* Boston: Houghton Mifflin.

Hanna, P. R., & Moore, J. T. (1953). Spelling—from spoken word to written symbol. *Elementary School Journal, 53,* 329–337.

Hannaford, A. E. (1983). Microcomputers in special education: Some new opportunities, some old problems. *The Computing Teacher, 10,* 11–17.

Hannaford, A. E., & Taber, F. M. (1982). Microcomputer software for the handicapped: Development and evaluation. *Exceptional Children, 49*(2), 137–144.

Haring, N. G., & Phillips, E. L. (1962). *Educating emotionally disturbed children.* New York: McGraw-Hill.

Harris, A. J. (1970). *How to increase reading ability.* New York: McKay.

Harris, A. J., & Sipay, E. R. (1985). *How to increase reading ability.* New York: Longman.

Harris, L., & Smith, C. (1976). *Reading instruction: Diagnosis teaching in the classroom* (2nd ed.). New York: Holt, Rinehart, & Winston.

Harris, T. L. (1960). Handwriting. In C. W. Harris (Ed.), *Encyclopedia of educational research* (3rd ed., pp. 616–624). New York: Macmillan.

Harris, W. J., & Schutz, P. N. B. (1986). *The special education resource program.* Columbus, OH: Merrill/Macmillan.

Hartwell, L. K., Wiseman, D. E., & Van Reusen, A. (1979). Modifying course content for mildly handicapped students at the secondary level. *Teaching Exceptional Children, 12*(1), 28–32.

Hasselbring, T. S., & Hamlett, C. L. (1984). Planning and managing instruction: Computer-based decision making. *Teaching Exceptional Children, 16*(4), 248–252.

Hassett, J., & Weisberg, A. (1973). *Open education.* Englewood Cliffs, NJ: Prentice-Hall.

Hebb, D. O. (1949). *The organization of behavior: A neuropsychological theory.* New York: Wiley.

Hebb, D. O. (1958). *A text book of psychology.* Philadelphia: Sauders.

Heckelman, R. C. (1966). Using the neurological impress remedial techniques. *Academic Therapy Quarterly, 1,* 235–239.

Heideman, C. (1975). A plea to teachers: Ten reasons for reading aloud. Unpublished manuscript. Madison, WI.

Heider, F. (1958). *The psychology of interpersonal relations.* New York: Wiley.

Heimer, R. T., & Trueblood, C. R. (1977). *Strategies for teaching children mathematics.* Menlo Park, CA: Addison-Wesley.

Heller, M. F. (1986, February). How do you know what you know? Metacognitive modeling in content areas. *Journal of Reading*, 415–422.

Henderson, E. (1985). *Teaching spelling*. Dallas, TX: Houghton Mifflin.

Hermann, K. (1959). *Reading disability: A medical study of word-blindness and related handicaps*. Springfield, IL: Charles C. Thomas.

Hewett, F. M. (1967). Educational engineering with emotionally disturbed children. *Exceptional Children, 33*(7), 459–471.

Hiebert, B., Wong, B., & Hunter, M. (1982). Affective influences on learning disabled adolescents. *Learning Disability Quarterly, 5*, 334–343.

Hinshelwood, J. (1917). *Congenital word blindness*. London: Lewis.

Hodges, R. E. (1966). *The psychological basis of spelling: Research on handwriting and spelling*. Champaign, IL: National Council of Teachers of English.

Hoffman, F. J., Sheldon, K. L., Minskoff, E. M., Sautter, S. W., Steidle, E. F., Baker, D. P., Bailey, M. B., & Echols, L. D. (1987). Needs of learning disabled adults. *Journal of Learning Disabilities, 20*(1), 43–53.

Hofmeister, A. M. (1982). Microcomputers in perspective. *Exceptional Children, 49*, 25–31.

Hoge, J. D. (1985). Four ways to end classroom computer neglect. *Principal, 65*(1), 41–43.

Hohman, L. B. (1922). Post-encephalitic behavior disorders in children. *Johns Hopkins Hospital Bulletin, 380*, 272–275.

Holborow, P. L., & Berry, P. S. (1986). Hyperactivity and learning difficulties. *Journal of Learning Disabilities, 19*, 426–431.

Homme, L. (1974). *How to use contingency contracting in the classroom*. Champaign, IL: Research Press.

HOPE (Harness Our Parent Energy). PTA project HOPE Committee of San Diego Unified PTA council

Hood-Smith, N. E., & Leffingwell, J. R. (1983). The impact of physical space alteration on destructive classroom behavior: A case study. *Education, 6*, 224–231.

Horvath, G. (1981). Issues in correctional education: A conundrum of conflict. *Journal of Correctional Education, 33*(4), 8–15.

Houck, C. K. (1984). *Learning disabilities*. Englewood Cliffs, NJ: Prentice-Hall.

Howell, K., & Morehead, M. (1987). *Curriculum based education for special and remedial education*. Columbus, OH: Merrill/Macmillan.

Huefner, D. S. (1988). The consulting teacher model: Risks and opportunities. *Exceptional Children, 54*(5), 403–414.

Huey, E. B. (1908/1968). *The psychology and pedogogy of reading*. Cambridge, MA: MIT Press.

Hughes, C. A., Schumaker, J. B., Deshler, D. D., & Mercer, C. D. (1988). *The test taking strategy*. Lawrence, KS: Excellent Enterprises.

Hughes, J. N. (1988). *Cognitive behavior therapy with children in schools*. New York: Pergamon Press.

Hughes, J. R., & Park, G. E. (1968). The EEG in dyslexia. In P. Kellaway & I. Petersen (Eds.), *Clinical electroencephalography of children* (pp. 307–327). Stockholm: Almquist & Wiksell.

Hull, C. L. (1951). *Essentials of behavior.* New Haven: Yale University.

Humes, C. W. (1978). School counselors and P.L.94–142. *School Counselor, 25*(3), 7–11.

Humphrey, M., Hoffman, E., & Crosby, B. (1984). Mainstreaming LD students. *Academic Therapy, 19*(4), 321–327.

Hunt, D. E. (1975). Person—environment interaction: A challenge found before it was tried. *Review of Educational Research, 45*(2), 209–230.

Idol, L. (1987). Group story mapping: A comprehension strategy for both skilled and unskilled readers. *Journal of Learning Disabilities, 20,* 196–205.

Idol, L., Paolucci-Whitcomb, P., & Nevin, A. (1986). *Collaborative Consultation.* Rockville, MD: Aspen.

Idol, L., & West, J. F. (1987). Consultation in special education (Part II): Training and practice. *Journal of Learning Disabilities, 20,* 388–408.

Idol-Maestas, L. A. (1981). A teacher training model: The resource/consulting teacher. *Behavioral Disorders, 6,* 108–121.

Idol-Maestas, L. A. (1983). *Special education: Consultation handbook.* Rockville, MD: An Aspen Publication.

Idol-Maestas, L. A. (1986). *Collaborative school consultation: Recommendations for state departments of education.* The National Task Force on School Consultation. The Teacher Education Division, The Council for Exceptional Children.

Idol-Maestas, L. A., & Ritter, S. (1985). A follow-up study of resource/consulting teachers: Factors that facilitate and inhibit teacher consultation. *Teacher Education and Special Education, 8*(3), 121–131.

Ingram, T. T. S. (1964). The dyslexic child. *Word Blind Bulletin, 1*(4), 1.

Inhelder, B., & Piaget, J. (1958). *The growth of logical thinking from childhood to adolescence.* New York: Basic Books.

Interagency committee on learning disabilities. (1987). *Learning disabilities: A report to the United States Congress.* Bethesda, MD: National Institue of Health.

Itard, J. M. (1962). *The wild boy of Aveyron* (translated by George & Muriel Humphrey). New York: Appelton Century-Crofts.

Jacobson, F. N. (1976). The juvenile court judge and learning disabilities. *Monograph of the National Council of Juvenile Court Judges.* Reno: University of Nevada.

Jackson, P. W., & Lahderne, H. M. (1967). Inequalities of teacher-pupil contact. *Psychology in the School, 3,* 4–11.

James, J. W. (1890). *The prinicples of psychology* (Vol. 1). New York: Holt.

Jenkins, J., & Jenkins, L. (1985). Peer tutoring in elementary and secondary programs. *Focus on Exceptional Children, 17*(6), 1–12.

Jenkins, J. R., & Mayhall, W. F. (1976). Development and evaluation of a resource teacher program. *Exceptional Children, 43,* 21–24.

Jenson, W. R., & Morgan, D. P. (1988). *Teaching behaviorally disordered students.* Columbus, OH: Merrill/Macmillan.

Johnson, A. B., Vickers, L. L., & Norman, J. E. (1984). The language experience approach with mildly handicapped learners: Emphasizing basic skills. *Reading Improvement, 21,* 66–67.

Johnson, D. J. (1988). Review of research on specific reading, writing, and mathematics disorders. In J. E. Kavanagh & T. J. Truss, Jr. (Eds.), *Learning disabilities: Proceedings of the national conference* (pp. 79–163). Parkton, MD: York Press.

Johnson, D. J., & Myklebust, H. R. (1967). *Learning disabilities: Educational principles and practices.* New York: Grune & Stratton.

Johnson, D. R., Bruininks, R. H., & Thurlow, M. L. (1987). Meeting the challenge of transition service planning through improved interagency cooperation. *Exceptional Children, 53*(6), 522–530.

Johnson, D. W., & Johnson, R. T. (1980). Integrating handicapped students into the mainstream. *Exceptional Children, 47*(2), 90–98.

Johnson, D. W., & Johnson, R. T. (1986). Mainstreaming and cooperative learning strategies. *Exceptional Children, 52*(6), 553–561.

Johnson, D. W., Johnson, R. T., & Maruyama, G. (1983). Interdependence and interpersonal attraction among heterogeneous and homogeneous individuals: A theoretical formulation and meta-analysis of the research. *Review of Educational Research, 53,* 5–54.

Johnson, D. W., Johnson, R. T., Warring, D., & Maruyama, G. (1986). Different cooperative learning procedures and cross-handicap relationships. *Exceptional Children, 53*(3), 247–252.

Johnson, L., & Bany, M. (1970). *Classroom management.* New York: Macmillan.

Johnson, S. W. (1979). *Arithmetic and learning disabilities.* Boston: Allyn & Bacon.

Jones, K. M., Torgesen, J. K., & Sexton, M. A. (1987). Using computer guided practice to increase decoding fluency in learning disabled children: A study using the hint and hunt I program. *Journal of Learning Disabilities, 20*(2), 122–128.

Jones, M. C. (1924). The elimination of children's fears. *Journal of Experimental Psychology, 7,* 382–390.

Justice, E. M. (1985). Metamemory: An aspect of metacognition in mentally retarded. In N. R. Ellis & N. W. Bray (Eds.), *International review of research in mental retardation* (Vol. 13, pp. 79–107). New York: Academic Press.

Kaluger, G., & Kolson, C. J. (1978). *Reading and learning disabilities* (2nd ed.). Columbus, OH: Merrill/Macmillan.

Kameya, L. I. (1972). Behavioral interventions in emotional disturbance. In W. C. Rhodes & M. L. Tracy (Eds.), *A study of child variance: Vol. 2. Interventions* (pp. 159–252). Ann Arbor: University of Michigan.

Kaminsky, S., & Powers, R. (1981). Remediation of handwriting difficulties: A practical approach. *Academic Therapy, 17*(1), 19–25.

Kauffman, J. (1985). *Characteristics of children's behavior disorders.* Columbus, OH: Merrill/Macmillan.

Kauffman, J. M., Gerber, M. M., & Semmel, M. I. (1988). Arguable assumptions underlying the regular education initiative. *Journal of Learning Disabilities, 21*(1), 6–11.

Kauffman, J. M., & Hallahan, D. P. (1976). *Teaching children with learning disabilities: Personal perspectives.* Columbus, OH: Merrill/Macmillan.

Kaufman, M. J., Gottlieb, J., Agard, J. A., & Kukic, M. B. (1975). Mainstreaming: Toward an explication of the construct. In E. L. Meyen, G. A. Vergason, & R. J.

Whelan (Eds.), *Alternatives for teaching exceptional children* (pp. 35–54). Denver, CO: Love.

Kavale, K. A. (1982). Psycholinguistic training programs: Are there differential treatment effects? *The Exceptional Child, 29*(1), 21–29.

Kavale, K. A. (Ed.). (1988). *Learning disabilities: State of the art and practice.* Boston: Little, Brown.

Kavale, K., & Forness, S. (1985). *The science of learning disabilities.* Boston: Little, Brown.

Kavale, K. A., Forness, S. R., & Bender, M. (1987). *Handbook of learning disabilities: Vol. I. Dimensions and diagnosis.* Boston: Little, Brown.

Kavale, K. A., Forness, S. R., & Bender, M. (1988a). *Handbook of learning disabilities: Vol. 2. Methods and interventions.* Boston: Little, Brown.

Kavale, K. A., Forness, S. R., & Bender, M. (1988b). *Handbook of learning disabilities: Vol. 3. Programs and practices.* Boston: Little, Brown.

Kavanagh, J. F. (Ed.). (1968). *Communication by language: The reading process.* Bethesda, MD: National Institute of Child Health and Human Development.

Kavanagh, J. F., & Truss, T. J., Jr. (1988). *Learning disabilities: Proceedings of the national conference.* Parkton, MD: York Press.

Kay, M. (1986). Overcoming passive behavior. *Academic Therapy, 22,* 35–39.

Kazdin, A. E. (1982). The token economy: A decade later. *Journal of Applied Behavior Analysis, 15,* 431–445.

Keefe, C. H. (1988). Social skills: A basic subject. *Academic Therapy, 23*(4), 367–373.

Keilitz, I., & Dunivant, N. (1986). The relationship between learning disability and juvenile delinquency: Current state of knowledge. *Remedial and Special Education, 7*(3), 18–26.

Kendall, P. C., & Hollon, S. D. (1979). Cognitive-behavioral interventions: Overview and current status. In P. C. Kendall & S. D. Hollon (Eds.), *Cognitive behavioral interventions: Theory, research and procedures* (pp. 1–9). New York: Academic Press.

Keogh, B. K. (1969). Early identification of children with potential learning problems: Introduction and overview. *Journal of Special Education, 4*(3), 307–311.

Keogh, B. K., (1986). Future of the LD field: Research and practice. *Journal of Learning Disabilities, 19*(8), 455–460.

Keogh, B. K., (1987). Learning disabilities: In defense of a construct. *Learning Disabilities Research, 3*(1), 4–9.

Keogh, B. K., (1988). Learning disability diversity in search of order. In M. C. Wang, M. C. Reynolds, & H. J. Walberg (Eds.), *Handbook of special education research and practice: Vol. 2. Mildly handicapped conditions* (pp. 225–251). New York: Pergamon.

Keogh, B. K. (1990). Definitional assumptions and research issues. In H. L. Swanson & B. K. Keogh (Eds.), *Learning disabilities: Theoretical and research issues* (pp. 13–19). Hillsdale, NJ: Earlbaum.

Keogh, B. K., & Becker, L. (1973). Early detection of learning problems: Questions, cautions, and guidelines. *Exceptional Children, 40,* 5–12.

Kephart, N. C. (1960). *The slow learner in the classroom.* Columbus, OH: Merrill/ Macmillan.

Kephart, N. C. (1968). *Learning disabilities: An educational adventure.* West Lafayette, IN: Kappa Delta Pi Press.

Kirk, S. A. (1958). *Early education of the mentally retarded: An experimental study.* Urbana: University of Illinois Press.

Kirk, S. A. (1962). *Educating exceptional children.* Boston: Houghton Mifflin.

Kirk, S. A. (1963). Behavioral diagnosis and remediation of learning disabilities. *Proceedings of the Annual Meeting of the Conference on Exploration into the Problems of Perceptually Handicapped child* (Vol. 1). Chicago: Perceptually Handicapped Children, Inc.

Kirk, S. A. (1971). Learning disabilities: The view from here. In D. D. Hammill & N. R. Bartel (Eds.), *Educational perspectives in learning disabilities* (pp. 20–25). New York: Wiley.

Kirk, S. A. (1972). *Educating exceptional children.* Boston: Houghton Mifflin.

Kirk, S. A. (1987). The learning disabled preschool child. *Teaching Exceptional Children, 19,* 78–81.

Kirk, S. A., & Chalfant, J. C. (1984). *Academic and developmental learning disabilities.* Denver: Love Publishing.

Kirk, S. A., & Kirk, W. D. (1971). *Psycholinguistic learning disabilities: Diagnosis and remediation.* Urbana: University of Illinois Press.

Kirk, S. A., McCarthy, J. J., & Kirk, W. D. (1968). *Illinois Test of Psycholinguistic Abilities* (Rev. ed.). Urbana: University of Illinois Press.

Kistinger, B. J., & Kerchner, L. B. (1984). Language processing/word processing: Written expression, computers and learning disabled students. *Learning Disability Quarterly, 7*(4), 329–335.

Knott, P. D., & Fathum, S. D. (1984). Denver academy: A program for learning disabled adolescents. In W. M. Cruickshank & J. M. Kliebhan (Eds.), *Early adolescence to early adulthood: Vol. 5. The best of ACLD* (pp. 137–175). Syracuse: Syracuse University Press.

Kohn, A. (1986, September). How to succeed without even vying. *Psychology Today,* pp. 22–28.

Kokaska, C. J., & Brolin, D. E. (1985). *Career education for handicapped individuals.* Columbus, OH: Merrill/Macmillan.

Kolich, E. M. (1985). Microcomputer technology with the learning disabled: A review of the literature. *Journal of Learning Disabilities, 18*(7), 428–451.

Kolligan, J., & Sternberg, R. J. (1987). Intelligence, information processing, and specific learning disabilities: A triarchic synthesis. *Journal of Learning Disabilities, 20*(1), 8–17.

Kosc, L. (1974). Developmental dyscalculia. *Journal of Learning Disabilities, 7*(3), 46–59.

Kriask, J., & Ross, S. (1981). An adaptive educational model for correctional education. *Journal of Correctional Education, 31*(4), 11–13.

Kronick, D. (1976). The importance of a sociological perspective towards learning disabilities. *Journal of Learning Disabilities, 9,* 115–119.

Kronick, D. (1978). An examination of psychosocial aspects of learning disabled adolescents. *Learning Disability Quarterly, 1*(4), 86–93.

Kronick, D. (1981). *Social development of learning disabled persons: Examining the effects and treatment of inadequate interpersonal skills.* San Francisco, CA: Jossey-Bass.

Kulik, J., Bangert, R. L., & Williams, G. W. (1983). Effects of computer-based teaching on secondary school students. *Journal of Educational Psychology, 75*, 19–26.

Kunzelmann, H. P., Cohen, M. A., Hulten, W. J., Martin, G. L., & Mingo, A. R. (1970). *Precision teaching.* Seattle, WA: Special Child Publications.

LaBerge, D., & Samuels, S. J. (1974). Toward a theory of automatic information processing in reading. *Cognitive Psychology, 6*, 293–323.

LaGreca, A. M., & Mesibov, G. B. (1979). Social skills interventions with learning disabled children: Selecting skills and implementing training. *Journal of Clinical Child Psychology, 8*, 234–241.

LaGreca, A. M., & Mesibov, G. B. (1981). Facilitating interpersonal functioning with peers in learning disabled children. *Journal of Learning Disabilities, 14*, 197–199.

Lamb, P., & Arnold, R. (Eds.). (1972). *Reading: Foundation and instructional strategies.* Belmont, CA: Wadsworth.

Lane, B. A. (1980). The relationship of learning disabilities to juvenile delinquency: Current status. *Journal of Learning Disabilities, 13*(8), 20–29.

Lanier, R. J., & Davis, A. P. (1972). Developing comprehension through teacher-made questions. *Reading Teacher, 26*(2), 153–157.

Larsen, B. L., & Roberts, B. B. (1986). The computer as a catalyst for mutual support and improvement among learning disabled students. *Journal of Learning Disabilities, 19*(1), 52–55.

Larsen, S. C., & Hammill, D. D. (1975). The relationship of selected visual-perceptual abilities to school learning. *Journal of Special Education, 9*, 281–291.

Larsen, S. C., Parker, R. M., & Hammill, D. D. (1982). Effectiveness of psycholinguistic training: A response to Kavale. *Exceptional Children, 49*(1), 60–66.

Learning Disabilities: A report to the U.S. Congress (1987). Washington, DC: Interagency Committee on learning disabilities, Department of Health and Human Services.

Lee, W. W. (1987). Microcomputer courseware production and evaluation guidelines for students with learning disabilities. *Journal of Learning Disabilities, 20*(7), 436–438.

Leitman, A., & Churchill, E. (1966). *A classroom of young children.* MA: Newton.

Lenz, B. K., Schumaker, J. B., Deshler, D. D., & Beals, V. L. (1984). *Learning strategies curriculum: The word identification strategy.* Lawrence, KS: University of Kansas.

Lenz, B. K., Warner, M. M., Alley, G. R., & Deshler, D. D. (1980). *A comparison of youths who have committed delinquent acts with learning disabled, low achieving, and normally achieving adolescents.* (DHEW/OE Project # USD 497). Washington, DC: Bureau of Education for the Handicapped (ERIC Document No. ED 217 641)

Lerner, J. W. (1985). *Children with learning disabilities.* Boston, MA: Houghton Mifflin.

Lerner, J. W. (1989). *Learning disabilities* (5th ed.). Boston: Houghton Mifflin.

Lerner, J. W., Evans, M. A., & Meyers, G. S. (1977). LD programs at the secondary level: A survey. *Academic Therapy, 13*(1), 5–22.

Levin, R., & Doyle, C. (1983). The microcomputer in the writing, reading/study lab. *Technology Horizons in Education, 10,* 77–79.

Lewis, E. R., & Lewis, H. P. (1965). An analysis of errors in the formation of manuscript letters by first grade children. *American Educational Research Journal, 2,* 25–35.

Lewis, R. S., Strauss, A., & Lehtinen, L. (1951). *The other child.* New York: Grune & Stratton.

Lieberman, L. M. (1986). Reconciling standards and individual differences. *Journal of Learning Disabilities, 19*(2) 127.

Lilly, M. S. (1970). A teapot in tempest. *Exceptional Children, 37,* 43–49.

Lilly, M. S. (1986). The relationship between general and special education: A new face on an old issue. *Counterpoint, 6*(1), 10.

Lilly, M. S., & Givens-Ogle, L. (1981). Teacher consultation: Present, past and future. *Behavior Disorders, 6,* 73–77.

Lindsay, G. A., & Wedell, K. (1982). The early identification of educationally "at risk" children revisited. *Journal of Learning Disabilities, 15*(4), 212–216.

Lindsley, O. R. (1963). Experimental analysis of social reinforcement: Terms and method. *American Journal of Orthopsychiatry, 33,* 624–633.

Lindsley, O. R. (1990). Precision teaching. *Teaching Exceptional Children, 22*(3), 10–15.

Linton, T. E. (1969, March). The french educateur approach to the reeducation of disturbed and maladjusted children. *American Journal of Orthopsychiatry.*

Lischio, M. A. (Ed.). (1984). *A guide to colleges for learning disabled students.* New York: Academic Press.

Lloyd, J. (1980). Academic instruction and cognitive behavior modification: The need for attack strategy training. *Exceptional Education Quarterly, 1,* 53–63.

Lloyd, J. (1984). How shall we individualize instruction—or should we? *Remedial and Special Education [RASE], 5*(1), 7–15.

Lloyd, J., & Kniedler, R. D. (1979). *The effect of verbalizing a decoding strategy on the word reading accuracy of children with learning disabilities.* Charlottesville: University of Virginia Learning Disabilities Research Institute.

Lloyd, J., Saltzman, N. J., & Kauffman, J. M. (1981). Predictable generalization in academic learning as a result of preskills and strategy training. *Learning Disability Quarterly, 4*(1), 203–216.

Loban, W. (1976). *Language development, kindergarten through grade twelve.* Urbana, IL: National Council of Teachers of English.

Loftus, E. (1975). Leading questions and eyewitness reports. *Cognitive Psychology, 7,* 560–575.

Loftus, L., & Walter, V. (1981, October). *For special educators: Tips for working with regular classroom teachers.* Office of Special Education and Rehabilitative Services, pp. 3–4.

Lombana, J. (1980). Fostering positive attitudes toward handicapped students: A guidance challenge. *The School Counselor, 27*(1), 176–182.

Love, W. C., & Bachara, G. H. (1975). The diagnostic team approach for juvenile delinquents with learning disabilities. *Juvenile Justice, 26,* 1, 6, 27–31.

Lovitt, T. C., & Curtis, K. A. (1968). Effects of manipulating an antecedent event on mathematics reponse rate. *Journal of Applied Behavior Analysis, 1,* 329–333.

Lund, K. A., Foster, G. E., & McCall-Perez, F. C. (1978). The effectiveness of psycholinguistic training: A re-evaluation. *Exceptional Children, 44,* 310–319.

Lundell, K., & Brown, W. (1979). Peer tutoring: An economical instructional model. *Academic Therapy,* January, 287–292.

Lynch, E. W., & Stein, R. (1982). Perspectives on parent participation in special education. *Exceptional Education Quarterly, 3*(2), 56–63.

Lyon, G. R. (1988). Subtype remediation. In K. A. Kavale, S. R. Forness, & M. Bender (Eds.), *Handbook of learning disabilities: Vol. 2. Methods and interventions* (pp. 33–58). Boston: Little, Brown.

Lyon, G. R., & Flynn, J. M. (1991). Assessing subtypes of learning abilities. In H. L. Swanson (Ed.), *Handbook on the assessment of learning disabilities* (pp. 59–74). Austin, TX: PRO-ED.

Lyon, G. R., & Moats, L. C. (1988). Critical issues in the instruction of the learning disabled. *Journal of Consulting and Clinical Psychology, 6,* 830–835.

Lysakowski, R. S., & Walberg, H. J. (1981). Classroom reinforcement and learning: A quantitative synthesis. *Journal of Educational Research, 75,* 69–77.

MacArthur, C. A. (1988). The impact of computers on the writing process. *Exceptional Children, 54*(6), 536–542.

MacArthur, C. A., & Graham, S. (1987). Learning disabled students' difficulties in learning to use word processor: Implications for instruction and software evaluation. *Journal of Learning Disabilities, 19,* 243–247.

MacArthur, C. A., & Schneiderman, B. (1986). Learning disabled students' difficulties in learning to use word processor: Implications for instruction and software evaluation. *Journal of Learning Disabilities, 19*(4), 248–253.

MacMillan, D. L., & Semmel, M. I. (1977). Evaluation of mainstreaming programs. *Focus on Exceptional Children, 9,* 1–14.

Madden, N. A., & Slavin, R. E. (1983). Mainstreaming students with mild handicaps: Academic and social outcomes. *Review of Educational Research, 53,* 519–570.

Mager, R. (1962). *Preparing instructional objectives.* Palo Alto, CA: Fearon.

Maher, C., & Bennett, R. (1982). *Planning and evaluating special education services.* Englewood Cliffs, NJ: Prentice-Hall.

Maisto, A. A., & Baumeister, A. A. (1984). Dissection of component processes in rapid information processing tasks: Comparison of retarded and non retarded people. In P. H. Brooks, R. Sperber, & C. McCauley (Eds.), *Learning and cognition in the mentally retarded* (pp. 165–188). New Jersey: Erlbaum.

Major, S. T. (1983). Written language. In C. T. Wren (Ed.), *Language learning disabilities* (pp. 297–325). Rockville, MD: Aspen.

Mangrum, C. T., & Strichart, S. S. (1984). *College and the learning disabled student.* New York: Grune & Stratton.

Mann, L. (1971). Psychometric phrenology and the new faculty psychology: The case against ability assessment and training. *Journal of Special Education, 5,* 3–14.

Mann, L., Goodman, L., & Wiederholt, J. L. (1978). *Teaching the learning-disabled adolescent.* Boston: Houghton Mifflin.

Mann, L., & Phillips, W. A. (1967). Fractional practices in special education: A critique. *Exceptional Children, 33,* 311–317.

Mann, L., & Sabatino, D. A. (1985). *Foundations of cognitive process in remedial special education.* Rockville: Aspen.

Mann, P. H., Suiter, P. A., & McClung, R. M. (1979). *Handbook in diagnostic-prescriptive teaching* (abridged 2nd ed.). Boston: Allyn & Bacon.

Mann, V. A. (1986). Why some children encounter reading problems: The contribution of difficulties with language processing and phonological sophistication to early reading disability. In J. K. Torgesen & B. Y. L. Wong (Eds.), *Psychological and educational perspectives on learning disabilities* (pp. 133–159). Orlando, FL: Academic Press.

Mann, V. A., Cowin, E., & Schoenheimer, J. (1990). Phonological processing, language comprehension, and reading ability. In J. K. Torgesen (Ed.), *Cognitive and behavioral characteristics of children with learning disabilities* (pp. 59–87). Austin, TX: PRO-ED.

Manning, B. H. (1984). A self-communication structure for learning mathematics. *School Science and Mathematics, 84*(1).

Manning, M. M., & Manning, G. L. (1986). *Improving spelling in the middle grades.* Washington, DC: NEA.

Markman, E. M. (1979). Realizing that you don't understand: Elementary school children's awareness of inconsistency. *Child Development, 50,* 643–655.

Marsh, G. E., Gearheart, C., & Gearheart, B. (1978). *The learning disabled adolescent.* St. Louis: Mosby.

Marsh, G. E., II, & Price, B. J. (1980). *Methods for teaching the mildly handicapped adolescent.* St. Louis: Mosby.

Martin, H. P. (1980). Nutrition, injury, illness, and minimal brain dysfunction. In H. Rie & E. Rie (Eds.), *Handbook of minimal brain dysfunction: A critical review* (pp. 169–184). New York: Wiley.

Mason, M. (1983). Language arts activities and microcomputers, k–12. *Microcomputers in K–12 Education, 4,* 43–47.

Mastropieri, M. A. (1988). Learning disabilities in early childhood. In K. A. Kavale (Ed.), *Learning disabilities: State of the art and practice* (pp. 161–179). Boston, MA: Little, Brown.

Mattingly, I. G. (1972). Reading, the linguistic process, and linguistic awareness. In J. F. Kavanagh & I. C. Mattingly (Eds.), *Language by ear and by eye* (pp. 133–148). Cambridge, MA: MIT Press.

Mauser, A. J. (1974). Learning disabilities and delinquent youth. *Academic Therapy, 9*(6), 389–400.

May, F. B. (1986). *Reading as communication.* Columbus, OH: Merrill/Macmillan.

Mayer, L. C. (1982). *Educational administration and special education: A handbook for school administrators.* Boston, MA: Allyn & Bacon.

McCarthy, J. M. (1971). Learning disabilities: Where have we been? Where are we going? In D. D. Hammill & N. R. Bartel (Eds.), *Educational perspectives in learning disability* (pp. 10–19). New York: Wiley.

McCarthy, J. M. (1989). Through my kaleidoscope—1989 elements from the past with promise for the future. *Learning Disabilities Focus, 4*(2), 67–83.

McCarthy, J. M., & Kirk, S. A. (1961). *Illinois test of psycholinguistic abilities.* Urbana: University of Illinois Press.

McClure, A. A. (1985). Predictable books: Another way to teach reading to learning disabled children. *Teaching Exceptional Children, 17*(4), 267–273.

McCue, P. M., Shelly, C., & Goldstien, G. (1986). Intellectual, academic and neuropsychological preformance levels in learning disabled adults. *Journal of Learning Disabilities, 19*(4), 233–236.

McDermott, P., & Watkins, M. (1983). Computerized vs. conventional remedial instruction for LD pupils. *Journal of Special Education, 17*(1), 81–88.

McDowell, F. E. (1986). Adaptive learning model fosters both equity and excellence. *School Administrator, 43*(1), 20–23.

McGuire, J. M., & Shaw, S. F. (1987). A decision-making process for the college-bound student: Matching learner, institution, and support program. *Learning Disability Quarterly, 10,* 106–111.

McGuire, J. M., & Shaw, S. F. (1989). *Learning disabilities in Connecticut colleges and universities.* Connecticut University: Storrs Postsecondary Learning Disability Technical Assistance Center.

McKinney, J. D. (1984). The search for subtypes of specific learning disability. *Journal of Learning Disabilities, 17,* 19–26.

McKinney, J. D. (1989). Longitudinal research on the behavioral characteristics of children with learning disabilities. *Journal of Learning Disabilities, 22*(3), 141–150.

McKinney, J. D., & Feagans, L. (1983). Adaptive classroom behavior of learning disabled children. *Journal of Learning Disabilities, 16,* 360–367.

McKinney, J. D., & Hocutt, A. M. (1982). Public school involvement of parents of learning-disabled children and average achievers. *Exceptional Children Quartely, 3,* 64–73.

McKinney, J. D., & Hocutt, A. M., (1988). The need for policy analysis in evaluating the regular education initiative. *Journal of Learning Disabilities, 21*(1), 12–18.

McKinney, L. D., McClure, S., & Feagans, L. (1982). Classroom behavior of learning disabled children. *Learning Disability Quarterly, 5,* 45–52.

McLoone, B. B., Scruggs, T. E., Mastropieri, M. A., & Zucker, S. F., (1986). Memory instruction and training with LD adolescent. *Learning Disabilities Research, 2*(1), 45–53.

McLoughlin, J. A., Edge, D., & Strenecky, B. (1978). Perspective on parent involvement in the diagnosis and treatment of learning disabled children. *Journal of Learning Disabilities, 11,* 32–37.

McLoughlin, J. A., & Lewis, R. (1990). *Assessing special students.* Columbus, OH: Merrill/Macmillan.

McManama, J. (1972). *An effective program for teacher-aide training.* West Nyack, NY: Parker.

McNutt, G., & Mandelbaum, L. H. (1980). General assessment competencies for special education teachers. *Exceptional Education Quarterly, 1*(3), 21–29.

Meichenbaum, D. (1977). *Cognitive-behavior modification: An integrative approach*. New York: Plenum Press.

Meichenbaum, D. (1983). Teaching thinking: A cognitive-behavioral approach. In D. Carnine, D. Elkind, A. D. Hendrickson, D. Meichenbaum, R. L. Sieben, & F. Smith (Eds.), *Interdisciplinary voices in learning disabilities and remedial education* (pp. 127–155). Austin, TX: PRO-ED.

Meichenbaum, D., Burland, S., Gruson, L., & Cameron, R. (1985). Metacognitive assessment. In S. R. Yussen (Ed.), *The growth of reflection in children* (pp. 3–30). New York: Academic Press.

Meichenbaum, D., & Goodman, J. (1971). Training impulsive children to talk to themselves: A means of developing self-control. *Journal of Abnormal Psychology, 77*, 115–126.

Meisgeier, C. (1976). A review of critical issues underlying mainstreaming. In L. Mann & D. A. Sabatino (Eds.), *The third review of special education* (pp. 245–269). New York: Grune & Stratton.

Mercer, C. D. (1987a). Beyond the traditional assessment. In S. Vaughn & C. S. Bos (Eds.), *Research in learning disabilities* (pp. 153–169). Boston, MA: College-Hill.

Mercer, C. D. (1987b). *Students with learning disabilities* (3rd ed.). Columbus, OH: Merrill/Macmillan.

Mercer, C. D., Algozzine, B., & Trifiletti, J. J. (1979). Early identification: Issues and considerations. *Exceptional Children, 52*, 52–54.

Mercer, C. D., Algozzine, B., & Trifiletti, J. J. (1988). Early identification—An analysis of the research. *Learning Disability Quarterly, 11*(3), 176–189. (Reprinted from 2(2), 1979)

Mercer, C. D., & Mercer, A. R. (1985). *Teaching students with learning problems* (2nd ed.). Columbus, OH: Merrill/Macmillan.

Meyen, E. L. (1982). *Exceptional children in today's American schools: An alternative resource book*. Denver, CO: Love Publishing.

Miller, S., Sabatino, D., & Larsen, R. (1980). Issues in the professional preparation of secondary school special educators. *Exceptional Children, 46*, 344–350.

Miller, W. H. (1978). *Diagnostic kit*. New York: The Center for Applied Research in Education.

Milne, N. (1982). Issues and concerns related to the education of exceptional bilingual students. In O. Thomas (Ed.), *Bilingual special education resource guide* (pp. 3–10). Phoenix, AZ: Oryx Press.

Minskoff, E. H. (1975). Research on psycholinguistic training: Critique and guidelines. *Exceptional Children, 42*, 136–143.

Minskoff, E. H. (1982). Training LD students to cope with the everyday world. *Academic Therapy, 17*, 311–316.

Minskoff, E. H., Sautter, S. W., Hoffman, F. J., & Hawks, R. (1987). Employer attitudes toward hiring the learning disabled. *Journal of Learning Disabilities, 20*(1), 53–57.

Mithaug, D. E., Martin, J. E., & Agran, M. (1987). Adaptability, instruction: The goal of transitional programing. *Exceptional Children, 53*(6), 500–507.

Monroe, M. (1932). *Children who cannot read*. Chicago: University of Chicago Press.

Montessori, M. (1912). [*The Montessori method: Scientific pedagogy as applied to child education in "the children's houses"*] (A. E. George, trans.). New York: Frederick Stokes.

Moore, P. J. (1983). Aspects of metacognitive knowledge about learning. *Journal of Research in Reading, 6*(2), 87–102.

Morgan, D. (1981a). *A primer on individualized education programs for exceptional children: Preferred strategies and practices.* Reston, VA: Foundation for Exceptional Children.

Morgan, D. (1981b). Characteristics of a quality IEP. *Education Unlimited, 3*(3), 12–17.

Morgan, D. J. (1979). Prevalence and types of handicapping conditions found in juvenile corrections: A national survey. *Journal of Special Education, 13,* 283–295.

Morgan, D. P., & Jenson, W. R. (1988). *Teaching behaviorally disordered students.* Columbus, OH: Merrill/Macmillan.

Mori, A. A. (1979). The handicapped child in the mainstream—new roles for the regular educator. *Education, 99,* 243–249.

Morocco, C. C., & Neuman, S. B. (1986). Word processors and the acquisition of writing strategies. *Journal of Learning Disabilities, 19*(4), 243–247.

Morsink, C. V., Soar, R. S., Soar, R. M., & Thomas, R. (1986). Research on teaching: Opening the door to special education classrooms. *Exceptional Children, 53*(1), 32–40.

Mowder, B. (1979). Assessing the bilingual handicapped student. *Psychology in the School, 16*(1), 43–50.

Mowder, B. (1980). A strategy for assessment of bilingual handicapped children. *Psychology in the School, 17*(1), 7–12.

Mowder, B. (1982). Assessing the bilingual child. In O. Thomas (Ed.), *Bilingual special education resource guide* (pp. 11–21). Phoenix, AZ: Oryx Press.

Murray, C. (1976). *The link between learning disabilities and juvenile delinquency: Current theory and knowledge.* Grant No. 76JN-99-0009, Juvenile Justice and Delinquency Prevention Operations Task Group, Law Enforcement Administration. Washington, DC: U.S. Department of Justice.

Myers, P. I., & Hammill, D. D. (1982). *Learning disabilities.* Austin, TX: PRO-ED.

Myklebust, H. R. (1954). *Auditory disorders in children.* New York: Grune & Stratton.

Myklebust, H. R. (1960). *The psychology of deafness.* New York: Grune & Stratton.

Myklebust, H. R. (1965). *Development and disorders of written language* (Vol. 1). New York: Grune & Stratton.

Myklebust, H. R. (Ed.). (1968). *Progress in learning disabilities* (Vol. 1). New York: Grune & Stratton.

Myklebust, H. R. (1973). *Development and disorders of written language: Vol. 2. Studies of normal and exceptional children.* New York: Grune & Stratton.

Myklebust, H. R., & Boshes, B. (1960). Psychoneurological learning disorders in children. *Archives of Pediatrics, 77,* 247–256.

Naidoo, S. (1972). *Specific dyslexia.* London: Pitman.

National Advisory Committee on Handicapped Children. (1968). *First annual report, special education for handicapped children.* Washington, DC: U.S. Office of Education. Department of Health, Education, & Welfare.

National Dissemination & Assessment Center. (1980). *The initial screening and diagnostic assessment of students of limited english proficiency*, pp. 7–12.

National Joint Committee on Learning Disabilities. (1985). Adults with learning disabilities: A call to action. Cited in *Learning Disability Quarterly*, 1986, 9, 164–167.

National Joint Committee on Learning Disabilities. (1988). [letter to NJCLD member organizations]

Neisser, U. (1967). *Cognitive psychology*. New York: Appleton-Century-Crofts.

Neisser, U. (1976). General, academic and artificial intelligence. In L. Resnick (Ed.), *The nature of intelligence* (pp. 135–144). Hillsdale, NJ: Erlbaum.

Nelson, C. M., & Rutherford, R. B. (1985). Timeout revisited: Guidelines for its use in special education. *Exceptional Education Quarterly*, 3, 56–67.

Nelson, H. E. (1980). Analysis of spelling errors in normal and dyslexic children. In U. Frith (Ed.), *Cognitive process in spelling* (pp. 475–493). New York: Academic Press.

Nelson, M. C. (1988). Social skills training for mildly handicapped students. *Teaching Exceptional Children*, 20(4), 19–23.

Neufeld, H. H. (1982). *Reading, writing, and algorithms: Computer literacy in the schools*. Paper presented at the Annual Meeting of the Claremont Reading Conference. (ERIC Document Reproduction Service, ED 211 459).

Newcomer, P. L. (1989). The new, improved holy grail. *Learning Disability Quarterly*, 12, 154–155.

Newcomer, P. L., & Hammill, D. D. (1975). ITPA and academic achievement. *The Reading Teacher*, 28, 731–741.

Newell, A. (1979). One final word. In D. T. Tuma & J. Reid (Eds.), *Problem solving and education: Issues in teaching and research* (pp. 175–189). Hillsdale, NJ: Erlbaum.

Newland, T. E. (1932). An analytical study of the development of illegibilities in handwriting from the lower grades to adulthood. *Journal of Educational Research*, 26, 249–258.

Newman, B. M., & Newman, P. R. (1986). *Adolescent development*. Columbus, OH: Merrill/Macmillan.

Ninness, H. A., & Glenn, S. S. (1988). *Applied behavior analysis and school psychology*. New York: Greenwood Press.

Nodine, B. F., Barenbaum, E., & Newcomer, P. (1985). Story composition by learning disabled, reading disabled, and normal children. *Learning Disability Quarterly*, 8, 167–181.

Noland, E. C., & Schuldt, W. J. (1971). Sustained attention and reading retardation. *Journal of Experimental Education*, 40(2), 73–76.

Oakland, J., & Matuzek, P. (1977). Using tests in nondiscriminatory assessment. In J. Oakland (Ed.), *Psychological and educational assessment of minority children* (pp. 52–69). New York: Brunner/Mazel.

O'Connor, T. (1984). Adolescent development and the learning disabled teenager: Implications for the classroom teacher. *English Journal*, 73(8), 33–35.

Oden, S., & Asher, S. (1977). Coaching children in social skills for friendship making. *Child Development*, 48, 495–506.

Okolo, C. M., & Sitlington, P. (1986). The role of special education in LD adolescents' transition from school to work. *Learning Disability Quarterly, 9*(2), 141–155.

O'Leary, K. D., & Drabman, R. (1971). Token reinforcement programs in the classroom: A review. *Psychological Bulletin, 75*, 379–398.

Olofsson, A., & Lundberg, I. (1982). *Can phonemic awareness be trained in kindergarten?* Unpublished manuscript. University of Umea, Sweden.

Olsen, J. L., Wong, B. Y. L., & Marx, R. W. (1983). Linguistic and metacognitive aspects of normal achieving and learning disabled children's communication process. *Learning Disability Quarterly, 6*, 289–304.

Orton, S. T. (1928). Specific reading disability—strephosymbolia. *Journal of the American Medical Association, 90*, 1095–1099.

Orton, S. T. (1937). *Reading, writing and speech problems in children.* New York: Norton.

Osgood, C. E. (1953). *Method and theory in experimental psychology.* New York: Oxford University Press.

Osgood, C. E. (1957). Motivational dynamics of language behavior. In M. Jones (Ed.), *Nebraska symposium on motivation* (pp. 348–424). Lincoln: University of Nebraska Press.

Osgood, C. E. (1963). Psycholinguistics. In S. Koch (Ed.), *Psychology: A study of a science* (Vol. 6, pp. 224–316). New York: McGraw-Hill.

Osguthorpe, R. (1984). Handicapped students as tutors for non-handicapped peers. *Academic Therapy, 19*(4), 473–483.

O'Sullivan, J. T., & Pressley, M. (1984). Completeness of instruction and strategy transfer. *Journal of Educational Psychology, 38*, 275–288.

Otto, W., McMenemy, R. M., & Smith, R. J. (1973). *Corrective and remedial teaching* (2nd ed.). Boston: Houghton Mifflin.

Outhred, L. (1989). Word processing: Its impact on children's writing. *Journal of Learning Disabilities, 22*(4), 262–264.

Owen, F. W. (1978). Dyslexia: Genetic aspects. In A. L. Benton & D. Pearl (Eds.), *Dyslexia: An appraisal of current knowledge* (pp. 265–284). New York: Oxford University Press.

Owen, F. W., Adams, P. A., Forrest, T., Stolz, L. M., & Fisher, S. (1971). Learning disorders in children: Sibling studies. *Monographs of the Society for Research in Child Development, 36* (Serial No. 144).

Owings, R. A., Peterson, G. A., Bransford, J. D., Morris, C. D., & Stein, B. S. (1980). Spontaneous monitoring and regulations of learning: A comparison of successful and less successful fifth graders. *Journal of Educational Psychology, 72*, 117–175.

Palincsar, A. S. (1986). Metacognitive strategy instruction. *Exceptional Children, 53*(2), 118–124.

Palincsar, A. S., & Brown, A. L. (1984). Reciprocal teaching of comprehension-fostering and monitoring activities. *Cognition and Instruction, 1*, 117–175.

Palincsar, A. S., & Brown, A. L. (1986). Interactive teaching to promote independent reading from text. *Reading Teacher, 39*(8), 771–777.

Palincsar, A. S., & Brown, D. A. (1987). Enhancing instructional time through attention to metacognition. *Journal of Learning Disabilities, 20*(2), 66–75.

Palincsar, A. S., Brown, A. L., & Campione, J. C. (1991). Dynamic assessment. In H. L. Swanson (Ed.), *Handbook on the assessment of learning disabilities: Theory, research, and practice* (pp. 75–94). Austin, TX: PRO-ED.

Palmer, J. (1985). Youth in transition: What parents should know. *The Exceptional Parent, 15,* 10–17.

Paolucci-Whitcomb, P., & Nevin, A. (1985). Preparing consulting teachers through a collaborative approach between university faculty and field based consulting teachers. *Teacher Education and Special Education, 8*(3), 132–143.

Paris, S. G., Cross, D. R., & Lipson, M. Y. (1984). Informed strategies for learning: A program to improve children's reading awareness and comprehension. *Journal of Educational Psychology, 76,* 1239–1252.

Paris, S. G., Lipson, M. Y., & Wixson, K. K. (1983). Becoming a strategic reader. *Contemporary Educational Psychology, 8,* 293–316.

Paris, S. G., & Myers, M. (1981). Comprehension monitoring, memory, and study strategies of good and poor readers. *Journal of Reading Behavior, 13,* 5–22.

Paris, S. G., & Oka, E. R. (1989). Strategies for comprehending text and coping with reading difficulties. *Learning Disability Quarterly, 12*(1), 32–42.

Parker, C. (1975). *Psychological consultation in the schools: Helping teachers meet special needs.* Reston, VA: Council for Exceptional Children.

Parrill-Burnstein, M. (1981). *Problem solving and learning disabilities: An information processing approach.* New York: Grune & Stratton.

Pasamanick, B., & Knobloch, H . (1960). Brain damage and reproductive causality. *American Journal of Orthopsychiatry, 30,* 229–305.

Pasamanick, B., & Knobloch, H. (1973). The epidemiology of reproductive causality. In S. G. Sapir & A. C. Nitzburg (Eds.), *Children with learning problems* (pp. 193–199). New York: Brunner/Mazel.

Pasternack, R., & Lyon, K. (1982). Clinical and empirical identification of learning disabled juvenile delinquents. *Journal of Correctional Education, 33*(2), 7–13.

Paul, J. L. (1987). Defining behavioral disorders in children. In B. C. Epanchin & J. L. Paul (Eds.), *Emotional problems of childhood and adolescence* (pp. 15–29). Columbus, OH: Merrill/Macmillan.

Payan, R. (1984). Language assessment for bilingual exceptional children. In L. M. Baca & H. T. Cervantes (Eds.), *The bilingual special education interface* (pp. 125–137). St. Louis, MO: The Mirror/Mosby.

Pearson, P. D., Hansen, J., & Gordon, C. (1979). The effect of background knowledge on young children's comprehension of explicit and implicit information. *Journal of Reading Behavior, 11,* 201–210.

Pearson, P. D., & Johnson, D. D. (1978). *Teaching reading comprehension.* New York: Rinehart & Winston.

Peck, D. G. (1981). Adolescent self-esteem, emotional learning disabilities, and significant others. *Adolescence, 16*(62), 443–451.

Perlmutter, B. F., Crocker, J., Cordray, D., & Garstecki, D. (1983). Sociometric status and related personality characteristics of mainstreamed learning disabled adolescents. *Learning Disability Quarterly, 6,* 20–30.

Perosa, L. M., & Perosa, S. L. (1981). The school counselor use of structured family therapy with learning disabled students. *School Counselor, 29*(2), 152–159.

Personke, C. R., & Yee, A. H. (1971). *Comprehensive spelling instruction: Theory, research, and application.* Scranton, PA: Index Educational Publishers.

Peterson, D., Mercer, C. D., & O'Shea, L. (1988). Teaching learning disabled students place value using the concrete to abstract sequence. *Learning Disabilities Research, 4*(1), 52–56.

Pfeiffer, S. I. (1980). The school-based interprofessional team: Recurring problems and some possible solutions. *Journal of School Psychology, 18,* 388–394.

Pfeiffer, S. I. (1981a). The problems facing multidisciplinary teams: As perceived by team members. *Psychology in the Schools, 18,* 330–333.

Pfeiffer, S. I. (1981b). Multidisciplinary team and nondiscriminatory assessment. *Arizona Personnel and Guidance Journal, 7*(1), 22–23.

Pfeiffer, S. I. (1982a). The superiority of team decision making. *Exceptional Children, 49,* 68–69.

Pfeiffer, S. I. (1982b). Special education placement decisions made by teams and individuals: A cross-cultural perspective. *Psychology in the Schools, 19,* 335–340.

Pflaum, S. W., & Pasarella, E. T. (1980). Interactive effects of prior reading achievement and training in context on the reading of learning disabled children. *Reading Research Quarterly, 16*(1), 138–158).

Piaget, J. (1926). *The language and thought of the child.* New York: Harcourt Brace.

Piaget, J. (1952). *The origins of intelligence.* New York: International University Press.

Piaget, J. (1963). *The origins of intelligence in children.* New York: Norton.

Piaget, J. (1966). *Judgment and reasoning in the child.* New Jersey: Littlefield, Adams.

Piaget, J. (1967). Development and learning. In E. Victor & M. S. Lerner (Eds.), *Readings in science education for the elementary school* (pp. 321–334). New York: Macmillan.

Piaget, J. (1970). Piaget's theory. In P. Mussen (Ed.), *Carmichael's manual of child psychology* (3rd ed., pp. 703–732). New York: Wiley.

Pihl, R. O., & McLarnon, L. (1984). Learning disabled children as adolescents. *Journal of Learning Disabilities, 17*(2), 96–100.

Plata, M. (1982). *Assessment, placement, programing of bilingual exceptional pupils: Practical approach.* Reston, VA: Council for Exceptional Children.

Platt, J., Wienke, W., & Tunich, R. (1982). The need for training in special education for correctional educators. *Journal of Correctional Education, 32*(4), 8–12.

Podboy, J. W., & Mallory, W. A. (1978). The diagnosis of specific learning disabilities in a juvenile delinquent population. *Federal Probation, 42,* 26–32.

Policy paper. (1980, April 30). Washington, DC: United States Department of Education.

Polloway, E. A. (1984). The integration of mildly retarded students in the schools: A historical review. *Remedial and Special Education, 5*(4), 18–28.

Popham, W. J. (1966). *Systematic instructional decision making.* Los Angeles, CA: Vimcet Associates.

Popham, W. J. (1974). An approaching peril: Cloud-referenced tests. *Phi Delta Kappan, 55*, 614–615.

Popham, W. J. (1978). *Criterion-referenced measurement.* Englewood Cliffs, NJ: Prentice-Hall.

Poplin, M. S., Gray, R., Larsen, S., Banikowski, A., & Mehring, T. (1980). A comparison of components of written expression abilities in learning disabled and non-learning disabled children at three grade levels. *Learning Disability Quarterly, 3,* 46–53.

Poteet, J. A. (1978). *Characteristics of written expression of learning disabled and non-learning disabled elementary school students.* Muncie, IN: Ball State University. (ERIC Document Reproduction Service No. ED 159 830)

Preiser, W. F. E., & Taylor, A. (1983). The habitability framework: Linking human behavior and physical environment in special education. *Exceptional Education Quarterly, 4*(2), 1–15.

Premack, D. (1965). Reinforcement theory. In D. Levine (Ed.), *Nebraska symposium on motivation* (pp. 123–180). Lincoln: University of Nebraska Press.

Pressley, M., Borkowski, J. G., & O'Sullivan, J. T. (1985). Children's metamemory and the teaching of memory strategies. In D. L. Forrest-Pressley, G. E. MacKinnon, & T. G. Waller (Eds.), *Metacognition, cognition, and human performance* (pp. 111–153). New York: Academic Press.

Pressley, M., Symons, S., Snyder, B. L., & Cariglia-Bull, T. (1989). Strategy instruction research comes of age. *Learning Disability Quarterly, 12*(1), 32–42.

Prout, H. T. (1981). The incidence of suspected exceptional education needs among youth in juvenile facilities. *Journal of Correctional Education, 32*(4), 22–24.

Pryzwansky, N. W. B. (1981). Mandated team participation: Implications for psychologists working in the schools. *Psychology in the School, 18,* 460–466.

Rabinowitz, M., & Chi, M. T. H. (1987). An interactive model of strategic processing. In S. J. Ceci (Ed.), *Handbook of cognitive, social, and neuropsychological aspects of learning disabilities* (Vol. 2, pp. 83–102). Hillsdale, NJ: Erlbaum.

Ragghianti, S., & Miller, R. (1982). The microcomputer and special education management. *Exceptional Children, 49*(2), 131–135.

Ranking, E., & Culhane, J. (1969). Comparable cloze and multiple-choice comprehension test scores. *Journal of Reading, 13,* 193–198.

Raphael, T. E., Kirschner, B. M., & Englert, C. S. (1989). Student's metacognitive knowledge about writing. *Research in the Teaching of English, 23,* 343–379.

Rappaport, P., & Savard, W. G. (1980). *Computer assisted instruction.* Research on school effectiveness project: Topics summary report. (ERIC Document Reproduction Service, ED 214 707)

Raver, S. A. (1991). *Strategies for teaching at-risk and handicapped infants and toddlers: A transdisciplinary approach.* New York: Macmillan.

Redl, F. (1959a). The concept of life space interview. *American Journal of Orthopsychiatry, 24,* 1–18.

Redl, F. (1959b). The concept of a therapeutic milieu. *American Journal of Orthopsychiatry, 24,* 721–734.

Reid, D. K. (1988). *Teaching the learning disabled.* Boston: Allyn & Bacon.

Reid, D. K., & Borkowski, G. J. (1987). Causal attributions of hyperactive children: Implications for teaching strategies and self-control. *Journal of Educational Psychology, 79,* 296–307.

Reinert, H. R. (1980). *Children in conflict* (2nd ed.). St. Louis: Mosby.

Reinert, H. R., & Huang, A. (1987). *Children in conflict* (3rd ed.). Columbus, OH: Merrill/Macmillan.

Report of the Joint Committee on Health Problems in Education (1939). Washington, DC: National Education Association.

Reynolds, C. R. (1984–1985). Critical measurement issues in learning disabilities. *Journal of Special Education, 18*(4).

Reynolds, M. C., & Birch, J. W. (1982). *Teaching exceptional children in all America's schools.* Reston, VA: The Council for Exceptional Children.

Reynolds, M. C., Wang, M. C., & Walberg, H. J. (in press). The knowledge bases for special and general education. *Remedial and Special Education (RASE).*

Rezmierski, V., & Kotre, J. (1972). A limited literature review of theory of the psychodynamic model. In W. C. Rhodes & M. L. Tracy (Eds.), *A study of child variance* (pp. 181–258). Ann Arbor: University of Michigan Press.

Rezmierski, V., Knoblock, P., & Bloom, R. B. (1982). The psychoeducational model: Theory and historical perspective. In R. L. McDowell, G. W. Adamson, & F. H. Wood (Eds.), *Teaching emotionally disturbed children* (pp. 47–69). Boston, MA: Little, Brown.

Richards, G. P., Samuels, S. J., Turnure, J. E., & Ysseldyke, J. E. (1990). Sustained and selective attention in children with learning disabilities. *Journal of Learning Disabilities, 23*(2), 129–136.

Richardson, S. O., Kloss, J. L., & Timmons, D. (1971). The parents talk to doctors. In J. I. Arena (Ed.), *The child with learning disabilities, his right to learn.* Selected papers on learning disabilities, Eighth annual international conference of the Association for Children with Learning Disabilities. Pittsburgh: Association for Children with Learning Disabilities.

Richey, D. D., & McKinney, J. D. (1978). Classroom behavior styles of learning disabled children. *Journal of Learning Disabilities, 11,* 38–43.

Rigney, J. W. (1980). Cognitive learning strategies and dualities in information processing. In R. E. Snow & W. E. Montague (Eds.), *Aptitude, learning, and instruction* (Vol. 1, pp. 315–343). Hillsdale, NJ: Erlbaum.

Roach, E., & Kephart, N. C. (1966). *Purdue perceptual-motor survey.* Columbus, OH: Merrill/Macmillan.

Roach, J., Paolucci-Whitcomb, P., Meyers, H., & Duncan, D. (1983). Comparative effects of peer tutoring in math by and for secondary special needs students. *Pointer, 27*(4), 20–24.

Robinson, M. E., & Schwartz, L. B. (1973). Visuo-motor skills and reading ability: A longitudinal study. *Developmental Medicine and Child Neurology, 15,* 281–286.

Robinson, S. L., & DePascale, C., & Roberts, F. C. (1989). Computer-delivered feedback in group-based instruction: Effects for learning disabled students in mathematics. *Learning Disabilities Focus, 5*(1), 28–35.

Rodriguez, R. F., Perieto, A. G., & Rueda, R. S. (1984). Issues in bilingual/multicultural special education. *National Association of Bilingual Education Journal, 8,* 55–65.

Rogers, H., & Saklofske, D. H. (1985). Self-concept, locus of control and performance expectations of learning disabled children. *Journal of Learning Disabilities, 18,* 273–278.

Rogers-Warren, A. K. (1977). Planned change: Ecobehaviorally based interventions. In A. Rogers-Warren & S. F. Warren (Eds.), *Ecological perspectives in behavior analysis* (pp. 197–210). Baltimore, MD: University Park Press.

Rogers-Warren, A. K. (1984). Ecobehavioral analysis. *Education and Treatment of Children, 7,* 283–303.

Rose, K. (1982). *Teaching language arts to children.* New York: Harcourt Brace Jovanovich.

Rosenshine, B. (1976). Classroom instruction. In N. Gage (Ed.), *The psychology of teaching methods* (Vol. 75, Pt. 1, pp. 335–371). Chicago, IL: University of Chicago Press.

Rosenthal, I. (1985). A career development program for learning disabled college students. *Journal of Counseling and Development, 63,* 308–310.

Rosenthal, I. (1986). New directions for service delivery to learning disabled youth and young adults. *Learning Disabilities Focus, 2*(1), 55–61.

Ross, A. O. (1976). *Psychological aspects of learning disabilities and reading disorders.* New York: McGraw-Hill.

Ross, D. M., & Ross, S. A. (1982). *Hyperactivity: Current issues, research, and therapy.* New York: Wiley.

Rude, R. T., & Oehlkers, W. J. (1984). *Helping students with reading problems.* Englewood Cliffs, NJ: Prentice-Hall.

Rueda, R. (1989). Refining mild disabilities with language-minority students. *Exceptional Children, 56*(2), 121–128.

Rusch, F. R., & Phelps, L. A. (1987). Secondary special education and transition from school to work: A national priority. *Exceptional Children, 53*(6), 487–492.

Russell, R. L., & Ginsburg, H. P. (1984). Cognitive analysis of children's mathematics difficulties. *Cognition and Instruction, 2,* 217–244.

Rust, J. O., Miller, L. S., & Wilson, W. H. (1978). Using a control group to evaluate a resource room program. *Psychology in the School, 15,* 503–506.

Ryan, D. (1984). Mainstreaming isn't just for students anymore. *Journal of Learning Disabilities, 17*(3), 167–169.

Sabatino, D. A. (1971). An evaluation of resource rooms for children with learning disabilities. *Journal of Learning Disabilities, 4,* 84–93.

Sabatino, D. A. (1981a). Secondary and postsecondary educational aspects of the learning disabled. In D. A. Sabatino, T. L. Miller, & C. Schmidt (Eds.), *Learning disabilities: Systematic teaching and service delivery* (pp. 385–460). Rockville, MD: Aspen.

Sabatino, D. A. (1981b). Are appropriate educational programs operationally achievable under mandated promises of P.L. 94–142? *Journal of Special Education, 15*(1), 9–23.

Sabatino, D. A., & Mauser, A. J. (1978). *Specialized education in today's secondary schools.* Boston: Allyn & Bacon.

Sabatino, D. A., Miller, T. L., & Schmidt, C. R. (1981). *Learning disabilities.* Rockville, MD: Aspen.

Sabatino, D. A., Sabatino, A. C., & Lester, M. (1983). *Discipline and behavioral management.* Rockville, MD: Aspen.

Salend, S. J., Brooks, L., & Salend, S. M. (1985). Identifying school districts policies for implementing mainstreaming. *The Pointer, 32*(1), 34–37.

Salend, S. J., & Lutz, J. G. (1984). Mainstreaming or mainlining: A competency-based approach to mainstreaming. *Journal of Learning Disabilities, 17,* 27–29.

Salend, S. J., & Salend, S. M. (1986). Competencies for mainstreaming secondary level learning disabled students. *Journal of Learning Disabilities, 19*(2), 91–94.

Salvia, J., & Ysseldyke, J. E. (1985). *Assessment in special and remedial education.* Boston, MA: Houghton Mifflin.

Samuels, S. J. (1987). Information processing abilities and reading. *Journal of Learning Disabilities, 20*(1), 18–22.

Sanacore, J. (1984). Metacognition and the improvement of reading: Some important links. *Journal of Reading, 27,* 706–712.

Sapir, (1985). *The clinical teaching model.* New York: Brunner/Mazel.

Sargent, L. R. (1981). Resource teacher time utilization. *Exceptional Children, 47*(6), 420–425.

Satz, P., & Van Nostrand, G. K. (1973). Developmental dyslexia: An evaluation of a theory. In P. Satz & J. Russ (Eds.), *The disabled learner: Early detection and intervention* (pp 121–148). Rotterdam: Rotterdam University Press.

Sawicki, D., & Schaeffer, B. (1979). An affirmative approach to the LD\JD link. *Juvenile and Family Court Journal, 30*(2), 11–16.

Scardamalia, M., & Bereiter, C. (1985). Helping students become better writers. *School Administrator, 24*(4), 16–26.

Schank, R. C., & Abelson, R. P. (1977). *Scripts, plans, goals, and understanding.* Hillsdale, NJ: Erlbaum.

Schiffman, G., Tobin, D., & Buchanan, D. (1982). Microcomputer instruction for the learning disabled. *Journal of Learning Disabilities, 15,* 557–561.

Schloss, P. J. (1984). *Social development of handicapped children and adolescents.* Rockville, MD: Aspen.

Schmidt, M., Weinstein, T., Niemic, R., & Walberg, H. J. (1985–1986). Computer-assisted instruction with exceptional children. *Journal of Special Education, 19*(4), 493–501.

Schniedewind, N., & Salend, S. J. (1987, Winter). Cooperative learning works. *Teaching Exceptional Children,* pp. 22–25.

Schultz, J. B., Carpenter, C. D., & Turnbull, A. P. (1991). *Mainstreaming exceptional students: A guide for classroom teachers.* Boston, MA: Allyn & Bacon.

Schultz, J. B., & Turnbull, A. P. (1984). *Mainstreaming handicapped students.* Boston: Allyn & Bacon.

Schulze, A. K., Rule, S., & Innocent, M. S. (1989). Coincidental teaching: Parents promoting social skills at home. *Teaching Exceptional Children, 21*(2), 24–27.

Schumaker, J. B., Denton, P. H., & Deshler, D. D. (1984). *Learning strategies curriculum: The paraphrasing strategy.* Lawrence, KS: University of Kansas.

Schumaker, J. B., & Deshler, D. D. (1984). Setting demand variables: A major factor in program planning for LD adolescents. *Topics in Language Disorders Journnal, 4,* 22–40.

Schumaker, J. B., & Deshler, D. D. (1988). Implementing the regular education initiative in secondary schools: A different ball game. *Journal of Learning Disabilities, 21*(1), 36–42.

Schumaker, J. B., Deshler, D. D., Alley, G. R., & Warner, M. M. (1983). Toward the development of an intervention model for learning disabled adolescents. *Exceptional Education Quarterly, 4*(1), 45–74.

Schumaker, J., Deshler, D., Alley, G., Warner, M., & Denton, P. (1984). Multipass: A learning strategy for improving reading comprehension. *Learning Disability Quarterly, 5*(2), 295–304.

Schumaker, J. B., Deshler, D. D., & Denton, P. H. (1984). An integrated system for providing content to learning disabled adolescents using audio tape format. In W. M. Cruickshank & J. M. Kliebhan (Eds.), *The best of ACLD: Vol. 5. Early adolescence to early adulthood* (pp. 79–113). Syracuse, NY: Syracuse University Press.

Schumaker, J. B., Deshler, D. D., & Ellis, E. S. (1986). Intervention issues related to the education of LD adolescents. In J. Torgesen & B. Wong (Eds.), *Psychological and educational perspectives on learning disabilities* (pp. 329–366). New York: Academic.

Schumaker, J. B., & Ellis, E. (1982). Social skills training of LD adolescents: A generalization study. *Learning Disability Quarterly, 5,* 409–414.

Schumaker, J. B., & Hazel, J. S. (1988). Social skills training. In K. A. Kavale, S. R. Forness, & M. Bender (Eds.), *Handbook of learning disabilities: Vol. 2. Methods and interventions* (pp. 111–153). Boston, MA: Little, Brown.

Schumaker, J. B., Pederson, C. S., Hazel, J. S., & Meyen, E. L. (1983). Social skills curricula for mildly handicapped adolescents: A review. *Focus on Exceptional Children, 16*(4), 1–16.

Schumaker, J. B., & Sheldon, J. (1985). *Learning strategies curriculum: The sentence writing strategy (Instructor's Manual).* Lawrence, KS: University of Kansas.

Schunk, D. H., & Rice, J. H. (1987). Enhancing comprehension skills and self-efficacy with strategy value information. *Journal of Reading Behavior, 3,* 285–302.

Scruggs, T. (1988). Nature of learning disabilities. In K. A. Kavale (Ed.), *Learning disabilities: State of the art and practice* (pp. 22–43). Boston: Little, Brown.

Scruggs, T., & Osguthorpe, R. (1985). *Tutoring interventions within special education: A comparison of cross age and peer tutoring.* Paper presented at the Annual Conference of the Council for Exceptional Children, Anaheim, CA. [ERIC Document Reproduction Service No. ED 258 419]

Seligman, M. E. P. (1975). *Helplessness: On depression, development and death.* San Francisco: Freeman.

Semmel, M. I., Abernathy, T. V., Butera, G., & Lesar, S. (1991). Teacher perceptions of the regular education initiative. *Exceptional Children, 58*(1), 9–24.

Semmel, M. I., & Bellard-Campbell, M. (1982, January). *Role delineation of the program specialist under the California Master Plan for Special Education.* Prepared under Grant No.42-3008-80-3293-7100 from the California State Department of Education, University of California, Santa Barbara.

Senf, G. M. (1972). An information-integration theory and its application to normal reading acquisition and reading disability. In N. D. Bryant & C. E. Kass (Eds.), *Leadership training institute in learning disabilities, Final report, Vol. 2* (pp. 305–391). Tuscon: University of Arizona.

Seguin, E. (1866). *Idiocy: Its treatment by the psychological method.* New York: William Wood.

Sever, J. (1985). Maternal infections. In C. C. Brown (Ed.), *Childhood learning disabilities and prenatal risk: An interdisciplinary data review for health care professionals and parents* (pp. 31–38). Skillman, NJ: Johnson & Johnson.

Shankweiler, D., & Liberman, I. Y. (1976). Exploring the relations between reading and speech. In R. M. Knights & D. J. Bakker (Eds.), *Neuropsychology of learning disorders: Theoretical approaches* (pp. 297–313). Baltimore: University Park Press.

Shaywitz, S. E., & Shaywitz, B. A. (1988). Attention deficit disorder: Current perspectives. In J. E. Kavanagh & J. Truss (Eds.), *Learning disabilities: Proceedings of the national conference* (pp. 369–546). Parkton, MD: York Press.

Shea, T. M., & Bauer, A. M. (1987). *Teaching children and youth with behavior disorders* (2nd ed.). Englewood Cliffs, NJ: Prentice-Hall.

Sheldon, J., Sherman, J. A., Schumaker, J. B., & Hazel, J. S. (1983). *Developing a social skills curriculum for mildly handicapped adolescents and young adults: Some problems and approaches.* Paper presented at the Minnesota Conference on Programing for the developmental needs of adolescents with behavioral disorders, Minneapolis. [ERIC Document Service no. EC 170 415].

Short, E. J., & Ryan, E. B. (1984). Metacognitive differences between skilled and less skilled readers: Remediating deficits through story grammar and attribution training. *Journal of Educational Psychology, 76,* 225–235.

Shrauger, J. S., & Osberg, T. M. (1982). Self-awareness: The ability to predict one's future behavior. In G. Underwood (Ed.), *Aspects of consciousness* (Vol. 3, pp. 267–313). New York: Academic Press.

Shuard, H. (1984). Contemporary trends in primary-school mathematics: Implications for teacher education. In R. Morris (Ed.), *Studies in mathematics education* (Vol. 3, pp. 23–50). UNESCO.

Siegel, E., & Gold, R. (1982). *Educating the learning disabled.* New York: Macmillan.

Siegel, M., & Clapp, E. (1981). *The development of plato computer-based instruction for the severly and profoundly developmentally disabled.* Illinois University, Urbana. Computer-based education research lab. (ERIC Document Reproduction Service ED 271 644)

Silver, L. B. (1988). A review of the federal government's Interagency Committee of Learning Disabilities Report to the U.S. Congress. *Learning Disabilities Focus, 3*(2), 73–80.

Silver, L. B. (1990). Attention deficit-hyperactivity disorder: It is a learning disability or a related disorder? *Journal of Learning Disabilities, 23*(7), 394–397.

Silver, L. B. (1991). The regular education initiative: A deja vu remembered with sadness and concern. *Journal of Learning Disabilities, 24*(7), 389–390.

Simeonsson, R. J. (1986). *Psychological and developmental assessment of special children.* Boston, MA: Allyn & Bacon.

Sinatra, R. C., Berg, D., & Dunn, R. (1985). Semantic mapping improves reading comprehension of learning disabled students. *Teaching Exceptional Children, 17*(4), 310–314.

Siperstein, G. N., Bopp, M. J., & Bak, J. (1978). Social status of learning disabled children. *Journal of Learning Disabilities, 11,* 98–102.

Siperstein, G. N., & Goding, M. J. (1983). Social integration of learning disabled children in regular classrooms. In K. Gadow & I. Bialer (Eds.), *Advances in learning and behavioral disabilities* (Vol. 2, pp. 227–264). Greenwich, CT: JAI Press.

Sisterhen, D. H., & Gerber, P. J. (1989). Auditory, visual, and multisensory nonverbal social perception in adolescents with and without learning disabilities. *Journal of Learning Disabilities, 22*(4), 245–259.

Sitko, M. C., & Gillespie, P. H. (1978). Language and speech difficulties. In L. Mann, L. Goodman, & J. L. Wiederholt (Eds.), *Teaching the learning disabled adolescent* (pp. 135–168). Boston: Houghton-Mifflin.

Skeels, H. M. (1966). Adult status of children with contrasting early life experience. *Monographs of the Society for Research in Child Development, 31*(3).

Skinner, B. F. (1938). *The behavior of organisms.* New York: D. Appleton Century.

Skinner, B. F. (1953). *Science and human behavior.* New York: Macmillan.

Skinner, B. F. (1961). *Are theories of learning necessary?* New York: Appleton-Century-Crofts.

Skinner, B. F. (1966). Operant behavior. In W. K. Honig (Ed.), *Operant behavior: Areas of research and application* (pp. 12–32). New York: Appleton-Century-Crofts.

Skinner, B. F. (1968a). *The technology of teaching.* New York: Appleton.

Skinner, B. F. (1968b). What is the experimental analysis of behavior? *Journal of Experimental Analysis of Behavior, 9*(3), 213–218.

Skrtic, T. M. (1987). An organizational analysis of special educational reform. *Counterpoint, 8*(2), 15–19.

Smiley, S. S., Oakley, D. D., Worthen, D., Campione, J. C., & Brown, A. L. (1977). Recall of thematically relevant materials of adolescent good and poor readers as a function of written versus oral presentation. *Journal of Educational Psychology, 69,* 381–388.

Smith, B. (1973). Is psychology relevant to new priorities? *American Pscyhologist, 28,* 463–471.

Smith, C. R. (1983). *Learning disabilities: The interaction of learner, task, and setting.* Boston: Little, Brown.

Smith, C. R. (1986). The future of the LD field: Intervention approaches. *Journal of Learning Disabilities, 19*(3), 461–472.

Smith, G. (1983). *Parallel alternate curriculum—a mainstreaming implementation program at the secondary level: Alternative teaching strategies combined with basic skills* (Report No. 229–964). Detroit, MI: Paper presented at the annual international convention of the council for exceptional children.

Smith, G. (1988). *The parallel alternative curriculum program: A secondary level mainstreaming program.* Mesa, AZ: Mesa Public Schools.

Smith, G., & Smith, D. (1985). A mainstreaming program that really works. *Journal of Learning Disabilities, 18*(6).

Smith, N. B. (1969). The many faces of reading comprehension. *Reading Teacher, 23*(3), 249–259.

Smith, P. L., & Friend, M. (1986). Training learning disabled adolescents in a strategy for using text structure to aid recall of instructional prose. *Learning Disabilities Research, 2*(1), 38–44.

Smith, R. J., & Johnson, O. D. (1980). *Teaching children to read.* Reading, MA: Addison-Wesley.

Smith, S. D., & Pennington, B. F. (1987). Genetic influences. In K. A. Kavale, S. R. Forness, & M. Bender (Eds.), *Handbook of learning disabilities: Vol. 1. Dimensions and diagnosis* (pp. 49–75). San Diego, CA: College-Hill.

Snowling, M. J. (1985). *Children's written language difficulties.* Windsor: NFER-Nelson Publishing.

Souviney, R. J. (1984). Working story problems. In R. Morris (Ed.), *Studies in mathematics education* (Vol. 3, pp. 145–151). UNESCO.

Sowell, P., Parker, R., Poplin, M., & Larsen, S. (1979). The effects of psycholinguistic training on improving psycholinguistic skills. *Learning Disability Quarterly, 2,* 69–77.

Spache, G. D. (1963). *Toward better reading.* Champaign, IL: Gerrard Press.

Spiro, O., & Myers, A. (1984). Individual differences and underlying cognitive processes. In P. D. Pearson (Ed.), *Handbook of reading research* (pp. 471–504). New York: Longman.

Spitzer, R. (1975). Taking the pressure off. *Journal of Reading, 19,* 198–200.

Spreen, O. (1981). The relationship between learning disabilities, neurological impairment, and delinquency: Results of a followup study. *Journal of Nervous and Mental Disease, 169*(12), 791–799.

Stainback, S., & Stainback, W. (1988). Letter to the editor. *Journal of Learning Disabilities, 21,* 452–453.

Stainback, W., & Stainback, S. (1984). A rationale for the merger of special and regular education. *Exceptional Children, 51*(2), 102–111.

Stainback, W., Stainback, S., Courtnace, L., & Jaben, T. (1985). Facilitating mainstreaming by modifying the mainstream. *Exceptional Children, 52*(2), 144–152.

Stanovich, K. E. (1980). Toward an interactive-compensatory model of individual differences in the development of reading fluency. *Reading Research Quarterly, 16,* 32–71.

Stanovich, K. E. (1986). Explaining the variance in reading ability in terms of psychological processes: What have we learned? *Annals of Dyslexia, 35,* 67–96.

Stein, N. L., & Glenn, C. G. (1978). An analysis of story comprehension in elementary school children. In R. O. Freedle (Ed.), *New directions in discourse processing* (Vol. 2, pp. 53–120). Norwood, NJ: Ablex.

Sternberg, R. J. (1987). A unified theory of intellectual exceptionality. In J. C. Day & J. G. Borkowski (Eds.), *Intelligence and exceptionality: New directions for theory, assessment, and instructional practices* (pp. 135–172). Norwood, NJ: Ablex.

Sternig-Babcock, S. H. (1987). *Learning disabilities and juvenile delinquency: Prevalence, family, schooling, and delinquency characteristics.* Unpublished doctoral dissertation, California State University-University of California, Los Angeles.

Stevens, G. D., & Birch, J. W. (1957). A proposal for clarification of the terminology used to describe brain-injured children. *Exceptional Children, 23,* 346–349.

Stevens, R. J. (1988). Effects of strategy training on the identification of the main idea of expository passages. *Journal of Educational Psychology, 80,* 21–26.

Stewart, O., & Tei, E. (1983). Some implications of metacognition for reading instruction. *Journal of Reading, 27,* 36–43.

Stone, W. L., & LaGreca, A. M. (1990). The social status of children with learning disabilities: A reexamination. *Journal of Learning Disabilities, 23*(1), 32–37.

Strain, P., & Odum, S. (1986). Peer social imitations: Effective intervention for social skills development of exceptional children. *Exceptional Children, 52*(6), 543–551.

Strang, R. (1978). The nature of reading. In J. Chapman & P. Czerniewska (Eds.), *Reading from process to practice* (pp. 61–94). London: Routledge & Kegan in association with Open University Press.

Strauss, A. A., & Kephart, N. C. (1955). *Psychopathology and education of the brain-injured child: Vol. II. Progress in theory and clinic.* New York: Grune & Stratton.

Strauss, A. A., & Lehtinen, L. E. (1947). *Psychopathology and education of the brain-injured child.* New York: Grune & Stratton.

Strauss, A. A., & Werner, H. (1943). Comparative psychopathology of the brain-injured child and the traumatic brain-injured adult. *American Journal of Psychiatry, 99,* 835–838.

Streissguth, A. (1983). Smoking and drinking. In C. C. Brown (Ed.), *Childhood learning disabilities and prenatal risk: An interdisciplinary data review for health care professionals and parents* (pp. 49–56). Skillman, NJ: Johnson & Johnson.

Super, D. E. (1976). Career education and the meanings of work. *Monographs on career education.* United States Department of Health, Education and Welfare, U.S. Office of Education.

Swanson, H. L. (Ed.). (1982a). Controversy: Strategy or capacity deficit [Special issue]. *Topics in Learning and Learning Disabilities, 2.*

Swanson, H. L. (1982b). A multidirectional model for assessing learning disabled student's intelligence. *Learning Disability Quarterly, 5,* 312–326.

Swanson, H. L. (1985). Assessing learning disabled children's intellectual performance: An information processing perspectives. In K. D. Gadow (Ed.), *Advances in learning and behavior disabilities* (Vol. 4, pp. 225–272). Connecticut: JAI Press.

Swanson, H. L. (1988a). Toward a metatheory of learning disabilities. *Journal of Learning Disabilities, 21*(4), 196–209.

Swanson, H. L. (1988b). Assessment practices in learning disabilities. In K. A. Kavale (Ed.), *Learning disabilities: State of the art and practice* (pp. 71–97). Boston, MA: Little, Brown.

Swanson, H. L. (1988c). A multidirectional model for assessing learning disabled student's intelligence: An information-processing framework. *Learning Disability Quarterly, 11*(3), 233–247.

Swanson, H. L. (1989). Strategy instruction: Overview of principles and procedures for effective use. *Learning Disability Quarterly, 12*(1), 3–15.

Swanson, H. L. (1990). Intelligence and learning disabilities: An introduction. In H. L. Swanson & B. K. Keogh (Eds.), *Learning disabilities: Theoretical and research issues* (pp. 23–39). Hillsdale, NJ: Earlbaum.

Swanson, H. L. (1991). Issues and concerns in the assessment of learning disabilities. In H. L. Swanson (Ed.), *Handbook on the assessment of learning disabilities* (pp. 1–19). Austin, TX: PRO-ED.

Swanson, H. L., & Keogh, B. K. (1990). *Learning disabilities: Theoretical and research issues.* Hillsdale, NJ: Earlbaum.

Swanson, H. L., & Reinert, H. R. (1984). *Teaching strategies for children in conflict* (2nd ed.). St. Louis, MO: Time Mirror/Mosby.

Swanson, H. L., & Watson, B. (1982). *Educational and psychological assessment of exceptional children.* St. Louis, MO: Mosby.

Swanstrom, W. J., Randle, C. W., & Offord, K. (1981). The frequency of LD: A comparison between JD seventh grade populations. *Journal of Correctional Education, 32* (3), 29–33.

Swap, S. M., Prieto, A. G., & Harth, R. (1982). Ecological perspectives of the emotionally disturbed child. In R. L. McDowell, G. W. Adamson, & F. H. Wood (Eds.), *Teaching emotionally disturbed children* (pp. 72–98). Boston, MA: Little, Brown.

Systma, J. (1984). Special education resource teacher, team facilitator and in-school consultant: A successful in-service/resource teacher model. *Special Education in Canada, 58,* 51–54.

Taber, F. M. (1981). *The microcomputer: Its applicability to special education: Selection and decision-making process.* Reston, VA: The Council for Exceptional Children.

Tallal, P. (1988). Developmental language disorders. In J. F. Kavanagh & T. J. Truss, Jr. (Eds.), *Learning disabilities: Proceedings of the National Conference* (pp. 181–272). Parkton, MD: York Press.

Tansley, P., & Panckhurst, J. (1981). *Children with specific learning difficulties.* Windsor: NFER-Nelson Publishing.

Tempest, F. (1982). A theoretical framework for bilingual instruction: How does it apply to students in special eduction. In A. M. Ochoa & J. Hurtado (Eds.), *Special education and the bilingual child* (pp. 9–27). San Diego State University: National Origin Desegregation Law Center.

Terman, L. M. (1916). *The measurement of intelligence.* Boston, MA: Houghton Mifflin.

Thompson, R. J. (1986). *Behavior problems in children with developmental and learning disabilities* [Monograph No. 3]. Ann Arbor: University of Michigan Press.

Thorndike, E. L. (1911). *Animal intelligence.* New York: Macmillan.

Thorndike, E. L. (1913). *The psychology of learning.* New York: Teachers College.

Thorndike, E. L. (1917). Reading as reasoning: A study of mistakes in paragraph reading. *Journal of Educational Psychology, 8,* 323–332.

Thornton, C. A., & Toohey, M. A. (1985). Basic math facts: Guidelines for teaching and learning. *Learning Disabilities Focus, 1,* 44–57.

Thornton, C. A., Tucker, B. F., Dossey, J. A., & Bazik, E. F. (1983). *Teaching mathematics to children with special needs.* Menlo Park, CA: Addison-Wesley.

Thurman, S. (1977). Congruence of behavioral ecologies: A model for special education programming. *Journal of Special Education, 11,* 329–334.

Tolman, E. C. (1933). *Purposive behavior in animals and men.* New York: Appleton-Century-Crofts.

Torgesen, J. K. (1977). The role of nonspecific factors in the task performance of learning disabled children: A theoretical assessment. *Journal of Learning Disabilities, 10*(1), 27–34.

Torgesen, J. K. (1978–1979). Performance of reading disabled children on serial memory tasks. *Reading Research Quarterly, 14*(1), 57–58.

Torgesen, J. K. (1979). What shall we do with psychological processes? *Journal of Learning Disabilities, 12,* 514–521.

Torgesen, J. K. (1980). Conceptual and educational implications of the use of efficient task strategies by learning disabled children. *Journal of Learning Disabilities, 13,* 364–371.

Torgesen, J. K. (1982). The learning disabled child as an inactive learner: Educational implications. *Topics in Learning and Learning Disabilities, 2,* 45–52.

Torgesen, J. K. (1988). Studies of children with learning disabilities who perform poorly on memory span tasks. *Journal of Learning Disabilities, 21*(10), 605–612.

Torgesen, J. K., Dahlem, W. E., & Gerenstein, J. (1987). Using verbatim text recordings to enhance reading comprehension in learning disabled adolescents. *Learning Disabilities Focus, 3*(1), 30–38.

Torgesen, J. K., & Kail, R. V. (1980). Memory processes in exceptional children. In B. K. Keogh (Ed.), *Advances in special education: Vol. 1. Basic constructs and theoretical orientations* (pp. 55–99). Greenwich, CT: JAI Press.

Torgesen, J. K., & Licht, B. (1983). The learning-disabled child as an inactive learner: Retrospect and prospects. In J. D. McKinney & L. Feagans (Eds.), *Topics in learning disabilities* (Vol. 1, pp. 3–31). Rockville, MD: Aspen Press.

Torgesen, J. K., & Wong, B. Y. L. (Eds.). (1986). *Psychological and educational perspectives on learning disabilities.* Orlando, FL: Academic.

Towle, M. (1978). Assessment and remediation of handwriting deficits for children with learning disabilities. *Journal of Learning Disabilities, 11*(6), 43–50.

Tucker, J. A. (1985). Curriculum based assessment: An introduction. *Exceptional Children, 52*(3), 199–204.

Turnbull, A. P., & Schultz, J. B. (1979). *Mainstreaming handicapped students: A guide for the classroom teacher.* Boston, MA: Allyn & Bacon.

Turnbull, A. P., Strickland, B., & Hammer, S. E. (1978). The individualized education program—Part I: Procedural guidelines. *Journal of Learning Disabilities, 11,* 40–46.

Ullmann, L. P., & Krasner, L. A. (1965). *Case studies in behavior modification.* New York: Holt, Rinehart, & Winston.

Unger, K. (1978). Learning disabilities and juvenile delinquency. *Journal of Juvenile and Family Courts, 29*(1), 25–30.

United States Department of Education Policy Paper 4/30/80, United States Department of Education. (1987). Ninth Annual Report to Congress.

Vacc, N. N., (1987). Word processor versus handwriting: A comparative study of writing samples produced by mildly mentally handicapped students. *Exceptional Children, 54*(2), 156–165.

Van Allen, R. (1968). How a language experience program works. In V. M. Howes & H. F. Darrow (Eds.), *Reading and the elementary school child: Selected readings on programs and practices* (pp. 262–268). New York: Macmillan.

Van Hiele, P. M. (1986). *Structure and insight: A theory of mathematics education.* New York: Academic Press.

Vasa, S. F., Steckelburg, A. L., & Ronning, L. V. (1982). *The special education resource teacher as a consultant: Fact or fantasy.* Paper presented at the annual meeting of the International Council of Exceptional Children. New York.

Vaughn, S. R. (1985). Why teach social skills to learning disabled students? *Journal of Learning Disabilities, 18*, 588–591.

Vaughn, S. R. (1987). TLC—Teaching learning and caring: Teaching interpersonal problem-solving skills to behaviorally disordered adolescent. *The Pointer, 31*(2), 25–30.

Vaughn, S. R., & Bos, C. S. (Eds.). (1987). *Research in learning disabilities: Issues and future directions.* Boston: Little, Brown.

Vaughn, S. R., & McIntosh, R. (1989). Interpersonal problem solving: A piece of the social competence puzzle for students with learning disabilities. *Journal of Reading, Writing, and Learning Disabilities International, 4*, 321–334.

Vautour, J. A. C. (1976). A study of placement decisions for exceptional children determined by child study teams and individuals. (Doctoral dissertation, University of Connecticut, 1975). *Dissertation Abstracts International, 36*, 6607A.

Vellutino, F. R. (1977). Alternative conceptualization of dyslexia: Evidence in support of verbal-deficit hypothsis. *Harvard Educational Review, 47*(3), 334–354.

Vellutino, F. R. (1978). Toward an understanding of dyslexia: Psychological factors in specific reading disability. In A. L. Benton & D. Pearl (Eds.), *Dyslexia: An appraisal of current knowledge* (pp. 61–111). New York: Oxford University Press.

Vellutino, F. R. (1986). Commentary: Linguistic and cognitive correlates of learning disabilities: Reaction to three reviews. In S. J. Ceci (Ed.), *Handbook of cognitive, social, and neurological aspects of learning disabilities* (Vol. 1, pp. 317–337). Hillsdale, NJ: Earlbaum.

Vellutino, F. R., & Scanlon, D. M. (1982). Verbal processing in poor and normal readers. In J. C. Brainerd & M. Pressley (Eds.), *Verbal processes in children* (pp. 189–265). New York: Springer-Verlag.

Vellutino, F. R., & Scanlon, D. M. (1985). Verbal memory in poor and normal readers: Developmental differences in the use of linguistic codes. In D. B. Gray & J. F.

Kavanagh (Eds.), *Biobehavioral measures of dyslexia* (pp. 174–214). Parkton, MD: York Press.

Vogel, S. A. (1982). On developing LD college programs. *Journal of Learning Disabilities, 15*(9), 518–528.

Wagner, R. K., & Sternberg, R. J. (1984). Alternative conceptions of intelligence and their implications for education. *Review of Educational Research, 54*(2), 179–223.

Wagoner, S. A. (1983). Comprehension monitoring: What is it and what we know about it. *Reading Research Quarterly, 17,* 328–346.

Walker, H. M. (1979). *The individualized education program (IEP) as a vehicle for delivery of special education and related services to handicapped children.* IEP developing criteria for evaluation of individualized education program provisions. Philadelphia: Research for Better Schools.

Walker, J. E., & Shea, T. M. (1988). *Behavior management: A practical approach for educators.* Columbus, OH: Merrill/Macmillan.

Wallace, G., Cohen, S. B., & Polloway, E. A. (1987). *Language arts: Teaching exceptional students.* Austin, TX: PRO-ED.

Wallace, G., & Kauffman, J. (1986). *Teaching students with learning and behavior problems* (3rd ed.). Columbus, OH: Merrill/Macmillan.

Wallace, G., & Larsen, S. C. (1978). *Educational assessment of learning problems: Testing for teaching.* Boston, MA: Allyn & Bacon.

Wallace, G., & McLoughlin, J. A. (1988). *Learning disabilities: Concepts and characteristics* (3rd ed.). Columbus, OH: Merrill/Macmillan.

Wanant, P. E. (1983). Social skills: An awareness program with learning disabled adolescents. *Journal of Learning Disabilities, 16*(1), 35–38.

Wang, M. C., & Birch, J. W. (1984a). Comparison of a full-time mainstreaming program and a resource room approach. *Exceptional Children, 51*(1), 33–40.

Wang, M. C., & Birch, J. W. (1984b). Effective special education in regular classes. *Exceptional Children, 50,* 391–397.

Wang, M. C., Gennari, P., & Waxman, H. (1985). The adaptive learning environments model: Design, implementation, and effects. In M. C. Wang & H. J. Walberg (Eds.), *Adapting instruction to individual differences* (pp. 192–235). Berkeley, CA: McCutchan.

Wang, M. C., Peverly, S., & Randolph, R. (1984). An investigation of the implementation of a full-time mainstreaming program. *Journal of Special and Remedial Education, 5*(6), 21–32.

Wang, M. C., & Reynolds, M. C. (1985). Avoiding the "catch 22" in special education reform. *Exceptional Children, 51*(6), 497–502.

Wang, M. C., Reynolds, M. C., & Walberg, H. J. (1986). Rethinking special education. *Educational Leadership, 44*(1), 26–31.

Wang, M. C., & Vaughn, E. D. (1985). *Handbook for the implementation of adaptive instruction programs.* Learning Research and Development Center, University of Pittsburgh, PA.

Wang, M. C., & Walberg, H. (1983). Adaptive instruction and classroom time. *American Educational Research Journal, 20,* 601–626.

Watson, A. E. (1935). *Experimental studies in the psychology and teaching of spelling.* Contributions to education, No. 638. New York: Teachers College, Columbia University.

Watson, J. B. (1913). Psychology as a behaviorist views it. *Psychology Review, 20,* 158–177.

Watson, J. B. (1919). *Psychology from the standpoint of a behaviorist.* Philadelphia: Lippincott.

Watson, J. B. (1928). *The ways of behaviorism.* New York: Harper.

Watson, J. B., & Rayner, R. (1920). Conditioned emotional reactions. *Journal of Experimental Psychology, 3,* 1–4.

Wechsler, D. (1974). *Wechsler intelligence scale for children—revised.* New York: Psychological Corporation.

Wehman, P., Kregel, J., & Baracus, J. (1985). From school to work: A vocational transition model for handicapped students. *Exceptional Children, 52*(1), 25–37.

Weinstein, C. (1982). Learning strategies: The metacurriculum. *Journal of Developmental and Remedial Education, 5*(2), 6–7, 10.

Weiss, H. G., & Weiss, M. S. (1976). *A survival manual: Case studies and suggestions for the learning disabled teenager.* Great Barrington, MA: Treehouse Associates.

Wellman, H. M. (1977). Preschoolers' understanding of memory-relevant variables. *Child Development, 48,* 1720–1723.

Wellman, H. M. (1985). The origins of metacognition. In D. L. Forrest-Pressley, G. E. MacKinnon, & T. G. Waller (Eds.), *Metacognition, cognition, and human performance: Vol. 1. Theoretical perspectives* (pp. 1–32). Orlando, FL: Academic Press.

Wepman, J. M. (1958). *Wepman test of auditory discrimination.* Chicago, IL: Language Research Associates.

Wepman, J. M. (1960). Auditory discrimination, speech and reading. *Elementary School Journal, 25,* 323–332.

Werner, H. (1957). The concept of development from a comparative and organismic point of view. In D. Harris (Ed.), *The concept of development: An issue in the study of human behavior* (pp. 125–148). Minneapolis: University of Minnesota Press.

West, J. F., & Idol, L. (1987). School consultation (Part I): An interdisciplinary perspective on theory, models and research. *Journal of Learning Disabilities, 20,* 388–408.

West, R. C. (1985). Let's teach our LD children social skills. *Academic Therapy, 21,* 61–67.

White, O. R. (1986). Precision teaching—precision learning. *Exceptional Children, 5*(6), 522–534.

White, W. J. (1985). Perspectives on the education and training of learning disabled adults. *Learning Disability Quarterly, 8,* 231–236.

White, W. J., Alley, G. R., Deshler, D. D., Schumaker, J. B., Warner, M. M., & Clark, F. L. (1982). Are there learning disabilities after high school? *Exceptional Children, 49,* 273–274.

Wiederholt, J. L. (1974). Historical perspectives on the education of the learning disabled. In L. Mann & D. A. Sabatino (Eds.), *The second review of special education* (pp. 103–152). Philadelphia, PA: JSE Press.

Wiederholt, J. L. (1978a). Educating the learning disabled adolescent: Some assumptions. *Learning Disability Quarterly, 1*(4), 11–23.

Wiederholt, J. L. (1978b). Adolescents with learning disabilities: The problem in perspective. In L. Mann, L. Goodman, & J. L. Wiederholt (Eds.), *Teaching the learning disabled adolescent* (pp. 9–27). Boston: Houghton-Mifflin.

Wiederholt, J. L., Hammill, D. D., & Brown, V. L. (1983). *The resource teacher: A guide for effective practice*. Austin, TX: PRO-ED.

Wiederholt, J. L., & McEntire, B. (1980). Educational options for handicapped adolescents. *Exceptional Children Quarterly, 1*(2), 1–10.

Wiener, N. (1948). *Cybernetics: Control and communication in the animal and the machine*. Cambridge, MA: MIT Press.

Wiens, J. W. (1983). Metacognition and the adolescent passive learner. *Journal of Learning Disabilities, 16*(3), 144–149.

Wiig, E. H., & Semel, E. M. (1984). *Language assessment and intervention for the learning disabled*. Columbus, OH: Merrill/Macmillan.

Wilcox, E. (1970). Identifying characteristics in NH adolescent. In L. E. Anderson (Ed.), *Helping the adolescent with the hidden handicap* (pp. 5–11). Los Angeles: California Association for Neurologically Handicapped Children.

Wilen, D. K., & Sweeting, C. V. M. (1986). Assessment of limited English proficient hispanic students. *School Psychology Review, 15*(1), 59–75.

Wilkins, G., & Miller, S. (1983). *Strategies for success*. New York: Columbia University, Teachers College.

Wilks, H. H., Bireley, J. K., & Schultz, J. J. (1979). Criteria for mainstreaming the learning disabled child into regular classes. *Journal of Learning Disabilities, 12*, 46–51.

Will, M. (1984). *OSERS programming for the transition of youth with disabilities: Bridges from school to working life*. Washington, DC: Office of Special Education and Rehabilitative Services (OSERS), U.S. Department of Education.

Will, M. C. (1984). Let us pause and reflect—but not too long. *Exceptional Children, 51*(1), 11–16.

Will, M. C. (1986). Educating children with learning problems: A shared responsibility. *Exceptional Children*, February, 411–415.

Wilson, R. M. (1972). *Diagnostic and remedial reading for classroom and clinic*. Columbus, OH: Merrill/Macmillan.

Wilson, R. M., & Hall, M. A. (1972). *Reading and the elementary school child*. New York: Van Nostrand Reinhold.

Winograd, T. (1975). Frame representations and the declarative/procedural controversy. In D. G. Bobrow & A. Collins (Eds.), *Representation and understanding* (pp. 185–210). New York: Academic Press.

Winograd, P. (1984). Strategic difficulties in summarizing texts. *Reading Research Quarterly, 19*(4), 404–425.

Witt, J. C., Miller, C. D., McIntyre, R. M., & Smith, D. (1984). Effects of variables on parental perceptions of staffings. *Exceptional Children, 51*(1), 27–32.

Wong, B. Y. L. (1979). Increasing retention of main ideas through questioning strategies. *Learning Disability Quarterly, 3*, 29–37.

Wong, B. Y. L. (Ed.). (1982a). Metacognition and learning disabilities. *Topics in Learning and Learning Disabilities, 2*(1), 1–17.

Wong, B. Y. L. (1982b). Understanding learning disabled students' reading problems: Contribution from cognitive psychology. *Topics in Learning and Learning Disabilities, 141*), 43–50.

Wong, B. Y. L. (1985a). Metacognition and learning disabilities. In D. L. Forrest-Pressley, G. E. MacKinnon, & T. G. Waller (Eds.), *Metacognition, cognition and human performance* (pp. 137–180). New York: Academic Press.

Wong, B. Y. L. (1985b). Self-questioning instructional research: A review. *Review of Educational Research, 55,* 227–265.

Wong, B. Y. L. (1986). A cognitive approach to teaching spelling. *Exceptional Children, 53*(2), 169–173.

Wong, B. Y. L., & Jones, W. (1982). Increasing metacomprehension in learning disabled and normally achieving students through self-questioning training. *Learning Disability Quarterly, 5,* 228–238.

Wood, J. W., & Carmen, M. (1982). A profile of a successful mainstreaming teacher. *The Pointer, 27*(1,), 21–23.

Woodcock, R. W., Clark, C. K., & Davies, C. O. (1979). *The Peabody rebus reading program.* Circle Pines, MN: American Guidance Service.

Woods, P. A., Sedlacek, W. E., & Boyer, S. P. (1990). Learning disability programs in large universities. *NASPA Journal, 27*(3), 248–256.

Wren, C. T. (Ed.). (1983). *Language learning disabilities.* Rockville, MD: Aspen.

Wyskoff, L. M. (1977). School volunteers face the issues. *Phi Delta Kappan, 58*(10), 755–756.

Yin, R. K., & Moore, G. B. (1987). The use of advanced technology in special education: Prospects for robotics, artificial intelligence, and computer simulation. *Journal of Learning Disabilities, 20*(1), 60–63.

Young, B. J., & Staebler, B. L. (1987). Learning disabilities and the developmental education program. In K. M. Ahrendt (Ed.), *New directions in the community colleges: Vol. 57. Teaching the developmental education student.* San Francisco, CA: Jossey-Bass.

Young, C. C. (1981). Children as instructional agents for handicapped peers. In P. S. Strain (Ed.), *The utilization of classroom peers as behavior change agents* (pp. 305–326). New York: Plenum Press.

Ysseldyke, J. E. (1979). Issues in psychoeducational assessment. In G. Phye & D. Reschly (Eds.), *School psychology: Perspectives and issues* (pp. 87–121). New York: Academic Press.

Ysseldyke, J. E. (1983). Current practices in making psychoeducational decisions about learning disabled students. *Journal of Learning Disabilities, 16,* 226–233.

Ysseldyke, J. E., & Algozzine, B. (1982). *Critical issues in special and remedial education.* Boston, MA: Houghton Mifflin.

Ysseldyke, J. E., & Salvia, J. (1974). Diagnostic-prescriptive: Two models. *Exceptional Children, 31*(3), 181–185.

Ysseldyke, J. E., & Thurlow, M. L. (1983). *Identification/classification research: An integrative summary of findings* (Research Report No. 142). Minneapolis: University of Minnesota, Institute for Research on Learning Disabilities.

Zaner-Bloser (1979). *Zaner-Bloser evaluation scales.* Columbus, OH: Author.

Zigmond, N., & Sansone, J. (1986). Designing a program for the learning disabled adolescent. *Remedial and Special Education, 7*(5), 13–17.

Zigmond, N., Sansone, J., Miller, S. E., Donahoe, K. A., & Kohnke, R. (1986). *Teaching learning disabled students at the secondary school level.* Reston, VA: The Council for Execptional Children.

Zimmerman, J., Rich, W. D., Kielitz, I., & Broder, P. K. (1981). Some observations of the link between learning disabilities and juvenile delinquency. *Journal of Criminal Justice, 9,* 1–17.

Zintz, M. V. (1981). *Corrective reading.* Dubuque, IA: Wm. C. Brown.

Author Index

Subject Index